W9-BNZ-588

EARLIER PUBLICATIONS IN THE SERIES
EDITED BY OSCAR KRISEN BUROS

TESTS IN PRINT

BARBARA A. PEACE
EDITORIAL ASSOCIATE

WILLIAM L. MATTS
EDITORIAL ASSISTANT

BF431
Z99
B8
c.2

TESTS IN PRINT

A COMPREHENSIVE BIBLIOGRAPHY
OF TESTS FOR USE IN
EDUCATION, PSYCHOLOGY, AND INDUSTRY

Edited by

OSCAR KRISEN BUROS

Professor of Education and
Director, The Institute of Mental Measurements
Rutgers, The State University

THE GRYPHON PRESS

HIGHLAND PARK · NEW JERSEY

101403

NOV 1965

DESIGNED BY LUELLA BUROS

COPYRIGHT 1961 BY OSCAR KRISEN BUROS. PUBLISHED BY THE GRYPHON PRESS
220 MONTGOMERY STREET, HIGHLAND PARK, NEW JERSEY

MANUFACTURED BY VAIL-BALLOU PRESS, INC., BINGHAMTON, NEW YORK
PRINTED IN THE UNITED STATES OF AMERICA

181.2916
18037F
c.7.

To the memory of

RUTH GRUNER THURLOW

CONTENTS

TESTS IN PRINT

PREFACE

It is with relief and something of surprise that I see this manuscript off to the printer, for the present volume (or at least a prototype of it) has been in preparation intermittently for the past 20 years. As far back as 1941 when but two volumes of *The Mental Measurements Yearbook* series, the 1938 and 1940 yearbooks, had appeared, we saw the need for a comprehensive bibliography of tests which also would serve as an index to the contents of the MMY volumes. Although the manuscript for such a bibliography was very nearly completed in 1941, it was not published because of the war. Following the publication of *The Third Mental Measurements Yearbook* in 1949 I began working on an updated second draft of the bibliography. This was never published because rising labor and production costs made it impossible for us to finance the manufacture and distribution of both the yearbook and the test bibliography. And so it was with the third draft upon which work was undertaken and then abandoned following the publication of *The Fourth Mental Measurements Yearbook* in 1953.

As each succeeding yearbook appeared, the need for an index and supplement to the series became more and more pressing. Despite the numerous cross references provided in the MMY's to critical reviews in earlier volumes, it became extremely difficult to locate quickly the relevant material in a series which now numbered four volumes. Furthermore, since each MMY stressed test developments in the period since the publication of the last volume, there was no way of knowing whether tests listed in earlier volumes but not included in the latest edition were still available. Their omission might mean that they had gone out of print, or it might mean simply that there had been no changes in them since their last listing and review in an MMY. Except in the case of very widely used tests, we saw no point in presenting new reviews of unrevised tests which had already been adequately reviewed. This characteristic of the MMY series has, we know, been a source of confusion and annoyance to many users. Had they stopped to realize what size the MMY volumes would have become had each volume listed all previously listed tests which were still available, in addition to presenting data and reviews on newly published or revised tests, their annoyance might have been lessened, but the confusion and inconvenience would have remained.

We have been aware of this limitation in the yearbook series since the publication of the second volume, *The 1940 Yearbook*. A noncritical test bibliography which also contained cross references to all material concerning each particular test to be found in any of the MMY volumes was, it seemed, the logical solution to the problem. We have toyed with other means of letting test users know what tests were still available; old friends in the test publishing field may recall our proposals for a union catalog of test publishers, which fell through because certain of the larger publishers did not wish to join in the project. They may also recall the title "Guide to Tests in Print" and other variations of the present title in the names of which we have requested materials and information over the years. In fact, some publishers may have begun to wonder if the "comprehensive bibliography of tests and assessment techniques" which we seem forever to be "preparing for publication" is not but a ruse to secure test materials in interim periods when no MMY is in preparation! We trust that the appearance of this volume will serve as proof of our motives.

In August 1959 *The Fifth Mental Measurements Yearbook* appeared, and with it information on 462 tests which had never before been listed, together with 495 which had appeared in previous volumes. But what of the many other tests listed in earlier volumes? Were they in or out of print? The reader had no way of knowing. In addition, in order to secure comprehensive coverage of the testing field, he might now need to consult five volumes in a series which now covered a 21 year time span, 1938–59. It was now imperative that something be done to assist him.

Thus, the preparation of *Tests in Print,* our fourth attempt to bring to publication a comprehensive test bibliography and index to the MMY series, was begun. With such a long history of unproductive effort and delay, the work was undertaken with many misgivings. Yet, with a new yearbook just published and with what seemed to be so much of the preparatory work already done in connection with it and with earlier drafts of the bibliography, we were encouraged to think that this would be a relatively simple task. Unfortunately, it turned out to be an extremely time consuming one. Test publication just does not stand still for many months, let alone over a period of several years. The status of tests checked in the past had all to be checked again. In addition, we decided to extend our scope to cover the status of many tests listed only in the early noncritical bibliographies which preceded *The 1938 Yearbook.* (These covered the period 1933–36.) A tremendous amount of correspondence was required to check on the status of old tests, to discover new tests, and to secure the latest information and materials for revised tests. With a few exceptions in cases where we have been unable to locate anyone once associated with a test (out-of-business publishers, deceased authors, and publishers who have refused repeatedly to reply to correspondence), every item of information in this bibliography has been checked in several ways including a final check of copy by the test publisher or author. No test has been listed as in print unless this proved to be so. As a result of the many precautions we have taken, we believe that this bibliography is unusually accurate and comprehensive as of June 1, 1961.

ACKNOWLEDGMENTS

I should like to acknowledge my debt to the more than four hundred test publishing organizations, author-publishers, and test distributors who have cooperated in this project by supplying materials for and information concerning their tests. Admittedly, this cooperation was reluctant in some cases. However, these cases are offset by the many, many publishers who have cooperated fully and unhesitatingly in this project and in past endeavors.

To them, particularly, are due my warm thanks. Perhaps it is not cricket to say thank you and to register a complaint in the same paragraph—particularly since the complaint is a 20 year old one. Nevertheless, we take this opportunity to ask what we have asked so many times before, and perhaps to make more clear our reasons for making the request. In short, our plea is that we receive *complete* examination materials for *all* new and revised tests, and *all* supplements to existing materials for them, *as they are published.* If *Tests in Print* is to become an established publication this is especially important. Many publishers seem quite willing to give us their full cooperation once we write to ask for it, but few have adopted the policy of sending us tests as they are published. In fact, after years of association with them, there are quite a few publishers who make us write each year to request their catalogs! We wonder if it is not more of a bother to publishers to receive constant letters of request from us than it would be to make arrangements to have newly published materials sent to us automatically. To such publishers, we say: (*a*) If you list in your catalog a test which you have not sent us previously or a new form, revised manual, or other supplement to an existing test, we will be writing to request it if you do not send it to us; (*b*) If you send us a specimen set (rather than a complete examination set; maybe we should call this an "MMY set"; it does not seem to have any good name in the jargon, and the "complete" part of "complete examination set" is too often overlooked) of one form of a test, we will be writing to request the alternate forms, keys, and other accessories; (*c*) If you send us one sample key for a test with multiple keys or scoring scales, we will be writing to request all the rest of the keys; (*d*) If, when you check copy for an MMY or *Tests in Print* entry, you update the publication dates shown and do not send us anything to warrant this updating, we will be writing to request it. These, it seems to us, are but simple facts which could save both of us much time and correspondence. But enough of this footnote to my thanks for your help in the present venture—solicited or, happily, not so.

It was most kind of the American Psychological Association and the American Educational Research Association, publishers of the *Technical Recommendations,* to give us permission to reprint these important committee reports despite the fact that both reports are still in print as separate booklets. We are grateful that they have permitted us to bring together test information with these valuable standards for test manual evaluation.

Many persons have worked with me on the various drafts of the test bibliographies which have been prepared over the past 20 years. I shall, however, refer only to those who have worked with me in preparing this volume. I have been most fortunate to have an unusually efficient part-time editorial and secretarial staff. Mrs. Margaret Hammond, Mrs. Doris Mc-Can, and Mrs. Minnie Yale—all of whom have worked with me on one or more *Mental Measurements Yearbooks*—have ably and conscientiously assisted me by typing, indexing, copyreading, proofreading, and performing the many miscellaneous functions which inevitably fall to versatile workers in a small office. Mrs. McCan was also of valuable assistance in helping to trace the current status of tests previously listed in the MMY; her proofreader's eye and flair for accuracy have served me well in this task, as they have in the preparation of the third, fourth, and fifth yearbooks. Mrs. Hammond and Mrs. McCan, together with Miss Peace, have been responsible for reading proof on the entire volume. Mr. James Weeks, an undergraduate student, assumed with exceptional efficiency responsibility for mimeographing and filing multiple copies of the more than three thousand pieces of paper which go to make up the manuscript of the test sections of this volume and for waging the eternal battle of trying to keep our test collection in some semblance of order. Much of the credit for the fact that we have been able to put out this volume with such a small staff is due to the efficiency and unstinting efforts of these four co-workers.

Special thanks are due to Mr. William L. Matts, a graduate student in school psychology, who served part-time as editorial assistant. Mr. Matts provided valuable assistance in corresponding with test publishers and in preparing many of the test entries which appear in this volume. My greatest debt is to my editorial associate, Miss Barbara A. Peace, who devoted full time to this project. Miss Peace, who was also an editorial associate for *The Fifth Mental Measurements Yearbook,* assumed a major role in the preparation of this bibliography and also was active in every phase of its manufacture. Seldom have I had on my staff a person to whom I could delegate so many of the functions with which I have been burdened in the past. In a small operation such as ours, she has had to handle editing, office management, and publishing—all tasks which she does extremely well. I could not ask for a more efficient or a more conscientious editorial associate.

I wish also to acknowledge my special gratitude to my wife, Luella, who has actively assisted me at many stages in the preparation of this manuscript, as she has in all previous publications. The typographic design of this volume has been one of her responsibilities. Others to whom thanks are due are the following: Mrs. Mildred R. Howley, Mr. John G. Rancy, Miss Beverly A. Richards, and Mr. Warner H. Thurlow.

Finally, I wish to acknowledge the encouragement and assistance which I have received from my university—Rutgers, The State University. I am especially grateful to the Graduate School of Education for providing us with editorial quarters in its Institute of Mental Measurements and for giving me support and encouragement in many other ways.

It is with sadness that this book has been dedicated to the memory of Mrs. Ruth Gruner Thurlow, a beloved friend and a talented editorial assistant who worked closely with my wife and me in the preparation of the third, fourth, and fifth yearbooks. Few have been more closely and more capably associated with the many problems we have faced over the years; few have been a greater source of cheer, comfort, and encouragement to me, and, I believe, to all who knew her. Unhappily she was permitted to work only a few short months on this manuscript. It is with a great sense of loss that I pay this small tribute to a truly remarkable woman. She is deeply missed.

OSCAR KRISEN BUROS

New Brunswick, N.J.
  September 1, 1961

INTRODUCTION

The objectives of *Tests in Print* are threefold: first, to present a comprehensive bibliography of tests—achievement, aptitude, intelligence, personality, and certain sensory-motor skills—published as separates and currently available in English-speaking countries; second, to serve as a classified index and supplement to the volumes of *The Mental Measurements Yearbook* series [1] published to date; third, to give a wider distribution to the excellent recommendations for improving test manuals made by committees of the American Psychological Association, the American Educational Research Association, and the National Council on Measurements Used in Education.

The first objective is approached from two directions: (*a*) by presenting, in the section "In Print Tests," a comprehensive listing of tests which are currently available; and (*b*) by presenting, in the section "Out of Print Tests," a listing of tests which have previously been listed in *The Mental Measurements Yearbook* series which are no longer available. The second objective is met through the presentation in both the in print and out of print test sections of detailed cross references to additional information and test reviews to be found in all of the yearbooks. The third objective is fulfilled through a complete reprinting of the *Technical Recommendations for Psychological Tests and Diagnostic Techniques* and the *Technical Recommendations for Achievement Tests*.

The reader may find it helpful to turn first to the Contents in order to gain an overall picture of the scope and organization of the book. In addition, the following explanations may be of assistance.

a) PAGE AND ENTRY NUMBERS. Page numbers appear in the running heads next to the *inside* margins throughout the book. In the test sections, entry numbers (i.e., the numbers assigned to specific tests) appear in the running heads next to the *outside* margins. The entry numbers on facing pages are the numbers corresponding to the first and last tests listed on these pages. The Contents refers to page numbers; the indexes and the cross references within *Tests in Print* refer to entry numbers. Except when using the Contents, the reader will have no need to use page numbers. Tests listed in the in print and out of print sections are numbered consecutively; numbers beyond 2104 refer to entries for out of print tests.

b) TEST CLASSIFICATION. Tests listed in both the in print and out of print sections are

---

[1] The eight earlier publications in the series, all edited by the present Editor and now published by The Gryphon Press (220 Montgomery Street, Highland Park, New Jersey), are as follows:
1. *The Fifth Mental Measurements Yearbook*. 1959. Pp. xxix, 1292. $22.50.
2. *The Fourth Mental Measurements Yearbook*. 1953. Pp. xxv, 1163. $18.00.
3. *The Third Mental Measurements Yearbook*. 1949. Pp. xv, 1047. $12.50.
4. *The Nineteen Forty Mental Measurements Yearbook*. 1941. Pp. xxv, 647. Out of print.
5. *The Nineteen Thirty Eight Mental Measurements Yearbook of the School of Education, Rutgers University*. 1938. Pp. xv, 415. Out of print.
6. *Educational, Psychological, and Personality Tests of 1936: Including a Bibliography and Book Review Digest of Measurement Books and Monographs of 1933–36*. 1937. Pp. 141. Paper. $0.60.
7. *Educational, Psychological, and Personality Tests of 1933, 1934, and 1935*. 1936. Pp. 83. Paper. $0.50.
8. *Educational, Psychological, and Personality Tests of 1933 and 1934*. 1935. Pp. 44. Paper. Out of print.

classified according to general area of measurement. Particularly in the cases of "Character and Personality" and "Intelligence" the classifications are broad, as they must be in order to remain workable. The classification scheme is much the same as that used in *The Fifth Yearbook*. A category for "specific" intelligence tests has been added in the in print section in order to separate tests of very specific intellectual functions from the more general categories of "Group" and "Individual" tests. Many of the rather ancient performance tests of specific factors fall within this category, which includes both group and individual tests. In the section "Vocations," we have gone back to our practice in *The Fourth Yearbook* of grouping tests in the section "Specific Vocations" by occupational category. Finally, two other new categories have been added: "Marriage and Courtship" in the miscellaneous section, and "Selection and Rating Forms" in the vocations section. The former tests were previously included under personality or health; the latter previously appeared under the miscellaneous category in the vocations section. Some may find fault with our classification scheme or take exception to our classification of specific tests. To them we can say only that it is the purpose of the scheme to provide organization for the test sections of the book and some general assistance to the user in locating materials in broad areas; it is not its purpose to provide a definitive subject index. Such an index was contemplated early in the preparation of this volume, but time has not permitted its development.

c) CATCHWORDS. The running heads include catchwords to assist readers in the location of particular materials. In the test sections these catchwords refer to the first subheading in the test classification scheme which appears on the facing pages, or, if none occurs, to the last subheading on preceding pages. In the section "Out of Print Tests," the subject catchwords are preceded by the words "OP Tests."

d) INDEXES. The book contains four indexes: the Publishers Directory and Index, which furnishes the addresses of all publishers of in print tests represented in this volume; the Distributors Directory and Index, which provides information on the availability of tests outside of their country of origin; the Title Index, wherein any test included in *Tests in Print* can be located if its exact title, or an alternate title also included in the test entry, is known; and the Name Index, in which are listed the names of all in print test authors and all reviewers of tests (both in and out of print) mentioned in the book. Additional information on the use of each index is contained in a footnote to the index title.

IN PRINT TESTS

The comprehensive bibliography of tests is presented in the section "In Print Tests." We have included in this section a complete listing of all tests about which we have been able to secure information which are sold or rented to test users in English-speaking countries. In addition, we have included numerous "confidential" tests which are neither sold nor rented but are administered under carefully controlled conditions by testing and professional organizations with only the scores reported to the test users, and several tests for use in industry which are restricted to use by the clients of the publisher. Examples of confidential tests are the *College Entrance Examination Board Scholastic Aptitude Test,* the *Law School Admission Test,* and the *Miller Analogies Test.* No attempt has been made to list all confidential or restricted tests; only those likely to be of general interest have been included. Tests designed for use in statewide testing programs have been included only when such tests are also sold to test users in other states. The bibliography does not include tests presented in journals, books, and theses unless the tests have also been made available —either through commercial publication or through their authors—in separately printed form. Nor does the bibliography include tests designed for use with specific textbooks and courses of study and tests designed primarily as practice or teaching devices.

The criteria for deciding whether or not a test should be listed in the section "In Print Tests" are essentially the same as the criteria used in the last two *Mental Measurements Yearbooks* with two exceptions: we have broadened the coverage to include tests which publishers and authors distribute for experimental or research use only, and we have been more lenient in listing tests which are obviously experimental although not so labeled.

A Word of Caution

The entries for research and experimental tests so labeled or identified by their authors or publishers include the warning "experimental form" or "for research use only." Test users are urged to heed these warnings. They are also urged to keep in mind that the section "In Print Tests" is completely nonevaluative and almost completely nonselective. Within the framework and limitations outlined in the preceding paragraphs, virtually the only requirement for inclusion in the section has been availability to potential users. This section presents a bibliography of what can be bought, borrowed, rented, or obtained upon request. The entry for the thoroughly researched and standardized test printed in faultless format is no different from the entry for the test printed in mimeographed form and distributed without norms or other interpretive material. The qualifications "experimental form" or "for research use only" are present only when these cautions appear on the test materials or are the expressed intentions of the author or publisher. It must be remembered that there are also tests without norms or other data which do not carry any such warnings. Therefore, the discriminating user of this section of the book will use it only as a source of "leads" to tests. He will not consider that listing implies approval. This has never been true of *The Mental Measurements Yearbooks;* because of its less selective nature, it is even more important that this point be recognized by the user of *Tests in Print*. The discriminating user will examine the test itself before he seriously considers it and, in cases where it has been reviewed in the MMY, he will study the reviewers' opinions. We realize that some test users will not be critical and discriminating in their selection and use of tests no matter what we or the most authoritative test critics, technicians, and users say. For such test users *Tests in Print* could conceivably perform a disservice by making known to them more tests from which to select indiscriminately.

CONTENTS

The section "In Print Tests" contains 2126 entries—2104 consecutively numbered entries and 22 inserts. Inserted entries are designated by a letter following the entry number, e.g., entry "[209a]" is inserted between entry 209 and entry 210. Of these 2126 entries, 1866 relate to tests which were originally published in English in the United States; 9 entries relate to tests originally published in English abroad but also published or stocked and distributed by a publisher in this country. One entry (Rorschach) covers tests in both of the preceding categories. The remaining 250 entries relate to tests published only outside of the United States.

Before presenting further statistics on the section "In Print Tests," we had better make clear what the figures represent. Each test is counted only once, even though it may be available in several countries in the same or very nearly the same form. If it is available in a foreign—that is, foreign to the country in which it was originally published—country in essentially the same form, this fact is mentioned in the entry only when the "foreign" edition is a United States edition. If the foreign edition of the test represents a fairly extensive revision or adaptation, we have given brief details concerning the revision within the entry for the original test. Only in cases where the revision or adaptation is substantial enough that the test might be considered a separate and distinct test have we prepared a separate entry for it. Except in these cases and cases in which two separate editions of a test (e.g., the original edition and a revision) are both being sold, each test entry covers all levels, parts, and editions of the test represented, as well as the existence of foreign adaptations. In some cases where the subtests of a test are also available in separate booklets, additional entries have been prepared for listing the subtests in their respective sections of the chapter. In other cases where the subtests, even though available in separate booklets, seemed designed to be used primarily as a battery, only the one entry is presented. Finally, in many cases we have used "group entries." Thus, all the various modifications and extensions of the Rorschach technique are grouped under the one entry, "Rorschach"; similarly, many of the entries in such sections as "Multi-Aptitude Batteries," "Record and Report Forms," and "Selection and Rating Forms" list several tests or rating techniques under one entry. Thus, since our unit for counting tests is the test entry, the actual number of different tests—not counting alternate forms as different tests—is greater than the number reported here. Since in the majority of cases an entry covers only one distinct test, we have frequently used the words "entries" and "tests" interchangeably.

Of the 2126 entries presented in the section "In Print Tests," 487 (22.9 per cent) represent new tests not previously listed in any of *The Mental Measurements Yearbooks;* 61 of these new tests are expressly for experimental or research use only. The new tests are indicated by stars preceding their titles. Four hundred and thirty-one tests (20.3 per cent) have been either revised or supplemented by the addition of new forms, manuals, norm booklets, or other accessories since their last listing in an MMY. The revised or supplemented tests are indicated by asterisks preceding their titles. The total number of new, revised, and supplemented tests is 918, 43.2 per cent of the total number of in print tests.

The large number of starred tests should not be interpreted to mean that there has been a sudden spurt in the number of new tests published since the publication of *The Fifth Yearbook.* To a large extent it reflects the painstaking search which we have made for tests which might otherwise have been missed. It is extremely difficult to locate the tests of small test publishers—frequently author-publishers of single tests. Our persistence in searching has resulted in our unearthing numerous obscure tests—most of which are probably of questionable value from any informed point of view. Possibly we have given too much importance to the goal of bibliographic completeness, which, of course, is not fully attainable. The near completeness which we have achieved has greatly increased the cost and time required to prepare the manuscript for *Tests in Print,* and, unfortunately, it is giving publicity to some poor tests which otherwise might have remained unknown to many test users. Nevertheless, we have decided to continue to seek comprehensiveness for *Tests in Print* without making any evaluations of specific tests. In contrast, the goal of *The Mental Measurements Yearbooks* will continue to be to encourage more discriminating use of tests through the presentation of frankly critical reviews of tests of every description. We can only hope that, in using *Tests in Print,* test users who are not prepared and willing to make critical evaluations of particular tests will refuse to use such tests unless, or until, the tests have been favorably reviewed in *The Mental Measurements Yearbook* and other professional publications.

TABLE 1.   IN PRINT TESTS BY MAJOR CLASSIFICATIONS

Classification	Number of Entries	Percentage of Entries	Entry Numbers
Character and Personality	306	14.4	99–397
Vocations	287	13.5	1819–2104
Intelligence	238	11.2	706–939
Miscellaneous	233	11.0	1138–1366
Mathematics	198	9.3	940–1137
English	192	9.0	398–584
Reading	159	7.5	1387–1544
Social Studies	113	5.3	1706–1818
Science	106	5.0	1545–1650
Foreign Languages	92	4.3	614–705
Sensory-Motor	55	2.6	1651–1705
Business Education	53	2.5	46–98
Achievement Batteries	45	2.1	1–45
Fine Arts	29	1.4	585–613
Multi-Aptitude Batteries	20	0.9	1367–1386
Total	2126	100.0	1–2104

Table 1 presents, in order of category size, the number of in print entries listed under each of the major classifications under which tests have been grouped. The classification with the largest number of tests is "Character and Personality"—the area in which assessment instruments have the least claim to validity. Two of the classifications with the smallest numbers of test entries—"Achievement Batteries" and "Multi-Aptitude Batteries"— actually represent a much larger number of individual tests since each entry usually represents more than one test. The achievement and multi-aptitude sections include many of the most widely used tests.

Tables 2 and 3 present statistics comparing test production in the United States with that in other countries. The test production figures for non-English-speaking countries, e.g., Sweden, refer only to tests which may be used with English-speaking subjects. These two tables probably reflect several facts—facts about our approach in preparing this bibliography, about our method of tallying tests, and about overseas testing practices themselves. First, our search for non-United States tests could not be as intensive as our search for tests originating in this country. For example, one source of information concerning new and hard-to-locate United States tests has been the Library of Congress's *Catalog of Copyright Entries;*

TABLE 2. IN PRINT TESTS PUBLISHED IN THE UNITED STATES
AND FOREIGN COUNTRIES BY MAJOR CLASSIFICATIONS [2]

Classification	United States		Foreign Countries		Total	
	Number	Percentage	Number	Percentage	Number	Percentage
Character and Personality	290	15.5	28	10.6	318	14.9
Vocations	259	13.8	28	10.6	287	13.4
Intelligence	153	8.2	85	32.3	238	11.1
Miscellaneous	219	11.7	14	5.3	233	10.9
Mathematics	154	8.2	44	16.7	198	9.3
English	171	9.1	21	8.0	192	9.0
Reading	137	7.3	22	8.4	159	7.4
Social Studies	112	5.9	1	0.4	113	5.3
Science	103	5.5	3	1.1	106	4.9
Foreign Languages	90	4.8	2	0.8	92	4.3
Sensory-Motor	51	2.7	4	1.5	55	2.6
Business Education	52	2.8	1	0.4	53	2.5
Achievement Batteries	41	2.2	4	1.5	45	2.1
Fine Arts	28	1.5	1	0.4	29	1.4
Multi-Aptitude Batteries	15	0.8	5	1.9	20	0.9
Total	1875	100.0	263	99.9	2138	100.0

TABLE 3. IN PRINT TESTS BY COUNTRIES [2]

Country	Number	Percentage
United States	1875	87.7
Great Britain	149	7.0
Canada	39	1.8
Australia	38	1.8
Union of South Africa	23	1.1
Switzerland	6	0.3
Holland	3	0.1
New Zealand	3	0.1
Sweden	2	0.1
Total	2138	100.0

obviously, no comparable search could be carried out for foreign tests.
Secondly, factors such as the additional cost of sending us materials, the
language differences, and the fact that the MMY's are less well known
overseas have undoubtedly made some foreign test publishers less anxious
to cooperate with us. This bibliography will, after all, have its widest circu-
lation in this country. Though the major overseas test publishers have
cooperated with us most fully, there may be smaller publishers whom we
were unable to locate and others whose failure to respond to correspondence

[2] In Tables 2 and 3, the 13 sublistings under Rorschach (entry 373) are tallied separately since
9 of these sublistings refer to tests of United States origin and 4 to tests of Swiss origin. Thus, in
Tables 2 and 3, the total tests (or entries) is increased to 2138. In all other tallies Rorschach is
treated as one entry, as are all other group entries.

means only that they did not quite see the relevance of our endeavor for their particular publications. We have no way of knowing how many, if any, lesser-known English-language tests originating in foreign countries may have been omitted because of these factors, though we suspect that the number is very small. Third, Tables 2 and 3 do not include adaptations of tests originating in the United States or other countries which have been prepared for use in foreign countries (unless the adaptation is substantial enough to warrant a separate entry), and they do not reflect the practice in foreign countries of importing overseas tests for use "as is." (For some information in these areas, the reader is referred to the Distributors Directory.) Fourth, *Tests in Print* covers only English-language tests; obviously the proportion of United States to foreign tests shown in Table 3 would be reduced if native-language tests were included. Finally, since *Tests in Print* does not attempt to cover the testing activities of overseas school examining boards and specific universities, there is a sizable area of testing, particularly in Great Britain, which is not represented. (But, incidentally, this area—i.e., tests of specific colleges, universities, and professional examining boards, and restricted state programs—is not covered for the United States either.)

Despite the above factors, it seems safe to say that English-language standardized tests are used relatively little in other English-speaking countries compared to their extensive use in this country. Of the 2126 in print test entries, 1867 (87.8 per cent) cover tests published in the United States. There can be no question but that we, as a nation, believe that considerable good results from our extensive use of tests.

IN PRINT TEST ENTRIES

Each test entry in the section "In Print Tests" consists of the bibliographic entry for the test itself and, whenever appropriate, a second paragraph containing cross references to relevant material to be found in *The Mental Measurements Yearbooks*. Whenever relevant, the following information has been reported, in the order given, for each test.

a) TITLE. The title is presented in boldface type. A star before the title indicates a new test not previously listed in an MMY. (Very old tests are not starred even though they have not appeared in an MMY.) An asterisk before the title indicates a test which has been revised or supplemented since it was last listed in an MMY. Subtitles and series titles have been included only when the main title alone does not appear to be sufficiently definitive. Where test booklet and manual titles differ, the better known of the two is used; when neither title seems especially preferable, the test booklet title is used. It should be emphasized that we try always to use the "official" title of a test. We seldom make use of variations, frequently incorporating the author's name, which are often used in the literature. To do so would, we think, only encourage what we regard as a confusing practice.

b) EXAMINEES AND LEVELS. A description of the subjects to whom the test may be administered is presented in a manner so as also to indicate the various levels represented by the test. For example, "Grades 1, 2-3, 4-6, 7-9" indicates that the test has four levels: one test booklet for grade 1, a second for grades 2-3, a third for grades 4-6, and a fourth for grades 7-9. Commas are used to separate levels. "High school and college" denotes a single test booklet for both levels; "High school, college" denotes two test booklets, one for high school and one for college.

c) PUBLICATION DATES. The publication dates reported represent the range of dates for the various editions, forms, and accessories making up the test. In a few instances where copyright date precedes the date of publication, a notation such as "1956, c1955" has been used. This means that the test was copyrighted in 1955 but not published until 1956. When publication or copyright dates do not appear on the test materials and they have been secured from correspondence, the dates are given in brackets.

d) SPECIAL COMMENTS. Examples of the type of information included under special comments follow: tests administered 3 times a year; new form usually issued annually; for research use only; revision of *Progressive Achievement Tests;* for Catholic schools; persistence [meaning that the test is said to be a measure of persistence]; and, reprinted from *Handbook of Tests for Use in Schools.* Whenever parts or subtests are also listed elsewhere in *Tests in Print,* cross references are given at this point in the entry following a notation such as, "subtests in arithmetic, English, and reading available as separates (see 432, 1033, and 1441)."

e) NUMBER OF SCORES. The number of scores is reported for each test along with a verbal description of what each score presumably represents. The absence of any reference to scores usually implies a single score.

f) AUTHORS. In all but a few instances, all test authors are listed with their names written in exactly the same form and order as they appear on the test booklets. When names do not appear on the test materials and information concerning authorship has been secured from other sources, the names are enclosed in brackets. Some or all authors have been omitted in the following cases: annual editions of tests with authors constantly changing; tests constructed by fairly large committees; and tests constructed by unnamed staff members, or by a long list of staff members, of the test publisher.

g) PUBLISHER. For each test the full name of its publisher or distributor (or a sufficient portion of it to enable the reader to locate the name in the Publishers Directory) is given. If the author and publisher are the same, a notation such as "the Author" or "the Council" is given as publisher. Brackets are used in cases where the publisher's name differs from the name reported on the test materials, and in cases where no publisher is reported and the information has been secured from correspondence. If a test is obtainable only from a distributor, the words "distributed by" precede the distributor's name. The distinction between distributors and publishers is important. Reputable test publishers generally do not require as high standards for tests which they distribute as they do for tests which they publish. The first listed publisher is the original publisher of the English-language version of the test. In the case of foreign tests which are also distributed or published in the United States, the United States distributor or publisher is given in parentheses.

h) FOREIGN ADAPTATIONS. Revisions and adaptations of tests for foreign use which are substantial enough to warrant separate mention but not substantial enough to warrant separate listing are given in parentheses following the description of the original edition. Only adaptations which remain in English are mentioned; translations to other languages are not included here. Within the parentheses whatever portions of the preceding information which are relevant are repeated for the foreign adaptation.

i) CLOSING ASTERISK. The asterisk immediately following the test publisher or distributor (or, when a foreign edition is described, immediately following the parenthesis ending this description) indicates that the test entry was prepared from an actual examination of the test materials. Unlike other test bibliographies, virtually every entry (all but six, representing "apparatus only" tests which it is impractical to request) in this bibliography is based upon first hand examination of at least part of the materials available for the test; in all but a few cases (18, including the 6 "apparatus only" tests mentioned previously) this has meant first hand examination of *all* non-apparatus accessories available for the test. In the 12 cases of non-apparatus tests (cases in which we have not seen the form, revised manual, or other accessory carrying the latest publication date reported; presumably the entry is correct in other particulars since we have seen other materials for the test), no asterisk follows the entry. With the exception of the six "apparatus-only" tests, *no* entries in this bibliography have been prepared from secondary sources. Many users of this bibliography, and perhaps many MMY users as well, may not be aware of the importance of this fact and of the service performed by the closing asterisk in indicating it. In the publishing business, delays and cancellations are inevitable. Even the most reputable of test publishers occasionally lists a test in his catalog which is not yet available. Sometimes a publisher will be forced to cancel entirely plans for publishing a new test, new form of an existing test, revised manual, or other new material which has been announced. Secondly, tests frequently go out of print before catalogs and other announcements concerning them can be revised or withdrawn. Preparers of test lists who use secondary sources are often mislead by this fact. For these reasons, we have, over the years, learned to be quite suspicious. We don't like to take a publisher's word for anything; we like to see for ourselves! (We certainly would not have wanted anyone to take *our* word for the date of publication of this volume!) The asterisk following the test entry means that we *have* seen for ourselves. Thus, for the reader, the closing asterisk performs the important function of assuring him that, as of the closing date of this bibliography (June 1, 1961), the materials described in the entry preceding it actually do exist in the editions, levels, and other particulars reported.

j) PARTS AND SUBTESTS. In the case of tests consisting of several booklets representing parts, subtests, or levels with distinctive titles, the booklet titles are listed in small capital letters immediately following the main part of the test entry. Whenever the parts or subtests are also listed elsewhere in the book, cross references are given. In cases in which a test is composed of numerous subtests, each in a separate booklet and each with a very brief and nondistinctive title (e.g., "Coding," "Letter Recognition"), we have occasionally conserved space by reporting these titles within the main part of the entry rather than listing them following it. In such cases the booklet titles are capitalized.

k) CROSS REFERENCES WITHIN *Tests in Print*. In addition to cross references within the entries to separately listed subtests, cross references are given when other entries in *Tests in Print* are relevant—e.g., an older or more recent edition of the test which is also available. Such cross references are given following the closing asterisk.

l) CROSS REFERENCES TO MMY LISTINGS. For tests which have been listed in the first five *Mental Measurements Yearbooks* (or in earlier publications if the information is still applicable), the entry includes a second paragraph consisting of cross references to relevant materials previously published in the series. When a title has an asterisk, indicating that it has been revised since its last appearance in the series, but no cross reference is given, it means that the information provided for the test (usually in one of the early bibliographies) is too outdated to be useful and, hence, the cross reference has been omitted. The cross references provide, wherever relevant, information on names of reviewers, number of references listed in the MMY for the test, and number of reviews excerpted from professional journals. The cross references list *The Mental Measurements Yearbooks* and earlier publications in the series in order of recency using the following code:

> 5:136 refers to entry 136 in *The Fifth Yearbook*
> 4:3 refers to entry 3 in *The Fourth Yearbook*
> 3:624 refers to entry 624 in *The Third Yearbook*
> 40:1287 refers to entry 1287 in *The 1940 Yearbook*
> 38:901 refers to entry 901 in *The 1938 Yearbook*
> 36:532 refers to entry 532 in *Educational, Psychological, and Personality Tests of 1936*
> 35:311 refers to entry 311 in *Educational, Psychological, and Personality Tests of 1933, 1934, and 1935*
> 34:172 refers to entry 172 in *Educational, Psychological, and Personality Tests of 1933 and 1934*

Cross references will be found useful even when no reviews are referred to; additional information on number of forms, administration time, group or individual test, lack of norms, some indication of prices from more recent books, and other particulars will be found in the more detailed MMY listings.

RELATION TO THE YEARBOOK SERIES

The cross references to entries, references, and reviews in *The Mental Measurements Yearbooks* will, we hope, be the most important contribution of *Tests in Print*. If much needed improvements in testing practices are to be brought about, test users will need to become more discriminating in selecting and using tests. Since the major objective of the yearbooks is to assist test users to choose and use tests more wisely, we hope that the references to MMY reviews will cause many more test users to turn to the reviews and to give them careful consideration.

At present, no matter how poor a test may be, if it is nicely packaged and if it promises to do all sorts of things which no test can do, the test will find many gullible buyers. When we initiated critical test reviewing in *The 1938 Yearbook,* we had no idea how difficult it would be to discourage the use of poorly constructed tests of unknown validity. Even the better informed test users who finally become convinced that a widely used test has no validity after all are likely to rush to use a new instrument which promises far more than any good test can possibly deliver. Counselors, personnel directors, psychologists, and school administrators seem to have an unshakable will to believe the exaggerated claims of test authors and publishers. If these test users were better informed regarding the merits and limitations of their testing instruments, they would probably be less happy and less successful in their work. The test user who has faith—however unjustified—can speak with confidence in interpreting test results and in making recommendations. The well informed test user cannot do this; he knows that the best of our tests are still highly fallible instruments which are extremely difficult to interpret with assurance in individual cases. Consequently, he must interpret test results cautiously and with so many reservations that others wonder whether he really knows what he is talking about. Children, parents, teachers, and school administrators are likely to have a greater respect and admiration for a school counselor who interprets test results with confidence even though his interpretations have no scientific justification. The same applies to psychologists and personnel directors. Highly trained psychologists appear to be as gullible as the less well trained school counselors. It pays to know only a little about testing; furthermore, it is much more fun for everyone concerned—the examiner, the examinee, and the examiner's employer.

We realize that the preceding paragraph may seem out of place in a test bibliography. Nevertheless, we are permitting it to stand. It probably reflects our discouragement at the little progress which has been made toward using tests more intelligently since we first started to publish frankly critical test reviews in *The 1938 Yearbook*. It is difficult to allocate the blame for the lack of greater progress. We think, however, that the major blame rests with test users. The better test publishers would like to make more moderate claims for their tests. Unfortunately, test buyers don't want tests which make only moderate claims. Consequently, even the best test publishers find themselves forced by competition to offer test users what they want. Bad usage of tests is probably more common than good usage. Must it always be this way? We are afraid so.

Although we think that test users will enjoy administering and interpreting tests more if they do not read the reviews which the tests have received in the MMY's, we hope that they will turn in ever increasing numbers to the MMY's and consider the reviews carefully. Some of the reviews are conflicting and some are not particularly good reviews. But on the whole, the reviews represent the best and most authoritative source of critical information about currently published tests. If at times some reviews seem hypercritical, keep in mind that we have reason to believe that for every reviewer who is overly critical, there are at least ten reviewers who pull their punches in assessing a test. It is, of course, more pleasant and more profitable to speak well of the work of others.

If *Tests in Print* causes many more test users to study carefully the test reviews in *The Mental Measurements Yearbooks,* we will feel that the arduous task of preparing this bibliography will have been worthwhile. If it were not for our hope that this would result, we would not have undertaken this task.

We have digressed enough; let us conclude our description of the section "In Print Tests" with a summary of its contents in relation to *Mental Measurements Yearbook* coverage. Table 4 presents this summary.

TABLE 4. NEW TESTS, REVISED OR SUPPLEMENTED TESTS, AND OTHER TESTS IN PRINT BY MAJOR CLASSIFICATIONS WITH MMY REVIEW COVERAGE

Classification	In Print Tests				No. of In Print Tests Reviewed	No. of In Print Test Reviews
	New	Revised or Supplemented	Others	Total		
Achievement Batteries	3	16	26	45	33	112
Business Education	11	20	22	53	22	40
Character and Personality	106	25	175	306	151	343
English	32	48	112	192	84	157
Fine Arts	4	4	21	29	23	51
Foreign Languages	24	29	39	92	42	72
Intelligence	34	34	170	238	141	309
Mathematics	33	46	119	198	104	199
Miscellaneous	65	47	121	233	58	87
Multi-Aptitude Batteries	2	6	12	20	15	56
Reading	15	29	115	159	101	220
Science	21	48	37	106	44	96
Sensory-Motor	16	3	36	55	14	22
Social Studies	21	43	49	113	37	62
Vocations	100	33	154	287	120	291
Total	487	431	1208	2126	989	2117

We previously mentioned that 22.9 per cent of the in print tests are new tests not previously listed in an MMY and that 20.3 per cent of the tests have been revised or supplemented since they were last listed in an MMY. Of the 1639 in print tests which have been listed in one or more MMY's, 989 (60.3 per cent) have been reviewed by one or more reviewers. These 989 tests received a total of 2117 reviews, an average of 2.1 reviews per test.

OUT OF PRINT TESTS

The section "Out of Print Tests" has been included for several reasons. (*a*) It serves as the second prong of our approach to the problem of letting MMY users know what has become of tests once listed in the yearbook and earlier publications. (*b*) It permits us a way out of the dilemma that, were it not for this section, users of *Tests in Print* would be left either to wonder whether, or to conclude that, any test not listed as in print was automatically out of print. Even without the limitations which we have placed upon tests selected for inclusion in the in print section, it is doubtful that any bibliography could ever claim with assurance that it included *all* currently available tests. (*c*) Even though the tests are out of print, students of testing are likely to find some of the material presented in the MMY entries and reviews to which they are referred of interest and value. (*d*) Some out of print tests are still being used by particular test users. For such users it may be worthwhile to know that the test is now considered out of print by its publisher and to have available a concise source of reference to critical reviews.

CONTENTS

The section "Out of Print Tests" contains 841 entries—844 consecutively numbered entries plus 2 inserted entries and less 1 double-numbered entry and 4 "now available" entries. The latter entries relate to tests originally planned for out of print listing but, very late in our preparations, found to be still available from their authors. Rather than renumber the sections in which they occur, we have said simply, "Now available," and referred the reader to an entry in the in print section. The section includes only tests which have previously been listed in an MMY or one of the earlier bibliographies, excluding, however, categories of tests no longer considered eligible for inclusion (e.g., tests constructed for use with specific textbooks) which were on occasion listed in earlier books. Tests listed in this section are out of print in separately printed form; they may, of course, still exist in books, journals, or other publications. In nearly all cases, the out of print status of tests listed as such has been confirmed by the test author or publisher. This has not been possible in cases of out-of-business publishers, deceased authors, and publishers who refuse to reply to correspondence. In such cases, we have felt justified in concluding that if the publisher or author cannot be reached his tests must be assumed to be no longer available.

TABLE 5: IN PRINT AND OUT OF PRINT TESTS BY MAJOR
CLASSIFICATIONS WITH MMY REVIEW COVERAGE
OF OUT OF PRINT TESTS

Classification	In Print Entries	Out of Print Entries	Total Entries	Percentage Out of Print	No. of OP Tests Reviewed	No. of OP Test Reviews
Achievement						
Batteries	45	13	58	22.4	6	19
Business Education	53	22	75	29.3	9	11
Character and						
Personality	306	102	408	25.0	48	91
English	192	95	287	33.1	34	52
Fine Arts	29	14	43	32.6	9	13
Foreign Languages	92	67	159	42.1	38	61
Intelligence	238	55	293	18.8	39	56
Mathematics	198	72	270	26.7	37	63
Miscellaneous	233	111	344	32.2	36	52
Multi-Aptitude	20	0	20	0.0	0	0
Reading	159	56	215	26.0	30	46
Science	106	61	167	36.5	34	52
Sensory-Motor	55	10	65	15.4	3	10
Social Studies	113	96	209	45.9	39	70
Vocations	287	67	354	18.9	25	49
Total	2126	841	2967	28.3	387	645

The total number of out of print entries, 841, is 28.3 per cent of the total number of all entries, both in and out of print, in *Tests in Print*. Table 5 presents a statistical summary of in and out of print tests in the various test categories and of MMY review coverage of out of print tests. The percentages which the out of print test entries are of total entries in *Tests in Print* vary from zero for multi-aptitude tests to 45.9 for social studies tests. Of the 841 out of print tests, 387 (46.0 per cent) have been reviewed one or more times (mean, 1.7 reviews per test) in the first five MMY's. Of the total of 2967 in print and out of print entries, 2480 (83.6 per cent) have appeared in the MMY series. Of these 2480 tests appearing in the yearbooks or the earlier bibliographies (where no review coverage was provided), 1286 (51.8 per cent) have been reviewed by one or more reviewers. These 1286 in print and out of print tests received a total of 2762 reviews—still an average of 2.1 reviews per test.

OUT OF PRINT TEST ENTRIES

The entries for out of print tests are extremely brief, including only title followed by cross references to additional information and reviews. Titles are given in italic type. When several tests or subtests of distinctive titles are subsumed under one main title, we have also given these subtitles in order that they might be included in the title index. Cross references to additional information and reviews in the MMY's and the earlier bibliographies are given in the same form and sequence as they are given for in print tests.

THE TECHNICAL RECOMMENDATIONS

The *Technical Recommendations* represent what we believe to be the most comprehensive and authoritative published standards for test manual writing and thus, indirectly, for test construction and evaluation. The *Technical Recommendations for Psychological Tests and Diagnostic Techniques,* first published in March 1954 and still available as a 38-page supplement to *Psychological Bulletin,* were prepared by a joint committee of the American Psychological Association, the American Educational Research Association, and the National Council on Measurements Used in Education. The original draft was prepared by the APA Committee on Test Standards.[3] Modifications were then made in cooperation with similar committees of the AERA and the NCMUE. The Committees on Test Standards of the last two organizations [4] also prepared a 36-page extension, *Technical Recommendations for Achievement Tests,* published in January 1955 by and still available from the AERA.

The two reports present recommendations as to what information should be presented in manuals for tests intended "for use in practical situations where the user is unlikely to validate the tests for himself." They present standards for evaluating the inclusiveness, and in some cases the methods of presentation, of the information reported in test manuals; they do not

[3] The APA Committee on Test Standards consisted of Edward S. Bordin, R. C. Challman, H. S. Conrad, Lee J. Cronbach (Chairman), Lloyd G. Humphreys, Paul E. Meehl, and Donald E. Super.
[4] The AERA Committee on Test Standards was composed of Herbert S. Conrad, Lee J. Cronbach, J. Raymond Gerberich, Jacob S. Orleans (Chairman), and Saul B. Sells; the NCMUE Committee on Test Standards consisted of Willis W. Clark, Robert L. Ebel (Chairman), J. Raymond Gerberich, Jacob S. Orleans, Henry D. Rinsland, Douglas E. Scates, David Segel, Arthur E. Traxler, and J. Wayne Wrightstone.

present standards for evaluating tests (although test manual evaluation is of necessity part and parcel of the process of test evaluation). A test manual may report all the information recommended by these reports and yet be worthless. The information still needs to be critically evaluated by persons competent in testing and in the areas represented by the test before judgments as to the goodness of the test can be made. Conscientious reporting of the kinds of information covered in these recommendations should, however, help to expose more openly than is frequently the case now the strengths and weaknesses of particular tests and it should help to reduce the bases upon which exaggerated claims for tests are frequently grounded. We hope that *Tests in Print* readers who have not previously studied these important standards will do so now. The test bibliography presented in the section "In Print Tests" will tell the test user what is available, but someone in his school, office, or clinic must still decide which test, from among the several which may appear to fill the bill, will best fit the particular needs. Critical test reviews in the MMY's will help the test user to make discriminating selections from among particular tests. These recommendations should be a valuable additional source of assistance to him in evaluating the kinds and extent of information presented in any test manual.

We are pleased to note that many of the newly published test manuals of the better publishers make some reference to these recommendations. Awareness of the recommendations is not, of course, fulfilling them, yet we firmly believe that it is a step in the right direction. We can only hope that more and more authors and publishers will take meaningful action in attempting to bring their tests and the manuals accompanying them closer to these standards. Many of the tests on the market today would cease to exist if these standards should become the accepted criterion for evaluating test manuals. We hope that our reprinting of them will help to encourage test users to examine tests more critically from the viewpoint of the essentials suggested for test manuals. If they will do this and if they will consider the evaluations of MMY reviewers of specific tests—which evaluations have for years been pointing out just such weaknesses as failure to comply with these recommendations reflects—we cannot see how anything but improvement in testing practices can result.

Both reports suggest that portions of the recommendations also be applied to test advertising literature and to books which are intended to perform the functions of test manuals. It is to be hoped that test publishers, authors, and researchers will make effective use of these applications of the standards. Both reports also state that the committees do not expect teachers to make much use of the recommendations. We would hope that, on the contrary, teachers who are in any way responsible for how tests are selected and used in their classrooms will make use of the standards. If they have responsibilities for test selection or interpretation they should have the minimum background knowledge necessary to understand the recommendations; if they do not have this knowledge, they should not be selecting or interpreting standardized tests.

In our opinion, there are, of course, areas in which the standards could be improved. Both reports recognize the need for periodic revision. (Committees are, in fact, now preparing revisions of the two reports.) It is not our purpose or prerogative to make specific criticisms here. We would hope, however, that in any forthcoming revision the committees would supplement their standards with more recommendations of specific requirements and that they would advise rather forcefully that their standards be applied rigorously in all areas to which a test manual is related—test planning, construction, standardization and validation, use, and interpretation. Understandably, there is a reluctance in a society such as ours to say that any standards of evaluation should be applied equally to all objects of a particular class. This reluctance, which is reflected to a certain degree in the present reports, stems from fears of stifling growth, discouraging innovation, or failing to recognize particular specific problems. We think it is high time that test users begin to insist that *all* operational tests conform to certain minimum standards—standards of which recommendations such as these might well form the basis. The so called "growth" which such an attitude would stifle *should* be stifled—the quicker the better. Innovation should be experimental before it is made—or more often just called—operational. As for particular problems (and the present recommendations do advise this at several points), test authors who claim to have produced operational tests should be held responsible for explaining and demonstrating why their tests should be exempt from any of the minimum standards. Many tests are criticized for being released prematurely, before they are ready for operational use. In our opinion, premature release is too often permitted to become established existence. Many of the tests on the market today whose manuals do not conform to minimum standards have been in existence for years. These are not simple cases of premature release; obviously the authors and publishers involved have no intention of revising or supplementing such tests and their manuals. It amazes us that after all the unfavorable reviews many such tests have received in the MMY's they continue to exist year after year. We are brought once again to our conclusion that the major blame for the existence of many bad tests lies with test users. Test reviewers cannot kill bad tests; only test users can do this by refusing to buy them. Test users will not refuse to buy bad tests until they have learned to heed the warnings of competent test critics writing in *The Mental Measurements Yearbooks* and other professional publications and until they have learned to apply rigorously standards such as those presented in the *Technical Recommendations* to the manuals for *all* operational tests which they are considering for practical use. It is our hope that *Tests in Print* will assist them in both areas.

IN PRINT TESTS

ACHIEVEMENT BATTERIES

[1]

★The American College Testing Program Examination. Grade 12; 1959–61; tests administered 3 times a year; 5 scores: English, mathematics, social studies reading, natural sciences reading, total; Science Research Associates, Inc. *

[2]

*American School Achievement Tests. Grades 1, 2–3, 4–6, 7–9; 1941–58; subtests in language-spelling, arithmetic readiness, arithmetic, reading, and social studies-science available as separates (see 400, 1017, 1018, 1391, and 1707); Willis E. Pratt, Robert V. Young, Miriam E. Wilt, and Clara Cockerille; Public School Publishing Co. *

For additional information and reviews by J. Raymond Gerberich and Virgil E. Herrick, see 5:1; for a review by Ralph C. Preston of an earlier edition, see 4:1; for reviews by Walter W. Cook and Gordon N. Mackenzie (with Glen Hass), see 3:1. For reviews of subtests, see 5:174, 5:455–6, and 5:620.

[3]

[Burt Scholastic Tests.] Variously ages 4–14; 1921–51; reprinted from *Handbook of Tests for Use in Schools, Second Edition* (see 4:B73) and *Mental and Scholastic Tests, Second Edition* (see 4:B74); 7 tests; Cyril Burt; Staples Press Ltd. *

a) TEST 1, READING VOCABULARY TEST. Ages 4–14; 1949.
b) TEST 3, READING SPEED AND ACCURACY: DISCONTINUOUS UNGRADED TEST: TWO- AND THREE-LETTER MONOSYLLABLES. Ages 4–14 with reading handicaps; 1951.
c) TEST 5, READING COMPREHENSION TEST. "Older and brighter pupils"; 1949.
d) TEST 6, SPELLING GRADED VOCABULARY TEST. Ages 5–14; 1951.
e) TEST 9, MECHANICAL ARITHMETIC GRADED TEST. Ages 7–14; 1949.
f) TEST 10, PROBLEM ARITHMETIC GRADED TEST. Ages 7–14; 1949.
g) TESTS 11–14, MECHANICAL ARITHMETIC, FUNDAMENTAL RULES. 1949.

[4]

California Achievement Tests, 1950 Edition. Grades 1–4.5, 4–6, 7–9, 9–14; 1933–51; revision of *Progressive Achievement Tests;* 10 scores: reading vocabulary, reading comprehension, total reading, arithmetic reasoning, arithmetic fundamentals, total arithmetic, mechanics of English and grammar, spelling, total language, total; tests in language, arithmetic, and reading available as separates (see 405, 1043, and 1394); Ernest W. Tiegs and Willis W. Clark; California Test Bureau. * For the 1957 edition entry, see 5; for the hand scoring edition entry, see 6.

For additional information and reviews by Warren G. Findley, Alvin W. Schindler, and J. Harlan Shores, see 4:2 (8 references); for a review by Paul

A. Witty of an earlier edition, see 3:15 (3 references); for reviews by C. W. Odell and Hugh B. Wood, see 40:1193 (1 reference); for a review by D. Welty Lefever, see 38:876 (1 excerpt). For reviews of subtests, see 4:151, 4:411, 4:530, 40:1292, 40:1459, 40:1563, 38:893, and 38:1110.

[5]

*California Achievement Tests, 1957 Edition. Grades 1–2, 3–4.5, 4–6, 7–9, 9–14; 1934–59; 11 scores: reading vocabulary, reading comprehension, reading total, arithmetic reasoning, arithmetic fundamentals, arithmetic total, mechanics of English, spelling, language total, total, handwriting; tests in language, arithmetic, and reading available as separates (see 406, 1044, and 1395); Ernest W. Tiegs and Willis W. Clark; California Test Bureau. * For the 1950 edition entry, see 4.

For additional information and a review by Charles O. Neidt, see 5:2 (10 references). For reviews of subtests, see 5:177 and 5:468.

[6]

California Basic Skills Tests. Grades 4–6, 7–9; 1933–54; hand scoring edition of Forms AA and DD of *California Achievement Tests, 1950 Edition* (see 4); 10 scores: vocabulary, reading (comprehension, total), arithmetic (reasoning, fundamentals, total), mechanics of English and grammar, spelling, total language, total; Ernest W. Tiegs and Willis W. Clark; California Test Bureau. *
For additional information, see 5:3.

[7]

California Tests in Social and Related Sciences. Grades 4–8, 9–12; 1946–55; revision of *Progressive Tests in Social and Related Sciences;* Georgia Sachs Adams, John A. Sexson, William E. Keeley, William B. Melchior, and Vesperella E. Ott; California Test Bureau. *
a) ELEMENTARY. Grades 4–8; 1946–53; 3 parts, 23 scores: social studies 1 (8 scores), social studies 2 (8 scores), related sciences (7 scores).
b) ADVANCED. Grades 9–12; 1954–55; 3 parts, 28 scores: American history through War between the States (8 scores), American history since War between the States (8 scores), related sciences (12 scores).
For additional information and a review by David R. Krathwohl, see 5:4; for reviews by Harry D. Berg and J. Raymond Gerberich of an earlier edition of the elementary level, see 4:23.

[8]

Cooperative General Achievement Tests. Grade 12 and college entrants; 1937–56; Cooperative Test Division. *
a) TEST I, SOCIAL STUDIES. See 1710.
b) TEST 2, NATURAL SCIENCE. See 1548.
c) TEST 3, MATHEMATICS. See 944.
For additional information and a review by Max D. Engelhart of Forms XX and YZ, see 5:6 (12 references); for a review by Paul L. Dressel of earlier forms, see 4:5 (9 references); for a review by John V. McQuitty, see 3:3. For reviews of individual tests, see 3:316, 3:548, and 3:596.

[9]

Cooperative General Culture Test. College; 1930–56; 6 scores: social studies, literature, science, fine arts, mathematics, total; Cooperative Test Division. *
For additional information and a review by Benjamin S. Bloom, see 5:7 (9

references); for a review by John V. McQuitty of earlier forms, see 4:6 (10 references); for reviews by Benjamin S. Bloom and H. T. Morse, see 3:4 (14 references); for reviews by Lavone A. Hanna, Edward S. Jones, and Hilda Taba, see 40:1184 (2 references); for a review by F. S. Beers, see 38:871.

[10]

Coordinated Scales of Attainment. Grades 1, 2, 3, 4, 5, 6, 7, 8; 1946–54; subtests for grades 4–8 in English, spelling, arithmetic, reading, science, geography, and history available as separates (see 415, 535, 1049, 1426, 1551, 1741, and 1767); James A. Fitzgerald, Dora V. Smith, Ethel V. Nelson, Victor L. Lohmann, [Marvin J. Van Wagenen], Edgar B. Wesley, Mendel E. Branom, Ellen Frogner, Leo J. Brueckner, Victor C. Smith, and August Dvorak; Educational Test Bureau. *

For additional information and a review by Alvin W. Schindler of the complete battery, see 4:8; for reviews by Roland L. Beck, Lavone A. Hanna, Gordon N. Mackenzie (with Glen Hass), and C. C. Ross of the batteries for grades 4–8, see 3:6.

[11]

*Eighth Grade Test.** Grade 8; 1934–61; new form usually issued annually; 5 scores: English, arithmetic, science, history, total; Ohio Scholarship Tests. *
For additional information, see 4:21.

[12]

Essential High School Content Battery. Grades 9–13; 1950–51; 5 scores: mathematics, science, social studies, English, total; David P. Harry and Walter N. Durost; [Harcourt, Brace & World, Inc.]. *
For additional information and reviews by Herbert S. Conrad, J. Thomas Hastings, and Gordon N. Mackenzie (with A. Harry Passow), see 4:9.

[13]

Every Pupil Primary Achievement Test. Grades 1–3; 1932–33; 7 scores: arithemetical computation, reading arithmetic, sentence spelling, word reading, sentence reading, paragraph reading, total; Kathryn Kayser and H. E. Schrammel; Bureau of Educational Measurements. *
For additional information and a review by C. C. Ross, see 3:7.

[14]

*General Scholarship Test for High School Seniors.** Grade 12; 1930–61; new form usually issued annually; 6 scores: English, history, mathematics, science, reading-language, total; Ohio Scholarship Tests. *
For additional information, see 5:9; for a review by C. C. Ross of the 1947 edition, see 3:14.

[15]

*The Graduate Record Examinations: The Area Tests.** Grades 14–17; 1954–61; available only in the Institutional Testing Program; 3 scores: social science, humanities, natural science; Educational Testing Service. * For the testing program entry, see 1353.

For additional information and reviews by Benjamin S. Bloom and Frederick B. Davis, see 5:10 (1 reference). For a review of the testing program, see 5:601.

[16]

*The Gray-Votaw-Rogers General Achievement Tests. Grades 1–3, 4–6, 5–9, 7–9; 1934–61; original edition called *New South Achievement Tests;* Hob Gray, David F. Votaw, and J. Lloyd Rogers; Steck Co. *

a) [COMPLETE EDITION.] Grades 1–3, 4–6, 7–9; 1934–61.

  1) *Primary*. Grades 1–3; 1934–61; 6 scores: reading comprehension, reading vocabulary, spelling, arithmetic reasoning, arithmetic computation, total.

  2) *Intermediate*. Grades 4–6; 1934–60; 11 scores: same as for primary level plus elementary science, language, literature, social studies, health and safety.

  3) *Advanced*. Grades 7–9; 1934–60; 11 scores: same as for intermediate level.

b) ABBREVIATED EDITION. Grades 5–9; 1939–51; 7 scores: elementary science, social studies, literature, language, reading, arithmetic, total.

  For additional information and reviews by Warren G. Findley and Douglas E. Scates, see 5:11 (1 reference); for a review by Oliver F. Anderhalter, see 4:12; for a review by Roland L. Beck of an earlier edition, see 3:9 (3 references); for reviews by Joseph E. Moore and C. C. Ross, see 40:1187 (1 reference).

[17]

Group Achievement Test: Dominion Tests, 1934 Edition. Grade 8; 1934–56; 2 parts; Department of Educational Research, Ontario College of Education, University of Toronto; distributed by Guidance Centre. *

a) PART 1. 3 scores: spelling, language usage, paragraph reading.

b) PART 2. 2 scores: arithmetic computation, arithmetic reasoning.

  For additional information, see 5:12.

[18]

Group Achievement Tests: Dominion Tests: Niagara Edition. Grade 3; 1949–56; 5 tests; F. W. Minkler, C. Howitt, C. R. MacLeod, W. A. Marshall, M. F. Pummell, N. Wightman, and the Department of Educational Research, Ontario College of Education, University of Toronto; distributed by Guidance Centre. *

a) TEST 1, VOCABULARY. 1949–50.

b) TEST 2, DIAGNOSTIC PARAGRAPH COMPREHENSION. 1950.

c) TEST 3, ENGLISH GRAMMAR. 1949–56.

d) TEST 4, SPELLING. 1950.

e) TEST 5, ARITHMETIC COMPUTATION. 1950.

  For additional information, see 5:13.

[19]

The Harlow Achievement Tests for Texas. Grades 1, 2, 3, 4, 5, 6, 7, 8; 1942–50; Harlow Publishing Corporation. *

a) FIRST GRADE. 1942; 7 scores: word recognition, sentence meaning, nature study, health, spelling, number work, total.

b) SECOND GRADE. 1942; 6 scores: word meaning, paragraph meaning, health, spelling, arithmetic, total.

c) THIRD GRADE. 1949; 9 scores: arithmetic computation, arithmetic reasoning, word meaning, paragraph meaning, correct use of words, spelling, geography, science, total.

d) FOURTH GRADE. 1949; 10 scores: same as for third grade plus health.

e) FIFTH GRADE. 1949; 10 scores: same as for third grade plus health.

f) SIXTH GRADE. 1949; 11 scores: same as for third grade plus hygiene, United States history.

g) SEVENTH GRADE. 1949; 11 scores: same as for third grade plus hygiene, United States history.

h) EIGHTH GRADE. 1949; 12 scores: same as for third grade plus hygiene, United States history, citizenship.

For additional information, see 4:13.

[20]

*The Harlow Battery Achievement Test. Grades 1–3, 4–6, 4–8, 7–9; 1945–60; Harlow Publishing Corporation. *

a) PRIMARY BATTERY. Grades 1–3; 7 scores: English, spelling, reading comprehension, word meaning, arithmetic computation, arithmetic reasoning, total.

b) INTERMEDIATE GRADE BATTERY. Grades 4–6; 11 scores: same as Primary Battery plus history, geography, hygiene, science.

c) UPPER GRADE BATTERY. Grades 4–8; 11 scores: same as intermediate level.

d) JUNIOR HIGH BATTERY. Grades 7–9; 11 scores: same as intermediate level.

For additional information, see 4:14.

[21]

*High School Fundamentals Evaluation Test. Grades 9–12; 1955–59; 6 scores: reading (vocabulary, comprehension), history and social studies, science, mathematics, total; David F. Votaw; Steck Co. *

For additional information and reviews by Victor H. Noll and Verner M. Sims, see 5:14.

[22]

Iowa Every-Pupil Tests of Basic Skills. Grades 3–5, 5–9; 1940–47; 4 tests; H. F. Spitzer, Ernest Horn, Maude McBroom, H. A. Greene, and E. F. Lindquist; Houghton Mifflin Co. *

a) TEST A, SILENT READING COMPREHENSION. See 1450.

b) TEST B, WORK-STUDY SKILLS. See 1544.

c) TEST C, BASIC LANGUAGE SKILLS. See 404.

d) TEST D, BASIC ARITHMETIC SKILLS. See 1038.

For additional information and reviews by Miriam M. Bryan and Anton Thompson, see 4:15 (4 references); for reviews by Frederic L. Ayer, Gustav J. Froehlich, and Ralph C. Preston, see 3:10 (8 references); for reviews by Harriet M. Barthelmess [Morrison], William A. Brownell, J. Murray Lee, and Charles W. Odell of an earlier edition, see 38:872 (3 references). For reviews of subtests, see 3:334 and 3:501.

[23]

Iowa High School Content Examination, 1943 Edition. Grades 11–13; 1924–43; 5 scores: English and literature, mathematics, science, history and social studies, total; D. B. Stuit, H. A. Greene, and G. M. Ruch; Bureau of Educational Research and Service. *

For additional information and a review by David V. Tiedeman, see 4:16 (4 references); for a review by Maurice E. Troyer, see 3:11 (7 references).

[24]

Iowa Tests of Basic Skills. Grades 3–9; 1955–56; 15 scores: vocabulary, reading comprehension, language (5 scores), work-study skills (4 scores), arithmetic skills (3 scores), total; E. F. Lindquist, A. N. Hieronymus, and others; Houghton Mifflin Co. *

For additional information and reviews by Virgil E. Herrick, G. A. V. Morgan, and H. H. Remmers, see 5:16 (1 excerpt).

[25]

*The Iowa Tests of Educational Development. Grades 9–13; 1942–59; 9 tests, 10 scores: 9 scores listed below and total of a–h; E. F. Lindquist and others; Science Research Associates, Inc. *

a) TEST 1, UNDERSTANDING OF BASIC SOCIAL CONCEPTS. See 1715.
b) TEST 2, GENERAL BACKGROUND IN THE NATURAL SCIENCES. See 1564.
c) TEST 3, CORRECTNESS AND APPROPRIATENESS OF EXPRESSION. See 447.
d) TEST 4, ABILITY TO DO QUANTITATIVE THINKING. See 959.
e) TEST 5, ABILITY TO INTERPRET READING MATERIALS IN THE SOCIAL STUDIES. See 1510.
f) TEST 6, ABILITY TO INTERPRET READING MATERIALS IN THE NATURAL SCIENCES. See 1511.
g) TEST 7, ABILITY TO INTERPRET LITERARY MATERIALS. See 506.
h) TEST 8, GENERAL VOCABULARY. See 568.
i) TEST 9, USE OF SOURCES OF INFORMATION. See 1526.

For additional information and reviews by J. Murray Lee and Stephen Wiseman, see 5:17 (9 references); for a review by Eric F. Gardner, see 4:17 (3 references); for reviews by Henry Chauncey, Gustav J. Froehlich, and Lavone A. Hanna, see 3:12.

[26]

Metropolitan Achievement Tests, [1947 Edition]. Grades 1, 2, 3–4, 5–7.5, 7–9.5; 1931–50; Gertrude H. Hildreth, Richard D. Allen, Harold H. Bixler, William L. Connor, and Frederick B. Graham; [Harcourt, Brace & World, Inc.]. * For the revised edition entry, see 27.

a) PRIMARY 1 BATTERY. Grade 1; 1931–48; 4 scores: word pictures, word recognition, word meaning, numbers.
b) PRIMARY 2 BATTERY. Grade 2; 1932–48; 5 scores: reading, word meaning, arithmetic (fundamentals, problems), spelling.
c) ELEMENTARY BATTERY. Grades 3–4; 1932–49; 6 scores: reading, vocabulary, arithmetic (fundamentals, problems), language usage, spelling.
d) INTERMEDIATE BATTERY. Grades 5–7.5; 1932–50; 6–10 scores: reading, vocabulary, arithmetic (fundamentals, problems), English, spelling, (complete battery only) literature, geography, history and civics, science.
e) ADVANCED BATTERY. Grades 7–9.5; 1932–50; 6–10 scores: same as for intermediate battery.

For additional information and a review by Warren G. Findley, see 4:18 (10 references); see also 3:13 (7 references); for reviews by E. V. Pullias and Hugh B. Wood of an earlier edition, see 40:1189 (3 references); for reviews by Jack W. Dunlap, Charles W. Odell, and Richard Ledgerwood, see 38:874. For reviews of subtests, see 4:416, 4:543, 40:1458.1, 40:1551, 38:892, and 38:1105.

[27]

*Metropolitan Achievement Tests, [1960 Edition]. Grades 1.5, 2, 3–4, 5–6, 7–9; 1960, c1958–59; subtests in arithmetic, reading, science, and social studies available as separates (see 1072, 1421, 1566, and 1716); Walter N. Durost, Harold H. Bixler, Gertrude H. Hildreth, Kenneth W. Lund, and J. Wayne Wrightstone; [Harcourt, Brace & World, Inc.]. * For an earlier edition entry and references to reviews, see 26.

a) PRIMARY BATTERY I. Grade 1.5; 4 scores: word knowledge, word discrimination, reading, arithmetic concepts and skills.

b) PRIMARY BATTERY 2. Grade 2; 7 scores: word knowledge, word discrimination, reading, spelling, arithmetic (concepts and problem solving, computation, total).

c) ELEMENTARY BATTERY. Grades 3–4; 9 scores: word knowledge, word discrimination, reading, spelling, language (usage, punctuation and capitalization, total), arithmetic (computation, problem solving and concepts).

d) INTERMEDIATE BATTERY. Grades 5–6; 11–13 scores: word knowledge, reading, spelling, language (usage, parts of speech, punctuation and capitalization, total), language study skills, arithmetic (computation, problem solving and concepts), social studies study skills, (complete battery only) social studies information, science.

e) ADVANCED BATTERY. Grades 7–9; 12–14 scores: same as for intermediate battery plus kinds of sentences under language.

[28]

Modern School Achievement Tests: Skills Edition. Grades 2–8; 1931–49; 6 scores: reading comprehension, reading speed, arithmetical computation, arithmetical reasoning, spelling, reading accuracy; Arthur I. Gates, Paul R. Mort, and Ralph B. Spence; Bureau of Publications. *

For additional information and a review by Charles R. Langmuir, see 4:19; for reviews by William A. Brownell, Herbert S. Conrad, and Herschel T. Manuel of the original edition, see 40:1190 (3 references).

[29]

Municipal Battery: National Achievement Tests. Grades 3–6, 6–8; 1938–55; subtests in English, arithmetic, reading, history-civics, and geography available as separates (see 432, 1033, 1441, 1713, and 1747); Robert K. Speer and Samuel Smith; Acorn Publishing Co. *

For additional information and a review by J. Murray Lee, see 5:18; for a review by Ralph C. Preston, see 4:20; for reviews by A. M. Jordan and Hugh B. Wood, see 40:1191. For reviews of subtests, see 5:790, 4:406, and 4:664.

[30]

National Achievement Tests. Grades 4–6, 7–9; 1954–58; 4 scores: language, mathematics, social studies-science-health, total; Lester D. Crow, Alice Crow, and William H. Bristow; Acorn Publishing Co. *

For additional information and a review by William E. Coffman, see 5:19.

[31]

★National Educational Development Tests. Grades 9–10; 1959–61; tests administered annually by individual schools; 6 scores: English usage, mathematics usage, social studies reading, natural sciences reading, word usage, total; E. F. Lindquist, Leonard S. Feldt, and others; Science Research Associates, Inc. *

[32]

*National Merit Scholarship Qualifying Test. Second semester juniors and first semester seniors seeking college scholarships; 1955–61; new forms issued annually; 6 scores: English usage, mathematics usage, social studies reading, natural sciences reading, word usage, total; tests administered annually by individual schools; Science Research Associates, Inc. *

For additional information and reviews by Benno G. Fricke and Roger T. Lennon of the 1958 test, see 5:20.

[33]

*Public School Achievement Tests. Grades 3–8; 1928–59; subtests in reading, arithmetic computation, arithmetic reasoning, language usage, grammar, and spelling available as separates (see 439, 453, 554, 1021, 1029, and 1439); Jacob S. Orleans; Public School Publishing Co. *

For additional information and reviews by Herbert S. Conrad and E. V. Pullias, see 40:1194 (2 references).

[34]

Public School Attainment Tests for High School Entrance: Examination of Abilities in Reading, English, and Mathematics. High school entrants; 1935; a battery assembled from previously published tests; 4 scores: reading, English, algebraic ability, total; Arthur E. Traxler, J. C. Tressler, Henry D. Rinsland, Roland L. Beck, and J. Murray Lee; Public School Publishing Co. *

For additional information and a review by Benjamin S. Bloom, see 3:17; for reviews by Harold Gulliksen and C. C. Ross, see 40:1195 (1 reference).

[35]

*SRA Achievement Series. Grades 1–2, 2–4, 4–6, 6–9; 1954–58; subtests in language arts, arithmetic, reading, and work-study skills available as separates (see 469, 1082, 1442, and 1532); Louis P. Thorpe, D. Welty Lefever, and Robert A. Naslund; Science Research Associates, Inc. *

For additional information and reviews by Warren G. Findley and Worth R. Jones, see 5:21. For reviews of subtests, see 5:200, 5:483, 5:649, 5:668, and 5:696.

[36]

*SRA High School Placement Test. Grades 8.5–9.5; 1957–61; new form issued annually; 5 or 6 scores: reasoning or educational ability, reading, arithmetic, language arts, composite, Catholic religion (optional); Science Research Associates, Inc. *

For additional information and reviews by Cyril J. Hoyt (with W. Wesley Tennyson) and William W. Turnbull, see 5:22.

[37]

Scholastic Achievement Series. Grades 1.5–2.5, 2.5–3, 4–6, 7–9; 1953–55; for Catholic schools; subtests in English-spelling and arithmetic available as separates (see 470 and 1083); Oliver F. Anderhalter, R. Stephen Gawkoski, and John O'Brien; Scholastic Testing Service, Inc. *

For additional information and reviews by William E. Coffman and James R. Hayden, see 5:23. For reviews of subtests, see 5:201 and 5:484.

[38]

★Secondary School Admission Tests: General School Ability and Reading Test. Students in grades 6–11 who are applying for admission to independent secondary schools; 1957–60; administered 3 times annually at centers established by the publisher; test consists of secure forms of *Cooperative School and*

College Ability Tests (see 743) and *Reading Comprehension: Cooperative English Test, [1960 Revision]* (see 1436); 7 scores: reading (vocabulary, speed, level, total), general school ability (verbal, quantitative, total); program administered for the Secondary School Admission Test Board by Educational Testing Service. *

[39]

*Sequential Tests of Educational Progress. Grades 4–6, 7–9, 10–12, 13–14; 1956–59; 7 tests: Essay Test (see 482), Listening (see 1284), Mathematics (see 974), Reading (see 1449), Science (see 1573), Social Studies (see 1719), Writing (see 483); Cooperative Test Division. *

For additional information and reviews by Robert W. B. Jackson and Wilbur L. Layton, see 5:24 (1 reference, 1 excerpt). For reviews of individual tests, see 5:206, 5:207, 5:438, 5:578, 5:653, 5:716, and 5:792.

[40]

Seven Plus Assessment: The Northumberland Series. Ages 7–8; 1951; 3 tests: spelling (see 555), arithmetic (see 1031), reading (see 1440); C. M. Lambert; University of London Press Ltd. *

For additional information and a review by Stanley D. Nisbet, see 4:24.

[41]

Standard Graduation Examination for Elementary Schools. Grade 8; 1930–33; 11 scores: spelling, reading, vocabulary, arithmetic computation, arithmetic reasoning, grammar, language usage, literature, history, geography, total; Arthur S. Otis and J. S. Orleans; [Harcourt, Brace & World, Inc.]. *

[42]

*Stanford Achievement Test, [1953 Revision]. Grades 1.9–3.5, 3–4, 5–6, 7–9; 1923–60; subtests in arithmetic, reading, study skills, science, and social studies available as separates (see 1090, 1453, 1536, 1574, and 1728); Truman L. Kelley, Richard Madden, Eric F. Gardner, Lewis M. Terman, and Giles M. Ruch; [Harcourt, Brace & World, Inc.]. *

For additional information and a review by N. L. Gage, see 5:25 (19 references); for reviews by Paul R. Hanna (with Claude E. Norcross) and Virgil E. Herrick of the previous edition, see 4:25 (20 references); for reviews by Walter W. Cook and Ralph C. Preston, see 3:18 (34 references). For reviews of subtests, see 5:487, 5:656, 5:698, 5:799, 4:419, 4:555, 4:593, 3:503, and 3:595.

[43]

Test for High School Entrants: [National Achievement Tests]. High school entrants; 1945–57; 5 scores: English, reading comprehension, arithmetic, general information, total; Lester D. Crow and Alice Crow; Acorn Publishing Co. *

For additional information and a review by Jacob S. Orleans, see 5:26; for a review by Benjamin S. Bloom, see 3:19.

[44]

Tests of General Educational Development. High school, college; 1944–57; 5 tests; United States Armed Forces Institute; Veterans' Testing Service. *

a) TEST I, CORRECTNESS AND EFFECTIVENESS OF EXPRESSION. See 417.

b) TEST 2, INTERPRETATION OF READING MATERIALS IN THE SOCIAL STUDIES. See 1509.

c) TEST 3, INTERPRETATION OF READING MATERIALS IN THE NATURAL SCIENCES.
See 1508.
d) TEST 4, INTERPRETATION OF LITERARY MATERIALS. See 505.
e) TEST 5, GENERAL MATHEMATICAL ABILITY. See 951.

For additional information and a review by Robert J. Solomon, see 5:27 (39
references); for a review by Gustav J. Froehlich, see 4:26 (27 references); for
reviews by Herbert S. Conrad and Warren G. Findley, see 3:20 (11 references).
For reviews of individual tests, see 3:122 and 3:528.

[45]

**Wide Range Achievement Test: Reading, Spelling, Arithmetic From Kin-
dergarten to College, 1946 Edition.** Ages 5 and over; 1940–46; 3 scores: reading, spelling, arithmetic; Joseph Jastak and Sidney Bijou; distributed by Psychological Corporation. *

For additional information and reviews by Paul Douglas Courtney, Verner
M. Sims, and Louis P. Thorpe, see 3:21.

BUSINESS EDUCATION

[46]

*Business Education: National Teacher Examinations. College seniors and
teachers; 1956–[59]; Educational Testing Service. * For the testing program
entry, see 1192.

For additional information, see 5:507. For reviews of the testing program,
see 5:538 and 4:802.

[47]

***Business Fundamentals and General Information Test: National Business
Entrance Tests.** Grades 12–16 and adults; 1938–60; Joint Committee on Tests
of the United Business Education Association and the National Office Management Association; United Business Education Association. * For the complete
battery entry, see 53.

For additional information, see 5:508; for reviews by Vera M. Amerson and
C. C. Upshall of the 1946 form, see 3:369. For reviews of the complete battery,
see 5:515 and 3:396.

[48]

***Business Relations and Occupations, Form 4: Achievement Examinations
for Secondary Schools.** High school; 1951–59; Forms 1–3 published by Educational Test Bureau are out of print; A. Donald Beattie; C. A. Gregory Co. *

For additional information concerning earlier forms, see 5:509.

[49]

**Business Relations and Occupations: Midwest High School Achievement
Examinations.** High school; 1952–55; A. Donald Beattie; Educational Test
Bureau. *

For additional information, see 5:510.

[50]

★General Business: Every Pupil Scholarship Test. High school; 1959;
Bureau of Educational Measurements. *

[51]

*General Office Clerical Test (Including Filing): National Business Entrance Tests. Grades 12–16 and adults; 1948–60; Joint Committee on Tests of the United Business Education Association and the National Office Management Association; United Business Education Association. * For the complete battery entry, see 53.

For additional information, see 5:511; for reviews by Arnold E. Schneider and C. C. Upshall of the 1946 form, see 3:379. For reviews of the complete battery, see 5:515 and 3:396.

[52]

General Test of Business Information. Grades 9–16; 1942–43; Stephen J. Turille; Bureau of Educational Measurements. *

For additional information and reviews by Vera M. Amerson and Herbert A. Tonne, see 3:380.

[53]

*National Business Entrance Tests. Grades 12–16 and adults; 1938–60; formerly called *National Clerical Ability Tests* and *United-NOMA Business Entrance Tests;* two series: General Testing Series (1938–57) and Official Testing Series (1938–60, tests administered at NBET Centers which may be established in any community); Joint Committee on Tests of the United Business Education Association and the National Office Management Association; United Business Education Association. *

a) BOOKKEEPING TEST. See 60.
b) BUSINESS FUNDAMENTALS AND GENERAL INFORMATION TEST. See 47.
c) GENERAL OFFICE CLERICAL TEST (INCLUDING FILING). See 51.
d) MACHINE CALCULATION TEST. See 65.
e) STENOGRAPHIC TEST. See 81.
f) TYPEWRITING TEST. See 95.

For additional information and reviews by Edward N. Hay, Jacob S. Orleans, and Wimburn L. Wallace, see 5:515; see also 4:453 (1 reference); for a review by Paul S. Lomax of the 1946 forms, see 3:396; see also 40:1476 (9 references). For reviews of individual tests, see 5:506, 5:508, 5:511, 5:514, 5:522, 5:526, 3:368–9, 3:379, 3:384, 3:391, and 3:394.

BOOKKEEPING

[54]

*Bookkeeping: Every Pupil Scholarship Test. High school; 1926–61; new form usually issued twice a year; Bureau of Educational Measurements. *

For additional information, see 5:503.

[55]

*Bookkeeping, Form 4: Achievement Examinations for Secondary Schools. High school; 1951–59; Forms 1–3 published by Educational Test Bureau are out of print; Helen L. Haberman; C. A. Gregory Co. *

For additional information concerning earlier forms, see 5:502.

[56]

Bookkeeping: Midwest High School Achievement Examinations. High school; 1952–55; Lois E. Hastings; Educational Test Bureau. *

For additional information and a review by I. David Satlow, see 5:504.

[57]

*Bookkeeping I: Every Pupil Test. 1 year high school; 1939–61; new form usually issued annually; Ohio Scholarship Tests. *
  For additional information, see 5:505.

[58]

★Bookkeeping I: Final District-State Scholarship Test. High school; 1938–61; Ohio Scholarship Tests. *

[59]

★Bookkeeping I: Preliminary District-State Scholarship Test. High school; 1947–61; Ohio Scholarship Tests. *

[60]

*Bookkeeping Test: National Business Entrance Tests. Grades 12–16 and adults; 1938–60; Joint Committee on Tests of the United Business Education Association and the National Office Management Association; United Business Education Association. * For the complete battery entry, see 53.
  For additional information, see 5:506; for reviews by Harvey A. Andruss and Ray G. Price of the 1946 form, see 3:368. For reviews of the complete battery, see 5:515 and 3:396.

[61]

*Bookkeeping Test: State High School Tests for Indiana. 1, 2, 3, 4 semesters high school; 1942–60; Department of Business Education, Ball State Teachers College; State High School Testing Service for Indiana. *
  For additional information concerning earlier forms, see 3:367.

[62]

*First Year Bookkeeping: Manchester Semester-End Achievement Tests. 1, 2 semesters high school; 1934–[61]; Bureau of Tests. *

[63]

Shemwell-Whitcraft Bookkeeping Test. 1, 2 semesters high school; 1937–38; E. C. Shemwell, John E. Whitcraft, and H. E. Schrammel; Bureau of Educational Measurements. *
  For additional information and a review by Arnold E. Schneider, see 3:387.

MISCELLANEOUS

[64]

★Commercial Law: Every Pupil Scholarship Test. High school; 1951; Bureau of Educational Measurements. *

[65]

*Machine Calculation Test: National Business Entrance Tests. Grades 12–16 and adults; 1941–61; earlier tests called *Key-Driven Calculating Machine Ability Tests;* Joint Committee on Tests of the United Business Education Association and the National Office Management Association; United Business Education Association. * For the complete battery entry, see 53.
  For additional information and review by Dorothy C. Adkins, see 5:514; for a review by Elizabeth Fehrer of the 1946 form, see 3:384. For reviews of the complete battery, see 5:515 and 3:396.

[66]

Parke Commercial Law Test. High school; 1933; L. A. Parke; Bureau of Educational Measurements. *
For additional information and a review by Ray G. Price, see 3:385.

STENOGRAPHY

[67]

★APT Dictation Test. Stenographers; 1955; distribution restricted to clients; Associated Personnel Technicians, Inc. *

[68]

★Byers' First-Year Shorthand Aptitude Tests. First year students in grades 9–13 and business school; 1959; 6 scores: total and 5 scores listed below; Edward E. Byers; Allied Publishers, Inc. *
a) PART 1. 2 scores: phonetic perception, retention ability.
b) PART 2. 3 scores: observation aptitude, pattern from parts, hand dexterity.

[69]

Commercial Education Survey Tests: Junior and Senior Shorthand. 1, 2 years high school; 1933; 7 scores: form knowledge (errors of principle, phrasing, total), dictation (transcript errors, spelling, punctuation), spelling; Edith V. Bisbee; Public School Publishing Co. *
For additional information, see 38:936 (2 references, 1 excerpt).

[70]

E.R.C. Stenographic Aptitude Test. High school and adults; 1944; 6 scores: speed of writing, word discrimination, phonetic spelling, vocabulary, dictation, total; Walter L. Deemer, Jr.; Science Research Associates, Inc. *
For additional information and reviews by Philip H. DuBois and Edward A. Rundquist, see 3:372 (1 reference).

[71]

Hiett Simplified Shorthand Test (Gregg). 1–2 semesters high school; 1951; Victor C. Hiett and H. E. Schrammel; Bureau of Educational Measurements. *
For additional information and a review by Gale W. Clark, see 5:512.

[72]

Personnel Research Institute Test of Shorthand Skills. Stenographers; 1951–54; title on test is *Otis and Laurent Test of Shorthand Skills;* [Jay L. Otis and Harry Laurent]; Personnel Research Institute. *
For additional information, see 5:517.

[73]

★Revised Standard Graded Tests for Stenographers. High school and business school; 1958–59, c1956–59; H. M. Overley; Atlantic Refining Co. *

[74]

The Seashore-Bennett Stenographic Proficiency Tests: A Standard Recorded Stenographic Worksample. Adults; 1946–56; Harold Seashore and George K. Bennett; Psychological Corporation. *
For additional information, see 5:519 (2 references); for a review by Harold F. Rothe, see 4:455 (1 reference); for a review by Ann Brewington, see 3:386.

[75]

Shorthand Aptitude Test. High school; 1953–54; V. Brownless, S. Dunn, and the Queensland Department of Public Instruction; Australian Council for Educational Research. *

For additional information and a review by James Lumsden, see 5:520.

[76]

***Shorthand I: Every Pupil Test.** 1 year high school; 1938–61; new form usually issued annually; Ohio Scholarship Tests. *

For additional information, see 5:521.

[77]

★Shorthand Test: Individual Placement Series (Area IV). Adults; 1960; J. H. Norman; the Author. *

[78]

***[Simplified] Shorthand Test: State High School Tests for Indiana.** 1, 2, 3, 4 semesters high school; 1950–[60]; Department of Business Education, Ball State Teachers College; State High School Testing Service for Indiana. *

For additional information concerning earlier forms, see 4:457.

[79]

Stenogauge. Stenographers and typists; 1922; 5 scores: dictation, typing, accuracy, spelling, total; Eugene J. Benge; Management Service Co. *

For additional information and a review by Beatrice J. Dvorak, see 3:389.

[80]

Stenographic Aptitude Test. Grades 9–16; 1939–46; 3 scores: transcription, spelling, total; George K. Bennett; Psychological Corporation. *

For additional information and reviews by Philip H. DuBois and Edward A. Rundquist, see 3:390 (1 reference); see also 40:1677 (1 reference).

[81]

***Stenographic Test: National Business Entrance Tests.** Grades 12–16 and adults; 1938–60; earlier tests called *Stenographic Ability Tests;* Joint Committee on Tests of the United Business Education Association and the National Office Management Association; United Business Education Association. * For the complete battery entry, see 53.

For additional information and a review by Edward B. Greene, see 5:522; for reviews by Ann Brewington and Elizabeth Fehrer of the 1946 form, see 3:391. For reviews of the complete battery, see 5:515 and 3:396.

[82]

Test for Stenographic Skill. Applicants for stenographic positions; 1950; Edward N. Hay; Aptitude Test Service. *

For additional information and reviews by Reign H. Bittner and Clifford E. Jurgensen, see 4:459.

[83]

Turse-Durost Shorthand Achievement Test (Gregg). 1–2 years high school; 1941–42; 4 scores: language skills, shorthand penmanship, shorthand principles,

total; Paul L. Turse and Walter N. Durost; [Harcourt, Brace & World, Inc.]. *
For additional information, see 3:392 (1 excerpt).

[84]

Turse Shorthand Aptitude Test. Grades 8 and over; 1937–40; 8 scores: strok-
ing, spelling, phonetic association, symbol transcription, word discrimination,
dictation, word sense, total; Paul L. Turse; [Harcourt, Brace & World, Inc.]. *
For additional information and a review by Leslie M. Haynes, see 4:460 (5
references); for a review by Philip H. DuBois, see 3:393.

TYPEWRITING

[85]

Commercial Education Survey Tests: Junior and Senior Typewriting. 1, 2
years high school; [1931]; Jane E. Clem; Public School Publishing Co. *
For additional information, see 40:1480 (1 excerpt).

[86]

***First-Year Typewriting: Manchester Semester-End Achievement Tests.** 1,
2 semesters high school; [1934–60]; Bureau of Tests. *

[87]

★International Typewriting Tests. High school and business college; 1950;
W. C. Maxwell; Educational Test Bureau. *

[88]

Kauzer Typewriting Test. 1, 2, 4 semesters high school; 1934; Adelaide
Kauzer and H. E. Schrammel; Bureau of Educational Measurements. *
For additional information and a review by E. G. Blackstone, see 3:382.

[89]

SRA Typing Adaptability Test. High school and adults; 1954–56; formerly
called *Columbia-Southern Typing Test;* 3 scores: time, error, total; Mary
Tydlaska and Clem White; Science Research Associates, Inc. *
For additional information and reviews by Gale W. Clark and Edward B.
Greene, see 5:518.

[90]

SRA Typing Skills. Grades 9–12 and adults; 1947; 2 scores: speed, accuracy;
Marion W. Richardson and Ruth A. Pedersen; Science Research Associates,
Inc. *
For additional information, see 3:388d.

[91]

**★The Tapping Test: A Predictor of Typing and Other Tapping Opera-
tions.** High school; 1959; John C. Flanagan, Grace Fivars, and Shirley A.
Tuska; [Psychometric Techniques Associates]. *

[92]

Test for Typing Skill. Typists; 1952; Edward N. Hay; Aptitude Test Service. *
For additional information and a review by Bernadine Meyer, see 5:523.

[93]

*Typewriting I: Every Pupil Test. 1 year high school; 1938–61; new form usually issued annually; 2 scores: speed, performance; Ohio Scholarship Tests. *
  For additional information, see 5:525.

[94]

*Typewriting I and II: Every Pupil Scholarship Test. 1 or 2 years high school; 1928–61; new form usually issued twice a year; Bureau of Educational Measurements. *
  For additional information, see 5:524.

[95]

*Typewriting Test: National Business Entrance Tests. Grades 12–16 and adults; 1941–60; earlier tests called *Typing Ability Test;* Joint Committee on Tests of the United Business Education Association and the National Office Management Association; United Business Education Association. * For the complete battery entry, see 53.
  For additional information and a review by Clifford E. Jurgensen, see 5:526; for reviews by E. G. Blackstone and Beatrice J. Dvorak of the 1946 form, see 3:394. For reviews of the complete battery, see 5:515 and 3:396.

[96]

*Typewriting Test: State High School Tests for Indiana. 1, 2, 3, 4 semesters high school; 1934–[60]; Department of Business Education, Ball State Teachers College; State High School Testing Service for Indiana. *
  For additional information concerning earlier forms, see 4:463.

[97]

★Typing Test: Individual Placement Series (Area IV). Adults; 1959; J. H. Norman; the Author. *

[98]

United Students Typewriting Tests, Volume 14. 1, 2, 3, 4 semesters; 1932–58; Committee on Tests, UBEA Research Foundation; United Business Education Association. *
  For additional information, see 5:527.

CHARACTER AND PERSONALITY

NONPROJECTIVE

[99]

A-S Reaction Study: A Scale for Measuring Ascendance-Submission in Personality. College and adults; 1928–39; Gordon W. Allport and Floyd H. Allport; Houghton Mifflin Co. *
  For additional information, see 5:28 (15 references); for a review by William U. Snyder, see 3:23 (11 references); for a review by Doncaster G. Humm of the 1928 edition, see 40:1198 (19 references); for a review by Doncaster G. Humm of an out of print revision for business use, see 40:1199 (4 references).

[100]

★Activity Rating Scale for Psychiatric Patients. Male psychiatric patients; 1959; 6 scores: deteriorated behavior, interpersonal tensions, emotional controls, resistive isolation, regressive activity, reality concern; for research use only; Wilson H. Guertin and Arnold D. Krugman; Cooperative Psychological Test Distributors. *

[101]

*Activity Vector Analysis. Adults; 1948–59; title on test is *Placement Analysis;* 5 scores: aggressiveness, sociability, emotional adjustment, social adaptability, activity level; [Walter V. Clarke]; Walter V. Clark Associates, Inc. *

For additional information and reviews by Brent Baxter and George K. Bennett, see 5:29 (11 references).

[102]

★The Adjective Check List. Grades 9–16; 1950–60; for research use only; Harrison G. Gough; the Author. *

[103]

*The Adjustment Inventory. Grades 9–16, adults; 1934–58; Hugh M. Bell; distributed by Consulting Psychologists Press, Inc. *
a) STUDENT FORM. Grades 9–16; 1934–39; 4 scores: home, health, social, emotional.
b) ADULT FORM. Adults; 1938–39; 5 scores: home, occupational, health, social, emotional.
c) REVISED STUDENT FORM, RESEARCH EDITION. Grades 9–16; 1958; 7 scores: home, health, social, emotional, economic background, attitude toward people, masculinity-femininity.

For additional information, see 5:30 (26 references); for reviews by Nelson G. Hanawalt and Theodore R. Sarbin, see 4:28 (104 references); for reviews by Raymond B. Cattell, John G. Darley, C. M. Louttit, and Percival M. Symonds of the Student Form, and reviews by S. J. Beck, J. P. Guilford, and Doncaster G. Humm of the Adult Form, see 40:1200 (15 references, 1 excerpt); for a review by Austin H. Turney of the Student Form, see 38:912.

[104]

Adjustment Questionnaire. Ages 12–17; 1951; 11 scores: self-confidence, sense of personal worth, sense of personal freedom, recognition, social relationships, nervous symptoms, moral attitudes, family relationships, school relationships, emotionality, total; National Bureau of Educational and Social Research. *

For additional information, see 5:31.

[105]

Affectivity Interview Blank. Ages 7–12; 1951; child feelings; Elizabeth Mechem Fuller; Child Development Laboratories, University of Michigan. *

For additional information and reviews by Morris Krugman and Verner M. Sims, see 4:29 (3 references).

[106]

The Alcadd Test. Adults; 1949; identification of alcoholic addicts and individuals with alcoholic problems; Morse P. Manson; Western Psychological Services. *

For additional information and reviews by Charles Honzik and Albert L. Hunsicker, see 4:30 (1 reference).

[107]

Aspects of Personality. Grades 4–9; 1937–38; 3 scores: ascendance-submission, extroversion-introversion, emotionality; Rudolf Pintner, John J. Loftus, George Forlano, and Benjamin Alster; [Harcourt, Brace & World, Inc.]. *

For additional information and reviews by C. M. Louttit and P. E. Vernon, see 40:1201 (4 references); see also 38:913 (1 excerpt).

[108]

★**Association Adjustment Inventory.** Normal and institutionalized adults; 1959; adaptation of the *Kent-Rosanoff Free Association Test* (see 358); 13 scores: juvenility, psychotic responses, depressed-optimistic, hysteric-nonhysteric, withdrawal-sociable, paranoid-naive, rigid-flexible, schizophrenic-objective, impulsive-restrained, sociopathic-empathetic, psychosomapathic-physical contentment, anxious-relaxed, total; Martin M. Bruce; the Author. *

[109]

Attitude-Interest Analysis Test. Early adolescents and adults; 1936; masculinity-femininity; also called *M-F Test;* Lewis M. Terman and Catherine Cox Miles; McGraw-Hill Book Co., Inc. *

For additional information and a review by Starke R. Hathaway, see 3:24 (20 references); for excerpts from related book reviews, see 40:B1094 (3 excerpts), 38:B498 (14 excerpts), and 36:B256 (8 excerpts).

[110]

★**Attitudes Toward Industrialization.** Adults; 1959; community attitude toward industrial expansion; Donald E. Kaldenberg; Psychometric Affiliates. *

[111]

Attitudes Toward Parental Control of Children. Adults; 1936; experimental form; Ralph M. Stogdill and Henry H. Goddard; Ralph M. Stogdill. *

For additional information, see 40:1205 (2 references).   ,

[112]

BEC Personality Rating Schedule. Grades 7–16; 1936; 9 ratings by teachers: mental alertness, initiative, dependability, cooperativeness, judgment, personal impression, courtesy, health, final summary; Philip J. Rulon, Elizabeth A. Nash, and Grace L. Woodward; distributed by Philip J. Rulon. *

For additional information and reviews by Francis F. Bradshaw and Theos A. Langlie, see 38:915 (1 reference).

[113]

*****Behavior Cards: A Test-Interview for Delinquent Children.** Delinquents having a reading grade score 4.5 or higher; 1941–50; Ralph M. Stogdill; distributed by C. H. Stoelting Co. *

For additional information and reviews by W. C. Kvaraceus and Simon H. Tulchin, see 3:25 (3 references).

[114]

★**The Behavior Interpretation Inventory.** Grades 13–14 and "young adults"; 1957–58; 4 motivation scores: escape, avoidance, social approval, self-approval; for research use only; Mortimer H. Applezweig and George Moeller; Mortimer H. Applezweig. *

[115]

Behavior Preference Record: What Would You Do? (A Study of Some Home and School Problems). Grades 4–6, 7–9, 9–12; 1953; 6 scores: cooperation, friendliness, integrity, leadership, responsibility, critical thinking; Hugh B. Wood; California Test Bureau. *

For additional information and reviews by J. Thomas Hastings and Edward Landy, see 5:32 (1 excerpt).

[116]

★[Behavior Rating Scales.] Mental patients; 1959–61; distributed by E. I. Burdock. *

a) WARD BEHAVIOR RATING SCALE. Adults; 1959–60; ratings by nurses or attendants, research workers after interview with patient and nurse; 3 scores: verbal behavior-appearance-deportment, adaptation to ward routine, total; E. I. Burdock, Anne S. Hardesty, G. Hakerem, and J. Zubin.

b) CLINICAL BEHAVIOR RATING SCALE. Adults; 1960; ratings by psychiatrists, psychologists, social workers, or sociologists; E. I. Burdock and Anne S. Hardesty.

c) INTERVIEW BEHAVIOR RATING SCALE. Adults; 1960; ratings by psychiatrists; 3 scores: verbal, nonverbal, total; E. I. Burdock and Anne S. Hardesty.

d) WORK BEHAVIOR RATING SCALE. Adults; 1960; ratings by supervisors, employers, or occupational therapists; E. I. Burdock and Anne S. Hardesty.

e) CHILDREN'S BEHAVIOR RATING SCALE. Ages 1–16; 1960–61; ratings by psychiatrists, psychologists, pediatricians, or remedial teachers; 3 scores: verbal, nonverbal, total; E. I. Burdock and Anne S. Hardesty.

[117]

★Billett-Starr Youth Problems Inventory. Grades 7–9, 10–12; 1961, c1953–61; problems checklist; 12 scores: physical health and safety, getting along with others, boy-girl relationships, home and family life, personal finance, interests and activities, school life, heredity, planning for the future, mental-emotional health, morality and religion, total; Roy O. Billett and Irving S. Starr; [Harcourt, Brace & World, Inc.]. *

[118]

★Biographical Inventory for Students: Experimental Form for Research in Testing. Grades 12–13; 1955–58; 10 scores: action, social activities, heterosexual activities, religious activities, literature-music-art, political activities, socioeconomic status, economic independence, dependence on home, social conformity; for research use only; Laurence Siegel; distributed by Educational Testing Service. *

[119]

Bonney-Fessenden Sociograph. Grades 4–12; 1955; Merl E. Bonney and Seth A. Fessenden; California Test Bureau. *

For additional information and reviews by Åke Bjerstedt and C. Robert Pace, see 5:33.

[120]

A Book About Me. Grades kgn–1; 1952; workbook for gathering data about children's background, maturity, interests, and attitudes; Edith Sherman Jay; Science Research Associates, Inc. *

For additional information and a review by Florence M. Teagarden, see 5:34.

[121]

Bristol Social-Adjustment Guides. Ages 5–15; 1956–58; D. H. Stott and E. G. Sykes; University of London Press Ltd. *
a) THE CHILD IN SCHOOL.
b) THE CHILD IN RESIDENTIAL CARE.
c) THE CHILD IN THE FAMILY.
   For additional information, see 5:35.

[122]

C-R Opinionaire. Grades 11–16 and adults; 1935; conservatism-radicalism; Theodore F. Lentz; Character Research Association. *
   For additional information and a review by George W. Hartmann, see 4:39 (5 references); for a review by Goodwin Watson, see 40:1212 (5 references); for a review by H. H. Remmers, see 38:899.

[123]

California Psychological Inventory. Ages 13 and over; 1956–57; 18 scores: dominance, capacity for status, sociability, social presence, self-acceptance, sense of well-being, responsibility, socialization, self-control, tolerance, good impression, communality, achievement via conformance, achievement via independence, intellectual efficiency, psychological-mindedness, flexibility, femininity; Harrison G. Gough; Consulting Psychologists Press, Inc. *
   For additional information and reviews by Lee J. Cronbach and Robert L. Thorndike, see 5:37 (33 references, 1 excerpt).

[124]

California Test of Personality, 1953 Revision. Grades kgn–3, 4–8, 7–10, 9–16, adults; 1939–53; 15 scores: self-reliance, sense of personal worth, sense of personal freedom, feeling of belonging, withdrawing tendencies, nervous symptoms, total personal adjustment, social standards, social skills, anti-social tendencies, family relations, school relations or occupational relations, community relations, total social adjustment, total adjustment; Louis P. Thorpe, Willis W. Clark, and Ernest W. Tiegs; California Test Bureau. *
   For additional information and a review by Verner M. Sims, see 5:38 (93 references); for reviews by Laurance F. Shaffer and Douglas Spencer of the original edition, see 3:26 (24 references, 1 excerpt); for reviews by Raymond B. Cattell, Percival M. Symonds, and P. E. Vernon of the elementary and secondary levels, see 40:1213 (1 excerpt).

[125]

The Cassel Group Level of Aspiration Test, 1957 Revision. Grades 5–16 and adults; 1952–57; 7 scores: clinical difference, Hausmann, aspiration difference, first goal, psychological response to failure, physiological response to failure, level of aspiration quotient; Russell N. Cassel; Western Psychological Services. *
   For additional information and reviews by W. Grant Dahlstrom, Harrison G. Gough, and J. P. Sutcliffe, see 5:39 (5 references, 2 excerpts).

[126]

The Cassel Psychotherapy Progress Record. Mental patients; 1953; 3 ratings: emotional development, barrier vulnerability development, overall psychotherapy development; Russell N. Cassel; Western Psychological Services. *
   For additional information, see 5:40.

[127]

Character-Conduct Self-Rating Scale for Students. Grades 7–12; 1931; Edwin J. Brown; Bureau of Educational Measurements. *

[128]

★**Child Behavior Rating Scale.** Grades kgn–3; 1960; experimental form; ratings by teachers; 6 adjustment scores: self, home, social, school, physical, total; Russell N. Cassel; the Author. *

[129]

Child Personality Scale. Grades kgn–9; 1951; ratings by classmates and teachers or self-ratings; 22 ratings: pep, intelligence, sociability, nervous-calmness, popularity, religiousness, punctuality, courtesy, cooperation, generosity, persistence, honesty, neatness, patience, interests, disposition, good sport, quietness, entertaining, thoughtfulness, sense of humor, dependability; Mary Amatora; C. A. Gregory Co. *

For additional information and reviews by Robert H. Bauernfeind and Dale B. Harris, see 5:41 (18 references).

[130]

*****Client-Centered Counseling Progress Record.** Adults and children undergoing psychotherapeutic counseling; 1950–60; Russell N. Cassel; Associated Publishers. *

For additional information, see 4:33.

[131]

The College Inventory of Academic Adjustment. College; 1949; 7 scores: curricular adjustment, maturity of goals and level of aspiration, personal efficiency-planning and use of time, study skills and practices, mental health, personal relations, total; Henry Borow; distributed by Consulting Psychologists Press, Inc. *

For additional information and reviews by Lysle W. Croft and Harrison G. Gough, see 4:34 (3 references).

[132]

Community Improvement Scale. Adults; 1955; community morale; Inez Fay Smith; Psychometric Affiliates. *

For additional information and a review by Wimburn L. Wallace, see 5:42.

[133]

Concept Formation Test. Normal and schizophrenic adults; 1940; Jacob Kasanin and Eugenia Hanfmann; C. H. Stoelting Co. *

For additional information and a review by Kate Levine Kogan (with William S. Kogan), see 4:35 (8 references); for a review by O. L. Zangwill, see 3:27 (19 references); for excerpts from related book reviews, see 3:28.

[134]

★*****Constant-Choice Perceptual Maze Attitude of Responsibility Test.** Ages 4 and over; 1938–60; "liking or disliking of required behavior"; 3 scores: intensity of quality, persistency of quality, reaction tendencies; John C. Park; the Author. *

[135]

Cornell Index. Ages 18 and over; 1944–49; psychosomatic and neuropsychiatric symptoms; Arthur Weider, Harold G. Wolff, Keeve Brodman, Bela Mittelmann, and David Wechsler; Psychological Corporation. *

For additional information, see 5:43 (7 references); for reviews by Hans J. Eysenck, Nelson G. Hanawalt, and Laurance F. Shaffer, see 4:37 (41 references).

[136]

Cornell Word Form 2. Adults; 1946-55; psychosomatic and neuropsychiatric symptoms; [Arthur Weider, Bela Mittelmann, David Wechsler, and Harold G. Wolff]; Cornell University Medical College. *

For additional information, see 5:44 (11 references).

[137]

★Cotswold Personality Assessment P. A. 1. Ages 11–16; [1960]; 6 scores: 3 preference scores (things, people, ideas) and 3 attitude scores (using one's hands, being with other people, talking about school); C. M. Fleming; Robert Gibson & Sons (Glasgow), Ltd. *

[138]

★Cowell Personal Distance Scale. Boys in grades 7–9; [1958]; title on scale is *Confidential Personal Distance Ballot;* social distance ratings of classmates in physical education classes; Charles C. Cowell; the Author. *

[139]

★Cowell Social Behavior Trend Index. Grades 7–9; [1958]; social adjustment as judged by teachers; Charles C. Cowell; the Author. *

[140]

DF Opinion Survey. Grades 12–16 and adults; 1954–56; 10 scores: need for attention, liking for thinking, adventure vs. security, self-reliance vs. dependence, aesthetic appreciation, cultural conformity, need for freedom, realistic thinking, need for precision, need for diversion; J. P. Guilford, Paul R. Christensen, and Nicholas A. Bond, Jr.; Sheridan Supply Co. *

For additional information and reviews by Andrew R. Baggaley, John W. French, and Arthur W. Meadows, see 5:45.

[141]

Detroit Adjustment Inventory. Ages 5–8, grades 3–6, 7–12; 1942–54; title on tests for grades 3–6 and 7–12 is *Telling What I Do;* Harry J. Baker; Public School Publishing Co. *

For additional information and a review by Laurance F. Shaffer, see 5:46 (1 reference); for a review by Albert Ellis of the form for grades 7–12, see 3:31.

[142]

★Dynamic Personality Inventory. Ages 17 and over with IQ's of 80 and over; 1960, c1956; 33 scores: hypocrisy, passivity, seclusion-introspection, orality, oral aggression, oral dependence, emotional independence, verbal aggression, impulsiveness, unconventionality, hoarding behavior, attention to details, conservatism, submissiveness, anal sadism, insularity, phallic symbol interest, narcissm, exhibitionism, active Icarus complex, passive Icarus complex, sensuality, Icarian exploits, sexuality, tactile impression enjoyment, creative interests, masculine sexual identification, feminine sexual identification, social role seeking, social activity interest, need to give affection, ego defense persistence, initiative; also available in abbreviated form, without scores for orality, phallic symbol interest, and sexuality, under the title *Likes and Interests Test* for use with apprentices and employee applicants ages 15 and over; T. G. Grygier; distributed by National Foundation for Educational Research in England and Wales. *

[143]

*Edwards Personal Preference Schedule. College and adults; 1953–59; 15 scores: achievement, deference, order, exhibition, autonomy, affiliation, intraception, succorance, dominance, abasement, nurturance, change, endurance, heterosexuality, aggression; Allen L. Edwards; Psychological Corporation. *
  For additional information and reviews by Frank Barron, Åke Bjerstedt, and Donald W. Fiske, see 5:47 (50 references, 2 excerpts).

[144]

The Ego Strength Q-Sort Test. Grades 9–16 and adults; 1956–58; 6 scores: ego-status, social status, goal setting and striving, good mental health, physical status, total; Russell N. Cassel; Psychometric Affiliates. *
  For additional information, see 5:48.

[145]

Embedded Figures Test. Ages 10 and over; 1950–57; Herman A. Witkin; the Author. *
  For additional information, see 5:49 (9 references).

[145a]

★Emo Questionnaire. Adults; 1958–59; 14 scores: rationalization, inferiority feelings, fear and anxiety, N vector (total of preceding 3 scores), depression, projection, unreality, withdrawal, Z vector (total of preceding 4 scores), hostility, sex, organic response, total diagnostic, buffer score; George O. Baehr and Melany E. Baehr; Education-Industry Service. *

[146]

★Emotional Maturity Test. High school; 1954; problems checklist; 4 scores: introductory, people, home, work or school; W. H. Winkler; Winkler Publications. *

[147]

The Empathy Test. Ages 13 and over; 1947–55; Willard A. Kerr and Boris J. Speroff; Psychometric Affiliates. *
  For additional information and a review by Robert L. Thorndike, see 5:50 (20 references).

[148]

★Employee Questionnaire. Industry; 1946–49; 9 scores: extraversion, drive, neuroticism, detail, objectivity, persecution, social dominance, emotion, unusual; distribution restricted to clients and former clients; [Harold Rothe]; Stevenson, Jordon & Harrison, Inc. *

[149]

Evaluation Modality Test. Adults; 1956; 4 scores: realism, moralism, individualism, total; Hugo O. Engelmann; Psychometric Affiliates. *

For additional information and a review by Wilson H. Guertin, see 5:51.

[150]

★Evaluation of Attitudes Toward Home and Family Life. Grades 7–9; 1952; Victor N. Phelps; Curriculum Bulletin. *

[151]

Every-Day Life: A Scale for the Measure of Three Varieties of Self-Reliance. High school; 1941; 3 scores: independence, resourcefulness, responsibility; Leland H. Stott; Sheridan Supply Co. *

For additional information and a review by Harold E. Jones, see 4:41; for a review by Albert Ellis, see 3:38 (6 references).

[152]

Examining for Aphasia: A Manual for the Examination of Aphasia and Related Disturbances, Revised Edition. Adolescents and adults; 1946–54; Jon Eisenson; Psychological Corporation. *

For additional information and a review by T. R. Miles, see 5:52 (3 references, 2 excerpts) ; for a review by D. Russell Davis, see 4:42 (2 excerpts) ; for a review by C. R. Strother, see 3:39 (1 excerpt).

[153]

★FIRO-B: [A Three-Dimensional Theory of Interpersonal Behavior]. Adults; 1958, c1957–58; William C. Schutz; Rinehart & Co., Inc. (manual) ; test materials distributed by Harvard Printing Office. *

For additional information concerning the manual, see 5:B375.

[154]

Family Adjustment Test. Ages 12 and over; 1952–54; title on test is *Elias Family Opinion Survey;* 11 scores: attitudes toward mother, attitudes toward father, father-mother attitude quotient, oedipal, struggle for independence, parent-child friction-harmony, interparental friction-harmony, family inferiority-superiority, rejection of child, parental qualities, total; Gabriel Elias; Psychometric Affiliates. *

For additional information and a review by Albert Ellis, see 5:53 (6 references).

[155]

★Famous Sayings. Grades 9–16 and business and industry; 1957–58; 4 scores: conventional mores, hostility, fear of failure, social acquiescence; Bernard M. Bass; Psychological Test Specialists. *

[156]

★Fantasy Scale. College; 1959; 13 daydream content scores: achievement, romance, hostility, past, defense, pleasure, realism, service, mysticism, dependence, exhibition, pathology, worry; experimental form; Horace A. Page and Seymour Epstein; Horace A. Page. *

[157]

Fatigue Scales Kit. Adults; 1944–54; [Willard A. Kerr]; Psychometric Affiliates. *

a) INDUSTRIAL SUBJECTIVE FATIGUE AND EUPHORIA SCALES. Adults; 1944–54.

b) RETROSPECTIVE WORK CURVE FEELINGS FOR NATIONAL RESEARCH PROGRAM ON EMPLOYEE FEELINGS AT WORK. Adults; 1954.
c) STUDY OF DAY [MOTHER'S DAY FATIGUE SCALE]. Housewives; 1954.
  For additional information, see 5:54.

[158]

Fels Parent Behavior Rating Scales. "For the use of the trained home visitor in appraising certain aspects of parent-child relationships"; 1937–49; 30 scores: adjustment of home, activeness of home, discord in home, sociability of family, coordination of household, child-centeredness of home, duration of contact with mother, intensity of contact with mother, restrictiveness of regulations, readiness of enforcement, severity of actual penalties, justification of policy, democracy of policy, clarity of policy, effectiveness of policy, disciplinary friction, quantity of suggestion, coerciveness of suggestion, accelerational attempt, general babying, general protectiveness, readiness of criticism, direction of criticism, readiness of explanation, solicitousness for welfare, acceptance of child, understanding, emotionality toward child, affectionateness toward child, rapport with child; Alfred L. Baldwin, Joan Kalhorn, Fay Huffman Breese, and Horace Champney; Fels Research Institute. *
  For additional information and a review by Dale B. Harris, see 4:43 (15 references).

[159]

The Freeman Anxiety Neurosis and Psychosomatic Test. Mental patients; 1952–55; 9 scores: anxiety neurosis, psychosomatic syndrome, and 7 subscores; M. J. Freeman; Grune & Stratton, Inc. *
  For additional information, see 5:55 (3 references).

[160]

Friend-Critic Statement. Adults; 1948; subject's essays on himself as seen by a good friend and by a strong critic; Aptitude Associates. *
  For additional information, see 5:56.

[161]

★**G. C. Personality Development Record.** High school; [1959]; ratings by teachers; Guidance Centre. *

[162]

★**Goal Preference Inventory.** College; 1958; 3 need scores: academic recognition, social recognition, social love and affection; for research use only; [Shephard Liverant]; the Author. *

[163]

Goldstein-Scheerer Tests of Abstract and Concrete Thinking. Adults; 1941–51; 5 tests; Kurt Goldstein and Martin Scheerer; Psychological Corporation. *
a) GOLDSTEIN-SCHEERER CUBE TEST. 1941–47.
b) GLEB-GOLDSTEIN COLOR SORTING TEST. 1941–51.
c) GOLDSTEIN-SCHEERER OBJECT SORTING TEST. 1941–51.
d) WEIGL-GOLDSTEIN-SCHEERER COLOR FORM SORTING TEST. 1941–45.
e) GOLDSTEIN-SCHEERER STICK TEST. 1941–47.
  For additional information, see 5:57 (21 references); for reviews by Kate Levine Kogan, C. R. Strother (with Ludwig Immergluck), and O. L. Zangwill, see 3:41 (28 references); for an excerpt from a related book review, see 3:42.

[164]

Gordon Personal Inventory. Grades 9–16 and adults; 1956, c1955–56; 4 scores: cautiousness, original thinking, personal relations, vigor; Leonard V. Gordon; [Harcourt, Brace & World, Inc.]. *

For additional information and reviews by Benno G. Fricke and John A. Radcliffe, see 5:58 (1 reference, 2 excerpts).

[165]

Gordon Personal Profile. Grades 9–16 and adults; 1953–54, c1951–53; 5 scores: ascendancy, responsibility, emotional stability, sociability, total; Leonard V. Gordon; [Harcourt, Brace & World, Inc.]. *

For additional information and reviews by Benno G. Fricke and John A. Radcliffe, see 5:59 (16 references, 1 excerpt).

[166]

The Grassi Block Substitution Test: For Measuring Organic Brain Pathology. Mental patients; 1947–53; formerly called *Fairfield Block Substitution Test;* Joseph R. Grassi; the Author. *

For additional information, see 5:60 (5 references, 2 excerpts).

[167]

The Grayson Perceptualization Test. Detection of cortical impairment; 1950–57; Harry M. Grayson; Western Psychological Services. *

For additional information and reviews by D. Russell Davis and William Schofield, see 5:61.

[168]

Group Cohesiveness: A Study of Group Morale. Adults; 1958, c1957–58; 5 scores: satisfaction of individual motives, satisfaction of interpersonal relations, homogeneity of attitude, satisfaction with leadership, total; Bernard Goldman; Psychometric Affiliates. *

For additional information, see 5:62.

[169]

★Group Dimensions Descriptions Questionnaire: Experimental Form for Research in Testing. College and adult groups; 1956; 13 group dimensions scores: autonomy, control, flexibility, hedonic tone, homogeneity, intimacy, participation, permeability, polarization, potency, stability, stratification, viscidity; for research use only; John K. Hemphill and Charles M. Westie; distributed by Educational Testing Service. *

[170]

★Guidance Inventory. High school; 1960; identification of problems related to underachievement and need for counseling; Ralph Gallagher; the Author. *

[171]

The Guilford-Martin Inventory of Factors GAMIN, Abridged Edition. Grades 10–16 and adults; 1943–48; 5 scores: general activity, ascendance-submission, masculinity-femininity, inferiority feelings, nervousness; [J. P. Guilford and H. G. Martin]; Sheridan Supply Co. *

For additional information, see 5:63 (33 references); for a review by Hubert E. Brogden, see 4:47 (18 references); for a review by H. J. Eysenck, see 3:43 (7 references); for a related review, see 3:45.

[172]

The Guilford-Martin Personnel Inventory. Grades 10–16 and adults; 1943–
46; 3 scores: objectivity, agreeableness, cooperativeness; [J. P. Guilford and
H. G. Martin]; Sheridan Supply Co. *

For additional information, see 5:64 (27 references); for a review by Neil
Van Steenberg, see 4:48 (20 references); for a review by Benjamin Shimberg,
see 3:44 (7 references); for a related review, see 3:45.

[173]

Guilford-Martin Temperament Profile Chart. College and adults; 1934–45;
for use with *Guilford-Martin Inventory of Factors GAMIN, Abridged Edition*
(see 171), *Guilford-Martin Personnel Inventory* (see 172), and *Inventory of
Factors STDCR* (see 201); J. P. Guilford and H. G. Martin; Sheridan Supply
Co. *

For additional information and a review by R. A. Brotemarkle, see 3:45.

[174]

The Guilford-Zimmerman Temperament Survey. Grades 9–16 and adults;
1949–55; revision and condensation of *Inventory of Factors STDCR* (see 201),
Guilford-Martin Inventory of Factors GAMIN (see 171), and *Guilford-Martin
Personnel Inventory* (see 172); J. P. Guilford and Wayne S. Zimmerman;
Sheridan Supply Co. *

For additional information and a review by David R. Saunders, see 5:65 (48
references); for reviews by William Stephenson and Neil Van Steenberg, see
4:49 (5 references, 1 excerpt).

[175]

[Re Guilford-Zimmerman Temperament Survey.] G-Z Temperament Map.
Grades 9–16 and adults; 1952; interpretation aid for *Guilford-Zimmerman
Temperament Survey;* P. C. Perry; Sheridan Supply Co. *

[176]

[Re Guilford-Zimmerman Temperament Survey.]   Falsification   Scales.
Grades 9–16 and adults; 1955; supplementary keys for *Guilford-Zimmerman
Temperament Survey;* 3 scales: gross-falsification, subtle-falsification, care-
lessness-deviancy; Alfred Jacobs and Allan Schlaff; Sheridan Supply Co. *

[177]

Haggerty-Olson-Wickman Behavior Rating Schedules. Grades kgn–12;
1930; 6 scores: behavior problems, behavior rating (intellectual, physical, social, emotional, total); M. E. Haggerty, W. C. Olson, and E. K. Wickman;
[Harcourt, Brace & World, Inc.]. *

For additional information and a review by Harold E. Jones, see 40:1222 (8
references).

[178]

★**The Handicap Problems Inventory.** Ages 16 and over with physical disabilities; 1960; 4 problem area scores: personal, family, social, vocational;
George N. Wright and H. H. Remmers; [University Book Store]. *

[179]

Heston Personal Adjustment Inventory. Grades 9–16 and adults; 1949; 6
scores: analytical thinking, sociability, emotional stability, confidence, personal

relations, home satisfaction; Joseph C. Heston; [Harcourt, Brace & World, Inc.]. *

For additional information, see 5:66 (11 references); for reviews by Albert Ellis, Hans J. Eysenck, and E. Lowell Kelly, see 4:50 (2 references, 1 excerpt).

[180]

★Holland Vocational Preference Inventory, Research Edition, Third Revision. College and adults; 1959, c1953-59; 13 scores: omitted items, infrequency, acquiescence, physical activity, intellectuality, social responsibility, conformity, verbal activity, emotionality, control, aggressiveness, masculinity-femininity, status; John L. Holland; Consulting Psychologists Press, Inc. *

[181]

★The Hooper Visual Organization Test. Adults; 1957-58; organic brain pathology; H. Elston Hooper; Western Psychological Services. *

[182]

Hospital Adjustment Scale. Mental patients; 1951-53; 4 ratings by psychiatric aides or nurses: communication and interpersonal relations, self-care and social responsibility, work and recreation, total; James T. Ferguson, Paul McReynolds, and Egerton L. Ballachey; [Consulting Psychologists Press, Inc.]. *

For additional information and a review by Maurice Lorr, see 5:67 (5 references).

[183]

★How Well Do You Know Yourself? High school, college, office and factory workers; 1959-61; 19 scores: irritability, practicality, punctuality, novelty-loving, vocational assurance, cooperativeness, ambitiousness, hypercriticalness, dejection, general morale, persistence, nervousness, seriousness, submissiveness, impulsiveness, dynamism, emotional control, consistency, test objectivity; Thomas N. Jenkins, John H. Coleman (manual) and Harold T. Fagin (manual); Executive Analysis Corporation. *

[184]

*Human Relations Inventory. Grades 9-16 and adults; 1954-59; social conformity; Raymond E. Bernberg; Psychometric Affiliates. *

For additional information and reviews by Raymond C. Norris and John A. Radcliffe, see 5:68 (2 references).

[185]

The Humm-Wadsworth Temperament Scale. Adults; 1935-56; Doncaster G. Humm and Guy W. Wadsworth, Jr.; Humm Personnel Consultants. *

For additional information, see 5:69 (20 references); for reviews by H. J. Eysenck, H. Meltzer, and Lorenz Misbach of the 1940 edition, see 3:48 (31 references); for reviews by Forrest A. Kingsbury and P. E. Vernon, see 40:1223 (13 references); for a review by Daniel A. Prescott of an earlier edition, see 38:920.

[186]

Hunt-Minnesota Test for Organic Brain Damage. Chronological ages 16-70 and mental ages 8 and over; 1943; 16 tests grouped in 3 divisions: the vocabulary test of Revised Stanford-Binet Intelligence Scale (see 909), interpolated tests, learning and recall; Howard F. Hunt; University of Minnesota Press. *

For additional information and a review by Seymour G. Klebanoff, see 4:51 (8 references); for reviews by Margaret Ives and O. L. Zangwill, see 3:49 (11 references).

[187]

*The IPAT Anxiety Scale. Ages 14 and over; 1957–60; title on test is *IPAT Self Analysis Form;* 6 scores: self sentiment development, ego strength, protension or paranoid trend, guilt proneness, ergic tension, total anxiety; Raymond B. Cattell and [Ivan H. Scheier]; Institute for Personality and Ability Testing. *

For additional information and reviews by J. P. Guilford and E. Lowell Kelly, see 5:70 (2 references, 1 excerpt)

[188]

★IPAT Children's Personality Questionnaire. Ages 8–12; 1959–60; title on test is *What You Do and What You Think;* 16 scores: reserved vs. easy going, less intelligent vs. more intelligent, emotionally unstable vs. emotionally mature, phlegmatic vs. excitable, submissive vs. dominant, serious vs. happy-go-lucky, frivolous vs. persevering, shy vs. venturesome, tough minded vs. tender minded, vigorous vs. internally restrained, simple vs. shrewd, complacent vs. self reproaching, lax vs. self controlled, composed vs. tense, anxiety vs. adjustment, extraversion vs. introversion; R. B. Porter and R. B. Cattell; Institute for Personality and Ability Testing. *

[189]

IPAT Contact Personality Factor Test. Grades 9–16 and adults; 1954–56; 2 scores: extraversion-introversion, distortion; Raymond B. Cattell, Joseph E. King, and A. K. Schuettler; Institute for Personality and Ability Testing. (Also published under the title *Employee Attitude Series: C.P.F.* by Industrial Psychology, Inc.) *

For additional information and reviews by Cecil D. Johnson and S. B. Sells, see 5:71 (1 reference).

[190]

★IPAT 8-Parallel-Form Anxiety Battery. Ages 16 and over; 1960; for research use only; Ivan H. Scheier and Raymond B. Cattell; Institute for Personality and Ability Testing. *

[191]

*IPAT High School Personality Questionnaire. Ages 12–18; 1953–60; formerly called *The Junior Personality Quiz;* 14 scores: schizothymia vs. cyclothymia, mental defect vs. general intelligence, general neuroticism vs. ego strength, phlegmatic temperament vs. excitability, submissiveness vs. dominance, desurgency vs. surgency, lack of rigid internal standards vs. super ego strength, threctia vs. parmia, harria vs. premsia, dynamic simplicity vs. neurasthenic self-critical tendency, confident adequacy vs. guilt proneness, group dependency vs. self-sufficiency, poor self sentiment formation vs. high strength of self sentiment, low ergic tension vs. high ergic tension; R. B. Cattell, H. Beloff, and R. W. Coan; Institute for Personality and Ability Testing. (Also published, with a manual revised for school use, under the title *Jr.-Sr. High School Personality Questionnaire* by Bobbs-Merrill Co., Inc.) *

For additional information, see 5:72 (4 references).

[192]

The IPAT Humor Test of Personality. Grades 9–16 and adults; 1949–52; formerly called *The C–L Humor Test (A Humor Rating Quiz);* 10 scores: debonair sexual and general uninhibitedness vs. anxious considerateness, good-natured play vs. dry wit, tough self-composure vs. reassurance in embarrassment, gruesomeness vs. flirtatious playfulness, hostile derogation vs. urbane pleasantness, resignation vs. impudent defiance of deceny, cold realism vs. theatricalism, ponderous humor vs. neat and lighthearted wit, whimsical retort vs. damaging retort, mistreatment humor vs. cheerful independence; R. B. Cattell, L. B. Luborsky, and [Donald Tollefson]; Institute for Personality and Ability Testing. *

For additional information and reviews by W. Grant Dahlstrom, Ardie Lubin, and J. R. Wittenborn, see 4:61 (5 references).

[193]

***IPAT Music Preference Test of Personality.** Ages 6 and over; 1952–60; 11 scores of which the following 8 are profiled: adjustment vs. frustrated emotionality, hypomanic self-centeredness vs. self-distrust and doubt, tough sociability vs. tenderminded individuality, introspectiveness vs. social contact, anxiety and concern vs. paranoid imperiousness, complex eccentricity vs. stability normality, resilience vs. withdrawn schizothymia, schizothyme tenacity vs. relaxed cyclothymia; Raymond B. Cattell and Herbert W. Eber; Institute for Personality and Ability Testing. *

For additional information and a review by Neil J. Van Steenberg, see 5:73 (4 references).

[194]

IPAT Neurotic Personality Factor Test. Grades 9–16 and adults; 1955; 2 scores: neuroticism, distortion; R. B. Cattell, J. E. King, and A. K. Schuettler; published jointly by Institute for Personality and Ability Testing and Industrial Psychology, Inc. (Industrial Psychology, Inc. distributes the test under the title *Employee Attitude Series: N.P.F.*) *

For additional information and reviews by S. B. Sells and William Stephenson, see 5:74.

[195]

★Insight Into Friction Between People. Ages 16 and over; 1948; W. H. Winkler; [Winkler Publications]. *

[196]

Institute of Child Study Security Test. Grades 4–8; 1957; title on test is *The Story of Jimmy;* 2 scores: consistency, security; Michael F. Grapko; distributed by Guidance Centre. *

For additional information and a review by Laurance F. Shaffer, see 5:75.

[197]

Interaction Chronograph. All ages; 1944–57; device for recording interaction between 2 individuals; used in a standardized interview to obtain ratings on 29 personality characteristics; Eliot D. Chapple; E. D. Chapple Co., Inc. *

For additional information and a review by Cecil A. Gibb, see 5:76 (20 references) ; see also 3:688 (5 references).

[198]

Interest Inventory for Elementary Grades: George Washington University Series. Grades 4–6; 1941; 11 scores: reading, movies, radio, games and toys, hobbies, things to own, school subjects, people, occupations, activities, total; Mitchell Dreese and Elizabeth Mooney; Center for Psychological Service. *

For additional information and reviews by Harold D. Carter and Lee J. Cronbach, see 3:52 (1 reference).

[199]

Inventory of Affective Tolerance. College and adults; 1942; Robert I. Watson and V. E. Fisher; Sheridan Supply Co. *

For additional information and reviews by Paul R. Farnsworth, E. Lowell Kelly, and William U. Snyder, see 3:54 (5 references).

[200]

★An Inventory of Certain Feelings. Applicants for employment; 1952; preoccupation with anxieties; Maurice H. Krout; distributed by Johanna Krout Tabin. *

[201]

An Inventory of Factors STDCR. Grades 9–16 and adults; 1934–46; 5 scores: social introversion-extraversion, thinking introversion-extraversion, depression, cycloid disposition, rhathymia; J. P. Guilford; Sheridan Supply Co. *

For additional information, see 5:78 (28 references); for a review by Hubert E. Brogden, see 4:59 (17 references); for a review by H. J. Eysenck, see 3:55 (10 references); for a related review, see 3:45.

[202]

★Inventory of Interest and Temperament Areas. Grades 9–12 and adults; [1941]–59; revision of an unpublished inventory by S. N. Stevens; 14 scores: variety, nervousness, carelessness, people, emotionality, thinking, detail, records, physical action, indecision, confidence, anti-conversational beliefs, sociable beliefs, total; W. H. Winkler; [Winkler Publications]. *

[203]

★It Scale for Children. Ages 5–6; 1956; sex role preference; for research use only; Daniel G. Brown; Psychological Test Specialists. *

[204]

Johnson Temperament Analysis. Grades 12–16 and adults; 1941–45; 9 scores: nervous-composed, depressive-gay-hearted, active-quiet, cordial-cold, sympathetic-hard-boiled, subjective-objective, aggressive-submissive, critical-appreciative, self-mastery-impulsive; Roswell H. Johnson; California Test Bureau. *

For additional information and a review by Albert Ellis, see 4:62 (6 references); for a review by H. Meltzer, see 3:57.

[205]

Jones Personality Rating Scale. Grades 9–12 and adults; 1939; 8 ratings: dependability, cultural refinement, leadership, industriousness, mental alertness, thoroughness, personal appearance, ability to get along with others; Harold J. Jones; [Jones Teaching Aids]. *

[206]

KD Proneness Scale and Check List. Grades 7–12, ages 7 and over; 1950–56; William C. Kvaraceus; [Harcourt, Brace & World, Inc.]. *
a) KD PRONENESS SCALE. Grades 7–12; also called *Delinquency Proneness Scale.*
b) KD PRONENESS CHECK LIST. Ages 7 and over; ratings by teachers.
    For additional information and a review by John W. M. Rothney, see 5:79 (6 references); for reviews by Douglas Courtney and Dale B. Harris, see 4:64.

[207]

★Kessler Passive-Dependency Scale. Adults; 1953; experimental form; Sydney Kessler; the Author. *

[208]

★Knowledge of People Inventory. High school; 1946–49; W. H. Winkler; Winkler Publications. *

[209]

Kuder Preference Record—Personal. Grades 9–16 and adults; 1948–54; 6 scores: group activity, stable situations, working with ideas, avoiding conflict, directing others, verification; G. Frederic Kuder; Science Research Associates, Inc. *
    For additional information and a review by Dwight L. Arnold, see 5:80 (5 references); see also 4:65 (4 references, 1 excerpt).

[209a]

★The Leadership Ability Evaluation. Grades 9–16 and adults; 1961; social climate created in influencing others; 5 scores: laissez faire, democratic-co-operative, autocratic-submissive, autocratic-aggressive, decision pattern; Russell N. Cassel and Edward J. Stancik; Western Psychological Services. *

[210]

★The Leadership Q-Sort Test (A Test of Leadership Values). Adults; 1958; Russell N. Cassel; Psychometric Affiliates. *

[211]

★The Leiter Profile. Adult mental patients; [1959]; also called *Leiter Nomenclature Profile;* 7 categories of mental illness based upon IQ patterns on *Wechsler Adult Intelligence Scale, Leiter Adult Intelligence Scale,* and *Porteus Maze Test;* Russell Graydon Leiter; [Psychological Service Center Press]. *

[212]

★The Level of Aspiration Board. Mental ages 12.5 and over; 1942–50; J. B. Rotter; distributed by Edward Butler. *

[213]

Life Adjustment Inventory. High school; 1951; 14 scores: adjustment to curriculum, reading and study skills, communication and listening skills, social skills and etiquette, boy-girl relationships, religion-moral-ethics, functional citizenship, vocational orientation and preparation, physical and mental health, family living, orientation to science, consumer education, art appreciation and creativity, use of leisure time; J. Wayne Wrightstone and Ronald C. Doll; Acorn Publishing Co. *
    For additional information and reviews by John W. M. Rothney and Helen Shacter, see 4:67.

[214]

Life Experience Inventory. Ages 13 and over; 1957; 4 scores: childhood, social, emotional, total; Gilbert L. Betts and Russell N. Cassel; the Authors. *

For additional information and reviews by Dan L. Adler and Douglas T. Kenny, see 5:81 (1 reference).

[215]

The MACC Behavioral Adjustment Scale: An Objective Approach to the Evaluation of Behavioral Adjustment of Psychiatric Patients. Mental patients; 1957; 5 ratings: affect, cooperation, communication, total adjustment, motility; Robert B. Ellsworth; Western Psychological Services. *

For additional information and a review by Maurice Lorr, see 5:82.

[216]

***[Re MACC Behavioral Adjustment Scale.] Behavior Charting Record.** Mental patients; 1959; record form for use with *The MACC Behavioral Adjustment Scale;* F. Harold Giedt; Western Psychological Services. *

[217]

★M-B History Record. Psychiatric patients; 1957–[59]; interview questionnaire for use with family informants; Peter F. Briggs; the Author. *

[218]

The Manson Evaluation. Adults; 1948; identification of alcoholics, potential alcoholics, and severely maladjusted adults; Morse P. Manson; Western Psychological Services. *

For additional information and reviews by Charles H. Honzik and Albert L. Hunsicker, see 4:68 (4 references).

[219]

★Maudsley Personality Inventory. College and adults; 1959; 2 scores: neuroticism, extraversion; H. J. Eysenck; University of London Press Ltd. *

[220]

★Maxfield-Buchholz Scale of Social Maturity for Use With Preschool Blind Children. Infancy–6 years; 1958; revision of the *Maxfield-Fjeld Adaptation of the Vineland Social Maturity Scale;* Kathryn E. Maxfield and Sandra Buchholz; American Foundation for the Blind, Inc. *

[221]

***Memory-for-Designs Test.** Ages 8.5 and over; 1946–60; presence of brain damage; Frances Graham and Barbara Kendall; Psychological Test Specialists. *

For additional information, see 4:69 (5 references).

[222]

***Mental Health Analysis, 1959 Revision.** Grades 4–8, 7–9, 9–16, adults; 1946–59; 13 scores: close personal relationships, inter-personal skills, social participation, satisfying work and recreation, adequate outlook and goals, total assets, behavioral immaturity, emotional instability, feelings of inadequacy, physical defects, nervous manifestations, total liabilities, total; Louis P. Thorpe and Willis W. Clark; California Test Bureau. *

For additional information and reviews by William E. Coffman, Henry E. Garrett, C. M. Louttit, James Maxwell, and Douglas Spencer of the original edition, see 3:59 (1 excerpt).

[223]

Minnesota Counseling Inventory. High school; 1953–57; 9 scores: family relationships, social relationships, emotional stability, conformity, adjustment to reality, mood, leadership, validity, question; Ralph F. Berdie and Wilbur L. Layton; Psychological Corporation. *

For additional information, see 5:85 (1 excerpt).

[224]

Minnesota Multiphasic Personality Inventory, Revised Edition. Ages 16 and over; 1943–51; 14 scores: hypochondriasis, depression, hysteria, psychopathic deviate, masculinity and femininity, paranoia, psychathenia, schizophrenia, hypomania, social introversion, question, lie, validity, test taking attitude; Starke R. Hathaway and J. Charnley McKinley; Psychological Corporation. *

For additional information and reviews by Albert Ellis and Warren T. Norman, see 5:86 (496 references); for a review by Arthur L. Benton, see 4:71 (211 references); for reviews by Arthur L. Benton, H. J. Eysenck, L. S. Penrose, and Julian B. Rotter, see 3:60 (72 references, 1 excerpt); for excerpts from related book reviews, see 5:B199, 5:B200, 5:B467, and 4:72.

[225]

Minnesota Rating Scale for Personal Qualities and Abilities, [Fourth Revision]. College and adults; 1925–38; revision of *Rating Scale for Teachers of Home Economics;* Clara M. Brown [Arny]; University of Minnesota Press. *

For additional information and a review by Dorothy M. Clendenen, see 5:88 (1 reference).

[226]

*Minnesota T-S-E Inventory. Grades 13–16 and adults; 1942–57; 3 introversion-extraversion scores: thinking, social, emotional; for research use only; Catharine Evans and T. R. McConnell; distributed by Educational Testing Service. *

For additional information and reviews by Philip Eisenberg and John W. French, see 3:62 (6 references).

[227]

Mooney Problem Check List, 1950 Revision. Grades 7–9, 9–12, 13–16, adults; 1941–50; Ross L. Mooney and Leonard V. Gordon; Psychological Corporation. * For adaptations for use with nurses and with rural students, see 260 and 261.

a) JUNIOR HIGH SCHOOL FORM. Grades 7–9; 1942–50; 7 scores: health and physical development, school, home and family, money-work-the future, boy and girl relations, relations to people in general, self-centered concerns.

b) HIGH SCHOOL FORM. 1941–50; 11 scores: health and physical development, finances-living conditions-employment, social and recreational activities, social-psychological relations, personal-psychological relations, courtship-sex-marriage, home and family, morals and religion, adjustment to school work, the future-vocational and educational, curriculum and teaching procedures.

c) COLLEGE FORM. Grades 13–16; 1941–50; 11 scores: same as for high school.
d) ADULT FORM. Adults; 1950; 9 scores: health, economic security, self-improvement, personality, home and family, courtship, sex, religion, occupation.

For additional information, see 5:89 (26 references); for reviews by Harold E. Jones and Morris Krugman, see 4:73 (13 references); for reviews by Ralph C. Bedell and Theodore F. Lentz of an earlier edition, see 3:67 (17 references).

[227a]

★The Mother-Child Relationship Evaluation. Mothers; 1961; 5 scores: acceptance, overprotection, overindulgence, rejection, confusion-dominance; experimental form; Robert M. Roth; Western Psychological Services. *

[228]

★Motivation Analysis Test, Research Edition. Ages 16 and over; 1961; 10 scores: career, home, fear, narcissism, super ego, self sentiment, sex, sadism, self assertion, wife-sweetheart; R. B. Cattell, J. L. Horn, J. A. Radcliffe, and A. B. Sweney; Institute for Personality and Ability Testing. *

[229]

★Multidimensional Scale for Rating Psychiatric Patients, Hospital Form. Hospitalized patients; 1953–54; revision of the *Northport Record* by Maurice Lorr, M. Singer, and H. Zobel; 12 factor scores: retarded depression vs. manic excitement, compliance vs. resistiveness, paranoid projection, activity level, melancholy agitation, perceptual distortion, motor disturbances, submissiveness vs. grandiose expansiveness, conceptual disorganization, hysterical conversion; Maurice Lorr, R. L. Jenkins, and J. Q. Holsopple; Veterans Administration. *

[230]

★Myers-Briggs Type Indicator. Grades 9–16 and adults; 1943–58; 4 scores·extraversion vs. introversion, sensation vs. intuition, thinking vs. feeling, judging vs. perceptive; for research use only; Katharine C. Briggs and Isabel Briggs Myers; distributed by Educational Testing Service. *

[231]

★The Neuroticism Scale Questionnaire. Ages 16 and over; 1961; 5 scores: depressiveness, submissiveness, overprotection, anxiety, neuroticism total; Ivan H. Scheier and Raymond B. Cattell; Institute for Personality and Ability Testing. *

[232]

New York Rating Scale for School Habits. Grades 1–9; 1927; 9 teacher ratings: attention, neatness, honesty, interest, initiative, ambition, persistence, reliability, stability; E. L. Cornell, W. W. Coxe, and J. S. Orleans; [Harcourt, Brace & World, Inc.]. *

[233]

Northampton Activity Rating Scale. Mental patients; 1951; Isidor W. Scherer; the Author. *

For additional information, see 4:74.

[234]

★Objective-Analytic (O-A) Anxiety Battery. Ages 14 and over; 1955–60; revision of anxiety-to-achieve battery (U.I. 24) of *Objective-Analytic Personality Test Batteries* (see 235); R. B. Cattell and I. H. Scheier; Institute for Personality and Ability Testing. *

[235]

Objective-Analytic Personality Test Batteries. Ages 11–16, adults; 1955; 18
single-factor batteries (plus 4 combinations as listed below): children and
adults-competent assertiveness (U.I. 16), restraint-timidity (U.I. 17), hypomanic overcompensation (U.I. 18), critical-dominant exactness (U.I. 19), sociable willingness (U.I. 20), energetic decisiveness (U.I. 21), nervous-alert re-
activity (U.I. 22), neural reserves vs. neuroticism (U.I. 23), anxiety-to achieve
(U.I. 24), accurate realism vs. psychoticism (U.I. 25), cultured introspective
self-control (U.I. 26), apathetic temperament (U.I. 27), sociable-emotional
evasiveness (U.I. 28), sympathetic mobilization of energy (U.I. 29), stolid
super ego satisfaction (U.I. 30), adults only-wary realism (U.I. 31), schizoid
tenacity (U.I. 32), dourness (U.I. 33); Raymond B. Cattell, A. R. Baggaley,
L. Checov, E. A. Cogan, D. Flint, W. Gruen, E. Husek, T. Meeland, D. R.
Saunders, and H. Schiff; Institute for Personality and Ability Testing. *

a) THE ADULT 18 0-A BATTERY. Ages 16 and over; 18 factors (U.I. 16–33).
b) THE ADULT 12 0-A BATTERY. Ages 16 and over; 12 factors (U.I. 16–27).
c) THE CHILDREN 14 0-A BATTERY. Ages 11–16; 14 factors (U.I. 16–26, 28–30).
d) THE CHILDREN 10 0-A BATTERY. Ages 11–16; 10 factors (U.I. 16, 17, 19–23,
26, 28, 29).

For additional information and a review by H. J. Eysenck, see 5:90 (6 references).

[235a]

Ohio College Association Rating Scale. High school; no date; ratings by
teachers; Ohio College Association. *

[235b]

P-S Experience Blank: Psycho-Somatic Inventory. Late adolescents and
adults; 1938; Ross A. McFarland and Clifford P. Seitz; [Ross A. McFarland]. *

For additional information and reviews by Doncaster G. Humm and Charles
I. Mosier, see 40:1234 (2 references).

[236]

★The Pauli Test, [N.I.P.R. Edition, Experimental Form]. Ages 12 and over;
1957; volitional aspects of personality; 12 scores yielding ratings for 6 factors:
speed of work, energy and endurance, accuracy and neatness, steadiness-vari-
ability, quick adaptation and unreserved exertion, motivation; revision of *Der
Pauli-Test* by Richard Pauli; H. Reuning; National Institute for Personnel
Research. *

[237]

The Personal and Social Development Program. Grades kgn–9; 1956; form
for recording behavior incidents in 8 areas: personal adjustment, responsibility
and effort, creativity and initiative, integrity, social adjustment, sensitivity to
others, group orientation, adaptability to rules and conventions; John C. Flanagan; Science Research Associates, Inc. *

For additional information and reviews by Edward Landy and C. Gilbert
Wrenn (with Roy D. Lewis), see 5:92.

[238]

Personal Audit. Grades 9–16 and adults; 1941–45; emotional adjustment in
6 (short form) or 9 (long form) areas: seriousness, firmness, frankness, tran-
quility, stability, tolerance, and (long form only) steadiness, persistence, con-

tentment; Clifford R. Adams and William M. Lepley; Science Research Associates, Inc. *

For additional information and a review by William Seeman, see 4:75 (3 references); for a review by Percival M. Symonds, see 3:64 (9 references).

[239]

★**Personal Experience and Attitude Questionnaire.** Ages 16 and over; 1956; 7 scores: criminalism, emotional instability, inadequate personality, sexual psychopathy, nomadism, other psychopathic traits, total; for research use only; Mortimer H. Applezweig, Andrew S. Dibner, and Raymond L. Osborne; Mortimer H. Applezweig. *

[240]

Personal Index. Boys in grades 7–9; 1933; "detection of attitudes indicative of problem-behavior"; Graham C. Loofbourow and Noel Keys; Educational Test Bureau. *

For additional information and reviews by J. B. Maller and Carl R. Rogers, see 40:1237 (5 references).

[241]

The Personal Preference Scale. Ages 15 and over; 1947–54; 10 scores: active-inactive, sociable-individualistic, permissive-critical, consistent-inconsistent, efficient-inefficient, self-effacing-egocentric, masculine-effeminoid, feminine-masculinoid, emotionally mature-emotionally immature, socially mature-socially immature; Maurice H. Krout and Johanna Krout Tabin; [Johanna Krout Tabin]. *

For additional information, see 5:93 (2 references).

[242]

★**Personal Relations Inventory.** Adults; 1953; 3 scores: sado-aggression, maso-submission, difference; for research use only; Raymond E. Bernberg; the Author. *

[243]

*Personality and Interest Inventory.** Grades 4–9; 1935–59; Gertrude Hildreth; Bureau of Publications. *

For additional information and a review by Stephen M. Corey, see 40:1238 (3 references); for a review by Jack W. Dunlap, see 38:924.

[244]

The Personality Evaluation Form: A Technique for the Organization and Interpretation of Personality Data. Ages 2 and over; 1955; Charlotte Buhler and Gertrude Howard; Western Psychological Services. *

For additional information and a review by Dorothy H. Eichorn, see 5:94 (1 excerpt).

[245]

Personality Index. Adults; 1945; 6 scores: job interest, social intelligence, leadership, planning, drive, follow through; Howard K. Morgan; La Rue Printing Co. *

For additional information and a review by Benjamin Shimberg, see 3:65.

[246]

The Personality Inventory. Grades 9–16 and adults; 1931–38; 6 scores: neurotic tendency, self-sufficiency, introversion-extroversion, dominance-submission, confidence, sociability; Robert G. Bernreuter; distributed by Consulting Psychologists Press, Inc. *

For additional information, see 5:95 (40 references); for a review by Leona E. Tyler, see 4:77 (188 references); for reviews by Charles I. Mosier and Theodore Newcomb, see 40:1239 (71 references); for excerpts from related book reviews, see 38:B358 and 36:B108.

[247]

★[Re The Personality Inventory.] Carlile's Scoring Bars. 1951; for scoring *The Personality Inventory;* A. B. Carlile; the Author. *

[248]

*Personality Record (Revised). Grades 7-12; 1941–58; 7 ratings by teachers: seriousness of purpose, industry, initiative, influence, concern for others, responsibility, emotional stability; also available in combination with either the *Secondary-School Record, Revised* (see 1318) or the *Junior High School Record* (see 1311); National Association of Secondary-School Principals. *

For additional information and a review by Verner M. Sims of the original edition, see 4:78 (1 reference)

[249]

Personality Report. High school and college; ratings by instructors; 1929; Committee on Personnel Methods of the American Council on Education; the Council. *

[250]

Personality Schedule, 1929 Edition. Grades 13–16 and adults; 1928–30; neurotic tendencies; L. L. Thurstone and Thelma Gwinn Thurstone; University of Chicago Press. *

For additional information and a review by J. P. Guilford, see 40:1243 (28 references).

[251]

★The Personnel Reaction Blank. Adults; 1954; worker dependability and conscientiousness; for research use only; Harrison G. Gough; the Author. *

[252]

The Philo-Phobe. Ages 10 and over; 1943–50; interview form for obtaining and analyzing data in 4 areas: aspiration, emotion, judgment and insight, ethico-moral development; John N. Buck; [Western Psychological Services]. *

For additional information and a review by Parker Davis, Jr., see 3:66 (3 references).

[253]

Pictorial Study of Values: Pictorial Allport-Vernon. Ages 14 and over; 1957; 7 scores: aesthetic, economic, political, religious, social, theoretical, strength of liking things in general; Charles Shooster; Psychometric Affiliates. *

For additional information and reviews by Andrew R. Baggaley and Harrison G. Gough, see 5:96.

[254]

★Polyfactorial Study of Personality. Adults; 1959; 11 scores: hypochrondriasis, sexual identification, anxiety, social distance, sociopathy, depression, compulsivity, repression, paranoia, schizophrenia, hyperaffectivity; Ronald H. Stark; Martin M. Bruce. *

[255]

★[Position Response Form and Response Form.] Industry; 1958; distribution restricted to clients; William F. Reiterman, Jr.; the Author. *
a) POSITION RESPONSE FORM. Management personnel; for recording personality requirements of a job.
b) RESPONSE FORM. Job applicants; for self-rating of on-the-job personality characteristics.

[256]

The Power of Influence Test. Grades 2–13; 1958; seating preference sociometric test; Roy Cochrane and Wesley Roeder; Psychometric Affiliates. *
For additional information, see 5:97.

[257]

Practical Policy Test. Adults; 1948; also called *Test of Cynicism;* Martin F. Fritz and Charles O. Neidt; Martin F. Fritz. *
For additional information, see 5:98 (9 references).

[258]

Pre-Counseling Inventory. Ages 8–14; 1949; 2 scores: adjustment, tension; Alfred Schmieding; Concordia Publishing House. *
For additional information and a review by Charles H. Honzik, see 4:80 (1 reference).

[259]

Primary Empathic Abilities. Grades 9–16 and adults; 1957–58; 7 scores: diplomacy, industrial, with insecure people, with conscientious middle class, with lower middle class, with stable young married people, with upper social levels; Willard Kerr; Psychometric Affiliates. *
For additional information and a review by Robert L. Thorndike, see 5:99.

[260]

Problem Check List: Form for Rural Young People. Ages 16–30; 1946–48; adaptation of an earlier edition of *Mooney Problem Check List, 1950 Revision,* College Form (see 227); 10 scores: health and physical, relationship with people, citizenship, education, vocation and economic, morals and religion, personal temperament, courtship-sex-marriage, social and recreational, home and family; Ralph E. Bender, Mary Alice Price, and Ross L. Mooney; Publication Office, Ohio State University. *
For additional information, see 4:81 (2 references).

[261]

Problem Check List: Form for Schools of Nursing. Student nurses; 1945–48; adaptation of an earlier edition of *Mooney Problem Check List, 1950 Revision,* College Form (see 227); 13 scores: health and physical development, finances and living conditions, social and recreational activities, social-psychological relations, personal-psychological relations, courtship-sex-marriage, home and family, morals and religion, adjustment to school of nursing, the future-professional and educational, curriculum and school program, adjustment to human relationships in nursing, adjustment to administration of nursing care;

Luella J. Morison, Mary Alice Price, and Ross L. Mooney; Publication Office, Ohio State University. *

For additional information, see 4:82 (1 reference).

[262]

★Problems Inventory (For Guidance Purposes Only). High school; 1953–56; also called *The Guidance Inventory;* checklist of problems in 8 areas: learning, conversation, self traits, people, sensing values, enjoying life, nervousness, home; W. H. Winkler; [Winkler Publications]. *

[263]

★Psychiatric History Form. Adult mental patients; 1958; Janet E. King; Division of Psychiatry, Medical School, University of Minnesota. *

[264]

★Psychometric Behavior Checklist. Adults; 1960; for recording unusual test-taking behavior; University Counseling Center, University of Maryland; the Center. *

[265]

★The Psychotic Reaction Profile (PRP): An Inventory of Patient Behavior for Use by Hospital Personnel. Mental patients; 1961; ratings by nurses or psychiatric aides; 4 scores: withdrawal, thinking disorganization, paranoid belligerence, agitated depression; Maurice Lorr, James P. O'Connor, and John W. Stafford; Western Psychological Services. *

[266]

Pupil Adjustment Inventory. Grades kgn–12; 1957; ratings in 7 areas: academic, social, emotional, physical, activities and interests, school's influence on pupil, home background; Houghton Mifflin Co. *

For additional information and reviews by Robert H. Bauernfeind and John Pierce-Jones, see 5:100 (1 excerpt).

[267]

*The Purdue Master Attitude Scales. Grades 7–16; 1934–60; 9 scales; *a–h* have space for insertion of any 5 attitude variables; series title for the first 8 scales was formerly listed as *Generalized Attitude Scales;* H. H. Remmers and others; University Book Store. *

a) A SCALE TO MEASURE ATTITUDE TOWARD ANY SCHOOL SUBJECT. 1934–60.

b) A SCALE FOR MEASURING ATTITUDES TOWARD ANY VOCATION. 1934–60.

c) A SCALE FOR MEASURING ATTITUDE TOWARD ANY INSTITUTION. 1934–60.

d) A SCALE FOR MEASURING ATTITUDE TOWARD ANY DEFINED GROUP. 1934–60; revision of *A Scale for Measuring Attitude Toward Races and Nationalities.*

e) A SCALE FOR MEASURING ATTITUDES TOWARD ANY PROPOSED SOCIAL ACTION. 1935–60.

f) A SCALE FOR MEASURING ATTITUDES TOWARD ANY PRACTICE. 1934–60.

g) A SCALE FOR MEASURING ATTITUDE TOWARD ANY HOME-MAKING ACTIVITY. 1934–60.

h) A SCALE FOR MEASURING INDIVIDUAL AND GROUP "MORALE." 1936–60.

i) HIGH SCHOOL ATTITUDE SCALE. 1935–60.

For additional information and reviews by Donald T. Campbell and Kenneth E. Clark, see 4:46 (37 references); for reviews by W. D. Commins and Theodore Newcomb, see 40:1202 (9 references); for a review by Stephen M. Corey, see 38:897; for a review by Lee J. Cronbach of *i*, see 3:46; for excerpts from related book reviews, see 40:B1050, 36:B215, and 36:B216.

[268]

The Purdue Rating Scale for Administrators and Executives. Administrators and executives; 1950–51; 36 ratings plus factor scores; H. H. Remmers and R. L. Hobson; [University Book Store]. *

a) REPORT FORM A. College administrators; 3 factor scores: fairness to subordinates, administrative achievement, democratic orientation.

b) REPORT FORM B. Business executives; 2 factor scores: social responsibility for subordinates and society, executive achievement.

c) REPORT FORM C. School administrators.

For additional information and reviews by John P. Foley, Jr. and Herbert A. Tonne, see 5:101 (1 reference); for a review by Kenneth L. Heaton, see 4:83 (7 references).

[269]

Rating Scale for Pupil Adjustment. Grades 3–9; 1950–53; [Gwen Andrew, Samuel W. Hartwell, Max L. Hutt, and Ralph E. Walton]; Science Research Associates, Inc. * For a complementary test, see 365.

For additional information and reviews by William E. Henry and Morris Krugman, see 5:102.

[270]

Report Form on Temperament and Social Behavior. Ages 2–7; 1940; for recording observations; C. W. Valentine; the Author. *

For additional information, see 40:1247 (1 reference).

[271]

★Russell Sage Social Relations Test. Classroom groups in grades 3–6; [1956]; group problem solving skills; for research use only; Dora E. Damrin; Educational Testing Service. *

[272]

★Rutgers Social Attribute Inventory. Adults; 1959; ratings of others on 24 traits: good natured-stubborn, intelligent-unintelligent, tense-relaxed, strongweak, childish-mature, old fashioned-modern, dominating-submissive, thin-fat, adventurous-cautious, lazy-ambitious, optimistic-pessimistic, masculine-feminine, young-old, responsible-irresponsible, crude-refined, tall-short, suspicious-trusting, talkative-quiet, thrifty-wasteful, dependent-self reliant, unsympathetic-sympathetic, good looking-plain, conventional-unconventional, rich-poor; William D. Wells; Psychometric Affiliates. *

[273]

SAQS Chicago Q Sort. College and adults; 1956–57; Raymond Corsini; Psychometric Affiliates. *

For additional information and reviews by William Stephenson and Clifford H. Swensen, Jr., see 5:103 (2 references).

[274]

SRA Junior Inventory. Grades 4–8; 1951–57; 5 scores: school, home, myself, people, health (Form A), general (Form S); H. H. Remmers and Robert H. Bauernfeind; Science Research Associates, Inc. *

For additional information and a review by Warren R. Baller, see 5:104 (2 excerpts); for a review by Dwight L. Arnold of Form A, see 4:90.

[275]

★SRA Survey of Interpersonal Values. Grades 9–16 and adults; 1960; 6 scores: support, conformity, recognition, independence, benevolence, leadership; Leonard V. Gordon; Science Research Associates, Inc. *

[276]

SRA Youth Inventory. Grades 7–12; 1949–56; 9 scores: school, future, myself, people, home, dates and sex, health, general, basic difficulty; H. H. Remmers, Benjamin Shimberg, and Arthur J. Drucker; Science Research Associates, Inc. *

For additional information, see 5:105 (12 references); for reviews by Kenneth E. Clark and Frank S. Freeman, see 4:91 (7 references).

[277]

★[School Characteristics Indexes.] Grades 9–13, 13–16, adults; 1957–61; environmental press; 30 press scores for each index: abasement, achievement, adaptiveness, affiliation-rejection, aggression-blame avoidance, change-sameness, conjunctivity-disjunctivity, counteraction-inferiority avoidance, deference, dominance, ego achievement, emotionality-placidity, energy-passivity, exhibitionism-inferiority avoidance, fantasied achievement, harm avoidance, humanism, impulsion-deliberation, narcissism, nurturance-rejection, objectivity, order, play, pragmatism, reflectiveness, scientism, sentience, sex-prudery, succorance-autonomy, understanding; distributed by Psychological Research Center. * For a related entry, see 296.

a) HIGH SCHOOL CHARACTERISTICS INDEX. Grades 9–13; 1960; experimental form; George G. Stern, John Dopyera, Vernon Woolston, Eva K. Woolfolk, and James Lyons.

b) COLLEGE CHARACTERISTICS INDEX. Grades 13–16; 1957–58; George G. Stern and C. Robert Pace.

c) EVENING COLLEGE CHARACTERISTICS INDEX. Adults; 1961; experimental form; George G. Stern, Clifford L. Winters, Jr., N. Sidney Archer, and Donald L. Meyer.

[278]

The School Inventory. High school; 1936; attitudes toward teachers and school; Hugh M. Bell; distributed by Consulting Psychologists Press, Inc. *

For additional information and a review by Ross W. Matteson, see 4:84 (3 references); for reviews by Robert G. Bernreuter and J. B. Maller, see 40:1252 (4 references); for related book reviews, see 40:B842, 38:B309, and 36:B30. and 36:B30.

[279]

★School Motivation Analysis Test, Research Edition. Ages 11–16; 1961; 15 scores: gregariousness, pugnacity, assertion, protectiveness, sex, curiosity, play-phantasy, narcissism, sensuality, construction, self sentiment, patriotism, religion, acquisitiveness, super ego; Arthur B. Sweney and Raymond B. Cattell; Institute for Personality and Ability Testing. *

[280]

Schrammel-Gorbutt Personality Adjustment Scale. Grades 7–16 and adults; 1943; H. E. Schrammel and Dorothy Gale Gorbutt; Bureau of Educational Measurements. *

For additional information and reviews by Raleigh M. Drake and Nelson G. Hanawalt, see 3:92.

[281]

The Science Research Temperament Scale. Grades 12–16 and adults; 1955; traits associated with research productivity; William C. Kosinar; Psychometric Affiliates. *

For additional information and reviews by John D. Black and David R. Saunders, see 5:106 (1 reference).

[282]

Security-Insecurity Inventory. Grades 9–16 and adults; 1945–52; title on test is *The S-I Inventory;* A. H. Maslow, E. Birsh, I. Honigmann, F. McGrath, A. Plason, and M. Stein; distributed by Consulting Psychologists Press, Inc. *

For additional information and reviews by Nelson G. Hanawalt and Harold Webster, see 5:107 (10 references).

[283]

Self-Analysis Inventory. Adults; 1945; title on test is *"How'm I Doin'?";* interviewing aid for locating maladjustment in 37 problem areas; Harry J. Baker; Public School Publishing Co. *

For additional information and reviews by Warren R. Baller and John W. Gustad, see 5:108.

[284]

★Self-Interview Inventory. Adult males; 1958; 10 scores: current complaints, emotional insecurity, guilt feelings, composite neurotic, prepsychotic or psychotic, behavior problems, childhood illness, composite maladjustment, validation (lack of carefulness, lack of truthfulness); H. Birnet Hovey; Psychometric Affiliates. *

[285]

Self-Perception Inventory: An Adjustment Survey With Special Reference to the Speech Situation. High school and college; 1940–54; formerly called *Personal-Social Adjustment Inventory;* 8 scores: self-centered introversion, objective introversion, self-centered extroversion, objective extroversion, self-centeredness, objectivity, introversion, extroversion; Lawrence W. Miller and Elwood Murray; University of Denver Bookstores. *

For additional information and a review by C. R. Strother, see 5:109.

[286]

Sense of Humor Test, Second Edition. Ages 16 and over; 1939–43; A. A. Roback; Sci-Art Publishers. *

[287]

The Sherman Mental Impairment Test. Adults; 1955–57; 2 scores: letter finding, reaction time; Murray H. Sherman; Western Psychologcial Services. *

For additional information and reviews by D. Russell Davis and William Schofield, see 5:110 (1 reference).

[288]

Shipley-Institute of Living Scale for Measuring Intellectual Impairment. Adults; 1939–46; formerly called *Shipley-Hartford Retreat Scale for Measuring*

Intellectual Impairment; 4 scores: vocabulary, abstractions, total, conceptual quotient; Walter C. Shipley; distributed by Mrs. Walter C. Shipley. *

For additional information, see 5:111 (23 references); for reviews by E. J. G. Bradford, William A. Hunt, and Margaret Ives, see 3:95 (26 references).

[289]

*Sixteen Personality Factor Questionnaire. Ages 16 and over; 1949–60; 16 or 17 scores: aloof vs. warm-outgoing; dull vs. bright, emotional vs. mature, submissive vs. dominant, glum-silent vs. enthusiastic, casual vs. conscientious, timid vs. adventurous, tough vs. sensitive, trustful vs. suspecting, conventional vs. eccentric, simple vs. sophisticated, confident vs. insecure, conservative vs. experimenting, dependent vs. self-sufficient, lax vs. controlled, stable vs. tense, motivational distortion scale (optional); R. B. Cattell, D. R. Saunders, and G. Stice; Institute for Personality and Ability Testing. (Also published, under the title *Employee Attitude Series: 16 P.F.,* by Industrial Psychology, Inc.) *

For additional information and a review by C. J. Adcock, see 5:112 (21 references); for reviews by Charles M. Harsh, Ardie Lubin, and J. Richard Wittenborn, see 4:87 (8 references).

[290]

★A Social Competence Inventory for Adults. Adults; 1960; behavior checklist for use with mentally retarded and senile persons; Katharine M. Banham; Family Life Publications, Inc. *

[291]

Social Intelligence Test: George Washington University Series, Revised Form. Grades 9–16 and adults; 1930–49; F. A. Moss, Thelma Hunt, K. T. Omwake, and L. G. Woodward; Center for Psychological Service. *

a) SECOND EDITION. 1930–49; 6 scores: judgment in social situations, recognition of the mental state of the speaker, memory for names and faces, observation of human behavior, sense of humor, total.

b) SHORT EDITION. 1944; 5 scores: same as for second edition except for memory for names and faces.

c) SP (SPECIAL) EDITION. 1947; 3 scores: judgment in social situations, observation of human behavior, total.

For additional information, see 4:89 (7 references); for reviews by Glen U. Cleeton and Howard R. Taylor, see 3:96 (9 references); for a review by Robert L. Thorndike, see 40:1253 (20 references).

[292]

Social Personality Inventory for College Women. College women; 1942; self-esteem; A. H. Maslow; distributed by Consulting Psychologists Press, Inc. *

For additional information and a review by Nelson G. Hanawalt, see 3:97 (10 references).

[293]

★Spiral Aftereffect Test. Ages 5 and over; 1958; detection of brain damage; Psychological Research & Development Corporation. *

[294]

★Stanford Hypnotic Susceptibility Scale. College and adults; 1959; André M. Weitzenhoffer and Ernest R. Hilgard; Consulting Psychologists Press, Inc. *

[295]

★[Stereopathy-Acquiescence Schedule.] College; [1960]; title on test booklets is *SSRC S-A Schedule;* 2 parts, 13 scores for each: stereopathic (violent
categorical, violent qualified, moderate categorical, moderate qualified, total),
nonstereopathic (same as for stereopathic plus antiviolent categorical, antiviolent qualified), total; for research use only; George Stern, Nevitt Sanford,
Hugh Lane, Harold Webster, and Richard Christie; distributed by Psychological
Research Center. *
a) FORM I [IDEOLOGICAL].
b) FORM P [PERSONALITY].

[296]

★Stern Activities Index. Grades 7-16 and adults; 1950–58; 30 need scores:
abasement, achievement, adaptiveness, affiliation-rejection, aggression-blame
avoidance, change-sameness, conjunctivity-disjunctivity, counteraction-inferiority avoidance, deference, dominance, ego achievement, emotionality-placidity,
energy-passivity, exhibitionism-inferiority avoidance, fantasied achievement,
harm avoidance, humanism, impulsion-deliberation, narcissism, nurturance-rejection, objectivity, order, play, pragmatism, reflectiveness, scientism, sentience,
sex-prudery, succorance-autonomy, understanding; George G. Stern; distributed
by Psychological Research Center. * For a related entry, see 277.

[297]

★Straus Rural Attitudes Profile. Adults; 1956–59; 5 scores: innovation proneness, rural life preference, primary group preference, economic motivation, total;
Murray A. Straus; Washington State University. *

[298]

★A Study of Choices. Ages 16 and over; 1948; 16 scores: 12 value scores (intellectual activity, home life, social service, personal improvement, friends, security, political power, comfort, excitement, wealth, society, religion) and 4
derived scores; Asahel D. Woodruff; the Author. *

[299]

*Study of Values: A Scale for Measuring the Dominant Interests in Per-
sonality, Third Edition. Grades 13 and over; 1931–60; 6 scores: theoretical,
economic, aesthetic, social, political, religious; Gordon W. Allport, Philip E.
Vernon, and Gardner Lindzey; Houghton Mifflin Co. *
   For additional information and a review by N. L. Gage of the Second Edition, see 5:114 (57 references); for reviews by Harrison G. Gough and William
Stephenson, see 4:92 (25 references, 1 excerpt); for a review by Paul E. Meehl
of the original edition, see 3:99 (61 references).

[300]

★Style of Mind Inventory: Trait, Value and Belief Patterns in Greek,
Roman and Judeo-Christian Perspectives. College and adults; 1958–61,
c1957–61; formerly called *The Fetler Test;* 3 scores (Greek, Roman, Judeo-
Christian) in each of 3 areas (traits, values, beliefs); Daniel Fetler; the Author. *

[301]

★Survey of Personal Attitude "SPA" (With Pictures): Individual Placement Series (Area III). Adults; 1960; 3 scores: social attitude, personal frankness, aggressiveness; for research use only; J. H. Norman; the Author. *

[302]

★**Syracuse Scales of Social Relations.** Grades 5–6, 7–9, 10–12; 1958–59; pupil ratings of need interactions with classmates and others; Eric F. Gardner and George Thompson; [Harcourt, Brace & World, Inc.]. *
a) ELEMENTARY LEVEL. Grades 5–6; 2 scores: succorance, achievement-recognition.
b) JUNIOR HIGH LEVEL. Grades 7–9; 2 scores: succorance, deference.
c) SENIOR HIGH LEVEL. Grades 10–12; 2 scores: succorance, playmirth.

[303]

Temperament and Character Test. College and adults; 1950–52; 11 scores: nervous, sentimental, choleric, passionate, sanguine, phlegmatic, amorphous, apathetic, emotivity, activity, perseveration; Institut pédagogique Saint-Georges. *
For additional information, see 5:115.

[303a]

★**Temperament Comparator.** Adults; 1958–61; revision of *Paired Comparison Temperament Schedule;* 18 trait scores (calm, cautious, decisive, demonstrative, emotionally stable, energetic, enthusiastic, even-tempered, lively, persevering, prompt starter, quick worker, seeks company, self-confident, serious, socially at ease, steady worker, talkative) and 5 factor scores (controlled vs. outgoing, stable vs. unstable, self-reliant vs. dependent, excitable vs. placid, sociable vs. solitary); Melany E. Baehr and R. W. Pranis; Education-Industry Service.*

[303b]

Test for Developmental Age in Girls. Girls ages 8–18; 1933–34; social maturity; test material must be reproduced from the manual, *A Scale for Measuring Developmental Age in Girls;* Celestine Sullivan; Catholic University of America Press. *
For additional information, see 38:1140; for an excerpt from a review of the manual, see 38:B495.

[304]

★**Test of Basic Assumptions.** Adults; 1959, c1957–59; 12 scores: 3 attitude scores (realist, idealist, pragmatist) for each of 4 "life areas" (organization of effort and problem solving, human abilities and the individual, general philosophy of life, economics and business); for research use only; James H. Morrison and Martin Levit; James H. Morrison. *

[305]

★**Test of Behavioral Rigidity, Research Edition.** Adolescents and adults; 1960, c1956–60; 4 scores: motor-cognitive rigidity, personality-perceptual rigidity, psychomotor speed, total; K. Warner Schaie; Consulting Psychologists Press, Inc. *

[306]

Test of Personality Adjustment. Ages 9–13; 1931; 5 scores: personal inferiority, social maladjustment, family maladjustment, daydreaming, total; Carl R. Rogers; Association Press. *
For additional information and reviews by Dan L. Adler and Harrison G. Gough, see 5:117 (19 references); for a review by C. M. Louttit, see 40:1258.

[307]

★**Test of Social Insight.** Grades 6–12, 13–16 and adults; 1959; 6 scores: withdrawal, passivity, cooperation, competition, aggression, total; Russell N. Cassel; Martin M. Bruce. *

[308]

★**Test of Work Competency and Stability.** Ages 21 and over; 1960; for predicting work capacity and identifying persons psychologically incapable of work; interview questionnaire (ego strength and, optionally, occupational stability) and 4 or 6 tests: 2 perceptual tests of intelligence (digits backward, picture arrangement), 2 psychomotor tests (tapping, steadiness), and (optionally) stress test (mirror drawing), digit symbol; A. Gaston Leblanc; Institut de Recherches Psychologiques. *

[309]

Thurstone Temperament Schedule. Grades 9–16 and adults; 1949–53; 7 scores: active, vigorous, impulsive, dominant, stable, sociable, reflective; L. L. Thurstone; Science Research Associates, Inc. *

For additional information and a review by Neil J. Van Steenberg, see 5:118 (12 references); for reviews by Hans J. Eysenck, Charles M. Harsh, and David G. Ryans, see 4:93 (1 excerpt).

[310]

★**Tucson YMCA Character Rating Scale.** Boys ages 12–17; 1958–59; ratings by youth group leaders; 18 ratings in 6 areas: justice or fairness, idealism, creativity, truth-seeking, inner consistency, respect or reverence; Character Guidance Committee, Lighthouse Branch, Tucson YMCA; Youth Character Research Institute. *

[311]

Tulane Factors of Liberalism-Conservatism. Social science students; 1946–55; 5 scores: political, economic, religious, social, aesthetic; Willard A. Kerr; Psychometric Affiliates.*

For additional information and reviews by Donald T. Campbell and C. Robert Pace, see 5:119 (2 references).

[312]

★**[VC Personality Test Battery.]** College women; 1956–57; 2 tests, 10 scores: total of *a* and *b* and 9 scores listed below; for research use only; Mary Conover Mellon Foundation. *

a) VC ATTITUDE INVENTORY. 1957; 7 scores: social maturity, developmental status, impulse expression, dominance and confidence, social integration, repression and suppression, masculine role; Nevitt Sanford and Harold Webster.

b) VC FIGURE PREFERENCE TEST. 1956–57; 2 scores: complex preference, masculine preference; Harold Webster.

[313]

★**Verbal Language Development Scale.** Birth to age 15; 1958–59; extension of the communication section of the *Vineland Social Maturity Scale* (see 314); Merlin J. Mecham; Educational Test Bureau. *

[314]

Vineland Social Maturity Scale. Birth to maturity; 1935–53; Edgar A. Doll; Educational Test Bureau. *

For additional information, see 5:120 (15 references) ; for reviews by William M. Cruickshank and Florence M. Teagarden, see 4:94 (21 references) ; for reviews by C. M. Louttit and John W. M. Rothney, see 3:107 (58 references, 1 excerpt) ; for reviews by Paul H. Furfey, Elaine F. Kinder, and Anna S. Starr of an experimental form, see 38:1143; for excerpts from related book reviews, see 5:B121.

[315]

★**The Visual-Verbal Test: A Measure of Conceptual Thinking.** Schizophrenic patients; 1959–60; Marvin J. Feldman and James Drasgow; Western Psychological Services. *

[316]

★**WLW Personal Attitude Inventory, Fifth Edition.** Business and industry; 1954–60; 6 scores: emotional stability, friendliness, aggressiveness, humility and insight, reliability, leadership; R. W. Henderson; William, Lynde & Williams. *

[317]

Washburne Social-Adjustment Inventory. Ages 12 and over; 1932–40; 9 scores: truthfulness, happiness, alienation, sympathy, purpose, impulse-judgment, control, wishes, total; John N. Washburne; [Harcourt, Brace & World, Inc.]. *

For additional information and a review by William Seeman, see 4:95 (12 references) ; see also 3:110 (11 references, 2 excerpts) and 40:1262 (4 references) ; for a review by Daniel A. Prescott of an earlier edition, see 38:928.

[318]

A Weighted-Score Likability Rating Scale. Ages 6 and over; 1946; 10 ratings: honesty, cooperation, courtesy, responsibility, initiative, industry, attentiveness, enthusiasm, perseverance, willingness; A. B. Carlile; the Author. *

For additional information, see 5:121.

[319]

★**Welsh Figure Preference Test, Research Edition.** Ages 6 and over; 1959, c1949–59; 27 scores: don't like total, repeat, conformance, *Barron-Welsh Art Scale,* revised art scale, male-female, neuropsychiatric, children, movement, 5 sex symbol scores, and 13 figure-structure preference scores; George S. Welsh; Consulting Psychologists Press, Inc. *

[320]

What I Like to Do: An Inventory of Children's Interests. Grades 4–7; 1954–58; 8 scores: art, music, social studies, active play, quiet play, manual arts, home arts, science; Louis P. Thorpe, Charles E. Meyers, and Marcella Ryser Sea [Bonsall] ; Science Research Associates, Inc. *

For additional information and reviews by John W. M. Rothney and Naomi Stewart, see 5:122 (1 excerpt).

[321]

★**William, Lynde & Williams Analysis of Personal Values, Second Edition.** Business and industry; 1958–60; 6 scores: theoretical, practical, social, personal power, aesthetic, mystic; R. W. Henderson; William, Lynde & Williams. *

[322]

Wilson Scales of Stability and Instability. Grades 9–16 and adults; 1941; 2 scores: stability, instability; Matthew H. Wilson; Bureau of Educational Measurements. *

For additional information and reviews by Paul E. Meehl and Katherine W. Wilcox, see 3:112.

[323]

The Wishes and Fears Inventory. Ages 4–8, 8–16; 1949; 8 scores: wishes, positive identifications, negative identifications, desired activities, undesired activities, changes desired in oneself, fears, earliest recollection; Martin L. Reymert; Mooseheart Laboratory for Child Research. *

For additional information, see 4:97.

[324]

Wittenborn Psychiatric Rating Scales. Mental patients; 1955; 9 ratings: acute anxiety, conversion hysteria, manic, depressed, schizophrenic, paranoid, paranoid schizophrenic, hebephrenic schizophrenic, phobic compulsive; J. Richard Wittenborn; Psychological Corporation. *

For additional information and reviews by H. J. Eysenck and Maurice Lorr, see 5:123 (15 references, 1 excerpt).

PROJECTIVE

[325]

The Auditory Apperception Test. Grades 9 and over; 1953; Western Psychological Services. *

For additional information and reviews by Kenneth L. Bean and Clifford H. Swensen, Jr., see 5:124 (3 references).

[326]

★**The Behavioral Complexity Test: A Test for Use in Research.** Ages 5 and over; 1955–61; revision of *The Adult-Child Interaction Test;* 7 scores: continuum (weighted total of scores for 5 complexity of response categories), highest category attained, symbolization (card stimuli, added stimuli), emotional expression (positive, negative, total); Theron Alexander; distributed by Campus Stores. *

For additional information concerning the earlier test, see 5:B31 (1 excerpt).

[327]

*[Bender-Gestalt Test.] Ages 4 and over; 1938–60.
a) VISUAL MOTOR GESTALT TEST. 1938–46; Lauretta Bender; American Orthopsychiatric Association, Inc. *
b) REVISED BENDER-GESTALT TEST. 1944–60; Max L. Hutt and Gerald J. Briskin; Grune & Stratton, Inc. *

For additional information concerning the original test, see 5:172 (118 references); for reviews by Arthur L. Benton and Howard R. White, see 4:144 (34 references); see also 3:108 (8 references); for excerpts from related book reviews, see 5:B330, 4:145, 3:109, and 40:B843.

[328]

The Blacky Pictures: A Technique for the Exploration of Personality Dynamics. Ages 5 and over; 1950; psychosexual development; Gerald S. Blum; Psychological Corporation. *

For additional information and a review by Kenneth R. Newton, see 5:125 (38 references, 1 excerpt); for a review by Albert Ellis, see 4:102 (7 references, 3 excerpts).

[329]

***Children's Apperception Test.** Ages 3–10; 1949–61; Leopold Bellak and Sonya Sorel Bellak; C.P.S. Co. *

a) CHILDREN'S APPERCEPTION TEST, FOURTH EDITION. 1949–61.

b) CHILDREN'S APPERCEPTION TEST—SUPPLEMENT. 1952–55.

For additional information and reviews by Douglas T. Kenny and Albert I. Rabin of the second edition, see 5:126 (15 references); for reviews by John E. Bell and L. Joseph Stone, see 4:103 (2 references, 5 excerpts); for excerpts from related book reviews, see 5:B63.

[330]

★**The Color- and Form-Personality Perceptual Personality Test.** Ages 7 and over; 1959; Sylvia S. Honkavaara; Color Institute. *

[331]

Controlled Projection for Children, Second Edition. Ages 6–12; 1945–51; John C. Raven; H. K. Lewis & Co. Ltd. * (United States distributor: Psychological Corporation.)

For additional information, see 5:127 (8 references, 3 excerpts); for reviews by Arthur L. Benton and Percival M. Symonds of the original edition, see 3:29 (5 excerpts).

[332]

Curtis Completion Form. Grades 11–16 and adults; 1950–53; emotional maturity and adjustment; James W. Curtis; Science Research Associates, Inc. *

For additional information and a review by Alfred B. Heilbrun, Jr., see 5:128 (1 reference).

[333]

Draw-A-Person Quality Scale. Ages 16–25; 1955; level of intellectual functioning; Mazie Earle Wagner and Herman J. P. Schubert; Herman J. P. Schubert. *

For additional information and a review by Philip L. Harriman, see 5:129 (3 references).

[334]

The Drawing-Completion Test: A Projective Technique for the Investigation of Personality. Ages 5 and over; 1952; based on the *Wartegg Test Blank;* G. Marian Kinget; Grune & Stratton, Inc. *

For additional information, see 5:130 (3 references, 4 excerpts).

[335]

★**The Driscoll Play Kit.** Ages 2–10; 1952; personality development and adjustment; Gertrude P. Driscoll; Psychological Corporation. *

[336]

The Eight Card Redrawing Test (8CRT). Ages 7 and over; 1950–57; Leopold Caligor; 8CRT. *

For additional information and reviews by Cherry Ann Clark and Philip L. Harriman, see 5:131 (6 references, 1 excerpt).

[337]

Family Relations Test: An Objective Technique for Exploring Emotional Attitudes in Children. Ages 3–7, 7–15; 1957; Eva Bene and James Anthony; distributed by National Foundation for Educational Research in England and Wales. *

For additional information and reviews by John E. Bell, Dale B. Harris, and Arthur R. Jensen, see 5:132 (1 reference).

[338]

The Five Task Test: A Performance and Projective Test of Emotionality, Motor Skill and Organic Brain Damage. Ages 8 and over; 1955; Charlotte Buhler and Kathryn Mandeville; Western Psychological Services. *

For additional information and reviews by Dorothy H. Eichorn and Bert R. Sappenfield, see 5:133 (1 excerpt).

[339]

The Forer Structured Sentence Completion Test. Ages 10–18, adults; 1957; Bertram R. Forer; Western Psychological Services. *

For additional information and reviews by Charles N. Cofer and Percival M. Symonds, see 5:134 (5 references).

[340]

The Forer Vocational Survey. "Young adolescents"; 1957; vocational adjustment; Bertram R. Forer; Western Psychological Services. *

For additional information and reviews by Benjamin Balinsky and Charles N. Cofer, see 5:135 (1 excerpt).

[341]

***Four Picture Test, Second Edition.** Ages 12 and over; 1948–58; D. J. van Lennep and R. Houwink; publisher and distributor in Holland and Belgium: Netherlands Institute of Industrial Psychology; distributor in all other countries: Martinus Nijhoff. *

For additional information and reviews by John E. Bell, E. J. G. Bradford, and Ephraim Rosen of the original edition, see 4:105 (3 references, 1 excerpt).

[342]

Franck Drawing Completion Test. Ages 6 and over; 1951–52; masculinity-femininity; Kate Franck; Australian Council for Educational Research. *

For additional information and a review by Arthur W. Meadows, see 5:136 (5 references).

[343]

The Graphomotor Projection Technique. Mental patients; 1948–54; Samuel B. Kutash and Raymond H. Gehl; C. H. Stoelting Co. *

For additional information and a review by Philip L. Harriman, see 5:137 (7 references, 2 excerpts).

[344]

★The Graphoscopic Scale: A Multi-Dimensional Projective Test of Personality. Ages 5 and over; 1956–59; 4 content categories: human, factory-made
objects, animals, houses; Justin Pikunas; [University of Detroit Bookstore]. *

[345]

★The Group Personality Projective Test. Ages 11 and over; 1961, c1958–61;
formerly called *Kahn Stick Figure Personality Test;* 7 scores: tension reduction
quotient, nurturance, withdrawal, neuroticism, affiliation, succorance, total;
Russell N. Cassel and Theodore C. Kahn; Psychological Test Specialists. *

[346]

★[Group] Picture Impressions. Groups of 3–12 people (ages 17–30); 1953;
group cohesiveness; Lester Libo; Research Center for Group Dynamics. *
For additional information concerning the manual, see 5:B267 (2 excerpts).

[347]

Group Projection Sketches for the Study of Small Groups. Groups of 3–40
people (ages 16 and over); 1949; William E. Henry and Harold Guetzkow;
William E. Henry. *
For additional information and a review by Cecil A. Gibb, see 5:138 (1 reference); for reviews by Robert R. Holt and N. W. Morton, see 4:106.

[348]

H-T-P: House-Tree-Person Projective Technique. Ages 5 and over; 1946–
56; John N. Buck and Isaac Jolles; Western Psychological Services. *
For additional information and a review by Philip L. Harriman, see 5:139 (61
references); for reviews by Albert Ellis and Ephraim Rosen, see 4:107 (14
references, 1 excerpt); for reviews by Morris Krugman and Katherine W.
Wilcox, see 3:47 (5 references); for excerpts from related book reviews, see
5:B234.

[349]

*Holtzman Inkblot Technique. Ages 5 and over; 1958–61; 22 scores: reaction
time, rejections, location, space, form definiteness, form appropriateness, color,
shading, movement, pathognomic verbalization, integration, content (human,
animal, anatomy, sex, abstract), anxiety, hostility, barrier, penetration, balance,
populars; Wayne H. Holtzman; Psychological Corporation. *
For additional information, see 5:140 (1 reference).

[350]

Horn-Hellersberg Test. Ages 3 and over; 1945–49; based upon drawings taken
from *Horn Art Aptitude Inventory;* "capacity to function or to adapt to a given
surrounding"; Elizabeth F. Hellersberg; the Author. *
For additional information and reviews by Philip L. Harriman and T. W.
Richards, see 4:108 (5 references); for excerpts from related book reviews, see
4:109.

[351]

The Howard Ink Blot Test. Adults; 1953; James W. Howard; *Journal of
Clinical Psychology.* *
For additional information and a review by C. R. Strother, see 5:141 (3 refer-
ences, 1 excerpt).

[352]

★The IES Test. Ages 10 and over; 1956–58; 4 tests, 3 scores each for *a–c:* impulses, ego, superego; Lawrence A. Dombrose and Morton S. Slobin; Psychological Test Specialists. *
a) ARROW-DOT TEST. 1957–58; reaction to goal barriers.
b) PICTURE STORY COMPLETION TEST. 1956–58; conception of outside world.
c) PHOTO-ANALYSIS TEST. 1956–58; desired self-gratifications.
d) PICTURE TITLE TEST. 1956–58; recognition and acceptance of ego pressures; 5 scores: impulses, ego, superego, defense, superego plus defense.

[353]

An Incomplete Sentence Test for Industrial Use. Adults; 1949; George Spache; [Reading Laboratory and Clinic]. *
For additional information and a review by Benjamin Balinsky, see 5:142.

[354]

The Insight Test: A Verbal Projective Test for Personality Study. Adults; 1944–53; Helen D. Sargent; Grune & Stratton, Inc. *
For additional information and a review by Richard Jessor, see 5:143 (8 references); for excerpts from related book reviews, see 5:B370.

[355]

Interpersonal Diagnosis of Personality. Adults; 1955–58; a combination of assessment procedures consisting of the *Minnesota Multiphasic Personality Inventory,* the *Interpersonal Check List,* and the *Thematic Apperception Test* or the *Interpersonal Fantasy Test;* Timothy Leary, Rolfe LaForge, and Robert Suczek; Psychological Consultation Service. *
For additional information, see 5:144 (11 references); for excerpts from related book reviews, see 5:B261.

[356]

*Kahn Test of Symbol Arrangement. Ages 6 and over; 1949–60; Theodore C. Kahn; Psychological Test Specialists. *
For additional information and reviews by Cherry Ann Clark and Richard Jessor, see 5:145 (16 references, 1 excerpt); for a review by Edward Joseph Shoben, Jr., see 4:110 (2 references).

[357]

★The Kell-Hoeflin Incomplete Sentence Blank: Youth-Parent Relations. College and adults; 1959; Ruth Hoeflin and Leone Kell; Child Development Publications of the Society for Research in Child Development, Inc. *

[358]

Kent-Rosanoff Free Association Test. Ages 4 and over; [1910]; G. H. Kent and A. J. Rosanoff; C. H. Stoelting Co. *

[359]

★The Kessler Structured Sentence Completion Test. Adults; 1955; for research use only; Sydney Kessler; the Author. *

[360]

The Lowenfeld Kaleidoblocs. Ages 2.5 and over; 1958; Margaret Lowenfeld; Badger Tests Co., Ltd. *
For additional information, see 5:146 (2 references).

[361]

Lowenfeld Mosaic Test. Ages 2 and over; 1930–58; Margaret Lowenfeld; Badger Tests Co., Ltd. *

For additional information and a review by C. J. Adcock, see 5:147 (43 references) ; see also 4:115 (13 references) ; for excerpts from related book reviews, see 5:B274.

[362]

Machover Draw-A-Person Test. Ages 2 and over; 1949; also called *Machover Figure Drawing Test;* Karen Machover; Charles C Thomas, Publisher. *

For additional information, see 5:148 (39 references) ; for reviews by Philip L. Harriman and Naomi Stewart, see 4:111 (13 references) ; for excerpts from related book reviews, see 4:112.

[363]

Make A Picture Story. Ages 6 and over; 1947–52; Edwin S. Shneidman; Psychological Corporation. *

For additional information, see 5:149 (19 references) ; for reviews by Albert I. Rabin and Charles R. Strother, see 4:113 (19 references) ; for excerpts from related book reviews, see 4:114.

[364]

★Make A Sentence Test. Adults; 1961; 11 scoring categories: paranoid, hostile, assertive, annoyed, conventional, avoidant, depressive, anxious, self-analytic, hypochrondriac, optimistic; for experimental use only; Edgar F. Borgatta; the Author. *

[365]

The Michigan Picture Test. Ages 8–14; 1953; Gwen Andrew, Samuel W. Hartwell, Max L. Hutt, and Ralph E. Walton; Science Research Associates, Inc. * For a complementary test, see 269.

For additional information and reviews by William E. Henry and Morris Krugman, see 5:150 (7 references, 2 excerpts).

[366]

★Myokinetic Psychodiagnosis (M.K.P.). Ages 10 and over; 1951–58; English edition ('58) translated from the French edition ('51) ; Emilio Mira y Lopez; Logos Press. *

[367]

The Object Relations Technique. Ages 11 and over; 1955; Herbert Phillipson; Tavistock Publications. * (United States distributor: Quadrangle Books, Inc.)

For additional information and a review by George Westby, see 5:151 (6 references) ; for excerpts from related book reviews, see 5:B338.

[368]

★Pain Apperception Test. Adults; 1956–58; for research use only; 2 scoring categories: intensity, duration; Donald V. Petrovich; the Author. *

[369]

The Picture Impressions: A Projective Technique for Investigating the Patient-Therapist Relationship. Adolescents and adults; 1956; Lester M.

Libo; Department of Psychiatry, School of Medicine, University of Maryland. *
For additional information, see 5:152 (1 reference, 1 excerpt).

[370]

The Picture World Test. Ages 6 and over; 1955–56; Charlotte Buhler and
Morse P. Manson; Western Psychological Services. *
For additional information and a review by Walter Kass, see 5:153 (1 excerpt).

[371]

★[Psychiatric Attitudes Battery.] Adults; 1955–59; attitudes toward mental
hospitals, psychiatrists, and psychiatric treatment; 5 parts; directions for administration and scoring are presented in *J Clin Psychol* 15:260–5 Jl '59; [Marvin Reznikoff, John Paul Brady, William W. Zeller, and Omneya Souelem (*d*)];
test materials available from the Institute of Living. *
a) [PICTURE ATTITUDES TEST.] 1959.
b) [SENTENCE COMPLETION ATTITUDES TEST.] 1959.
c) [MULTIPLE CHOICE ATTITUDES QUESTIONNAIRE.] 1959.
d) [SOUELEM ATTITUDE SCALE.] 1955–59.
e) [DEGREE OF IMPROVEMENT RATING SCALE.] 1959; ratings by psychiatrists.

[372]

★**Rock-A-Bye, Baby: A Group Projective Test for Children.** Ages 5–10;
[1959]; 6 scores: self concept, jealousy index, aggression to parents, guilt
index, anxiety index, index of obsessive trends; Mary R. Haworth and Adolf
G. Woltmann; distributed by Psychological Cinema Register. *

[373]

*Rorschach. Ages 3 and over; 1921–60.
a) BEHN-RORSCHACH TEST. 1941–56; a parallel set of ink blots; Hans Zulliger;
Hans Huber. * (United States distributor: Grune & Stratton, Inc.)
b) THE BUHLER-LEFEVER RORSCHACH DIAGNOSTIC SIGN LIST AND RECORD OF THE
RORSCHACH STANDARDIZATION STUDIES FOR THE DETERMINATION AND EVALUATION OF THE BASIC RORSCHACH SCORE. 1954; Charlotte Buhler, Karl Buhler, and
D. Welty Lefever; Western Psychological Services. *
c) HARROWER'S GROUP RORSCHACH. Ages 12 and over; 1941–45; the original
Rorschach ink blots on slides; M. R. Harrower and M. E. Steiner; Psychological Corporation. *
d) HARROWER'S MULTIPLE CHOICE TEST. Ages 12 and over; 1943–45; M. R.
Harrower; Psychological Corporation. *
e) PSYCHODIAGNOSTIC INKBLOTS. 1945–60; a parallel set of ink blots; M. R.
Harrower and M. E. Steiner; Grune & Stratton, Inc. *
f) PSYCHODIAGNOSTIC PLATES, FIFTH EDITION. 1921–54; Hermann Rorschach;
Hans Huber. * (United States distributor: Grune & Stratton, Inc.)
g) RORSCHACH COMBINED LOCATION RECORD FORM. 1957; Nicholas De Palma;
the Author. *
h) THE RORSCHACH EVALOGRAPH. 1954; Morse P. Manson and George A. Ulett;
Western Psychological Services. *
i) RORSCHACH LOCATION CHARTS (BECK'S SCORING AREAS). 1951–54; Julian C.
Davis; Hans Huber. * (United States distributor: Grune & Stratton, Inc.)
j) RORSCHACH METHOD OF PERSONALITY DIAGNOSIS, REVISED EDITION. 1939–60;
record blank; Bruno Klopfer and Helen H. Davidson; [Harcourt, Brace &
World, Inc.]. *

k) THE RORSCHACH MINIATURE INK BLOTS: A LOCATION CHART. 1955; Morse P. Manson; Western Psychological Services. *

★*l*) THE RORSCHACH INDEX OF REPRESSION. 1958–60; a scoring system; Murray Levine and George Spivack; Devereaux Foundation. *

m) STRUCTURED-OBJECTIVE RORSCHACH TEST: PRELIMINARY EDITION. See 382.

★*n*) RORSCHACH: PSYCHODIAGNOSTICS SCHEMABLOCK (RECORDING BLANKS). 1947; Hans Huber. *

For additional information and reviews by Samuel J. Beck, H. J. Eysenck, Raymond J. McCall, and Laurance F. Shaffer, see 5:154 (1078 references); for a review by Helen Sargent, see 4:117 (621 references); for reviews by Morris Krugman and J. R. Wittenborn, see 3:73 (451 references); see also 40:1246 (147 references); for excerpts from related book reviews, see 5:B32, 5:B34, 5:B40-1, 5:B60, 5:B73, 5:B79, 5:B190, 5:B247-8, 5:B337, 5:B369, 5:B372, 5:B402, 4:118-28, and 3:74-91.

[374]

Rosenzweig Picture-Frustration Study. Ages 4–13, 14 and over; 1944–49; 15 scores: direction of aggression (extrapunitive, intropunitive, impunitive), type of aggression (obstacle dominance, ego-defense, need-persistence), 9 combinations of the preceding categories; Saul Rosenzweig; the Author. *

For additional information and reviews by Richard H. Dana and Bert R. Sappenfield, see 5:155 (109 references); for reviews by Robert C. Challman and Percival M. Symonds, see 4:129 (77 references).

[375]

The Rotter Incomplete Sentences Blank. Grades 9–12, 13–16, adults; 1950; Julian B. Rotter and Janet E. Rafferty; Psychological Corporation. *

For additional information, see 5:156 (18 references); for reviews by Charles N. Cofer and William Schofield, see 4:130 (6 references, 1 excerpt).

[376]

★**The Ruth Fry Symbolic Test.** Ages 14 and over; 1959–61; experimental form; Ruth Thacker Fry; C. G. Jung Educational Center. *

[377]

Self Valuation Test. Ages 7–15, adults; 1957; verbal and nonverbal projective test employing several stimuli simultaneously; John Liggett; J. & P. Bealls Ltd. *

For additional information, see 5:157 (2 references).

[378]

Sentence Completions Test. Ages 12 and over; 1940–57; revision of *Payne Sentence Completion Blank* ('29); Amanda R. Rohde; Western Psychological Services. *

For additional information, see 5:158 (1 reference); for reviews by Charles N. Cofer and Charles R. Strother of an earlier edition, see 4:131 (3 references, 1 excerpt); for excerpts from related book reviews, see 5:B358.

[379]

★**The South African Picture Analysis Test.** Ages 5–13; 1960, c1959; 8 interpretive categories: condition of hero, environmental pressure, needs, reactions, characteristics of stories (4 categories); B. F. Nel and A. J. K. Pelser; Swets & Zeitlinger. *

[380]

★**Spatial Comprehension Schedule.** Grades 9–16 and adults; 1959; experimental form; 4 scores: symmetry, perspective, motion, inadequacy; John H. Pflaum; the Author. *

[381]

★**Structured Doll Play Test.** Ages 2–6; 1959–60; David B. Lynn; Test Developments. *

[382]

Structured-Objective Rorschach Test: Preliminary Edition. Adults; 1958; also called *S-O Rorschach Test;* 15 scores (for deriving 26 traits): whole blot, major details, minor details, white space, form resemblance, poor form resemblance, human movement, animal movement, color and form resemblance, color and poor form resemblance, shading, animal figure, human figure, modal responses, rare responses; Joics B. Stone; California Test Bureau. *
    For additional information, see 5:159.

[383]

Symbol Elaboration Test. Ages 6 and over; 1950–53; Johanna Krout [Tabin]; the Author. *
    For additional information and a review by Richard H. Dana, see 5:160 (1 reference).

[384]

Symonds Picture-Story Test. Grades 7–12; 1948; Percival M. Symonds; Bureau of Publications. *
    For additional information and reviews by Walter Kass and Kenneth R. Newton, see 5:161 (2 references); for a review by E. J. G. Bradford, see 4:132 (2 references, 1 excerpt); for excerpts from related book reviews, see 4:133.

[385]

Szondi Test. Ages 4 and over; 1937–52; 8 factors, 4 vectors (each vector is a total of 2 factors): homosexual, sadistic, sexual vector, epileptic, hysteric, paroxysmal vector, catatonic, paranoic, schizophrenic vector, depressive, manic, contact vector; Lipot Szondi; Hans Huber. * (United States distributor: Grune & Stratton, Inc.)
    For additional information, see 5:162 (74 references); for reviews by Ardie Lubin and Albert I. Rabin, see 4:134 (64 references); for a review by Susan K. Deri, see 3:100; for excerpts from related book reviews, see 5:B418 and 4:135.

[386]

A Test of Family Attitudes. Ages 6–12; 1952; Lydia Jackson; Methuen & Co. Ltd. *
    For additional information and a review by John E. Bell, see 5:163 (2 references).

[387]

Thematic Apperception Test. Ages 4 and over; 1936–43; Henry A. Murray; Harvard University Press. *
    For additional information and reviews by Leonard D. Eron and Arthur R.

Jensen, see 5:164 (311 references) ; for a review by Arthur L. Benton, see 4:136 (198 references) ; for reviews by Arthur L. Benton, Julian B. Rotter, and J. R. Wittenborn, see 3:103 (101 references, 1 excerpt) ; for excerpts from related book reviews, see 5:B63, 5:B204, 5:B395, 4:137–41, 3:104, and 3:104a.

[388]

[Re Thematic Apperception Test.] Bellak TAT and CAT Blank, Short Form. Ages 3–10; 1955; form for recording and analyzing responses to the *Thematic Apperception Test* and the *Children's Apperception Test* (see 329) ; Leopold Bellak; C.P.S. Co. *

[389]

[Re Thematic Apperception Test.] Bellak TAT Blank. Ages 7 and over; 1947; for recording and analyzing responses to the *Thematic Apperception Test;* Leopold Bellak; Psychological Corporation. *

For additional information, see 4:137 (1 excerpt).

[390]

[Re Thematic Apperception Test.] TAT Summary Record Blank. 1952; for use with *Thematic Apperception Test;* Pauline G. Vorhaus; [Harcourt, Brace & World, Inc.]. *

[391]

Thematic Apperception Test for African Subjects. Ages 10 and over; 1953; S. G. Lee; University of Natal Press. *

For additional information and a review by Mary D. Ainsworth, see 5:165 (1 reference).

[392]

Thematic Apperception Test: Thompson Modification. Negroes ages 4 and over; 1949, c1943–49; Charles E. Thompson; Harvard University Press. *

For additional information and a review by Mary D. Ainsworth, see 5:166 (4 references) ; see also 4:138 (5 references, 3 excerpts).

[393]

*The Tomkins-Horn Picture Arrangement Test. Ages 10 and over; 1942–58; Silvan S. Tomkins, Daniel Horn, and John B. Miner (manual) ; Springer Publishing Co., Inc. *

For additional information and reviews by Donald W. Fiske, John W. Gittinger, and Wayne H. Holtzman, see 5:167 (6 references, 1 excerpt).

[394]

The Toy World Test. Ages 2 and over; 1941–55; formerly called *The World Test;* Charlotte Buhler; distributed by Joyce B. Baisden. *

For additional information and a review by L. Joseph Stone, see 5:168 (11 references) ; see also 4:147 (6 references).

[395]

The Travis Projective Pictures. Ages 4 and over; 1949–57; revision of *The Travis-Johnston Projective Test: For the Exploration of Parent-Child Relationships;* [Lee E. Travis]; Griffin-Patterson Co., Inc. *

For additional information and a review by Edwin S. Shneidman, see 5:169 (1 reference) ; for a review by Robert R. Holt of the original edition, see 4:142 (3 references).

[396]

The Tree Test. Ages 9 and over; 1949–52; Charles Koch; Hans Huber. *
(United States distributor: Grune & Stratton, Inc.)

For additional information, see 5:170 (2 references); for excerpts from related book reviews, see 5:B251.

[397]

Twitchell-Allen Three-Dimensional Personality Test. Ages 3 and over
(sighted and sightless); 1948–58; formerly called *Twitchell-Allen Three-Dimensional Apperception Test;* Doris Twitchell-Allen; C. H. Stoelting Co. *

For additional information, see 5:171 (3 references); for a review by Edward
Joseph Shoben, Jr., see 4:143.

ENGLISH

[398]

A.C.E.R. English Usage Tests. Ages 10–13.0; 1951; 2 scores: word usage,
sentence structure; Australian Council for Educational Research. *

For additional information and a review by J. A. Richardson, see 5:173.

[399]

Ability for English (Language): Fife Tests of Ability, Test I. Secondary
school entrants; 1947; Frank M. Earle; University of London Press Ltd. * For
the complete battery entry, see 1374.

For additional information, see 3:114 (1 reference). For reviews of the complete battery, see 4:713 and 3:8.

[400]

American School Achievement Tests: Part 3, Language and Spelling.
Grades 4–6, 7–9; 1941–58; 2 scores: language, spelling; Willis E. Pratt and
Robert V. Young; Public School Publishing Co. * For the complete battery
entry, see 2.

For additional information and reviews by M. A. Brimer and Clarence Derrick, see 5:174. For reviews of the complete battery, see 5:1, 4:1, and 3:1.

[401]

*****Analytical Survey Test in English Fundamentals.** Grades 9–13; 1932–57;
formerly called *Diagnostic Survey Test in English Fundamentals;* J. Helen
Campbell and Walter Scribner Guiler; C. A. Gregory Co. *

[402]

*****Barrett-Ryan English Test.** Grades 7–13; 1926–58; E. R. Barrett, Teresa M.
Ryan, M. W. Sanders, H. E. Schrammel, and E. R. Wood; Bureau of Educational Measurements. *

For additional information and a review by J. Raymond Gerberich, see
5:175 (1 reference).

[403]

Barrett-Ryan-Schrammel English Test, New Edition. Grades 9–13; 1938–
54; 6 scores: grammar, sentence, punctuation, vocabulary, pronunciation, total;
E. R. Barrett, Teresa M. Ryan, and H. E. Schrammel; [Harcourt, Brace &
World, Inc.]. *

For additional information and reviews by Leonard S. Feldt and Cleveland

A. Thomas, see 5:176 (1 reference) ; for reviews by G. Frederic Kuder, Robert
C. Pooley, and Charles Swain Thomas of the original edition, see 40:1267.

[404]

Basic Language Skills: Iowa Every-Pupil Tests of Basic Skills, Test C.
Grades 3–5, 5–9; 1940–47; 5 or 6 scores: punctuation, capitalization, usage,
spelling, sentence sense (elementary level only), total; H. F. Spitzer, Ernest
Horn, Maude McBroom, H. A. Greene, and E. F. Lindquist; Houghton Mifflin
Co. * For the complete battery entry, see 22.

For additional information, see 4:150; see also 3:116 (2 references). For
reviews of the complete battery, see 4:15, 3:10, and 38:872.

[405]

California Language Test, 1950 Edition. Grades 1–4.5, 4–6, 7–9, 9–14; 1933–
50; revision of *Progressive Language Tests;* subtest of *California Achievement
Tests, 1950 Edition* (see 4) ; 3 scores: mechanics of English and grammar,
spelling, total; Ernest W. Tiegs and Willis W. Clark; California Test Bureau. *
For the 1957 edition entry, see 406.

For additional information and reviews by Gerald V. Lannholm and Robert
C. Pooley, see 4:151; for reviews by Harry A. Greene and J. Paul Leonard of
an earlier edition, see 40:1292. For reviews of the complete battery, see 4:2,
3:15, 40:1193, and 38:876.

[406]

*California Language Test, 1957 Edition. Grades 1–2, 3–4.5, 4–6, 7–9, 9–14;
1933–59; subtest of *California Achievement Tests, 1957 Edition* (see 5) ; 4
scores: mechanics of English, spelling, total, handwriting; Ernest W. Tiegs
and Willis W. Clark; California Test Bureau. * For the 1950 edition entry, see
405.

For additional information and reviews by Constance M. McCullough and
Winifred L. Post, see 5:177 (3 references). For a review of the complete battery, see 5:2.

[407]

The Clapp-Young English Test: The Clapp-Young Self-Marking Tests.
Grades 5–12; 1929; Frank L. Clapp and Robert V. Young; Houghton Mifflin
Co. *

For additional information and a review by Gerald V. Lannholm, see 3:117.

[408]

College English Test: National Achievement Tests. Grades 12–13; 1937–43;
7 scores: punctuation, capitalization, language usage, sentence structure, modifiers, miscellaneous principles, total; A. C. Jordan; Acorn Publishing Co. *

For additional information and a review by Osmond E. Palmer, see 5:178; for
reviews by Constance M. McCullough and Robert W. Howard, see 40:1269.1.

[409]

***College Entrance Examination Board Advanced Placement Examination:
Literature and English Composition.** Candidates desiring credit for college
level courses or admission to advanced courses; 1954–61; program administered
for the College Entrance Examination Board by Educational Testing Service. *
For the testing program entry, see 1346.

For additional information and a review by Robert C. Pooley of Form EBP of English composition (formerly a separate test), see 5:205; for a review by John S. Diekhoff of Form FBP of literature (formerly a separate test), see 5:211.

[410]

College Placement Test in English. College; 1941–43; 8 scores: grammar, punctuation, sentence structure, reading, syntax, vocabulary, theme, total; Hector H. Lee; Turner E. Smith & Co. *

For additional information and a review by Charlotte Croon Davis, see 4:153.

[411]

College Preparatory Test in English. High school; 1943; 8 scores: grammar, sentence revision, comprehension of reading, syntax, vocabulary, sentence structure, punctuation, total; Hector H. Lee; Turner E. Smith & Co. *

For additional information and a review by Charlotte Croon Davis, see 4:154.

[412]

Columbia Research Bureau English Test. Grades 11–16; 1925–26; 5 scores: spelling, mechanical accuracy in composition, vocabulary, literary knowledge, total; Harrison R. Steeves, Allan Abbott, and Ben D. Wood; [Harcourt, Brace & World, Inc.]. *

For additional information and reviews by L. K. Shumaker and Louis C. Zahner, see 40:1270.

[413]

***Cooperative English Tests, [1960 Revision].** Grades 9–12, 13–14; 1940–60; revision of *Cooperative English Test: Lower and Higher Levels;* 6 scores: vocabulary, level of comprehension, speed of comprehension, reading total, English expression, total; subtests in reading and English available as separates (see 424 and 1436); Clarence Derrick, David P. Harris, and Biron Walker; Cooperative Test Division. *

For additional information concerning the earlier edition, see 5:179 (58 references); for a review by Chester W. Harris of Forms S, T, Y, and RX, see 4:155 (53 references); for reviews by J. Paul Leonard, Edward S. Noyes, and Robert C. Pooley of Forms R, S, and T, see 3:120 (29 references); see also 40:1276 (2 references).

[414]

***Cooperative English Test: Usage, Spelling, and Vocabulary.** Grades 7–16; 1932–51; 4 scores: usage, spelling, vocabulary, total; M. F. Carpenter, E. F. Lindquist, W. W. Cook, D. G. Paterson, F. S. Beers, and Geraldine Spaulding; Cooperative Test Division. *

For additional information and reviews by Carleton C. Jones, Jeanette McPherrin, Louis C. Zahner, Henry D. Rinsland, and L. K. Shumaker of Form PM and earlier forms, see 40:1271 (11 references); for reviews by John M. Stalnaker, Charles S. Thomas, and John H. Thompson, see 38:961.

[415]

Coordinated Scales of Attainment: English. Grades 4, 5, 6, 7, 8; 1946–54; Dora V. Smith; Educational Test Bureau. * For the complete battery entry, see 10.

For additional information, see 5:180. For reviews of the complete battery, see 4:8 and 3:6.

[416]

Correct English Usage Test. Grades 9–12; 1944; 6 scores: nouns-pronouns-verbs, adjectives-adverbs-prepositions-conjunctions, capitalization and punctuation, contractions-spelling-usage, vocabulary, total; Doris Taylor; Harlow Publishing Corporation. *

For additional information, see 4:156.

[417]

Correctness and Effectiveness of Expression. High school, college; 1944–57; subtest of *Tests of General Educational Development* (see 44); United States Armed Forces Institute; Veterans' Testing Service. *

For additional information, see 5:181; for a review by Charlotte W. Croon [Davis] of the college level, see 3:122. For reviews of the complete battery, see 5:27, 4:26, and 3:20.

[418]

Cotswold Junior English Ability Test. Ages 8–9; 1949–52; C. M. Fleming; Robert Gibson & Sons (Glasgow), Ltd. *

For additional information and reviews by M. A. Brimer and John C. Daniels, see 5:182.

[419]

***Cotswold Measurement of Ability: English.** Ages 10–12.5; 1947–59, c1947–55; C. M. Fleming and J. W. Jenkins; Robert Gibson & Sons (Glasgow), Ltd. *

For additional information and reviews by M. A. Brimer and S. C. Richardson, see 5:183.

[420]

Cross English Test. Grades 9–13; 1923–26; 9 scores: spelling, pronunciation, recognizing sentences, punctuation, verb forms, pronoun forms, idiomatic expressions, miscellaneous faulty expressions, total; E. A. Cross; [Harcourt, Brace & World, Inc.]. *

For additional information and reviews by Roland L. Beck and Edward S. Noyes, see 40:1272 (3 references).

[420a]

Diagnostic Tests in English Composition. Grades 7–12; 1923; 4 tests: Capitalization, Punctuation, Grammar, Sentence Structure; S. L. Pressey, L. C. Pressey, F. R. Conkling, E. V. Bowers, Helen Ruhlen, and Blythe Pearce; Public School Publishing Co. *

For additional information and reviews by Harry A. Greene and Jean Hoard, see 40:1274.

[421]

The Eaton Diagnostic-Accomplishment Tests in English. Grades 7–12; 1928; 11 tests on specific areas of grammar and usage; Harold T. Eaton; [Ridge Manor Publishing Co.]. *

[422]

***Eleventh Year English Fundamentals: Manchester Semester-End Achievement Tests.** 1 semester grade 11; 1934–[47]; Bureau of Tests. *

[423]

*English: Every Pupil Scholarship Test. Grades 2–4, 5–6, 7–8, 9–12; 1926–60; new form usually issued twice a year; Bureau of Educational Measurements. *

For additional information, see 5:184.

[424]

*English Expression: Cooperative English Tests, [1960 Revision]. Grades 9–12, 13–14; 1940–60; revision of *Mechanics of Expression: Cooperative English Test: Lower and Higher Levels, Test A* and *Effectiveness of Expression: Cooperative English Test: Lower and Higher Levels, Tests B1 and B2;* Geraldine Spaulding, Herbert Danzer, W. W. Cook, Janet Afflerbach, Miriam M. Bryan, Paula Thibault, and Catherine Dodd; revision by Clarence Derrick, David P. Harris, and Biron Walker; Cooperative Test Division. *

For the complete battery entry and reference to reviews, see 413.

[425]

★English IX–XII: Final District-State Scholarship Test. High School; 1938–61; Ohio Scholarship Tests. *

[426]

*English IX–XII, Form 4: Achievement Examinations for Secondary Schools. Grades 9, 10, 11, 12; 1951–59; Forms 1–3 published by Educational Test Bureau are out of print; Carl Towley, Ina Engburg, and Winifred Murray; C. A. Gregory Co. *

For additional information concerning earlier forms, see 5:185.

[427]

★English IX–XII: Preliminary District-State Scholarship Test. High school; 1947–61; Ohio Scholarship Tests. *

[428]

English: Northumberland Standardised Tests (1925 Series). Ages 10–14; [1925]; Cyril Burt; University of London Press Ltd. *

[429]

*English Progress Tests A–F. Ages 8, 8.5–10.0, 9, 10, 11, 12, 13; 1952–60; A. F. Watts and M. A. Brimer; published for the National Foundation for Educational Research in England and Wales; Newnes Educational Publishing Co. Ltd. *

For additional information and reviews by Neil Gourlay and Stanley Nisbet, see 5:187.

[430]

English Survey Test: Ohio Scholarship Tests: Ohio Senior Survey Tests. Grade 12; 1935–54; 6 scores: grammar, spelling, capitalization, punctuation, sentence structure, total; Mary H. Hutchison; Ohio Scholarship Tests. *

For additional information, see 5:188; for reviews by Charlotte W. Croon Davis and J. Paul Leonard of the original edition, see 3:125 (1 reference).

[431]

*English Test (Adv.). Ages 12–13; 1954–60; published for the National Foundation for Educational Research in England and Wales; Newnes Educational Publishing Co. Ltd. *

For additional information, see 5:189.

[432]

English Test: Municipal Tests: National Achievement Tests. Grades 3–6, 6–8; 1938–56; subtest of *Municipal Battery* (see 29); 5 scores: language usage-words, language usage-sentences, punctuation and capitalization, expressing ideas, total; Robert K. Speer and Samuel Smith; Acorn Publishing Co. *

For additional information, see 5:190. For reviews of the complete battery, see 5:18, 4:20, and 40:1191.

[433]

English Test: National Achievement Tests. Grades 3–8, 7–12; 1936–57; Robert K. Speer and Samuel Smith; Acorn Publishing Co. *
a) GRADES 3–8. 1936–38; 7 scores: capitalization, punctuation, language usage (sentences), language usage (words), expressing ideas, letter writing, total.
b) GRADES 7–12. 1936–57; 7 scores: word usage, punctuation, vocabulary, language usage (sentences), expressing ideas, expressing feeling, total.

For additional information, see 5:191; for a review by Winifred L. Post, see 4:162; for a review by Harry A. Greene, see 3:126.

[434]

***English Tests 1, 3–10.** Ages 10 to 11–11; 1951–60; G. A. V. Morgan, M. A. Brimer, and A. E. Davies; published for the National Foundation for Educational Research in England and Wales; Newnes Educational Publishing Co. Ltd. *

For additional information concerning tests 1 and 3–8, see 5:193.

[435]

English Test 2. Ages 12–13; 1952; G. A. V. Morgan; published for the National Foundation for Educational Research in England and Wales; Newnes Educational Publishing Co. Ltd. *

For additional information and reviews by Reginald Edwards, S. C. Richardson, and Cleveland A. Thomas, see 5:192.

[436]

English: Thanet Mental Tests. Ages 10–12; 1937; W. P. Alexander; University of London Press Ltd. *

For additional information and a review by C. Ebblewhite Smith, see 40:1279.

[437]

***English Usage: Every Pupil Test.** 1, 2 semesters in grades 3–4, 5–6, 7–9, 10–12; 1929–61; new form usually issued twice a year; Ohio Scholarship Tests. *

For additional information, see 5:194; for a review by J. R. Gerberich of the 1946 forms, see 3:127 (1 reference).

[438]

Essentials of English Tests. Grades 7–12; 1939–44; 6 scores: spelling, grammatical usage, word usage, sentence structure, punctuation and capitalization, total; Dora V. Smith and Constance M. McCullough; Educational Test Bureau. *

For additional information and reviews by Charlotte W. Croon Davis and Gerald V. Lannholm, see 3:128 (1 excerpt).

[439]

*Grammar: Public School Achievement Tests. Grades 6–8; 1928–59; Jacob
S. Orleans; Public School Publishing Co. * For the complete battery entry, see
33.
For additional information and reviews of the complete battery, see 40:1194.

[440]

Greene-Stapp Language Abilities Test. Grades 9–13; 1952–54; 5 scores:
capitalization, spelling, sentence structure, punctuation, usage; Harry A. Greene
and Helen I. Stapp; [Harcourt, Brace & World, Inc.]. *
For additional information and reviews by Richard A. Meade and Osmond
E. Palmer, see 5:195 (1 reference).

[441]

Hoyum-Schrammel English Essentials Tests. Grades 3–4, 5–6, 7–8; 1955–56;
Vera Davis Hoyum and H. E. Schrammel; Bureau of Educational Measurements. *
For additional information and reviews by Worth R. Jones and Ruth Strickland, see 5:196.

[442]

Iowa Grammar Information Test. Grades 7–12; 1935; Fred D. Cram and
Harry A. Greene; Bureau of Educational Research and Service. *
For additional information and a review by Robert C. Pooley, see 4:164.

[443]

Iowa Language Abilities Test. Grades 4–7, 7–10; 1948, c1946–48; H. A. Greene
and H. L. Ballenger; [Harcourt, Brace & World, Inc.]. *
a) ELEMENTARY TEST. Grades 4–7; 6 scores: spelling, word meaning, language
usage, capitalization, punctuation, total.
b) INTERMEDIATE TEST. Grades 7–10; 8 scores: same as for elementary test
plus grammatical form recognition, sentence sense.
For additional information and a review by Margaret G. McKim, see 4:165.

[444]

Iowa Placement Examinations: English Aptitude: Series EA1, Revised.
Grades 12–13; 1925–26; M. F. Carpenter and G. D. Stoddard; Bureau of Educa-
tional Research and Service. *
For additional information and reviews by Clarence Derrick and W. C.
Kvaraceus, see 4:166 (5 references); for a review by Robert C. Pooley, see
3:115 (9 references).

[445]

Iowa Placement Examinations: English Training. Grades 12–13; 1925–44;
Bureau of Educational Research and Service. *
a) SERIES ET-1, REVISED. 1925–26; M. F. Carpenter and G. D. Stoddard.
b) NEW SERIES ET-2, REVISED. 1925–44; M. F. Carpenter, G. D. Stoddard, L. W.
Miller, and D. B. Stuit.
For additional information and reviews by Clarence Derrick and W. C.
Kvaraceus, see 4:167 (5 references); for a review by Robert C. Pooley, see
3:131 (15 references).

[446]

Iowa Primary Language Test. Grades 1–3; 1936; 9 scores: filling in forms, informal conversation, oral composition, telephone conversation, correct usage, recorded composition, miscellaneous social responses, letter writing, total; Lou A. Shepherd and Harry A. Greene; Bureau of Educational Research and Service. *

[447]

*****The Iowa Tests of Educational Development: Test 3, Correctness and Appropriateness of Expression.** Grades 9–13; 1942–59; E. F. Lindquist and others; Science Research Associates, Inc. * For the complete battery entry, see 25.

For additional information, see 5:197. For reviews of the complete battery, see 5:17, 4:17, and 3:12.

[448]

Kirby Grammar Test: University of Iowa Standard Tests and Scales. Grades 7–12; 1920; Thomas J. Kirby; Bureau of Educational Research and Service. *

[449]

*****Language Arts IX–XII: Midwest High School Achievement Examinations.** Grades 9, 10, 11, 12; 1955–61; earlier forms called *English IX–XII: Midwest High School Achievement Examinations;* Educational Test Bureau. *

For additional information and a review by Roger A. Richards of earlier forms, see 5:186.

[450]

★**Language Battery: National Institute for Personnel Research High Level Battery.** Adults with at least 12 years of education; 1960–[61]; combination of tests in reading comprehension and vocabulary from *National Institute for Personnel Research High Level Battery* (see 1382); National Institute for Personnel Research.

[451]

★**Language Battery: National Institute for Personnel Research Normal Battery.** Standards 6–10 (grades 8–12) and job applicants with 8–11 years of education; 1960–[61]; combination of tests in reading comprehension, vocabulary, and spelling from *National Institute for Personnel Research Normal Battery* (see 1383); National Institute for Personnel Research.

[452]

Language Essentials Tests. Grades 4–8; 1941; 5 scores: punctuation, capitalization, sentence structure, correct usage, total; H. E. Schrammel and Vera Davis; Educational Test Bureau. *

For additional information and a review by Harry A. Greene, see 3:133.

[453]

*****Language Usage: Public School Achievement Tests.** Grades 3–8; 1928–59; Jacob S. Orleans; Public School Publishing Co. * For the complete battery entry, see 33.

For additional information and reviews of the complete battery, see 40:1194.

[454]

Linguistic Awareness Test. High school; 1938; Elmer R. Smith; Turner E. Smith & Co. *
For additional information, see 40:1287.

[455]

***Mechanics of Written English: State High School Tests for Indiana.**
Grades 9–12; 1940–[59]; 6 scores: punctuation, recognition of non-standard usage, capitalization, vocabulary, spelling, total; State High School Testing Service for Indiana. *
For additional information, see 4:169.

[456]

★Moray House English Tests. Ages 8.5–10.5, 10 to 12-0, 12 to 14-0; 1935–61; Department of Education, University of Edinburgh; University of London Press Ltd.
a) MORAY HOUSE ENGLISH TEST 2. Ages 8.5–10.5; 1952–58. *
b) MORAY HOUSE ENGLISH TEST 33. Ages 10 to 12-0; 1935–61.
c) MORAY HOUSE ENGLISH TEST (ADV. 2). Ages 12 to 14-0; 1956–58. *

[457]

Nelson's High School English Test: The Clapp-Young Self-Marking Tests.
Grades 7–12; 1931–32; 5 scores: word usage, sentence structure, grammar, punctuation, total; M. J. Nelson; Houghton Mifflin Co. *
For additional information and reviews by Frank P. De Lay and Jacob S. Orleans, see 40:1290.

[458]

The New Purdue Placement Test in English. Grades 11–16; 1931–55; 8 scores: punctuation, grammar, sentence structure, reading (study), reading (pleasure), vocabulary, spelling, total; G. S. Wykoff, J. H. McKee, and H. H. Remmers; Houghton Mifflin Co. * For the original edition entry, see 467.
For additional information and reviews by Gerald V. Lannholm and M. J. Wantman, see 5:199 (5 references).

[459]

***Ninth Year English Fundamentals: Manchester Semester-End Achievement Tests.** 1 semester grade 9; 1934–[47]; Bureau of Tests. *

[460]

***Novelty Grammar Tests, Second Revision.** High school; 1936–61; volume of 74 short tests on specific areas of grammar; Clarine Coffin and Frank Connor; J. Weston Walch, Publisher. *

[461]

★Objective Test in Constructive English. Grades 7, 8, 9, 10–12; 1955; Gunnar Horn; Perfection Form Co. *

[462]

Objective Test in Grammar. Grades 10–12; 1950; Nellie F. Falk; Perfection Form Co. *
For additional information, see 4:171.

[463]

Objective Tests in English [Grammar]. Grades 7–9; 1950; Gunnar Horn; Perfection Form Co. *

For additional information, see 4:172.

[464]

★**Objective Tests in Punctuation.** Grades 7, 8, 9, 10–12; 1955; Gunnar Horn; Perfection Form Co. *

[465]

★**The Pribble-Dallmann Diagnostic Tests in Elementary Language Skills.** Grades 3–4, 5–6, 7–8; 1948–49; tests for grades 7–8 called *Pribble-Dallmann Diagnostic Tests in Basic English Skills;* 8 scores: sentences, verbs, nouns, pronouns and modifiers, spelling, capitalization, punctuation, total; Evalin Pribble and Martha Dallmann; Lyons & Carnahan. *

[466]

★**The Pribble-McCrory Diagnostic Tests in Practical English Grammar.** Grades 9–10, 11–13; 1942–44; 8 scores: sentences, verbs, pronouns, adjectives and adverbs, nouns, redundancy, punctuation, total; Evalin E. Pribble and John R. McCrory; Lyons & Carnahan. *

[467]

The Purdue Placement Test in English: The Clapp-Young Self-Marking Tests. Grades 11–13; 1931–48; 8 scores: punctuation, grammatical classification, recognition of grammatical errors, sentence structure, reading, vocabulary, spelling, total; G. S. Wykoff, J. H. McKee, and H. H. Remmers; Houghton Mifflin Co. * For the revised edition entry, see 458.

For additional information, see 4:173 (9 references).

[468]

*****Rinsland-Beck Natural Test of English Usage.** Grades 9–13; 1934–58; 4 scores: total plus 3 scores listed below; Henry D. Rinsland, Betty Shrock Beck, and Roland L. Beck; Public School Publishing Co. *
a) TEST I [MECHANICS].
b) TEST II [GRAMMAR].
c) TEST III [RHETORIC].

For additional information and reviews by John M. Stalnaker and Charles Swain Thomas, see 40:1293 (3 references, 1 excerpt).

[469]

SRA Achievement Series: Language Arts. Grades 2–4, 4–6, 6–9; 1954–57; 3 scores: capitalization-punctuation, grammatical usage, spelling; Louis P. Thorpe, D. Welty Lefever, and Robert A. Naslund; Science Research Associates, Inc. * For the complete battery entry, see 35.

For additional information and reviews by Constance M. McCullough and Winifred L. Post, see 5:200. For reviews of the complete battery, see 5:21.

[470]

Scholastic Achievement Series: English-Spelling. Grades 2.5–3, 4–6, 7–9; 1954–55; for Catholic schools; 4 scores: punctuation and capitalization, correct usage, English total, spelling; Oliver F. Anderhalter, R. Stephen Gawkoski, and John O'Brien; Scholastic Testing Service, Inc. * For the complete battery entry, see 37.

For additional information and reviews by Geraldine Spaulding and Ruth Strickland, see 5:201. For reviews of the complete battery, see 5:23.

[471]

The Schonell Diagnostic English Tests. Ages 9.5–16; 1940; 5 scores: English usage, capital letters and punctuation, vocabulary, sentence structure, composition; F. Eleanor Schonell; Oliver & Boyd Ltd. *

For additional information and reviews by John Cohen and Robert H. Thouless, see 3:135.

[472]

***Senior English Fundamentals: Manchester Semester-End Achievement Tests.** 1 semester grade 12; [1936–47]; Gletha Mae Noffsinger; Bureau of Tests. *

[473]

★Survey of Language Achievement: California Survey Series. Grades 7–9, 9–12; 1959; abbreviated combinations of items from various forms of the appropriate level of *California Language Test, 1957 Edition;* 2 scores: English, spelling; Ernest W. Tiegs and Willis W. Clark; California Test Bureau. *

[474]

Survey Tests of English Usage. Grades 9–13; 1947–49; some forms entitled *Achievement Test of English Usage;* L. J. O'Rourke; Psychological Institute. *

For additional information, see 5:202.

[475]

***Tenth Year English Fundamentals: Manchester Semester-End Achievement Tests.** 1 semester grade 10; 1934–[47]; Bureau of Tests. *

[476]

Test of English Usage. High school and college; 1950; 4 scores: mechanics of writing, use of words, sentences and paragraphs, total; Henry D. Rinsland, Raymond W. Pence, Betty S. Beck, and Roland L. Beck; California Test Bureau. *

For additional information and a review by Charlotte Croon Davis, see 4:175.

[477]

Tests of Language Usage: Active Vocabulary and Expression: Cooperative Inter-American Tests. Grades 8–13; 1950; English and Spanish editions; 3 scores: active vocabulary, expression, total; Committee on Modern Languages of the American Council on Education; [Guidance Testing Associates]. * For the complete battery entry, see 1347.

For additional information and a review by Walter V. Kaulfers, see 4:176 (3 references).

[478]

Tressler English Minimum Essentials Tests, Revised Edition. Grades 8–12; 1932–56; J. C. Tressler; Public School Publishing Co. *

For additional information, see 5:203.

[479]

20th Century Test for English—9th Grade. Grade 9; 1948–49; [Ardis Sanders]; Benton Review Publishing Co., Inc. *

For additional information, see 4:159.

[480]

20th Century Test for English—10th Grade. Grade 10; 1950; Ardis Sanders; Benton Review Publishing Co., Inc. *

For additional information, see 4:160.

COMPOSITION

[480a]

*College Entrance Examination Board Achievement Test in English Composition. Candidates for college entrance; 1943–61; program administered for the College Entrance Examination Board by Educational Testing Service. * For the testing program entry, see 1345.

For additional information, see 5:204 (14 references); for a review by Charlotte Croon Davis of earlier forms, see 4:178 (6 references).

[481]

★College Entrance Examination Board Writing Sample. Candidates for college entrance; 1960–61; program administered for the College Entrance Examination Board by Educational Testing Service. For the testing program entry, see 1345.

[482]

*Sequential Tests of Educational Progress: Essay Test. Grades 4–6, 7–9, 10–12, 13–14; 1957–59; Cooperative Test Division. * For the complete battery entry, see 39.

For additional information and reviews by John S. Diekhoff, John M. Stalnaker, and Louis C. Zahner, see 5:206 (1 reference). For reviews of the complete battery, see 5:24.

[483]

*Sequential Tests of Educational Progress: Writing. Grades 4–6, 7–9, 10–12, 13–14; 1956–59; Cooperative Test Division. * For the complete battery entry, see 39.

For additional information and reviews by Charlotte Croon Davis and John M. Stalnaker, see 5:207. For reviews of the complete battery, see 5:24.

[484]

★A Test of Creative Writing Aptitude and Ability. High school; 1942; tentative form; 4 scores: recognition of creative writing, synonyms, style preferences, use of figures of speech and modifiers; Elinor Hatch; Curriculum Bulletin. *

LITERATURE

[485]

American Literature: Every Pupil Scholarship Test. High School; 1958; Bureau of Educational Measurements. *

For additional information, see 5:208.

[486]

*American Literature: Every Pupil Test. High school; 1934–61; new form usually issued annually; Ohio Scholarship Tests. *
For additional information, see 5:209.

[487]

An Awareness Test in 20th Century Literature. Grades 9–16; 1937–40; Elmer R. Smith; Turner E. Smith & Co. *
For additional information, see 4:182; for reviews by H. H. Giles and Ann L. Gebhardt, see 40:1296.

[488]

Barrett-Ryan Literature Test. Grades 9–16; 1933; E. R. Barrett, Teresa M. Ryan, and H. E. Schrammel; Bureau of Educational Measurements. *
For additional information and a review by Chester W. Harris, see 3:139.

[489]

★Book Review Tests. High school; 1953–60; 115 tests on specific literary works; Perfection Form Co. *

[490]

Carroll Prose Appreciation Test. Grades 7–9, 10–12, 13–16; 1932–35; Herbert A. Carroll; Educational Test Bureau. *
For additional information and a review by Chester W. Harris, see 3:140 (4 references).

[491]

★Catholic Book Tests. Grades 7–10, 10–12, 1954; 60 tests at each level on specific Catholic literary works; teachers and librarians of the U. S. Province Brothers of Holy Cross; Bruce Publishing Co. *

[492]

Center-Durost Literature Acquaintance Test. Grades 11–13; 1953, c1952–53; Stella S. Center and Walter N. Durost; [Harcourt, Brace & World, Inc.]. *
For additional information and a review by Holland Roberts, see 5:210 (1 reference).

[493]

Cooperative Literary Comprehension and Appreciation Test. Grades 10–16; 1935–51; Mary Willis, Hyman Eigerman, Frederick B. Davis, and H. A. Domincovich; Cooperative Test Division. *
For additional information, see 4:184 (1 reference); for a review by Holland Roberts, see 3:142 (3 references).

[494]

*Davis-Roahen-Schrammel American Literature Test. High school and college; 1938–58; V. A. Davis, R. L. Roahen, and H. E. Schrammel; Bureau of Educational Measurements. *
For additional information and reviews by Paul B. Diederich and Violet Hughes, see 40:1300.

[495]

The Eaton Book-Report System. High school; 1934–37; 7 parts; Harold T. Eaton; [Ridge Manor Publishing Co.]. *

a) FORM A, FOR NOVELS, DRAMAS, ETC.
b) FORM B, FOR SHORT STORIES, ESSAYS, ETC.
c) FORM C, THE BOOK REVIEW.
d) FORM D, THE PHOTOPLAY REVIEW.
e) FORM E, BIOGRAPHY.
f) FORM F, TRAVEL.
g) EATON BOOK REPORT RECORD CARDS.

For additional information and a review by Paul B. Diederich, see 38:972.

[496]

The Eaton Literature Tests and **The New Eaton Literature Tests.** High school; 1928–37; 38 tests on specific literary works; Harold T. Eaton; [Ridge Manor Publishing Co.]. *

For additional information, see 38:978.

[497]

*Elementary Literature: Every Pupil Scholarship Test.** Grades 7–8; 1928–61; new form usually issued twice a year; Bureau of Educational Measurements. *

For additional information, see 5:218.

[498]

*English Language and Literature: National Teacher Examinations.** College seniors and teachers; 1940–61; Educational Testing Service. * For the testing program entry, see 1192.

For additional information, see 5:212. For reviews of the testing program, see 5:538 and 4:802.

[499]

English Language and Literature: Teacher Education Examination Program. College seniors preparing to teach secondary school; 1957; Educational Testing Service. * For the testing program entry, see 1205.

For additional information, see 5:213. For a review of the testing program, see 5:543.

[500]

*English Literature: Every Pupil Test.** High school; 1934–61; new form usually issued annually; Ohio Scholarship Tests. *

For additional information, see 5:214.

[501]

English Tests for Outside Reading. Grades 9–10, 11–12; 1939; 100 tests on specific literary works; Henrietta Silliman; the Author. *

For additional information, see 40:1301.

[502]

★**500 Outside Reading Tests for Freshmen and Sophomores.** Grades 9–10; 1956; volume of short tests on 500 specific books; Christobel M. Cordell; J. Weston Walch, Publisher. *

[503]

★**500 Outside Reading Tests for Juniors and Seniors, Revised Edition.** Grades 11–12; 1950–58; volume of short tests on 500 specific books; Christobel M. Cordell; J. Weston Walch, Publisher. *

[504]

*The Graduate Record Examinations Advanced Tests: Literature. Grades 16–17; 1939–60; Educational Testing Service. * For the testing program entry, see 1353.

For additional information and a review by Robert C. Pooley of Form EGR, see 5:215. For a review of the testing program, see 5:601.

[505]

Interpretation of Literary Materials. High school, college; 1944–57; subtest of *Tests of General Educational Development* (see 44); United States Armed Forces Institute; Veterans' Testing Service. *

For additional information, see 5:216. For reviews of the complete battery, see 5:27, 4:26, and 3:20.

[506]

*The Iowa Tests of Educational Development: Test 7, Ability to Interpret Literary Materials. Grades 9–13; 1942–59; E. F. Lindquist and others; Science Research Associates, Inc. * For the complete battery entry, see 25.

For additional information, see 5:217. For reviews of the complete battery, see 5:17, 4:17, and 3:12.

[507]

Literature Appreciation Tests. High school; 1936–40; 13 tests on specific literary works; Turner E. Smith & Co. *

For additional information, see 4:190; for a review by Paul B. Diederich, see 38:976.

[508]

*Literature: Every Pupil Scholarship Test. Grades 9–12; 1928–61; new form usually issued twice a year; Bureau of Educational Measurements. *

For additional information, see 5:218.

[509]

Literature Test: National Achievement Tests. Grades 7–12; 1937–57; 5 scores: recognizing effects, recognizing qualities, analyzing moods, miscellaneous facts, total; Robert K. Speer and Samuel Smith; Acorn Publishing Co. *

For additional information, see 5:219; for reviews by H. H. Giles and Robert C. Pooley, see 40:1304.

[510]

★Objective Test in American Anthology. High school; 1959–61; 5 tests on specific periods in American literature and a final examination; Carl H. Larson; Perfection Form Co. *

[511]

★Objective Test in English Anthology. High school; 1959; 7 tests on specific periods in English literature and a final examination; Carl H. Larson; Perfection Form Co. *

[512]

Objective Tests in American Literature. High school; 1931; a general test and 6 tests on specific literary periods; Hazel Call; [Ridge Manor Publishing Co.]. *

[513]

Objective Tests in English Literature. High school; 1932; 4 tests on specific literary periods; Hazel Call; [Ridge Manor Publishing Co.]. *

[514]

*Objective Tests in English [Perfection Form Co.]. High school; 1929–61; 88 tests on specific literary works; Perfection Form Co. *
For additional information, see 4:193.

[515]

Objective Tests in English [Turner E. Smith & Co.]. High school; 1926–41; 47 tests on specific literary works; Mabel S. Satterfield and others; Turner E. Smith & Co. *
For additional information, see 4:194.

[516]

★**Outside Reading Tests for Junior High Schools.** Grades 7–9; 1959; volume of short tests on 350 specific books; Christobel M. Cordell; J. Weston Walch, Publisher. *

[517]

Rigg Poetry Judgment Test. Grades 9–16; 1937–42; Melvin G. Rigg; Bureau of Educational Research and Service. *
For additional information and reviews by John S. Diekhoff and Louis C. Zahner, see 3:146 (2 references).

[518]

Survey Test in American Literature. High school and college; 1940; Salibelle Royster; Turner E. Smith & Co. *
For additional information, see 3:147.

[519]

Survey Test in English Literature. High school and college; 1940; Elmer R. Smith; Turner E. Smith & Co. *
For additional information and a review by John S. Diekhoff, see 4:196.

[520]

Test of Literary Essentials. Grades 10–12; 1938; Elmer R. Smith; Turner E. Smith & Co. *
For additional information, see 4:217.

[521]

Ullman-Clark Test on Classical References and Allusions. Grades 8–12; 1938; B. L. Ullman and Grace W. Clark; Bureau of Educational Research and Service. *
For additional information, see 4:197.

SPEECH

[522]

★**Evaluating the Effectiveness of Oral English.** High school; 1942; tentative form; 2 parts; Kenneth Larson; Curriculum Bulletin. *
a) FORM I: STUDENT INVENTORY. 11 scores: voice control, understanding vo-

cabulary, writing vocabulary, speaking vocabulary, conversational success, fluency total, poise, pronounciation, diction, mastery total, total.

b) FORM II: TEACHER'S INVENTORY AND CONFERENCE GUIDE. Teacher's observation and interview record for above score areas plus grammatical structure.

[523]

*The Graduate Record Examinations Advanced Tests: Speech.** Grades 16–17; 1953–59; available only in the Institutional Testing Program; Educational Testing Service. * For the testing program entry, see 1353.

For additional information, see 5:220. For a review of the testing program, see 5:601.

[524]

★The Houston Test for Language Development.** Ages 6–36 months; 1958; Margaret Crabtree; the Author. *

[524a]

★An Integrated Articulation Test for Use With Children With Cerebral Palsy.** Ages 3–16; 1961; Orvis C. Irwin; *Cerebral Palsy Review.* *

[525]

★Speech Articulation Test for Young Children, Revised Edition.** Ages 3.5–8.5; 1955–59; Merlin J. Mecham; University Press, Brigham Young University. *

[526]

★[Speech Correction Records.]** Grades 1–12; 1958; Severina E. Nelson, Frances L. Johnson, and Jane B. Archer; Randolph School Supply Co. *

a) CASE HISTORY FOLDER.

b) PHONETIC CHART.

c) SPEECH RECORD.

[527]

Speech Defect Questionnaire. Ages 6 and over; 1933; Samuel D. Robbins; Expression Co. *

[528]

Speech Diagnostic Chart. Grades 1–8; 1937–51; test words and sentences contained in the author's book, *Better Speech and Better Reading: A Practice Book;* Lucille D. Schoolfield; Expression Co. *

[529]

★Templin-Darley Screening and Diagnostic Tests of Articulation.** Ages 3–8; 1960; Mildred C. Templin and Frederic L. Darley; Bureau of Educational Research and Service. *

[530]

Weidner-Fensch Speech Screening Test. Grades 1–3; 1955; William E. Weidner and Edwin A. Fensch; Psychometric Affiliates. *

For additional information and a review by Robert S. Cathcart (with Louise B. Scott), see 5:221.

SPELLING

[531]

A.C.E.R. Spelling Test (Form C). Grades 3–4, 4–5, 5–6, 6–7, 7; 1946–51; Australian Council for Educational Research. *
For additional information and reviews by J. A. Richardson and D. K. Wheeler, see 5:222.

[532]

A.C.E.R. Spelling Tests. Ages 8–13.5; 1935–36; Australian Council for Educational Research. *
For additional information and a review by David H. Russell, see 40:1309 (1 reference).

[533]

Ayer Standardized Spelling Test. Grades 9–12; 1950; Fred C. Ayer; Steck Co. *
For additional information and a review by Harold H. Bixler, see 4:198 (1 reference).

[534]

Buckingham Extension of the Ayers Spelling Scale. Grades 2–9; [1918?]; B. R. Buckingham; Public School Publishing Co. *

[535]

Coordinated Scales of Attainment: Spelling. Grades 4, 5, 6, 7, 8; 1946–54; James A. Fitzgerald; Educational Test Bureau. * For the complete battery entry, see 10.
For additional information, see 5:223. For reviews of the complete battery, see 4:8 and 3:6.

[536]

Davis-Schrammel Spelling Test. Grades 1–9; 1935–36; Vera Davis and H. E. Schrammel; Bureau of Educational Measurements. *
For additional information and a review by Anton Thompson, see 4:199; for reviews by Walter W. Cook and Joseph C. Dewey, see 40:1311 (1 reference).

[537]

***Gates-Russell Spelling Diagnosis Test.** Grades 2–6; 1937–40; 9 scores: spelling words orally, word pronunciation, giving letters for letter sounds, spelling one syllable, spelling two syllables, word reversals, spelling attack, auditory discrimination, visual-auditory-kinaesthetic and combined study methods; Arthur I. Gates and David H. Russell; Bureau of Publications. *
For additional information and a review by George Spache, see 4:200 (1 reference); for reviews by John C. Almack and Thomas G. Foran, see 38:1159.

[538]

Graded Word Spelling Test. Ages 5–15; 1950–55; Fred J. Schonell; Oliver & Boyd Ltd. *
For additional information and a review by John Nisbet, see 5:224.

[538a]

★Group Diagnostic Spelling Test. Grade 13; [1958]; Thomas G. Kemp; Reading Laboratory and Clinic. *

[539]

[Iowa Dictation Exercise and Spelling Test.] Grades 3–4, 5–6, 7–8; [pre-1937]; words selected in part from *Iowa Spelling Scales* (see 540); H. A. Greene; Bureau of Educational Research and Service. *

[540]

The Iowa Spelling Scales. Grades 2, 3, 4, 5, 6, 7, 8; 1921–45; Ernest J. Ashbaugh; Bureau of Educational Research and Service. *

[541]

Kansas Spelling Test. Grades 1–3, 4–6, 7–9; 1941; H. E. Schrammel, O. M. Rasmussen, Nathan Budd, Wayne Gordon, and Fayrene Reiff; Bureau of Educational Measurements. *
For additional information and reviews by Henry D. Rinsland and Guy M. Wilson, see 3:153.

[542]

Kelvin Measurement of Spelling Ability. Ages 7–12; 1933; C. M. Fleming; Robert Gibson & Sons (Glasgow), Ltd. *
For additional information, see 38:1160.

[543]

*Lincoln Diagnostic Spelling Tests, [Educational Records Bureau Edition]. Grades 2–4, 5–8, 8–12; 1941–60; A. L. Lincoln; Educational Records Bureau. *
a) LINCOLN PRIMARY SPELLING TEST. Grades 2–4; 1960.
b) LINCOLN INTERMEDIATE SPELLING TEST. Grades 5–8; 1941–49.
c) LINCOLN DIAGNOSTIC SPELLING TEST [ADVANCED]. Grades 8–12; 1941–49.
For additional information, see 5:225 (2 references) ; for reviews by Walter Scribner Guiler and George Spache of *b* and *c*, see 4:203 and 4:202.

[544]

Lincoln Diagnostic Spelling Tests, [Public School Publishing Company Edition]. Grades 5–8, 9–12; 1941–56; A. L. Lincoln; Public School Publishing Co. *
For additional information, see 5:225 (2 references) ; for reviews of the Educational Records Bureau Edition, see 4:202 and 4:203.

[545]

Morrison-McCall Spelling Scale. Grades 2–8; 1923; J. Cayce Morrison and William A. McCall; [Harcourt, Brace & World, Inc.]. *
For additional information and a review by Anton Thompson, see 4:205 (2 references).

[546]

★The New Iowa Spelling Scale. Grades 2–8; [1954]; Harry A. Greene; Bureau of Educational Research and Service. *

[547]
The New Standard High School Spelling Scale. Grades 7–12; 1925–49;
Ernest P. Simmons and Harold H. Bixler; Turner E. Smith & Co. *
For additional information, see 4:206.

[548]
Phonovisual Diagnostic Spelling Test, [1949 Edition]. Grades 3–12; 1949;
Lucille D. Schoolfield and Josephine B. Timberlake; Phonovisual Products,
Inc. * For the later edition entry, see 549.
For additional information, see 5:226.

[549]
***Phonovisual Diagnostic Spelling Test, [1958 Edition].** Grades 3–12; 1958;
Lucille D. Schoolfield and Josephine B. Timberlake; Phonovisual Products,
Inc. * For the earlier edition entry, see 548.

[550]
Rich-Engelson Spelling Test. Grades 9–13; 1947; Vernita Rich, Ieleen Engel-
son, and H. E. Schrammel; Bureau of Educational Measurements. *
For additional information and a review by Henry D. Rinsland, see 4:207.

[551]
***Spelling and Vocabulary: Every Pupil Test.** 1, 2 semesters in grades 3–4,
5–6, 7–9, 10–12; 1948–61; new form usually issued twice a year; Ohio Scholarship Tests. *
For additional information, see 5:227.

[552]
Spelling Errors Test. Grades 2–4, 5–6, 7–8; 1948–55; George Spache; [Read-
ing Laboratory and Clinic]. *
For additional information, see 5:228 (1 reference).

[553]
***Spelling: Every Pupil Scholarship Test.** Grades 3, 4–6, 7–8, 9–12; 1928–61;
new form usually issued twice a year; Bureau of Educational Measurements. *
For additional information, see 5:229.

[554]
***Spelling: Public School Achievement Tests.** Grades 3–8; 1928–59; Jacob S.
Orleans; Public School Publishing Co. * For the complete battery entry, see 33.
For additional information and reviews of the complete battery, see 40:1194.

[555]
Spelling: Seven Plus Assessment: Northumberland Series. Ages 7–8;
1951; C. M. Lambert; University of London Press Ltd. * For the complete battery entry, see 40.
For additional information, see 4:210. For a review of the complete battery,
see 4:24.

[556]
**Spelling Test for Clerical Workers: [Personnel Research Institute Clerical
Battery].** Stenographic applicants and high school; 1947; Jay L. Otis, David J.

Chesler, and Irene Salmi; Personnel Research Institute. * For the complete battery entry, see 1846.

For additional information and a review by Harold H. Bixler, see 4:211. For reviews of the complete battery, see 4:729.

[557]

Spelling Test: National Achievement Tests. Grades 3–4, 5–8, 7–9, 10–12; 1936–57; Robert K. Speer and Samuel Smith; Acorn Publishing Co. *

For additional information and a review by James A. Fitzgerald, see 5:230; for a review by W. J. Osburn, see 38:1161.

[558]

Traxler High School Spelling Test. Grades 9–12; 1937–55; Arthur E. Traxler; C. A. Gregory Co. *

For additional information, see 5:231; for a review by Henry D. Rinsland, see 4:212.

[559]

Wellesley Spelling Scale. Grades 9–16; 1944–57; Thelma G. Alper and Edith B. Mallory; California Test Bureau. *

For additional information and a review by Janet G. Afflerbach, see 5:232 (1 reference); for reviews by Henry D. Rinsland and Guy M. Wilson, see 3:157.

VOCABULARY

[560]

[A.C.E.R.] Word Knowledge Test: Adult Form B. Ages 18 and over; 1957; identical with word knowledge subtest of *A.C.E.R. Silent Reading Tests* (see 1387) except for directions and norms; Australian Council for Educational Research. *

For additional information and a review of the reading test, see 5:616.

[561]

★**Bruce Vocabulary Test.** Business and industry; 1959; Martin M. Bruce; the Author. *

[562]

★**The College Vocabulary Test.** College and adults; 1954; for research use only; Harrison G. Gough and Harold Sampson; Harrison G. Gough. *

[563]

Cooperative Vocabulary Test. Grades 7–16; 1940–53; Frederick B. Davis, F. S. Beers, D. G. Paterson, Mary Willis, and Charlotte Croon Davis; Cooperative Test Division. *

For additional information, see 4:213 (4 references); for reviews by Edgar Dale and Henry D. Rinsland of Form Q and earlier forms, see 3:160.

[564]

Durost-Center Word Mastery Test. Grades 9–12; 1951–52, c1950–52; 3 scores: vocabulary, vocabulary in context, use of context; Walter N. Durost and Stella S. Center; [Harcourt, Brace & World, Inc.]. *

For additional information and a review by A. N. Hieronymus, see 5:233.

[565]

English Vocabulary Tests for High School and College Students. Grades 9–16; 1928; W. T. Markham; Public School Publishing Co. *

[565a]

★Gulick Vocabulary Survey. College and superior high school seniors; 1961, c1954–61; Sidney L. Gulick; Chandler Publishing Co. *

[566]

Holborn Vocabulary Test for Young Children. Ages 3.5–8.5; 1944–49; reprinted from *The Language and Mental Development of Children;* A. F. Watts; George G. Harrap & Co. Ltd. *

For additional information and a review by C. M. Fleming, see 4:215 (1 reference).

[567]

The Inglis Tests of English Vocabulary. Grades 9–16; 1923–51; Alexander Inglis and Ralph W. Walter; Ginn & Co. * For a related entry, see 571.

For additional information, see 5:234 (3 references); for a review by Henry D. Rinsland, see 3:163 (7 references).

[568]

*The Iowa Tests of Educational Development: Test 8, General Vocabulary. Grades 9–13; 1942–59; E. F. Lindquist and others; Science Research Associates, Inc. * For the complete battery entry, see 25.

For additional information, see 5:235. For reviews of the complete battery, see 5:17, 4:17, and 3:12.

[569]

*Johnson O'Connor English Vocabulary Worksamples 95, 176, and 180. Grades 3–5, 6–10, 11–16, "high vocabulary students and adults"; 1931–60; Johnson O'Connor; [Johnson O'Connor Research Foundation Inc.]. *

[570]

Kansas Vocabulary Test. Grades 4–8; 1940; H. E. Schrammel, Otho M. Rasmussen, Anna Huebert, and Donald J. Tate; Bureau of Educational Measurements. *

For additional information and a review by Harold H. Bixler, see 3:164.

[571]

A Lower Extension of the Inglis Tests of English Vocabulary. Grades 6–10; 1932; Chester Miller Downing and Charles Swain Thomas; Ginn & Co. *

For additional information, see 35:225 (1 reference). For a review of the upper level, see 3:163.

[572]

Michigan Vocabulary Profile Test. Grades 9–16 and adults; 1937–49; 9 scores: human relations, commerce, government, physical sciences, biological sciences, mathematics, fine arts, sports, total; Edward B. Greene; [Harcourt, Brace & World, Inc.].

For additional information and a review by David Segel, see 4:216 (7 references); for a review by Joseph E. King, see 3:166 (6 references); for a review

by Herbert A. Landry, see 40:1320 (2 references, 1 excerpt); for reviews by
John G. Darley, Richard Ledgerwood, John M. Stalnaker, M. R. Trabue, and
Arthur E. Traxler of an earlier edition, see 38:1171.

[573]

*New Standard Vocabulary Test. Grades 7–12; 1955–59; Miriam M. Bryan,
Janet G. Afflerbach, and Herbert A. Landry; Educational Division, Reader's
Digest Services, Inc. *
    For additional information and reviews by Richard A. Meade and Osmond E.
Palmer, see 5:236.

[574]

Purdue Industrial Supervisors Word-Meaning Test. Supervisors; 1952;
Joseph Tiffin and Donald A. Long; University Book Store. *
    For additional information and reviews by Jerome E. Doppelt and Bernadine
Meyer, see 5:237 (2 references).

[575]

Quick-Scoring Vocabulary Test: Dominion Tests. Grades 9–13; 1958; Department of Educational Research, Ontario College of Education, University of
Toronto; distributed by Guidance Centre. *
    For additional information, see 5:238.

[576]

Schrammel-Wharton Vocabulary Test. Grades 7–12; 1938; H. E. Schrammel
and LaVerna P. Wharton; Bureau of Educational Measurements. *
    For additional information and a review by Arthur E. Traxler, see 40:1321.

[577]

Sentence Vocabulary Scale. Grades 3–8, 7–12; 1919; Charles E. Holley; Public School Publishing Co. *

[578]

Survey Test of Vocabulary. Grades 3–12; 1931–48; L. J. O'Rourke; Psychological Institute. *
    For additional information, see 5:239 (3 references); for reviews by Verner
M. Sims and Clifford Woody, see 3:167 (1 reference).

[579]

*Vocabulary: Every Pupil Scholarship Test. High school; 1935–61; new
form usually issued twice a year; Bureau of Educational Measurements. *
    For additional information, see 5:240.

[580]

★Vocabulary Test. Adults; 1949; Eugene J. Benge; Management Service Co. *

[581]

★Vocabulary Test-GT. Ages 21 and over; 1957–60; Robert L. Thorndike,
George Gallup, and Irving Lorge; Institute of Psychological Research. *

[582]

Vocabulary Test: National Achievement Tests. Grades 3–8, 7–12; 1939–57;
Robert K. Speer and Samuel Smith; Acorn Publishing Co. *
    For additional information, see 5:241; for a review by Clifford Woody, see
3:168.

[583]

Wide Range Vocabulary Test. Ages 8 and over; 1937–45; C. R. Atwell and F. L. Wells; Psychological Corporation. *
For additional information and a review by Paul S. Burnham, see 3:169 (1 reference).

[584]

Word Dexterity Test. Grades 7–16; 1942–50; Shailer Peterson; the Author. *
For additional information, see 4:218; see also 3:170 (2 references).

FINE ARTS

[585]

★**Oberlin Test of Music and Art.** College; [1960]; experimental form for use in evaluating college music and art programs; 2 scores: music, art; Oberlin College; distributed by Educational Testing Service. *

ART

[586]

★**Art Education: National Teacher Examinations.** College seniors and teachers; 1961; Educational Testing Service. * For the testing program entry and references to reviews, see 1192.

[587]

★**The Cooper Union Art School Imagination Test.** Entering college students of art and architecture; [1949]; for research use only; Walter S. Watson; Cooper Union for the Advancement of Science and Art. *

[588]

Graves Design Judgment Test. Grades 7–16 and adults; 1948; Maitland Graves; Psychological Corporation. *
For additional information and reviews by William B. Michael and Edwin Ziegfeld, see 4:220 (2 references, 1 excerpt).

[589]

Horn Art Aptitude Inventory. Grades 12–16 and adults; 1939–53; 2 scores: scribbling and doodling, imagery; Charles C. Horn; C. H. Stoelting Co. *
For additional information and a review by Orville Palmer, see 5:242; for a review by Edwin Ziegfeld, see 3:171 (1 reference).

[590]

Knauber Art Ability Test. Grades 7–16; 1932–35; Alma Jordan Knauber, the Author. *
For additional information and a review by Edwin Ziegfeld, see 4:222; for a review by Norman C. Meier, see 40:1323 (4 references).

[591]

Knauber Art Vocabulary Test. Grades 7–16; 1932–35; Alma Jordan Knauber; the Author. *
For additional information and a review by Edwin Ziegfeld, see 4:223 (2 references); for reviews by Ray Faulkner and Joseph E. Moore, see 40:1324 (4 references).

[592]

Measuring Scale for Freehand Drawing. Grades kgn–8; 1922–33; 2 scales: representation, design and composition; Linus W. Kline and Gertrude L. Carey; Johns Hopkins Press. *

For additional information, see 38:896.

[593]

The Meier Art Tests: I, Art Judgment. Grades 7–16 and adults; 1929–42; revision of *Meier-Seashore Art Judgment Test;* Norman Charles Meier; Bureau of Educational Research and Service. *

For additional information and a review by Harold A. Schultz, see 4:224 (9 references); for a review by Edwin Ziegfeld, see 3:172 (4 references); for reviews by Paul R. Farnsworth and Aulus Ward Saunders of the original edition, see 40:1326 (15 references).

[594]

Tests in Fundamental Abilities of Visual Arts. Grades 3–12 and first year art students; 1927; 3 parts; Alfred S. Lewerenz; California Test Bureau. *
a) PART 1. 2 scores: recognition of proportion, originality of line drawing.
b) PART 2. 3 scores: observation of light and shade, subject matter vocabulary, visual memory of proportion.
c) PART 3. 4 scores: analysis of perspective (3 scores), recognition of color.

For additional information and reviews by Ray Faulkner and Aulus Ward Saunders, see 40:1329 (6 references).

MUSIC

[595]

Aliferis Music Achievement Test: College Entrance Level. Entering freshman music students; 1954, c1947–54; 4 scores: melody, harmony, rhythm, total; James Aliferis; University of Minnesota Press. *

For additional information and a review by Herbert D. Wing, see 5:243 (5 references).

[596]

Beach Music Test. Grades 4–16; 1920–39; Frank A. Beach and H. E. Schrammel; Bureau of Educational Measurements. *

For additional information and a review by James L. Mursell, see 3:174.

[597]

Diagnostic Tests of Achievement in Music. Grades 4–12; 1950; 11 scores: diatonic syllable names, chromatic syllable names, number names, time signatures, major and minor keys, note and rest values, letter names, signs and symbols, key names, song recognition, total; M. Lela Kotick and T. L. Torgerson; California Test Bureau. *

For additional information and reviews by William S. Larson and Herbert D. Wing, see 4:226.

[598]

Drake Musical Aptitude Tests. Ages 8 and over; 1954–57; 2 scores: musical memory (identical with *Drake Musical Memory Test*), rhythm; Raleigh M. Drake; Science Research Associates, Inc. *

For additional information and reviews by Robert W. Lundin and James Mainwaring, see 5:245 (1 reference); for a review by William S. Larson of the *Drake Musical Memory Test,* see 3:175 (2 references) ; for reviews by Paul R. Farnsworth and James L. Mursell, see 40:1330; see also 38:1083 (1 excerpt).

[599]

The Farnum Music Notation Test. Grades 7–9; 1953; Stephen E. Farnum; Psychological Corporation. *

For additional information and reviews by Kenneth L. Bean and William S. Larson, see 5:246 (1 reference).

[600]

*The Graduate Record Examinations Advanced Tests: Music. Grades 16–17; 1951–60; available only in the Institutional Testing Program; Educational Testing Service. * For the testing program entry, see 1353.

For additional information and a review by William S. Larson of Form ZGR, see 5:247. For a review of the testing program, see 5:601.

[601]

★Jones Music Recognition Test. Grades 4–8, 9–16; 1949; Archie N. Jones; Carl Fischer, Inc. *

[602]

Knuth Achievement Tests in Music: For Recognition of Certain Rhythmic and Melodic Aspects. Grades 3–4, 5–6, 7–12; 1936; William E. Knuth; Educational Test Bureau. *

For additional information and a review by Carl E. Seashore, see 40:1332 (1 reference) ; for reviews by Jay W. Fay and James L. Mursell, see 38:1085.

[603]

Kwalwasser-Dykema Music Tests. Grades 4–16 and adults; 1930; 11 scores: tonal memory, quality discrimination, intensity discrimination, tonal movement, time discrimination, rhythm discrimination, pitch discrimination, melodic taste, pitch imagery, rhythm imagery, total; Jacob Kwalwasser and Peter W. Dykema; Carl Fischer, Inc. *

For additional information and a review by William S. Larson, see 3:176 (29 references).

[604]

Kwalwasser Music Talent Test. Grades 4–6, 7–16 and adults; 1953; Jacob Kwalwasser; Mills Music, Inc. *

For additional information and reviews by Paul R. Farnsworth and Kate Hevner Mueller, see 5:248.

[605]

Kwalwasser Test of Music Information and Appreciation. High school and college; 1927; Jacob Kwalwasser; Bureau of Educational Research and Service. *

For additional information and reviews by Raleigh M. Drake and Karl W. Gehrkens, see 40:1334 (1 reference).

[606]

Kwalwasser-Ruch Test of Musical Accomplishment. Grades 4–12; 1924–27; Jacob Kwalwasser and G. M. Ruch; Bureau of Educational Research and Service. *

For additional information and reviews by William S. Larson and James L. Mursell, see 40:1333 (1 reference).

[607]

*Music Education: National Teacher Examinations.** College seniors and teachers; 1957–[60]; Educational Testing Service. * For the testing program entry, see 1192.

For additional information, see 5:249. For reviews of the testing program, see 5:538 and 4:802.

[608]

Musical Aptitute Test: Series A. Grades 4–10; 1950; 4 scores: rhythm, pitch, melody, total; Harvey S. Whistler and Louis P. Thorpe; California Test Bureau. *

For additional information and a review by Robert W. Lundin, see 5:250 (2 references); for a review by William S. Larson, see 4:228.

[609]

*Seashore Measures of Musical Talents, Revised Edition.** Grades 4–16 and adults; 1919–60; 6 scores: pitch, loudness, rhythm, time, timbre, tonal memory; Carl E. Seashore, Don Lewis, and Joseph G. Saetveit; Psychological Corporation. *

For additional information, see 5:251 (9 references); for reviews by John McLeish and Herbert D. Wing, see 4:229 (16 references); for reviews by Paul R. Farnsworth, William S. Larson, and James L. Mursell, see 3:177 (46 references); see also 40:1338 (60 references).

[610]

Strouse Music Test. Grades 4–16; 1937; Catherine E. Strouse; Bureau of Educational Measurements. *

For additional information and reviews by Clara J. McCauley and Carl E. Seashore, see 40:1339 (1 reference); for a review by Paul R. Farnsworth, see 38:1087.

[611]

Test of Musicality, Fourth Edition. Grades 4–12; 1942–58; E. Thayer Gaston; Odell's Instrument Service. *

For additional information and reviews by Paul R. Farnsworth and Kate Hevner Mueller, see 5:252 (1 reference).

[612]

Watkins-Farnum Performance Scale: A Standardized Achievement Test for All Band Instruments. Music students; 1942–54; John G. Watkins and Stephen E. Farnum; Hal Leonard Music, Inc. *

For additional information and a review by Herbert D. Wing, see 5:253 (2 references); for related reviews, see 3:1228.

[613]

*Wing Standardised Tests of Musical Intelligence.** Ages 8 and over; 1939–60; 8 scores: chord analysis, pitch change, memory, rhythmic accent, harmony, intensity, phrasing, total; H. D. Wing; distributed by National Foundation for Educational Research in England and Wales. *

For additional information, see 5:254 (4 references); for a review by John McLeish of an earlier edition, see 4:230 (6 references); for excerpts from related book reviews, see 4:231.

FOREIGN LANGUAGES

[614]

*Foreign Language Prognosis Test. Grades 8–9; 1930–59; Percival M. Symonds; Bureau of Publications. *
a) FORM A. 5 scores: English inflection, word translation-English to Esperanto, sentence translation-Esperanto to English, related words, total.
b) FORM B. 5 scores: word translation-Esperanto to English, artificial language, sentence translation-English to Esperanto, formation of parts of speech in English, total.
   For additional information and a review by William B. Michael, see 4:232; for a review by Walter V. Kaulfers, see 40:1340 (6 references).

[615]

Iowa Placement Examinations: Foreign Language Aptitude. Grades 12–13; 1925–44; Bureau of Educational Research and Service. *
a) SERIES FAI, REVISED. 1925–26; G. D. Stoddard and G. E. Vander Beke.
b) NEW SERIES FA-2, REVISED. 1925–44; G. D. Stoddard, Grace Cochran, J. R. Nielson, and D. B. Stuit.
   For additional information and a review by H. E. Brogden, see 3:178 (7 references).

[616]

Luria-Orleans Modern Language Prognosis Test. Grades 7–13; 1928–30; Max A. Luria and Jacob S. Orleans; [Harcourt, Brace & World, Inc.]. *
   For additional information and a review by Walter V. Kaulfers, see 40:1341 (3 references).

[617]

★MLA Foreign Language Proficiency Tests for Teachers and Advanced Students. Foreign language teachers and students in grades 15–17; 1961; 31 tests; 1 common examination (*Professional Preparation Test*) and 6 tests in each of 5 areas: French (see 648), German (see 658), Italian (see 664), Russian (see 686), Spanish (see 698); Modern Language Association of America and Educational Testing Service; program administered by Educational Testing Service. *

[618]

★Modern Language Aptitude Test. Grades 9–16 and adults; 1958–59, c1955–58; 4–6 scores: number learning (long form only), phonetic script (long form only), spelling clues, words in sentences, paired associates, total; John B. Carroll and Stanley M. Sapon; Psychological Corporation. *

ENGLISH

[619]

Diagnostic Test for Students of English as a Second Language. Applicants from non-English language countries for admission to American colleges; 1953; A. L. Davis; Educational Services. *
   For additional information and reviews by Nelson Brooks and Herschel T. Manuel, see 5:255.

[620]

English Examinations for Foreign Students. Applicants from non-English language countries for admission to American colleges; 1947–56; Educational Testing Service. *

a) BOOK I. 4 scores: reading comprehension, aural comprehension, pronunciation, total.

b) BOOK 2 [ENGLISH COMPOSITION].

c) BOOK 3. Title on test is *English Examination for Foreign Students (Including a Test of Non-Verbal Reasoning)*; 2 scores: scientific vocabulary, non-verbal reasoning.

For additional information and reviews by Ralph Bedell, John A. Cox, Jr., and Charles R. Langmuir, see 5:256.

[621]

English Language Test for Foreign Students. Applicants from non-English language countries for admission to American colleges; 1951; Robert Lado; distributed for English Language Institute by Follett's Michigan Book Store, Inc. *

For additional information and a review by John A. Cox, Jr., see 5:257 (1 reference); for a review by Clarence E. Turner, see 4:234 (2 references).

[622]

An English Reading Test for Students of English as a Foreign Language. College entrants; 1956; Harold V. King and Russell N. Campbell; Washington Publications. *

For additional information and reviews by Ralph Bedell and John A. Cox, Jr., see 5:258.

[623]

*English Usage Test for Non-Native Speakers of English. Non-native speakers of English; 1955–60; distribution restricted to the International Cooperation Administration or the Bureau of Educational and Cultural Affairs of the U. S. Department of State; A. L. Davis, Kenneth Croft, Harry Freeman, David P. Harris, and Winifred E. Jones; American University Language Center. *

For additional information, see 5:259.

[624]

Examination in Structure (English as a Foreign Language). Entering foreign college freshmen; 1947; English Language Institute, University of Michigan; distributed by Follett's Michigan Book Store, Inc. *

For additional information, see 5:260.

[625]

★Rating Language Proficiency in Speaking and Understanding English. Non-native speakers of English; [1959]; also called *AULC Interview Rating Form;* 6 ratings by interviewers: comprehension, pronunciation, grammar and word-order, vocabulary, general speed of speech and sentence length, total; distribution restricted to the International Cooperation Administration or the Bureau of Educational and Cultural Affairs of the U.S. Department of State; [David P. Harris]; American University Language Center. *

[626]

Test of Aural Comprehension. Applicants from non-English language coun-
tries for admission to American colleges; 1946–57; Robert Lado; distributed for
English Language Institute by Follett's Michigan Book Store, Inc. *
    For additional information and reviews by Herschel T. Manuel and Clarence
E. Turner, see 5:261.

[627]

★Test of Aural Perception in English for Japanese Students. Japanese students in American colleges; 1950–58; for research use only; Robert Lado and
R. D. Andrade; distributed for English Language Institute by Follett's Michigan Book Store, Inc. *

[628]

Test of Aural Perception in English for Latin-American Students. Latin-
American students of English; 1947–57; Robert Lado; distributed for English
Language Institute by Follett's Michigan Book Store, Inc. *
    For additional information, see 5:262.

[629]

**★A Vocabulary and Reading Test for Students of English as a Second
Language, Experimental Edition.** Non-native speakers of English; 1960; dis-
tribution restricted to the International Cooperation Administration or the
Bureau of Educational and Cultural Affairs of the U. S. Department of State;
David P. Harris; American University Language Center. *

FRENCH

[630]

American Council Beta French Test. Grades 7–11; 1926–27; 4 scores: vocabulary, comprehension, grammar, total; Jacob Greenberg and Ben D. Wood;
[Harcourt, Brace & World, Inc.]. *
    For additional information and a review by Bateman Edwards, see 40:1344
(2 references).

[631]

Cohen French Test. 1–3 years secondary school; 1944–49; 4 scores: vocabulary, silent reading, grammar, aural comprehension; S. W. Cohen; Australian
Council for Educational Research. *
    For additional information and a review by Mary E. Turnbull, see 4:236.

[632]

*College Entrance Examination Board Achievement Test in French. Candidates for college entrance with 2–4 years high school French; 1901–61; program administered for the College Entrance Examination Board by Educational
Testing Service. * For the testing program entry, see 1345.
    For additional information, see 5:263 (2 references); for a review by Walter
V. Kaulfers of earlier forms, see 4:237 (7 references).

[633]

**★College Entrance Examination Board Achievement Test in French
Listening Comprehension.** Candidates for college entrance with 2–4 years

French; 1960–61; program administered for the College Entrance Examination Board by Educational Testing Service. * For the testing program entry, see 1345.

[634]
*College Entrance Examination Board Advanced Placement Examination: French. Candidates desiring credit for college level courses or admission to advanced courses; 1954–61; program administered for the College Entrance Examination Board by Educational Testing Service. * For the testing program entry, see 1346.
For additional information, see 5:264.

[635]
Cooperative French Listening Comprehension Test. 2–5 semesters high school or college; 1955; Nelson Brooks; Cooperative Test Division. *
For additional information and reviews by Walter V. Kaulfers and Kathleen N. Perret, see 5:265 (1 reference).

[636]
Cooperative French Test. 1–4 semesters high school or 1–2 semesters college, more than 4 semesters high school or more than 2 semesters college; 1932–41; 4 scores: reading, vocabulary, grammar, total; Geraldine Spaulding, Jacob Greenberg, and Paul Vaillant; Cooperative Test Division. *
For additional information, see 3:181 (3 references); for reviews by C. E. Ficken, Harry Heller, and Joseph F. Jackson of an earlier form of the advanced level, see 40:1349 (4 references); for reviews by Warren S. Holmes and James B. Tharp of an earlier form of the elementary level, see 40:1350 (6 references); for a review by Nelson Brooks, see 38:985; for a review by Walter V. Kaulfers, see 38:986.

[637]
★Dents' Modern Language Tests: French Grammar. High school; 1944; H. E. Ford and R. K. Hicks; J. M. Dent & Sons (Canada) Ltd. *

[638]
First Year French Test. High school and college; 1956; Minnie M. Miller, Jean Leblon, and Marguerite Rice Crain; Bureau of Educational Measurements. *
For additional information and reviews by Nelson Brooks and Mary E. Turnbull, see 5:266.

[639]
*French, First Year—Second Semester: State High School Tests for Indiana. 2 semesters high school; 1948–[59]; revision of *French Recognition Vocabulary Test;* Oliver Andrews, Jr., Anne D. Belfort, and Rolande G. ErSelcuk; State High School Testing Service for Indiana. *
For additional information and a review by Clarence E. Turner of the earlier test, see 4:240 (1 reference).

[640]
★French I and II: Final District-State Scholarship Test. High school; 1938–61; Ohio Scholarship Tests. *

[641]

*French I and II, Form 4: Achievement Examinations for Secondary Schools. 1 or 2 years high school; 1951–59; Forms 1–3 published by Educational Test Bureau are out of print; Lee Stark; C. A. Gregory Co. *

For additional information concerning earlier forms, see 5:267; for a review by Elton Hocking, see 4:239.

[642]

*French I and II: Midwest High School Achievement Examinations. 2 years high school; 1951–60; Lee Stark; Educational Test Bureau. *

For additional information and a review by Mary E. Turnbull of earlier forms, see 5:268.

[643]

★French I and II: Preliminary District-State Scholarship Test. High school; 1947–61; Ohio Scholarship Tests. *

[644]

French: Teacher Education Examination Program. College seniors preparing to teach secondary school; 1957; Educational Testing Service. * For the testing program entry, see 1205.

For additional information, see 5:269. For a review of the testing program, see 5:543.

[645]

*The Graduate Record Examinations Advanced Tests: French. Grades 16–17; 1939–60; Educational Testing Service. * For the testing program entry, see 1353.

For additional information and a review by Walter V. Kaulfers of Form GGR, see 5:270. For a review of the testing program, see 5:601.

[646]

Iowa Placement Examinations: French Training: Series FT1, Revised. Grades 12–13; 1925–26; G. E. Vander Beke, G. D. Stoddard, and C. E. Young; Bureau of Educational Research and Service. *

For additional information and a review by Geraldine Spaulding, see 3:189 (4 references).

[647]

Lundeberg-Tharp Audition Test in French. High school and college; 1934; James B. Tharp and Olav K. Lundeberg; James B. Tharp. *

For additional information and a review by Nelson Brooks, see 40:1354 (3 references).

[648]

★MLA Foreign Language Proficiency Tests for Teachers and Advanced Students: French. French teachers and students in grades 15–17; 1961; 7 tests; Modern Language Association of America and Educational Testing Service; program administered by Educational Testing Service. *

a) LISTENING COMPREHENSION TEST: FRENCH.

b) SPEAKING TEST: FRENCH.

c) READING TEST: FRENCH.

d) WRITING TEST: FRENCH.
e) APPLIED LINGUISTICS TEST: FRENCH.
f) CIVILIZATION AND CULTURE TEST: FRENCH.
g) PROFESSIONAL PREPARATION TEST.

[649]

Second Year French Test. High school and college; 1956; Minnie M. Miller, Jean Leblon, and Marguerite Rice Crain; Bureau of Educational Measurements. *

For additional information and reviews by Geraldine Spaulding and Clarence E. Turner, see 5:271.

[650]

Standard French Test: Vocabulary, Grammar, and Comprehension. High school; 1929; Peter Sammartino and Carl A. Krause; Public School Publishing Co. *

For additional information and a review by Laura B. Johnson, see 40:1356 (2 references).

GERMAN

[651]

*College Entrance Examination Board Achievement Test in German. Candidates for college entrance with 2–4 years high school German; 1901–61; program administered for the College Entrance Examination Board by Educational Testing Service. * For the testing program entry, see 1345.

For additional information and a review by Harold B. Dunkel of Form FAC, see 5:272 (3 references); for a review by Herbert Schueler of earlier forms, see 4:244 (3 references).

[652]

★College Entrance Examination Board Achievement Test in German Listening Comprehension. Candidates for college entrance with 2–4 years German; 1960–61; program administered for the College Entrance Examination Board by Educational Testing Service. * For the testing program entry, see 1345.

[653]

*College Entrance Examination Board Advanced Placement Examination: German. Candidates desiring credit for college level courses or admission to advanced courses; 1954–61; 2 tests; program administered for the College Entrance Examination Board by Educational Testing Service. * For the testing program entry, see 1346.
a) INTERMEDIATE GERMAN. 3 years high school, including the equivalent of an intermediate college level course.
b) ADVANCED GERMAN: INTRODUCTION TO GERMAN LITERATURE. 4 years high school, including the equivalent of a college level German literature course.

For additional information and a review by Herbert Schueler of an earlier form of *a*, see 5:273.

[654]

First Year German Test. High school and college; 1933; J. R. Aiken and Cora Held; Bureau of Educational Measurements. *

For additional information and a review by Herbert Schueler, see 5:274.

[655]

*German I and II, Form 4: Achievement Examinations for Secondary Schools. 1 or 2 years high school; 1951–59; Forms 1–3 published by Educational Test Bureau are out of print; Emma Marie Birkmaier; C. A. Gregory Co. *

For additional information concerning the earlier forms, see 5:275.

[656]

*German I and II: Midwest High School Achievement Examinations. 2 years high school; 1951–60; Educational Test Bureau. *

For additional information and a review by Harold B. Dunkel of earlier forms, see 5:276.

[657]

Lundeberg-Tharp Audition Test in German. High school and college; 1929; Olav K. Lundeberg, James B. Tharp, and C. A. Williams; James B. Tharp. *

For additional information and a review by Harold B. Dunkel, see 3:194.

[658]

★MLA Foreign Language Proficiency Tests for Teachers and Advanced Students: German. German teachers and students in grades 15–17; 1961; 7 tests; Modern Language Association of America and Educational Testing Service; program administered by Educational Testing Service. *

a) LISTENING COMPREHENSION TEST: GERMAN.

b) SPEAKING TEST: GERMAN.

c) READING TEST: GERMAN.

d) WRITING TEST: GERMAN.

e) APPLIED LINGUISTICS TEST: GERMAN.

f) CIVILIZATION AND CULTURE TEST: GERMAN.

g) PROFESSIONAL PREPARATION TEST.

GREEK

[659]

*College Entrance Examination Board Achievement Test in Greek. Candidates for college entrance with 2–4 years Greek; 1901–61; program administered for the College Entrance Examination Board by Educational Testing Service. * For the testing program entry, see 1345.

For additional information and a review by Konrad Gries of Form FAC, see 5:277.

HEBREW

[660]

★College Entrance Examination Board Achievement Test in Hebrew. Candidates for college entrance with 2–4 years high school Hebrew; 1961; program administered for the College Entrance Examination Board by Educational Testing Service. * For the testing program entry, see 1345.

[661]

★Test on the Fundamentals of Hebrew. Pupils in grades 2–5, 3–6, and 4–7 who attend Hebrew school 6 hours a week or more; 1955–59; 4–5 scores:

sentences (grades 3–6 and 4–7 only), vocabulary, stories, grammar, total; Committee on Tests of the American Association for Jewish Education; the Association. *

ITALIAN

[662]

★College Entrance Examination Board Achievement Test in Italian Listening Comprehension. Candidates for college entrance with 2–4 years Italian; 1961; program administered for the College Entrance Examination Board by Educational Testing Service. * For the testing program entry, see 1345.

[663]

*College Entrance Examination Board Achievement Test: Italian Reading and Essay. Candidates for college entrance with 2–4 years Italian; 1924–61; program administered for College Entrance Examination Board by Educational Testing Service. * For the testing program entry, see 1345.

For additional information concerning earlier forms, see 5:279.

[664]

★MLA Foreign Language Proficiency Tests for Teachers and Advanced Students: Italian. Italian teachers and students in grades 15–17; 1961; 7 tests; Modern Language Association of America and Educational Testing Service; program administered by Educational Testing Service. *
a) LISTENING COMPREHENSION TEST: ITALIAN.
b) SPEAKING TEST: ITALIAN.
c) READING TEST: ITALIAN.
d) WRITING TEST: ITALIAN.
e) APPLIED LINGUISTICS TEST: ITALIAN.
f) CIVILIZATION AND CULTURE TEST: ITALIAN.
g) PROFESSIONAL PREPARATION TEST.

LATIN

[665]

Cicero Test. High school and college; 1937; Mary Alice Seller Peterson and H. E. Schrammel; Bureau of Educational Measurements. *
For additional information and a review by S. D. Atkins, see 40:1363.

[666]

*College Entrance Examination Board Achievement Test in Latin. Candidates for college entrance with 2–4 years high school Latin; 1901–61; program administered for the College Entrance Examination Board by Educational Testing Service. * For the testing program entry, see 1345.

For additional information and a review by Konrad Gries of Form FAC, see 5:280 (1 reference); for a review by Harold B. Dunkel of earlier forms, see 4:250 (2 references).

[667]

*College Entrance Examination Board Advanced Placement Examination: Latin. Candidates with 4, 5 years Latin desiring credit for college level courses or admission to advanced courses; 1954–61; program administered for the

College Entrance Examination Board by Educational Testing Service. * For the testing program entry, see 1346.

For additional information, see 5:281.

[668]

Cooperative Latin Test. 1–4 semesters high school or 1–2 semesters college, more than 4 semesters high school or more than 2 semesters college; 1932–41; 4 scores: reading, vocabulary, grammar, total; George A. Land; Cooperative Test Division. *

For additional information, see 3:204 (1 reference); for reviews by Harold B. Dunkel and John Flagg Gummere of an earlier form of the elementary level, see 40:1365; for a review by S. D. Atkins, see 38:1065; for a review by Norman T. Pratt, Jr. of an earlier form of the advanced level, see 38:1064.

[669]

*First Year Latin: Every Pupil Scholarship Test. 1 year high school; 1926–61; new form usually issued twice a year; Bureau of Educational Measurements. *

For additional information, see 5:282.

[670]

*First Year Latin: Manchester Semester-End Achievement Tests. 1, 2 semesters high school; 1934–[46]; Bureau of Tests. *

[671]

Holtz Vergil Test. High school and college; 1937; W. L. Holtz and H. E. Schrammel; Bureau of Educational Measurements. *

For additional information and reviews by W. L. Carr and Norman T. Pratt, Jr., see 40:1366.

[672]

Kansas First Year Latin Test. 1, 2 semesters high school; 1935–56; Helen Pearson; Bureau of Educational Measurements. *

For additional information, see 5:283; for a review by Hazel M. Toliver of an earlier edition, see 3:206; for a review by John Flagg Gummere, see 40:1368 (1 reference).

[673]

Kansas Second Year Latin Test. 1, 2 semesters high school; 1935–36; W. L. Holtz and H. E. Schrammel; Bureau of Educational Measurements. *

For additional information and a review by W. C. Kvaraceus, see 4:254; for a review by W. L. Carr, see 40:1369 (1 reference).

[674]

*Latin I and II: Every Pupil Test. 1 or 3, 2 or 4 semesters high school; 1929–61; new form usually issued twice a year; Ohio Scholarship Tests. *

For additional information, see 5:285.

[675]

★Latin I and II: Final District-State Scholarship Test. High school; 1938–61; Ohio Scholarship Tests. *

[676]

*Latin I and II, Form 4: Achievement Examinations for Secondary Schools. 1 or 2 years high school; 1951–59; Forms 1–3 published by Educa-

tional Test Bureau are out of print; Margaret M. Forbes; C. A. Gregory Co. *
For additional information concerning earlier forms, see 5:284.

[677]

*Latin I and II: Midwest High School Achievement Examinations. 2 years
high school; 1951–59; Educational Test Bureau. *
For additional information and a review by Mary E. Turnbull of earlier forms,
see 5:286.

[678]

★Latin I and II: Preliminary District-State Scholarship Test. High school;
1947–61; Ohio Scholarship Tests. *

[679]

*Latin Test: State High School Tests for Indiana. 1, 2, 3, 4 semesters high
school; 1934–[59]; Josephine Lillian Lee and Inez Painter; State High School
Testing Service for Indiana. *
For additional information concerning earlier forms, see 4:252 and 4:257.

[680]

Orleans-Solomon Latin Prognosis Test. High school and college; 1926; Jacob
S. Orleans and Michael Solomon; [Harcourt, Brace & World, Inc.]. *
For additional information and a review by C. W. Odell, see 3:207.

[681]

Powers Diagnostic Latin Test. Grades 9–12; 1930; 7 scores: English-Latin
translation, nouns and adjectives, verbs, vocabulary, comprehension and syntax,
derivatives, total; Francis F. Powers; Public School Publishing Co. *
For additional information and reviews by Paul B. Diederich and Norman
T. Pratt, Jr., see 40:1370.

[682]

*Second Year Latin: Every Pupil Scholarship Test. 2 years high school;
1939–61; new form usually issued twice a year; Bureau of Educational Measurements. *

[683]

*Second Year Latin: Manchester Semester-End Achievement Tests. 3, 4
semesters high school; 1934–[46]; Bureau of Tests. *

[684]

Ullman-Kirby Latin Comprehension Test. High school; 1922; B. L. Ullman
and T. J. Kirby; Bureau of Educational Research and Service. *

RUSSIAN

[685]

★College Entrance Examination Board Achievement Test in Russian. Candidates for college entrance with 2–4 years high school Russian; 1961; program
administered for the College Entrance Examination Board by Educational Testing Service. * For the testing program entry, see 1345.

[686]

★MLA Foreign Language Proficiency Tests for Teachers and Advanced
Students: Russian. Russian teachers and students in grades 15–17; 1961; 7

tests; Modern Language Association of America and Educational Testing Service; program administered by Educational Testing Service. *

a) LISTENING COMPREHENSION TEST: RUSSIAN.

b) SPEAKING TEST: RUSSIAN.

c) READING TEST: RUSSIAN.

d) WRITING TEST: RUSSIAN.

e) APPLIED LINGUISTICS TEST: RUSSIAN.

f) CIVILIZATION AND CULTURE TEST: RUSSIAN.

g) PROFESSIONAL PREPARATION TEST.

SPANISH

[687]

*College Entrance Examination Board Achievement Test in Spanish. Candidates for college entrance with 2–4 years high school Spanish; 1902–61; program administered for the College Entrance Examination Board by Educational Testing Service. * For the testing program entry, see 1345.

For additional information, see 5:287 (1 reference); see also 4:259 (3 references).

[688]

★College Entrance Examination Board Achievement Test in Spanish Listening Comprehension. Candidates for college entrance with 2–4 years Spanish; 1960–61; program administered for the College Entrance Examination Board by Educational Testing Service. * For the testing program entry, see 1345.

[689]

*College Entrance Examination Board Advanced Placement Examination: Spanish. Candidates desiring credit for college level courses or admission to advanced courses; 1954–61; program administered for the College Entrance Examination Board by Educational Testing Service. * For the testing program entry, see 1346.

For additional information, see 5:288.

[690]

Cooperative Spanish Test: Elementary and Advanced Forms. 1–4 semesters high school or 1–2 semesters college, more than 4 semesters high school or more than 2 semesters college; 1932–40; 4 scores: reading, vocabulary, grammar, total; Robert H. Williams, Geraldine Spaulding, Jacob Greenberg, and E. Herman Hespelt; Cooperative Test Division. *

For additional information and a review by Christian O. Arndt of Form P of the elementary level, see 40:1374; for reviews by Lawrence Andrus and Harry J. Russell of Form P of the advanced level, see 40:1373 (3 references); for a review by Walter V. Kaulfers of an earlier form of the elementary level, see 38:1156.

[691]

*First Year Spanish Test: State High School Tests for Indiana. 1, 2 semesters high school; [1945–60]; D. H. Patterson; State High School Testing Service for Indiana. *

For additional information concerning earlier forms, see 4:261.

[692]

Furness Test of Aural Comprehension in Spanish. 1–3 years high school or 1–2 years college; 1945–51; 2 editions; Edna Lue Furness; Banks Upshaw & Co. *

a) [ORIGINAL EDITION.] 1945–46; 4 scores: vocabulary, completion, identification, total.

b) [RECORDED EDITION.] 1951; 5 scores: vocabulary, completion, identification, question-answer, total.

For additional information, see 4:262; for reviews by Frederick B. Agard and Walter V. Kaulfers, see 3:213.

[693]

*The Graduate Record Examinations Advanced Tests: Spanish. Grades 16–17; 1946–60; Educational Testing Service. * For the testing program entry, see 1353.

For additional information, see 5:289. For a review of the testing program, see 5:601.

[694]

Iowa Placement Examinations: Spanish Training: Series ST1, Revised. Grades 12–13; 1925–26; G. E. Vander Beke and G. D. Stoddard; Bureau of Educational Research and Service. *

For additional information and a review by Harry J. Russell, see 3:212 (2 references).

[695]

Kansas First Year Spanish Test. 1 year high school or college; 1947; Minnie M. Miller; Bureau of Educational Measurements. *

For additional information, see 4:264.

[696]

Kansas Second Year Spanish Test. High school and college; 1953; Helen Johnson; Bureau of Educational Measurements. *

For additional information, see 5:290.

[697]

Lundeberg-Tharp Audition Test in Spanish. High school and college; 1929; Olav K. Lundeberg and James B. Tharp; James B. Tharp. *

For additional information and reviews by Frederick B. Agard and Walter V. Kaulfers, see 3:211 (1 excerpt).

[698]

★MLA Foreign Language Proficiency Tests for Teachers and Advanced Students: Spanish. Spanish teachers and students in grades 15–17; 1961; 7 tests; Modern Language Association of America and Educational Testing Service; program administered by Educational Testing Service. *

a) LISTENING COMPREHENSION TEST: SPANISH.
b) SPEAKING TEST: SPANISH.
c) READING TEST: SPANISH.
d) WRITING TEST: SPANISH.
e) APPLIED LINGUISTICS TEST: SPANISH.
f) CIVILIZATION AND CULTURE TEST: SPANISH.
g) PROFESSIONAL PREPARATION TEST.

[699]

Spanish and Latin American Life and Culture. 2 years high school or 1 year college; 1956; Minnie M. Miller and Beulah Aiken; Bureau of Educational Measurements. *

For additional information and a review by Kathleen N. Perret, see 5:291.

[700]

★Spanish I and II: Final District-State Scholarship Test. High school; 1938–61; Ohio Scholarship Tests. *

[701]

*Spanish I and II, Form 4: Achievement Examinations for Secondary Schools. 1 or 2 years high school; 1951–59; Forms 1–3 published by Educational Test Bureau are out of print; Emma Marie Birkmaier and Walter Pederson; C. A. Gregory Co. *

For additional information concerning earlier forms, see 5:292.

[702]

*Spanish I and II: Midwest High School Achievement Examinations. 2 years high school; 1951–60; Educational Test Bureau. *

For additional information concerning earlier forms, see 5:293.

[703]

★Spanish I and II: Preliminary District-State Scholarship Test. High school; 1947–61; Ohio Scholarship Tests. *

[704]

[Spanish Reading and Vocabulary Tests.] 1–6 and 1–8 semesters high school or 1–2 semesters college; 1927; María de la Soledad S. Contreras, Eustace Broom, and Walter Kaulfers; Public School Publishing Co. *

a) A TEST OF SPANISH VOCABULARY.

b) A SILENT READING TEST IN SPANISH.

[705]

Spanish: Teacher Education Examination Program. College seniors preparing to teach secondary school; 1957; Educational Testing Service. * For the testing program entry, see 1205.

For additional information, see 5:294. For a review of the testing program, see 5:543.

INTELLIGENCE
GROUP

[706]

A.C.E.R. Advanced Test B40. Ages 13 and over; 1940–53; title on test is *Adult Test (B40)*; Australian Council for Educational Research. *

For additional information and a review by C. Sanders, see 5:296 (3 references).

[707]

A.C.E.R. Advanced Tests AL and AQ. College and superior adults; 1953–55; 2 tests: linguistic, quantitative; D. Spearritt; Australian Council for Educational Research. *

For additional information and a review by Duncan Howie, see 5:295.

[708]

*A.C.E.R. Higher Tests. Ages 13 and over; 1944–59; formerly called *A.C.E.R. General Ability Test: Advanced M;* 2 parts, 3 scores: linguistic, quantitative, total; D. Spearritt and M. L. Clark; Australian Council for Educational Research. *

a) FORMS ML AND WL [LINGUISTIC].

b) FORMS MQ AND WQ [QUANTITATIVE].

For additional information and a review by C. Sanders, see 5:297.

[709]

*A.C.E.R. Intermediate Test A. Ages 10–14; 1938–61; test essentially the same as *A.C.E.R. General Test A;* Australian Council for Educational Research. *

For additional information concerning the earlier test, see 4:269; for excerpts from related book reviews, see 3:1110 and 40:B1005.

[710]

A.C.E.R. Intermediate Test D. Ages 10–14.0; 1947–58; Australian Council for Educational Research. *

For additional information and a review by James Lumsden, see 5:298 (2 references).

[711]

*A.C.E.R. Junior A Test. Ages 8.5–12.0; 1946–[58]; formerly called *General Test T;* Australian Council for Educational Research. *

For additional information and a review by R. Winterbourn, see 5:299.

[712]

*A.C.E.R. Junior B Test. Ages 8.5–12.0; 1948–58; Australian Council for Educational Research. *

For additional information and a review by R. Winterbourn, see 5:300 (1 reference).

[713]

A.C.E.R. Junior Non-Verbal Test. Ages 8.5–12.0; 1949–53; D. Spearritt; Australian Council for Educational Research. *

For additional information and a review by D. A. Pidgeon, see 5:301 (1 reference).

[714]

★A.C.E.R. Test W.N.V. Ages 13-6 to 16-11; [1960]; pictorial general ability test; Australian Council for Educational Research. *

[715]

APT Performance Test. Adults; 1954–57; distribution restricted to clients; Bentley Barnabas; Associated Personnel Technicians, Inc. *

For additional information, see 5:302.

[716]

★Academic Alertness "AA": Individual Placement Series (Area I). Adults; 1957–59; 7 scores: general knowledge, arithmetic, vocabulary, reasoning ability, logical sequence, accuracy, total; J. H. Norman; the Author. *

[717]

Academic Aptitude Test: Non-Verbal Intelligence: Acorn National Aptitude Tests. Grades 7–16 and adults; 1943–57; 4 scores: spatial relations, physical relations, graphic relations, total; Andrew Kobal, J. Wayne Wrightstone, and Karl R. Kunze; Acorn Publishing Co. *

For additional information, see 5:303; for a review by William B. Schrader, see 4:274.

[718]

Academic Aptitude Test: Verbal Intelligence: Acorn National Aptitude Tests. Grades 7–16 and adults; 1943–52; 4 scores: general information, mental alertness, comprehension of relations, total; Andrew Kobal, J. Wayne Wrightstone, and Karl R. Kunze; Acorn Publishing Co. *

For additional information, see 5:304; for a review by William B. Schrader, see 4:275; for a review by Marion A. Bills, see 3:215.

[719]

Adaptability Test. Job applicants; 1942–54; Joseph Tiffin and C. H. Lawshe; Science Research Associates, Inc. *

For additional information and a review by John M. Willits, see 5:305 (13 references); for reviews by Anne Anastasi and Marion A. Bills, see 3:216 (3 references).

[720]

*Advanced Personnel Test. High-level employees in business; 1926–60; identical with Form H of *Miller Analogies Test* (see 794); distribution restricted and test administered at licensed testing centers; W. S. Miller; Psychological Corporation. *

For additional information, see 5:306.

[721]

Advanced Test N. Ages 15 and over; 1951–52; Australian Council for Educational Research.*

For additional information and reviews by A. E. G. Pilliner and C. Sanders, see 5:307.

[722]

American Council on Education Psychological Examination for College Freshmen. Grade 13; 1924–54; 3 scores: quantitative, linguistic, total; L. L. Thurstone, Thelma Gwinn Thurstone, and Educational Testing Service; Cooperative Test Division. *

For additional information and reviews by Hanford M. Fowler and William B. Michael, see 5:308 (163 references); see also 4:277 (133 references); for reviews by W. D. Commins and J. P. Guilford of an earlier edition, see 3:217 (95 references); for reviews by Jack W. Dunlap and Robert L. Thorndike, see 40:1377 (48 references); for reviews by Anne Anastasi and David Segel, see 38:1037.

[723]

American Council on Education Psychological Examination for High School Students. Grades 9–12; 1933–54; 3 scores: quantitative, linguistic, total; L. L. Thurstone, Thelma Gwinn Thurstone, and Educational Testing Service; Cooperative Test Division. *

For additional information and a review by William B. Michael, see 5:309 (1 reference); see also 4:278 (2 references); for a review by Carl I. Hovland of an earlier edition, see 3:218 (7 references); for a review by A. H. Turney, see 40:1378 (2 references); for a review by V. A. C. Henmon, see 38:1038.

[723a]

★**American School Intelligence Test.** Grades 4–6, 7–9; 1961; Willis E. Pratt, M. R. Trabue, Rutherford B. Porter, and George A. W. Stouffer, Jr.; Bobbs-Merrill Co., Inc. *

[724]

★**Analysis of Relationships.** Grades 12–16 and adults; 1960; Edwin E. Ghiselli; Consulting Psychologists Press, Inc. *

[725]

*****Army General Classification Test, First Civilian Edition.** Grades 9–16 and adults; 1940–60; identical with Form 1a of the Army edition; test by Personnel Research Section, the Adjutant General's Office, War Department; Science Research Associates, Inc. *

For additional information, see 5:310 (17 references); for a review by John T. Dailey, see 4:280 (15 references); see also 3:219 (14 references, 1 excerpt).

[726]

Army Group Examination Alpha. Grades 5–16 and adults; 1919–39; manual by H. E. Schrammel and E. R. Wood; Psychology Committee of the National Research Council; Bureau of Educational Measurements. * For revisions, see 725, 727, 796, and 847.

For additional information and reviews by John T. Dailey and Willis C. Schaefer, see 4:281 (12 references); see also 3:220 (75 references).

[727]

Army Group Examination Alpha: Schrammel-Brannan Revision. Grades 7–16 and adults; 1935–38; H. E. Schrammel and Christine V. Brannan; Bureau of Educational Measurements. *

For additional information and a review by W. D. Commins, see 38:1040; see also 3:220 (75 references for *Army Group Examination Alpha* and revisions).

[728]

[Benge Employment Tests.] Adults; 1942; 6 scores for each test level: memory, numbers, vocabulary, spatial perception, reasoning, total; Eugene J. Benge; Management Service Co. *

a) EMPLOYMENT TEST, FORM B. Adults with an eighth grade education or less.
b) BASIC EMPLOYMENT TEST. Adults with more than an eighth grade education.

For additional information and reviews by Brent Baxter and Marion A. Bills, see 3:221.

[729]

California Analogies and Reasoning Test. Grades 10–13; 1958; Claude Mitchell; California Test Bureau. *

For additional information, see 5:312.

[730]

California Capacity Questionnaire. Grades 7–16 and adults; 1941–42; abbreviated adaptation of an earlier edition of *California Test of Mental Maturity;* 3 scores: nonlanguage, language, total; Elizabeth T. Sullivan, Willis W. Clark, and Ernest W. Tiegs; California Test Bureau. *

For additional information, see 4:282e; for reviews by Anne Anastasi and Emily T. Burr, see 3:222.

[731]

*California Short-Form Test of Mental Maturity. Grades kgn–1, 1–3, 4–8, 7–9, 9–13, 10–16 and adults; 1938–58; 7 scores: spatial relationships, logical reasoning, numerical reasoning, verbal concepts, language, nonlanguage, total; Elizabeth T. Sullivan, Willis W. Clark, and Ernest W. Tiegs; California Test Bureau. * For the regular edition entry, see 732.

For additional information and a review by Cyril Burt, see 5:313 (15 references) ; see also 4:282 (1 excerpt). For reviews of the regular edition, see 5:314, 3:223, 40:1384, and 38:1042.

[732]

California Test of Mental Maturity, 1957 Edition. Grades kgn–1, 1–3, 4–8, 7–9, 9–13, 10–16 and adults; 1936–57; 8 scores: memory, spatial relationships, logical reasoning, numerical reasoning, verbal concepts, language, nonlanguage, total; Elizabeth T. Sullivan, Willis W. Clark, and Ernest W. Tiegs; California Test Bureau. * For the abbreviated edition entry, see 731.

For additional information and reviews by Frank S. Freeman and John E. Milholland, see 5:314 (34 references) ; see also 4:282 (24 references, 1 excerpt) ; for a review by Henry E. Garrett of an earlier edition, see 3:223 (10 references, 2 excerpts) ; for reviews by Raymond B. Cattell and F. Kuhlmann, see 40:1384 (5 references, 1 excerpt) ; for reviews by W. D. Commins, Rudolf Pintner, and Arthur E. Traxler, see 38:1042 (1 excerpt).

[733]

*Cattell Culture Fair Intelligence Test. Ages 4–8 and mentally defective adults, 8–13 and average adults, grades 10–16 and superior adults; 1933–60; title on tests is *Test of g: Culture Fair;* formerly called *IPAT Culture Free Intelligence Test;* Raymond B. Cattell and A. K. S. Cattell; Institute for Personality and Ability Testing. (Scales 2 and 3 also published, with manuals revised for school use, in 1960 by Bobbs-Merrill Co., Inc.) *
a) SCALE 1. Ages 4–8 and mentally defective adults; 1933–60; identical with *Cattell Intelligence Tests, Scale O: Dartington Scale* (see 734).
b) SCALE 2. Ages 8–13 and average adults; 1949–58.
c) SCALE 3. Grades 10–16 and superior adults; 1950–59.

For additional information and a review by I. Macfarlane Smith, see 5:343 (11 references) ; for reviews by Raleigh M. Drake and Gladys C. Schwesinger, see 4:300 (2 references).

[734]

Cattell Intelligence Tests. Mental ages 4–8, 8–11, 11–15, 15 and over; 1930–52; R. B. Cattell; George G. Harrap & Co. Ltd. *
a) SCALE O (DARTINGTON SCALE). Mental ages 4–8; 1933.
b) SCALE 1 (NON-VERBAL), NEW EDITION, REVISED. Mental ages 8–11; 1930–52.
c) SCALE 2, NEW EDITION, REVISED. Mental ages 11–15; 1930–52.
d) SCALE 3, NEW EDITION, REVISED. Mental ages 15 and over; 1930–52.

For additional information and a review by I. Macfarlane Smith, see 5:315 (9 references) ; for a review by Godfrey H. Thomson, see 40:1386 (3 references).

[735]

Chicago Non-Verbal Examination. Ages 6 and over; 1936–54; Andrew W. Brown, Seymour P. Stein, and Perry L. Rohrer; Psychological Corporation. *

For additional information and a review by Raleigh M. Drake, see 5:316 (10 references) ; for reviews by Robert G. Bernreuter, Myrtle Luneau Pignatelli, and S. D. Porteus, see 40:1387.

[736]

Classification Test 40-A. Job applicants; 1957; Public Personnel Association. *
For additional information, see 5:317.

[737]

Cole-Vincent Group Intelligence Test for School Entrants. Grades kgn–1;
1924–28; Lawrence W. Cole and Leona E. Vincent; Bureau of Educational Measurements. *
For additional information and a review by Ruth W. Washburn, see 3:226.

[738]

***College Entrance Examination Board Scholastic Aptitude Test.** Candidates
for college entrance; 1926–61; 2 scores: verbal, mathematical; program administered for the College Entrance Examination Board by Educational Testing
Service. * For the testing program entry, see 1345.
For additional information and a review by John T. Dailey, see 5:318 (20
references); for a review by Frederick B. Davis of earlier forms, see 4:285 (22
references).

[739]

College Placement Test. College entrants; 1957; 3 scores: verbal, quantitative,
total; Science Research Associates, Inc. *
For additional information and reviews by Gustav J. Froehlich and David V.
Tiedeman, see 5:319.

[740]

***College Qualification Tests.** Grades 11–13; 1955–60; 6 scores: total and 5
scores listed below; George K. Bennett, Marjorie G. Bennett, Wimburn L. Wallace, and Alexander G. Wesman; Psychological Corporation. *
a) TEST V [VERBAL].
b) TEST N [NUMERICAL].
c) TEST I [INFORMATION]. 3 scores: science information, social science information, total.
For additional information and reviews by Gustav J. Froehlich, A. E. G. Pilliner, and David V. Tiedeman, see 5:320.

[741]

Comprehension Tests: Supplementary Mentality Tests for Superior Adults.
Adults; 1925–44; A. A. Roback; [Sci-Art Publishers]. *

[742]

Concept Mastery Test. Grades 15–16 and graduate students and applicants for
executive and research positions; 1956, c1950; Lewis M. Terman; Psychological
Corporation. *
For additional information and reviews by J. A. Keats and Calvin W. Taylor,
see 5:321 (4 references).

[743]

Cooperative School and College Ability Tests. Grades 4–6, 6–8, 8–10, 10–12,
12–14; 1955–57; 3 scores: verbal, quantitative, total; Cooperative Test Division. *
For additional information and reviews by Frederick B. Davis, Hanford M.
Fowler, and Julian C. Stanley, see 5:322 (7 references).

[744]

Cotswold Junior Ability Tests. Ages 8–9; 1949–51; C. M. Fleming; Robert Gibson & Sons (Glasgow), Ltd. *
For additional information, see 5:323.

[745]

***Cotswold Measurement of Mental Ability.** Ages 10–12.5; 1947–59; C. M. Fleming and J. W. Jenkins; Robert Gibson & Sons (Glasgow), Ltd. *
For additional information and a review by A. W. Heim, see 5:324.

[746]

Daneshill Intelligence Test. Ages 9.5–11.5; 1950–51; R. MacDonald; University of London Press Ltd. *
For additional information and reviews by A. W. Heim and F. W. Warburton, see 5:325.

[747]

Davis-Eells Test of General Intelligence or Problem-Solving Ability. Grades 1–2, 3–6; 1953, c1952–53; title on test is *Davis-Eells Games;* Allison Davis and Kenneth Eells; [Harcourt, Brace & World, Inc.]. *
For additional information and reviews by Cyril Burt, Raleigh M. Drake, and J. P. Guilford, see 5:326 (36 references); for excerpts from related book reviews, see 5:B140.

[748]

Dawson Mental Test. Ages 11–12; 1936; Shepherd Dawson; George G. Harrap & Co. Ltd. *
For additional information and reviews by Raymond B. Cattell and Percival Smith, see 40:1389; see also 38:1043 (2 excerpts).

[749]

Deeside Picture Puzzles. Ages 6.5–8.5; 1956–58; W. G. Emmett; George G. Harrap & Co. Ltd. *
For additional information and reviews by Charlotte E. K. Banks and M. L. Kellmer Pringle, see 5:327.

[750]

Detroit Advanced First-Grade Intelligence Test. Grades 1–2; 1928, c1925–28; Harry J. Baker; [Harcourt, Brace & World, Inc.]. *
For additional information and a review by A. M. Jordan, see 40:1392.

[751]

Detroit Beginning First-Grade Intelligence Test (Revised). First grade entrants; 1921–37; revision of the *Detroit First-Grade Intelligence Test;* Anna M. Engel and Harry J. Baker; [Harcourt, Brace & World, Inc.]. *
For additional information and a review by Psyche Cattell, see 38:1044 (1 excerpt).

[752]

Detroit General Intelligence Examination. Grades 7–12; 1938–54; Harry J. Baker and Paul H. Voelker; Public School Publishing Co. *
For additional information, see 5:328.

[753]

[Detroit Intelligence Tests.] Grades 2–4, 5–8, 9–16; 1924–56; Harry J. Baker; Public School Publishing Co. *
a) PUBLIC SCHOOL PRIMARY INTELLIGENCE TEST. Grades 2–4; revision of *Detroit Primary Intelligence Test.*
b) DETROIT ALPHA INTELLIGENCE TEST. Grades 5–8.
c) DETROIT ADVANCED INTELLIGENCE TEST. Grades 9–16.
   For additional information, see 5:329 (9 references) ; see also 4:288 (2 references) ; for a review by W. Line, see 40:1393.

[754]

The Dominion Group Test of Intelligence. Ages 13 and over; 1945; adaptation for Australian use of Form B of the advanced level of *Group Test of Learning Capacity: The Dominion Tests* (see 770) ; also called *The Dominion Higher Test;* Australian Council for Educational Research. *
   For additional information, see 5:330.

[755]

Doppelt Mathematical Reasoning Test. Graduate students and high level employees; 1958, c1954; distribution restricted and test administered at licensed testing centers; Jerome E. Doppelt; Psychological Corporation. *
   For additional information, see 5:331.

[756]

Duplex Series of Ability Tests. Ages 10, 11, 12, 13; 1947–50; 6 scores: verbal ability, logical reasoning, numerical reasoning, spatial relationships, nonlanguage factors, total; Frank M. Earle; George G. Harrap & Co. Ltd. *
   For additional information and reviews by W. G. Emmett and Stanley D. Nisbet, see 4:289 (2 references, 1 excerpt).

[757]

Easel Age Scale. Ages 4–8.5; 1955; Beatrice Lantz; California Test Bureau. *
   For additional information and reviews by Naomi Stewart and Florence M. Teagarden, see 5:332.

[758]

The Essential Intelligence Test. Ages 7–12; 1940–52, c1940–48; Fred J. Schonell and R. H. Adams; Oliver & Boyd Ltd. *
   For additional information and a review by R. Winterbourn, see 5:333; for a review by F. W. Warburton, see 4:290.

[759]

Figure Reasoning Test: A Non-Verbal Intelligence Test. Ages 10 and over; 1949; John C. Daniels; Crosby Lockwood & Son Ltd. *
   For additional information and reviews by E. J. G. Bradford and James Maxwell, see 4:291 (1 reference, 1 excerpt).

[760]

General Intelligence: Northumberland Standardised Tests (1925 Series). Ages 10–14; [1925] ; Cyril Burt; University of London Press Ltd. *

[761]

*General Verbal Practice Tests G1 and G2. Ages 10 to 11–11; 1954–59; published for the National Foundation for Educational Research in England and Wales; Newnes Educational Publishing Co. Ltd. *
For additional information, see 5:334.

[762]

★The Gestalt Continuation Test. Illiterate and semi-literate industrial workers; 1960; H. Hector; National Institute for Personnel Research. *

[763]

Goodenough Intelligence Test. Grades kgn–3; 1926; also called *Draw-a-Man;* Florence L. Goodenough; [Harcourt, Brace & World, Inc.]. *
For additional information, see 5:335 (34 references); for a review by Naomi Stewart, see 4:292 (60 references).

[764]

*The Graduate Record Examinations Aptitude Test. Grades 16–17; 1949–61; Educational Testing Service. * For the testing program entry, see 1353.
For additional information and a review by John T. Dailey of Form EGR, see 5:336 (7 references); for reviews by J. P. Guilford and Carl I. Hovland of Forms XGR and YGR, see 4:293 (2 references). For a review of the testing program, see 5:601.

[765]

Group Tests 33 and 33B. Ages 14 and over; 1923–56; verbal intelligence; National Institute of Industrial Psychology. *
For additional information, see 5:339 (9 references); see also 4:295 (2 references).

[766]

Group Test 36. Ages 10–14; 1937–45; verbal intelligence; National Institute of Industrial Psychology. *
For additional information, see 4:296.

[767]

Group Test 70. Ages 14 and over; 1939–50; nonverbal intelligence; National Institute of Industrial Psychology. *
For additional information and a review by George Westby, see 4:297 (5 references).

[768]

Group Test 75. Ages 12–0 to 13–11; 1957; nonverbal intelligence; National Institute of Industrial Psychology. *
For additional information, see 5:338.

[769]

Group Test 90A. Adults; 1947–48; verbal intelligence; National Institute of Industrial Psychology. *
For additional information and a review by John Liggett, see 5:340.

[770]

Group Test of Learning Capacity: Dominion Tests. Grades kgn–1, 4–6, 7–9, 10–13 and adults; 1934–56; formerly called *Group Test of Intelligence;* Department of Educational Research, Ontario College of Education, University of Toronto; distributed by Guidance Centre. * For the quick scoring edition entry, see 834.

For additional information, see 5:341; for a review by W. G. Emmett, see 4:294 (3 references); for a review by F. T. Tyler, see 3:231.

[771]

Henmon-Nelson Tests of Mental Ability: The Clapp-Young Self-Marking Tests. Grades 3–8, 7–12, 12–16; 1931–50; V. A. C. Henmon and M. J. Nelson; Houghton Mifflin Co. * For the revised edition entry, see 772.

For additional information and a review by H. M. Fowler, see 4:299 (25 references); for reviews by Anne Anastasi, August Dvorak, Howard Easley, and J. P. Guilford, see 40:1398 (1 excerpt).

[772]

*The Henmon-Nelson Tests of Mental Ability, Revised Edition. Grades 3–6, 6–9, 9–12, 13–17; 1931–61; Tom A. Lamke, M. J. Nelson, and Paul C. Kelso (college level); 3 scores for college level: quantitative, verbal, total; Houghton Mifflin Co. * For the original edition entry, see 771.

For additional information and reviews by D. Welty Lefever and Leona E. Tyler, see 5:342 (14 references, 1 excerpt).

[773]

*High School Placement Test. Entering freshmen; 1955–59; for Catholic schools; 9 scores: verbal ability, quantitative ability, total ability, IQ, arithmetic, language, reading, religion, total; [Oliver F. Anderhalter and Robert Sullivan]; Scholastic Testing Service, Inc. *

For additional information and reviews by William C. Cottle and Robert A. Jones of an earlier edition, see 5:15.

[774]

Inductive Reasoning Test. Grades 9–12 and adults; 1946; G. Bernard Baldwin; Educational Test Bureau. *

For additional information and a review by Charles R. Langmuir, see 3:232.

[775]

Jenkins Non-Verbal Test. Ages 10–14.0; 1949–53; adaptation of *Non-Verbal Test 1* (see 804); Australian Council for Educational Research. *

For additional information, see 5:344 (2 references).

[776]

★Job Alertness Tests. Grades 9–12 and adults; 1943–44; 2 tests; W. H. Winkler; Winkler Publications. *

a) ARITHMETIC TEST. 1947–55.

b) TEST OF ABILITY TO UNDERSTAND INSTRUCTIONS. 1943–44; also called *Word Alertness Test.*

[777]

Junior Scholastic Aptitude Test, Revised Edition. Grades 7–9; 1935–59; 2 scores: verbal, numerical; Secondary Education Board (original edition) and Geraldine Spaulding (revision); Educational Records Bureau. *

For additional information, see 5:345 (7 references); see also 3:233 (3 references).

[778]

Junior School Grading Test. Age 7 or junior school entrants; 1937; W. P. Alexander; University of London Press Ltd. *
For additional information and a review by E. Patricia Hunt, see 40:1400.

[779]

Kelvin Measurement of Ability in Infant Classes. Ages 5–8; 1935; C. M. Fleming; Robert Gibson & Sons (Glasgow), Ltd. *
For additional information, see 5:346.

[780]

Kelvin Measurement of Mental Ability. Ages 8–12; 1933; C. M. Fleming; Robert Gibson & Sons (Glasgow), Ltd. *
For additional information, see 38:1047.

[781]

*Kentucky Classification Battery. Grades 9–11, 12–13; 1948–59; 4 scores: general ability, English, mathematics, total; Kentucky Cooperative Counseling and Testing Service. *
a) LOWER LEVEL. Grades 9–11; 1951.
b) [UPPER LEVEL.] Grades 12–13; 1948–59; consists of revisions of *Kentucky General Ability Test* ('32–46, formerly called *Kentucky General Scholastic Ability Test* and *Kentucky Classification Test*), *Kentucky English Test* ('37–46), and *Kentucky Mathematics Test* ('45).
For additional information and a review by David V. Tiedeman of an earlier edition of *b*, see 4:301 (1 reference); see also 40:1402 (3 references). For a review by Richard Ledgerwood of the general ability test, see 38:1048; see also 35:338 (2 references). For a review by Henry D. Rinsland of the English test, see 38:966.

[782]

The Kingston Test of Intelligence. Ages 10–12; 1953–54; M. E. Highfield; George G. Harrap & Co. Ltd. *
For additional information and a review by A. W. Heim, see 5:347.

[783]

Kuhlmann-Anderson Intelligence Tests, Sixth Edition. Grades kgn, 1, 2, 3, 4, 5, 6, 7–8, 9–12; 1927–52; F. Kuhlmann and Rose G. Anderson; Personnel Press, Inc. * For the seventh edition entry, see 784.
For additional information, see 5:348 (15 references); for reviews by Henry E. Garrett and David Segel, see 4:302 (10 references); for reviews by W. G. Emmett and Stanley S. Marzolf of an earlier edition, see 3:236 (25 references); for a review by Henry E. Garrett, see 40:1404 (15 references); for reviews by Psyche Cattell, S. A. Courtis, and Austin H. Turney, see 38:1049.

[784]

*Kuhlmann-Anderson Intelligence Tests, Seventh Edition. Grades 7–9, 9–12; 1927–60; 3 scores: verbal, quantitative, total; F. Kuhlmann and Rose G. Anderson; Personnel Press, Inc. * For the sixth edition entry and references to reviews, see 783.

[785]

*Kuhlmann-Finch Tests. Grades 1, 2, 3, 4, 5, 6, 7–9, 10–12; 1951–60; Frank H. Finch; American Guidance Service, Inc. *

For additional information and reviews by Walter N. Durost, Henry E. Garrett, and Charles O. Neidt, see 5:349 (3 references).

[786]

Laycock Mental Ability Test. Grades 4–10; 1933–35; S. R. Laycock; University of Saskatchewan Bookstore. *

For additional information and reviews by George A. Ferguson and F. T. Tyler, see 3:237.

[787]

*The Lorge-Thorndike Intelligence Tests. Grades kgn–1, 2–3, 4–6, 7–9, 10–12; 1954–59; Irving Lorge and Robert L. Thorndike; Houghton Mifflin Co. *
a) NONVERBAL BATTERY. Grades kgn–1, 2–3, 4–6, 7–9, 10–12.
b) VERBAL BATTERY. Grades 4–6, 7–9, 10–12.

For additional information and reviews by Frank S. Freeman, John E. Milholland, and D. A. Pidgeon, see 5:350 (6 references).

[788]

★Lowry-Lucier Reasoning Test Combination. Grades 5–16 and adults; 1956–59; Ellsworth Lowry and Omer Lucier; distributed by Rowland & Co. *
a) TEST A: [SEQUENTIAL RELATIONS].
b) TEST B: [SPATIAL RELATIONS].

[789]

★Maddox Verbal Reasoning Test. Ages 9.5–10.5; 1960; H. Maddox; Oliver & Boyd Ltd. *

[790]

*Manchester General Ability Tests (Senior). Ages 12–14.5, 13.5–15; 1952–59; Stephen Wiseman; University of London Press Ltd. *

For additional information and a review by A. E. G. Pilliner of the lower level, see 5:351.

[791]

★Mental Alertness: National Institute for Personnel Research High Level Battery. Adults with at least 12 years of education; 1960–[61]; National Institute for Personnel Research. For the complete battery entry, see 1382.

[792]

★Mental Alertness: National Institute for Personnel Research Normal Battery. Standards 6–10 and job applicants with 8–11 years of education; 1960; National Institute for Personnel Research. * For the complete battery entry, see 1383.

[793]

*Mill Hill Vocabulary Scale. Ages 4–14, 11–14, 14 and over; 1943–58; J. C. Raven; H. K. Lewis & Co. Ltd. * For a complementary test, see 831.

For additional information, see 4:303 (7 references); for a review by David Wechsler, see 3:239 (3 references).

[794]

*Miller Analogies Test.** Candidates for graduate school; 1926–60; also available under the title *Advanced Personnel Test* (see 720); tests administered at licensed testing centers; W. S. Miller; Psychological Corporation. *

For additional information and a review by John T. Dailey, see 5:352 (28 references); for reviews by J. P. Guilford and Carl I. Hovland, see 4:304 (16 references).

[795]

★Mitchell Vocabulary Test.** Adults; 1958; instructions contained in manual for *Diagnostic Performance Tests* (see 886); A. Mitchell; distributed by National Foundation for Educational Research in England and Wales. *

[796]

Modified Alpha Examination Form 9. Grades 7–12 and adults; 1941–51; 3 scores: numerical, verbal, total; F. L. Wells; Psychological Corporation. *

For additional information and a review by Dael Wolfle, see 4:305 (5 references); see also 3:220 (75 references for *Army Group Examination Alpha* and revisions).

[797]

*Moray House Intelligence Tests.** Ages 8.5–10.5, 10–12, 12–14, 13.5–17.5; 1930–61; Department of Education, University of Edinburgh; University of London Press Ltd.

a) MORAY HOUSE JUNIOR REASONING TEST 2 FOR NINE-YEAR-OLDS. Ages 8.5–10.5; 1947–58. *

b) MORAY HOUSE VERBAL REASONING TEST 67. Ages 10–12; 1930–61.

c) MORAY HOUSE VERBAL REASONING TEST (ADV.) 10. Ages 12–14; 1940–56. *

d) MORAY HOUSE ADULT TEST 1. Ages 13.5–17.5; 1952. *

For additional information, see 5:353 (2 references); for a review by Patrick Slater of earlier forms, see 3:241 (2 references); for a review by C. Ebblewhite Smith of an earlier form of *b*, see 40:1409 (1 reference).

[798]

Moray House Picture Intelligence Test 1. Ages 6.5–8.5; 1944–48; Margaret A. Mellone; University of London Press Ltd. *

For additional information and reviews by Gertrude Keir and M. L. Kellmer Pringle, see 4:306 (5 references).

[799]

★Multi-Racial Picture Intelligence Tests Suitable for Use in African and Asian Schools.** Ages 10–11.5; [1955]; Y. K. Lule; A. Wheaton & Co., Ltd. *

[800]

★[N. B. Group Tests.]** Ages 5–6, 7–8; [1958]; National Bureau of Educational and Social Research. *

a) N. B. GROUP TEST FOR FIVE AND SIX YEAR OLDS.

b) N. B. GROUP TEST FOR SEVEN AND EIGHT YEAR OLDS.

[801]

New Rhode Island Intelligence Test. Ages 3–6; 1923–55; G. E. Bird, Clara R. Craig, and G. L. Betts; [G. L. Betts]. *

For additional information and a review by Raymond C. Norris, see 5:354 (6 references).

[802]

New South African Group Test. Ages 8–11, 10–14, 13–18; 1931–56; 3 scores: verbal, nonverbal, total; National Bureau of Educational and Social Research. *
  For additional information, see 5:355.

[803]

Non-Language Multi-Mental Test. Grades 2 and over; 1942; E. L. Terman, William A. McCall, and Irving Lorge; Bureau of Publications. *
  For additional information and a review by Carroll A. Whitmer, see 3:243 (1 reference).

[804]

***Non-Verbal Tests.** Ages 8 to 11–0, 10 to 12–11, 10 to 15–0, 12 to 13–11; 1947–58; published for the National Foundation for Educational Research in England and Wales; Newnes Educational Publishing Co. Ltd. *
  a) NON-VERBAL TEST 1. Ages 10 to 12–11; 1947–51; title on test is *A Scale of Non-Verbal Mental Ability;* J. W. Jenkins.
  b) NON-VERBAL TEST 2. Ages 10 to 12–11; 1948–51; D. M. Lee and J. W. Jenkins.
  c) NON-VERBAL TEST 3. Ages 10 to 15–0; 1953–58; B. Calvert and I. Macfarlane Smith.
  d) NON-VERBAL TEST 4. Ages 12 to 13–11; 1951.
  e) NON-VERBAL TEST 5. Ages 8 to 11–0; 1953–58; D. A. Pidgeon.
  For additional information and a review by Cyril A. Rogers of tests 1–3, see 5:356 (1 reference); for a review by E. A. Peel of the original edition of tests 1 and 2, see 4:307 (3 references).

[805]

The "Northern" Test of Educability. Mental ages 9.5–14.5; 1932; T. P. Tomlinson; University of London Press Ltd. *

[806]

The Northumberland Mental Tests. Ages 10–12.5, 11–16; 1922; Godfrey H. Thomson; George G. Harrap & Co. Ltd. *

[807]

The Ohio Penal Classification Test. Penal institutions; 1952–54; 5 scores: block counting, digit-symbol, number series, memory span, total; DeWitt E. Sell; Psychometric Affiliates. (Special edition for industrial use entitled *Ohio Classification Test* ('57) also available; manual by the author and Robert W. Scollay and Leroy N. Vernon.) *
  For additional information and a review by Norman Eagle, see 5:358.

[808]

***Ohio State University Psychological Test.** Grades 9–16 and adults; 1919–59; 4 scores: same-opposites, analogies, reading comprehension, total; Herbert A. Toops; Ohio College Association. (Form 21 also published by Science Research Associates, Inc.) *
  For additional information and a review by Cyril J. Hoyt (with W. Wesley Tennyson) of Form 25, see 5:359 (29 references); for a review by George A. Ferguson of Form 24, see 4:308 (23 references); for a review by J. P. Guilford of Form 21, see 3:244 (28 references); for reviews by Louis D. Hartson, Theos A. Langlie, and Rudolf Pintner of Form 20, see 38:1051.

[809]

An Orally Presented Group Test of Intelligence for Juniors. Ages 8–11; 1952; J. Cornwell; Methuen & Co. Ltd. *
For additional information and a review by Elizabeth D. Fraser, see 5:360 (2 references).

[810]

O'Rourke General Classification Test, Senior Grade. Grades 12–13 and adults; 1927–42; L. J. O'Rourke; Psychological Institute. *
For additional information and a review by Marion A. Bills, see 3:246 (3 references).

[811]

The "Orton" Intelligence Test, No. 4. Ages 10–14; 1931; Robert Gibson & Sons (Glasgow), Ltd. *
For additional information, see 38:1052.

[812]

Otis Classification Test, Revised. Grades 4–8; 1923–41; 3 scores: mental ability, achievement, total; mental ability subtest identical with Beta Test of *Otis Quick-Scoring Mental Ability Tests* (see 816); Arthur S. Otis; [Harcourt, Brace & World, Inc.]. *
For additional information, see 3:247 (3 references, 1 excerpt).

[813]

Otis Employment Tests. Applicants for employment; 1943, c1922; tests identical with Forms A and B of the *Otis Self-Administering Tests of Mental Ability* (see 818); Arthur S. Otis; [Harcourt, Brace & World, Inc.]. *
For additional information, see 4:310.

[814]

Otis General Intelligence Examination: Designed Especially for Business Institutions. Applicants for clerical and executive positions; 1920; Arthur S. Otis; [Harcourt, Brace & World, Inc.]. *
For additional information and a review by Frederic Kuder, see 3:248.

[815]

Otis Group Intelligence Scale. Grades kgn–4, 5–16 and adults; 1918–40; Arthur S. Otis; [Harcourt, Brace & World, Inc.]. (English edition: Ages 6–10, 10 and over; 1921–48; tests identical with American edition; George G. Harrap & Co. Ltd.) *

[816]

Otis Quick-Scoring Mental Ability Tests. Grades 1.5–4, 4–9, 9–16; 1936–54; tests for grades 4 and over are revisions of *Otis Self-Administering Tests of Mental Ability* (see 818); Arthur S. Otis; [Harcourt, Brace & World, Inc.]. (English edition: ages 7–10; nonverbal section of *a* only; 1936–39; tests identical with American edition; George G. Harrap & Co. Ltd.) * For the new edition entry, see 817.
a) ALPHA TEST. Grades 1.5–4; 1936–39; 3 scores: nonverbal, verbal, total.
b) BETA TEST. Grades 4–9; 1937–54.
c) GAMMA TEST. Grades 9–16; 1937–54.
For additional information, see 5:361; for a review by Frederic Kuder, see

3:249 (9 references); for reviews by F. Kuhlmann and C. Spearman, see 40:1413; for reviews by Psyche Cattell and R. Pintner, see 38:1053 (2 excerpts).

[817]

Otis Quick-Scoring Mental Ability Tests, New Edition. Grades 1.5–4, 4–9, 9–16; 1936–54; Arthur S. Otis; [Harcourt, Brace & World, Inc.]. * For the original edition entry, see 816.

For additional information and reviews by D. Welty Lefever and Alfred Yates, see 5:362 (33 references).

[818]

Otis Self-Administering Tests of Mental Ability. Grades 4–9, 9–16; 1922–29; Arthur S. Otis and Thomas N. Barrows; [Harcourt, Brace & World, Inc.]. (Australian adaptation: ages 9–14, 12.5 and over; 1936–55; manuals by D. Spearritt; Australian Council for Educational Research. New Zealand adaptation: ages 9–15, 12–18; 1937–53; New Zealand Council for Educational Research; distributed by Educational Books.) * For the later edition entries, see 816 and 817.

For additional information, see 5:363 (52 references); for a review by Frederic Kuder, see 3:250 (71 references). For the Australian edition, see 40:1412.

[819]

Pattern Perception Test. Ages 6 and over; 1943; L. S. Penrose; Galton Laboratory, University College. *

For additional information and a review by Alice W. Heim, see 4:312 (3 references).

[820]

★Performance Alertness "PA" (With Pictures): Individual Placement Series (Area I). Adults; 1961; J. H. Norman; the Author. *

[821]

★Personal Classification Test. Business and industry; 1953–59; W. E. Brown, W. H. E. Geiger, R. W. Henderson, and L. C. Steckle; William, Lynde & Williams. *

[822]

Personnel Research Institute Classification Test. Adults; 1943–54; formerly called *Classification Test for Industrial and Office Personnel;* Jay L. Otis, Evelyn Katz, Robert W. Henderson, Mary Aiken, David J. Chesler, and Gardner E. Lindzey; Personnel Research Institute. *

For additional information, see 5:364; see also 4:284 (1 reference).

[823]

Personnel Research Institute Factory Series Test. Applicants for routine industrial positions; 1950–56; Jay L. Otis and Alfred H. Exton; Personnel Research Institute. *

For additional information, see 5:365.

[824]

Personnel Tests for Industry. Trade school and adults; 1945–54; 3 tests; Psychological Corporation. *

a) PTI-VERBAL TEST. 1952–54; Alexander G. Wesman.

b) PTI-NUMERICAL TEST. 1952–54; Jerome E. Doppelt.
c) PTI-ORAL DIRECTIONS TEST. 1945–54; Charles R. Langmuir.

For additional information and a review by Erwin K. Taylor, see 5:366; for reviews by Charles D. Flory, Irving Lorge, and William W. Turnbull of the original edition of *c,* see 3:245; see also 4:309 (1 reference).

[825]

*Picture Intelligence Test 1. Ages 7 to 8–1; 1955–58; Joan E. Stuart; published for the National Foundation for Educational Research in England and Wales; Newnes Educational Publishing Co. Ltd. *

For additional information and reviews by Charlotte E. K. Banks and M. L. Kellmer Pringle, see 5:367.

[826]

Pintner General Ability Tests: Non-Language Series. Grades 4–9; 1945, c1941–45; Rudolf Pintner; [Harcourt, Brace & World, Inc.]. *

For additional information and a review by Carroll A. Whitmer, see 3:254.

[827]

Pintner General Ability Tests: Verbal Series. Grades kgn–2, 2–4, 4–9, 9–12 and over; 1923–46; Rudolf Pintner, Bess V. Cunningham, and Walter N. Durost; [Harcourt, Brace & World, Inc.]. *

a) PINTNER-CUNNINGHAM PRIMARY TEST. Grades kgn–2; 1923–46; revision of *Pintner-Cunningham Primary Mental Test.*
b) PINTNER-DUROST ELEMENTARY TEST. Grades 2–4; 1940–41; 3 scores: picture content, reading content; total.
c) PINTNER INTERMEDIATE TEST. Grades 4–8; 1931–42; revision of *Pintner Intelligence Test.*
d) PINTNER ADVANCED TEST. Grades 9–12 and over; 1938–42.

For additional information, see 5:368 (10 references); for reviews by Stanley S. Marzolf and D. A. Worcester, see 3:255 (13 references); see also 40:1416 (3 excerpts).

[828]

★Preliminary Scholastic Aptitude Test. Grades 11–12; 1959–60; abbreviated adaptation of the *College Entrance Examination Board Scholastic Aptitude Test* (see 738) for guidance and scholarship testing; administered locally on dates established by the publisher; 2 scores: verbal, mathematical; program administered for the College Entrance Examination Board by Educational Testing Service. *

[829]

[Pressey Classification and Verifying Tests.] Grades 1–2, 3–6, 7–12; 1922–58; S. L. Pressey and L. C. Pressey; Public School Publishing Co. *

a) PRIMARY CLASSIFICATION TEST. Grades 1–2; 1922.
b) INTERMEDIATE CLASSIFICATION TEST. Grades 3–6; 1922.
c) INTERMEDIATE VERIFYING TEST. Grades 3–6; 1923.
d) PRESSEY SENIOR CLASSIFICATION TEST. Grades 7–12; 1922–58.
e) PRESSEY SENIOR VERIFYING TEST. Grades 7–12; 1923–58.

[830]

*Primary Verbal Tests. Ages 8 to 10-6, 9 to 11-6; 1953–59; published for the National Foundation for Educational Research in England and Wales; Newnes Educational Publishing Co. Ltd. *

a) PRIMARY VERBAL TEST 1. Ages 8 to 10-6; 1953–58; formerly called *Primary*

School Verbal Intelligence Test 1; adaptation of *A.C.E.R. Junior A Test* (see 711) and *A.C.E.R. Junior B Test* (see 712) ; D. A. Pidgeon.
b) PRIMARY VERBAL TEST. Ages 9 to 11-6; [1959]; Valerie Land.

For additional information and reviews by John Nisbet and F. W. Warburton of Test 1, see 5:369.

[831]

Progressive Matrices. Ages 5 and over; 1938–56; J. C. Raven; H. K. Lewis & Co. Ltd. * (United States distributor: Psychological Corporation.) For complementary tests, see 793 and 883.
a) PROGRESSIVE MATRICES (1938), 1956 REVISION. Ages 6 and over; 1938–56; title on test is *Standard Progressive Matrices.* (Australian edition: ages 10 and over; 1943–58; test identical with British edition; manual by V. T. Brownless and M. L. Clark; Australian Council for Educational Research.)
b) COLOURED PROGRESSIVE MATRICES, [(1947), 1956 REVISION]. Ages 5–11 and mental patients and senescents; 1947–56.
c) ADVANCED PROGRESSIVE MATRICES. Ages 11 and over; 1943–47; formerly called *Progressive Matrices (1947).* (Australian edition: college; [1948]; tests identical with British edition; Australian Council for Educational Research.)

For additional information, see 5:370 (62 references) ; for reviews by Charlotte Banks, W. D. Wall, and George Westby, see 4:314 (32 references) ; for reviews by Walter C. Shipley and David Wechsler of the 1938 edition, see 3:258 (13 references) ; for a review by T. J. Keating, see 40:1417 (8 references).

[832]

Proverbs Test. Grades 5–16 and adults; 1954–56; 2 scores: abstract, concrete; Donald R. Gorham; Psychological Test Specialists. *
For additional information and reviews by Eugene L. Gaier and Alfred B. Heilbrun, Jr., see 5:371 (4 references).

[833]

Purdue Non-Language Test. Grades 9–12 and adults; 1957–58; Joseph Tiffin, Alin Gruber, and Kay Inaba; Science Research Associates, Inc. *
For additional information, see 5:372.

[834]

Quick-Scoring Test of Learning Capacity: Dominion Tests. Grades 7–9, 10–13 and adults; 1934–58; quick scoring edition of *Group Test of Learning Capacity: The Dominion Tests* (see 770) ; Department of Educational Research, Ontario College of Education, University of Toronto; distributed by Guidance Centre. *
For additional information, see 5:373.

[835]

Reasoning Tests for Higher Levels of Intelligence. College entrants; 1954; C. W. Valentine; Oliver & Boyd Ltd. *
For additional information and a review by Reginald R. Dale, see 5:374.

[836]

Revised Beta Examination. Ages 16 and over; 1931–57; revision of *Army Group Examination Beta* ('20); D. E. Kellogg, N. W. Morton, Robert M. Lindner, and Milton Gurvitz; Psychological Corporation. *
For additional information, see 5:375 (14 references) ; for reviews by Raleigh

M. Drake and Walter C. Shipley, see 3:259 (5 references); for reviews by S.
D. Porteus and David Wechsler, see 40:1419 (4 references).

[837]

Roback Mentality Tests for Superior Adults, Eighth Edition. Adults; 1920–
47; A. A. Roback; Sci-Art Publishers. *

[838]

The Ryburn Group Intelligence Tests. Ages 6.5–12.5, 9.5–15.5; [1936–40];
H. V. Clark; Robert Gibson & Sons (Glasgow), Ltd. *
  For additional information, see 40:1421.

[839]

SRA College Classification Tests. College entrants; 1958; 6 scores: English
usage, mathematics usage, social studies reading, natural science reading, word
usage, composite; Science Research Associates, Inc. *
  For additional information, see 5:376.

[840]

SRA Non-Verbal Form. Ages 12 and over; 1946–47; formerly called *SRA
Non-Verbal Classification Form;* Robert N. McMurry and Joseph E. King;
Science Research Associates, Inc. *
  For additional information and a review by W. D. Commins, see 4:318; see
also 3:261 (1 excerpt).

[841]

SRA Tests of Educational Ability. Grades 4–6, 6–9, 9–12; 1957–58; 4 or 5
scores: language, reasoning, quantitative, total, nonreading total (grades 4–6);
L. L. Thurstone and Thelma Gwinn Thurstone; Science Research Associates,
Inc. *
  For additional information and reviews by Joshua A. Fishman, William B.
Michael, and E. A. Peel of test for grades 9–12, see 5:377.

[842]

★SRA Tests of General Ability. Grades kgn–2, 2–4, 4–6, 6–9, 9–12; 1957–60;
2 or 4 scores: IQ, grade expectancy and (optional) information, non-cultural
reasoning; John C. Flanagan; Science Research Associates, Inc. *

[843]

SRA Verbal Form. Ages 12 and over; 1946–56; formerly called *SRA Verbal
Classification Form;* abbreviated adaptation of *Thurstone Test of Mental Alert-
ness* (see 865); 3 scores: quantitative, linguistic, total; Thelma Gwinn
Thurstone and L. L. Thurstone; Science Research Associates, Inc. *
  For additional information, see 5:378; for reviews by W. D. Commins and
Willis C. Schaefer, see 4:319.

[844]

Scholastic Mental Ability Tests. Grades kgn–1, 2–3, 4–9; 1953–54; for
Catholic schools; 6 scores in grades 2–9: linguistic, non-linguistic, total, logical
reasoning, numerical reasoning, fluency; Oliver F. Anderhalter; Scholastic
Testing Service, Inc. *
  For additional information and reviews by Walter N. Durost and Alexander
G. Wesman, see 5:380.

[845]

School Aptitude Test: Thanet Mental Tests. Ages 10–12; 1937; W. P. Alexander; University of London Press Ltd. *
   For additional information and a review by C. Ebblewhite Smith, see 40:1422.

[846]

Schrammel General Ability Test. Grades 9 and over; 1953–55; based in part upon *Army Group Examination Alpha* and revisions; H. E. Schrammel; Bureau of Educational Measurements. *
   For additional information and a review by Henry E. Garrett, see 5:381.

[847]

Schubert General Ability Battery. Grades 12–16 and adults; 1946–53; 5 scores: vocabulary, analogies, arithmetic problems, syllogisms, total; Herman J. P. Schubert; the Author. *
   For additional information and a review by William B. Schrader, see 5:382.

[848]

Scientific Ingenuity and Juristic Aptitude Test. Adults; 1931–51; A. A. Roback; [Sci-Art Publishers]. *
a) TEST 1, PROBLEM TEST. 1935.
b) TEST 2, CATEGORY TEST. 1951.
c) TEST 3, DISCRIMINATION TEST. 1931–39.
d) TEST 4, REFUTATION TEST. 1931–39.

[849]

Scott Company Mental Alertness Test. Applicants for office positions; 1923; Scott Co.; C. H. Stoelting Co. *

[850]

★Secondary Verbal Test 1. Ages 11.5–13.5; [1960]; Olive Wood and Valerie Land; published for the National Foundation for Educational Research in England and Wales; Newnes Educational Publishing Co. Ltd. *

[851]

★Selective Service System College Qualification Test. Draft registrants desiring deferment as college students; 1951–60; tests administered annually at centers established by the publisher; Educational Testing Service. *

[852]

Ship Destination Test. Grades 9 and over; 1955–56; general reasoning; Paul R. Christensen and J. P. Guilford; Sheridan Supply Co. *
   For additional information and a review by C. J. Adcock, see 5:383 (1 reference).

[853]

The Simplex GNV Intelligence Tests. Ages 11–13; 1952–57; C. A. Richardson; George G. Harrap & Co. Ltd. *
   For additional information, see 5:384 (2 references).

[854]

The Simplex Group Intelligence Scale. Ages 10 and over; 1922–39; C. A. Richardson; George G. Harrap & Co. Ltd. *
   For additional information and a review by James Mainwaring, see 5:385.

[855]

[The Simplex Junior Intelligence Tests.] Ages 7–14; 1932–51; C. A. Richardson; George G. Harrap & Co. Ltd. *
a) THE SIMPLEX JUNIOR INTELLIGENCE SCALE. 1932.
b) THE SIMPLEX JUNIOR 'A' INTELLIGENCE TEST. 1950–51.
   For additional information and a review by Arthur B. Royse, see 5:386 (1
reference) ; see also 4:322 (2 references).

[856]

Sleight Non-Verbal Intelligence Test. Ages 6–10; George F. Sleight; George
G. Harrap & Co. Ltd. *
   For additional information and reviews by John C. Daniels and M. L. Kellmer
Pringle, see 5:387.

[857]

The Southend Test of Intelligence. Ages 10–12; 1939–53; revision of Southend Group Test of Intelligence; M. E. Hebron and W. Stephenson; George G.
Harrap & Co. Ltd. *
   For additional information and a review by James Mainwaring, see 5:388;
for a review by Gertrude Keir of the original edition, see 4:323 (1 reference) ;
see also 40:1423 (1 excerpt).

[858]

*Survey of Mental Maturity: California Survey Series. Grades 7–9, 10–adult;
1959; tests are combinations of items from various levels of California Test of
Mental Maturity, 1957 Edition (see 732) ; 3 scores: language, nonlanguage,
total; Willis W. Clark, Elizabeth T. Sullivan, and Ernest W. Tiegs; California
Test Bureau. *

[859]

Terman Group Test of Mental Ability. Grades 7–12; 1920; Lewis M. Terman; [Harcourt, Brace & World, Inc.]. * For the revised edition entry, see
860.
   For additional information and reviews by Anne Anastasi and Howard Easley,
see 40:1424 (25 references).

[860]

Terman-McNemar Test of Mental Ability. Grades 7–12; 1941–42; revision
of Terman Group Test of Mental Ability (see 859) ; Lewis M. Terman and
Quinn McNemar; [Harcourt, Brace & World, Inc.]. *
   For additional information, see 4:324 (12 references) ; for reviews by Carl I.
Hovland and Robert L. Thorndike, see 3:263 (25 references).

[861]

Test of General Knowledge. Ages 14 and over; 1938; 7 scores: comprehension,
mathematics, information, vocabulary, estimation, reasoning, total; Eugene J.
Benge; Management Service Co. *
   For additional information, see 40:1425 (1 reference).

[862]

Test of Word-Number Ability. Grades 10–16; 1939–57; formerly called Word-
Number Test of Scholastic Aptitude; 3 scores: word, number, total; H. T.

Manuel, James Knight, J. A. Floyd, R. C. Jordan, Lulu Vinson, Marjorie L. Bagley, and B. F. Johnson, Jr.; Steck Co. *

For additional information and reviews by I. David Satlow and John M. Willits, see 5:389 (1 reference); for a review by Jane Loevinger of an earlier edition, see 4:333.

[863]

Tests AH4 and AH5. Ages 10 and over, 13 and over; 1955–56; A. W. Heim; distributed by National Foundation for Educational Research in England and Wales. *

a) TEST AH4: GROUP TEST OF INTELLIGENCE. Ages 10 and over; 1955.

b) TEST AH5: GROUP TEST OF HIGH-GRADE INTELLIGENCE. Ages 13 and over; 1956.

For additional information and reviews by George A. Ferguson of *a* and J. A. Keats of *b*, see 5:390 (11 references).

[864]

Tests of General Ability: Cooperative Inter-American Tests. Grades 1–3, 4–7, 8–13; 1950; English and Spanish editions; Committee on Modern Languages of the American Council on Education; [Guidance Testing Associates]. *
For the complete battery entry, see 1347.

a) PRIMARY LEVEL. Grades 1–3; 2 scores: oral vocabulary, total.

b) INTERMEDIATE LEVEL. Grades 4–7; 3 scores: nonverbal, verbal, total.

c) ADVANCED LEVEL. Grades 8–13; 3 scores: same as for *b*.

For additional information and reviews by Raleigh M. Drake and Walter N. Durost, see 4:325 (8 references).

[865]

Thurstone Test of Mental Alertness, Revised Edition. Grades 9–12 and adults; 1943–53; abbreviated adaptation of 1940 edition of *American Council on Education Psychological Examination for High School Students* (see 723); 3 scores: quantitative, linguistic, total; Thelma Gwinn Thurstone and L. L. Thurstone; Science Research Associates, Inc. *

For additional information and a review by Joshua A. Fishman, see 5:391; see also 4:326 (3 references); for reviews by Anne Anastasi and Emily T. Burr of an earlier edition, see 3:265.

[866]

The Tomlinson Junior School Test. Ages 7–12.0; 1953; T. P. Tomlinson; University of London Press Ltd. *

For additional information and a review by John C. Daniels, see 5:392.

[867]

Verbal and Non-Verbal Test 1. Ages 12 to 13-11; 1951–53; published for the National Foundation for Educational Research in England and Wales; Newnes Educational Publishing Co. Ltd. *

For additional information and a review by T. R. Miles, see 5:393.

[868]

Verbal Capacity Sampler. Adults; 1950–52; Byron B. Harless and Gerald P. Bodily; Harless & Kirkpatrick Associates, Inc. *

For additional information, see 5:394.

[869]

*Verbal Test (Adv.) 1, 2, 3, 4. Ages 12 to 13–11; 1954–60; D. A. Pidgeon; published for the National Foundation for Educational Research in England and Wales; Newnes Educational Publishing Co. Ltd. *

For additional information, see 5:396.

[870]

*Verbal Tests 1–2, 4–10. Ages 10 to 11–11; 1951–60; I. Macfarlane Smith and M. A. Brimer; published for the National Foundation for Educational Research in England and Wales; Newnes Educational Publishing Co. Ltd. *

For additional information concerning tests 1–2 and 4–8, see 5:397.

[871]

Vocabulary Tests. Ages 10–15; 1931–35; Frank Watts; University of London Press Ltd. *

a) VOCABULARY TEST NO. 1, 100 COMMON NAMES.
b) VOCABULARY TEST NO. 2, 100 COMMON CLASS NAMES.
c) VOCABULARY TEST NO. 3, 100 COMMON VERBS.
d) VOCABULARY TEST NO. 4, 100 COMMON ADJECTIVES (LIST A).
e) VOCABULARY TEST NO. 5, 100 COMMON ADJECTIVES (LIST B).

For additional information and a review by John Nisbet, see 5:398.

[872]

Wesman Personnel Classification Test. Grades 8–16 and adults; 1946–51; 3 scores: verbal, numerical, total; Alexander G. Wesman; Psychological Corporation. *

For additional information, see 5:399 (8 references); for reviews by John C. Flanagan and Erwin K. Taylor, see 4:331 (3 references); see also 3:253 (1 excerpt).

[873]

The "West Riding" Tests of Mental Ability. Ages 9–14; 1925; T. P. Tomlinson; University of London Press Ltd. *

For a review by Ll. Wynn Jones, see 40:1430.

[874]

"West Yorkshire" Group Test of Intelligence. Ages 7.5–15; 1940; T. P. Tomlinson; University of London Press Ltd. *

For additional information, see 4:332.

[875]

*Wonderlic Personnel Test. Adults; 1939–59; E. F. Wonderlic; the Author. *

For additional information, see 5:400 (59 references); for reviews by H. E. Brodgen, Charles D. Flory, and Irving Lorge, see 3:269 (7 references); see also 40:1415 (2 references).

INDIVIDUAL

[876]

Alexander Performance Scale: A Performance Scale for the Measurement of Practical Ability. Ages 8–18; 1935–46; 3 tests: *The Passalong Test* (see 904) and modifications of Kohs' *Block-Design Test* (see 918) and the *Cube*

Construction Test (see 921); W. P. Alexander; distributed by National Foundation for Educational Research in England and Wales. *

For additional information and a review by Charles A. Strickland, see 4:334 (4 references); for a review by John Cohen, see 3:270 (1 reference, 2 excerpts); for a review by J. M. Blackburn, see 40:1376 (3 references); for excerpts from related book reviews, see 38:B293 and 36:B3. For reviews of *The Passalong Test,* see 40:1414.

[877]

Arthur Point Scale of Performance Tests. Ages 4.5 or 5.5 to superior adults; 1925–47; Grace Arthur. *

a) FORM I. Ages 5.5 to superior adults; 1925–43; 10 tests: *Knox Cube Test (Arthur Revision), Seguin Form Board (Arthur Revision), Two-Figure Form Board, Casuist Form Board, Manikin Test, Feature Profile Test, Mare and Foal Formboard, Healy Pictorial Completion Test I, Porteus Maze Test (1924 Series), The Block-Design Test (Arthur Modification)*; C. H. Stoelting Co.

b) REVISED FORM II. Ages 4.5 to superior adults; 1933–47; 5 tests: *Knox Cube Test (Arthur Revision), Seguin Form Board (Arthur Revision), Arthur Stencil Design Test I, Porteus Maze Test (Arthur Revision), Healy Pictorial Completion Test II;* Psychological Corporation.

For additional information and a review by William R. Grove, see 4:335 (12 references); for reviews by Andrew W. Brown and Carroll A. Whitmer, see 40:1379 (16 references, 1 excerpt); see also 3:271 (19 references, 1 excerpt); for excerpts from related book reviews, see 40:B830, 38:B304, and 36:B19.

[878]

Canadian Intelligence Examination, 1947 Revision. Ages 3–16; 1940–47; modification of the *Stanford-Binet Scale* ('16); Harry Amoss, Charles G. Stogdill, and Carman E. Stothers; Ryerson Press. *

For additional information and a review by Gwen F. Arnold, see 4:336; see also 3:272 (1 reference, 2 excerpts).

[879]

Carl Hollow Square Scale. Ages 10 and over; 1939–45; George P. Carl; Psychological Service, Institute of the Pennsylvania Hospital. *

For additional information and a review by Grace H. Kent, see 3:273 (3 references); for a review by T. J. Keating, see 40:1385 (2 references).

[880]

Cattell Infant Intelligence Scale. Ages 3–30 months; 1940; downward extension of the *Revised Stanford-Binet Intelligence Scale, Second Revision* (see 909); Psyche Cattell; Psychological Corporation. *

For additional information and reviews by Florence M. Teagarden and Beth L. Wellman, see 3:281 (2 references, 1 excerpt).

[881]

★**Children's Picture Information Test.** Ages 2–6 with motor handicaps; [1959]; Kate L. Kogan and Richard L. Crager; Spastic Aid Council, Inc. *

[882]

*****Columbia Mental Maturity Scale, Revised Edition.** Mental ages 3–12; 1954–59; Bessie B. Burgemeister, Lucille Hollander Blum, and Irving Lorge; [Harcourt, Brace & World, Inc.]. *

For additional information concerning the original edition, see 5:402 (13 references).

[883]

Crichton Vocabulary Scale. Ages 4–11; 1950; J. C. Raven; H. K. Lewis & Co. Ltd. * For a complementary test, see 831.

For additional information and reviews by Charlotte Banks and W. D. Wall, see 4:337.

[884]

Detroit Kindergarten Test. Kindergarten entrants; 1922–25, c1921–25; Harry J. Baker and H. J. Kaufmann; [Harcourt, Brace & World, Inc.]. *

For additional information and reviews by Psyche Cattell and Ruth W. Washburn, see 3:274 (1 reference).

[885]

Detroit Tests of Learning Aptitude. Ages 3 and over; 1935–55; 20 scores: pictorial absurdities, verbal absurdities, pictorial opposites, verbal opposites, motor speed and precision, auditory attention span (for unrelated words, for related syllables), oral commissions, social adjustment A, visual attention span (for objects, for letters), orientation, free association, memory for designs, number ability, social adjustment B, broken pictures, oral directions, likenesses and differences, total; Harry J. Baker and Bernice Leland; Public School Publishing Co. *

For additional information, see 5:403; for a review by F. L. Wells, see 3:275 (1 reference); for reviews by Anne Anastasi and Henry Feinberg of an earlier edition, see 38:1058 (1 excerpt).

[886]

★Diagnostic Performance Tests. Adults; 1958; 5 tests; Boris Semeonoff and Eric Trist; distributed by National Foundation for Educational Research in England and Wales. *
a) SEMEONOFF-VIGOTSKY TEST. Adaptation of *Concept Formation Test* (see 133).
b) TRIST-HARGREAVES TEST.
c) TRIST-MISSELBROOK-KOHS TEST. Modification of Kohs' *Block-Design Test* (see 918).
d) CARL HOLLOW SQUARE TEST. Essentially the same as *Carl Hollow Square Scale* (see 879).
e) THE REVISED PASSALONG TEST. Modification of *The Passalong Test* (see 904).
  For additional information concerning the manual, see 5:B393.

[887]

Full-Range Picture Vocabulary Test. Ages 2 and over; 1948; Robert B. Ammons and Helen S. Ammons; Psychological Test Specialists. *

For additional information and reviews by William D. Altus and William M. Cruickshank, see 4:340 (10 references).

[888]

Gesell Developmental Schedules, 1940 Series. Ages 4 weeks to 6 years; 1925–49; also called *Gesell Maturity Scale, Gesell Norms of Development, Gesell Tests, Preschool Child Development Scale, Preschool Child Test, Yale Psycho-Clinic Developmental Schedules, Yale Tests of Child Development,* and other variations; Arnold Gesell and others; Psychological Corporation. *

For additional information, see 4:341 (5 references); for reviews by Nancy Bayley and Florence M. Teagarden, see 3:276 (28 references); for excerpts from related book reviews, see 3:277–80 and 40:B912–6.

[889]

[Re Gesell Developmental Schedules.] Blum-Fieldsteel Development Charts. Birth to 72 months; 1952–53; based on the *Gesell Developmental Schedules;* Lucille Hollander Blum and Nina D. Fieldsteel; [Harcourt, Brace & World, Inc.]. *

For additional information, see 5:585 (1 reference).

[890]

The Griffiths Mental Development Scale for Testing Babies From Birth to Two Years. 1951–55; 6 scores: locomotor, personal-social, hearing and speech, eye and hand, performance, total; Ruth Griffiths; the Author. *

For additional information and a review by Nancy Bayley, see 5:404 (3 references).

[891]

The Immediate Test: A Quick Verbal Intelligence Test. Adults; 1951; Raymond J. Corsini; Sheridan Supply Co. *

For additional information and reviews by Jerome E. Doppelt and Ivan Norman Mensh, see 4:342 (1 reference).

[892]

Intelligence Tests for Children. Ages 1.5–15; 1945–58; C. W. Valentine; Methuen & Co. Ltd. *

For additional information and reviews by Elizabeth D. Fraser and G. A. V. Morgan, see 5:405 (2 references); see also 4:343 (3 references); for excerpts from related book reviews, see 4:344, 4:345, and 3:283.

[893]

★Kahn Intelligence Tests: Experimental Form. Ages 1 month and over; 1960; test materials identical with those of *Kahn Test of Symbol Arrangement* (see 356); main scale plus 6 optional scales: brief scale, concept formation, recall, motor coordination, scale for use with the deaf, scale for use with the blind; Theodore C. Kahn; Psychological Test Specialists. *

[894]

Kent Series of Emergency Scales. Ages 5–7, 6–8, 6.5–10, 9–14; 1932–46; Grace H. Kent; Psychological Corporation. *
a) SCALE A. Ages 5–7; 1944–46; formerly called *Andover School-Entrance Test.*
b) SCALES B AND C. Ages 6–8, 6.5–10; 1946.
c) SCALE D. Ages 9–14; 1932–46; revision of *Emergency Test* (also called *Kent E-G-Y Test*).

For additional information and a review by Ivan Norman Mensh, see 4:346 (8 references); for a review by Charles N. Cofer, see 3:284 (26 references).

[895]

★The Leiter Adult Intelligence Scale. Adults; 1956–59; includes *The FR-CR Test, Pathways Test, The Leiter Adaptation of Arthur's Stencil Design Test,* and *The Leiter Adaptation of the Painted Cube Test;* 3 scores: language, non-language, total; Russell Graydon Leiter; C. H. Stoelting Co. *

For additional information, see 5:406 (1 reference); for additional information and a review by George K. Bennett of the *Pathways Test,* see 4:355 (1 reference, 1 excerpt); for additional information regarding the other subtests, see 4:347 (1 reference, 1 excerpt), 4:348 (1 reference, 1 excerpt), and 4:339.

[896]

Leiter International Performance Scale. Ages 2–18; 1936–52; Russell Gray-don Leiter; C. H. Stoelting Co. *

For additional information, see 5:408 (17 references); for a review by Gwen F. Arnold, see 4:349 (25 references, 1 excerpt); for a related review, see 40:B989.

[897]

Leiter International Performance Scale: Arthur Adaptation. Ages 2–12; 1952–55; test materials consist of Trays 1 and 2 (ages 2–12) of *Leiter International Performance Scale* (see 896); Grace Arthur; C. H. Stoelting Co. *

For additional information, see 5:407.

[898]

Merrill-Palmer Scale of Mental Tests. Ages 24–63 months; 1926–31; 15 tests: *Stutsman Color-Matching Test, Wallin Peg Boards, Stutsman Buttoning Test, Stick-and-String Test, Stutsman Language Test, Stutsman Picture Formboard, Mare and Foal Formboard,* modification of *Seguin-Goddard Formboard, Manikin Test, Decroly Matching Game, Stutsman Nested Cubes, Action Agent Test* (modification of *Action-Agent Association Test* ['11] by R. S. Woodworth and F. L. Wells), *Copying Test, Pyramid Test,* and *Little Pink Tower Test;* Rachel Stutsman; C. H. Stoelting Co. *

For additional information and reviews by Nancy Bayley, B. M. Castner, Florence L. Goodenough, and Florence M. Teagarden, see 40:1406 (13 references); for excerpts from related book reviews, see 40:B1123.

[899]

Minnesota Preschool Scale. Ages 1.5–6; 1932–40; 3 scores: verbal, nonverbal, total; Florence L. Goodenough, Katherine M. Maurer, and M. J. Van Wagenen; Educational Test Bureau. *

For additional information, see 4:351 (2 references); for a review by Beth L. Wellman, see 3:286 (2 references); for reviews by Rachel Stutsman Ball, Nancy Bayley, and Florence M. Teagarden of the original edition, see 40:1407 (3 references); for excerpts from related book reviews, see 4:352, 3:287, and 3:288.

[900]

Nebraska Test of Learning Aptitude. Deaf and hearing children ages 4–10; 1941–55; Marshall S. Hiskey; the Author. *

For additional information and a review by William Sloan, see 5:409 (8 references); for a review by Mildred C. Templin of an earlier edition, see 4:353 (1 reference); see also 3:289 (3 references).

[901]

Non-Verbal Intelligence Tests for Deaf and Hearing Subjects. Ages 3–16; 1939–58; J. Th. Snijders and N. Snijders-Oomen; J. B. Wolters. * (Distributor outside of Holland: Swets & Zeitlinger.)

For additional information, see 5:410.

[902]

The Northwestern Intelligence Tests: For Measuring Adaptation to the Physical and Social Environment. Ages 13–36 weeks; 1943–51; revision of

Gilliland-Shotwell Intelligence Scale ('43); A. R. Gilliland; Houghton Mifflin Co. *

For additional information and a review by Nancy Bayley, see 5:411; for a review by Mildred C. Templin, see 4:354 (9 references, 1 excerpt).

[903]

Ontario School Ability Examination. Children ages 3–15 who are deaf, non-native speakers of English, or handicapped in language development; 1936; Harry Amoss; Ryerson Press. *

For additional information and a review by W. Line, see 40:1411 (2 references).

[904]

The Passalong Test: A Performance Test of Intelligence. Ages 8 and over; 1932–37; subtest of *Alexander Performance Scale* (see 876); revision appears in *Diagnostic Performance Tests* (see 886); W. P. Alexander; distributed by National Foundation for Educational Research in England and Wales. * (United States publisher: C. H. Stoelting Co.)

For additional information and reviews by James Drever, T. J. Keating, and Grace H. Kent, see 40:1414 (5 references). For reviews of the complete Alexander battery, see 4:334, 3:270, and 40:1376.

[905]

★**Peabody Picture Vocabulary Test.** Ages 2.5–18; 1959; Lloyd M. Dunn; American Guidance Service, Inc. *

[906]

Performance Tests of Intelligence: A Series of Non-Linguistic Tests for Deaf and Normal Children, Third Edition. Ages 5–6, 7–16; 1928–44; James Drever and Mary Collins; A. H. Baird (test materials), and Oliver & Boyd Ltd. (manual). *

a) SERIES A. Ages 7–16; 10 tests: modification of *The Block-Design Test, Knox Cube Test: Pintner Modification,* Drever-Collins *Domino Test,* Drever-Collins *Size and Weights Test, Manikin Test, Feature Profile Test: Pintner-Paterson Modification,* modification of *Two-Figure Formboard,* modification of *Healy-Fernald Puzzle Box A, Cube Construction Test,* and Drever-Collins *Picture Completion Test.*

b) SERIES B. Ages 5–6; 6 tests: size test from *Size and Weights Test, Knox Cube Test: Pintner Modification, Dearborn Formboard 4 (Triangle Board), Seguin Formboard: Pintner-Paterson Modification, Manikin Test,* and *Mare and Foal Formboard.*

For additional information, see 3:290 (2 references); for excerpts from related book reviews, see 36:B87.

[907]

*The Porteus Maze Test.** Ages 3 and over; 1914–59; 2 scores: quantitative, qualitative; Stanley D. Porteus. *

a) VINELAND REVISION. Ages 3 and over; 1914–24; C. H. Stoelting Co.

b) VINELAND REVISION: NEW SERIES. Ages 3 and over; 1914–59; Psychological Corporation.

c) PORTEUS MAZE EXTENSION. Ages 14 and over; 1953–59; Psychological Corporation.

d) PORTEUS MAZE SUPPLEMENT. Ages 7 and over; 1959; a retesting series; Psychological Corporation.

For additional information, see 5:412 (28 references); for reviews by C. M.

Louttit and Gladys C. Schwesinger, see 4:356 (56 references). For excerpts from reviews of the 1950 manual, see 4:357. For excerpts from reviews of the 1933 manual, see 38:B453 and 36:B210.

[908]

Randall's Island Performance Series. Ages 2–4; 1931–53; Louise E. Poull, Ada S. Bristol, Helen B. King, and Lillie B. Peatman; test materials, formerly published by C. H. Stoelting Co., out of print; manual, with adaptations for testing deaf children, distributed for Central Institute for the Deaf by Volta Bureau. *

[909]

Revised Stanford-Binet Intelligence Scale, Second Revision. Ages 2 and over; 1916–37; revision of *Stanford-Binet Scale* ('16); Lewis M. Terman and Maud A. Merrill; Houghton Mifflin Co. * For a later revision entry, see 910.

For additional information and reviews by Mary R. Haworth and Norman D. Sundberg, see 5:413 (127 references); for a review by Boyd R. McCandless, see 4:358 (142 references); see also 3:292 (217 references) and 40:1420 (134 references, 3 excerpts); for reviews by Francis N. Maxfield, J. W. M. Rothney, and F. L. Wells, see 38:1062; for excerpts from related book reviews, see 3:293, 3:294, 40:B1093, and 38:B497.

[910]

***Revised Stanford-Binet Intelligence Scale, Third Revision.** Ages 2 and over; 1916–60; Lewis M. Terman and Maud A. Merrill; Houghton Mifflin Co. * For the earlier edition entry and references to reviews, see 909.

[911]

Tests of Mental Development. Ages 3 months and over; 1939; 7 scores: mental age, intelligence quotient (below age 16), percent of average, speed, speed quotient, accuracy, variability; F. Kuhlmann; Educational Test Bureau. *

For additional information and reviews by Grace H. Kent, Francis N. Maxfield, Myrtle Luneau Pignatelli, and F. L. Wells, see 40:1426 (1 reference, 2 excerpts).

[912]

Wechsler Adult Intelligence Scale. Ages 16 and over; 1939–55; revision of Form 1 of *Wechsler-Bellevue Intelligence Scale* (see 913); 14 scores: verbal (information, comprehension, arithmetic, similarities, digit span, vocabulary, total), performance (digit symbol, picture completion, block design, picture arrangement, object assembly, total), total; David Wechsler; Psychological Corporation. *

For additional information and reviews by Nancy Bayley and Wilson H. Guertin, see 5:414 (42 references). For reviews of the Wechsler-Bellevue Scale, see 5:415, 4:361, 3:298, and 40:1429. For excerpts from related book reviews, see 3:299, 3:300, 3:301, and 40:B1121.

[913]

Wechsler-Bellevue Intelligence Scale. Ages 10 and over; 1939–47; 14 scores: verbal (general information, general comprehension, digit span, arithmetic, similarities, vocabulary, total), performance (picture arrangement, picture completion, block design, object assembly, digit symbol, total), total; David Wechsler; Psychological Corporation. (South African adaptation: ages 18–44; [1960];

National Institute for Personnel Research.) * For the revised edition entry, see 912.

For additional information, see 5:415 (254 references); for reviews by Murray Aborn and William D. Altus, see 4:361 (250 references); for a review by Robert I. Watson, see 3:298 (119 references); for a review by F. L. Wells, see 40:1429 (2 references, 2 excerpts); for excerpts from related book reviews, see 5:B332, 4:362, 3:299–301, and 40:B1121.

[914]
Wechsler Intelligence Scale for Children. Ages 5–15; 1949; downward extension of Form 2 of *Wechsler-Bellevue Intelligence Scale* (see 913); 13–15 scores: verbal (information, comprehension, arithmetic, similarities, vocabulary, digit span—optional, total), performance (picture completion, picture arrangement, block design, object assembly, coding, mazes—optional, total), total; David Wechsler; Psychological Corporation. *

For additional information and reviews by Elizabeth D. Fraser, Gerald R. Patterson, and Albert I. Rabin, see 5:416 (111 references); for reviews by James M. Anderson, Harold A. Delp, and Boyd R. McCandless, see 4:363 (22 references, 1 excerpt).

[915]
★**Williams Intelligence Test for Children with Defective Vision.** Ages 5–15; [1956]; M. Williams; University of Birmingham Institute of Education. *

SPECIFIC

[916]
★**Alternate Uses.** Grades 7–16 and adults; 1960; experimental form; spontaneous flexibility; Paul R. Christensen, J. P. Guilford, Philip R. Merrifield, and Robert C. Wilson; Sheridan Supply Co. *

[917]
Benton Visual Retention Test, Revised Edition. Ages 8 and over; 1946–55; Arthur L. Benton; distributed by Psychological Corporation. *

For additional information and a review by Nelson G. Hanawalt, see 5:401 (5 references); for reviews by Ivan Norman Mensh, Joseph Newman, and William Schofield of the original edition, see 4:360 (3 references); see also 3:297 (1 excerpt).

[918]
The Block-Design Test. Mental ages 5–20; [1919]; also called *Kohs' Block-Design Test;* modifications appear in *Alexander Performance Scale* (see 876), *Arthur Point Scale of Performance Tests* (see 877), *Performance Tests of Intelligence* (see 906), *Diagnostic Performance Tests* (see 886), and *General Adaptability Battery* (see 1822); S. C. Kohs; C. H. Stoelting Co. *

[919]
★**Christensen-Guilford Fluency Tests.** Grades 7–16 and adults; 1957–59; Paul R. Christensen and J. P. Guilford; Sheridan Supply Co. *
a) WORD FLUENCY.
b) IDEATIONAL FLUENCY I.
c) ASSOCIATIONAL FLUENCY I.
d) EXPRESSIONAL FLUENCY.

[919a]

★Concealed Figures: A Test of Flexibility of Closure. Grades 9–16 and industrial employees; 1956–59; revision of *Gottschaldt Figures;* L. L. Thurstone and T. E. Jeffrey; Education-Industry Service. *

[920]

★Consequences. Grades 7–16 and adults; 1958; 2 scores: remote responses (originality), obvious responses (ideational fluency); P. R. Christensen, P. R. Merrifield, and J. P. Guilford; Sheridan Supply Co. *

[921]

Cube Construction Test. Ages 14–16; [1918]; modifications appear in *Alexander Performance Scale* (see 876) and *Performance Tests of Intelligence* (see 906); E. A. Doll; C. H. Stoelting Co. *

[922]

Feature Profile Test: Pintner-Paterson Modification. Ages 4 and over; [1917–23]; modification of *Knox-Kempf Feature Profile Test* ['14]; subtest of *Arthur Point Scale of Performance Tests* (see 877) and *Performance Tests of Intelligence* (see 906); R. Pintner and D. G. Paterson; C. H. Stoelting Co.

[923]

[Fernald Weights Discrimination Test.] Ages 6 and over; [1930]; G. M Fernald; C. H. Stoelting Co.

[924]

Foster Mazes. Ages 5 and over; [1923]; William S. Foster; C. H. Stoelting Co. *

[924a]

★Gestalt Completion: A Test of Speed of Closure. Grades 9–16 and industrial employees; 1956–59; L. L. Thurstone and T. E. Jeffrey; Education-Industry Service. *

[925]

Healy Pictorial Completion Tests. Ages 5 and over; [1914–21]; William Healy; C. H. Stoelting Co. *
a) TEST I. 1914; subtest of *Performance Tests of Intelligence* (see 906) and, with modifications, *Arthur Point Scale of Performance Tests* (see 877).
b) TEST II. [1917–21]; subtest of *Arthur Point Scale of Performance Tests* and *Performance Tests of Intelligence.*

[926]

★Jensen Alternation Board. Ages 5 and over; [1959]; learning age; Milton B. Jensen; Lafayette Instrument Co. *

[927]

Knox Cube Test: Arthur Revision. Ages 4.5 and over; [1925]; modification of *Knox Cube Imitation Test* ('14); subtest of *Arthur Point Scale of Performance Tests* (see 877); Grace Arthur; C. H. Stoelting Co.

[928]

Manikin Test. Ages 2 and over; [1917]; subtest of *Merrill-Palmer Scale of Mental Tests* (see 898), *Performance Tests of Intelligence* (see 906), and *Ar-*

thur Point Scale of Performance Tests, Form 1 (see 877) ; R. Pintner; C. H. Stoelting Co.

[929]

Mare and Foal Formboard. Ages 2–15; [1911]; modifications appear in *Arthur Point Scale of Performance Tests* (see 877), *Merrill-Palmer Scale of Mental Tests* (see 898), and *Performance Tests of Intelligence* (see 906) ; William Healy and G. M. Fernald; C. H. Stoelting Co.

[930]

Meyer Finger Mazes. Ages 12 and over; date unknown; C. H. Stoelting Co.

[931]

Nufferno Tests of Speed and Level. Mental ages 11 and over; 1956; W. D. Furneaux; distributed by National Foundation for Educational Research in England and Wales. *

For additional information and reviews by John Liggett and E. A. Peel, see 5:357 (3 references).

[931a]

★**Perceptual Speed (Identical Forms).** Grades 9–16 and industrial employees; 1956–59; L. L. Thurstone and T. E. Jeffrey; Education-Industry Service. *

[932]

★**Pertinent Questions.** Grades 9–16 and adults; 1960; experimental form; conceptual foresight; Raymond M. Berger and J. P. Guilford; Sheridan Supply Co. *

[933]

★**The Rutgers Drawing Test.** Ages 3–7, 7–10; 1952–61; Anna Spiesman Starr; the Author. *

[934]

Seguin-Goddard Formboard. Ages 5–14; [1911]; modifications appear in *Arthur Point Scale of Performance Tests* (see 877), *Merrill-Palmer Scale of Mental Tests* (see 898), and *Performance Tests of Intelligence* (see 906) ; [E. Seguin, H. H. Goddard, and N. Norsworthy] ; C. H. Stoelting Co.

[935]

Stencil Design Test I. Ages 4 to superior adults; 1944–47; subtest of *Arthur Point Scale of Performance Tests, Revised Form II* (see 877) ; adaptation in *Leiter Adult Intelligence Scale* (see 895) ; Grace Arthur; Psychological Corporation. *

For additional information and a review by Benjamin Balinsky, see 4:359 (4 references) ; for a review by James M. Anderson, see 3:295.

[936]

★**Subsumed Abilities Test.** Ages 9 and over; 1957–58; 4 scores: recognition, abstraction, conceptualization, total; for research use only; Joseph R. Sanders; Martin M. Bruce. *

[937]

Time Appreciation Test. Ages 10 and over; 1943–46; title on test is *JNB Time Test;* John N. Buck; Western Psychological Services. *

For additional information and reviews by E. J. G. Bradford and Charles N. Cofer, see 3:266 (2 references).

[938]

Two-Figure Formboard. Ages 4 and over; [1917]; modifications appear in *Arthur Point Scale of Performance Tests* (see 877) and *Performance Tests of Intelligence* (see 906); R. Pintner; C. H. Stoelting Co.

[939]

Wechsler Memory Scale. Adults; 1945; David Wechsler and Calvin P. Stone; Psychological Corporation. *

For additional information and reviews by Ivan Norman Mensh and Joseph Newman, see 4:364 (6 references); for a review by Kate Levine Kogan, see 3:302 (3 references).

MATHEMATICS

[940]

★**Business Mathematics: Every Pupil Scholarship Test.** High school; 1956; Bureau of Educational Measurements. *

[941]

*****College Entrance Examination Board Achievement Test in Advanced Mathematics.** Candidates for college entrance; 1936–61; program administered for the College Entrance Examination Board by Educational Testing Service. * For the testing program entry, see 1345.

For additional information, see 5:417 (3 references); for a review by Paul L. Dressel of earlier forms, see 4:367 (4 references).

[942]

*****College Entrance Examination Board Achievement Test in Intermediate Mathematics.** Candidates for college entrance; 1936–61; program administered for the College Entrance Examination Board by Educational Testing Service. * For the testing program entry, see 1345.

For additional information, see 5:418 (3 references); for a review by Paul J. Blommers of earlier forms, see 4:368 (2 references).

[943]

*****College Entrance Examination Board Advanced Placement Examination: Mathematics.** Candidates desiring credit for college level courses or admission to advanced courses; 1954–61; program administered for the College Entrance Examination Board by Educational Testing Service. * For the testing program entry, see 1346.

For additional information and a review by Paul L. Dressel of Form FBP, see 5:419 (1 reference).

[944]

Cooperative General Achievement Tests: Test 3, Mathematics. Grade 12 and college entrants; 1937–56; Paul J. Burke and Bernice Orshansky; Cooperative Test Division. * For the complete battery entry, see 8.

For additional information, see 5:420; see also 4:379 (2 references); for a review by John F. Randolph of earlier forms, see 3:316. For reviews of the complete battery, see 5:6, 4:5, and 3:3.

[945]

Cooperative General Mathematics Test for High School Classes. High school; 1933–51; H. T. Lundholm and L. P. Siceloff; Cooperative Test Division. *

For additional information and a review by L. B. Kinney, see 40:1432 (1 reference); for a review by Maurice Hartung of an earlier form, see 38:1072.

[946]

Cooperative Mathematics Pre-Test for College Students. College entrants; 1936–48; Committee on Tests of the Mathematical Association of America; Cooperative Test Division. *

For additional information and a review by E. P. Starke, see 4:369; for reviews by M. W. Richardson and S. S. Wilks of earlier forms, see 38:1073.

[947]

Cooperative Mathematics Tests for Grades 7, 8, and 9. Grades 7–9; 1938–50; 5 scores: skills, facts-terms-concepts, application, appreciation, total; H. Vernon Price and Bernice Orshansky; Cooperative Test Division. *

For additional information and a review by Gordon Fifer, see 5:421 (1 reference); see also 4:370 (2 references); for a review by M. L. Hartung of earlier forms, see 3:305 (1 reference); for reviews by Richard M. Drake, Judson W. Foust, and G. M. Ruch, see 40:1433 (2 references).

[948]

Davis Test of Functional Competence in Mathematics. Grades 9–12; 1951–52, c1950–51; David J. Davis; [Harcourt, Brace & World, Inc.]. *

For additional information and reviews by Paul L. Dressel and Tom A. Lamke, see 5:422 (2 references).

[949]

★ERB Mathematics Tests, Experimental Form. High school; 1961; 4 tests; Subcommittee on Mathematics Tests of the Educational Records Bureau; Educational Records Bureau. *

a) TEST I: ANALYTICAL GEOMETRY TEST.
b) TEST II: SETS, EQUATIONS, INEQUALITIES, AND NUMBER CONCEPTS.
c) TEST III: PROBABILITY AND STATISTICS.
d) TEST IV: INTRODUCTORY CALCULUS.

[950]

Functional Evaluation in Mathematics. Grades 4–6, 7–9; 1952; 3 tests; Ben A. Sueltz; Educational Test Bureau. *

a) QUANTITATIVE UNDERSTANDING.
b) PROBLEM SOLVING.
c) BASIC COMPUTATIONS.

For additional information and a review by Charles S. Ross, see 4:372.

[951]

General Mathematical Ability. High school; 1944–57; subtest of high school level of *Tests of General Educational Development* (see 44); United States Armed Forces Institute; Veterans' Testing Service. *

For additional information, see 5:426. For reviews of the complete battery, see 5:27, 4:26, and 3:20.

[952]

*General Mathematics: Every Pupil Scholarship Test. High school; 1926–61; new form usually issued twice a year; Bureau of Educational Measurements. *

For additional information, see 5:423.

[953]

*General Mathematics: Midwest High School Achievement Examinations. High school; 1955–61; Educational Test Bureau. *

For additional information concerning earlier forms, see 5:424.

[954]

*General Mathematics III, Form 4: Achievement Examinations for Secondary Schools. High school; 1951–59; Forms 1–3 published by Educational Test Bureau are out of print; J. R. Schunert and Wallace M. Bernards; C. A. Gregory Co. *

For additional information concerning earlier forms, see 5:425.

[955]

Graded Arithmetic-Mathematics Test. Ages 7–21; 1949; P. E. Vernon; University of London Press Ltd. *

For additional information and a review by Stanley Nisbet, see 5:476.

[956]

*The Graduate Record Examinations Advanced Tests: Mathematics. Grades 16–17; 1939–61; Educational Testing Service. * For the testing program entry, see 1353.

For additional information and a review by Eric F. Gardner, see 5:427 (1 reference). For a review of the testing program, see 5:601.

[957]

Iowa Placement Examinations: Mathematics Aptitude. Grades 12–13; 1925–44; Bureau of Educational Research and Service. *

a) SERIES MAI, REVISED. 1925–26; G. D. Stoddard and E. W. Chittenden.

b) NEW SERIES MA-2, REVISED. 1925–44; G. D. Stoddard, L. W. Miller, E. W. Chittenden, and D. B. Stuit.

For additional information and reviews by Edmund P. Churchill and Paul L. Dressel, see 3:308 (18 references).

[958]

Iowa Placement Examinations: Mathematics Training: Series MT1, Revised. Grades 12–13; 1925–26; G. D. Stoddard and E. W. Chittenden; Bureau of Educational Research and Service. *

For additional information and reviews by Edmund P. Churchill and Paul L. Dressel, see 3:309 (8 references).

[959]

*The Iowa Tests of Educational Development: Test 4, Ability to Do Quantitative Thinking. Grades 9–13; 1942–59; E. F. Lindquist and others; Science Research Associates, Inc. * For the complete battery entry, see 25.

For additional information, see 5:428. For reviews of the complete battery, see 5:17, 4:17, and 3:12.

[960]

Junior High School Mathematics Test: Acorn Achievement Tests. Grades
7–9; 1942–52; 4 scores: concepts, problem analysis, problems, total; Harry
Eisner; Acorn Publishing Co. *

For additional information and a review by Myron F. Rosskopf, see 5:429;
for a review by William Betz, see 3:310.

[961]

Kansas Mathematics Test, Revised Edition. Grades 9–13; 1937–55; 2 scores:
arithmetic, algebra; H. E. Schrammel; Bureau of Educational Measurements. *

For additional information and a review by Paul Blommers, see 5:430.

[962]

Mathematical Ability Test. Grades 4 and over; 1937; Harry Amoss; Ryerson
Press. *

For additional information, see 38:1075.

[963]

**Mathematical Literacy for High School Seniors: A Test of Basic Skills and
Abilities: [Ohio Senior Survey Tests].** Grade 12; 1946–53; revision of *Mathematics for High School Seniors: A Screening Test in Basic Skills;* 4 scores:
terms and formulas, computational skills, solving problems, total; Ohio Scholarship Tests. *

For additional information, see 5:431.

[964]

***Mathematics: Every Pupil Test.** 1, 2 semesters in grades 7–8; 1930–61; new
form usually issued twice a year; Ohio Scholarship Tests. *

For additional information, see 5:432.

[965]

***Mathematics: National Teacher Examinations.** College seniors and teach-
ers; 1940–61; Educational Testing Service. * For the testing program entry,
see 1192.

For additional information, see 5:433. For reviews of the testing program,
see 5:538 and 4:802.

[966]

Mathematics: Teacher Education Examination Program. College seniors
preparing to teach secondary school; 1957; Educational Testing Service. * For
the testing program entry, see 1205.

For additional information, see 5:434. For a review of the testing program,
see 5:543.

[967]

***Mathematics Test (Adv.).** Ages 12–14.0; 1954–60; D. A. Pidgeon; published
for the National Foundation for Educational Research in England and Wales;
Newnes Educational Publishing Co. Ltd. *

For additional information, see 5:435.

[968]

Mathematics Test 1. Ages 12 to 13-11; 1951–52; I. Macfarlane Smith; published for the National Foundation for Educational Research in England and Wales; Newnes Educational Publishing Co. Ltd. *

For additional information and a review by Jack Wrigley, see 5:436.

[969]

The Morgan Achievement Test in Mathematics for Employee Selection. Adults; 1942–46; formerly called *Rogers Achievement Test in Mathematics for Technical and Industrial Schools;* William J. Morgan; Aptitude Associates. *

For additional information and a review by Marion F. Shaycoft, see 5:437.

[970]

★**Portland Prognostic Tests for Mathematics.** Grades 8, 9; 1960; Ernest Hayes; [Hayes Educational Test Laboratory]. *

[971]

Purdue Industrial Mathematics Test. Adults; 1946; C. H. Lawshe, Jr. and Dennis H. Price; University Book Store. *

For additional information and reviews by Clyde H. Coombs and C. C. Upshall, see 3:314.

[972]

★**The Purdue Mathematics Training Test: Arithmetic and Algebra.** Grade 13; 1958–60, c1951–60; M. W. Keller, H. F. S. Jonah, H. H. Remmers, and P. C. Baker; University Book Store. *

[973]

Rasmussen General Mathematics Test. High school and college; 1942; Otho M. Rasmussen and H. E. Schrammel; Bureau of Educational Measurements. *

For additional information and a review by William G. Mollenkopf, see 3:315 (1 reference).

[974]

*Sequential Tests of Educational Progress: Mathematics.** Grades 4–6, 7–9, 10–12, 13–14; 1956–59; Cooperative Test Division. * For the complete battery entry, see 39.

For additional information and reviews by Paul L. Dressel, Gordon Fifer, and Tom A. Lamke, see 5:438. For reviews of the complete battery, see 5:24.

[975]

Snader General Mathematics Test. Grades 9–13; 1951–54, c1950–51; Daniel W. Snader; [Harcourt, Brace & World, Inc.]. *

For additional information, see 5:439; for reviews by Paul J. Blommers and Howard F. Fehr, see 4:378.

[976]

★**Survey of Mathematics Achievement: California Survey Series.** Grades 9–12; 1959; abbreviated combination of items from various forms of *California*

Mathematics Test, 1957 Edition (see 1044); Ernest W. Tiegs and Willis W. Clark; California Test Bureau. *

[977]
Test of Mathematical Fundamentals for Grades 7 to 12. Grades 7–12; 1944; H. R. Beattie; distributed by Guidance Centre. *
For additional information and a review by Frances E. Crook, see 5:440.

ALGEBRA

[978]
Ability for Algebra: Fife Tests of Ability, Test 3. Entrants to secondary schools; 1947; Frank M. Earle; University of London Press Ltd. * For the complete battery entry, see 1374.
For additional information and a review by William G. Mollenkopf, see 4:380 (3 references). For reviews of the complete battery, see 4:713 and 3:8.

[979]
*Advanced Algebra, Form 4: Achievement Examinations for Secondary Schools. High school; 1951–59; Forms 1–3 published by Educational Test Bureau are out of print; Harvey O. Jackson; C. A. Gregory Co. *
For additional information concerning earlier forms, see 5:441.

[980]
*Advanced Algebra: Midwest High School Achievement Examinations. High school; 1952–60; Educational Test Bureau. *
For additional information and a review by Emma Spaney of earlier forms, see 5:442.

[981]
★Advanced Algebra (II): Final District-State Scholarship Test. High school; 1938–61; Ohio Scholarship Tests. *

[982]
★Advanced Algebra (II): Preliminary District-State Scholarship Test. High school; 1947–61; Ohio Scholarship Tests. *

[983]
*Advanced Algebra Test: State High School Tests for Indiana. 3 semesters high school; 1934–59; Paul C. Baker; State High School Testing Service for Indiana. *
For additional information, see 4:382.

[984]
Algebra Readiness Test. Grades 8–9; 1947; 6 scores: fundamental operations, fractions, decimals, problem solving, general numbers, total; William R. Lueck; Public School Publishing Co. *
For additional information and a review by Harold Gulliksen, see 4:384.

[985]
★Algebra Test for Engineering and Science: National Achievement Tests. College entrants; 1958–61; A. B. Lonski; Acorn Publishing Co. *

[986]

Blyth Second-Year Algebra Test. 4 semesters high school; 1953–54; M. Isobel
Blyth; [Harcourt, Brace & World, Inc.]. *
For additional information and reviews by Paul Blommers and Myron F.
Rosskopf, see 5:443.

[987]

Breslich Algebra Survey Test. 1, 2 semesters high school; 1930–31; 7 scores:
algebraic concepts, simplifying expressions, solving equations, deriving equations, formulas and graphs, factoring, total; E. R. Breslich; Public School Publishing Co. *
For additional information and a review by John R. Clark, see 40:1435.

[988]

California Algebra Aptitude Test. High school; 1940–58; Noel Keys and
Muriel McCrum; American Guidance Service, Inc. *
For additional information, see 5:444; for a review by William G. Mollenkopf,
see 4:385; for a review by David Segel, see 3:320.

[989]

Colvin-Schrammel Algebra Test. 1, 2 semesters high school; 1937–38; Edgar
S. Colvin and H. E. Schrammel; Bureau of Educational Measurements. *
For additional information and a review by J. H. Minnick, see 40:1437; for
a review by Maurice Hartung, see 38:879.

[990]

Cooperative Algebra Test: Elementary Algebra Through Quadratics. High
school; 1932–51; Margaret P. Martin, Marion F. Shaycoft, Robert S. Lankton,
and Bernice Orshansky; Cooperative Test Division. *
For additional information and a review by Stanley Clark, see 4:387 (4 references); for a review by W. C. Brenke of earlier forms, see 3:321; for reviews
by Harl R. Douglass and Harold Fawcett, see 40:1438; for reviews by William Betz, Helen Walker, and S. S. Wilks, see 38:880.

[991]

Cooperative Intermediate Algebra Test: Quadratics and Beyond. High
school; 1933–51; Margaret P. Martin, Marion F. Shaycoft, M. Isobel Blyth,
and Bernice Orshansky; Cooperative Test Division. *
For additional information and reviews by Lucien B. Kinney and E. P.
Starke, see 4:388 (3 references); for a review by L. B. Plumlee of Form T and
earlier forms, see 3:322; for reviews by Albert A. Bennett and Earle R. Hedrick of earlier forms, see 40:1439; for reviews by J. O. Hassler and S. S. Wilks,
see 38:881.

[992]

Diagnostic Test in Basic Algebra. 2, 3 semesters high school; 1956; John H.
Henshaw; Australian Council for Educational Research. *
For additional information and a review by Stanley Clark, see 5:445.

[993]

*Elementary Algebra: Every Pupil Test. 1, 2 semesters high school; 1929–61;
new form usually issued twice a year; Ohio Scholarship Tests. *
For additional information, see 5:447.

[994]

*Elementary Algebra, Form 4: Achievement Examinations for Secondary Schools. High school; 1951–59; Forms 1–3 published by Educational Test Bureau are out of print; Lyle M. Eakins; C. A. Gregory Co. *

For additional information concerning earlier forms, see 5:446.

[995]

*Elementary Algebra: Midwest High School Achievement Examinations. High school; 1955–61; Educational Test Bureau. *

For additional information and a review by Lynnette B. Plumlee of earlier forms, see 5:448.

[996]

First Year Algebra: Every Pupil Scholarship Test. 1 year high school; 1926–58; Bureau of Educational Measurements. *

For additional information, see 5:449.

[997]

*First Year Algebra: Manchester Semester-End Achievement Tests. 1, 2 semesters high school; 1934–[50]; Bureau of Tests. *

[998]

★First-Year Algebra (I): Final District-State Scholarship Test. High school; 1938–61; Ohio Scholarship Tests. *

[999]

★First-Year Algebra (I): Preliminary District-State Scholarship Test. High school; 1947–61; Ohio Scholarship Tests. *

[1000]

★First Year Algebra Test: National Achievement Tests. 1 year high school; 1958–59; Ray Webb and Julius H. Hlavaty; Acorn Publishing Co. *

[1001]

*First Year Algebra Test: State High School Tests for Indiana. 1, 2 semesters high school; 1933–59; Paul C. Baker; State High School Testing Service for Indiana. *

For additional information, see 4:391.

[1002]

Garman-Schrammel Algebra Test. 3 semesters high school; 1934–40; Helen R. Garman, H. E. Schrammel, and O. M. Rasmussen; Bureau of Educational Measurements. *

For additional information and reviews by Paul Blommers and E. H. C. Hildebrandt, see 3:326.

[1003]

Illinois Algebra Test. 1, 1.5, 2 semesters high school; 1956–58; formerly called *Chicago Algebra Test;* Charles H. Schutter; C. A. Gregory Co. *

For additional information and reviews by Stanley Clark and Theodore E. Kellogg, see 5:450.

[1004]

Iowa Algebra Aptitude Test, Revised Edition. High school; 1929–42; 5 scores: arithmetic, abstract computation, numerical series, dependence and variation, total; Harry A. Greene and Alva H. Piper; Bureau of Educational Research and Service. *

For additional information and reviews by Harold Gulliksen and Emma Spaney, see 4:393; for a review by David Segel, see 3:327 (2 references); for reviews by Richard M. Drake and M. W. Richardson of an earlier edition, see 40:1441 (1 reference).

[1005]

Lankton First-Year Algebra Test. 1 year high school; 1951–54, c1950–51; Robert Lankton; [Harcourt, Brace & World, Inc.]. *

For additional information and a review by Emma Spaney, see 5:451; for a review by Stanley Clark, see 4:394.

[1006]

Larson-Greene Unit Tests in First-Year Algebra. High school; 1947; 6 tests (20 scores): test 1 (literal notation, simple equations and formulas, simple graphs, directed numbers, total), test 2 (fundamental operations, first degree equations-one unknown, total), test 3 (first degree equations-two unknowns, special products and factoring, total), test 4 (fractions, fractional equations, total), test 5 (variation, indirect measurement, total), test 6 (powers-roots-radicals, quadratic equations, total); Robert E. Larson and Harry A. Greene; Bureau of Educational Research and Service. *

For additional information, see 4:395.

[1007]

Lee Test of Algebraic Ability. Grade 9; 1930; J. Murray Lee; Public School Publishing Co. *

For additional information and a review by S. S. Wilks, see 40:1443 (1 reference).

[1008]

Orleans Algebra Prognosis Test, Revised Edition. High school; 1928–51; Joseph B. Orleans; [Harcourt, Brace & World, Inc.]. *

For additional information and reviews by Harold Gulliksen and Emma Spaney, see 4:396 (1 reference); for a review by S. S. Wilks of the original edition, see 40:1444 (4 references).

[1009]

Seattle Algebra Test. 1 semester high school; 1951–54; Harold B. Jeffery, Earl E. Kirschner, Philip Stucky, John R. Rushing, David B. Scott, and Otie P. Van Orsdall; [Harcourt, Brace & World, Inc.]. *

For additional information and a review by Albert E. Meder, Jr., see 5:452.

[1010]

***Second Year Algebra: Manchester Semester-End Achievement Tests.** 3, 4 semesters high school; 1936–[61]; Bureau of Tests. *

[1011]

★Survey Test of Algebraic Aptitude: California Survey Series. Grade 8; 1959; Robert E. Dinkel; California Test Bureau. *

[1012]

20th Century Test for First Year Algebra. 1, 2 semesters high school; 1949; [Ardis Sanders]; Benton Review Publishing Co., Inc. *

For additional information, see 4:392.

[1013]

*The Votaw Algebra Test: Elementary Algebra. High school; 1939–59; David F. Votaw, Sr. and David F. Votaw, Jr.; Steck Co. *

For additional information and reviews by Richard M. Drake and Nathan Morrison, see 3:329.

ARITHMETIC

[1014]

A.C.E.R. Arithmetic Tests. Grades 3–8; 1931–51; 6 parts: addition, subtraction, multiplication, division, arithmetical processes, terms and relations; Australian Council for Educational Research. *

For additional information, see 4:398.

[1015]

A.C.E.R. Arithmetic Tests: Standardized for Use in New Zealand. Ages 9–12; 1957; identical with corresponding parts of *A.C.E.R. Arithmetic Tests* (see 1014); 4 tests: addition, multiplication, subtraction, division; manual by A. E. Fieldhouse; New Zealand Council for Educational Research; distributed by Educational Books. *

For additional information, see 5:453 (the 2 references listed for this test are incorrectly placed and are for 5:454).

[1016]

A.C.E.R. Number Test. Ages 13.5 and over; 1942–55; D. Spearritt; Australian Council for Educational Research. *

For additional information, see 5:454 (2 references for this test are incorrectly placed under 5:453); for a review by Leslie M. Haynes of the original edition, see 4:399.

[1017]

American School Achievement Tests: Arithmetic Readiness. Grades kgn–1; 1941–55; identical with the numbers test of the Primary Battery I of *American School Achievement Tests* (see 2); Robert V. Young, Willis E. Pratt, and Frank Gatto; [Public School Publishing Co.]. *

For additional information and a review by Harold E. Moser, see 5:455. For reviews of the complete battery, see 5:1, 4:1, and 3:1.

[1018]

American School Achievement Tests: Part 2, Arithmetic. Grades 4–6, 7–9; 1941–58; 3 scores: computation, problems, total; Willis E. Pratt and Robert V. Young; Public School Publishing Co. * For the complete battery entry, see 2.

For additional information and reviews by Joseph Justman and J. Fred Weaver, see 5:456. For reviews of the complete battery, see 5:1, 4:1, and 3:1.

[1019]

Analytical Scales of Attainment: Arithmetic. Grades 3–4, 5–6, 7–8; 1933; 4 scores: quantitative relationships, problems, arithmetic vocabulary, funda-

mental operations; L. J. Brueckner, Martha Kellogg, and M. J. Van Wagenen; Educational Test Bureau. *
For additional information and reviews by R. L. Morton, W. J. Osburn, and G. M. Wilson, see 40:1447.

[1020]

Analytical Survey Test in Computational Arithmetic. Grades 7–12; 1930–57; H. C. Christofferson and W. S. Guiler; C. A. Gregory Co. *
For additional information and a review by Emma Spaney, see 5:457.

[1021]

***Arithmetic Computation: Public School Achievement Tests.** Grades 3–8; 1928–59; Jacob S. Orleans; Public School Publishing Co. * For the complete battery entry, see 33.
For additional information and reviews of the complete battery, see 40:1194.

[1022]

Arithmetic Essentials Test. Grades 3, 4, 5, 6, 7, 8, 9–12; 1949–56; James T. Shea; Steck Co. *
For additional information and a review by J. Wayne Wrightstone, see 5:458; for reviews by Foster E. Grossnickle and Charles S. Ross of the original edition, see 4:400.

[1023]

***Arithmetic: Every Pupil Scholarship Test.** Grades 4–6, 7–8; 1928–61; new form usually issued twice a year; Bureau of Educational Measurements. *
For additional information, see 5:459.

[1024]

***Arithmetic: Every Pupil Test.** 1, 2 semesters in grades 3, 4, 5–6; 1930–61; new form usually issued twice a year; Ohio Scholarship Tests. *
For additional information, see 5:460.

[1025]

Arithmetic Fundamentals Test: State High School Tests for Indiana. High school; 1944–45; Doyle T. French and Albert R. Mahin; State High School Testing Service for Indiana. *
For additional information, see 4:402.

[1026]

Arithmetic: Northumberland Standardised Tests (1925 Series). Ages 10–14; [1925]; Cyril Burt; University of London Press Ltd. *

[1027]

Arithmetic Progress Test. Ages 9 to 10-8, 10 to 11-6; 1952–58; G. A. V. Morgan; published for the National Foundation for Educational Research in England and Wales; Newnes Educational Publishing Co. Ltd. *
For additional information and reviews by William Curr and John Sutherland of the higher level, see 5:461.

[1028]

Arithmetic Reasoning. Grades 9 and over; 1941; B. V. Moore; the Author. *
For additional information and a review by Jacob S. Orleans, see 3:331.

[1029]

*Arithmetic Reasoning: Public School Achievement Tests. Grades 3–8; 1928–59; Jacob S. Orleans; Public School Publishing Co. * For the complete battery entry, see 33.

For additional information and reviews of the complete battery, see 40:1194.

[1030]

Arithmetic Reasoning Test: [Personnel Research Institute Clerical Battery]. Clerical applicants and high school; 1948; Jay L. Otis and David J. Chesler; Personnel Research Institute. * For the complete battery entry, see 1846.

For additional information, see 4:403. For reviews of the complete battery, see 4:729.

[1031]

Arithmetic: Seven Plus Assessment: Northumberland Series. Ages 7–8; 1951; C. M. Lambert; University of London Press Ltd. * For the complete battery entry, see 40.

For additional information, see 4:404. For a review of the complete battery, see 4:24.

[1032]

Arithmetic Test: Fundamental Operations: Dominion Tests. Grades 4–8; 1934–56; Department of Educational Research, Ontario College of Education, University of Toronto; distributed by Guidance Centre. *

For additional information and a review by Harry L. Stein, see 5:462; for a review by C. L. Thiele, see 3:332.

[1033]

Arithmetic Test (Fundamentals and Reasoning): Municipal Tests: National Achievement Tests. Grades 3–6, 6–8; 1938–56; subtest of *Municipal Battery* (see 29); Robert K. Speer and Samuel Smith; Acorn Publishing Co. *

For additional information, see 5:463; for reviews by Foster E. Grossnickle and Charles S. Ross, see 4:406. For reviews of the complete battery, see 5:18, 4:20, and 40:1191.

[1034]

Arithmetic Test: National Achievement Tests. Grades 3–8; 1936–55; 2 tests; Robert K. Speer and Samuel Smith; Acorn Publishing Co. *
a) FUNDAMENTALS. 1938–55; 4 scores: fundamentals-speed, number comparisons, fundamentals-skills, total.
b) REASONING. 1936–54; 5 scores: comparisons, problem analysis, finding problem key, problems, total.

For additional information, see 5:464; for reviews by R. L. Morton and Leroy H. Schnell, see 40:1449; for reviews by William A. Brownell and W. J. Osburn, see 38:889.

[1035]

*Arithmetic Tests 1–2, 4–7, 7E, 8–10, 10E. Ages 10 to 11-11; 1951–60; G. A. V. Morgan and M. A. Brimer; published for the National Foundation for Educational Research in England and Wales; Newnes Educational Publishing Co. Ltd. *

For additional information concerning tests 1–7E, see 5:465.

[1036]
Arithmetic: Thanet Mental Tests. Ages 10–12; 1937; W. P. Alexander; University of London Press Ltd. *
For additional information and reviews by Fred J. Schonell and C. Ebblewhite Smith, see 40:1450.

[1037]
★**Arithmetical Problems: National Institute for Personnel Research High Level Battery.** Adults with at least 12 years of education; 1956–[61]; revision of *Test A/68: Arithmetical Problems* (see 1094); National Institute for Personnel Research. For the complete battery entry, see 1382.

[1038]
Basic Arithmetic Skills: Iowa Every-Pupil Tests of Basic Skills, Test D. Grades 3–5, 5–9; 1940–47; 4 scores: fundamental knowledge, fundamental operations, problems, total; H. F. Spitzer, Ernest Horn, Maude McBroom, H. A. Greene, and E. F. Lindquist; Houghton Mifflin Co. * For the complete battery entry, see 22.
For additional information, see 4:408; for reviews by William A. Brownell and Leroy H. Schnell, see 3:334. For reviews of the complete battery, see 4:15, 3:10, and 38:872.

[1039]
Basic Number Skills Test for Employee Selection. Job applicants; 1951–52; William J. Morgan and Antonia Morgan; Aptitude Associates. *
For additional information and reviews by Dorothy C. Adkins and Marion F. Shaycoft, see 5:466.

[1040]
Basic Skills in Arithmetic Test. Grades 6–12; 1945; William L. Wrinkle, Juanita Sanders, and Elizabeth H. Kendel; Science Research Associates, Inc. *
For additional information and reviews by Jacob S. Orleans and F. Lynwood Wren, see 3:335.

[1041]
A Brief Survey of Arithmetic Skills, Revised Edition. Grades 5–12, 7–12; 1947–53; 3 scores: computation, reasoning, total; Arthur E. Traxler. *
a) [EDUCATIONAL RECORDS BUREAU EDITION.] Grades 5–12; Educational Records Bureau.
b) [C. A. GREGORY CO. EDITION.] Grades 7–12; C. A. Gregory Co.
For additional information and a review by H. Vernon Price, see 5:467 (1 reference); for reviews by William A. Brownell and Henry Van Engen of the original edition, see 4:409.

[1042]
[Brueckner Diagnostic Arithmetic Tests.] Grades 4–8, 5–8; 1926–43; 4 scores for each test: addition, subtraction, multiplication, division; L. J. Brueckner, H. W. Distad, and Abbie Chestek; Educational Test Bureau. *
a) BRUECKNER DIAGNOSTIC TEST IN DECIMALS. Grades 5–8; 1926–42.
b) BRUECKNER DIAGNOSTIC TEST IN FRACTIONS. Grades 5–8; 1926–43.
c) BRUECKNER DIAGNOSTIC TEST IN WHOLE NUMBERS. Grades 4–8; 1926–42.
For additional information and a review by Herbert F. Spitzer, see 4:410.

[1043]

California Arithmetic Test, 1950 Edition. Grades 1–4.5, 4–6, 7–9, 9–14; 1933–50; revision of *Progressive Arithmetic Tests;* subtest of *California Achievement Tests, 1950 Edition* (see 4) ; advanced level called *California Mathematics Test, 1950 Edition;* 3 scores: reasoning, fundamentals, total; Ernest W. Tiegs and Willis W. Clark; California Test Bureau. * For the 1957 edition entry, see 1044.

For additional information and a review by Robert L. Burch, see 4:411; see also 4:366 (1 reference) ; for reviews by C. L. Thiele and Harry Grove Wheat of an earlier edition, see 40:1459; for a review by William A. Brownell, see 38:893. For reviews of the complete battery, see 4:2, 3:15, 40:1193, and 38:876.

[1044]

***California Arithmetic Test, 1957 Edition.** Grades 1–2, 3–4.5, 4–6, 7–9, 9–14; 1933–59; subtest of *California Achievement Tests, 1957 Edition* (see 5) ; advanced level called *California Mathematics Test, 1957 Edition;* 3 scores: reasoning, fundamentals, total; Ernest W. Tiegs and Willis W. Clark; California Test Bureau. * For the 1950 edition entry, see 1043.

For additional information and a review by Robert D. North, see 5:468 (1 reference). For a review of the complete battery, see 5:2.

[1045]

The Clapp-Young Arithmetic Test: The Clapp-Young Self-Marking Tests. Grades 5–8; 1930–31, c1927–31; Frank L. Clapp and Robert V. Young; Houghton Mifflin Co. *

For additional information and a review by Leroy H. Schnell, see 3:339.

[1046]

***Commercial Arithmetic: Manchester Semester-End Achievement Tests.** 1, 2 semesters high school; 1934–[38] ; Bureau of Tests. *

[1047]

Commercial Arithmetic Test: State High School Tests for Indiana. High school; 1944–51; Charlotte Henderson and Philip Peak; State High School Testing Service for Indiana. *

For additional information, see 4:448.

[1048]

★Computation Test A/67. Job applicants with at least 8 years of education; [1956] ; multiplication; National Institute for Personnel Research. *

[1049]

Coordinated Scales of Attainment: Arithmetic. Grades 4, 5, 6, 7, 8; 1946–54; Leo J. Brueckner; Educational Test Bureau. * For the complete battery entry, see 10.

For additional information, see 5:469. For reviews of the complete battery, see 4:8 and 3:6.

[1050]

Cotswold Junior Arithmetic Ability Test. Ages 8–9; 1949–52; C. M. Fleming; Robert Gibson & Sons (Glasgow), Ltd. *

For additional information and reviews by William Curr and George W. Sturrock, see 5:470.

[1051]

*Cotswold Measurement of Ability: Arithmetic. Ages 10–12.5; 1947–59, c1947–55; C. M. Fleming and J. W. Jenkins; Robert Gibson & Sons (Glasgow), Ltd. *

For additional information, see 5:471; for a review by W. L. Sumner, see 4:412.

[1052]

★Diagnostic Arithmetic Tests. Standards 1–8 (ages 8–15); 1951–57; 9 tests in separate booklets: addition, subtraction, multiplication, division, money, weights and measures, fractions, decimals, percentages; National Bureau of Educational and Social Research. *

[1053]

Diagnostic Chart for Fundamental Processes in Arithmetic. Grades 2–8; 1925; G. T. Buswell and Lenore John; Public School Publishing Co. *

For additional information and a review by Leo J. Brueckner, see 4:413; for reviews by H. E. Benz and Foster E. Grossnickle, see 40:1456.

[1054]

Diagnostic Tests and Self-Helps in Arithmetic. Grades 3–12; 1955; Leo J. Brueckner; California Test Bureau. *
a) SCREENING TESTS. Grades 4–6, 5–6, 6, 7 and over.
b) DIAGNOSTIC TESTS. Grades 3, 4, 5, 6, 7.

For additional information and a review by Harold E. Moser, see 5:472.

[1055]

Diagnostic Tests in Arithmetic Fundamentals, Revised Edition: Dominion Tests. Grades 2, 3, 4, 5, 6; 1945–57; Department of Educational Research, Ontario College of Education, University of Toronto; distributed by Guidance Centre. *

For additional information and a review by John Sutherland, see 5:473; for a review by Leo J. Brueckner of the original edition, see 3:341.

[1056]

★Diagnostic Tests in Money. Ages 10–12; 1960; 5 scores: addition, subtraction, multiplication, division, changing money; F. J. Schonell, J. A. Richardson, and K. P. O'Connor; Oliver & Boyd Ltd. *

[1057]

Diagnostic Tests in Vulgar Fractions, Decimal Fractions and Percentages. Ages 10–14; 1956; Fred J. Schonell, J. Richardson, and K. P. O'Connor; Oliver & Boyd Ltd. *

For additional information and a review by Reginald Edwards, see 5:474.

[1058]

★Easy Steps in Arithmetic. Ages 8–14; 1951–58; E. W. Seville; Australian Council for Educational Research. *
a) DIAGNOSTIC ARITHMETIC TESTS. 1951–52.
   1) *Diagnostic Arithmetic Test 1:* [*Addition, Subtraction, Simple Multiplication, Simple Division*]. Ages 8–14.
   2) *Diagnostic Arithmetic Test 2:* [*Long Multiplication, Long Division*]. Ages 10–14.

b) DIAGNOSTIC MONEY TESTS. 1952.

   1) *Diagnostic Money Test 1*: [*Addition, Subtraction, Simple Multiplication, Simple Division*]. Ages 8–14.

   2) *Diagnostic Money Test 2*: [*Long Multiplication, Long Division*]. Ages 9–14.

   3) *Diagnostic Money Test 3*: [*Reduction*]. Ages 10–14.

c) DIAGNOSTIC FRACTIONS TESTS. Ages 9–14; 1957–58.

[1059]

[**Essential Arithmetic Tests.**] Ages 7–12, 7–14; 1945–47; 2 parts; Fred J. Schonell; Oliver & Boyd Ltd. *

a) THE ESSENTIAL MECHANICAL ARITHMETIC TEST. Ages 7–12.

b) THE ESSENTIAL PROBLEM ARITHMETIC TEST. Ages 7–14.

   For additional information and reviews by John Cohen and Stephen Wiseman, see 3:342.

[1060]

Gilbert Business Arithmetic. High school; 1941; Marc D. Gilbert and Otho M. Rasmussen; Bureau of Educational Measurements. *

   For additional information and a review by William L. Schaaf, see 4:450.

[1061]

Group Test of Speed and Accuracy in Arithmetic Computation: Dominion Tests. Grades 5–10; 1955–56; 3 scores: speed, accuracy, achievement; Department of Educational Research, Ontario College of Education, University of Toronto; distributed by Guidance Centre. *

   For additional information and reviews by Frances E. Crook and William Harrison Lucow, see 5:477.

[1062]

Hundred Problem Arithmetic Test. Grades 7–12; 1926–44; revision of *Schorling-Clark-Potter Arithmetic Test, Revised Edition;* 6 scores: addition, subtraction, multiplication, division, fractions-decimals-per cent, total; Raleigh Schorling, John R. Clark, and Mary A. Potter; [Harcourt, Brace & World, Inc.]. *

   For additional information and a review by William Betz, see 3:344 (2 references, 1 excerpt); for a review by W. J. Osburn of an earlier edition, see 40:1462.

[1063]

★**Intermediate Diagnostic Arithmetic Test 1.** Ages 10-0 to 12-6; 1959; Roy Harris; published for the National Foundation for Educational Research in England and Wales; Newnes Educational Publishing Co. Ltd. *

[1064]

Kansas Arithmetic Test. Grades 3–5, 6–8; 1934; 3 scores: computation, problem solving, total; H. E. Schrammel, Ruth E. Otterstrom, Mildred Peak, and Dodds M. Turner; Bureau of Educational Measurements. *

   For additional information and reviews by H. E. Benz and W. J. Osburn, see 40:1457.

[1065]

Kansas Primary Arithmetic Test. Grades 1–3; 1935; 6 scores: addition and subtraction, multiplication and division, miscellaneous problems, basic number concepts, simple reasoning problems, total; Charlotte Foster, Emma Humble, Gladys Kemp, Mildred Miller, and H. E. Schrammel; Bureau of Educational Measurements. *

For additional information and reviews by W. J. Osburn and G. M. Ruch, see 40:1458.

[1066]

Kelvin Measurement of Ability in Arithmetic. Ages 7–12; 1933; C. M. Fleming; Robert Gibson & Sons (Glasgow), Ltd. *

For additional information, see 38:891.

[1067]

Lee-Clark Arithmetic Fundamentals Survey Test: High School Edition. Grades 7–12; 1944; J. Murray Lee and Willis W. Clark; California Test Bureau. *

For additional information and reviews by Monica M. Hoye and F. Lynwood Wren, see 3:345.

[1068]

Los Angeles Diagnostic Tests: Fundamentals of Arithmetic. Grades 2–8; 1925–47; Caroline Armstrong and Willis W. Clark; California Test Bureau. *

For additional information, see 4:415.

[1069]

Los Angeles Diagnostic Tests: Reasoning in Arithmetic. Grades 3–9; 1926; Caroline Armstrong; California Test Bureau. *

[1070]

Madden-Peak Arithmetic Computation Test. Grades 7 and over; 1954–57; 6 scores: addition and subtraction, multiplication and division, common fractions, decimal fractions-mixed decimals-percentages, mental computation and estimation, total; Richard Madden and Philip Peak; [Harcourt, Brace & World, Inc.]. *

For additional information and reviews by Theodore E. Kellogg and Albert E. Meder, Jr., see 5:478.

[1071]

★**Manchester Mechanical Arithmetic Test (Sen.)** 1. Ages 13.5–15; 1959; Jack Wrigley and Stephen Wiseman; University of London Press Ltd. *

[1072]

*****Metropolitan Achievement Tests: [Arithmetic, 1960 Edition].** Grades 3–4, 5–6, 7–9; 1933–60, c1933–59; 2 scores: computation, problem solving and concepts; Walter N. Durost, Harold H. Bixler, Gertrude H. Hildreth, Kenneth W. Lund, and J. Wayne Wrightstone; [Harcourt, Brace & World, Inc.]. *
For the complete battery entry, see 27.

For additional information and a review by Robert L. Burch of the 1947 edition, see 4:416; for reviews by Peter L. Spencer and Harry Grove Wheat of an earlier edition, see 40:1458.1; for reviews by Foster E. Grossnickle and Guy M. Wilson, see 38:892. For reviews of earlier editions of the complete battery, see 4:18, 40:1189, and 38:874.

[1073]

Milne Arithmetic Test. Standards 2–8 (ages 7–17); 1946–54; based on F. T. Milne's *Witwatersrand Test;* 2 tests; National Bureau of Educational and Social Research. *

a) FUNDAMENTAL PROCESSES. 4 scores: addition, subtraction, multiplication, division.

b) MECHANICAL COMPUTATION AND PROBLEMS. 2 scores: computation, problems.
For additional information, see 5:479.

[1074]

*Moray House Arithmetic Tests. Ages 8.5–10.5, 10 to 12-0, 12 to 14-0; 1935–61; Department of Education, University of Edinburgh; University of London Press Ltd.

a) MORAY HOUSE JUNIOR ARITHMETIC TEST 2. Ages 8.5–10.5; 1952–58. *

b) MORAY HOUSE ARITHMETIC TEST 33. Ages 10-0 to 12-0; 1935–61.

c) MORAY HOUSE ARITHMETIC TEST (ADV.) 2. Ages 12-0 to 14-0; 1956–58. *

For additional information and a review by John Cohen of earlier forms of *b*, see 3:346.

[1075]

New York Test of Arithmetical Meanings. Grades 1.5–2, 2.5–3; 1956; J. Wayne Wrightstone, Joseph Justman, Morris Pincus, and Ruth H. Lowe; [Harcourt, Brace & World, Inc.]. *
For additional information and a review by Charles S. Ross, see 5:480.

[1076]

Number Fact Check Sheet. Grades 5–8; 1946–47; Roy Cochrane; California Test Bureau. *
For additional information and a review by Miriam M. Bryan, see 4:417.

[1077]

Oral Diagnostic Test in Addition: Analysis of Errors in Addition: Dominion Tests. Grades 4–6; 1945; Department of Educational Research, Ontario College of Education, University of Toronto; distributed by Guidance Centre. *
For additional information and a review by Leo J. Brueckner, see 3:348.

[1078]

Otis Arithmetic Reasoning Test. Grades 4–12; 1918–23; subtest of the Advanced Examination of *Otis Group Intelligence Scale* (see 815); Arthur S. Otis; [Harcourt, Brace & World, Inc.]. *

[1079]

*Primary Arithmetic: Every Pupil Scholarship Test. Grades 1, 2–3; 1935–61; new form usually issued twice a year; Bureau of Educational Measurements. *
For additional information, see 5:481.

[1080]

★Readiness and Achievement Tests in Arithmetic. Grades 1, 2; 1960; Leo J. Brueckner and Elda L. Merton; [Holt, Rinehart & Winston, Inc.]. *

[1081]

Revised Southend Attainment Test in Mechanical Arithmetic. Ages 7–15; 1939–50; [M. E. Hebron]; George G. Harrap & Co. Ltd. * For the original edition entry and references to reviews, see 1087.

[1082]

*SRA Achievement Series: Arithmetic. Grades 1–2, 2–4, 4–6, 6–9; 1954–58; 3 scores: reasoning, concepts and usage, computation; Louis P. Thorpe, D. Welty

Lefever, and Robert A. Naslund; Science Research Associates, Inc. * For the complete battery entry, see 35.

For additional information and reviews by Robert D. North and J. Fred Weaver, see 5:483. For reviews of the complete battery, see 5:21.

[1083]

Scholastic Achievement Series: Arithmetic. Grades 2.5–3, 4–6, 7–9; 1954–55; for Catholic schools; 3 scores: computation, reasoning, total; Oliver F. Anderhalter, R. Stephen Gawkoski, and John O'Brien; Scholastic Testing Service, Inc. * For the complete battery entry, see 37.

For additional information and reviews by Joseph Justman and Charles S. Ross, see 5:484. For reviews of the complete battery, see 5:23.

[1084]

Schonell Diagnostic Arithmetic Tests. Ages 7–13; 1936–57; 12 scores: combinations (addition, subtraction, multiplication, division, miscellaneous), graded addition, graded subtraction, graded multiplication, graded division (2 tests), graded mental arithmetic; Fred J. Schonell; Oliver & Boyd Ltd. *

For additional information and a review by John Sutherland, see 5:485 (1 reference); see also 3:350 (1 reference); for a review by C. Ebblewhite Smith of an earlier edition, see 40:1461 (2 references).

[1085]

***Schrammel-Otterstrom Arithmetic Test.** Grades 4–6, 7–8; 1945–52; 4 scores: computation, comprehension, problems, total; H. E. Schrammel, Ruth E. Otterstrom, and Virginia Reed; Bureau of Educational Measurements. *

For additional information and a review by William A. Brownell, see 3:351.

[1086]

★Seeing Through Arithmetic Tests. Grades 3, 4, 5, 6; 1960; 7 scores: problem solving, computation, selecting equations, solving equations, information, concepts, total; Maurice L. Hartung, Henry Van Engen, E. Glenadine Gibb, and Lois Knowles; Scott, Foresman & Co. *

[1087]

Southend Attainment Test in Mechanical Arithmetic. Ages 6, 7, 8, 9, 10, 11, 12, 13; 1939; [M. E. Hebron]; George G. Harrap & Co. Ltd. * For the revised edition entry, see 1081.

For additional information and a review by Stephen Wiseman, see 3:352 (1 reference).

[1088]

★Speed and Diagnostic Tests of Arithmetic. Ages 7–9; [1959]; 4 tests: addition, subtraction, multiplication, division; A. L. Hinshaw; Owen Martin Pty. Ltd. *

[1089]

The Staffordshire Arithmetic Test. Ages 7–15; 1938–58; identical in part with *Revised Southend Attainment Test in Mechanical Arithmetic* (see 1081); M. E. Hebron; George G. Harrap & Co. Ltd. *

For additional information, see 5:486.

[1090]

Stanford Achievement Test: Arithmetic. Grades 3–4, 5–6, 7–9; 1922–55; 2 scores: arithmetic reasoning, arithmetic computation; Truman L. Kelley, Richard Madden, Eric F. Gardner, Lewis M. Terman, and Giles M. Ruch; [Harcourt, Brace & World, Inc.]. * For the complete battery entry, see 42.

For additional information, see 5:487 (1 reference); for a review by Robert L. Burch of the previous edition, see 4:419 (1 reference). For reviews of the complete battery, see 5:25, 4:25, and 3:18.

[1091]

★Survey of Arithmetic Achievement: California Survey Series. Grades 7–9; 1959; abbreviated combinations of items from various forms of *California Arithmetic Test, 1957 Edition* (see 1044); Ernest W. Tiegs and Willis W. Clark; California Test Bureau. *

[1092]

Survey Test of Arithmetic Fundamentals: Dominion Tests. Grades 3–5, 5–8; 1957–58; Department of Educational Research, Ontario College of Education, University of Toronto; distributed by Guidance Centre. *
a) GRADES 3–5. 7 scores: addition, subtraction, multiplication, division, measurement, fractions, total.
b) GRADES 5–8. 5 scores: whole numbers, fractions, decimals and percentage, measurement, total.
For additional information and a review by Frances E. Crook, see 5:488.

[1093]

★Test A/8: Arithmetic. Technical college students and applicants for clerical and trade positions with 8–12 years of education; [1943–44]; National Institute for Personnel Research. *

[1094]

★Test A/68: Arithmetical Problems. Job applicants with at least 10 years of education; [1956]; National Institute for Personnel Research. *

[1095]

Tests of Mechanical Arithmetic. Ages 7 to 8-8, 8 to 9-2, 8 to 10-0; 1949–58; Miriam E. Highfield and [G. A. V. Morgan]; published for the National Foundation for Educational Research in England and Wales; Newnes Educational Publishing Co. Ltd. *
For additional information and reviews by George W. Sturrock and Jack Wrigley, see 5:489.

[1096]

The Tiedeman Arithmetical Knowledge and Information Test. Grades 7–13; 1957; H. R. Tiedeman; Western Psychological Services. *
For additional information and a review by James H. Ricks, Jr., see 5:490.

[1097]

★Understanding the Meanings in Arithmetic: A Diagnostic Test. Grades 7–12; 1959; David Rappaport; Science Research Associates, Inc. *

[1098]

The Wilson General Survey Tests in Arithmetic. Grades 5–10; 1945–46; Guy M. Wilson; [Ridge Manor Publishing Co.]. *

[1099]

The Wilson Inventory and Diagnostic Tests in Arithmetic. Grades 3–9; 1936–38; Guy M. Wilson; [Ridge Manor Publishing Co.]. *

GEOMETRY

[1100]

Ability for Geometry: Fife Tests of Ability, Test 4. Secondary school entrants; 1947; Frank M. Earle; University of London Press Ltd. * For the complete battery entry, see 1374.

For additional information, see 3:356 (2 references). For reviews of the complete battery, see 4:713 and 3:8.

[1101]

American Council Solid Geometry Test. Grades 11–15; 1928–29; Henry W. Raudenbush, L. Parker Siceloff, and Ben D. Wood; [Harcourt, Brace & World, Inc.]. *

[1102]

Becker-Schrammel Plane Geometry. 1, 2 semesters high school; 1934–35; Ida S. Becker and H. E. Schrammel; Bureau of Educational Measurements. *

For additional information and reviews by Harold Fawcett and Judson W. Foust, see 40:1465 (1 reference).

[1103]

Cooperative Plane Geometry Test. High school; 1932–51; Margaret P. Martin, H. Vernon Price, and Bernice Orshansky; Cooperative Test Division. *

For additional information and a review by Cyril J. Hoyt and Theodore E. Kellogg of Forms Y and Z, see 4:423 (1 reference); for reviews by Harold P. Fawcett and C. O. Oakley of Form T and earlier forms, see 3:357; for a review by Leroy H. Schnell of an earlier form, see 40:1467; for reviews by Charles C. Weidemann and S. S. Wilks, see 38:993.

[1104]

Cooperative Solid Geometry Test. High school; 1932–39; H. T. Lundholm, John A. Long, and L. P. Siceloff; Cooperative Test Division. *

For additional information and reviews by J. O. Hassler and Earle R. Hedrick, see 40:1468.

[1105]

Geometry Attainment Test. Ages 11–14; 1948; R. D. Walton; University of London Press Ltd. *

For additional information and reviews by I. Macfarlane Smith and W. L. Sumner, see 4:424.

[1106]

*Geometry: Every Pupil Test. 1, 2 semesters high school; 1929–61; new form usually issued twice a year; Ohio Scholarship Tests. *

For additional information, see 5:492.

[1107]

Geometry Survey Test. 1, 2 semesters high school; 1930–31; E. R. Breslich; Public School Publishing Co. *

[1108]

Illinois Plane Geometry Test. .5, 1, 1.5, 2 semesters high school; 1957; formerly called *Chicago Plane Geometry Test;* Charles H. Schutter; C. A. Gregory Co. *

For additional information and a review by Lynnette B. Plumlee, see 5:491.

[1109]

Iowa Plane Geometry Aptitude Test, Revised Edition. High school; 1935–42; 5 scores: reading of geometry content, algebraic computations, arithmetical and algebraic reasoning, visualization, total; Harry A. Greene and Harold W. Bruce; Bureau of Educational Research and Service. *

For additional information and a review by Philip H. DuBois, see 3:360; for reviews by Edward E. Cureton and Charles C. Weidemann of an earlier edition, see 40:1469.

[1110]

Lane-Greene Unit Tests in Plane Geometry, 1944 Edition. High school; 1929–44; 6 tests: fundamental ideas of geometry, parallel lines and triangles (5 scores), rectilinear figures (5 scores), the circle (5 scores), proportion and similar polygons (5 scores), areas of polygons (5 scores); Ruth O. Lane and Harry A. Greene; Bureau of Educational Research and Service. *

For additional information, see 4:426.

[1111]

Lee Test of Geometric Aptitude. High school students who have studied no geometry; 1931; Dorris M. Lee and J. Murray Lee; California Test Bureau. *

For additional information and reviews by Edward E. Cureton and Charles C. Weidemann, see 40:1470 (1 reference).

[1112]

Orleans Geometry Prognosis Test, Revised Edition. High school; 1929–51; Joseph B. Orleans; [Harcourt, Brace & World, Inc.]. *

For additional information, see 4:427 (2 references); for reviews by Edward E. Cureton and Charles C. Weidemann of the original edition, see 40:1471 (3 references).

[1113]

*Plane Geometry: Every Pupil Scholarship Test. High school; 1926–61; new form usually issued twice a year; Bureau of Educational Measurements. *

For additional information, see 5:494.

[1114]

★Plane Geometry: Final District-State Scholarship Test. High school; 1938–61; Ohio Scholarship Tests. *

[1115]

*Plane Geometry, Form 4: Achievement Examinations for Secondary Schools. High school; 1951–59; Forms 1–3 published by Educational Test Bureau are out of print; Emil J. Berger; C. A. Gregory Co. *

For additional information concerning earlier forms, see 5:493.

[1116]

*Plane Geometry: Manchester Semester-End Achievement Tests. 1, 2 semesters high school; 1934–[45]; Bureau of Tests. *

[1117]

*Plane Geometry: Midwest High School Achievement Examinations. High school; 1955–61; Educational Test Bureau. *

For additional information and a review by Harold P. Fawcett of earlier forms, see 5:495.

[1118]

★Plane Geometry: National Achievement Tests. High school; 1958–59; Ray
Webb and Julius H. Hlavaty; Acorn Publishing Co. *

[1119]

★Plane Geometry: Preliminary District-State Scholarship Test. High school;
1947–61; Ohio Scholarship Tests. *

[1120]

*Plane Geometry Test: State High School Tests for Indiana. 1, 2 semes-
ters high school; 1933–59; Philip Peak, Douglass Brown, Margaret Goodson,
Pryce Noe, and Reino Takala; State High School Testing Service for Indiana. *
    For additional information, see 4:429.

[1121]

Schrammel-Reed Solid Geometry Test. High school; 1950–52; H. E. Schrammel and Virginia M. Reed; Bureau of Educational Measurements. *
    For additional information and a review by H. Vernon Price, see 5:496.

[1122]

Seattle Plane Geometry Test. 1 semester high school; 1951–54; Harold B.
Jeffery, S. L. Merriam, Clifton T. Smith, Roy D. Kellogg, and Richard E. Bennett; [Harcourt, Brace & World, Inc.]. *
    For additional information and a review by Harold P. Fawcett, see 5:497.

[1123]

Seattle Solid Geometry Test Series. High school; 1927; 11 tests: lines and
planes (2 tests), dihedral and polyhedral angles, prisms and parallelopipeds—
volumes, pyramids, cylinders and cones (2 tests), spherical polygons and spherical areas, spherical volumes and areas, Scale B (Preliminary Examination),
Scale A (Final Examination); M. E. Morgan, W. T. Wait, and August Dvorak;
Public School Publishing Co. *

[1124]

Shaycoft Plane Geometry Test. 1 year high school; 1951–54, c1950–51; Marion
F. Shaycoft; [Harcourt, Brace & World, Inc.]. *
    For additional information, see 5:498; for reviews by Harold P. Fawcett and
Cyril J. Hoyt (with Theodore E. Kellogg), see 4:433.

[1125]

*Solid Geometry, Form 4: Achievement Examinations for Secondary
Schools. High school; 1951–59; Forms 1–3 published by Educational Test Bureau are out of print; Emil J. Berger; C. A. Gregory Co. *
    For additional information concerning earlier forms, see 5:499.

[1126]

*Solid Geometry: Manchester Semester-End Achievement Tests. 1 semester
high school; [1936–47]; J. E. Dotterer and Albert E. Harshbarger; Bureau of
Tests. *

[1127]

*Solid Geometry: Midwest High School Achievement Examinations. High
school; 1952–61; Educational Test Bureau. *
    For additional information concerning earlier forms, see 5:500.

[1128]

★Solid Geometry: National Achievement Tests. High school; 1958–59; Ray Webb and Julius H. Hlavaty; Acorn Publishing Co. *

[1129]

*Solid Geometry Test: State High School Tests for Indiana. High school; 1934–59; Philip Peak, Douglass Brown, Margaret Goodson, and Pryce Noe; State High School Testing Service for Indiana. *
    For additional information, see 4:435.

[1130]

20th Century Test for Plane Geometry. 1, 2 semesters high school; 1949; Benton Review Publishing Co., Inc. *
    For additional information, see 4:430.

TRIGONOMETRY

[1131]

American Council Trigonometry Test, Revised. Grades 11–15; 1928–30; Joseph B. Orleans, Henry W. Raudenbush, L. Parker Siceloff, and Ben D. Wood; [Harcourt, Brace & World, Inc.]. *
    For additional information and reviews by J. O. Hassler and G. E. Hawkins, see 40:1473.

[1132]

Cooperative Plane Trigonometry Test. High school and college; 1932–51; John A. Long, L. P. Siceloff, and others; Cooperative Test Division. *
    For additional information, see 4:438; for a review by G. E. Hawkins of an earlier form, see 40:1474 (1 reference); for reviews by J. O. Hassler and S. S. Wilks, see 38:1074.

[1133]

★Plane Trigonometry: National Achievement Tests. Grades 10–12 and college; 1958–59; Ray Webb and Julius H. Hlavaty; Acorn Publishing Co. *

[1134]

Rasmussen Trigonometry Test. High school and college; 1940; Otho M. Rasmussen; Bureau of Educational Measurements. *
    For additional information and a review by Lynnette B. Plumlee, see 5:501.

[1135]

★Trigonometry: Manchester Semester-End Achievement Tests. 1, 2 semesters high school; 1960–61; Bureau of Tests. *

[1136]

★Trigonometry: Midwest High School Achievement Examinations. High school; 1961; Sol Mastbaum; Educational Test Bureau. *

[1137]

*Trigonometry Test: State High School Tests for Indiana. High school; 1944–59; M. W. Keller; State High School Testing Service for Indiana. *
    For additional information, see 4:440.

MISCELLANEOUS

[1138]

★Creative Ability Inventory (Preventive-Imagination and Constructive-Imagination). Grades 9–12 and adults; 1961; checklist of specific areas of "preventive-imagination" (cautions) and "optimistic-imagination" (ability to see opportunities) believed necessary for the solution of any selected problem or the development of any selected ability; W. H. Winkler; [Winkler Publications]. *

[1139]

How Well Can You Read Lips? Deaf and hard of hearing children and adults with a reading level of grade 3 or over; 1946; Jean Utley; [American Film Registry]. *

For additional information, see 5:579 (2 references).

[1140]

★Inventory of Satisfactions in Home Life. Ages 16 and over; 1950; W. H. Winkler; [Winkler Publications]. *

[1141]

What Do You Know About Photography? Photography students; 1953; Martin M. Bruce and Jack Bernard; Martin M. Bruce. *

For additional information, see 5:580.

[1142]

★Worth of People to Each Other Inventory. Ages 16 and over; 1949–[60]; W. H. Winkler; [Winkler Publications]. *

AGRICULTURE

[1143]

*Agriculture: Every Pupil Scholarship Test. High school; 1927–57; Bureau of Educational Measurements. *

[1144]

Animal Husbandry Test: State High School Tests for Indiana. High school; 1932; R. W. Gregory, K. W. Kiltz, W. A. Smith, S. S. Cromer, and H. H. Remmers; State High School Testing Service for Indiana. *

For additional information, see 3:365.

[1145]

Farm Shop Tools: Recognition and Use: State High School Tests for Indiana. High school; 1942–43; Nelson M. Parkhurst; State High School Testing Service for Indiana. *

For additional information and a review by M. Ray Karnes, see 4:441 (1 reference).

COMPUTATIONAL AND SCORING DEVICES

[1146]

Age and IQ Calculator. 1940–52; for determining IQ's from MA's between 3 and 32 and CA's of 5 and over; California Test Bureau. *

[1147]

Baltimore Age Calculator. 1924–52; for determining CA's from birthdates falling in 1938 through 1959; John L. Stenquist; [Harcourt, Brace & World, Inc.]. *

[1148]

The Bowman I.Q. Kalculator. 1957; for determining IQ's from MA's and CA's between 4 and 22; Personnel Press, Inc. *
  For additional information, see 5:528.

[1149]

★**Dominion Table for Converting Mental Age to I.Q.** 1948; for determining IQ's from MA's and CA's between 5 and 17; Department of Educational Research, Ontario College of Education, University of Toronto; distributed by Guidance Centre. *

[1150]

★**The EB Punch-Key Scoring and Answer Sheet System.** 1958; special answer sheets and equipment for perforating them for hand scoring; Edvin Brye; the Author. *

[1150a]

★**Grade-O-Mat.** [1960]; portable machine for scoring IBM punch answer cards; Grade-O-Mat Division, Burgess Cellulose Co. *

[1151]

★**Hammond Matrix Sorter.** 1953; a device to facilitate the analysis of matrices by shifting rows and columns; S. B. Hammond; Australian Council for Educational Research. *

[1152]

Hankes' Answer Sheets. 1946; special answer sheets and scoring services available for *Strong Vocational Interest Blank* (see 1887 and 1888), *The Personality Inventory* (see 246), and *Minnesota Multiphasic Personality Inventory* (see 224); E. J. Hankes; Testscor. *
  For additional information, see 5:529 (1 reference); see also 4:466 (5 references).

[1153]

IBM Test Scoring Machine. 1937–58; for scoring IBM answer sheets; formerly called *International Test Scoring Machine;* International Business Machines Corporation. *
  For additional information, see 5:530 (15 references); for a review by Arthur E. Traxler, see 3:397 (22 references); for reviews by John G. Darley and H. T. Manuel, see 40:1492 (14 references).

[1154]

★**I.Q. Calculator.** 1952; for determining IQ's from MA's and CA's between 3.5 and 20; Milo M. Bolstad; Educational Test Bureau. *

[1155]

Inglis Intelligence Quotient Values, Second Revised Edition. 1921–38; for determining IQ's from CA's between 3-0 and 16-11 and MA's between 1 and 17; Alexander Inglis; [Harcourt, Brace & World, Inc.]. *

[1156]

Jensen I.Q. Dial. 1930; for determining IQ's from MA's and CA's between 3 and 18; Carl Christian Jensen; Public School Publishing Co. *

[1157]

★[**MRC Test Processing Service.**] 1956–60; special answer sheets and scoring services, available through the test publishers, for the following tests: *Essential High School Content Battery* (see 12), *Flanagan Aptitude Classification Tests* (see 1375), *Iowa Tests of Basic Skills* (see 24), *Iowa Tests of Educational Development* (see 25), *Lorge-Thorndike Intelligence Tests* (see 787), *Metropolitan Achievement Tests, [1960 Edition]* (see 27), and *Stanford Achievement Test, [1953 Revision]* (see 41); sponsors of large-scale testing programs may arrange for MRC scoring of other tests; Measurement Research Center, Inc. *

[1158]

★**The Multiple Purpose Self Trainer.** High school and adults; 1951–54; a teaching-testing pull-tab device for use with any set of objective questions keyed to the given answer pattern; Charles W. Nelson; Management Research Associates. *
a) [SCALE OF VALUES FORM.]
b) [TRUE-FALSE FORM.]

[1159]

Normal Percentile Chart. 1924–38; for graphic representation of test scores; revision of *Universal Percentile Graph;* Arthur S. Otis; [Harcourt, Brace & World, Inc.]. *

[1160]

The Tweeddale I.Q. Conversion Tables. 1950; for determining IQ's, reading quotients, or arithmetic quotients from MA's, reading ages, or arithmetic ages and CA's between 5-0 and 16-11; B. B. Mager; Oliver & Boyd Ltd. *
For additional information, see 4:469.

[1161]

[**V.G.C. Answer Strips and Scoring Sleeves.**] Grades 3–16; 1950; answer sheets and scoring devices for use with teacher-constructed true-false or multiple choice tests; Guidance Centre. *
For additional information, see 4:470.

DRIVING AND SAFETY EDUCATION

[1162]

*[**American Automobile Association Driver Testing Apparatus.**] Drivers; 1939–60; 13 tests; Traffic Engineering and Safety Department, American Automobile Association; the Association. *
a) AUTOMATIC REACTION TIME. 1958–60; braking reaction to electrically operated signals.
b) COLOR VISION. 1947–60.
c) COMPLEX REACTION TIME. 1940–49; braking and turning reactions to electrically operated signals.
d) DETONATORS. 1939–60; braking reaction and distance.

e) DISTANCE JUDGMENT. 1939–60.
f) DISTANCE JUDGMENT AND VISION. 1940; incorporates essential features of *e* and *m*.
g) DRIVER EVALUATOR. 1950–60; incorporates essential features of *b, e, h,* and *m*.
h) FIELD OF VISION. 1939–60.
i) JERK RECORDER. 1950.
j) NIGHT SIGHT METER. 1952–60; 3 scores: glare vision, night vision, recovery.
k) [SIMPLE] REACTION TIME. 1943–60; braking reaction to manually operated signals.
l) STEADINESS. 1939–60.
m) VISUAL ACUITY. 1943–60.
For additional information, see 4:521.

[1162a]

★Bicycle Safety Performance and Skill Tests, [1958 Revision]. Ages 10–16; 1940–58; tests 1, 2, 4, and 6 are modifications of the *National Bicycle Tests* by Alfred L. Lorenz; 12 tests, 13 scores: Balance Test (Straight Lane), Pedaling and Braking, Straight Line Test, Signalling-Mounting-Dismounting, Single Obstacle Test, Double Obstacle Test, Double Zig-Zag Obstacle Test, Figure-Eight Steering, Figure-Eight Balance Test, Turning Around, Emergency Turn and Stop, Cruising Test, total; Ben W. Miller; National Safety Council. *

[1163]

★Driver Scalogram. Drivers; [1955]; self rating of driving practices; Herbert J. Stack; Center for Safety Education. *

[1164]

Examination for Driving Instructors. College students preparing to teach high school driving instruction; 1951; Traffic Engineering and Safety Department, American Automobile Association; the Association. *
For additional information, see 4:522.

[1165]

General Test on Traffic and Driving Knowledge. Drivers; 1949–50; Traffic Engineering and Safety Department, American Automobile Association; the Association. *
For additional information, see 5:922.

[1166]

★Hannaford Industrial Safety Attitude Scales. Industry; 1959; Earle S. Hannaford; Center for Safety Education. *
a) INDUSTRIAL SAFETY ATTITUDE SCALE FOR MALE EMPLOYEES.
b) INDUSTRIAL SAFETY ATTITUDE SCALE FOR MALE SUPERVISORS.

[1167]

★Knowledge Test for Automobile Drivers. Student drivers; 1940–["late 40's"]; most items selected from *Abercrombie Driver Test* by Stanley A. Abercrombie; Center for Safety Education. *

[1168]

Lauer Driver Reaction Inventory. Drivers; 1948–57; revision of *Driving Attitude Inventory;* A. R. Lauer; Iowa State University Press. *
For additional information, see 5:593 (2 references).

[1169]

Rating Scale for Automobile-Driver Skills: The Abercrombie Driver Test.
Student drivers; 1940; Stanley A. Abercrombie; Center for Safety Education. *
For additional information, see 4:524.

[1170]

Revere Safety Test, Second Edition. Industrial employees especially in the
nonferrous metal industries; 1947–50; 5 scores: general safety, piling-carrying-
traffic, tools, machine operation, total; for research use only; Revere Copper
& Brass, Inc., and the Psychological Evaluation and Services Center, Syracuse
University; Revere Copper & Brass, Inc. *
For additional information and reviews by Willard A. Kerr and Harold G.
Seashore, see 4:525.

[1171]

Road Test Check List for Passenger Car Drivers. Passenger car drivers;
1947–55; formerly called *Road Test in Traffic for Passenger Car Drivers;* 3
scores: specific driving errors, general attitude and driving practices, total;
Amos E. Neyhart; published jointly by American Automobile Association and
Institute of Public Safety. *
For additional information, see 5:594.

[1172]

Rogers-Lauer Driver Rating Inventory. Drivers; 1935–57; formerly called
Rogers-Lauer Driver Training Inventory; 3 scores: behavior patterns, basic
skills, total; A. R. Lauer; Iowa State University Press. *
For additional information, see 5:595.

[1173]

★Safety Education: Manchester Semester-End Achievement Tests. 1 semester high school; [1937–46]; Bureau of Tests. *

[1174]

*Siebrecht Attitude Scale. Grades 9–16 and adults; 1941–58; attitude toward
safe driving practices; Elmer B. Siebrecht; Center for Safety Education. *
For additional information, see 3:458 (2 references).

[1175]

★Student Record in Driver Education. Student drivers; [1956]; Earl D.
Heath; Center for Safety Education. *

[1176]

★Test of Safety Mindedness. Adults; 1943–[55]; a battery consisting of *Test
of Ability to Understand Instructions: Job Alertness Tests* (see 776), *Observation Test* (see 1964), and the carelessness score from *Interest Inventory* (an abbreviated edition of *Inventory of Interest and Temperament Areas,* see 202);
W. H. Winkler; Winkler Publications. *

EDUCATION

[1177]

Academic Freedom Survey. College students and faculty; 1954; 3 scores: stu-
dent, faculty, total; Paul Slivnick and Academic Freedom Committee, Illinois
Division, American Civil Liberties Union; Psychometric Affiliates. *
For additional information, see 5:531.

[1178]

Aptitude Test for Elementary School Teachers-in-Training. Prospective elementary school teachers; 1946–51; Henry Bowers; J. M. Dent & Sons (Canada) Ltd. *

For additional information and reviews by Robert M. W. Travers and Edwin Wandt, see 4:792 (2 references, 1 excerpt).

[1179]

The Case of Mickey Murphy: A Case-Study Instrument in Evaluation, [Third Edition]. Teachers; 1942–55; 3 scores: interpretation of data, hasty conclusions, planning; Warren R. Baller; University of Nebraska Press. *

For additional information and a review by Dwight L. Arnold, see 5:533 (2 references); for a review by Frank S. Freeman of the second edition, see 4:794.

[1180]

*Case Study Tests in Human Growth and Development, Revised Edition. Psychologists and social workers and teachers in training and in service; 1946–60; revision of *Tests of Human Growth and Development;* 5 tests; 3 scores each for *b-e:* diagnostic total, remedial total, total; John E. Horrocks, Winifred B. Horrocks, and Maurice E. Troyer; Charles E. Merrill Books, Inc. * For a related entry, see 1204.

a) A TEST OF KNOWLEDGE OF FACT AND PRINCIPLE: ADOLESCENT DEVELOPMENT.
b) A STUDY OF CONNIE CASEY.
c) A STUDY OF SAM SMITH.
d) A STUDY OF BARRY BLACK.
e) A STUDY OF MURRAY MURSELL.

For additional information and reviews by Harold E. Jones and Goodwin Watson of the original edition, see 3:406 (3 references).

[1181]

★Class Activity-Analysis Chart. Teachers; 1941; supervisory observations; Edwin J. Brown; Bureau of Educational Measurements. *

[1182]

Diagnostic Teacher-Rating Scale. Grades 4–12; 1938–52; ratings by pupils; 8 ratings: liking for teacher, ability to explain, kindness-friendliness-understanding, fairness in grading, discipline, work required, liking for lessons, total; Mary Amatora; [Employers' Tests and Services Associates]. *

For additional information and a review by Dorothy M. Clendenen, see 5:534 (5 references); see also 4:795 (2 references).

[1183]

Educational Aptitude Test: George Washington University Series. Entrants to teacher training institutions; 1940; 7 scores: vocabulary, research judgment, logical reasoning, information, comprehension, arithmetic, total; Thelma Hunt and James Harold Fox; Center for Psychological Service. *

For additional information and reviews by A. S. Barr and Harl R. Douglass, see 3:400 (3 references).

[1184]

Educational Interest Inventory. Prospective students of education; 1958; 10 scores: counselor, elementary teacher, high school teacher, elementary principal,

high school principal, superintendent of schools, supervisor, psychologist, research worker, college professor; Percival M. Symonds, Arthur R. Jensen, Gordon Fifer, and Robert Drummond; Bureau of Publications. *
For additional information, see 5:535.

[1185]

Faculty Morale Scale for Institutional Improvement. College faculty; 1954–56; A Local Chapter Committee, American Association of University Professors; Psychometric Affiliates. *
For additional information, see 5:536.

[1186]

*The Graduate Record Examinations Advanced Tests: Education. Grades 16–17; 1946–60; Educational Testing Service. * For the testing program entry, see 1353.
For additional information and a review by Harry N. Rivlin of Form CGR, see 5:537; see also 4:797 (2 references). For a review of the testing program, see 5:601.

[1187]

How I Counsel. Counselors and prospective counselors; 1950; Stanley C. Benz and H. H. Remmers; University Book Store. *
For additional information and reviews by Clifford P. Froehlich and Milton E. Hahn, see 4:798 (4 references).

[1188]

How I Teach: Analysis of Teaching Practices. Teachers; 1942; also called *Purdue Teachers Examination;* Ida B. Kelley and Keith J. Perkins; Educational Test Bureau. *
For additional information and reviews by May V. Seagoe and D. A. Worcester, see 4:799 (4 references); for a review by David G. Ryans, see 3:403.

[1189]

Howe-Kyte Diagnostic Record of Teaching. Student and experienced teachers; 1932; ratings by supervisors; Mary E. Howe and George C. Kyte; Houghton Mifflin Co. *

[1190]

[Illinois Opinion Inventories.] Grades 9–12, adults; 1948; opinion on schools; directions and interpretive procedures are presented in *What People Think About Their Schools;* Harold C. Hand, Gilbert C. Finlay, and Ardwin J. Dolio; [Harcourt, Brace & World, Inc.]. *
a) ILLINOIS INVENTORY OF PUPIL OPINION.
b) ILLINOIS INVENTORY OF PARENT OPINION.
c) ILLINOIS INVENTORY OF TEACHER OPINION. Must be reproduced locally.
For additional information and a review by Kenneth E. Clark, see 4:52 (1 reference); for an excerpt from a related book review, see 4:53.

[1191]

Minnesota Teacher Attitude Inventory. Elementary or secondary school teachers and teachers in training and high school seniors; 1951; Walter W. Cook, Carroll H. Leeds, and Robert Callis; Psychological Corporation. *
For additional information and reviews by Dwight L. Arnold and Lee J. Cronbach, see 4:801 (9 references).

[1192]

*National Teacher Examinations. College seniors and teachers; 1940–61; tests administered annually at centers established by the publisher and locally by arrangement; Educational Testing Service. *

a) COMMON EXAMINATIONS. 6 scores: professional information, English expression, social studies-literature-fine arts, science and mathematics, nonverbal reasoning, total.

b) OPTIONAL EXAMINATIONS. 13 tests: Education in the Elementary School, Early Childhood Education, Biology and General Science, English Language and Literature, Industrial Arts Education, Mathematics, Chemistry-Physics-General Science, Social Studies, Physical Education, Business Education, Home Economics Education, Art Education, Music Education.

For additional information and reviews by William A. Brownell (Forms CNT, ENT, and FNT), Walter W. Cook (Forms CNT, DNT, and GNT), and Lawrence G. Derthick (Forms CNT, ENT, and FNT), see 5:538 (6 references); for a review by Harry N. Rivlin of earlier forms, see 4:802 (43 references).

[1193]

Ohio Teaching Record: Anecdotal Observation Form, Second Revised Edition. Teachers; 1940–45; ratings by supervisors; Publication Office, Ohio State University. *

For additional information, see 3:402 (1 reference, 1 excerpt).

[1194]

★Problem Check List for Student Teachers and Intern Teachers, [Experimental Edition]. Grades 13–16 and adults; 1958–61; 11 problem area scores: philosophy of education, responsibilities as staff member, use of materials of instruction, subject matter, materials for guidance, management of scheduling, classroom management-discipline, interpersonal relationships, professional responsibility and improvement, home and family relationships, total; Thelma A. McIntosh; the Author.

[1195]

A Pupil's Rating Scale of an Instructor. High school and college; 1952–57; Russell M. Eidsmoe; Morningside College. *

For additional information, see 5:539.

[1196]

★Purdue Instructional Television Attitude Scale. Adults; 1957–58; Purdue Research Foundation; distributed by TV Program Research Unit. *

[1197]

★The Purdue Instructor Performance Indicator. College teachers; 1960; ratings by students; John H. Snedeker and H. H. Remmers; University Book Store. *

[1198]

*The Purdue Rating Scale for Instruction. College teachers; 1927–60; student ratings on 26 characteristics of the instructor and teaching situation; H. H. Remmers and D. N. Elliott; University Book Store. *

For additional information and a review by Kenneth L. Heaton, see 4:803 (26 references).

[1199]

★Remmlein's School Law Test. Teacher education classes in school law; 1957; 3 or 4 scores: acquaintance with legal terms, knowledge of principles and cases, use of law books (optional), total; [Madaline Kinter Remmlein]; Interstate Printers & Publishers, Inc. *

[1200]

SRA Educators Opinion Inventory. Teachers; 1953; 19 ratings: work demands, working conditions, curriculum materials, pay, benefits, friendliness and cooperation of fellow employees, relations with immediate superior, confidence in administration, confidence in school board members, technical skills of immediate superior, effectiveness of school administration, adequacy of communication, personal freedom and community relations, security of job and work relations, professional satisfaction, identification with the school and its program, adequacy of provision for pupil individual differences, opportunity for growth and advancement, reactions to the inventory; Science Research Associates, Inc. *
For additional information, see 5:540.

[1201]

A Self Appraisal Scale for Teachers. Teachers; 1957; Howard Wilson; Administrative Research Associates. *
For additional information, see 5:541.

[1202]

★Sizing Up Your School Subjects. Grades 9–12; 1958; reactions to instruction by television; Henry S. Dyer and Anne H. Ferris; Educational Testing Service. *

[1203]

★Survey of Educational Leadership Practices. Teachers; 1955; J. J. Valenti and Charles W. Nelson; Management Research Associates. *

[1204]

*Syracuse Test Series in Human Growth and Development. Guidance counselors in training; 1955; extension of the original edition of *Case Study Tests in Human Growth and Development* (see 1180); George E. Schlesser; the Author. *
a) A STUDY OF BEN BLYTHE.
b) A STUDY OF JOE JARVEY.

[1205]

Teacher Education Examination Program. College seniors preparing to teach; 1957; tests administered by participating teacher training institutions; Educational Testing Service. *
a) GENERAL PROFESSIONAL EXAMINATIONS. 7 scores: foundations of education, child development and educational psychology, guidance and measurement, instructional methods, English, history-literature-fine arts, science and mathematics.
b) TEACHING FIELD TESTS. 11 tests: Early Childhood Education, Elementary School Education, English Language and Literature, Social Studies, Biological Science, Physical Science, Mathematics, French, Spanish, Industrial Arts, Physical Education.
For additional information and a review by Walter W. Cook of Form FTC, see 5:543.

[1206]

Teacher Opinionaire on Democracy. Teachers; 1949; democratic aspects of teacher philosophy; Enola Ledbetter and Theodore F. Lentz; Character Research Association. *

For additional information and reviews by George W. Hartmann and C. Robert Pace, see 4:805.

[1207]

★Teacher Preference Schedule. Elementary school teachers and prospective teachers; [1960]; experimental form; unconscious motivations for teaching; 2 parts, 10 scores for each: practical, status-striving, nurturant, non-directive, rebellious, preadult fixated, orderliness, dependency, exhibition, dominance; George G. Stern and Joseph M. Masling; distributed by Psychological Research Center. *

a) FORM A [ATTITUDES].
b) FORM G [GRATIFICATIONS].

[1208]

Teaching Aptitude Test: George Washington University Series. Grades 12–16; 1927; F. A. Moss, T. Hunt, and F. C. Wallace; Center for Psychological Service. *

For additional information and a review by May V. Seagoe, see 4:806; for a review by A. S. Barr, see 3:405 (8 references).

[1209]

The Teaching Evaluation Record. Teachers; 1953–56; ratings by supervisors; Dwight E. Beecher; Educators Publishing Co. *

For additional information, see 5:542.

[1210]

A Test on Adult Attitudes Toward Children. Classes in child development and teachers and parents; 1957; David F. Votaw; Steck Co. *

For additional information, see 5:544.

[1211]

What Would You Do? Perplexing Incidents in Human Relations. Teachers; 1955; Willard S. Elsbree and others; Bureau of Publications. *

For additional information, see 5:545.

[1212]

The Wilson Teacher-Appraisal Scale. Teachers; 1948–57; ratings by students in grades 7–12, 12–16; Howard Wilson; Administrative Research Associates. *

For additional information, see 5:546.

ETIQUETTE

[1213]

Furbay-Schrammel Social Comprehension Test. Grades 9–16; 1941–42; 15 scores: social calls, teas-receptions-parties, introductions, invitations, table etiquette, dress and personal habits, public courtesies, correspondence, house guests, conversation, traveling, funerals, dances and balls, courtships-engagements-weddings, miscellaneous; John H. Furbay and H. E. Schrammel; Bureau of Educational Measurements. *

For additional information and a review by James H. Ricks, Jr., see 4:472 (1 reference).

[1214]

The New Century Social Conduct Test. Grades 9 and over; 1939–45; Century School Crafts.

For additional information, see 5:547.

[1215]

Parsons Social Comprehension Test. Grades 9–12; 1953; Verlin Parsons; Bureau of Educational Measurements. *

For additional information, see 5:548.

[1216]

Test on Social Usage. High school and college; 1935–57; Margaret Stephenson and Ruth Millett; McKnight & McKnight Publishing Co. *

For additional information, see 5:549.

HANDWRITING

[1217]

The American Handwriting Scale. Grades 2–8; 1929–49; Paul V. West; A. N. Palmer Co. *

[1218]

Ayres Measuring Scale for Handwriting. Grades 5–8; 1912–40; also called *Ayres Handwriting Scale: Gettysburg Edition;* 2 scores: quality, speed; Leonard P. Ayres; Cooperative Test Division. *

For additional information, see 5:550; for a review by Worth J. Osburn, see 4:475 (9 references).

[1219]

Evaluation Scales for Guiding Growth in Handwriting. Grades 1, 2, 3, 4, 5, 6, 7, 8–9; 1958; Frank N. Freeman; Zaner-Bloser Co. *

For additional information, see 5:551.

[1220]

Metropolitan Primary Cursive Handwriting Scale and **Metropolitan Primary Manuscript Handwriting Scale.** Grades 1–3; 1933; Gertrude H. Hildreth; [Harcourt, Brace & World, Inc.]. *

[1221]

Normal Handwriting Scale. Grades 4–8; 1947; Albert Grant; Zaner-Bloser Co. *

For additional information, see 4:476.

HEALTH AND PHYSICAL EDUCATION

[1222]

★AAHPER Youth Fitness Test. Grades 5–12; 1958; 8–9 scores: pull-up, sit-up, shuttle run, standing broad jump, 50-yard dash, softball throw, 600-yard

run-walk, fitness average, swimming (optional); AAHPER Youth Fitness
Project; American Association for Health, Physical Education, and Recreation. *

[1223]

★Attitude Inventory. College women; [1959]; attitudes about values of
physical education; 5 scores: spiritual, sociological, psychological, general,
total; June P. Galloway; the Author. *

[1224]

Brewer-Schrammel Health Knowledge and Attitude. Grades 4–8; 1935;
John W. Brewer and H. E. Schrammel; Bureau of Educational Measure-
ments. *
    For additional information and reviews by John C. Almack and Frederick
Rand Rogers, see 40:1499 (1 reference).

[1225]

Byrd Health Attitude Scale. Grades 10–14; 1940–41; Oliver E. Byrd; Stanford University Press. *
    For additional information and reviews by Mayhew Derryberry and H. H.
Remmers, see 3:418 (1 reference, 1 excerpt).

[1226]

*College Health Knowledge Test, Personal Health. College; 1950–59; 12
scores: social and biological background, nutrition and diet, excretion and
cleanliness, exercise and body mechanics, fatigue and rest, mental hygiene, reproduction and heredity, prevention and control of disease, eye-ear-teeth hygiene, hygiene of environment, use of medical care, total; Terry H. Dearborn;
Stanford University Press. *
    For additional information and a review by H. Harrison Clarke of an earlier
edition, see 4:478 (1 reference).

[1227]

Cornell Medical Index—Health Questionnaire. Ages 14 and over; 1949–56;
Keeve Brodman, Albert J. Erdmann, Jr., and Harold G. Wolff; Cornell University Medical College. *
    For additional information, see 5:552 (2 references).

[1228]

*Elementary Health: Every Pupil Scholarship Test. Grades 6–8; 1933–61;
new form usually issued twice a year; Bureau of Educational Measurements. *
    For additional information, see 5:553.

[1229]

Gill-Schrammel Physiology Test. High school; 1936–37; Ethan M. Gill and
H. E. Schrammel; Bureau of Educational Measurements. *
    For additional information and a review by Clarence H. Nelson, see 5:554.

[1230]

Health and Safety Education Test: National Achievement Tests. Grades
3–6; 1947–56; 5 scores: good habits, cause and effect, facts, application of rules,
total; Lester D. Crow and Loretta C. Ryan; Acorn Publishing Co. *
    For additional information and a review by Clarence H. Nelson, see 5:555.

[1231]

*Health and Safety Education Test: State High School Tests for Indiana.
1, 2 semesters high school; 1945–59; Shelby Gallien and Hilda Schwehn; State
High School Testing Service for Indiana. *
For additional information, see 3:420.

[1232]

*Health Education and Hygiene: Every Pupil Test. 1, 2 semesters in grades
7–9; 1935–61; new form usually issued twice a year; Ohio Scholarship Tests. *
For additional information, see 5:556.

[1233]

Health Education Test: Knowledge and Application: Acorn National
Achievement Tests, Revised Edition. Grades 7–13; 1946–56; 3 scores: knowl-
edge, application, total; John H. Shaw and Maurice E. Troyer; Acorn Pub-
lishing Co. *
For additional information, see 5:557 (1 reference); for reviews by H. H.
Remmers and Mabel E. Rugen, see 3:421.

[1234]

Health Inventory for High School Students. Grades 9–12; 1942; 9 scores:
health status, health practice, public health, first aid, prevention of disease,
proper health habits, diet, mental hygiene, health knowledge total; Gerwin
Neher; California Test Bureau. *
For additional information and reviews by Mayhew Derryberry and Mabel
E. Rugen, see 3:422 (1 reference).

[1235]

Health Knowledge Test for College Freshmen: National Achievement
Tests. Grade 13; 1956; A. Frank Bridges; Acorn Publishing Co. *
For additional information and a review by James E. Bryan, see 5:558 (3
references).

[1236]

*Health: Manchester Semester-End Achievement Tests. 1 semester high
school; 1934–[59]; formerly called Twelfth Year Health; Bureau of Tests. *

[1237]

Health Practice Inventory. Grades 12–16 and adults; 1943–52; 14 scores:
personal health, nutrition, dental health, physical activity, rest-sleep-relaxation,
communicable disease, chronic disease, stimulants and depressants, mental
health, family health, consumer health, community health, safety education,
total; Edward B. Johns and Warren L. Juhnke; Stanford University Press. *
For additional information and a review by James E. Bryan, see 5:559 (2
references); for a review by Thomas Kirk Cureton of the original edition, see
3:423 (2 references).

[1238]

Health Test: National Achievement Tests. Grades 3–8; 1937–57; 5 scores:
recognizing best habits, health comparisons, causes and effects, health facts,
total; Robert K. Speer and Samuel Smith; Acorn Publishing Co. *
For additional information and a review by Benno G. Fricke, see 5:560; for
a review by Jacob S. Orleans, see 4:485.

[1239]

*High School Health: Every Pupil Scholarship Test. High school; 1938(?)–
61; new form usually issued twice a year; Bureau of Educational Measurements. *
    For additional information, see 5:561.

[1240]

Indiana University Motor Fitness Index. Boys and men in grades 10–16;
1943; Karl W. Bookwalter and Carolyn W. Bookwalter; distributed by Indiana
University Bookstore. *
    For additional information, see 3:424 (4 references).

[1241]

Kilander Health Knowledge Test. High school; 1936–51; H. F. Kilander;
[Harcourt, Brace & World, Inc.]. * For the college level entry, see 1242.
    For additional information, see 5:562 (3 references); see also 40:1503 (2
excerpts).

[1242]

★Kilander Health Knowledge Test [for College Students]. College; 1936–
61; H. Frederick Kilander; the Author. * For the high school level entry, see
1241.

[1243]

*Patient's Self-History Form, Second Edition. Patients; 1948–58; Oliver E.
Byrd; Stanford University Press. *
    For additional information, see 4:486.

[1244]

*Physical Education: National Teacher Examinations. College seniors and
teachers; 1954–61; Educational Testing Service. * For the testing program
entry, see 1192.
    For additional information, see 5:563. For reviews of the testing program,
see 5:538 and 4:802.

[1245]

Physical Education: Teacher Education Examination Program. College
seniors preparing to teach secondary school; 1957; Educational Testing Service. * For the testing program entry, see 1205.
    For additional information, see 5:564. For a review of the testing program,
see 5:543.

[1246]

Physical Education Tests. College women; 1955; 7 tests: badminton, basketball, bowling, field hockey, softball, tennis, volleyball; Gail M. Hennis; the
Author. *
    For additional information, see 5:565 (1 reference).

[1247]

★Smoking Habits Questionnaire. Grades 7–12; [1959]; V. J. Sallak; the
Author. *

[1248]

★Stimulants and Depressants. Grades 9–16 and adults; 1957, c1959; knowledge of effects of drugs; for research use only; H. Frederick Kilander; the
Author. *

[1249]

Trusler-Arnett Health Knowledge Test. Grades 9–16; 1940; V. T. Trusler,
C. E. Arnett, and H. E. Schrammel; Bureau of Educational Measurements. *
    For additional information and a review by Thomas Kirk Cureton, see 3:426.

[1250]

★Veenker Health Knowledge Test for the Seventh Grade. Grade 7; 1960;
C. H. Veenker; the Author. *

[1251]

[Wetzel Grid Charts.] Ages birth–3, 2–18; 1940–48; a chart for evaluating
physical growth and development; Norman C. Wetzel; NEA Service, Inc. *
a) THE BABY GRID: A GUIDE TO INDIVIDUAL PROGRESS DURING INFANCY. Ages
birth–3; 1946–48.
b) GRID FOR EVALUATING PHYSICAL FITNESS IN TERMS OF PHYSIQUE (BODY
BUILD), DEVELOPMENTAL LEVEL AND BASAL METABOLISM—A GUIDE TO INDIVIDUAL
PROGRESS FROM INFANCY TO MATURITY. Ages 2–18; 1940–48.
    For additional information, see 4:489 (9 references).

[1252]

Width-Weight Tables, Second Revised Edition. Ages 1 and over; 1936–40;
Helen B. Pryor; Stanford University Press. *
    For additional information, see 4:490 (1 reference); for excerpts from re-
views of the original edition, see 38:B455 and 36:B211.

[1253]

[Winsberg Tests: Examinations for Physical Education Major Students.]
College; 1952; 15 tests: badminton, basketball, body mechanics, bowling, canoe-
ing, folk dancing, golf, hockey, rhythms, soccer, softball, stunts and tumbling,
swimming, tennis, volleyball; Shirley Winsberg; Department of Physical Education for Women, State University of Iowa. *
    For additional information, see 5:567.

HOME ECONOMICS

[1254]

Assisting With Care and Play of Children: State High School Tests for
Indiana. Grades 7–8; 1946–47; Alice Stair and Muriel G. McFarland; State
High School Testing Service for Indiana. *
    For additional information and a review by Helen C. Dawe, see 3:427.

[1255]

Assisting With Clothing Problems: State High School Tests for Indiana.
Grades 7–8; 1945–46; Elizabeth Anderson, Muriel G. McFarland, and Kathleen
McGillicuddy; State High School Testing Service for Indiana. *
    For additional information, see 3:428.

[1256]

Chart for Diagnosing Defects in Buttonholes. High school; [1923]; Hazel K. Stiebeling and Dean A. Worcester; Bureau of Educational Measurements. *

[1257]

Child Development: State High School Tests for Indiana. High school; 1945; Roberta Kelly, Muriel G. McFarland, and Alice Stair; State High School Testing Service for Indiana. *
For additional information and a review by Helen C. Dawe, see 3:429.

[1258]

*Clothing: Every Pupil Scholarship Test.** High school; 1927–61; new form usually issued annually; Bureau of Educational Measurements. *
For additional information, see 5:568.

[1259]

Clothing I: State High School Tests for Indiana. High school; 1946–47; Mary I. Healey, Jeannette O. Parvis, Muriel G. McFarland, and M. Jean Wilson; State High School Testing Service for Indiana. *
For additional information, see 3:430.

[1260]

Clothing II: State High School Tests for Indiana. High school; 1946–47; Mary I. Healey, Ruth Davis Moutoux, Jeannette O. Parvis, and Muriel G. McFarland; State High School Testing Service for Indiana. *
For additional information, see 3:431.

[1261]

*Foods: Every Pupil Scholarship Test.** High school; 1927–61; new form usually issued annually; Bureau of Educational Measurements. *
For additional information, see 5:569.

[1262]

*Foods I, Food Selection and Preparation: State High School Tests for Indiana.** High school; 1934–[59]; Audrey M. Finn and Muriel G. McFarland; State High School Testing Service for Indiana. *
For additional information concerning earlier forms, see 4:495; for a review by Hester Chadderdon, see 38:1029.

[1263]

*Foods II, Planning for Family Food Needs: State High School Tests for Indiana.** High school; 1941–[59]; Audrey M. Finn and Muriel G. McFarland; State High School Testing Service for Indiana. *
For additional information concerning earlier forms, see 4:496.

[1264]

Helping With Food in the Home: State High School Tests for Indiana. Grades 7–8; 1941–48; Elizabeth Anderson and Muriel G. McFarland; State High School Testing Service for Indiana. *
For additional information and a review by Jean D. Amberson, see 4:498.

[1265]

Helping With the Housekeeping: State High School Tests for Indiana.
Grades 7–8; 1941–45; Evelyn Swaim, Kathleen McGillicuddy, and Muriel G.
McFarland; State High School Testing Service for Indiana. *
For additional information and a review by Hester Chadderdon, see 4:499.

[1266]

★Home Art Placement Test. First year students of college home economics;
1958; test materials must be assembled locally; [Hazel M. Hatcher, Laura D.
Kivlin, and Christine Salmon]; College of Home Economics, Pennsylvania
State University. *

[1267]

Home Care of the Sick Test: State High School Tests for Indiana. High
school; 1941–48; Louise Gentry, Gleela Ratcliffe, and Muriel G. McFarland;
State High School Testing Service for Indiana. *
For additional information, see 4:500.

[1268]

★Home Economics Education: National Teacher Examinations. College
seniors and teachers; 1960–61; Educational Testing Service. * For the testing
program entry and references to reviews, see 1192.

[1269]

★Homemaking I and II: Every Pupil Scholarship Test. 1, 2 years high
school; 1947–57; Bureau of Educational Measurements. *

[1270]

*Housing the Family: State High School Tests for Indiana. High school;
1941–[60]; Lois Rhinesperger and Muriel G. McFarland; State High School
Testing Service for Indiana. *
For additional information and a review by Jean D. Amberson of an earlier
form, see 4:501.

[1271]

Johnson Home Economics Interest Inventory. College women majoring in
home economics; 1955; 14 scores: clothing merchandising, designing, county
extension work, food product promotion, food service directing, social welfare
and public health work, home service, hospital dietetics, interior decorating,
journalism or radio, restaurant or tearoom managing, secondary school teaching, textile testing, work with young children; Hildegarde Johnson; Iowa State
University Press. *
For additional information and reviews by John D. Black and Leona E. Tyler,
see 5:570 (6 references).

[1272]

Minnesota Check List for Food Preparation and Serving, Third Edition.
Grades 7–16 and adults; 1938–51; Clara Brown Arny; University of Minnesota Press. *
For additional information, see 5:571; see also 40:1509 (1 reference, 1 excerpt).

[1273]
*Ninth Year Home Economics: Manchester Semester-End Achievement
Tests. 1, 2 semesters grade 9; [1934–51]; Bureau of Tests. *
a) [FOODS.] First semester.
b) [CLOTHING.] Second semester.

[1274]
*Nutrition Information Test. Grades 9–16 and adults; 1942–[57]; for research
use only; H. Frederick Kilander; the Author. *
For additional information, see 3:425 (1 reference).

[1275]
Unit Scales of Attainment in Foods and Household Management. Grades
7–9; 1933; Ethel B. Reeve and Clara M. Brown [Arny]; Educational Test
Bureau. *
For additional information and reviews by Norma A. Albright and Hester
Chadderdon, see 40:1511.

INDUSTRIAL ARTS

[1276]
★General Shop Woodworking: Manchester Semester-End Achievement
Tests. High school; [1944]; Bureau of Tests. *

[1277]
*Industrial Arts Education: National Teacher Examinations. College seniors
and teachers; 1947–61; Educational Testing Service. * For the testing program
entry, see 1192.
For additional information, see 5:574. For reviews of the testing program,
see 5:538 and 4:802.

[1278]
*Industrial Arts: Every Pupil Scholarship Test. High school; 1926–61; new
form usually issued twice a year; Bureau of Educational Measurements. *
For additional information, see 5:575.

[1279]
Industrial Arts: Teacher Education Examination Program. College seniors
preparing to teach secondary school; 1957; Educational Testing Service. *
For the testing program entry, see 1205.
For additional information, see 5:576. For a review of the testing program,
see 5:543.

[1280]
Mechanical Drawing. High school; 1937; Charles Schoonover, Jr., C. L.
Jackson, and H. E. Schrammel; Bureau of Educational Measurements. *
For additional information and a review by Dean M. Schweickhard, see
40:1513.

[1281]
Mechanical Drawing Test: State High School Tests for Indiana. High
school; 1944–45; Justus Rising; State High School Testing Service for Indiana. *
For additional information and a review by William J. Micheels, see 4:503.

[1282]

Middleton Industrial Arts Test. High school; 1951; Jean Ellis Middleton and
H. E. Schrammel; Bureau of Educational Measurements. *
   For additional information and a review by William J. Micheels, see 4:504.

LISTENING COMPREHENSION

[1283]

Brown-Carlsen Listening Comprehension Test. Grades 9–13; 1953–55; James
I. Brown and G. Robert Carlsen; [Harcourt, Brace & World, Inc.]. *
   For additional information and reviews by E. F. Lindquist and Irving Lorge,
see 5:577 (13 references).

[1284]

***Sequential Tests of Educational Progress: Listening.** Grades 4–6, 7–9, 10–
12, 13–14; 1956–59; Cooperative Test Division. * For the complete battery
entry, see 39.
   For additional information and reviews by E. F. Lindquist and Irving Lorge,
see 5:578 (1 reference). For reviews of the complete battery, see 5:24.

MARRIAGE AND COURTSHIP

[1285]

★A Courtship Analysis. Adults; [1961]; for analysis of the attitudes and behavior traits of each partner as seen by the other; experimental form; Gelolo
McHugh; Family Life Publications, Inc. *

[1286]

★A Dating Problems Checklist. High school and college; [1961]; experimental form; Gelolo McHugh; Family Life Publications, Inc. *

[1287]

★Individual and Marriage Counseling Inventory. Adult counselees; 1956;
Aaron L. Rutledge; Merrill-Palmer Institute. *

[1288]

★Information Test on Human Reproduction. Grades 9–16 and adults;
[1959]; for research use only; H. Frederick Kilander; the Author. *

[1289]

★A Marriage Adjustment Form. Adults; 19(?)–[61]; problems checklist;
Ernest W. Burgess; distributed by Family Life Publications, Inc. *

[1290]

A Marriage Prediction Schedule. Adults; 1939–58; reprinted from *Predicting
Success or Failure in Marriage;* Ernest W. Burgess; Family Life Publications,
Inc. *
   For additional information, see 5:84 (8 references).

[1290a]

★Otto Pre-Marital Counseling Schedules. Adults; 1961; Herbert A. Otto;
Consulting Psychologists Press, Inc. *

[1291]

Sex Knowledge Inventory, Experimental Edition. Sex education classes in high school and college and adults; 1950–56; 2 tests; Gelolo McHugh; Family Life Publications, Inc. *
a) SEX KNOWLEDGE INVENTORY: FOR MARRIAGE COUNSELING. 1950–52.
b) SEX KNOWLEDGE INVENTORY: VOCABULARY AND ANATOMY, SECOND REVISION. 1950–56.
For additional information, see 5:566 (1 reference); for a review by Albert Ellis, see 4:488 (1 excerpt).

[1292]

★**Sex Knowledge Test.** Adults, particularly marriage counselees; 1958; medical advisors of *Sexology Magazine;* Sexology Corporation. *

PHILOSOPHY

[1293]

*****The Graduate Record Examinations Advanced Tests: Philosophy.** Grades 16–17; 1939–61; Educational Testing Service. * For the testing program entry, see 1353.
For additional information, see 5:581. For a review of the testing program, see 5:601.

[1294]

*****The Graduate Record Examinations Advanced Tests: Scholastic Philosophy.** Seniors in Catholic colleges; 1951–61; available only in the Institutional Testing Program; Educational Testing Service. * For the testing program entry, see 1353.
For additional information, see 4:506. For a review of the testing program, see 5:601.

PSYCHOLOGY

[1295]

Engle Psychology Test. High school; 1952–54, c1950–53; T. L. Engle; [Harcourt, Brace & World, Inc.]. *
For additional information and a review by Harold Seashore, see 5:582.

[1296]

*****The Graduate Record Examinations Advanced Tests: Psychology.** Grades 16–17; 1939–60; Educational Testing Service. * For the testing program entry, see 1353.
For additional information and a review by Harold Seashore, see 5:583. For a review of the testing program, see 5:601.

[1297]

Hogan Psychology Test. High school and college; 1951; Irene Hogan and H. E. Schrammel; Bureau of Educational Measurements. *
For additional information and a review by Harold Seashore, see 5:584.

[1298]

★**The Psychological Vocabulary and Information Test.** Senior psychology majors and graduate students; 1954; 11 scores: applied, comparative, developmental, experimental, general, personality, physiological, social, statistics, total psychology, vocabulary; Harrison G. Gough and Harold Sampson; Harrison G. Gough. *

[1299]
*Psychology Test: Every Pupil Scholarship Test. High school; 1932–59; Bureau of Educational Measurements. *

RECORD AND REPORT FORMS

[1300]
★A9 Cumulative Record Folder. Grades kgn–12; [1951]; American Guidance Service, Inc. *

[1301]
American Council on Education Cumulative Record Folders. Grades 1–3, 4–6, 7–12, 13–16; 1928–47; Committee on Cumulative Records of the American Council on Education; the Council. *
 For additional information and reviews by Warren R. Baller and Arthur H. Brayfield of the folders for grades 1–3 and 4–6, see 4:510; for a review by Herbert A. Toops of the folders for grades 7–12 and 13–16, see 3:444–5.

[1302]
★[Ayer's Cumulative Records]: Ayer Integrated Child Accounting Series. Grades 1–12; 1948–52; Steck Co. *
a) PUPIL'S CUMULATIVE RECORD: ELEMENTARY, JUNIOR, AND SENIOR HIGH SCHOOL. 1952.
b) PUPIL'S CUMULATIVE RECORD: ELEMENTARY SCHOOL. 1948.
c) PUPIL'S CUMULATIVE RECORD: HIGH SCHOOL. 1948.
d) PUPIL'S CUMULATIVE RECORD: ELEMENTARY AND HIGH SCHOOL. 1948.

[1303]
*[California Cumulative Record and Health Insert.] Grades 1–12; 1944–58; A. Carlisle & Co. *
a) CALIFORNIA CUMULATIVE RECORD. Grades 1–8, 9–12; 1944–55.
b) HEALTH INSERT. Grades 1–12; 1957–58, c1943–58; Noelle Anderson, Patricia Hill, Margaret Leonard, and David Van der Slice.
 For additional information and a review by Warren R. Baller of the original edition, see 4:511.

[1303a]
The Cassel Developmental Record. Birth to death; 1954; profile of 6 areas of development (physiological, emotional, psycho-sexual, intellectual, social, educational) and average development; Russell N. Cassel; the Author. *
 For additional information and a review by William E. Henry, see 5:586.

[1304]
Cumulative Personnel Record. Grades 7–12; 1946; National Association of Secondary-School Principals. *
 For additional information, see 4:513.

[1305]
*Florida Cumulative Guidance Record, Revised. Grades 1–12; 1950–59; H. & W. B. Drew Co. *

[1306]

G. C. Anecdotal Record Form. Teachers' recordings of student actions; 1943; Guidance Centre. *

[1307]

***G.C. Cumulative Record Folder, Revised Edition,** Grades 7–13; 1944–55; M. D. Parmenter; Guidance Centre. *

[1308]

G.C. Interview Record Form. Grades 7–13; 1943–44; M. D. Parmenter; Guidance Centre. *

[1309]

***G.C. Student Information Form, Revised.** Grades 1–12; 1943–47; M. D. Parmenter; Guidance Centre. *

[1310]

★**[Guidance Cumulative Folder and Record Forms.]** Grades kgn–12; 1941–[61]; 4 parts; Chronicle Guidance Publications, Inc. *
a) INTERVIEW RECORD SHEET.
b) OBSERVATION RECORD SHEET. Reports by teachers.
c) PERSONALITY REPORT SHEET. Ratings by teachers.
d) FOUR YEAR EDUCATIONAL PLAN.

[1311]

★**Junior High School Record.** Grades 7–10; 1955; also available in combination with the *Personality Record (Revised)* (see 248); National Association of Secondary-School Principals. *

[1312]

★**The Merrill-Palmer Logarithmic Developmental Graph.** Ages birth–18 years; 1955; for comparing chronological age with age equivalent on a developmental variable when both are expressed logarithmically; Charles G. Jennings and S. Idell Pyle; Merrill-Palmer Institute. *

[1313]

***Ontario School Record System, 1960 Revision.** Grades kgn–8, 9–13; 1950–60; Guidance Centre. *
a) ONTARIO SCHOOL RECORD FOLDERS 1 AND 2. Grades kgn–8, 9–13.
b) ONTARIO SCHOOL OFFICE RECORDS 1 AND 2. Grades kgn–8, 9–13.
c) ONTARIO SCHOOL RECORD STUDENT INFORMATION FORM. Grades 9–13.

[1314]

Permanent Record. Grades 9–12; [1941–51]; [National Association of Secondary-School Principals]. *

[1315]

A Pre-School Record Form. Ages 2–5; 1940–52; for recording ratings in 5 areas: gross motor development, language, general emotional development, social adjustment to adults, social adjustment to children; Agatha H. Bowley; E. & S. Livingstone Ltd. *

For additional information, see 5:587; for excerpts from related book reviews, see 3:776.

[1316]

★[Ready Record Forms.] Grades 1–12; [1949]; Educational Test Bureau. *
a) PERMANENT ELEMENTARY SCHOOL RECORD. Grades 1–8.
b) PERMANENT HIGH SCHOOL RECORD. Grades 9–12.
c) ALUMNI AND EX-STUDENT RECORD. Ages 12 to adult.
d) HEALTH RECORD CARD. Grades 1–12.

[1317]

★[School Records.] Grades 1–12; [1956–60]; School Administrator's Service. *
a) CUMULATIVE RECORD. Grades 1–8; [1959].
b) EDUCATIONAL PLAN. Grades 8–12; [1960].
c) PHYSICAL EDUCATION RECORD. Grades 1–12; [1956].
d) HEALTH AND PHYSICAL EXAMINATION RECORD. Grades 1–12; [1956].

[1318]

*Secondary-School Record (Revised). Grades 9–12; 1941–58; also available in combination with the *Personality Record (Revised)* (see 248); Joint Committee on School-College Relations of the National Association of Secondary-School Principals and the American Association of Collegiate Registrars and Admissions Officers; National Association of Secondary-School Principals. *

[1319]

Standard Profile Chart. Schools and industry; 1947; form for graphically presenting 18 test scores and ratings; Clifford E. Jurgensen; Educational Test Bureau. *
For additional information and a review by Charles R. Langmuir, see 3:448.

[1320]

★Steck Cumulative Record Folder. Grades 1–12; 1942; Charles A. Cate; Steck Co. *

[1321]

★Universal Cumulative Record, Revised. Grades kgn–8, 1–12; [1944–60]; E. H. Mellon; Randolph School Supply Co. *

RELIGIOUS EDUCATION

[1322]

★Achievement Test for Weekday Afternoon Congregational Schools. End of grade 3; 1959–[61]; 3 tests; Jewish Education Committee of New York, Inc.; Jewish Education Committee Press. *
a) THE JEWISH PEOPLE.
b) JEWISH LIFE AND OBSERVANCES.
c) HEBREW LANGUAGE.

[1323]

Attitude Inventory. Grades 5–12; 1952–54; religious attitudes; Walter O. Kraeft, Oliver E. Graebner, Elmer F. Pflieger, and Ernest E. Yunghans; Concordia Publishing House. *
For additional information, see 5:588 (1 reference).

[1324]

Bible History Tests. Grades 5–8; 1952–53; for Catholic schools; John A.
O'Brien and Gaston Benedict; Loyola University Press. *
   For additional information, see 5:589.

[1325]

My Ideas About Religion. Grades 7–9; 1933; [G. H. Betts]; Garrett Biblical
Institute. *

[1326]

Northwestern University Religious Education Tests. Grades 4–12; 1927–29;
2 tests for each of the titles below: information test, comprehension test; [Divi-
sion of Research, Northwestern University]; distributed by Garrett Biblical
Institute. *
a) LIFE AND TEACHINGS OF JESUS.
b) OLD TESTAMENT TEACHINGS.
c) THE ACTS AND EPISTLES.

[1327]

Peters Biblical Knowledge Test. Grades 9–16 and adults; 1948; 2 tests; Frank
C. Peters; Bureau of Educational Measurements. *
a) TEST I, OLD TESTAMENT.
b) TEST II, NEW TESTAMENT.
   For additional information and a review by Janet G. Afflerbach, see 5:590.

[1328]

Religion Test for Grades Two and Three. Grades 2–3; 1951–52; for Catholic
schools; M. Providencia; Loyola University Press. *
   For additional information, see 5:591.

[1329]

Religion Test for High Schools. Grades 9–12; 1953–55; for Catholic schools;
4 scores: the Creed, the Commandments, the Means of Grace, total; Austin G.
Schmidt and O. F. Anderhalter; Loyola University Press. *
   For additional information, see 5:592.

[1330]

★**The Southern Baptist Theological Seminary Bible Tests.** Ages 9 and over;
1958–60; 2 tests; R. L. Bishop; distributed by Sunday School Board of the
Southern Baptist Convention. *
a) LIFE AND TEACHINGS OF CHRIST: INFORMATION.
b) LIFE AND TEACHINGS OF CHRIST: INTERPRETATION.

[1331]

★**Standardized Bible Content Test.** Bible college; 1956–60; Standardized Bible
Content Test Committee of the Accrediting Association of Bible Colleges; distributed by Clarence E. Mason, Jr. *

[1332]

Test in Religious Instruction for High School Students. High school; 1938;
for Catholic schools; Alfred Schnepp; Bruce Publishing Co. *
   For additional information, see 40:1520.

[1333]

★**Test on Biblical Information.** Grades 6–8; 1954–55; 2 tests; Martin J. Maehr, Theodore G. Stelzer, and Herbert E. Kaiser; Concordia Publishing House. *
a) NEW TESTAMENT.
b) OLD TESTAMENT.

[1334]

★**Unit Tests on Luther's Catechism.** Grades 6–9; 1952–54; 7 tests, 11 scores for each: knowledge and skill (locating Bible references, spelling related words, quotations, applying quotations, Bible stories, vocabulary, understanding, ethical insight, total), attitudes, performance; Committee on Tests and Measurements of the Board for Parish Education, Lutheran Church—Missouri Synod; Concordia Publishing House. *

[1335]

Wilson Tests of Religious Aptitude. Grades 9–16 and adults; 1935–42; 6 tests; Matthew H. Wilson and H. E. Schrammel; Bureau of Educational Measurements. *
a) TEST OF RELIGIOUS APTITUDE CONCERNING PARENTS.
b) TEST OF RELIGIOUS APTITUDE CONCERNING TREES.
c) TEST OF RELIGIOUS APTITUDE CONCERNING FLOWERS.
d) TEST OF RELIGIOUS APTITUDE CONCERNING PRAYER.
e) TEST OF RELIGIOUS APTITUDE CONCERNING FRIENDS.
f) COMPOSITE TEST OF RELIGIOUS APTITUDE.
For additional information and a review by Goodwin Watson, see 3:456 (1 reference).

SOCIO-ECONOMIC STATUS

[1336]

The American Home Scale. Grades 8–16; 1942; socio-economic status; 5 scores: cultural, aesthetic, economic, miscellaneous, total; W. A. Kerr and H. H. Remmers; Psychometric Affiliates. *
For additional information, see 5:596 (2 references); for reviews by Henry S. Maas and Verner M. Sims, see 3:417 (7 references).

[1337]

★**The Home Index.** Grades 4–12; 1949–53; for research use only; Harrison G. Gough; the Author. *

[1338]

The Minnesota Home Status Index: A Scale for Measuring Urban Home Environment. Parents of students in grades 1–16; 1936; A. M. Leahy; University of Minnesota Press. *
For additional information and a review by Verner M. Sims, see 38:983 (1 reference, 4 excerpts); for excerpts from related book reviews, see 38:B411.

[1339]

Sims SCI Occupational Rating Scale. Grades 9–16 and adults; 1952; social class identification; Verner M. Sims; [Harcourt, Brace & World, Inc.]. *
For additional information and a review by Henry Weitz, see 5:597 (10 references).

[1340]

The Social Status Scale, 1952 Revision. Social workers and researchers; 1933–52; checklist for rating the socio-economic status of the living room of a home; F. Stuart Chapin; University of Minnesota Press. *
  For additional information, see 5:598 (7 references).

TEST PROGRAMS AND SERIES

[1341]

*Achievement Examinations for Secondary Schools, Form 4.** High school; 1951–59; Forms 1–3 published by Educational Test Bureau are out of print; 20 tests: Advanced Algebra (see 979), American History (see 1756), Biology (see 1581), Bookkeeping (see 55), Business Relations and Occupations (see 48), Chemistry (see 1608), Economic Geography (see 1742), Elementary Algebra (see 994), English IX–XII (see 426), French I and II (see 641), General Mathematics III (see 954), General Science III (see 1562), German I and II (see 655), Introduction to Social Studies (see 1714), Latin I and II (see 674), Modern World History (see 1777), Physics (see 1644), Plane Geometry (see 1115), Solid Geometry (see 1125), Spanish I and II (see 701); C. A. Gregory Co. *

[1342]

Acorn National Aptitude Tests. Grades 7–16 and adults; 1943–57; 5 tests; Andrew J. Kobal, J. Wayne Wrightstone, and Karl R. Kunze; Acorn Publishing Co. *
a) ACADEMIC APTITUDE TEST: NON-VERBAL INTELLIGENCE. See 717.
b) ACADEMIC APTITUDE TEST: VERBAL INTELLIGENCE. See 718.
c) CLERICAL APTITUDE TEST. See 1831.
d) INVENTORY OF VOCATIONAL INTERESTS. See 1873.
e) MECHANICAL APTITUDE TEST. See 1923.

[1343]

★The Affiliation Testing Program for Catholic Secondary Schools.** Grades 9–12 and seniors who are candidates for the high school diploma issued by the Catholic University of America; 1949–61; 13 tests; new form issued annually; tests administered annually at individual schools; Program of Affiliation, Catholic University of America. *
a) RELIGION TEST (FOUR-YEAR COURSE). Grade 12.
b) ENGLISH TEST (FOUR-YEAR COURSE). Grade 12.
c) LATIN TEST (TWO-YEAR COURSE). Grades 10–12.
d) SPANISH TEST (TWO-YEAR COURSE). Grades 10–12.
e) FRENCH TEST (TWO-YEAR COURSE). Grades 10–12.
f) ELEMENTARY ALGEBRA TEST. Grades 9–12.
g) PLANE GEOMETRY TEST. Grades 9–12.
h) NATURAL SCIENCE EXAMINATION: BIOLOGY. Grades 9–12.
i) NATURAL SCIENCE EXAMINATION: CHEMISTRY. Grades 9–12.
j) NATURAL SCIENCE EXAMINATION: PHYSICS. Grades 9–12.
k) SOCIAL STUDIES EXAMINATION: AMERICAN HISTORY. Grades 9–12.
l) SOCIAL STUDIES EXAMINATION: WORLD HISTORY. Grades 9–12.
m) SOCIAL STUDIES EXAMINATION: CHRISTIAN DEMOCRACY (CIVICS, SOCIOLOGY, ECONOMICS). Grades 9–12.

[1344]

★**California Survey Series.** Variously grades 7–12; 1959; 11 tests; California Test Bureau. *

a) SURVEY OF MENTAL MATURITY. See 858.

b) SURVEY OF LANGUAGE ACHIEVEMENT. See 473.

c) SURVEY OF ARITHMETIC ACHIEVEMENT. See 1091.

d) SURVEY OF MATHEMATICS ACHIEVEMENT. See 976.

e) SURVEY TEST OF ALGEBRAIC APTITUDE. See 1011.

f) SURVEY OF READING ACHIEVEMENT. See 1455.

g) SURVEY TEST IN INTRODUCTORY SCIENCE. See 1575.

h) SURVEY TEST IN BIOLOGICAL SCIENCE. See 1594.

i) SURVEY TEST IN PHYSICAL SCIENCE. See 1576.

j) SURVEY TEST IN GEOGRAPHY. See 1750.

k) SURVEY TEST IN INTRODUCTORY AMERICAN HISTORY. See 1784.

[1345]

*College Entrance Examination Board Admissions Testing Program.
Candidates for college entrance; 1901–61; tests (except those under *c* below) administered from 1 to 5 times annually, depending on the test, at centers established by the publisher; program administered for the College Entrance Examination Board by Educational Testing Service. *

a) SCHOLASTIC APTITUDE TEST. See 738.

b) ACHIEVEMENT TESTS. 14 tests: Advanced Mathematics (see 941), Biology (see 1586), Chemistry (see 1612), English Composition (see 480a), French (see 632), German (see 651), Hebrew (see 660), Intermediate Mathematics (see 942), Latin (see 666), Physics (see 1630), PSSC Physics (see 1629), Russian (see 685), Social Studies (see 1709), Spanish (see 687), and Writing Sample (see 481).

c) SUPPLEMENTARY ACHIEVEMENT TESTS. Administered locally on a date established by the publisher; 6 tests: French Listening Comprehension (see 633), German Listening Comprehension (see 652), Greek (see 659), Italian Listening Comprehension (see 662), Italian Reading and Essay (see 663), Spanish Listening Comprehension (see 688).

For additional information, see 5:599 (3 references); see also 4:526 (9 references). For reviews of individual tests, see 5:272, 5:277, 5:280, 5:318, 5:418, 5:725, 5:742, 5:749, 4:178, 4:237, and 4:367.

[1346]

*College Entrance Examination Board Advanced Placement Examinations.
Candidates desiring credit for college level courses or admission to advanced courses; 1954–61; 11 tests: American History (see 1761), Biology (see 1587), Chemistry (see 1613), European History (see 1762), French (see 634), German (see 653), Latin (see 667), Literature and English Composition (see 409), Mathematics (see 943), Physics (see 1631), Spanish (see 689); tests administered annually at centers established by the publisher; program administered for the College Entrance Examination Board by Educational Testing Service. *

For additional information, see 5:600. For reviews of individual tests, see 5:205, 5:211, 5:273, 5:419, 5:726, 5:743, 5:750, and 5:812.

[1347]

Cooperative Inter-American Tests. Grades 1–3, 4–7, 8–13; 1950; 5 tests; Committee on Modern Languages of the American Council on Education; [Guidance Testing Associates]. *

a) TESTS OF GENERAL ABILITY. See 864.

b) TESTS OF LANGUAGE USAGE: ACTIVE VOCABULARY AND EXPRESSION. See 477.
c) TESTS OF NATURAL SCIENCES: VOCABULARY AND INTERPRETATION OF READING MATERIALS. See 1513.
d) TESTS OF READING. See 1458.
e) TESTS OF SOCIAL STUDIES: VOCABULARY AND INTERPRETATION OF READING MATERIALS. See 1514.

For additional information and reviews of individual tests, see 4:176, 4:325, 4:557, 4:576, and 4:577.

[1348]

★**Cooperative Intercollegiate Examination Program.** Applicants for admission to member colleges of the United Negro College Fund; 1951–60; tests administered annually at centers established by the E.T.S.; 2 tests; program administered by Educational Testing Service; Cooperative Intercollegiate Examination Program. *
a) COOPERATIVE SCHOOL AND COLLEGE ABILITY TESTS. See 743.
b) READING COMPREHENSION: COOPERATIVE ENGLISH TESTS, [1960 REVISION]. See 1436.

[1349]

Dominion Tests. Variously grades kgn–12; 1934–58; 11 tests; Department of Educational Research, Ontario College of Education, University of Toronto; distributed by Guidance Centre. *
a) ACHIEVEMENT TEST IN SILENT READING. See 1390.
b) ARITHMETIC TEST: FUNDAMENTAL OPERATIONS. See 1032.
c) DIAGNOSTIC TESTS IN ARITHMETIC FUNDAMENTALS. See 1055.
d) GROUP ACHIEVEMENT TEST, 1934 EDITION. See 17.
e) GROUP ACHIEVEMENT TESTS, NIAGARA EDITION. See 18.
f) GROUP TEST OF LEARNING CAPACITY. See 770.
g) GROUP TEST OF READING READINESS. See 1496.
h) GROUP TEST OF SPEED AND ACCURACY IN ARITHMETIC COMPUTATION. See 1061.
i) ORAL DIAGNOSTIC TEST IN ADDITION: ANALYSIS OF ERRORS IN ARITHMETIC. See 1077.
j) QUICK-SCORING TEST OF LEARNING CAPACITY. See 834.
k) SURVEY TEST OF ARITHMETIC FUNDAMENTALS. See 1092.

[1350]

*Evaluation and Adjustment Series.** Variously grades 7 and over; 1936–61; 25 tests; [Harcourt, Brace & World, Inc.]. *
a) ANDERSON CHEMISTRY TEST. See 1604.
b) BILLETT-STARR YOUTH PROBLEMS INVENTORY. See 117.
c) BLYTH SECOND-YEAR ALGEBRA TEST. See 986.
d) BROWN-CARLSEN LISTENING COMPREHENSION TEST. See 1283.
e) CENTER-DUROST LITERATURE ACQUAINTANCE TEST. See 492.
f) CRARY AMERICAN HISTORY TEST. See 1768.
g) CUMMINGS WORLD HISTORY TEST. See 1769.
h) DAVIS TEST OF FUNCTIONAL COMPETENCE IN MATHEMATICS. See 948.
i) DIMOND-PFLIEGER PROBLEMS OF DEMOCRACY TEST. See 1802.
j) DUNNING PHYSICS TEST. See 1634.
k) DUROST-CENTER WORD MASTERY TEST. See 564.
l) ENGLE PSYCHOLOGY TEST. See 1295.
m) GREENE-STAPP LANGUAGE ABILITIES TEST. See 440.

n) KELLEY-GREENE READING COMPREHENSION TEST. See 1415.
o) KILANDER HEALTH KNOWLEDGE TEST. See 1241.
p) LANKTON FIRST-YEAR ALGEBRA TEST. See 1005.
q) MADDEN-PEAK ARITHMETIC COMPUTATION TEST. See 1070.
r) NELSON BIOLOGY TEST. See 1592.
s) PELTIER-DUROST CIVICS AND CITIZENSHIP TEST. See 1811.
t) READ GENERAL SCIENCE TEST. See 1570.
u) SEATTLE ALGEBRA TEST. See 1009.
v) SEATTLE PLANE GEOMETRY TEST. See 1122.
w) SHAYCOFT PLANE GEOMETRY TEST. See 1124.
x) SNADER GENERAL MATHEMATICS TEST. See 975.
y) SPITZER STUDY SKILLS TEST. See 1535.

[1351]

*Every Pupil Scholarship Tests. Variously grades 1 through high school; 1926–61; new forms usually issued annually; 47 tests: Agriculture (see 1143), American Government (see 1797), American History (see 1753), American Literature (see 485), Ancient History (see 1760), Arithmetic (see 1023), Biology (see 1578), Bookkeeping (see 54), Business Mathematics (see 940), Chemistry (see 1605), Citizenship (see 1708), Clothing (see 1258), Commercial Law (see 64), Constitution (see 1800), Current Affairs (see 1730), Elementary Health (see 1228), Elementary Literature (see 497), Elementary Reading (see 1404), Elementary Science (see 1553), English (see 423), First Year Algebra (see 996), First Year Latin (see 669), Foods (see 1261), General Business (see 50), General Mathematics (see 952), General Science (see 1555), Geography (see 1745), High School Health (see 1239), History (see 1772), Homemaking I and II (see 1269), Industrial Arts (see 1278), Kansas History (see 1774), Literature (see 508), Physical Geography (see 1749), Physics (see 1641), Plane Geometry (see 1113), Primary Arithmetic (see 1079), Primary Reading (see 1429), Psychology (see 1299), Second Year Latin (see 682), Social Studies (see 1721), Sociology (see 1818), Spelling (see 553), Typewriting I and II (see 94), Vocabulary (see 579), World Geography (see 1752), World History (see 1788); Bureau of Educational Measurements. *

[1352]

*Every Pupil Tests. Variously grades 2 through high school; 1929–61; new forms usually issued annually; 27 tests: American Government and Citizenship (see 1796), American History (see 1754), American Literature (see 486), Arithmetic (see 1024), Biology (see 1579), Bookkeeping I (see 57), Chemistry (see 1606), Contemporary Affairs (see 1729), Elementary Algebra (see 993), Elementary Reading (see 1405), Elementary Science and Health (see 1552), English Literature (see 500), English Usage (see 437), General Science (see 1556), Geography (see 1746), Geometry (see 1106), Health Education and Hygiene (see 1232), Latin I and II (see 675), Mathematics (see 964), Ohio History (see 1779), Physics (see 1642), Primary Reading (see 1430), Shorthand I (see 76), Spelling and Vocabulary (see 551), Techniques in Reading Comprehension for Junior-Senior High School (see 1457), Typewriting I (see 93), World History (see 1789); Ohio Scholarship Tests. *

[1353]

*Graduate Record Examinations. College through graduate school; 1937–61; two programs: National Program for Graduate School Selection (graduate school entrants; 1942–61; tests administered 5 times annually at centers established by the publisher) and Institutional Testing Program (college and graduate school; 1937–61; tests available at any time except during administration of National Program) ; Educational Testing Service. *

a) APTITUDE TEST. See 764.

b) THE AREA TESTS. See 15.

c) ADVANCED TESTS. 19 tests: Biology (see 1591), Chemistry (see 1619), Economics (see 1737), Education (see 1186), Engineering (see 2003), French (see 645), Geology (see 1627), Government (see 1804), History (see 1771), Literature (see 504), Mathematics (see 956), Music (see 600), Philosophy (see 1293), Physics (see 1637), Psychology (see 1296), Scholastic Philosophy (see 1294), Sociology (see 1816), Spanish (see 693), Speech (see 523).

For additional information and a review by Harold Seashore, see 5:601 (12 references) ; see also 4:527 (24 references). For reviews of individual tests, see 5:10, 5:215, 5:220, 5:247, 5:270, 5:336, 5:427, 5:537, 5:583, 5:727, 5:754, 5:818, and 5:835.

[1354]

Iowa Placement Examinations. Grades 12–13; 1925–44; Bureau of Educational Research and Service. *

a) NEW SERIES 2, REVISED. 1925–44; 5 tests: Chemistry Aptitude (see 1620), English Training (see 445), Foreign Language Aptitude (see 615), Mathematics Aptitude (see 957), Physics Aptitude (see 1638).

b) SERIES I, REVISED. 1925–26; 11 tests: same as for *a*, plus Chemistry Training (see 1621), English Aptitude (see 444), French Training (see 646), Spanish Training (see 694), Mathematics Training (see 958), Physics Training (see 1639).

For additional information and reviews of individual tests, see 4:166, 4:167, 4:621, 4:622, 4:638, 4:639, 3:115, 3:131, 3:178, 3:189, 3:212, 3:308, 3:309, 3:566, 3:567, and 3:587.

[1355]

*Manchester Semester-End Achievement Tests. High school; 1934–60; 25 tests: Biology (see 1582), Commercial Arithmetic (see 1046), Eleventh Year English Fundamentals (see 422), First Year Algebra (see 997), First Year Bookkeeping (see 62), First Year Chemistry (see 1617), First Year Latin (see 670), First Year Typewriting (see 86), General Shop Woodworking (see 1276), Health (see 1236), High School Economics (see 1738), Ninth Year Home Economics (see 1273), Ninth Year English Fundamentals (see 459), Physics (see 1645), Plane Geometry (see 1116), Safety Education (see 1173), Second Year Algebra (see 1010), Second Year Latin (see 683), Senior English Fundamentals (see 472), Solid Geometry (see 1126), Tenth Year English Fundamentals (see 475), Trigonometry (see 1135), United States Government (see 1815), United States History (see 1787), World History (see 1791) ; Bureau of Tests. *

[1356]

Mental Tests. Ages 6–10, 9–14; 1920; reprinted from the author's *Mental Tests;* *a* and *b* also appear in *The "New Examiner" Tests* (see 1361) ; 3 tests; P. B. Ballard; University of London Press Ltd. *

a) ONE MINUTE READING TEST. Ages 6–10.

b) SILENT READING TEST. Ages 9–14.

c) THREE-MINUTE ARITHMETIC TEST. Ages 9–14.

[1357]

*Midwest High School Achievement Examinations. High school; 1951–61; 22 tests: Advanced Algebra (see 980), Biology (see 1583), Bookkeeping (see 56), Business Relations and Occupations (see 49), Chemistry (see 1609), Economic Geography (see 1743), Elementary Algebra (see 995), Language Arts IX–XII (see 449), French I and II (see 642), General Mathematics (see 953), General Science III (see 1563), German I and II (see 656), Latin I and II (see 677), Physics (see 1646), Plane Geometry (see 1117), Social Studies IX (see 1722), Social Studies X (American History) (see 1782), Social Studies XI (World History) (see 1783), Social Studies XII (see 1723), Solid Geometry (see 1127), Spanish I and II (see 702), Trigonometry (see 1136); Educational Test Bureau. *

[1358]

*National Achievement Tests, [Series Entry]. Variously grades 2 through college; 1936–61; 30 tests: National Achievement Tests (see 30), Municipal Battery (see 29), Algebra Test for Engineering and Science (see 985), American History Test (see 1758), Arithmetic Test (see 1034), College English Test (see 408), Elementary Science Test (see 1554), English Test (see 433), First Year Algebra Test (see 1000), General Biology Test (see 1590), General Chemistry Test (see 1618), General Physics Test (see 1636), General Science Test (see 1560), Geography Test (see 1748), Health Test (see 1238), Health Knowledge Test for College Freshmen (see 1235), Health and Safety Education Test (see 1230), Health Education Test (see 1233), High School Reading Test (see 1412), Literature Test (see 509), Plane Geometry Test (see 1118), Plane Trigonometry (see 1133), Reading Comprehension (see 1437 and 1438), Social Studies Test (see 1724 and 1725), Solid Geometry (see 1128), Spelling (see 557), World History (see 1793), Vocabulary Test (see 582); Acorn Publishing Co. *

[1359]

★National Guidance Testing Program. Grades 4–14; 1958–60; program consists of one or more of the *Cooperative School and College Ability Tests* (see 743) and *Sequential Tests of Educational Progress* (see 39); tests administered at any time by individual schools; scoring 3 times a year by publisher; Cooperative Test Division. *

[1360]

★[National Science Foundation Testing Program.] Applicants for N.S.F. fellowships for graduate study in the sciences; [1951]–60; program consists of 2 tests from the National Program of the *Graduate Record Examinations* (see 1353): the Aptitude Test and 1 Advanced Test (Biology, Chemistry, Engineering, Geology, Mathematics, Physics, or Psychology); program administered for the National Science Foundation by Educational Testing Service. *

[1361]

The "New Examiner" Tests. Ages 9–14 except for *i* and *j;* 1920–23; reprinted from the author's *The New Examiner;* *a* and *j* also appear in *Mental Tests* (see 1356); 10 tests; P. B. Ballard; University of London Press Ltd. *
a) SILENT READING TEST.
b) ENGLISH (COMPREHENSION) TEST.
c) ENGLISH (CONSTRUCTION) TEST.
d) MECHANICAL ARITHMETIC TEST.

e) REASONING ARITHMETIC TEST.
f) ALGEBRA TEST.
g) GEOGRAPHY TEST.
h) HISTORY TEST.
i) [ONE-MINUTE ORAL ADDITION AND SUBTRACTION TESTS.] Ages 5–13.
j) ONE-MINUTE READING SCALE. Ages 6–10.

[1362]
★Ohio District-State Scholarship Tests. High school; 1938–61; 2 series of achievement tests available annually following use in Ohio; 15 tests in each series: Advanced Algebra (see 981 and 982), American History (see 1755 and 1757), Biology (see 1580 and 1584), Bookkeeping I (see 58 and 59), Chemistry (see 1607 and 1610), English (see 425 and 427), First-Year Algebra (see 998 and 999), French I and II (see 640 and 643), General Science (see 1557 and 1558), Latin I and II (see 676 and 678), Physics (see 1643 and 1647), Plane Geometry (see 1114 and 1119), Senior Social Studies (see 1717 and 1718), Spanish I and II (see 700 and 703), World History (see 1790 and 1792) ; Ohio Scholarship Tests. *
a) PRELIMINARY DISTRICT-STATE SCHOLARSHIP TESTS. 1947–61.
b) FINAL DISTRICT-STATE SCHOLARSHIP TESTS. 1938–61.

[1363]
Ohio Senior Survey Tests. Grade 12; 1934–54; 5 tests: English (see 430), mathematics (see 963), reading (see 1411, 1517, and 1534) ; Ohio Scholarship Tests. *

[1364]
★Project Talent Test Battery: A National Inventory of Aptitudes and Abilities. Grades 9–12; 1960–61; 8 booklets (22 tests and 3 questionnaires) ; for research use and normative studies only; University of Pittsburgh Project Talent Office. *
a) TEST BOOKLET A. 3 tests, 27 scores.
  1) *Information Test—Part 1.* 16 scores: screening, vocabulary, literature, music, social studies, mathematics, physical science, biological science, scientific attitude, aeronautics and space, electricity and electronics, mechanics, farming, home economics, sports, total.
  2) *Student Activities Inventory.* 10 scores: sociability, social sensitivity, impulsiveness, vigor, calmness, tidiness, culture, leadership, self-confidence, mature personality.
  3) [*Preferences Test.*] Characteristics preferred in friends and associates.
b) TEST BOOKLET B. 3 tests, 28 scores.
  1) *Interest Inventory.* 16 scores: science, computation, mechanical-technical, skilled trades, literary-linguistic, social service, public service, musical, artistic, business management, sales, office work, labor, farming, outdoor recreation, sports.
  2) *Information Test—Part 2.* 12 scores: art, law, medicine, engineering, architecture, military, accounting-business-sales, Bible, hunting and fishing, other outdoor activities, theater and ballet, total.
  3) *Student Information Blank.* Personal and family background data, activities, experiences, and plans.
c) TEST BOOKLET CI-X. 1 test (arithmetic computation) plus study materials for memory for words and memory for sentences below.
d) TEST BOOKLET CI. 4 tests, 12 scores: memory for words, memory for sentences,

mathematics (arithmetic reasoning, introductory, advanced, total), English (usage, effective expression, punctuation, spelling, capitalization, total).

e) TEST BOOKLET C2. 11 tests: abstract reasoning, mechanical reasoning, disguised words, creativity, clerical checking, visualization in 2 dimensions, reading comprehension, visualization in 3 dimensions, word functions in sentences, table reading, object inspection.

f) SCHOOL QUESTIONNAIRE: GENERAL SCHOOL CHARACTERISTICS. Principals.

g) SCHOOL QUESTIONNAIRE: GUIDANCE PROGRAM. Guidance counselors.

h) SCHOOL QUESTIONNAIRE: COUNSELOR'S QUESTIONNAIRE. Guidance counselors.

[1365]

Purdue Personnel Tests. Trade school and industry; 1945–58; 9 tests; University Book Store. *

a) PURDUE CLERICAL ADAPTABILITY TEST, REVISED EDITION. See 1848.

b) PURDUE INDUSTRIAL MATHEMATICS TEST. See 971.

c) PURDUE INDUSTRIAL SUPERVISORS WORD-MEANING TEST. See 574.

d) PURDUE MECHANICAL ADAPTABILITY TEST. See 1937.

e) PURDUE READING TEST FOR INDUSTRIAL SUPERVISORS. See 1434.

f) PURDUE TRADE INFORMATION TEST FOR SHEETMETAL WORKERS. See 2085.

g) PURDUE TRADE INFORMATION TEST IN CARPENTRY. See 2086.

h) PURDUE TRADE INFORMATION TEST IN ENGINE LATHE OPERATION. See 2087.

i) PURDUE TRADE INFORMATION TEST IN WELDING, REVISED EDITION. See 2088.

[1366]

*State High School Tests for Indiana. High school; 1932–60; 39 tests: Advanced Algebra (see 983), Animal Husbandry (see 1144), American History (see 1759), Arithmetic Fundamentals (see 1025), Biology (see 1585), Bookkeeping (see 61), Care and Play of Children (see 1254), Chemistry (see 1611), Child Development (see 1257), Clothing I (see 1259), Clothing II (see 1260), Clothing Problems (see 1255), Commercial Arithmetic (see 1047), Economics (see 1736), Farm Shop Tools (see 1145), First Year Algebra (see 1001), Food in the Home (see 1264), Foods I (see 1262), Foods II (see 1263), French (see 639), General Science (see 1561), Health and Safety Education (see 1231), Home Care of the Sick (see 1267), Housekeeping (see 1265), Housing the Family (see 1270), Junior High School Civics (see 1805), Latin (see 679), Mechanical Drawing (see 1281), Mechanics of Written English (see 455), Plane Geometry (see 1120), Physics (see 1648), Senior High School Civics (see 1812 and 1813), Simplified Shorthand (see 78), Solid Geometry (see 1129), Spanish (see 691), Trigonometry (see 1137), Typewriting (see 96), World History (see 1794); State High School Testing Service for Indiana. *

MULTI-APTITUDE BATTERIES

[1367]

[Aptitude-Intelligence Tests.] Job applicants; 1947–57; former title, *Factored Aptitude Series,* still on test booklets; 15 tests: Office Terms, Sales Terms, Tools, Numbers, Perception, Judgment, Precision, Fluency, Memory, Parts, Blocks, Dimension, Dexterity, Motor, Factory Terms; Joseph E. King; Industrial Psychology, Inc. *

For additional information and a review by Harold P. Bechtoldt, see 5:602; for a review by D. Welty Lefever of an earlier edition, see 4:712 (1 reference, 1 excerpt).

[1368]

Aptitude Tests for Occupations. Grades 9–13 and adults; 1951; 6 tests; Wesley S. Roeder and Herbert B. Graham; California Test Bureau. *
a) PERSONAL-SOCIAL APTITUDE.
b) MECHANICAL APTITUDE.
c) GENERAL SALES APTITUDE.
d) CLERICAL ROUTINE APTITUDE.
e) COMPUTATIONAL APTITUDE.
f) SCIENTIFIC APTITUDE.
　For additional information and a review by Lloyd G. Humphreys, see 5:891; for a review by Clifford P. Froehlich, see 4:710 (1 excerpt).

[1369]

Detroit General Aptitudes Examination. Grades 6–12; 1938–54; assembled from *Detroit Mechanical Aptitudes Examination, Detroit Clerical Aptitudes Examination,* and *Detroit Advanced Intelligence Test;* 20 scores: intelligence, mechanical, clerical, total, and 16 subtest scores; Harry J. Baker, Alex C. Crockett, and Paul H. Voelker; Public School Publishing Co. *
　For additional information, see 5:603; for reviews by G. Frederic Kuder, Irving Lorge, and John Gray Peatman, see 40:1654.

[1370]

Differential Ability Tests. Ages 10–17 (standards 5–10); 1951; 7 tests; National Bureau of Educational and Social Research. *
a) SILENT READING TEST (REVISED EDITION): SENIOR. See 1451.
b) VERBAL REASONING TEST.
c) NON-VERBAL REASONING.
d) ARITHMETIC TEST. 2 scores: mechanical arithmetic, problems.
e) MEMORY TEST.
f) SPACE PERCEPTION.
g) MECHANICAL COMPREHENSION TEST.
　For additional information, see 5:604.

[1371]

*****Differential Aptitude Tests.** Grades 8–12 and adults; 1947–59; 7 booklets, 9 scores: scholastic aptitude (total of *a* and *b*) and 8 scores listed below; George K. Bennett, Harold G. Seashore, and Alexander G. Wesman; Psychological Corporation. *
a) VERBAL REASONING.
b) NUMERICAL ABILITY.
c) ABSTRACT REASONING.
d) SPACE RELATIONS.
e) MECHANICAL REASONING.
f) CLERICAL SPEED AND ACCURACY.
g) LANGUAGE USAGE. 2 scores: spelling, sentences.
　For additional information and reviews by John B. Carroll and Norman Frederiksen, see 5:605 (49 references); for reviews by Harold Bechtoldt, Ralph F. Berdie, and Lloyd G. Humphreys, see 4:711 (28 references); see also 3:620 (1 excerpt).

[1372]

*****Differential Test Battery.** Ages 11 to "top university level" (range for *a* extends downward to age 7); 1955–59; 12 tests in 7 booklets; J. R. Morrisby;

distributed by National Foundation for Educational Research in England and Wales. *

a) COMPOUND SERIES TEST. 1955.
b) GENERAL ABILITY TESTS: VERBAL. 1955.
c) GENERAL ABILITY TESTS: NUMERICAL. 1955.
d) GENERAL ABILITY TESTS: PERCEPTUAL. 1955.
e) SHAPES TEST. 1955.
f) MECHANICAL ABILITY TEST. 1955.
g) SPEED TESTS. 1955–59; 6 tests: routine number and name checking, perseveration, word fluency, ideational fluency, motor speed, motor skill.

For additional information and reviews by E. A. Peel, Donald E. Super, and Philip E. Vernon, see 5:606.

[1373]

Employee Aptitude Survey. Ages 16 and over; 1952–58; 10 tests; G. Grimsley, F. L. Ruch, N. D. Warren, and J. S. Ford; Psychological Services, Inc. *

a) TEST 1, VERBAL COMPREHENSION.
b) TEST 2, NUMERICAL ABILITY.
c) TEST 3, VISUAL PURSUIT.
d) TEST 4, VISUAL SPEED AND ACCURACY.
e) TEST 5, SPACE VISUALIZATION.
f) TEST 6, NUMERICAL REASONING.
g) TEST 7, VERBAL REASONING.
h) TEST 8, WORD FLUENCY.
i) TEST 9, MANUAL SPEED AND ACCURACY.
j) TEST 10, SYMBOLIC REASONING.

For additional information and reviews by Dorothy C. Adkins and S. Rains Wallace, see 5:607.

[1374]

Fife Tests of Ability. Secondary school entrants; 1947; 4 tests; Frank M. Earle; University of London Press Ltd. *

a) TEST 1, ABILITY FOR ENGLISH (LANGUAGE). See 399.
b) TEST 2, ABILITY FOR SCIENCE. See 1545.
c) TEST 3, ABILITY FOR ALGEBRA. See 978.
d) TEST 4, ABILITY FOR GEOMETRY. See 1100.

For additional information and a review by I. Macfarlane Smith, see 4:713 (3 references); for a review by James Maxwell, see 3:8. For a review of *c,* see 4:380.

[1375]

*Flanagan Aptitude Classification Tests. Grades 9–12 and adults; 1941–60; John C. Flanagan; Science Research Associates, Inc. *

a) [SEPARATE BOOKLET EDITION.] 1951–60; 16 tests.
   1) *Fact 1A, Inspection.* 1953–56, c1951–56.
   2) *Fact 2A and 2B, Coding.* 1953–56, c1951–56.
   3) *Fact 3A and 3B, Memory.* 1953–56, c1951–56.
   4) *Fact 4A, Precision.* 1953–56, c1951–56.
   5) *Fact 5A, Assembly.* 1953–56, c1951–56.
   6) *Fact 6A, Scales.* 1953–56, c1951–56.
   7) *Fact 7A, Coordination.* 1953–56, c1951–56.
   8) *Fact 8A, Judgment and Comprehension.* 1953–56, c1951–56.
   9) *Fact 9A, Arithmetic.* 1953–56, c1951–56.

10) *Fact 10A, Patterns.* 1953–56, c1951–56.
11) *Fact 11A, Components.* 1953–56, c1951–56.
12) *Fact 12A, Tables.* 1953–56, c1951–56.
13) *Fact 13A and 13B, Mechanics.* 1953–56, c1951–56.
14) *Fact 14A, Expression.* 1953–56, c1951–56.
15) *Fact 15A, Reasoning.* 1960, c1957–60.
16) *Fact 16A, Ingenuity.* 1960, c1957–60.
b) [TWO-BOOKLET EDITION.] 1957–59; 2 booklets, 19 tests: same as for *a* plus vocabulary, planning, alertness.

For additional information and reviews by Harold P. Bechtoldt, Ralph F. Berdie, and John B. Carroll, see 5:608 (2 references).

[1376]

*General Aptitude Test Battery. Grades 9–12 and adults; 1946–59; 12 tests, 9 scores: intelligence, verbal, numerical, spatial, form perception, clerical perception, motor coordination, finger dexterity, manual dexterity; program administered through State Employment Service offices; tests available to nonprofit institutions for counseling purposes; United States Employment Service. * (Materials for *d* and *e* distributed by Specialty Case Manufacturing Co. and by Warwick Products Co.)
a) BOOK 1. 4 tests: name comparison, computation, three-dimensional space, vocabulary.
b) BOOK 2. 3 tests: tool matching, arithmetic reasoning, form matching.
c) PART 8. 1 test: mark making.
d) PEGBOARD. 2 tests: place, turn.
e) FINGER DEXTERITY BOARD. 2 tests: assemble, disassemble.

For additional information and reviews by Andrew L. Comrey, Clifford P. Froehlich, and Lloyd G. Humphreys, see 5:609 (176 references); for reviews by Milton L. Blum, Edward B. Greene, and Howard R. Taylor, see 4:714 (33 references).

[1377]

The Guilford-Zimmerman Aptitude Survey. Grades 9–16 and adults; 1947–50; 7 tests; J. P. Guilford and Wayne S. Zimmerman; Sheridan Supply Co. *
a) PART I, VERBAL COMPREHENSION.
b) PART II, GENERAL REASONING.
c) PART III, NUMERICAL OPERATIONS.
d) PART IV, PERCEPTUAL SPEED.
e) PART V, SPATIAL ORIENTATION.
f) PART VI, SPATIAL VISUALIZATION.
g) PART VII, MECHANICAL KNOWLEDGE.

For additional information and reviews by Anne Anastasi, Harold Bechtoldt, John B. Carroll, and P. E. Vernon, see 4:715 (15 references).

[1378]

Holzinger-Crowder Uni-Factor Tests. Grades 7–12; 1952–55; 5 scores: verbal, spatial, numerical, reasoning, scholastic aptitude; Karl J. Holzinger and Norman A. Crowder; [Harcourt, Brace & World, Inc.]. *
For additional information and reviews by Anne Anastasi, Benjamin Fruchter, and Philip E. Vernon, see 5:610 (3 references).

[1379]

*The Jastak Test of Potential Ability and Behavior Stability. Grades 7–9; 1958–59; 16 scores: 10 direct scores (coding, picture reasoning, arithmetic, vocabulary, space series, social concept, verbal reasoning, number series, space completion, spelling) and 6 derived scores (language, reality, motivation, psychomotor, intelligence, capacity) ; J. F. Jastak; Educational Test Bureau. *

For additional information, see 5:611.

[1380]

The Multi-Aptitude Test. College courses in testing; 1955; miniature battery of 10 tests for instructional use; Edward E. Cureton, Louise Witmer Cureton, and students; Psychological Corporation. *

For additional information and a review by H. H. Remmers, see 5:612 (1 reference).

[1381]

***Multiple Aptitude Tests, 1959 Edition.** Grades 7–13; 1955–60; 14 scores: scholastic potential plus 13 scores listed below; David Segel and Evelyn Raskin; California Test Bureau. *

a) FACTOR 1, VERBAL COMPREHENSION. 3 scores: word meaning, paragraph meaning, total.

b) FACTOR 2, PERCEPTUAL SPEED. 3 scores: language usage, routine clerical facility, total.

c) FACTOR 3, NUMERICAL REASONING. 3 scores: arithmetic reasoning, arithmetic computation, total.

d) FACTOR 4, SPATIAL VISUALIZATION. 4 scores: applied science and mechanics, 2-dimensional spatial relations, 3-dimensional spatial relations, total.

For additional information and reviews by Ralph Berdie and Benjamin Fruchter of the original edition, see 5:613 (2 references).

[1382]

★**National Institute for Personnel Research High Level Battery.** Adults with at least 12 years of education; 1960–[61] ; 4 tests: mental alertness, arithmetical problems, reading comprehension, vocabulary; subtests in mental alertness, arithmetical problems, and reading comprehension-vocabulary available as separates (see 450, 791, and 1037) ; National Institute for Personnel Research. *

[1383]

★**National Institute for Personnel Research Normal Battery.** Standards 6–10 and job applicants with 8–11 years of education; 1960–[61] ; 5 tests: mental alertness, comprehension, vocabulary, spelling, computation; subtests in mental alertness and comprehension-vocabulary-spelling available as separates (see 792 and 451) ; National Institute for Personnel Research. *

[1384]

SRA Primary Mental Abilities. Grades kgn–1, 2–6, 7–12; 1946–58; earlier editions titled *Tests for Primary Mental Abilities* and *Chicago Tests of Primary Mental Abilities;* L. L. Thurstone and Thelma Gwinn Thurstone; Science Research Associates, Inc. *

a) FOR AGES 5 TO 7. Grades kgn–1; 1946–53; 6 scores: verbal, perception, quantitative, motor, space, total.

b) ELEMENTARY: AGES 7 TO 11. Grades 2–6; 1948–56; 13 scores: 5 factor scores (verbal, space, reasoning, perception, number), IQ, nonreading IQ, reading aptitude, arithmetic aptitude, and 4 part scores.

c) INTERMEDIATE: AGES 11 TO 17. Grades 7–12; 1947–58; 5 or 6 scores: verbal, spatial, reasoning, number, word-fluency (optional), total.

For additional information and reviews by Norman Frederiksen and Albert

K. Kurtz, see 5:614 (59 references); for reviews by Anne Anastasi, Ralph F. Berdie, John B. Carroll, Stuart A. Courtis, and P. E. Vernon, see 4:716 (42 references); for reviews by Cyril Burt, Florence L. Goodenough, James R. Hobson, and F. L. Wells of an earlier edition, see 3:225 (50 references) and 3:264 (2 references); for reviews by Henry E. Garrett, Truman L. Kelley, C. Spearman, Godfrey H. Thomson, and Robert C. Tryon, see 40:1427 (10 references, 3 excerpts); for excerpts from related book reviews, see 40:B1099 and 38:B503.

[1385]

[United States Employment Service Special Aptitude Tests.] Ages 16 and over; 1935–44; tests *a, b, d–g,* and *o* adapted from *MacQuarrie Test for Mechanical Ability* (see 1922) published by California Test Bureau, from whom they must be purchased; 15 tests; program administered through State Employment Service offices; nonprofit institutions may purchase tests but must employ testing supervisors trained by U.S.E.S.; United States Employment Service. *

a) CI [MOTOR SPEED]. 1942.
b) C2 [AIMING]. 1942.
c) C9 [NUMBER WRITING]. 1939.
d) C14 [FIGURE COPYING]. 1942.
e) C15 [PLOTTING]. 1942.
f) C16 [SPATIAL]. 1942.
g) C17 [MAZE]. 1942.
h) C19 [ARITHMETIC]. 1939.
i) C29 [NUMBER COMPARISON]. 1939.
j) C32 [SUBSTITUTION]. 1939.
k) C43 [AUTOMOTIVE]. 1944.
l) C55 [SERIES COMPARISON]. 1941.
m) C57 [3-DIMENSIONAL SPACE RELATIONS]. 1941.
n) C86 [MECHANICAL INFORMATION]. 1941.
o) C101 [LOCATION]. 1942.
   For additional information, see 4:717.

[1386]

Yale Educational Aptitude Test Battery. Grades 9–16; 1946–53; 7 tests in 3 booklets: verbal comprehension, artificial language, verbal reasoning, quantitative reasoning, mathematical aptitude, spatial relations, mechanical ingenuity; Albert B. Crawford and Paul S. Burnham; distributed by Educational Records Bureau. *
   For additional information and reviews by Anne Anastasi and Ruth Churchill, see 5:615 (4 references); see also 4:718 (7 references).

READING

[1387]

A.C.E.R. Silent Reading Tests, Forms A and B. Grades 3–8 and adults (Part 1, Form B only); 1933–57; 5 parts; Australian Council for Educational Research. *
a) PART 1, WORD KNOWLEDGE.
b) PART 2, SPEED OF READING.
c) PART 3, READING FOR GENERAL SIGNIFICANCE.

d) PART 4, READING TO NOTE DETAILS.
e) PART 5, READING FOR INFERENCE.
For additional information and a review by Fred J. Schonell, see 5:616.

[1388]

A.C.E.R. Silent Reading Test, Form C. Grades 4–6; 1946–50; 3 parts; Australian Council for Educational Research. *
a) PART 1, WORD KNOWLEDGE.
b) PART 2, SPEED OF READING.
c) PART 3, READING FOR MEANING.
For additional information and reviews by Fred J. Schonell and D. K. Wheeler, see 5:617 (1 reference).

[1389]

A.C.E.R. Silent Reading Tests: Standardized for Use in New Zealand. Ages 9–12; 1955; tests for *a* and *c* identical with corresponding parts of *A.C.E.R. Silent Reading Test,* Form C (see 1388); test for *b* identical with corresponding part of *A.C.E.R. Silent Reading Tests,* Form B (see 1387); manual by A. E. Fieldhouse; New Zealand Council for Educational Research; distributed by Educational Books. *
a) PART 1, WORD KNOWLEDGE.
b) PART 2, SPEED OF READING.
c) PART 3, READING FOR MEANING.
For additional information, see 5:618.

[1390]

Achievement Test in Silent Reading: Dominion Tests. Grades 1, 2, 2–3, 3–4, 4–6, 5–6; 1941–57; 6 tests; Department of Educational Research, Ontario College of Education, University of Toronto; distributed by Guidance Centre. *
a) TYPE 1, WORD RECOGNITION. Grade 1; 1941–57.
b) TYPE 2, PHRASE AND SENTENCE READING. Grade 1; 1941–53.
c) TYPE 3, PARAGRAPH READING. Grade 1; 1943–53.
d) TYPE 4, DIAGNOSTIC TEST IN WORD RECOGNITION. Grade 1; 1943–53.
e) TYPE 1, VOCABULARY. Grades 2–3, 4–6; 1943–56.
f) TYPE 2, DIAGNOSTIC TEST IN PARAGRAPH READING. Grades 2, 3–4, 5–6; 1943–56.
For additional information and reviews by Harry L. Stein and Magdalen D. Vernon, see 5:619; for a review by Henry P. Smith, see 4:529; for a review by Margaret G. McKim, see 3:476.

[1391]

American School Achievement Tests: Part 1, Reading. Grades 2–3, 4–6, 7–9; 1941–58; 3 scores: sentence and word meaning, paragraph meaning, total; Willis E. Pratt and Robert V. Young; Public School Publishing Co. * For the complete battery entry, see 2.
For additional information and reviews by Russell G. Stauffer and Agatha Townsend, see 5:620. For reviews of the complete battery, see 5:1, 4:1, and 3:1.

[1392]

American School Reading Tests. Grades 10–13; 1955; 3 scores: vocabulary, reading rate, comprehension; Willis E. Pratt and Stanley W. Lore; Public School Publishing Co. *
For additional information and reviews by Henry S. Dyer and Donald E. P. Smith, see 5:621.

[1393]

Buffalo Reading Test for Speed and Comprehension. Grades 9–16; 1933–44;
3 scores: speed, comprehension, total; Mazie Earle Wagner; the Author. *
For additional information and reviews by Holland Roberts and William W.
Turnbull, see 3:477.

[1394]

California Reading Test, 1950 Edition. Grades 1–4.5, 4–6, 7–9, 9–14; 1933–50;
revision of *Progressive Reading Tests;* subtest of *California Achievement Tests,
1950 Edition* (see 4); 3 scores: reading vocabulary, reading comprehension,
total; Ernest W. Tiegs and Willis W. Clark; California Test Bureau. * For
the 1957 edition entry, see 1395.
For additional information and reviews by John C. Flanagan and James R.
Hobson, see 4:530 (1 excerpt); for a review by Frederick B. Davis of an earlier
edition, see 40:1563; for reviews by Ivan A. Booker and Joseph C. Dewey, see
38:1110. For reviews of the complete battery, see 4:2, 3:15, 40:1193, and 38:876.

[1395]

***California Reading Test, 1957 Edition.** Grades 1–2, 3–4.5, 4–6, 7–9, 9–14;
1933–59; subtest of *California Achievement Tests, 1957 Edition* (see 5); 3
scores: vocabulary, comprehension, total; Ernest W. Tiegs and Willis W.
Clark; California Test Bureau. * For the 1950 edition entry, see 1394.
For additional information, see 5:622 (5 references). For a review of the
complete battery, see 5:2.

[1396]

Chapman Reading Comprehension Test. Grades 5–12; 1924–53; formerly
called *Chapman Unspeeded Reading Comprehension Test;* J. C. Chapman; Educational Test Bureau. *
For additional information and a review by Russell P. Kropp, see 5:623.

[1397]

Commerce Reading Comprehension Test. Grades 12–16 and adults; 1956–58;
Irma T. Halfter and Raymond J. McCall; Department of Psychological Testing,
DePaul University. *
For additional information, see 5:624.

[1398]

Davis Reading Test. Grades 11–13; 1956–58; Frederick B. Davis and Charlotte
Croon Davis; Psychological Corporation. *
For additional information and a review by Benjamin Rosner, see 5:625.

[1399]

Detroit Reading Test. Grades 2, 3, 4–6, 7–9; 1927; Claudia M. Parker and
Eveline A. Waterbury; [Harcourt, Brace & World, Inc.]. *

[1400]

Detroit Word Recognition Test. Grades 1–3; 1925–29; Eliza F. Oglesby;
[Harcourt, Brace & World, Inc.]. *

[1401]

***Developmental Reading Tests.** Grades 1.5, 1.5–2.5, 2.5–3, 4–6; 1955–59; [Guy
L. Bond, Theodore Clymer, and Cyril Hoyt]; Lyons & Carnahan. *
a) [PRIMARY READING.] Grades 1.5, 1.5–2.5, 2.5–3; 1955.

1) *Part 1, Basic Vocabulary.*
2) *Part 2, General Comprehension.*
3) *Part 3, Specific Comprehension.*

b) [INTERMEDIATE READING.] Grades 4–6; 1959; 6 scores: basic vocabulary, reading to retain information, reading to organize, reading to evaluate-interpret, reading to appreciate, average comprehension.

For additional information concerning *a,* see 5:626.

[1402]

Diagnostic Reading Test: Pupil Progress Series. Grades 1.9–2.1, 2.2–3, 4–6, 7–8; 1956–57; some subtests also appear in *Scholastic Diagnostic Reading Test* (see 1445) for Catholic schools; Oliver F. Anderhalter, R. Stephen Gawkoski, and Ruth Colestock; Scholastic Testing Service, Inc. *

a) PRIMARY TEST I. Grades 1.9–2.1; 9 scores: vocabulary (word recognition, word to content relation, words in use, total), rate of reading for meaning, comprehension (recalling information, locating information, reading for descriptions, total).

b) PRIMARY TEST II. Grades 2.2–3; 10 scores: vocabulary (words in use, word meaning, total), rate of reading for meaning, comprehension (same as for *a* plus following directions, reading for meaning).

c) ELEMENTARY TEST. Grades 4–6; 13 scores: knowledge and use of sources (functions, best sources, use of index, use of table of contents, total), rate of reading for meaning, comprehension (same as for *a* plus word meaning, reading for meaning, reading for directions or procedures).

d) ADVANCED TEST. Grades 7–8; 13 scores: same as for *c.*

For additional information, see 5:627.

[1403]

*****Diagnostic Reading Tests.** Grades kgn–4, 4–8, 7–13; 1947–60; Committee on Diagnostic Reading Tests, Inc. (Tests *b* and *c* also published by Science Research Associates, Inc.) *

a) SURVEY SECTION: KINDERGARTEN—FOURTH GRADE. Grades kgn–1, 1, 2, 3–4; 1957.

1) *Reading Readiness Booklet.* Grades kgn–1; 5 scores: relationships, eye-hand coordination, visual discrimination, auditory discrimination, vocabulary.

2) *Booklet 1.* Grade 1; 13 scores: visual discrimination, auditory discrimination (3 subscores plus total), vocabulary (3 subscores plus total), story reading (2 subscores plus total), total.

3) *Booklets 2 and 3.* Grades 2, 3–4; 3 scores: word recognition, comprehension, total.

b) SURVEY SECTION: LOWER LEVEL. Grades 4–8; 1952–60.

1) *Booklet 1, Word Recognition and Comprehension.* 2 scores: word recognition, comprehension.

2) *Booklet 2, Vocabulary-Story Reading.* 3 scores: vocabulary, rate of reading, story comprehension.

c) SURVEY SECTION: [UPPER LEVEL]. Grades 7–13; 1947–60; 5 scores: rate of reading, comprehension check, vocabulary, total comprehension, total.

d) DIAGNOSTIC READING TESTS. 1947–60.

1) *Section 1, Vocabulary (Revised).* Grades 7–13; 6 scores: general, English, mathematics, science, social studies, total.

2) *Section 2, Comprehension: Silent and Auditory.* Grades 7–13.

3) *Section 3, Rates of Reading.* Grades 7–13; 1947–60.

(*a*) Part 1, General. 4 scores: normal rate of reading, comprehension at

normal rate, maximum rate of reading, comprehension at maximum rate.
   (*b*) Part 2, Social Studies. 2 scores: rate of reading, comprehension.
   (*c*) Part 3, Science. 2 scores: rate of reading, comprehension.
 4) *Section 4, Word Attack.* 1947–60.
   (*a*) Part 1, Oral. Grades 1–8, 7–13.
   (*b*) Part 2, Silent. Grades 4–13; 3 scores: identification of sounds, syllabication, total.
For additional information and reviews by Frederick B. Davis, William W. Turnbull, and Henry Weitz, see 4:531 (19 references).

[1404]

*Elementary Reading: Every Pupil Scholarship Test.** Grades 4–6, 7–8; 1928–61; new form usually issued twice a year; Bureau of Educational Measurements. *
For additional information, see 5:628.

[1405]

*Elementary Reading: Every Pupil Test.** 1, 2 semesters in grades 4–6; 1936–61; new form usually issued twice a year; 2 parts; Ohio Scholarship Tests. *
a) GENERAL ABILITY.
b) SPEED AND COMPREHENSION. 2 scores: speed, comprehension.
For additional information, see 5:629.

[1406]

Emporia Silent Reading Test. Grades 3–8; 1933–35; H. E. Schrammel and W. H. Gray; Bureau of Educational Measurements. *
For additional information and reviews by M. E. Broom and Harriet Barthelmess Morrison, see 40:1534.

[1407]

Gates Advanced Primary Reading Tests. Grades 2.5–3; 1926–58; 2 tests; Arthur I. Gates; Bureau of Publications. *
a) TYPE AWR, WORD RECOGNITION.
b) TYPE APR, PARAGRAPH READING.
For additional information, see 5:630 (3 references); for reviews by Virginia Seavey and George Spache of an earlier edition, see 3:484.

[1408]

Gates Basic Reading Tests. Grades 3.5–8; 1926–58; revision of *Gates Silent Reading Tests;* 5 tests; Arthur I. Gates; Bureau of Publications. *
a) TYPE GS, READING TO APPRECIATE GENERAL SIGNIFICANCE.
b) TYPE UD, READING TO UNDERSTAND PRECISE DIRECTIONS.
c) TYPE ND, READING TO NOTE DETAILS.
d) TYPE RV, READING VOCABULARY.
e) TYPE LC, LEVEL OF COMPREHENSION.
For additional information and a review by S. S. Dunn, see 5:631 (1 reference); for reviews by George Spache, Herbert F. Spitzer, and T. L. Torgerson of an earlier edition, see 3:485 (2 references); for reviews by Joseph C. Dewey and James R. Hobson of the original edition, see 40:1539 (5 references, 1 excerpt).

[1409]

Gates Primary Reading Tests. Grades 1–2.5; 1926–58; 3 tests; Arthur I. Gates; Bureau of Publications. *
a) TYPE PWR, WORD RECOGNITION.

b) TYPE PSR, SENTENCE READING.
c) TYPE PPR, PARAGRAPH READING.
   For additional information, see 5:632 (2 references); for reviews by William
S. Gray and George Spache of an earlier edition, see 3:486 (7 references).

[1410]
*Gates Reading Survey. Grades 3.5–10, 4–10; 1939–58; 5 scores: speed and
accuracy, accuracy, vocabulary, level of comprehension, total; Arthur I. Gates;
Bureau of Publications. *
   For additional information, see 5:633 (2 references); for reviews by Dorothy
E. Holberg and Herbert F. Spitzer of an earlier edition, see 3:487.

[1411]
General Reading Test: [Ohio Senior Survey Tests]. Grade 12; 1934–53; 4
scores: paragraph meaning, general vocabulary, outlining, total; S. L. Pressey
and Maurice E. Troyer; Ohio Scholarship Tests. *
   For additional information, see 4:534.

[1412]
High School Reading Test: National Achievement Tests. Grades 7–12; 1939–
52; 6 scores: vocabulary, word discrimination, sentence meaning, noting details,
interpreting paragraphs, total; Robert K. Speer and Samuel Smith; Acorn Publishing Co. *
   For additional information and a review by Victor H. Noll, see 5:634; for a
review by Holland Roberts, see 4:536; for a review by Robert L. McCaul, see
3:488.

[1413]
*Iowa Silent Reading Tests: New Edition. Grades 4–8, 9–14; 1927–56; H. A.
Greene, A. N. Jorgensen, and V. H. Kelley; [Harcourt, Brace & World, Inc.]. *
a) ELEMENTARY TEST. Grades 4–8; 1933–56; 9 scores: rate, comprehension, directed reading, word meaning, paragraph comprehension, sentence meaning,
alphabetizing, use of index, total.
b) ADVANCED TEST. Grades 9–14; 1927–43; 10 scores: rate, comprehension, directed reading, poetry comprehension, word meaning, sentence meaning, paragraph comprehension, use of index, selection of key words, total.
   For additional information and reviews by Frederick B. Davis and William
W. Turnbull, see 3:489 (21 references, 2 excerpts); for reviews by Ivan A.
Booker and Holland D. Roberts of an earlier edition, see 40:1547 (6 references).

[1414]
Kansas Primary Reading Test. Grades 1–3; 1935; 4 scores: sentence reading,
word knowledge, paragraph comprehension, total; Alma Hoag, Emma Humble,
Bertha Robinson, Adeline Wipf, and H. E. Schrammel; Bureau of Educational
Measurements. *
   For additional information and a review by Nila Banton Smith, see 4:539;
for a review by Alice K. Liveright, see 40:1549.

[1415]
Kelley-Greene Reading Comprehension Test. Grades 9–13; 1953–55, c1952–
55; 5 scores: paragraph comprehension, directed reading, retention of details,

reading rate, total; Victor H. Kelley and Harry A. Greene; [Harcourt, Brace & World, Inc.]. *

For additional information and reviews by Russell P. Kropp and Magdalen D. Vernon, see 5:636 (1 reference).

[1416]

Kelvin Measurement of Reading Ability. Ages 8–12; 1933; C. M. Fleming; Robert Gibson & Sons (Glasgow), Ltd. *

For additional information, see 38:1103.

[1417]

The Kingston Test of Silent Reading. Ages 7–11; 1953–54; M. E. Highfield; George G. Harrap & Co. Ltd. *

For additional information and reviews by Neil Gourlay and Magdalen D. Vernon, see 5:637.

[1418]

Lee-Clark Reading Test, 1958 Revision. Grades 1, 1–2; 1931–58; J. Murray Lee and Willis W. Clark; California Test Bureau. *

a) PRIMER. Grade 1; 4 scores: auditory stimuli, visual stimuli, following directions, total.

b) FIRST READER. Grades 1–2; 6 scores: same as for primer level plus completion, inference.

For additional information, see 5:638; for a review by Ruth Lowes of an earlier edition of the primer level, see 3:490.

[1419]

Los Angeles Elementary Reading Test. Grades 3–8; 1926–31; Jessie E. Ingraham; California Test Bureau. *

For additional information and a review by Henry P. Smith, see 4:541.

[1420]

★**Manchester Reading Comprehension Test (Sen.)** 1. Ages 13.5–15; 1959; Stephen Wiseman and Jack Wrigley; University of London Press Ltd. *

[1421]

*Metropolitan Achievement Tests: [Reading, 1960 Edition].** Grades 3–4, 5–6, 7–9; 1933–60, c1933–59; 2 scores: word knowledge, reading; Walter N. Durost, Harold H. Bixler, Gertrude H. Hildreth, Kenneth W. Lund, and J. Wayne Wrightstone; [Harcourt, Brace & World, Inc.]. * For the complete battery entry, see 27.

For additional information and reviews by James R. Hobson and Margaret G. McKim of the 1947 edition, see 4:543 (2 references); for a review by D. A. Worcester of an earlier edition, see 40:1551; for reviews by Ivan A. Booker and Joseph C. Dewey, see 38:1105. For reviews of earlier editions of the complete battery, see 4:18, 40:1189, and 38:874.

[1422]

Minnesota Reading Examination for College Students. Grades 9–16; 1930–35; 2 scores: vocabulary, paragraph reading; Melvin E. Haggerty and Alvin C. Eurich; University of Minnesota Press. *

For additional information and a review by James M. McCallister, see 3:491

(3 references) ; for a review by W. C. McCall, see 40:1554 (3 references) ; for
a review by Ruth Strang, see 38:1106.

[1423]

Monroe's Standardized Silent Reading Tests. Grades 3–5, 6–8, 9–12; 1919–
59; 2 scores: rate, comprehension; Walter S. Monroe; Public School Publishing
Co. *

[1424]

**The Nelson-Denny Reading Test: Vocabulary and Paragraph: The Clapp-
Young Self-Marking Tests.** Grades 9–16; 1929–38; 3 scores: vocabulary, para-
graph comprehension, total; M. J. Nelson and E. C. Denny; Houghton Mifflin
Co. * For the revised edition entry, see 1425.
   For additional information and a review by Ivan A. Booker, see 4:544 (17
references) ; for a review by Hans C. Gordon, see 40:1557 (6 references).

[1425]

***The Nelson-Denny Reading Test: Vocabulary-Comprehension-Rate.**
Grades 9–16 and adults; 1929–60; 4 scores: vocabulary, comprehension, total,
rate; M. J. Nelson, E. C. Denny, and James I. Brown; Houghton Mifflin Co. *
For an earlier edition entry and references to reviews, see 1424.

[1426]

Nelson-Lohmann Reading Test. Grades 4, 5, 6, 7, 8; 1946–54; identical with
reading sections of *Coordinated Scales of Attainment* (see 10); Ethel V. Nelson, Victor L. Lohmann, and Marvin J. Van Wagenen; Educational Test Bureau. *
   For additional information, see 5:639.

[1427]

**The Nelson Silent Reading Test: Vocabulary and Paragraph: The Clapp-
Young Self-Marking Tests.** Grades 3–9; 1931–39; 5 scores: vocabulary, general paragraph comprehension, ability to note details, ability to predict probable
outcome, total; M. J. Nelson; Houghton Mifflin Co. *
   For additional information and a review by William D. Sheldon, see 4:545
(1 reference) ; for a review by Constance M. McCullough, see 3:492; see also
40:1558 (1 excerpt).

[1428]

Pressey Diagnostic Reading Tests. Grades 3–9; 1929; 4 scores: speed, vocabulary, paragraph meaning, total; S. L. Pressey and L. C. Pressey; Public School
Publishing Co. *

[1429]

***Primary Reading: Every Pupil Scholarship Test.** Grades 1, 2–3; 1935–61;
new form usually issued twice a year; Bureau of Educational Measurements. *
   For additional information, see 5:640.

[1430]

***Primary Reading: Every Pupil Test.** 1, 2 semesters in grades 2–3; 1936–61;
new form usually issued annually; Ohio Scholarship Tests. *
   For additional information, see 5:641; for reviews by William S. Gray and
Virginia Seavey of earlier forms, see 3:493.

[1431]

Primary Reading Test. Grade 1; 1939–40; 5 scores: word recognition, word meaning, sentence meaning, paragraph meaning, total; Albert G. Reilley; Houghton Mifflin Co. *

For additional information and a review by Ruth Lowes, see 3:494 (1 reference).

[1432]

Primary Reading Test: Acorn Achievement Tests. Grades 2–3; 1943–57; 5 scores: word recognition, words-similar meaning, word meaning-opposites, story-paragraph-sentence meaning, total; Winifred E. Stayton, Frances C. Ranson, and Roland L. Beck; Acorn Publishing Co. *

For additional information, see 5:642; for a review by Alice N. Jameson, see 3:495.

[1433]

The Purdue Reading Test. Grades 7–16; 1928–53; H. H. Remmers, John M. Stalnaker, and P. C. Baker; distributed by State High School Testing Service for Indiana. *

For additional information, see 5:643; for a review by Albert J. Harris, see 3:496.

[1434]

Purdue Reading Test for Industrial Supervisors. Supervisors; 1955; Joseph Tiffin and Roy Dunlap; University Book Store. *

For additional information and reviews by Jerome E. Doppelt and Louis C. Nanassy, see 5:644 (1 reference).

[1435]

★**Reading Adequacy "READ" Test: Individual Placement Series.** Adults; 1961; 3 scores: reading rate, per cent of comprehension, corrected rate; J. H. Norman; the Author. *

[1436]

*Reading Comprehension: Cooperative English Tests, [1960 Revision].** Grades 9–12, 13–14; 1940–60; revision of *Reading Comprehension: Cooperative English Test: Lower and Higher Levels, C1 and C2;* 4 scores: vocabulary, level of comprehension, speed of comprehension, total; Frederick B. Davis, Mary Willis, Clarence Derrick, Harry R. Neville, Jeanne M. Bradford, Geraldine Spaulding, and Charlotte Croon Davis; revision by Clarence Derrick, David P. Harris, and Biron Walker; Cooperative Test Division. (Australian edition of the Higher Level of the earlier edition: 1958; manual by M. L. Clark; Australian Council for Educational Research.) *

For additional information concerning the earlier edition, see 5:645 (21 references) and 4:547 (20 references); for reviews by Robert Murray Bear and J. B. Stroud, see 3:497 (15 references); see also 40:1564 (2 references). For reviews of the earlier edition of the complete battery, see 4:155 and 3:120.

[1437]

Reading Comprehension Test: National Achievement Tests [Crow, Kuhlmann, and Crow]. Grades 4–6, 4–9; 1953–57; Lester D. Crow, Martha J. Kuhlmann, and Alice Crow; Acorn Publishing Co. *

For additional information, see 5:647.

[1438]

Reading Comprehension Test: National Achievement Tests [Speer and Smith]. Grades 3–8; 1938–57; 4 scores: following directions, sentence meaning, paragraph meaning, total; Robert K. Speer and Samuel Smith; Acorn Publishing Co. *

For additional information, see 5:646; for a review by James R. Hobson, see 3:498.

[1439]

*****Reading: Public School Achievement Tests.** Grades 3–8; 1928–59; Jacob S. Orleans; Public School Publishing Co. * For the complete battery entry, see 33.

For additional information and reviews of the complete battery, see 40:1194.

[1440]

Reading: Seven Plus Assessment: Northumberland Series. Ages 7–8; 1951; C. M. Lambert; University of London Press Ltd. * For the complete battery entry, see 40.

For additional information, see 4:548. For a review of the complete battery, see 4:404.

[1441]

Reading Test (Comprehension and Speed): Municipal Tests: National Achievement Tests. Grades 3–6, 6–8; 1938–57; subtest of *Municipal Battery* (see 29) ; 5 scores: following directions, sentence meaning, paragraph meaning, reading speed, total; Robert K. Speer and Samuel Smith; Acorn Publishing Co. *

For additional information, see 5:648. For reviews of the complete battery, see 5:18, 4:20, and 40:1191.

[1442]

*****SRA Achievement Series: Reading.** Grades 1–2, 2–4, 4–6, 6–9; 1954–58; 2 or 4 scores: comprehension, vocabulary, (grades 1–2 only) verbal-pictorial association, language perception; Louis P. Thorpe, D. Welty Lefever, and Robert A. Naslund; Science Research Associates, Inc. * For the complete battery entry, see 35.

For additional information and reviews by N. Dale Bryant and Clarence Derrick, see 5:649. For reviews of the complete battery, see 5:21.

[1443]

*****SRA Reading Record.** Grades 6–12; 1947–59; 5 scores: reading rate, comprehension, everyday reading skills, vocabulary, total; Guy T. Buswell; Science Research Associates, Inc. *

For additional information and a review by William W. Turnbull, see 4:550 (2 references) ; for a review by Frances Oralind Triggs, see 3:502 (1 excerpt).

[1444]

Sangren-Woody Reading Test. Grades 4–8; 1927–28; 8 scores: word meaning, rate, fact material, total meaning, central thought, following directions, organization, total; Paul V. Sangren and Clifford Woody; [Harcourt, Brace & World, Inc.]. *

For additional information and a review by David H. Russell, see 4:551; for a review by Alice K. Liveright, see 40:1565 (7 references).

[1445]

Scholastic Diagnostic Reading Test. Grades 1–3, 4–6, 7–9; 1953–55; for Catholic schools; some subtests also appear in *Diagnostic Reading Test: Pupil Progress Series* (see 1402) for non-Catholic schools; Oliver F. Anderhalter, Ruth Colestock, and R. Stephen Gawkowski; Scholastic Testing Service, Inc. *
a) PRIMARY TEST. Grades 1–3; 11 scores: vocabulary (word recognition, word meaning, word use, total), rate, comprehension (reading for recall, reading for location of information, reading for meaning, reading for directions or procedures, reading for descriptions, total).
b) ELEMENTARY TEST. Grades 4–6; 13 scores: knowledge and use of sources (functions, best sources, use of index, use of table of contents, total), rate of reading for meaning, comprehension (same as for *a* plus word meaning).
c) ADVANCED TEST. Grades 7–9; 13 scores: same as for *b*.
   For additional information and reviews by Russell G. Stauffer and Arthur E. Traxler, see 5:650.

[1446]

The Schonell Reading Tests. Ages 5–15, 6–9, 7–11, 9–13; 1942–55; 7 tests; *e*, *f*, and *g* available only as presented in the author's *Diagnostic and Attainment Testing, Third Edition* ('56); Fred J. Schonell; Oliver & Boyd Ltd. *
a) TEST R1, GRADED WORD READING TEST. Ages 5–15; 1942; also called *Graded Reading Vocabulary Test.*
b) TEST R2, SIMPLE PROSE READING TEST. Ages 6–9; 1942; also called *My Dog Test.*
c) TEST R3, SILENT READING TEST A. Ages 7–11; 1942.
d) TEST R4, SILENT READING TEST B. Ages 9–13; 1942.
e) TEST R5, TEST OF ANALYSIS AND SYNTHESIS OF WORDS CONTAINING COMMON PHONIC UNITS.
f) TEST R6, TEST OF DIRECTIONAL ATTACK ON WORDS.
g) TEST R7, VISUAL WORD DISCRIMINATION TEST.
   For additional information and a review by R. W. McCulloch, see 5:651 (4 references); for a review by M. L. Kellmer Pringle, see 4:552 (3 references); for a review by Edith I. M. Thomson, see 3:499.

[1447]

Schrammel-Gray High School and College Reading Test. Grades 7–16; 1940–42; 3 scores: gross-comprehension, comprehension-efficiency, rate; H. E. Schrammel and W. H. Gray; Public School Publishing Co. *
   For additional information and reviews by James M. McCallister and Robert L. McCaul, see 3:500 (1 excerpt).

[1448]

***Sentence Reading Test 1.** Ages 7-6 to 11-1; 1956–60; A. F. Watts; published for the National Foundation for Educational Research in England and Wales; Newnes Educational Publishing Co. Ltd. *
   For additional information and reviews by Reginald R. Dale and Stephen Wiseman, see 5:652.

[1449]

***Sequential Tests of Educational Progress: Reading.** Grades 4–6, 7–9, 10–12, 13–14; 1956–59; Cooperative Test Division. * For the complete battery entry, see 39.
   For additional information and reviews by Eric F. Gardner, James R. Hobson,

and Stephen Wiseman, see 5:653. For reviews of the complete battery, see 5:24.

[1450]

Silent Reading Comprehension: Iowa Every-Pupil Tests of Basic Skills, Test A. Grades 3–5, 5–9; 1940–47; 3 scores: reading comprehension, vocabulary, total; H. F. Spitzer, Ernest Horn, Maude McBroom, H. A. Greene, and E. F. Lindquist; Houghton Mifflin Co. * For the complete battery entry, see 22.

For additional information, see 4:554; for reviews by James R. Hobson and Constance M. McCullough, see 3:501. For reviews of the complete battery, see 4:15, 3:10, and 38:872.

[1451]

***Silent Reading Tests.** Standards 1–3 (ages 7–10), 3–5 (ages 10–12), 6–10 (ages 13–17); 1947–58; National Bureau of Educational and Social Research. *
a) SILENT READING TEST, [ELEMENTARY]. Standards 1–3; [1947–54]; 4 tests.
  1) *Paragraphs.*
  2) *Sentences.*
  3) *Vocabulary.*
  4) *Speed.*
b) SILENT READING TESTS (REVISED EDITION). Standards 3–5, 6–10; [1947–58].
  1) *Junior.* Standards 3–5; [1947–58]; 4 scores: vocabulary, paragraphs, sentences, language usage.
  2) *Senior.* Standards 6–10; [1951–58]; 3 scores: vocabulary, paragraphs, language usage.
For additional information concerning *a* and an earlier edition of *b*, see 5:654.

[1452]

The Standard Reading Tests. Reading ages up to 9-0; 1958; 12 tests; J. C. Daniels and Hunter Diack; Chatto & Windus Ltd. (Record blanks published by Philip & Tacey Ltd.) *
a) TEST 1, THE STANDARD TEST OF READING SKILL.
b) TEST 2, COPYING ABSTRACT FIGURES.
c) TEST 3, COPYING A SENTENCE.
d) TEST 4, VISUAL DISCRIMINATION AND ORIENTATION TEST.
e) TEST 5, LETTER-RECOGNITION TEST.
f) TEST 6, AURAL DISCRIMINATION TEST.
g) TEST 7, DIAGNOSTIC WORD-RECOGNITION TEST.
h) TEST 8, ORAL WORD-RECOGNITION TEST.
i) TEST 9, PICTURE WORD-RECOGNITION TEST.
j) TEST 10, SILENT PROSE-READING AND COMPREHENSION TEST.
k) TEST 11, GRADED SPELLING TEST.
l) TEST 12, GRADED TEST OF READING EXPERIENCE.
For additional information, see 5:655 (1 reference).

[1453]

Stanford Achievement Test: Reading. Grades 3–4, 5–6, 7–9; 1922–55; 2 scores: paragraph meaning, word meaning; Truman L. Kelley, Richard Madden, Eric F. Gardner, Lewis M. Terman, and Giles M. Ruch; [Harcourt, Brace & World, Inc.]. * For the complete battery entry, see 42.

For additional information and reviews by Helen M. Robinson and Agatha Townsend, see 5:656; for a review by James R. Hobson of the previous edition, see 4:555 (4 references) ; for a review by Margaret G. McKim, see 3:503. For reviews of the complete battery, see 5:25, 4:25, and 3:18.

[1454]

Stone-Webster Test in Beginning Reading. Grade 1; 1936–37; 3 scores: word recognition, sentence comprehension, total; Clarence R. Stone; Webster Publishing Co. *

For additional information and a review by Ruth Lowes, see 3:504 (1 reference).

[1455]

★Survey of Reading Achievement: California Survey Series. Grades 7–9, 9–12; 1959; abbreviated combinations of items from various forms of the appropriate level of *California Reading Test, 1957 Edition* (see 1395) ; Ernest W. Tiegs and Willis W. Clark; California Test Bureau. *

[1456]

Survey Tests of Reading. Grades 3–6, 7–13; 1931–32; 2 tests; L. J. O'Rourke; Psychological Institute. *
a) CENTRAL THOUGHT TEST. Grades 3–6, 7–13; 1931–32.
b) POWER TEST. Grades 3–13; 1931.

[1457]

*Techniques in Reading Comprehension for Junior-Senior High School: Every Pupil Test. 1, 2 semesters in grades 7–12; 1937–61; new form usually issued twice a year; Ohio Scholarship Tests. *

For additional information, see 5:657; for reviews by Ivan A. Booker and James M. McCallister of earlier forms, see 3:505.

[1458]

Tests of Reading: Cooperative Inter-American Tests. Grades 1–3, 4–7, 8–13; 1950; English and Spanish editions; 3 scores: vocabulary, comprehension, total; Committee on Modern Languages of the American Council on Education; [Guidance Testing Associates]. * For the complete battery entry, see 1347.

For additional information and reviews by Jacob S. Orleans and Frederick L. Westover, see 4:557 (4 references).

[1459]

Traxler High School Reading Test. Grades 10–12; 1938–42; 5 scores: reading rate, story comprehension, main ideas, total comprehension, total; Arthur E. Traxler; Public School Publishing Co. *

For additional information and a review by Harold D. Carter, see 4:559 (4 references) ; for reviews by Alvin C. Eurich, Constance M. McCullough, and C. Gilbert Wrenn, see 40:1578 (2 excerpts).

[1460]

Traxler Silent Reading Test. Grades 7–10; 1934–42; 6 scores: reading rate, story comprehension, word meaning, paragraph meaning, total comprehension, total; Arthur E. Traxler; Public School Publishing Co. *

For additional information and a review by J. Thomas Hastings, see 4:560 (2 references) ; for reviews by Robert L. McCaul and Miles A. Tinker of an earlier edition, see 40:1579 (3 references, 1 excerpt) ; for reviews by Frederick B. Davis and Spencer Shank, see 38:1114.

[1461]

Williams Primary Reading Test. Grades 1, 2–3; 1926–55; Allan J. Williams;
Public School Publishing Co. *
  For additional information, see 5:658; for a review by Alice N. Jameson of
the original edition, see 3:508.

[1462]

Williams Reading Test for Grades 4–9. Grades 4–9; 1929; Allan J. Williams;
Public School Publishing Co. *

MISCELLANEOUS

[1463]

Basic Sight Word Test. Grades 1–2; 1942; Edward W. Dolch; Garrard Press. *

[1464]

***Cumulative Reading Record, 1956 Revision.** Grades 9–12; 1933–56; revision
of a record by Margaret M. Skinner; National Council of Teachers of English. *

[1465]

**Diagnostic Reading Examination for Diagnosis of Special Difficulty in
Reading.** Grades 1–4; [1928–29]; a combination of assessment procedures con-
sisting of the *Revised Stanford-Binet Scale,* Gray's *Standardized Oral Reading
Paragraphs, Monroe's Standardized Silent Reading Tests,* an adaptation of *Ayres
Spelling Scale,* the arithmetic computation subtest of *Stanford Achievement Test:
Arithmetic,* and 9 additional tests: alphabet repeating and reading, *Iota Word
Test,* letter naming, recognition of orientation, mirror reading, mirror writing,
number reversals, word discrimination, sounding; Marion Monroe [Cox]; C. H.
Stoelting Co. *

[1466]

Doren Diagnostic Reading Test of Word Recognition Skills. Grades 1–9;
1956; 12 scores: letter recognition, beginning sounds, whole word recognition,
words within words, speech consonants, ending sounds, blending, rhyming,
vowels, sight words, discriminate guessing, total; Margaret Doren; Educational
Test Bureau. *
  For additional information and reviews by B. H. Van Roekel and Verna L.
Vickery, see 5:659.

[1467]

Durrell Analysis of Reading Difficulty, New Edition. Grades 1–6; 1937–55,
c1933–55; Donald D. Durrell; [Harcourt, Brace & World, Inc.]. *
  For additional information and reviews by James Maxwell and George D.
Spache, see 5:660; for a review by Helen M. Robinson of the original edition,
see 4:561 (2 references); for reviews by Guy L. Bond and Miles A. Tinker, see
40:1533; for a review by Marion Monroe [Cox], see 38:1098.

[1468]

Durrell-Sullivan Reading Capacity and Achievement Tests. Grades 2.5–4.5,
3–6; 1937–45; 2 tests, 3–5 scores: word meaning, paragraph meaning, total, spell-

ing (optional), written recall (optional); Donald D. Durrell and Helen Blair Sullivan; [Harcourt, Brace & World, Inc.]. *

a) READING CAPACITY TEST.

b) READING ACHIEVEMENT TEST.

For additional information and a review by James Maxwell, see 5:661 (5 references); for a review by Helen M. Robinson, see 4:562 (4 references); for reviews by William S. Gray and Marion Monroe [Cox] of the original edition, see 38:1099 (1 excerpt).

[1469]

★Functional Readiness Questionnaire for School and College Students. Grades 1–16; 1957; reports by pupil and teacher on physical and emotional problems related to reading difficulties and school problems; Earl A. Taylor and Harold A. Solan; Reading and Study Skills Center, Inc. *

[1470]

Gates Reading Diagnostic Tests. Grades 1–8; 1926–53; Arthur I. Gates; Bureau of Publications. *

For additional information and a review by George D. Spache, see 5:662; for a review by Worth J. Osburn, see 4:563 (2 references); for related reviews, see 4:564 (2 excerpts); for a review by T. L. Torgerson, see 3:510 (3 references).

[1471]

Individual Reading Test. Ages 5.5–8.5; 1935–36; 3 tests: oral word reading, comprehension, speed; L. W. Allen; Australian Council for Educational Research. *

For additional information and a review by R. W. McCulloch, see 5:663.

[1472]

★Learning Methods Test. Grades kgn, 1, 2, 3; 1954–55; comparative effectiveness of 4 methods of teaching new words: visual, phonic, kinesthetic, combination; Robert E. Mills; Mills Center, Inc. *

[1473]

McGuffey Diagnostic Reading Test. Grades 4–6; 1955; 5 scores: syllables, sound value recognition, vocabulary, appreciation, understanding; Ullin W. Leavell; [American Guidance Service, Inc.]. *

For additional information, see 5:664.

[1474]

Primary Reading Profiles, [Revised Edition]. Grades 1, 2; 1953–57; 6 scores: reading aptitude, auditory association, word recognition, word attack, reading comprehension, total; James B. Stroud and Albert N. Hieronymus; Houghton Mifflin Co. *

For additional information and reviews by James R. Hobson and Verna L. Vickery, see 5:665.

[1475]

★The Reader Rater. Ages 15 and over; 1959; self-administered survey of reading skills; 12 scores: speed, comprehension, reading habits, reading for details, reading for inferences, reading for main ideas and adjusting speed, summarizing, skimming, recall of information read, unspeeded vocabulary, speeded vocabulary, total; Better Reading Program, Inc. *

[1476]
Reading Diagnostic Record for High School and College Students. High school and college; 1938–52; Ruth Strang, Margaret M. Conant, Margaret G. McKim, and Mary Alice Mitchell; Bureau of Publications. *

For additional information and reviews by Marvin D. Glock and Donald E. P. Smith, see 5:666; for reviews by Robert Murray Bear and Carolyn M. Welch of the original edition, see 3:509; for a review by Henry D. Rinsland, see 40:1535 (3 excerpts).

[1477]
★[The Reading Eye Test Selections.] Grades 1, 2, 3, 4, 5, 6, 7–8, 9–16 and adults; 1959–60; for use with the publisher's eye movement camera; 9 scores (grade level of fundamental reading skill, fixations, regressions, average span of recognition, average duration of fixation, rate with comprehension, comprehension, relative efficiency, directional attack) and 2 diagnostic categories (visual adjustment, general adjustment to reading); Stanford E. Taylor and [Helen Frackenpohl]; Educational Development Laboratories, Inc. *

[1478]
Roswell-Chall Diagnostic Reading Test of Word Analysis Skills. Grades 2–6; 1956–58; Florence G. Roswell and Jeanne S. Chall; Essay Press. *

For additional information and a review by Byron H. Van Roekel, see 5:667 (1 reference).

[1479]
★Silent Reading Diagnostic Tests: Developmental Reading Tests. Grades 3–8; 1955; Guy L. Bond, Theodore Clymer, and Cyril J. Hoyt; Lyons & Carnahan. *

For additional information, see 5:669.

[1480]
★Southgate Group Reading Tests: Test 1—Word Selection. Ages 6–7.5; 1959; Vera Southgate; University of London Press Ltd. *

[1481]
Stanford Diagnostic Phonics Survey, Research Edition. High school and college; 1956–58; ability to relate printed sounds to spoken sounds; experimental form; Grace M. Brown and Alice B. Cottrell; Consulting Psychologists Press, Inc. *

For additional information, see 5:670.

ORAL

[1482]
★Flash-X Sight Vocabulary Test. Grades 1–2; 1961; 2 scores: sight vocabulary, experience vocabulary; George D. Spache and Stanford E. Taylor; Educational Development Laboratories, Inc. *

[1483]

Gilmore Oral Reading Test. Grades 1–8; 1951–52; 3 scores: accuracy, comprehension, rate; John V. Gilmore; [Harcourt, Brace & World, Inc.]. *
For additional information and reviews by Lydia A. Duggins and Maynard C. Reynolds, see 5:671 (1 reference).

[1484]

Graded Word Reading Test. Ages 5–14, 6 and over; 1923–38; P. E. Vernon; University of London Press Ltd. *
a) THE BURT (REARRANGED) READING TEST. Ages 5–14; 1923–38; adaptation of Cyril Burt's *Graded Word Reading Test.*
b) GRADED WORD READING TEST. Ages 6 and over; 1938.

[1485]

Holborn Reading Scale. Ages 5.5–11.0; 1948; 2 scores: word recognition, comprehension; A. F. Watts; George G. Harrap & Co. Ltd. *
For additional information and a review by Stanley Nisbet, see 5:635 (1 reference); for a review by C. M. Fleming, see 4:537.

[1486]

Leavell Analytical Oral Reading Test. Grades 1–10; 1952–53; [Ullin W. Leavell]; [American Guidance Service, Inc.]. *
For additional information and reviews by Lydia A. Duggins and Maynard C. Reynolds, see 5:672.

[1487]

★Neale Analysis of Reading Ability. Ages 6–12; 1957–58; 3 scores: accuracy, comprehension, rate of reading; Marie D. Neale; Macmillan & Co. Ltd. *
(United States publisher: St. Martin's Press, Inc.)

[1488]

Oral Diagnostic Test of Word-Analysis Skills, Primary: Dominion Tests. Grades 1–2; 1947; Department of Educational Research, Ontario College of Education, University of Toronto; distributed by Guidance Centre. *
For additional information and a review by S. A. Rayner, see 5:673; for a review by Nila Banton Smith, see 4:565.

[1489]

Oral Word Reading Test. Ages 7–11; 1952; A. E. Fieldhouse and the New Zealand Council for Educational Research; distributed by Educational Books. *
For additional information and reviews by S. A. Rayner and D. K. Wheeler, see 5:674.

[1490]

★Standardized Oral Reading Check Tests. Grades 1–2, 2–4, 4–6, 6–8; 1923–55; 2 scores: rate, accuracy; William S. Gray; Public School Publishing Co. *
For additional information and reviews by David H. Russell and Clarence R. Stone, see 40:1570 (1 reference).

[1491]

Standardized Oral Reading Paragraphs. Grades 1–8; 1915; William S. Gray; Public School Publishing Co. *
For additional information and reviews by David Kopel and Clarence R. Stone, see 40:1571 (7 references).

READINESS

[1492]

American School Reading Readiness Test. First grade entrants; 1941–55; 9 scores: vocabulary, discrimination of letter forms, discrimination of letter combinations, word selection, word matching, discrimination of geometric forms, following directions, memory of geometric forms, total; Willis E. Pratt, Robert V. Young, and Carroll A. Whitmer; Public School Publishing Co. *

For additional information and reviews by Joan Bollenbacher and Helen M. Robinson, see 5:675 (3 references); for reviews by David H. Russell and Paul A. Witty, see 3:513.

[1493]

Binion-Beck Reading Readiness Test for Kindergarten and First Grade. Grades kgn–1; 1945; Harriet Seay Binion and Roland L. Beck; Acorn Publishing Co. *

For additional information and reviews by Irving H. Anderson and Paul A. Witty, see 3:514 (1 reference).

[1494]

Classification Test for Beginners in Reading. First grade entrants; 1933; Clarence R. Stone and Clifford C. Grover; Webster Publishing Co. *

For additional information and reviews by Marion Monroe Cox and David H. Russell, see 3:515 (2 references).

[1495]

*Gates Reading Readiness Tests. Grade 1; 1939–42; 5 scores: picture directions, word matching, word-card matching, rhyming, letters and numbers; Arthur I. Gates; Bureau of Publications. (Australian edition: 1949; identical with American edition except for norms; Australian Council for Educational Research.) *

For additional information and a review by F. J. Schonell of the Australian edition, see 4:566; for reviews by Marion Monroe Cox and Paul A. Witty of the American edition, see 3:516 (3 references); see also 40:1537 (5 references, 2 excerpts).

[1496]

*Group Test of Reading Readiness: Dominion Tests. Grades kgn, kgn–1; 1949–59; 6 scores: discrimination of objects-symbols-words, listening-remembering-observing, familiarity with word forms, memory for word forms, motor coordination, total; Department of Educational Research, Ontario College of Education, University of Toronto; distributed by Guidance Centre. *

For additional information and a review by N. Dale Bryant, see 5:676.

[1497]

The Harrison-Stroud Reading Readiness Profiles. Grades kgn–1; 1949–56; 7 scores: using symbols, making visual discriminations (2 scores), using the context, making auditory discriminations, using context and auditory clues, giving the names of letters; M. Lucile Harrison and James B. Stroud; Houghton Mifflin Co. *

For additional information and a review by S. S. Dunn, see 5:677 (2 references); for a review by William S. Gray of an earlier edition, see 4:568.

[1498]

Lee-Clark Reading Readiness Test, 1951 Revision. Grades kgn–1; 1931–51; 4 scores: letter symbols, concepts, word symbols, total; J. Murray Lee and Willis W. Clark; California Test Bureau. *

For additional information and a review by James R. Hobson, see 5:678; for reviews by Marion Monroe Cox and David H. Russell of the 1943 edition, see 3:517 (2 references).

[1499]

*Maturity Level for School Entrance and Reading Readiness. Grades kgn–1; 1950–59; revision of *School Readiness Inventory;* 2 scores: maturity level, reading readiness; Katharine M. Banham; Educational Test Bureau. *

For additional information and a review by David H. Russell of the original edition, see 4:572.

[1500]

Metropolitan Readiness Tests. End of kgn and first grade entrants; 1933–50; 3 or 4 scores: reading readiness, number readiness, total, drawing-a-man (optional); Gertrude H. Hildreth and Nellie L. Griffiths; [Harcourt, Brace & World, Inc.]. (New Zealand adaptation of the original edition: ages 5-0 to 5-2; 1942–43; 7–9 scores: similarities, copying, vocabulary, sentences, information, numbers, total, (optional) drawing-a-man, writing name; New Zealand Council for Educational Research; distributed by Educational Books.) *

For additional information and a review by Eric F. Gardner, see 4:570 (3 references, 1 excerpt); for a review by Irving H. Anderson of the original edition, see 3:518 (5 references); for a review by W. J. Osburn, see 40:1552 (10 references).

[1501]

Murphy-Durrell Diagnostic Reading Readiness Test. First grade entrants; 1949, c1947–49; 3 scores: auditory, visual, learning rate; Helen A. Murphy and Donald D. Durrell; [Harcourt, Brace & World, Inc.]. *

For additional information and reviews by Joan Bollenbacher and S. S. Dunn, see 5:679 (2 references); see also 4:571 (2 references).

[1502]

Reading Aptitude Tests. Grades kgn–1; 1935; 5 scores: visual, auditory, motor, articulation, language; Marion Monroe [Cox]; Houghton Mifflin Co. *

For additional information and a review by Irving H. Anderson, see 3:519 (5 references).

[1503]

Reading Readiness Test. Grades kgn–1; 1957; David F. Votaw and Peggy Lou Moses; Steck Co. *

For additional information, see 5:680 (1 reference).

[1504]

★Reversal Test. Age 6.5; 1954; Åke W. Edfeldt; Skandinaviska Testförlaget AB. *

[1505]

Scholastic Reading Readiness Test. Grades kgn–1; 1953; for Catholic schools; Oliver F. Anderhalter and Ruth Colestock; Scholastic Testing Service, Inc. *

For additional information, see 5:681.

[1506]

★Watson Reading-Readiness Test. Grades kgn–1; 1960; 3 scores: subjective
test (teacher's ratings of physical, social, emotional, and psychological readiness), objective test, total; G. Milton Watson; Book Society of Canada Ltd. *
(United States publisher: C. S. Hammond & Co.)

[1507]

Webster Reading-Readiness Test. Grades kgn–1.5; 1950; 5 scores: verbal
discrimination, memory of word forms, auditory discrimination, vocabulary and
comprehension, total; Clarence R. Stone and Mary Nila; Webster Publishing
Co. *
  For additional information, see 5:682.

SPECIAL FIELDS

[1508]

Interpretation of Reading Materials in the Natural Sciences. High school,
college; 1944–57; subtest of *Tests of General Educational Development* (see
44); United States Armed Forces Institute; Veterans' Testing Service. *
  For additional information, see 5:683. For reviews of the complete battery,
see 5:27, 4:26, and 3:20.

[1509]

Interpretation of Reading Materials in the Social Studies. High school,
college; 1944–57; subtest of *Tests of General Educational Development* (see
44); United States Armed Forces Institute; Veterans' Testing Service. *
  For additional information, see 5:684; for reviews by W. E. Hall and C.
Robert Pace of the college level, see 3:528 (1 reference). For reviews of the
complete battery, see 5:27, 4:26, and 3:20.

[1510]

★The Iowa Tests of Educational Development: Test 5, Ability to Interpret
Reading Materials in the Social Studies. Grades 9–13; 1942–59; E. F. Lindquist and others; Science Research Associates, Inc. * For the complete battery
entry, see 25.
  For additional information, see 5:685. For reviews of the complete battery,
see 5:17, 4:17, and 3:12.

[1511]

★The Iowa Tests of Educational Development: Test 6, Ability to Interpret
Reading Materials in the Natural Sciences. Grades 9–13; 1942–59; E. F.
Lindquist and others; Science Research Associates, Inc. * For the complete
battery entry, see 25.
  For additional information, see 5:686. For reviews of the complete battery,
see 5:17, 4:17, and 3:12.

[1512]

[Robinson-Hall Reading Tests.] College; 1940–49; 4 tests; Francis P. Robinson and Prudence Hall; Publication Office, Ohio State University. *
  a) A TEST OF READING ABILITY FOR ART.
  b) A TEST OF READING ABILITY FOR GEOLOGY.
  c) A TEST OF READING ABILITY FOR HISTORY.

d) A TEST OF READING ABILITY FOR FICTION.
For additional information and a review by Robert Murray Bear, see 4:575
(2 references) ; see also 3:533 (3 references).

[1513]
**Tests of Natural Sciences: Vocabulary and Interpretation of Reading Ma-
terials: Cooperative Inter-American Tests.** Grades 8–13; 1950; English and
Spanish editions; 3 scores: vocabulary, interpretation of reading materials,
total; Committee on Modern Languages of the American Council on Education; [Guidance Testing Associates]. * For the complete battery entry, see 1347.
For additional information and a review by Clarence H. Nelson, see 4:576
(4 references).

[1514]
**Tests of Social Studies: Vocabulary and Interpretation of Reading Ma-
terials: Cooperative Inter-American Tests.** Grades 8–13; 1950; English and
Spanish editions; 3 scores: vocabulary, interpretation of reading materials, total;
Committee on Modern Languages of the American Council on Education;
[Guidance Testing Associates]. * For the complete battery entry, see 1347.
For additional information and reviews by Gustav J. Froehlich and Martha
E. Layman, see 4:577 (4 references).

SPEED

[1515]
Chapman-Cook Speed of Reading Test. Grades 4–8; 1923–24; J. C. Chapman
and Sidney Cook; Educational Test Bureau. *
For additional information and a review by Eason Monroe, see 3:522 (1
reference).

[1516]
Minnesota Speed of Reading Test for College Students. Grades 12–16; 1936;
Alvin C. Eurich; University of Minnesota Press. *
For additional information and a review by J. R. Gerberich, see 40:1555 (2
references) ; for reviews by Frederick B. Davis and Ruth Strang, see 38:1107.

[1517]
Reading Speed and Comprehension: Ohio Senior Survey Tests. Grade 12;
1935–53; 2 scores: speed, comprehension; S. L. Pressey and J. W. Sherburne;
Ohio Scholarship Tests. *
For additional information and reviews by J. B. Stroud and Miles A. Tinker,
see 3:524.

[1518]
Tinker Speed of Reading Test. Grades 7–16 and adults; 1955, c1947–55; Miles
A. Tinker; University of Minnesota Press. *
For additional information and a review by Leonard S. Feldt, see 5:687.

STUDY SKILLS

[1519]
★Ability to Learn (Exploratory and Corrective Inventory). High school;
1953; W. H. Winkler; [Winkler Publications]. *

[1520]

Bennett Use of Library Test. High school and college; 1947; Alma Bennett and H. E. Schrammel; Bureau of Educational Measurements. *

For additional information and a review by Louis Shores, see 4:578.

[1521]

Brown-Holtzman Survey of Study Habits and Attitudes. High school and college; 1953–56; William F. Brown and Wayne H. Holtzman; Psychological Corporation. *

For additional information and reviews by James Deese and C. Gilbert Wrenn (with Roy D. Lewis), see 5:688 (14 references).

[1522]

California Study Methods Survey. Grades 7–13; 1958; 5 scores: attitudes toward school, mechanics of study, planning and system, total, verification; Harold D. Carter; California Test Bureau. *

For additional information, see 5:689 (7 references).

[1523]

Cooperative Dictionary Test. Grades 7–12; 1951–52; 5 scores: alphabetizing, spelling, pronunciation, meaning, total; S. D. Melville, Clarence Derrick (manual), and Frances Swineford (manual); Cooperative Test Division. *

For additional information and a review by A. N. Hieronymus, see 5:690.

[1524]

Edmiston How to Study Test. Grades 7–13; 1947–49; R. W. Edmiston; the Author. *

For additional information, see 4:580.

[1525]

Evaluation Aptitude Test. Candidates for college and graduate school entrance; 1951–52; 5 scores: neutral syllogisms, emotionally toned syllogisms, total, emotional bias, indecision; DeWitt E. Sell; Psychometric Affiliates. *

For additional information and reviews by J. Thomas Hastings and Walker H. Hill, see 5:691.

[1526]

*The Iowa Tests of Educational Development: Test 9, Use of Sources of Information. Grades 9–13; 1942–59; E. F. Lindquist and others; Science Research Associates, Inc. * For the complete battery entry, see 25.

For additional information, see 5:692. For reviews of the complete battery, see 5:17, 4:17, and 3:12.

[1527]

*A Library Orientation Test for College Freshmen, 1955 Edition. Grade 13; 1950–61; Ethel M. Feagley, Dorothy W. Curtiss, Mary V. Gaver, and Esther Greene; Bureau of Publications. *

For additional information and reviews by Janet G. Afflerbach (with Lois Grimes Afflerbach) and J. Wayne Wrightstone, see 5:693.

[1528]

Library Usage Test. Grades 11–13; 1940; Elmer R. Smith; Turner E. Smith & Co. *

For additional information and a review by J. Wayne Wrightstone, see 3:537.

[1529]

Logical Reasoning. Grades 9–16 and adults; 1955; Alfred F. Hertzka and J. P. Guilford; Sheridan Supply Co. *

For additional information and reviews by Duncan Howie and Charles R. Langmuir, see 5:694 (1 reference).

[1530]

Peabody Library Information Test. Grades 4–8, 9–12, 13–16; 1938–40; Louis Shores and Joseph E. Moore; Educational Test Bureau. *
a) ELEMENTARY LEVEL. Grades 4–8; 1940.
b) HIGH SCHOOL LEVEL. Grades 9–12; 1940.
c) COLLEGE LEVEL, REVISED EDITION. Grades 13–16; 1938–40; 9 scores: the book, arrangement of books, catalog, dictionary, encyclopedia, periodicals and indexes, special reference books, bibliography, total.

For additional information and a review by Douglas E. Scates, see 3:538 (2 references, 2 excerpts).

[1531]

Pictographic Self Rating Scale. High school and college; 1955–57; attitude toward classroom and study activities; Einar R. Ryden; Acorn Publishing Co. *
For additional information, see 5:695 (2 references).

[1532]

SRA Achievement Series: Work-Study Skills. Grades 4–6, 6–9; 1954–57; 2 scores: references, charts; Louis P. Thorpe, D. Welty Lefever, and Robert A. Naslund; Science Research Associates, Inc. * For the complete battery entry, see 35.

For additional information and reviews by Robert L. Ebel and Ruth M. Strang, see 5:696. For reviews of the complete battery, see 5:21.

[1533]

★Senior High School Library and Reference Skills Test. Grades 9–12; 1960; 8 scores: alphabetization, uses of the dictionary, the card catalogue, research vocabulary, reference books, Dewey Decimal System, periodicals, total; Claude E. Stephenson; Perfection Form Co. *

[1534]

Special Reading Test: Ohio Senior Survey Tests. Grade 12; 1935–41; 5 scores: English vocabulary, foreign words, dictionary, graphs and maps, total; S. L. Pressey and J. W. Sherburne; Ohio Scholarship Tests. *
For additional information and a review by Miles A. Tinker, see 3:539.

[1535]

Spitzer Study Skills Test. Grades 9–13; 1954–55; 6 scores: dictionary, index, graphs-tables-maps, sources of information, total, note taking; Herbert F. Spitzer; [Harcourt, Brace & World, Inc.]. *
For additional information and a review by James Deese, see 5:697 (1 reference).

[1536]

Stanford Achievement Test: Study Skills. Grades 5–6, 7–9; 1953–54, c1952–54; Truman L. Kelley, Richard Madden, Eric F. Gardner, Lewis M. Terman, and Giles M. Ruch; [Harcourt, Brace & World, Inc.]. * For the complete battery entry, see 42.

For additional information and reviews by Robert L. Ebel and Ruth M. Strang, see 5:698. For reviews of the complete battery, see 5:25, 4:25, and 3:18.

[1537]

Study Habits Inventory, Revised Edition. Grades 12–16; 1934–41; C. Gilbert Wrenn; distributed by Consulting Psychologists Press, Inc. *

For additional information and a review by Douglas E. Scates, see 3:540 (8 references); for reviews by Edward S. Jones and William A. McCall, see 40:1574.

[1538]

Study Performance Test. High school and college; 1934–43; Herbert A. Toops, Grace Shover, and others; Ohio College Association. *

[1539]

Survey of Study Habits, Experimental Edition. Grades 8–14; 1944; Arthur E. Traxler; Educational Records Bureau. *

For additional information and a review by Warren R. Baller, see 4:583 (1 reference).

[1540]

Test of Critical Thinking. Grades 7–9; 1951; 7 scores: inquiry, interest, relationships, openmindedness, generalizations, accuracy, total; M. T. Macy and Hugh B. Wood; [Curriculum Bulletin]. *

For additional information, see 4:584.

[1541]

A Test of Study Skills. Grades 4–9; 1940–41; J. W. Edgar and H. T. Manuel; Steck Co. *

For additional information and a review by Marvin D. Glock, see 5:699; for a review by Douglas E. Scates, see 3:542.

[1541a]

★A Test on Use of the Dictionary. High school and college; [1955]; 6 scores: pronunciation, meaning, spelling, derivation, usage, total; George D. Spache; Reading Laboratory and Clinic. *

[1542]

Tyler-Kimber Study Skills Test. Grades 9–16; 1937; 9 scores: finding what you want in a book, using an index, using general reference books, recognizing common abbreviations, using the library card catalog, interpreting maps, current periodical literature, interpreting graphs, total; Henry T. Tyler and George C. Kimber; distributed by Consulting Psychologists Press, Inc. *

For additional information and reviews by William A. McCall and Rachel Salisbury, see 40:1580 (1 reference); for reviews by Edward S. Jones and C. Gilbert Wrenn, see 38:1166.

[1543]

Watson-Glaser Critical Thinking Appraisal. Grades 9–16 and adults; 1942–56; 6 scores: inference, assumptions, deduction, interpretation, arguments, total;

Goodwin **Watson** and Edward Maynard Glaser; [Harcourt, Brace & World, Inc.]. *

For additional information and reviews by Walker H. Hill and Carl I. Hovland, see 5:700 (8 references); for a review by Robert H. Thouless of the original edition, see 3:544 (3 references, 1 excerpt).

[1544]

Work-Study Skills: Iowa Every-Pupil Tests of Basic Skills, Test B. Grades 3–5, 5–9; 1940–47; 6 scores: map reading, use of references, use of index, use of dictionary, alphabetizing (grades 3–5) or graphing (grades 5–9), total; H. F. Spitzer, Ernest Horn, Maude McBroom, H. A. Greene, and E. F. Lindquist; Houghton Mifflin Co. * For the complete battery entry, see 22.

For additional information, see 4:588; for a review by J. Wayne Wrightstone, see 3:545. For reviews of the complete battery, see 4:15, 3:10, and 38:872.

SCIENCE

[1545]

Ability for Science: Fife Tests of Ability, Test 2. Secondary school entrants; 1947; Frank M. Earle; University of London Press Ltd. * For the complete battery entry, see 1374.

For additional information, see 3:546 (2 references). For reviews of the complete battery, see 4:713 and 3:8.

[1546]

***Biology and General Science: National Teacher Examinations.** College seniors and teachers; 1940–60; Educational Testing Service. * For the testing program entry, see 1192.

For additional information, see 5:701. For reviews of the testing program, see 5:538 and 4:802.

[1547]

***Chemistry, Physics, and General Science: National Teacher Examinations.** College seniors and teachers; 1940–60; Educational Testing Service. * For the testing program entry, see 1192.

For additional information, see 5:702. For reviews of the testing program, see 5:538 and 4:802.

[1548]

Cooperative General Achievement Tests: Test 2, Natural Science. Grade 12 and college entrants; 1937–56; Paul J. Burke, Carl A. Pearson, and John Zimmerman; Cooperative Test Division. * For the complete battery entry, see 8.

For additional information, see 5:703; see also 4:595 (1 reference); for a review by Palmer O. Johnson of earlier forms, see 3:548. For reviews of the complete battery, see 5:6, 4:5, and 3:3.

[1549]

Cooperative General Science Test. High school; 1932–51; Paul E. Kambly and Carl A. Pearson; Cooperative Test Division. *

For additional information and a review by John S. Richardson, see 4:623 (1 reference); for a review by G. W. Hunter of an earlier form, see 40:1601; for reviews by W. B. Meldrum and Alvin W. Schindler, see 38:1125.

[1550]

Cooperative Science Test for Grades 7, 8, and 9. Grades 7–9; 1941–51; 4 scores: informational background, terms and concepts, comprehension and interpretation, total; Paul E. Kambly; Cooperative Test Division. *

For additional information and a review by R. Will Burnett, see 4:624; for reviews by Hans C. Gordon and Herbert A. Thelen of earlier forms, see 3:571.

[1551]

Coordinated Scales of Attainment: Science. Grades 4, 5, 6, 7, 8; 1946–54; Victor C. Smith; Educational Test Bureau. * For the complete battery entry, see 10.

For additional information, see 5:704. For reviews of the complete battery, see 4:8 and 3:6.

[1552]

***Elementary Science and Health: Every Pupil Test.** 1, 2 semesters in grades 4–6; 1935–61; new form usually issued twice a year; Ohio Scholarship Tests. *

For additional information, see 5:705.

[1553]

***Elementary Science: Every Pupil Scholarship Test.** Grades 5–8; 1926–61; new form usually issued twice a year; Bureau of Educational Measurements. *

For additional information, see 5:706.

[1554]

***Elementary Science Test: National Achievement Tests.** Grades 4–6; 1948–58; 6 scores: practical applications, cause and effect relationships, miscellaneous facts, simple identifications, evaluation of statements, total; Lester D. Crow and W. L. Shuman; Acorn Publishing Co. *

For additional information and a review by William Harrison Lucow, see 5:707.

[1555]

***General Science: Every Pupil Scholarship Test.** High school; 1926–61; new form usually issued twice a year; Bureau of Educational Measurements. *

For additional information, see 5:708.

[1556]

***General Science: Every Pupil Test.** 1, 2 semesters high school; 1929–61; new form usually issued twice a year; Ohio Scholarship Tests. *

For additional information, see 5:709.

[1557]

★General Science: Final District-State Scholarship Test. High school; 1938–61; Ohio Scholarship Tests. *

[1558]

★General Science: Preliminary District-State Scholarship Test. High school; 1947–61; Ohio Scholarship Tests. *

[1559]

General Science Scales. Grades 7–12; 1924; August Dvorak; Public School Publishing Co. *

[1560]

General Science Test: National Achievement Tests. Grades 7–9; 1936–50; 7 scores: general concepts, identifications, men of science, definitions, use of objects, miscellaneous facts, total; Robert K. Speer, Lester D. Crow, and Samuel Smith; Acorn Publishing Co. *

For additional information and a review by Robert M. W. Travers, see 5:712; for reviews by Francis D. Curtis and G. W. Hunter, see 40:1602.

[1561]

***General Science Test: State High School Tests for Indiana.** 1, 2 semesters high school; 1934–59; Geraldine Shontz, David G. Koch, and Russell McDougal; State High School Testing Service for Indiana. *

For additional information, see 4:592.

[1562]

***General Science III, Form 4: Achievement Examinations for Secondary Schools.** High school; 1951–59; Forms 1–3 published by Educational Test Bureau are out of print; Victor C. Smith; C. A. Gregory Co. *

For additional information concerning the earlier forms, see 5:711.

[1563]

***General Science III: Midwest High School Achievement Examinations.** High school; 1955–61; Educational Test Bureau. *

For additional information concerning earlier forms, see 5:710.

[1564]

***The Iowa Tests of Educational Development: Test 2, General Background in the Natural Sciences.** Grades 9–13; 1942–59; E. F. Lindquist and others; Science Research Associates, Inc. * For the complete battery entry, see 25.

For additional information, see 5:713. For reviews of the complete battery, see 5:17, 4:17, and 3:12.

[1565]

McDougal General Science Test. 1, 2 semesters high school; 1941; Clyde R. McDougal and H. E. Schrammel; Bureau of Educational Measurements. *

For additional information and reviews by Hans C. Gordon and Herbert A. Thelen, see 3:576.

[1566]

***Metropolitan Achievement Tests: [Science, 1960 Edition].** Grades 5–6, 7–9; 1932–60; Walter N. Durost, Harold H. Bixler, Gertrude H. Hildreth, Kenneth W. Lund, and J. Wayne Wrightstone; [Harcourt, Brace & World, Inc.]. *

For the complete battery entry, see 27.

[1567]

Physical Science Aptitude Examination, Special Edition. Grades 12–13; 1943; 5 scores: mathematics, formulation, number series, information, total; C. J. Lapp, E. W. Chittenden, and D. B. Stuit; Bureau of Educational Research and Service. *

For additional information and reviews by Jack W. Dunlap and John C. Flanagan, see 3:547.

[1568]

Physical Science: Teacher Education Examination Program. College seniors preparing to teach secondary school; 1957; Educational Testing Service. * For the testing program entry, see 1205.

For additional information, see 5:714. For a review of the testing program, see 5:543.

[1569]

★Purdue Physical Science Aptitude Test. Grades 9–13; 1943–60; formerly called *Purdue Science Aptitude Test for High School and College;* H. H. Remmers and Ned A. Rosen; University Book Store. *

[1570]

Read General Science Test. Grades 9–13; 1951–54, c1950–51; John G. Read; [Harcourt, Brace & World, Inc.]. *

For additional information, see 5:715 (1 reference); for reviews by Benjamin S. Bloom and John S. Richardson, see 4:628.

[1571]

★Science Aptitude Examination. Grade 12; 1942–60; new form issued annually following use in the Science Talent Search program for Westinghouse scholarships and awards; Harold A. Edgerton, Steuart Henderson Britt, and Frederick O. Carleton; Science Service, Inc. *

[1572]

★Science Background: A Science Service Test to Identify Potential Scientific and Technical Talent. Grades 4–9; 1957–58; 2 tests; experimental form; Science Service, Inc. *
a) SCIENCE BACKGROUND—IA: THINGS DONE.
b) SCIENCE BACKGROUND—2A: VOCABULARY.

[1573]

★Sequential Tests of Educational Progress: Science. Grades 4–6, 7–9, 10–12, 13–14; 1956–59; Cooperative Test Division. * For the complete battery entry, see 39.

For additional information and reviews by Palmer O. Johnson, Julian C. Stanley (with M. Jacinta Mann), and Robert M. W. Travers, see 5:716. For reviews of the complete battery, see 5:24.

[1574]

Stanford Achievement Test: Intermediate and Advanced Science Test. Grades 5–9; 1941–54, c1940–54; items identical with those in science sections of *Stanford Achievement Test* (see 42); Truman L. Kelley, Richard Madden, Eric F. Gardner, Lewis M. Terman, and Giles M. Ruch; [Harcourt, Brace & World, Inc.]. *

For additional information, see 5:717; for reviews by Bertram Epstein and Paul E. Kambly of the previous edition, see 4:593. For reviews of the complete battery, see 5:25, 4:25, and 3:18.

[1575]

★Survey Test in Introductory Science: California Survey Series. Grades 7–9; 1959; identical with subtest 6 of the elementary level of *California Tests in Social and Related Sciences,* Form AA; Georgia Sachs Adams, William E. Keeley, and John A. Sexson; California Test Bureau. *

[1576]

★Survey Test in Physical Science: California Survey Series. Grades 7–10; 1959; identical with subtest 5 of the advanced level of *California Tests in Social and Related Sciences,* Form AA; Georgia Sachs Adams, William E. Keeley, and John A. Sexson; California Test Bureau. *

BIOLOGY

[1577]

Biological Science: Teacher Education Examination Program. College seniors preparing to teach secondary school; 1957; Educational Testing Service. * For the testing program entry, see 1205.

For additional information, see 5:718. For a review of the testing program, see 5:543.

[1578]

*Biology: Every Pupil Scholarship Test. High school; 1926–61; new form usually issued twice a year; Bureau of Educational Measurements. *

For additional information, see 5:720.

[1579]

*Biology: Every Pupil Test. 1, 2 semesters high school; 1935–61; new form usually issued twice a year; Ohio Scholarship Tests. *

For additional information, see 5:721.

[1580]

★Biology: Final District-State Scholarship Test. High school; 1938–61; Ohio Scholarship Tests. *

[1581]

*Biology, Form 4: Achievement Examinations for Secondary Schools. High school; 1951–59; Forms 1–3 published by Educational Test Bureau are out of print; B. R. Whitinger; C. A. Gregory Co. *

For additional information concerning the earlier forms, see 5:719.

[1582]

*Biology: Manchester Semester-End Achievement Tests. 1, 2 semesters high school; 1934–[45]; Bureau of Tests. *

[1583]

*Biology: Midwest High School Achievement Examinations. High school; 1955–61; Educational Test Bureau. *

For additional information concerning earlier forms, see 5:722.

[1584]

★Biology: Preliminary District-State Scholarship Test. High school; 1947–61; Ohio Scholarship Tests. *

[1585]

*Biology Test: State High School Tests for Indiana. 1, 2 semesters high school; 1934–59; Avis Risk and S. A. Rifenburgh; State High School Testing Service for Indiana. *

For additional information, see 4:598.

[1586]

*College Entrance Examination Board Achievement Test in Biology. Candidates for college entrance; 1915–61; program administered for the College Entrance Examination Board by Educational Testing Service. * For the testing program entry, see 1345.

For additional information and a review by Elizabeth Hagen of Form FAC, see 5:723 (2 references); for a review by Clark W. Horton of earlier forms, see 4:600.

[1587]

*College Entrance Examination Board Advanced Placement Examination: Biology. Candidates desiring credit for college level courses or admission to advanced courses; 1956–61; program administered for the College Entrance Examination Board by Educational Testing Service. * For the testing program entry, see 1346.

For additional information and a review by Clark W. Horton of Form FBP, see 5:724.

[1588]

Cooperative Biology Test. High school; 1933–51; Paul E. Kambly; Cooperative Test Division. *

For additional information and a review by Leland P. Johnson, see 4:601; for a review by C. W. Horton of earlier forms, see 3:550 (1 reference); for a review by Ralph W. Tyler, see 40:1585; for reviews by Francis D. Curtis and George W. Hunter, see 38:907.

[1589]

Cooperative Biology Test: Educational Records Bureau Edition. High school; 1941–58; Committee on Biology Tests of the Educational Records Bureau; Educational Records Bureau. *

For additional information, see 5:725 (1 reference); see also 4:602 (2 references).

[1590]

General Biology Test: National Achievement Tests. High school; 1951; 4 scores: uses-processes-results, biologists, miscellaneous facts, total; Lester D. Crow and James G. Murray; Acorn Publishing Co. *

For additional information and reviews by Elizabeth Hagen and Clark W. Horton, see 5:726.

[1591]

*The Graduate Record Examinations Advanced Tests: Biology. Grades 16–17; 1939–60; Educational Testing Service. * For the testing program entry, see 1353.

For additional information and a review by Clark W. Horton of Form FGR, see 5:727. For a review of the testing program, see 5:601.

[1592]

Nelson Biology Test. Grades 9–13; 1951–54, c1950–51; Clarence H. Nelson; [Harcourt, Brace & World, Inc.]. *

For additional information, see 5:728; for reviews by Clark W. Horton and Leland P. Johnson, see 4:605.

[1593]

*Semester Test for Biology. 1, 2 semesters high school; 1948–59; formerly called *20th Century Test for Biology;* Benton Review Publishing Co., Inc. *
  For additional information, see 4:599.

[1594]

★Survey Test in Biological Science: California Survey Series. Grades 7–10; 1959; identical with subtest 6 of the advanced level of *California Tests in Social and Related Sciences,* Form AA; Georgia Sachs Adams, William E. Keeley, and John A. Sexson; California Test Bureau. *

[1595]

Williams Biology Test. High school; 1934; John R. Williams and H. E. Schrammel; Bureau of Educational Measurements. *
a) TEST I [STRUCTURAL ANIMAL BIOLOGY].
b) TEST II [HUMAN BIOLOGY].
c) TEST III [PLANT BIOLOGY].
  For additional information and reviews by Clark W. Horton, Victor H. Noll, and Dael L. Wolfle, see 40:1589 (1 reference).

CHEMISTRY

[1596]

*A.C.S. Cooperative Examination in Biochemistry. 1–2 semesters college; 1947–59; Examinations Committee, Division of Chemical Education, American Chemical Society.
  For additional information, see 5:731.

[1597]

*A.C.S. Cooperative Examination in General Chemistry. 1 year college; 1934–60; 4 scores: information, application of principles, quantitative application of principles, total; Examinations Committee, Division of Chemical Education, American Chemical Society. *
  For additional information and reviews by Frank P. Cassaretto and Palmer O. Johnson, see 5:732 (2 references); for a review by Kenneth E. Anderson of earlier forms, see 4:610 (1 reference); for reviews by Sidney J. French and Florence E. Hooper, see 3:557 (3 references); see also 40:1593 (5 references).

[1598]

A.C.S. Cooperative Examination in Physical Chemistry. College; 1946–55; 4 scores: states of matter and solutions, thermodynamics-equilibrium-electrochemistry, structure of matter and kinetics, total; Examinations Committee, Division of Chemical Education, American Chemical Society. *
  For additional information, see 5:734; see also 4:612 (1 reference); for a review by Alfred S. Brown of an earlier form, see 3:559.

[1599]

★A.C.S. Cooperative Examination: Inorganic Chemistry. College; 1961; 3 scores: theory and periodicity, nomenclature and properties, total; Examinations Committee, Division of Chemical Education, American Chemical Society. *

[1600]

*[A.C.S. Cooperative Examinations in Organic Chemistry.] College; 1942–61; earlier tests called *A.C.S. Cooperative Organic Chemistry Test;* Examina-

tions Committee, Division of Chemical Education, American Chemical Society. *
a) A.C.S. COOPERATIVE EXAMINATION IN ORGANIC CHEMISTRY. 2 semesters college; 1953–58.
b) A.C.S. COOPERATIVE EXAMINATION FOR THE BRIEF COURSE IN ORGANIC CHEM-
ISTRY. 1 semester college; 1956–61.
For additional information, see 5:733; for a review by Shailer Peterson of an
earlier form, see 3:558 (1 reference).

[1601]

*[A.C.S. Cooperative Examinations in Qualitative Analysis.] 1–2 semesters
college; 1943–61; Examinations Committee, Division of Chemical Education,
American Chemical Society. *
a) A.C.S. COOPERATIVE EXAMINATION : QUALITATIVE ANALYSIS. 1943–60; formerly
called A.C.S. Cooperative Chemistry Test in Qualitative Analysis; 4 scores:
information-balancing equations, qualitative application of principles, quantitative application of principles, total.
b) A.C.S. COOPERATIVE EXAMINATION : BRIEF QUALITATIVE ANALYSIS. 1961.
c) [QUALITATIVE ANALYSIS SUPPLEMENT FOR GENERAL CHEMISTRY.] See 1624.
For additional information, see 5:730; for a review by William Rieman III
of Forms Y and Z of a, see 4:608 (2 references); for reviews by William B.
Meldrum and William Rieman III of an earlier form, see 3:562.

[1602]

A.C.S. Cooperative Examination in Quantitative Analysis. College; 1944–
57; Examinations Committee, Division of Chemical Education, American Chemical Society. *
For additional information, see 5:735 (1 excerpt); for reviews by William B.
Meldrum and William Rieman III of an earlier form, see 3:563.

[1603]

*A.C.S.-N.S.T.A. Cooperative Examination in High School Chemistry. High
school; 1957–61; Examinations Committee, Division of Chemical Education,
American Chemical Society. *
For additional information and reviews by Edward G. Rietz and Willard G.
Warrington, see 5:729.

[1604]

Anderson Chemistry Test. Grades 11–13; 1951–54, c1950–51; Kenneth E.
Anderson; [Harcourt, Brace & World, Inc.]. *
For additional information and a review by Theo. A. Ashford, see 5:737; for
a review by William Rieman III, see 4:613.

[1605]

*Chemistry: Every Pupil Scholarship Test. High school; 1928–61; new form
usually issued twice a year; Bureau of Educational Measurements. *
For additional information, see 5:739.

[1606]

*Chemistry: Every Pupil Test. 1, 2 semesters high school; 1929–61; new form
usually issued twice a year; Ohio Scholarship Tests. *
For additional information, see 5:740.

[1607]

★Chemistry: Final District-State Scholarship Test. High school; 1938–61; Ohio Scholarship Tests. *

[1608]

*Chemistry, Form 4: Achievement Examinations for Secondary Schools. High school; 1951–59; Forms 1–3 published by Educational Test Bureau are out of print; Harry E. Pulver; C. A. Gregory Co. *

For additional information concerning the earlier forms, see 5:738.

[1609]

*Chemistry: Midwest High School Achievement Examinations. High school; 1955–61; Educational Test Bureau. *

For additional information and a review by Edward G. Rietz of earlier forms, see 5:741.

[1610]

★Chemistry: Preliminary District-State Scholarship Test. High school; 1947–61; Ohio Scholarship Tests. *

[1611]

*Chemistry Test: State High School Tests for Indiana. 1, 2 semesters high school; 1934–59; Ezra A. Miller; State High School Testing Service for Indiana. *

For additional information, see 4:616; for a review by Fred P. Frutchey of an earlier form, see 38:931.

[1612]

*College Entrance Examination Board Achievement Test in Chemistry. Candidates for college entrance; 1901–61; program administered for the College Entrance Examination Board by Educational Testing Service. * For the testing program entry, see 1345.

For additional information and a review by Max D. Engelhart of Form FAC, see 5:742 (2 references); see also 4:617 (4 references).

[1613]

*College Entrance Examination Board Advanced Placement Examination: Chemistry. Candidates desiring credit for college level courses or admission to advanced courses; 1954–61; program administered for the College Entrance Examination Board by Educational Testing Service. * For the testing program entry, see 1346.

For additional information and a review by Theo. A. Ashford of Form FBP, see 5:743.

[1614]

Cooperative Chemistry Test. High school; 1933–50; Paul J. Burke and Joseph F. Castka; Cooperative Test Division. *

For additional information and reviews by Frank P. Cassaretto and Willard G. Warrington, see 5:744; see also 4:618 (4 references); for a review by John H. Daugherty of an earlier form, see 3:561; for reviews by Charles L. Bickel and Louis M. Heil, see 40:1592; for reviews by Edward E. Cureton and W. B. Meldrum, see 38:932.

[1615]

Cooperative Chemistry Test: Educational Records Bureau Edition. High school; 1941–58; Committee on Chemistry Tests of the Educational Records Bureau; Educational Records Bureau. *

For additional information, see 5:745 (1 reference); see also 4:619 (2 references).

[1616]

***Cooperative Objective Unit Tests in Organic Chemistry, 1949-50 Series.** 1, 2 semesters college; 1939–49; 24 tests: 10 first semester and 12 second semester tests on specific topics plus a final examination for each semester; Ed. F. Degering and others; Ed. F. Degering. *

[1617]

***First Year Chemistry: Manchester Semester-End Achievement Tests.** 1, 2 semesters high school; 1934–[46]; Bureau of Tests. *

[1618]

★General Chemistry Test: National Achievement Tests. Grades 10–12 and college; 1958–59; 4 scores: uses-processes-results, formulae and valence, miscellaneous facts, total; Lester D. Crow and Roy S. Cook; Acorn Publishing Co. *

[1619]

***The Graduate Record Examinations Advanced Tests: Chemistry.** Grades 16–17; 1939–59; Educational Testing Service. * For the testing program entry, see 1353.

For additional information, see 5:746. For a review of the testing program, see 5:601.

[1620]

Iowa Placement Examinations: Chemistry Aptitude. Grades 12–13; 1925–44; Bureau of Educational Research and Service. *
a) SERIES CAI, REVISED. 1925–26; G. D. Stoddard and Jacob Cornog.
b) NEW SERIES CA2, REVISED. 1925–44; G. D. Stoddard, Jacob Cornog, and D. B. Stuit.

For additional information and a review by Kenneth E. Anderson, see 4:621 (5 references); for a review by Theodore A. Ashford, see 3:566 (15 references).

[1621]

Iowa Placement Examinations: Chemistry Training: Series CT1, Revised. Grades 12–13; 1925–26; G. D. Stoddard and J. Cornog; Bureau of Educational Research and Service. *

For additional information and a review by Kenneth E. Anderson, see 4:622 (1 reference); for a review by Theodore A. Ashford, see 3:567 (14 references).

[1622]

A Junior Chemistry Test. 2 years secondary school; 1957; C. M. Goldburg; University of Queensland Press. *

For additional information and reviews by Roy W. Stanhope and Mervyn L. Turner, see 5:747.

[1623]

Kirkpatrick Chemistry Test. 1, 2 semesters high school; 1940–41; Ernest L. Kirkpatrick and H. E. Schrammel; Bureau of Educational Measurements. *

For additional information and a review by Theodore A. Ashford, see 3:568 (1 reference).

[1624]

Qualitative Analysis Supplement for General Chemistry. 1–2 semesters college; 1953; identical with Part 1 of *A.C.S. Cooperative Chemistry Test in Qualitative Analysis,* Form H (see 1601); Examinations Committee, Division of Chemical Education, American Chemical Society. *

For additional information and reviews by Frank P. Cassaretto and Palmer O. Johnson of the complete test, see 5:732 (2 references).

[1625]

★Toledo Chemistry Placement Examination. College entrants with 1 year high school chemistry and algebra; 1959; 7 scores: arithmetic and algebra, general knowledge, formulas and nomenclature, equations, algebraic formulations, chemical problems, total; Nelson W. Hovey and Albertine Krohn; distributed by Research Foundation, University of Toledo. *

MISCELLANEOUS

[1626]

★The Facts About Science Test: Experimental Form for Research in Testing. High school; 1958; 3 scores: understanding of science as an institution, knowledge of scientists as an occupational group, total; for research use only; Glen Stice and others; Educational Testing Service. *

[1627]

*The Graduate Record Examinations Advanced Tests: Geology. Grades 16–17; 1939–60; Educational Testing Service. * For the testing program entry, see 1353.

For additional information, see 5:748. For a review of the testing program, see 5:601.

[1628]

Measurement of Observation and Understanding of Physical Phenomena and Life Processes. Grades 9–10; 1952; Annette M. Wright and Hugh B. Wood; [Curriculum Bulletin]. *

For additional information, see 4:631.

PHYSICS

[1629]

★College Entrance Examination Board Achievement Test in PSSC Physics. Candidates for college entrance who have completed or are enrolled in the physics course prepared by the Physical Science Study Committee; 1961; program administered for the College Entrance Examination Board by Educational Testing Service. * For the testing program entry, see 1345.

[1630]

*College Entrance Examination Board Achievement Test in Physics. Candidates for college entrance; 1901–61; program administered for the College Entrance Examination Board by Educational Testing Service. * For the testing program entry, see 1345.

For additional information and a review by Theodore G. Phillips of Form FAC, see 5:749 (2 references) ; for a review by Palmer O. Johnson of earlier forms, see 4:633 (3 references).

[1631]

*College Entrance Examination Board Advanced Placement Examination: Physics. Candidates desiring credit for college level courses or admission to advanced courses; 1954–61; program administered for the College Entrance Examination Board by Educational Testing Service. * For the testing program entry, see 1346.

For additional information and a review by Leo Nedelsky of Form FBP, see 5:750.

[1632]

Cooperative Physics Test. High school; 1932–51; Paul J. Burke and others; Cooperative Test Division. *

For additional information and a review by Theodore G. Phillips, see 5:751 (1 reference) ; see also 4:634 (2 references) ; for a review by G. P. Cahoon of earlier forms, see 3:581 ; for reviews by Andrew Longacre, Alvin W. Schindler, and Ralph K. Watkins, see 40:1608 ; for reviews by Ernest E. Bayles and A. W. Hurd, see 38:1088.

[1633]

Cooperative Physics Test: Educational Records Bureau Edition. High school; 1941–58; Committee on Physics Tests of the Educational Records Bureau; Educational Records Bureau. *

For additional information, see 5:752 (1 reference) ; see also 4:635 (2 references).

[1634]

Dunning Physics Test. Grades 11–13; 1951–54, c1950–54; Gordon M. Dunning; [Harcourt, Brace & World, Inc.]. *

For additional information and a review by Robert M. W. Travers, see 5:753 ; for a review by G. P. Cahoon, see 4:636.

[1635]

Fulmer-Schrammel Physics Test. High school; 1934; V. G. Fulmer and H. E. Schrammel; Bureau of Educational Measurements. *
a) TEST I [MECHANICS].
b) TEST II [HEAT, MAGNETISM, ELECTRICITY, AND SOUND].

For additional information and reviews by Palmer O. Johnson and Alvin W. Schindler, see 40:1610.

[1636]

★General Physics Test: National Achievement Tests. Grades 10–12 and college; 1958; Lester D. Crow and Roy S. Cook; Acorn Publishing Co. *

[1637]

*The Graduate Record Examinations Advanced Tests: Physics. Grades 16–
17; 1939–60; Educational Testing Service. * For the testing program entry,
see 1353.

For additional information and a review by Leo Nedelsky of Form FGR, see
5:754. For a review of the testing program, see 5:601.

[1638]

Iowa Placement Examinations: Physics Aptitude. Grades 12–13; 1925–44;
Bureau of Educational Research and Service. *
a) SERIES PAI, REVISED. 1925–26; G. D. Stoddard and C. J. Lapp.
b) NEW SERIES PA-2, REVISED. 1925–44; G. D. Stoddard, C. J. Lapp, and D. B.
Stuit.

For additional information and a review by John W. French, see 4:638 (2
references) ; for a review by Robert M. W. Travers, see 3:587 (4 references).

[1639]

Iowa Placement Examinations: Physics Training: Series PT1, Revised.
Grades 12–13; 1925–26; C. J. Lapp and G. D. Stoddard; Bureau of Educational
Research and Service. *

For additional information and a review by G. P. Cahoon, see 4:639 (2 references).

[1640]

A Junior Physics Test. 2 years secondary school; 1956; R. A. Squire; University of Queensland Press. *

For additional information and reviews by Roy W. Stanhope and Mervyn L.
Turner, see 5:755.

[1641]

*Physics: Every Pupil Scholarship Test. High school; 1926–61; new form
usually issued twice a year; Bureau of Educational Measurements. *

For additional information, see 5:757.

[1642]

*Physics: Every Pupil Test. 1, 2 semesters high school; 1929–61; new form
usually issued twice a year; Ohio Scholarship Tests. *

For additional information, see 5:758.

[1643]

★Physics: Final District-State Scholarship Test. High school; 1938–61; Ohio
Scholarship Tests. *

[1644]

*Physics, Form 4: Achievement Examinations for Secondary Schools. High
school; 1951–59; Forms 1–3 published by Educational Test Bureau are out of
print; Clarence H. Boeck; C. A. Gregory Co. *

For additional information concerning the earlier forms, see 5:756.

[1645]

*Physics: Manchester Semester-End Achievement Tests. 1, 2 semesters
high school; 1934–[50]; Bureau of Tests. *

[1646]

*Physics: Midwest High School Achievement Examinations. High school; 1955–61; Educational Test Bureau. *

For additional information, see 5:759.

[1647]

★Physics: Preliminary District-State Scholarship Test. High school; 1947–61; Ohio Scholarship Tests. *

[1648]

*Physics Test: State High School Tests for Indiana. 1, 2 semesters high school; 1934–59; James F. Mackell; State High School Testing Service for Indiana. *

For additional information, see 4:642; for a review by A. W. Hurd of an earlier form, see 38:1092.

[1649]

★Tests of the Physical Science Study Committee. High school students taking the physics course developed by the Physical Science Study Committee; 1959; 10 tests: 8 tests listed below plus a comprehensive test on each half of the course; Frederick L. Ferris, Jr., Sherman Frankel, Walter C. Michels, and Thomas H. Wood; Cooperative Test Division. *

a) TEST 1: SPACE, TIME, AND MOTION.
b) TEST 2: MASS AND MATTER.
c) TEST 3: THE BEHAVIOR OF LIGHT.
d) TEST 4: LIGHT AND WAVE MOTION.
e) TEST 6: FORCE AND MOMENTUM.
f) TEST 7: ENERGY.
g) TEST 8: ELECTRICITY AND MAGNETISM.
h) TEST 9: THE ATOM.

[1650]

20th Century Test for Physics. 1, 2 semesters high school; 1949; Benton Review Publishing Co., Inc. *

For additional information, see 4:643.

SENSORY-MOTOR

[1651]

Harris Tests of Lateral Dominance. Ages 7 and over; 1947–58; Albert J. Harris; distributed by Psychological Corporation. *

For additional information, see 5:761 (1 reference); for reviews by William G. Peacher and Miles A. Tinker of an earlier edition, see 4:644; see also 3:466 (1 excerpt).

[1652]

★Leavell Hand-Eye Coordinator Tests. Ages 8–14; 1958; Ullin W. Leavell; Keystone View Co. *

[1653]

Moore Eye-Hand Coordination and Color-Matching Test. Ages 2–6, 7 and over; 1949–55; Joseph E. Moore; Joseph E. Moore and Associates. *

a) THE MOORE EYE-HAND COORDINATION TEST: PRE-SCHOOL FORM. Ages 2–6.

b) MOORE EYE-HAND COORDINATION AND COLOR-MATCHING TEST. Ages 7 and over; 2 scores: eye-hand coordination, color matching.

For additional information, see 5:872 (1 reference); for reviews by Norman Frederiksen and Jay L. Otis, see 4:750 (6 references).

[1654]

Pre-Tests of Vision, Hearing, and Motor Coordination. Grades kgn–1, 1–3, 4–8, 7–10, 9–12 and adults; 1936–51; formerly a part of *California Test of Mental Maturity;* Elizabeth T. Sullivan, Willis W. Clark, and Ernest W. Tiegs; California Test Bureau. *

For additional information, see 4:645.

HEARING

[1655]

★**Ambco Audiometers.** Ages 6 and over; 1954–61; Ambco, Inc. *
a) OTOMETER, MODEL 600. [1954]; for screening and threshold testing.
b) OTO-CHEK AUDITORY SCREENER, MODELS 700 and 800. [1956]; for single- and two-frequency screening; Howard P. House and Aram Glorig.
c) DIAGNOSTIC AUDIOMETER, MODEL 1150. [1958].
d) SPEECH AUDIOMETER, MODEL A-17. [1958]; for live and recorded voice testing.
e) SCREENING AUDIOMETERS, MODELS 1122 AND 1135. [1960–61].

[1656]

★**Ambco Speech Test Record.** Ages 3 and over; [1958]; for use with a speech audiometer for testing speech reception thresholds and discrimination; Ambco, Inc. *

[1657]

★**Auditory Discrimination Test.** Ages 5–8; 1958; Joseph M. Wepman; [Language Research Associates.]. *

[1658]

*****Auditory Tests.** Grades 2 and over; 1951; recorded adaptation of *Auditory Test No. 9* developed by Harvard University Psycho-Acoustic Laboratory; Central Institute for the Deaf; Technisonic Studios, Inc. *
a) AUDITORY TESTS W-1 AND W-2: SPONDAIC WORD LISTS. Auditory threshold for speech.
b) AUDITORY TEST W-22: PHONETICALLY-BALANCED WORD LISTS. Auditory discrimination for speech at levels above threshold.

For additional information, see 4:646.

[1659]

*****Maico Audiometers.** Grades kgn and over; 1949–59; Maico Electronics, Inc. *
a) PROFESSIONAL AUDIOMETER, MODEL H-1B. 1950.
b) PORTABLE AUDIOMETER, MODEL MA-2. 1956.
c) OFFICE AUDIOMETER, MODEL MA-5. 1958.
d) TWO-TONE HEARING CHECK, MODEL MA-7. 1959.
e) HEARING EVALUATOR, MODEL MA-8. 1959–60.

For additional information, see 5:763 (4 references).

[1660]

★**Maico Hearing Impairment Calculator.** 1959; for calculating percentage of single-ear or binaural impairment; Maico Electronics, Inc. *

[1661]

The Massachusetts Hearing Test. Grades 1–16 and adults; 1948; method of group screening using prescribed forms of scoring, signal presentation, and calibration with any pure tone audiometer; method of testing and instructions for scoring and interpretation are presented in *J Acoust Soc Am* 20:697–703 S '48; Philip W. Johnston; standardized instructions for administering available from Massachusetts Department of Public Health, Division of Maternal and Child Health Services. *

[1662]

★**Metricon Decibel Meter.** Hard of hearing subjects; 1958–60; 3 ratings for hearing aid specifications: most comfortable loudness, best audible pressure, maximum tolerable pressure; Vicon Instrument Co. *

[1663]

★**Pressurelog Hearing Chart.** 1959; for converting readings of any pure tone threshold audiometer from relative to real pressures; John A. Victoreen; Vicon Instrument Co. *

[1664]

Robbins Speech Sound Discrimination and Verbal Imagery Type Tests. Ages 4–8, 8 and over; 1948–58; Samuel D. Robbins and Rosa Seymour Robbins; Expression Co. *

a) VERBAL IMAGERY TYPE TEST FOR YOUNG CHILDREN. Ages 4–8; 1948–58.

b) PICTURE SPEECH SOUND DISCRIMINATION TEST FOR YOUNG CHILDREN. Ages 4–8; 1948–58.

c) SPEECH SOUND DISCRIMINATION TESTS FOR OLDER CHILDREN. Ages 8 and over; 1948.

For additional information, see 5:764.

[1665]

★[Rush Hughes (PB 50): Phonetically Balanced Lists 5–12.] Grades 2 and over; 1951; Technisonic Studios, Inc. *

[1666]

Sonotone Pure-Tone Audiometers. Ages 6 and over; 1941–57; Sonotone Corporation. *

a) MODELS 91M AND 91B. For use by physicians.

b) MODELS 91D AND 91S. For schools and industry.

For additional information, see 5:765; for an earlier model, see 4:648 (1 reference).

[1667]

★**Stycar Hearing Tests.** Ages 6–14 months, 14–18 months, 18–24 months, 2, 3–4, 5–7; 1958–59; Mary D. Sheridan; distributed by National Foundation for Educational Research in England and Wales. *

MOTOR

[1668]

Edmiston Motor Capacity Test. Grades 1–12 and adults; 1948; R. W. Edmiston; the Author. *

a) HAND-EYE COORDINATION. Grades 1–12.

b) ESTIMATE OF DISTANCE. Grades 7–12 and adults.
c) EYE COORDINATION AND JUDGMENT, 1. Grades 7–12 and adults.
d) EYE COORDINATION AND JUDGMENT, 2. Grades 7–12 and adults.
   For additional information, see 4:649.

[1669]

The Lincoln-Oseretsky Motor Development Scale. Ages 6–14; 1948–56; revision of *Oseretsky Tests of Motor Proficiency* (see 1670); William Sloan; C. H. Stoelting Co. *
   For additional information and a review by Anna Espenschade, see 5:767 (10 references).

[1670]

Oseretsky Tests of Motor Proficiency: A Translation From the Portuguese Adaptation. Ages 4–16; 1946; original test by N. Oseretsky published in Russian in 1923; Portuguese adaptation by Maria Irene Leite da Costa published in 1943; English translation by Elizabeth Joan Fosa; Educational Test Bureau. * For the revised edition entry, see 1669.
   For additional information and a review by Anna Espenschade, see 4:650 (10 references); for an excerpt from a related review, see 4:651; see also 3:472 (6 references, 1 excerpt).

[1671]

Perrin Motor Coordination Test. Adults; [1921]; F. A. C. Perrin; C. H. Stoelting Co. *

[1672]

The Rail-Walking Test. Ages 5 and over; 1941–44; locomotor coordination and general motor control; specifications for making rails and directions for administration, scoring, and interpretation are presented in *Am J Psychol* 57:482–99 O '44; S. Roy Heath, Jr.; norms may be obtained from the Author. *
   For additional information and a review by William Sloan, see 4:652.

[1673]

Smedley Hand Dynamometer. Ages 6–18; [1920(?)–53]; strength of grip; F. Smedley; C. H. Stoelting Co. *

[1674]

[Steadiness Tests.] Ages 9–14; various titles used by the manufacturers.
a) STEADINESS TESTER. [1946]; Lafayette Instrument Co. *
b) NINE-HOLE STEADINESS TEST. [1927?]; Marietta Apparatus Co. *
c) STEADINESS TEST. "About 1921"; C. H. Stoelting Co.

[1675]

★**Trankell's Laterality Tests: A Battery of Diagnostic Tests for the Determination of Degree of Left-Hand Preference and Asymmetry of Motor Skill.** Left-handed children in grades 1–2; [1951]; 3 tests; Arne Trankell; Skandinaviska Testförlaget AB. *
a) IMPULSE SCALE. 3 scores: hand, foot, eye.
b) TAPPING. 3 scores: right, left, asymmetri index.
c) TRACING. 3 scores: same as for *b* above.

[1676]

[Whipple Tapping Apparatus.] Various titles used by the manufacturers; [G. M. Whipple].
a) TAPPING BOARD. Ages 8 and over; [1946]; Lafayette Instrument Co. *
b) TAPPING TEST. Ages 8 and over; [1927]; Marietta Apparatus Co. *
c) WHIPPLE TAPPING BOARD. Ages 10 and over; date unknown; C. H. Stoelting Co.

VISION

[1677]

A-B-C Vision Test for Ocular Dominance. Ages 5 or 6 and over; 1927–46; Walter R. Miles; Psychological Corporation. *
For additional information and a review by Miles A. Tinker, see 4:654; see also 3:459 (5 references).

[1678]

AO H-R-R Pseudoisochromatic Plates, Second Edition. Ages 4 and over; 1940–57; formerly called *Pseudo-Isochromatic Plates for Testing Color Vision;* LeGrand H. Hardy, Gertrude Rand, and M. Catherine Rittler; American Optical Co. *
For additional information, see 5:768 (11 references); see also 4:661 (8 references) and 3:473 (9 references, 1 excerpt).

[1679]

AO School Vision Screening Test. Grades kgn–12; 1955; modification of *Massachusetts Vision Test* (see 1695); Massachusetts Department of Public Health, Hollis M. Leverett, and Evelyn A. Backer; American Optical Co. *
For additional information, see 5:769 (4 references).

[1680]

AO Sight Screener. Adults; 1945–56; American Optical Co. *
For additional information, see 5:770 (8 references); for reviews by Henry A. Imus and F. Nowell Jones, see 3:460 (7 references).

[1681]

Burnham-Clark-Munsell Color Memory Test. Adults; 1955–56; also called *Test of Hue Memory;* Robert W. Burnham and Joyce R. Clark; Munsell Color Co., Inc. *
For additional information, see 5:771 (1 reference).

[1682]

The Color Aptitude Test. Ages 16 and over; 1952; Walter A. Woods; Industrial Psychological Laboratory. *
For additional information, see 5:772.

[1683]

★Dvorine Animated Fusion Training Charts. Ages 5 and over; 1934–51; Israel Dvorine; Scientific Publishing Co. *

[1684]

Dvorine Pseudo-Isochromatic Plates, Second Edition. Ages 3 and over; 1944–55; revision of *Dvorine Color Perception Testing Charts;* Israel Dvorine;

Scientific Publishing Co. (Record blanks available from Western Psychological Services.) *

For additional information, see 5:773 (13 references, 3 excerpts); for the original edition, see 3:462 (4 references, 6 excerpts).

[1685]

Eames Eye Test. Grades kgn–16 and adults; 1938–50; Thomas H. Eames; [Harcourt, Brace & World, Inc.]. *

For additional information and a review by Magdalen D. Vernon, see 5:774 (2 references); see also 3:463 (5 references).

[1686]

★**Eye Movement Camera.** Ages 10 and over; [1950]; [Herman F. Brandt]; C. H. Stoelting Co. *

[1687]

Farnsworth Dichotomous Test for Color Blindness: Panel D–15. Ages 12 and over; 1947; Dean Farnsworth; Psychological Corporation. *

For additional information and a review by Elsie Murray, see 4:656 (2 references); see also 3:464 (1 excerpt).

[1688]

The Farnsworth-Munsell 100-Hue Test for the Examination of Color Discrimination. Mental ages 12 and over; 1942–57; Dean Farnsworth; Munsell Color Co., Inc. *

For additional information, see 5:775 (1 reference); for a review by Elsie Murray, see 4:657 (2 references).

[1689]

Freeman Acuity-Tester. Ages 4 and over; 1954; instrument for testing vision to screen for professional eye examination; Ellis Freeman; Freeman Technical Associates. *

For additional information, see 5:776.

[1690]

Freeman Protometer. Ages 6 and over; 1952; instrument for testing vision for screening for professional eye examination; Ellis Freeman; Freeman Technical Associates. *

For additional information, see 5:777.

[1691]

The Illuminant-Stable Color Vision Test, Second Edition. Ages 4 and over; 1949–54; Ellis Freeman; Freeman Technical Associates. *

For additional information, see 5:778 (2 references); for a review by Elsie Murray of the original edition, see 4:659 (2 references).

[1692]

Inter-Society Color Council Color Aptitude Test, 1953 Edition. Adults; 1944–53; Color Aptitude Test Committee, Inter-Society Color Council; Federation of Societies for Paint Technology. *

For additional information, see 5:779 (5 references).

[1693]

★**Keystone Tests of Binocular Skill: An Adaptation to the Keystone Telebinocular of the Oral Reading Check Tests.** Grades 1–2, 2–4, 4–6, 6 and over;

1938–49; based on the *Standardized Oral Reading Check Tests* (see 1490) by William S. Gray; Keystone View Co. *

[1694]

[Keystone Visual Tests.] Ages 5 and over; 1933–58; all tests involve the use of a *Keystone Telebinocular* or the *Keystone Periometer;* Keystone View Co. *
a) KEYSTONE VISUAL SURVEY SERVICE FOR SCHOOLS AND COLLEGES. 1933–58; originally called *Betts Ready to Read Tests.*
b) KEYSTONE OCCUPATIONAL VISUAL SERVICE. 1935–52.
c) KEYSTONE DRIVER VISION SERVICE. 1950.
    For additional information, see 5:780 (18 references); for a review by F. Nowell Jones of the *Keystone Occupational Telebinocular,* see 3:467 (43 references, 1 excerpt); for reviews by I. H. Anderson, David Kopel, Marion Monroe Cox, and Guy Wagner of the *Betts Ready to Read Tests,* see 38:1097.

[1695]

Massachusetts Vision Test. Grades kgn–16; 1942–54; Massachusetts Department of Public Health; Welch Allyn, Inc. *
    For additional information, see 5:781 (14 references); see also 3:468 (5 references, 1 excerpt).

[1696]

New Test for the Detection of Colorblindness. 1941; P. B. Wiltberger; Long's College Book Co. *
    For additional information, see 3:469 (2 excerpts).

[1697]

New York School Vision Tester. Grades kgn and over; 1957; Bausch & Lomb Inc. *
    For additional information, see 5:782 (1 reference).

[1698]

Ortho-Rater. Adults; 1942–58; 12 scores for each model: binocular action of the eyes (4 tests), fineness of visual discrimination (6 tests), perception of depth, color discrimination; Bausch & Lomb Inc. *
a) MASTER ORTHO-RATER. 1942–58.
b) MODIFIED ORTHO-RATER. 1952–58.
    For additional information, see 5:783 (59 references); for reviews by Henry A. Imus and F. Nowell Jones, see 3:471 (30 references).

[1699]

*Perceptual Forms Test. Ages 6–8.5; 1955–60; revision of *Children's Perceptual Achievement Forms;* visual development; Eyesight Conservation Committee, Winter Haven Lions Club; Winter Haven Lions Research Foundation, Inc.
    For additional information concerning the earlier edition, see 5:760.

[1700]

Spache Binocular Reading Test. Nonreaders and grade 1, grades 1.5–2, grades 3 and over; 1943–55; George D. Spache; Keystone View Co. *
    For additional information, see 5:784 (4 references); for a review by Albert J. Harris of the upper level, see 3:461 (4 references).

[1701]

★Stycar Vision Test. Ages 3–5, 5–7; 1960; Mary D. Sheridan; distributed by National Foundation for Educational Research in England and Wales. *

[1702]

★T/O Vision Testers. Ages 3–5 and retarded children, grades 1–6, 7–12 and adults; 1958–[60]; Titmus Optical Co., Inc. *
a) T/O SCHOOL VISION TESTER. Acuity.
  1) *Michigan Pre-School T/O Vision Tests.* Ages 3–5 and retarded children; [1960].
  2) [*School Vision Tests.*] Grades 1–6; 1958; modification of *Massachusetts Vision Test* (see 1695).
b) T/O PROFESSIONAL VISION TESTER. Grades 7–12 and adults; 1959; 11 tests: acuity (6 tests), stereopsis, color discrimination, vertical phoria, lateral phoria (2 tests).

[1703]

★Test for Colour-Blindness. Ages 6 and over; ["early 1930's"–1960?]; Shinobu Ishihara; distributed by H. K. Lewis & Co. Ltd. *

[1704]

Test of Color Blindness. 1944; short form of *New Test for the Detection of Colorblindness* (see 1696); P. B. Wiltberger; Long's College Book Co. *

[1705]

Visual Reaction Timer. Adults; [1946]; C. H. Stoelting Co. *

SOCIAL STUDIES

[1706]

American History—Government—Problems of Democracy: Acorn Achievement Tests. Grades 9–16; 1942–53; 6 scores: growth of a national spirit, growth of democracy, the Constitution, foreign policy, problems of American democracy, total; Vincent McGarrett; Acorn Publishing Co. *
  For additional information and a review by Richard E. Gross, see 5:785; for a review by Howard R. Anderson, see 3:590.

[1707]

American School Achievement Tests: Part 4, Social Studies and Science. Grades 4–6, 7–9; 1941–58; 2 scores: social studies, science; Willis E. Pratt and Clara Cockerille; Public School Publishing Co. * For the complete battery entry and references to reviews, see 2.

[1708]

★Citizenship: Every Pupil Scholarship Test. Grades 8–9; 1951–57; Bureau of Educational Measurements. *

[1709]

*College Entrance Examination Board Achievement Test in Social Studies. Candidates for college entrance; 1937–61; program administered for the College

Entrance Examination Board by Educational Testing Service. * For the testing program entry, see 1345.

For additional information and a review by Ralph W. Tyler of Form FAC, see 5:786 (3 references); for a review by Robert L. Thorndike of an earlier form, see 4:662 (6 references).

[1710]

Cooperative General Achievement Tests: Test 1, Social Studies. Grade 12 and college entrants; 1937–56; formerly called *A Test of General Proficiency in the Field of Social Studies;* Jeanne M. Bradford and Elaine Forsyth Cook; Cooperative Test Division. * For the complete battery entry, see 8.

For additional information, see 5:787; see also 4:668 (3 references); for a review by Harry D. Berg of earlier forms, see 3:596. For reviews of the complete battery, see 5:6, 4:5, and 3:3.

[1711]

Cooperative Social Studies Test for Grades 7, 8, and 9. Grades 7–9; 1941–51; Harry Berg, Elaine Forsyth Cook, and Eunice Ann Lloyd; Cooperative Test Division. *

For additional information and a review by Hilda Taba, see 4:663; for reviews by Robert A. Davis and Edgar B. Wesley of earlier forms, see 3:592.

[1712]

The Greig Social Studies Test. Grades 6–8; 1957; for Catholic schools; Mary E. Greig; Scholastic Testing Service, Inc. *

For additional information and a review by David R. Krathwohl, see 5:788.

[1713]

History and Civics Test: Municipal Tests: National Achievement Tests. Grades 3–6, 6–8; 1938–55; subtest of *Municipal Battery* (see 29); 3 scores: lessons of history, historical facts, total; Robert K. Speer and Samuel Smith; Acorn Publishing Co. *

For additional information and a review by Howard R. Anderson, see 5:790; for a review by Harry D. Berg, see 4:664. For reviews of the complete battery, see 5:18, 4:20, and 40:1191.

[1714]

*Introduction to Social Studies, Form 4: Achievement Examinations for Secondary Schools. High school; 1951–59; Forms 1–3 published by Educational Test Bureau are out of print; Kenneth D. Seeling; C. A. Gregory Co. *

For additional information concerning earlier forms, see 5:789.

[1715]

*The Iowa Tests of Educational Development: Test 1, Understanding of Basic Social Concepts. Grades 9–13; 1942–59; E. F. Lindquist and others; Science Research Associates, Inc. * For the complete battery entry, see 25.

For additional information, see 5:791. For reviews of the complete battery, see 5:17, 4:17, and 3:12.

[1716]

*Metropolitan Achievement Tests: [Social Studies, 1960 Edition]. Grades 5–6, 7–9; 1932–60; 2 scores: information, study skills; Walter N. Durost, Harold H. Bixler, Gertrude H. Hildreth, Kenneth W. Lund, and J. Wayne Wrightstone; [Harcourt, Brace & World, Inc.]. * For the complete battery entry, see 27.

[1717]

★Senior Social Studies: Final District-State Scholarship Test. High school; 1938–61; Ohio Scholarship Tests. *

[1718]

★Senior Social Studies: Preliminary District-State Scholarship Test. High school; 1947–61; Ohio Scholarship Tests. *

[1719]

*Sequential Tests of Educational Progress: Social Studies. Grades 4–6, 7–9, 10–12, 13–14; 1956–59; Cooperative Test Division. * For the complete battery entry, see 39.
For additional information and reviews by Richard E. Gross, S. A. Rayner, and Ralph W. Tyler, see 5:792. For reviews of the complete battery, see 5:24.

[1720]

Shearer Social Studies Test. Grades 7–9; 1952; Lois Shearer; Bureau of Educational Measurements. *
For additional information and a review by Raymond C. Norris, see 5:793 (1 reference).

[1721]

*Social Studies: Every Pupil Scholarship Test. Grades 7–8; 1935–61; new form usually issued twice a year; Bureau of Educational Measurements. *
For additional information, see 5:794.

[1722]

★Social Studies IX: Midwest High School Achievement Examinations. Grade 9; 1961; Educational Test Bureau. *

[1723]

*Social Studies XII: Midwest High School Achievement Examinations. Grade 12; 1955–61; Educational Test Bureau. *
For additional information concerning earlier forms, see 5:795.

[1724]

Social Studies Test: Acorn National Achievement Tests. Grades 7–9; 1946–50; 5 scores: human relations and life situations, products and places, social ideas and facts, application of knowledge, total; Lester D. Crow and Everett F. Augspurger; Acorn Publishing Co. *
For additional information and a review by Edgar B. Wesley, see 4:666.

[1725]

Social Studies Test: National Achievement Tests. Grades 4–6, 7–9; 1937–57; Robert K. Speer and Samuel Smith; Acorn Publishing Co. *
a) GRADES 4–6. 6 scores: human relations, life situations, social problems, products and peoples, meaning of events, total.
b) GRADES 7–9. 7 scores: human relations, life situations, social interpretations, values of products, social ideas, miscellaneous facts, total.
For additional information, see 5:798; for a review by Ray G. Wood, see 3:594.

[1726]

*Social Studies: National Teacher Examinations. College seniors and teachers; 1940–60; Educational Testing Service. * For the testing program entry, see 1192.

For additional information, see 5:796. For reviews of the testing program, see 5:538 and 4:802.

[1727]

Social Studies: Teacher Education Examination Program. College seniors preparing to teach secondary school; 1957; Educational Testing Service. * For the testing program entry, see 1205.

For additional information, see 5:797. For a review of the testing program, see 5:543.

[1728]

Stanford Achievement Test: Intermediate and Advanced Social Studies Test. Grades 5–9; 1940–54; items identical with those in social studies sections of *Stanford Achievement Test* (see 42); Truman L. Kelley, Richard Madden, Eric F. Gardner, Lewis M. Terman, and Giles M. Ruch; [Harcourt, Brace & World, Inc.]. *

For additional information and a review by Harry D. Berg, see 5:799; for a review by Ray G. Wood of the previous edition, see 3:595. For reviews of the complete battery, see 5:25, 4:25, and 3:18.

CONTEMPORARY AFFAIRS

[1729]

*Contemporary Affairs: Every Pupil Test. 1 semester in grades 7–12, 2 semesters in grades 11–12; 1939–61; new form usually issued twice a year; Ohio Scholarship Tests. *

For additional information, see 5:5.

[1730]

*Current Affairs: Every Pupil Scholarship Test. High school; 1935–61; new form usually issued twice a year; Bureau of Educational Measurements. *

For additional information, see 5:8.

[1731]

*Current Affairs Test. Grades 9–12 and adults; 1935–61; new test usually issued twice a year; Time, Inc. *

[1732]

★New York Times Current Affairs Test. High school; 1947–61; issued monthly during school year as part of School Service Program; New York Times. *

[1733]

★New York Times Current Affairs Test for Colleges. College; 1947–61; issued monthly during school year as part of School Service Program; New York Times. *

[1734]

★Newsweek Current News Test. Grades 9–12; 1951–60; new test usually issued twice a year; Newsweek Educational Division. *

[1735]

★Newsweek NewsQuiz. Grades 9–12; 1951–61; formerly called *Newsweek Monthly Objective Test;* new test issued monthly during school year; Newsweek Educational Division. *

ECONOMICS

[1736]

Economics Test: State High School Tests for Indiana. High school; 1934–50; Richard H. Gemmecke; State High School Testing Service for Indiana. *
  For additional information, see 4:670.

[1737]

*The Graduate Record Examinations Advanced Tests: Economics. Grades 16–17; 1939–60; Educational Testing Service. * For the testing program entry, see 1353.
  For additional information, see 5:800. For a review of the testing program, see 5:601.

[1738]

*High School Economics: Manchester Semester-End Achievement Tests. 1 semester high school; [1934–46]; Bureau of Tests. *

[1739]

Hills Economics Test. High school and college; 1940; John R. Hills and H. E. Schrammel; Bureau of Educational Measurements. *
  For additional information, see 4:673.

[1740]

★A Standard Achievement Test in Economic Understanding for Secondary Schools, Sixth Revision. High school; 1954–57; E. C. Alft and the Illinois Council on Economic Education; Joint Council on Economic Education. *

GEOGRAPHY

[1741]

Coordinated Scales of Attainment: Geography. Grades 6, 7, 8; 1946–54; Mendel E. Branom; Educational Test Bureau. * For the complete battery entry, see 10.
  For additional information, see 5:801. For reviews of the complete battery, see 4:8 and 3:6.

[1742]

*Economic Geography, Form 4: Achievement Examinations for Secondary Schools. High school; 1951–59; Forms 1–3 published by Educational Test Bureau are out of print; Helen Haberman; C. A. Gregory Co. *
  For additional information concerning earlier forms, see 5:802.

[1743]

*Economic Geography: Midwest High School Achievement Examinations. High school; 1952–61; Educational Test Bureau. *
  For additional information concerning earlier forms. see 5:803.

[1744]

Emporia Geography Test. Grades 4–7; 1937; H. E. Schrammel, E. J. Calkins, Harold Bechtoldt, Forrest Frease, and LaVerna Wharton; Bureau of Educational Measurements. *

For additional information and reviews by Edwin H. Reeder and Agatha Townsend, see 3:598.

[1745]

*Geography: Every Pupil Scholarship Test.** Grades 5–7; 1933–61; new form usually issued twice a year; Bureau of Educational Measurements. *

For additional information, see 5:804.

[1746]

*Geography: Every Pupil Test.** 1, 2 semesters in grades 4, 5, 6, 7; 1935–61; new form usually issued twice a year; Ohio Scholarship Tests. *

For additional information, see 5:805.

[1747]

Geography Test: Municipal Tests: National Achievement Tests. Grades 3–6, 6–8; 1938–52; subtest of *Municipal Battery* (see 29); 3 scores: geographical ideas and comparisons, miscellaneous facts, total; Robert K. Speer and Samuel Smith; Acorn Publishing Co. *

For additional information, see 5:806; for a review by Edwin H. Reeder, see 4:676. For reviews of the complete battery, see 5:18, 4:20, and 40:1191.

[1748]

Geography Test: National Achievement Tests. Grades 6–8; 1938–49; 6 scores: geographical ideas, locating products, uses of products and instruments, economic and human relations, miscellaneous problems, total; Robert K. Speer, Lester D. Crow, and Samuel Smith; Acorn Publishing Co. *

For additional information, see 4:677; for a review by Elaine Forsyth [Cook], see 3:600.

[1749]

★Physical Geography: Every Pupil Scholarship Test.** High school; 1943; Bureau of Educational Measurements. *

[1750]

★Survey Test in Geography: California Survey Series.** Grades 7–9; 1959; identical with subtest 3 of the elementary level of *California Tests in Social and Related Sciences,* Form AA; Georgia Sachs Adams and John A. Sexson; California Test Bureau. *

[1751]

Tate Economic Geography Test. Grades 9–16; 1940–41; Donald J. Tate; Bureau of Educational Measurements. *

For additional information and a review by Marguerite Uttley, see 3:601.

[1752]

★World Geography: Every Pupil Scholarship Test.** High school; 1952–59; Bureau of Educational Measurements. *

HISTORY

[1753]

*American History: Every Pupil Scholarship Test. High school; 1926–61; new form usually issued twice a year; Bureau of Educational Measurements. *
  For additional information, see 5:808.

[1754]

*American History: Every Pupil Test. 1, 2 semesters in grades 7–8, 11–12; 1931–61; new form usually issued twice a year; Ohio Scholarship Tests. *
  For additional information, see 5:809.

[1755]

★American History: Final District-State Scholarship Test. High school; 1938–61; Ohio Scholarship Tests. *

[1756]

*American History, Form 4: Achievement Examinations for Secondary Schools. High school; 1951–59; Forms 1–3 published by Educational Test Bureau are out of print; M. J. Haggerty; C. A. Gregory Co. *
  For additional information concerning earlier forms, see 5:807.

[1757]

★American History: Preliminary District-State Scholarship Test. High school; 1947–61; Ohio Scholarship Tests. *

[1758]

American History Test: National Achievement Tests. Grades 7–8; 1937–56; 5 scores: lessons of history, time concepts, historical associations, miscellaneous problems, total; Robert K. Speer, Lester D. Crow, and Samuel Smith; Acorn Publishing Co. *
  For additional information, see 5:811; for reviews by Jacob S. Orleans and Wallace Taylor, see 40:1630.

[1759]

*American History Test: State High School Tests for Indiana. 1, 2 semesters high school; 1934–59; Easdale Pickett; State High School Testing Service for Indiana. *
  For additional information, see 4:682.

[1760]

* Ancient History: Every Pupil Scholarship Test. High school; 1933–58; Bureau of Educational Measurements. *

[1761]

*College Entrance Examination Board Advanced Placement Examination: American History. Candidates desiring credit for college level courses or admission to advanced courses; 1956–61; program administered for the College Entrance Examination Board by Educational Testing Service. * For the testing program entry, see 1346.
  For additional information and reviews by James A. Field, Jr. and Christine McGuire, see 5:812.

[1762]

*College Entrance Examination Board Advanced Placement Examination: European History.** Candidates desiring credit for college level courses or admission to advanced courses; 1956–61; program administered for the College Entrance Examination Board by Educational Testing Service. * For the testing program entry, see 1346.

For additional information, see 5:813.

[1763]

Cooperative American History Test. High school and college; 1932–51; Harry D. Berg; Cooperative Test Division. *

For additional information and reviews by Dorothy C. Adkins and Martha E. Layman, see 4:684 (2 references); see also 3:604 (3 references); for a review by Margaret Willis of an earlier form, see 40:1633; for a review by Edgar B. Wesley, see 38:1014.

[1764]

Cooperative Ancient History Test. High school; 1933–51; Howard R. Anderson, E. F. Lindquist, Wallace Taylor, and Charlotte Croon Davis; Cooperative Test Division. *

For additional information, see 4:685; for a review by S. P. McCutchen of Form P, see 40:1634; for a review by Wilbur F. Murra of an earlier form, see 38:1015.

[1765]

Cooperative Modern European History Test. High school and college; 1932–51; Frederick H. Stutz; Cooperative Test Division. *

For additional information, see 4:686; for a review by Lavone A. Hanna of an earlier form, see 40:1635; for reviews by A. C. Krey and S. P. McCutchen, see 38:1016.

[1766]

Cooperative World History Test. High school; 1934–51; Wallace Taylor and Frederick H. Stutz; Cooperative Test Division. *

For additional information and a review by David K. Heenan, see 5:814; for a review by Kenneth E. Gell of an earlier form, see 40:1636; for a review by R. M. Tryon, see 38:1017.

[1767]

Coordinated Scales of Attainment: History. Grades 4, 5, 6, 7, 8; 1946–54; Edgar B. Wesley; Educational Test Bureau. * For the complete battery entry, see 10.

For additional information, see 5:815. For reviews of the complete battery, see 4:8 and 3:6.

[1768]

Crary American History Test. Grades 9–13; 1950–54; Ryland W. Crary; [Harcourt, Brace & World, Inc.]. *

For additional information and a review by Frederick H. Stutz, see 5:816 (2 references); for a review by Edgar B. Wesley, see 4:688.

[1769]

Cummings World History Test. Grades 9–13; 1950–54; Howard H. Cummings; [Harcourt, Brace & World, Inc.]. *
For additional information, see 5:817 (1 reference) ; for reviews by Dorothy C. Adkins and Howard R. Anderson, see 4:689.

[1770]

Emporia History Test. Grades 5–6, 7–8; 1937–39; H. E. Schrammel, E. J. Calkins, Harold Bechtoldt, Forrest Frease, and LaVerna Wharton; Bureau of Educational Measurements. *
For additional information, see 38:1018.

[1771]

***The Graduate Record Examinations Advanced Tests: History.** Grades 16–17; 1939–60; Educational Testing Service. * For the testing program entry, see 1353.
For additional information and a review by Robert H. Ferrell of Form EGR, see 5:818. For a review of the testing program, see 5:601.

[1772]

***History: Every Pupil Scholarship Test.** Grades 5–6, 7–8; 1933–61; new form usually issued twice a year; Bureau of Educational Measurements. *
For additional information, see 5:819.

[1773]

Kansas American History Test. 1, 2 semesters high school; 1938; Arthur Hartung, C. Stewart Boertman, and H. E. Schrammel; Bureau of Educational Measurements. *
For additional information and a review by W. H. Cartwright, see 3:610; for a review by Wilbur F. Murra, see 40:1639.

[1774]

***Kansas History: Every Pupil Scholarship Test.** Grades 7–12; 1934(?)–52; Bureau of Educational Measurements. *

[1775]

Kansas Modern European History Test. 1, 2 semesters high school; 1938–40; Alvin L. Hasenbank, H. E. Schrammel, and B. A. Hamilton; Bureau of Educational Measurements. *
For additional information and a review by Frederick H. Stutz, see 3:611; for a review by Clinton C. Conrad, see 40:1640.

[1776]

Kansas United States History Test. 1, 2 semesters in grades 7–8; 1957; Shirley Meares and M. W. Sanders; Bureau of Educational Measurements. *
For additional information and reviews by Wayne A. Frederick and John Manning, see 5:820.

[1777]

***Modern World History, Form 4: Achievement Examinations for Secondary Schools.** High school; 1951–59; Forms 1–3 published by Educational Test Bureau are out of print; Lola Fay and M. J. Haggerty; C. A. Gregory Co. *
For additional information concerning earlier forms, see 5:821.

[1778]

★Objective Tests in American History. 1, 2 semesters high school; 1960; 13 tests: 6 first semester tests and 4 second semester tests on specific topics plus 2 semester-end tests and a final examination; Earl Bridgewater; Perfection Form Co. *

[1779]

★Ohio History: Every Pupil Test. Grades 7–8; 1948–61; new form usually issued annually; Ohio Scholarship Tests. *

[1780]

*Semester Test for American History. 1, 2 semesters high school; 1938–59; formerly called *20th Century Test for American History;* Benton Review Publishing Co., Inc. *
For additional information, see 4:683.

[1781]

*Semester Test for High School World History. 1, 2 semesters high school; 1937–59; formerly called *20th Century Test for World History;* Benton Review Publishing Co., Inc. *
For additional information, see 4:697.

[1782]

*Social Studies X (American History): Midwest High School Achievement Examinations. Grade 10; 1955–61; earlier forms called *American History: Midwest High School Achievement Examinations;* Educational Test Bureau. *
For additional information and a review by Howard R. Anderson of earlier forms, see 5:810.

[1783]

*Social Studies XI (World History): Midwest High School Achievement Examinations. Grade 11; 1955–61; earlier forms called *Modern World History: Midwest High School Examinations;* Educational Test Bureau. *
For additional information concerning earlier forms, see 5:822.

[1784]

★Survey Test in Introductory American History: California Survey Series. Grades 7–9; 1959; identical with subtest 1 of the elementary level of *California Tests in Social and Related Sciences,* Form AA; Georgia Sachs Adams and John A. Sexson; California Test Bureau. *

[1785]

Taylor-Schrammel World History Test. 1, 2 semesters high school; 1935–36; Wallace Taylor and H. E. Schrammel; Bureau of Educational Measurements. *
For additional information and a review by J. R. Gerberich, see 40:1641.

[1786]

Understanding of American History, 1940 Revision. Grades 8–12; 1922–40; 5 scores: character judgment, historical vocabulary, sequence of events, cause and effect relationships, total; Luella Cole and R. C. Richards; Public School Publishing Co. *
For additional information and a review by Elizabeth C. Adams, see 4:693.

[1787]

*United States History: Manchester Semester-End Achievement Tests. 1, 2 semesters high school; 1934–56; C. Ray Keim; Bureau of Tests. *

[1788]

*World History: Every Pupil Scholarship Test. High school; 1926–61; new form usually issued twice a year; Bureau of Educational Measurements. *
   For additional information, see 5:823.

[1789]

*World History: Every Pupil Test. 1, 2 semesters high school; 1933–61; new form usually issued twice a year; Ohio Scholarship Tests. *
   For additional information, see 5:824.

[1790]

★World History: Final District-State Scholarship Test. High school; 1938–61; Ohio Scholarship Tests. *

[1791]

*World History: Manchester Semester-End Achievement Tests. 1, 2 semesters high school; 1934–[56]; Neal Merritt; Bureau of Tests. *

[1792]

★World History: Preliminary District-State Scholarship Test. High school; 1947–61; Ohio Scholarship Tests. *

[1793]

World History Test: Acorn National Achievement Tests. High school and college; 1948–57; 6 scores: social studies terms, world geography, contributions of world peoples to civilization, political history, economic-social-cultural history, total; Vincent McGarrett and Edward H. Merrill; Acorn Publishing Co. *
   For additional information and a review by John Manning, see 5:825.

[1794]

World History Test: State High School Tests for Indiana. 1, 2 semesters high school; 1934–51; Donald P. Knott, Paul C. Baker, Lawrie F. Davis, Harold Hargrave, and Frankie Jones; State High School Testing Service for Indiana. *
   For additional information, see 4:696.

POLITICAL SCIENCE

[1795]

American Civics and Government Tests for High Schools and Colleges, Revised Edition. High school and college; 1930–54; F. A. Magruder, R. J. Clinton, and M. M. Chambers; Public School Publishing Co. *
   For additional information, see 5:826.

[1796]

*American Government and Citizenship: Every Pupil Test. Grades 11–12; 1935–61; new form usually issued annually; Ohio Scholarship Tests. *
   For additional information, see 5:827; for a review by Elizabeth C. Adams of an earlier form, see 4:699.

[1797]

*American Government: Every Pupil Scholarship Test. High school; 1930–61; new form usually issued annually; Bureau of Educational Measurements. *
For additional information, see 5:828.

[1798]

Bear Test on United States Constitution. Grades 8–13; 1930; M. V. Bear; Public School Publishing Co. *

[1799]

Civic Vocabulary Test. High school; 1951; S. A. Rayner; Australian Council for Educational Research. *
For additional information and a review by I. G. Meddleton, see 5:830 (1 reference).

[1800]

*Constitution: Every Pupil Scholarship Test. High school; 1926–61; new form usually issued annually; Bureau of Educational Measurements. *
For additional information, see 5:831.

[1801]

Cooperative American Government Test. High school; 1947–51; John Haefner; Cooperative Test Division. *
For additional information and a review by Frederic L. Ayer, see 4:702.

[1802]

Dimond-Pflieger Problems of Democracy Test. High school; 1952–54; Stanley E. Dimond and Elmer F. Pflieger; [Harcourt, Brace & World, Inc.]. *
For additional information and reviews by John H. Haefner and Douglas E. Scates, see 5:833 (1 reference).

[1803]

★Duke University Political Science Information Test (American Government). Grade 13; 1958; materials may be borrowed or reproduced locally; 5 scores: federal government, constitutional system, politics, programs and policies, total; Robert H. Connery, Richard H. Leach, and Henry Weitz; Richard H. Leach. *

[1804]

*The Graduate Record Examinations Advanced Tests: Government. Grades 16–17; 1939–61; Educational Testing Service. * For the testing program entry, see 1353.
For additional information and a review by Christine McGuire of Form EGR, see 5:835. For a review of the testing program, see 5:601.

[1805]

Junior High School Civics Test: State High School Tests for Indiana. Grades 7–9; 1934–46; Florise Hunsucker; State High School Testing Service for Indiana. *
For additional information, see 4:704.

[1806]

The Kansas Constitution Test. High school and college; 1957; Louise Gardner and M. W. Sanders; Bureau of Educational Measurements. *
For additional information and a review by David K. Heenan, see 5:836.

[1807]

Mordy-Schrammel American Government Test. High school and college; 1940–45; Francis E. Mordy and H. E. Schrammel; Bureau of Educational Measurements. *

[1808]

Patterson Test or Study Exercises on the Constitution of the United States. Grades 9–16 and adults; 1931–53; Raymond G. Patterson; Public School Publishing Co. *
For additional information, see 5:838.

[1809]

Patterson Test or Study Exercises on the Declaration of Independence. Grades 9–16 and adults; 1931–52; Raymond G. Patterson; Public School Publishing Co. *
For additional information, see 5:839.

[1810]

Patterson's Tests on the Federal Constitution. Grades 9–14; 1927–37; Raymond G. Patterson; [Ridge Manor Publishing Co.]. *
For additional information, see 4:705.

[1811]

Peltier-Durost Civics and Citizenship Test. High school; 1958; 2 scores: achievement, attitude; Charles L. Peltier and Walter N. Durost; [Harcourt, Brace & World, Inc.]. *
For additional information, see 5:840.

[1812]

*****Senior High School Civics Test: For a One-Semester Course: State High School Tests for Indiana.** 1 semester high school; 1949–59; Meribah Clark; State High School Testing Service for Indiana. *
For additional information, see 4:706.

[1813]

*****Senior High School Civics Test: State High School Tests for Indiana.** 1, 2 semesters high school; 1934–59; Meribah Clark and Olis G. Jamison; State High School Testing Service for Indiana. *
For additional information, see 4:707.

[1814]

20th Century Test for Civics. 1, 2 semesters high school; 1935–49; Gale Smith; Benton Review Publishing Co., Inc. *
For additional information, see 4:701.

[1815]

*****United States Government: Manchester Semester-End Achievement Tests.** 1, 2 semesters high school; [1934–56]; C. Ray Keim; Bureau of Tests. *

SOCIOLOGY

[1816]

*The Graduate Record Examinations Advanced Tests: Sociology. Grades
16–17; 1939–61; Educational Testing Service. * For the testing program entry,
see 1353.
 For additional information, see 5:842. For a review of the testing program, see
5:601.

[1817]

Sare-Sanders Sociology Test. High school and college; 1958; Harold Sare
and Merritt W. Sanders; Bureau of Educational Measurements. *
 For additional information, see 5:843.

[1818]

Sociology: Every Pupil Scholarship Test. High school; 1935–58; Bureau of
Educational Measurements. *
 For additional information, see 5:844.

VOCATIONS

[1819]

★[APT Test Batteries.] Applicants for managerial or administrative, sales,
accountant or office worker, clerical or secretarial positions; [1947–60]; batteries consist of various combinations of the tests listed below; distribution restricted to clients; Associated Personnel Technicians, Inc. *
a) APT PERFORMANCE TEST. See 715.
b) THE PERSONALITY INVENTORY. See 246.
c) MINNESOTA MULTIPHASIC PERSONALITY INVENTORY, REVISED EDITION. See
224.
d) STRONG VOCATIONAL INTEREST BLANK FOR MEN, REVISED. See 1887.
e) STRONG VOCATIONAL INTEREST BLANK FOR WOMEN, REVISED. See 1888.
f) TESTS OF MECHANICAL COMPREHENSION. See 1946.
g) MINNESOTA CLERICAL TEST. See 1841.
h) WIDE RANGE VOCABULARY TEST. See 583.
i) WONDERLIC PERSONNEL TEST. See 875.
j) STRUCTURED-OBJECTIVE RORSCHACH TEST: PRELIMINARY EDITION. See 382.

[1820]

★[Aptitude Inventory.] Employee applicants; 1957–59; 1 test published in essentially the same form under 3 titles; 4 scores for each test: intelligent job
performance, leadership qualities, proper job attitudes, relations with others;
John C. Denton; Psychological Business Research. *
a) MANAGEMENT APTITUDE INVENTORY, [1959 REVISION]. Applicants for management and supervisory positions; 1957–59.
b) EMPLOYMENT APTITUDE INVENTORY. Applicants for office and factory positions; 1957.
c) SALES APTITUDE INVENTORY. Applicants for sales positions; 1958.

[1821]

★ETSA Tests. Adults; 1960, c1957–60; formerly called *Aptitests;* 8 tests; S.
Trevor Hadley and George A. W. Stouffer, Jr.; Employers' Tests and Services
Associates. *

a) ETSA TEST 1A, GENERAL MENTAL ABILITY TEST.
b) ETSA TEST 2A, OFFICE ARITHMETIC TEST.
c) ETSA TEST 3A, GENERAL CLERICAL ABILITY TEST.
d) ETSA TEST 4A, STENOGRAPHIC SKILLS TEST.
e) ETSA TEST 5A, MECHANICAL FAMILIARITY TEST.
f) ETSA TEST 6A, MECHANICAL KNOWLEDGE TEST.
g) ETSA TEST 7A, SALES APTITUDE TEST.
h) ETSA TEST 8A, PERSONAL ADJUSTABILITY TEST.

[1822]

★**General Adaptability Battery.** Illiterate and semi-literate job applicants; 1949–58; National Institute for Personnel Research. *
a) GENERAL CLASSIFICATION BATTERY. Illiterate and semi-literate applicants for semi-skilled and laboring jobs; 8 tests: *Nuts and Bolts, Sorting Test 1 (Mechanical Parts), Sorting Test 2 (Letters and Numbers),* [*N.I.P.R.*] *Cube Construction Test, Tripod Assembly Test, Formboards Test,* 2 modifications of Kohs' *Block-Design Test.*
b) [BOSSBOY SELECTION TESTS]. Illiterate and semi-literate applicants for bossboy and supervisory jobs who score in top category of *a* above; supervisory ability; 3 tests, called *Leaderless Group Test.*

[1823]

★**Individual Placement Series.** Adults; 1957–61; 8 tests; J. H. Norman; the Author. *
a) ACADEMIC ALERTNESS "AA." See 716.
b) PERFORMANCE ALERTNESS "PA" (WITH PICTURES). See 820.
c) SURVEY OF CLERICAL SKILLS (SOCS). See 1852.
d) OCCUPATIONAL INTEREST SURVEY (WITH PICTURES). See 1879.
e) SURVEY OF PERSONAL ATTITUDE "SPA." See 301.
f) READING ADEQUACY "READ" TEST. See 1435.
g) SHORTHAND TEST. See 77.
h) TYPING TEST. See 97.

[1824]

Personnel Selection and Classification Test. Adults; 1942–44; 7 scores: reading, arithmetic, verbal intelligence, mechanical dexterity, social adaptability, dependability-persistence, oral directions; Willis W. Clark, Ernest W. Tiegs, Louis P. Thorpe, T. W. MacQuarrie, and Elizabeth T. Sullivan; California Test Bureau. *
For additional information and reviews by Dorothy C. Adkins, George K. Bennett, and George A. Ferguson, see 3:690.

[1825]

★**Screening Tests for Apprentices.** Standards 5–10 (ages 14–20); [1957–60]; 8 scores: arithmetic (computations, problems), form relations (form perception, two dimensions, three dimensions), synonyms (Afrikaans, English), mechanical aptitude; National Bureau of Educational and Social Research. *

[1826]

Thurstone Employment Tests. Applicants for clerical and typing positions; 1922; 3 scores for each test: speed, accuracy, total; L. L. Thurstone; [Harcourt, Brace & World, Inc.]. *
a) EXAMINATION IN CLERICAL WORK.

b) EXAMINATION IN TYPING.

For additional information and reviews by John M. Willits and E. F. Wonderlic of *a,* see 3:632 (6 references).

[1827]

Vocational Aptitude Examination, Type E-A, Revised 1946. Grades 13–16; 1935–47; 8 scores (general information, arithmetical reasoning, judgment in estimating, symbolic relationships, reading comprehension, vocabulary, interest, social responsiveness) related to 4 occupational areas: sales, executive, accounting, technical; Glen U. Cleeton and Charles W. Mason; McKnight & McKnight Publishing Co. *

For additional information and reviews by D. Welty Lefever and Benjamin Shimberg, see 3:695 (1 reference); for reviews by Harold D. Carter and M. R. Trabue of an earlier edition, see 40:1679 (3 references).

CLERICAL

[1828]

*****A.C.E.R. Short Clerical Test.** Ages 13 and over; 1953–60; 2 scores: checking, arithmetic; Australian Council for Educational Research. *

For additional information, see 5:845.

[1829]

A.C.E.R. Speed and Accuracy Tests. Ages 13.5 and over; 1942–57; 2 tests: number checking, name checking; Australian Council for Educational Research. *

For additional information, see 5:846 (2 references); for a review by D. W. McElwain of an earlier form, see 4:719.

[1830]

★**Beginner's Clerical Test.** Applicants for clerical positions; 1958; abbreviated adaptation of N.I.I.P. *Group Test 25 (Clerical)* (see 1838); Herbert Moore; Guidance Centre. *

[1831]

Clerical Aptitude Test: Acorn National Aptitude Tests. Grades 7–16 and adults; 1943–50; 4 scores: business practice, number checking, date-name-address checking, total; Andrew Kobal, J. Wayne Wrightstone, and Karl R. Kunze; Acorn Publishing Co. *

For additional information, see 5:847 (1 reference); for reviews by Marion A. Bills, Donald G. Paterson, Henry Weitz, and E. F. Wonderlic, see 3:623.

[1832]

Clerical Perception Test. Grades 9–12; 1947; 2 scores: number checking, name checking; G. Bernard Baldwin; Educational Test Bureau. *

For additional information and reviews by Edward N. Hay, Raymond A. Katzell, Erwin K. Taylor, and E. F. Wonderlic, see 3:624 (1 excerpt).

[1833]

Clerical Test D: Extending—Verifying—Checking—Classifying. Ages 14 and over; 1922; Eugene J. Benge; Management Service Co. *

For additional information and reviews by Donald G. Paterson and John M. Willits, see 3:625.

[1834]

Clerical Tests 1 and 2. Ages 12–14.0; 1952–54; M. K. B. Richards and G. A. V. Morgan; published for the National Foundation for Educational Research in England and Wales; Newnes Educational Publishing Co. Ltd. *

For additional information, see 5:848.

[1835]

★Cross Reference Test. Clerical job applicants; 1959: James W. Curtis; Psychometric Affiliates. *

[1836]

Detroit Clerical Aptitudes Examination. Grades 9–12; 1937–44; 12 scores: motor (circles, classification, total), visual imagery (likenesses and differences, disarranged pictures, total), trade information, educational (handwriting, arithmetic, alphabetizing, total), total; includes *Ayres Measuring Scale for Handwriting* (see 1218); Harry J. Baker and Paul H. Voelker; Public School Publishing Co. *

For additional information and a review by E. F. Wonderlic, see 3:626 (1 reference); for reviews by Irving Lorge and M. W. Richardson of an earlier edition, see 40:1655.

[1837]

Group Test 20. Ages 15 and over; 1936; 2 scores: speed, accuracy; National Institute of Industrial Psychology. *

For additional information and a review by E. G. Chambers, see 4:723 (2 references).

[1838]

Group Test 25 (Clerical). Ages 14 and over; 1925–44; 7 scores: checking, classification, arithmetic, copying, filing, problems, oral instructions; National Institute of Industrial Psychology. *

For additional information and a review by E. G. Chambers, see 4:724 (1 reference).

[1839]

[Hay Tests for Clerical Aptitude.] Applicants for clerical positions; 1941–55; Edward N. Hay; Aptitude Test Service. *

a) TEST 1 : THE WARM UP.

b) NUMBER PERCEPTION TEST.

c) NUMBER SERIES COMPLETION TEST.

d) HAY NAME FINDING TEST.

For additional information, see 5:849 (2 references); for reviews by Reign H. Bittner and Edward E. Cureton, see 4:725 (8 references).

[1840]

Martin Office Aptitude Tests. Clerical employees and applicants for clerical positions; 1947–52; 10 tests; Howard G. Martin; Martin Publishing Co. *

a) MARTIN NUMBER CHECKING TEST. 1947–52.

b) MARTIN NAME CHECKING TEST. 1947–52.

c) MARTIN NUMBER FACILITY TEST. 1947–52.

d) MARTIN NUMERICAL OPERATIONS TEST. 1951–52.

e) MARTIN VOCABULARY TEST. 1947–52.

f) MARTIN ARITHMETIC REASONING TEST. 1950–52.
g) MARTIN ALPHABETIZING TEST. 1951–52.
h) MARTIN NUMERICAL ORDER TEST. 1951–52.
i) MARTIN STENOGRAPHIC TEST. 1949–52.
j) MARTIN TYPING TEST. 1949–52.

For additional information and reviews by D. Welty Lefever and Ross W. Matteson, see 4:726.

[1841]

*Minnesota Clerical Test. Grades 8–12 and adults; 1933–59; formerly called *Minnesota Vocational Test for Clerical Workers;* 2 scores: number comparison, name comparison; Dorothy M. Andrew, Donald G. Paterson, and Howard P. Longstaff; Psychological Corporation. *

For additional information and a review by Donald E. Super, see 5:850 (46 references); for reviews by Thelma Hunt, R. B. Selover, Erwin K. Taylor, and E. F. Wonderlic, see 3:627 (22 references); for a review by W. D. Commins, see 40:1664 (18 references).

[1842]

*National Institute of Industrial Psychology Clerical Test (North American Revision). Ages 16 and over; 1934–[60]; revision of *Group Test 25 (Clerical)* (see 1838); 8 scores: oral instructions, classification, arithmetic, copying, checking, filing, problems, total; J. H. Moore; Guidance Centre. *

For additional information and a review by R. B. Selover, see 3:628 (4 references); for a review by Donald G. Paterson, see 40:1665 (2 references).

[1843]

Office Worker Test 30–A. Office workers; 1956–58; 11 scores: reading, vocabulary, reasoning, arithmetic, checking, filing, spelling, punctuation, usage, information, total; Public Personnel Association. *

For additional information, see 5:516.

[1844]

O'Rourke Clerical Aptitude Test, Junior Grade. Applicants for clerical positions; 1926–58; L. J. O'Rourke; Psychological Institute. *

a) CLERICAL PROBLEMS. 1926–35.
b) REASONING TEST. 1926–58.

For additional information, see 5:851 (1 reference); for a review by Raymond A. Katzell, see 3:629 (3 references).

[1845]

Personnel Institute Clerical Tests. Applicants for office positions; 1957–58; Personnel Institute, Inc. *

a) BATTERY A: FOR TYPIST-STENOGRAPHERS. 5 tests; *EM-AY Inventory* (reprint of *Otis Employment Tests*, Test 2, Form A), *Grammar Test, Spelling Test, Test of Typewriting Ability,* and *Personal History Inventory.*
b) BATTERY B: FOR CLERICAL PERSONNEL. 5 tests: *EM-AY Inventory, Comparing Names Test, Copying Numbers Test, Arithmetic Test,* and *Personal History Inventory.*

For additional information, see 5:852.

[1846]

*[Personnel Research Institute Clerical Battery.] Applicants for clerical positions; 1945–54; 8 tests; Personnel Research Institute. *

a) PERSONNEL RESEARCH INSTITUTE CLASSIFICATION TEST. 1943–54; Jay L. Otis,

Evelyn Katz, Robert W. Henderson, Mary Aiken, David J. Chesler, and Gardner E. Lindzey.

b) NUMBER COMPARISON TEST FOR CLERICAL AND INDUSTRIAL INSPECTION OPERATIONS. 1945–46; Jay L. Otis and Louise W. Garman.

c) NAME COMPARISON TEST FOR CLERICAL AND INDUSTRIAL INSPECTION OPERATIONS. 1945–46; Jay L. Otis and Louise W. Garman.

d) TABULATION TEST. 1947; Jay L. Otis and David J. Chesler.

e) FILING TEST. 1947; Jay L. Otis and David J. Chesler.

f) ALPHABETIZING TEST. 1947; David J. Chesler.

g) ARITHMETIC REASONING TEST. 1948; Jay L. Otis and David J. Chesler.

h) SPELLING TEST FOR CLERICAL WORKERS. 1947; Jay L. Otis, David J. Chesler, and Irene Salmi.

For additional information and reviews by Louise Witmer Cureton and Albert K. Kurtz, see 4:729. For a review of *h*, see 4:211.

[1847]

Psychological Corporation General Clerical Test. Grades 9–16 and clerical job applicants; 1944–50; revision of *General Clerical Test, PCI Selection Form 20* ('42) ; 4 scores: clerical speed and accuracy, numerical ability, verbal facility, total; Psychological Corporation. *

For additional information and reviews by Edward E. Cureton and G. A. Satter, see 4:730 (4 references) ; for reviews by Edward N. Hay, Thelma Hunt, Raymond A. Katzell, and E. F. Wonderlic, see 3:630.

[1848]

Purdue Clerical Adaptability Test, Revised Edition. Applicants for clerical positions; 1949–56; 6 scores: spelling, computation, checking, word meaning, copying, reasoning; C. H. Lawshe, Joseph Tiffin, and Herbert Moore; distributed by University Book Store. *

For additional information and reviews by Mary Ellen Oliverio and Donald Spearritt, see 5:853 (2 references) ; for reviews by Edward N. Hay, Joseph E. Moore, and Alec Rodger of the previous edition, see 4:731.

[1849]

SRA Clerical Aptitudes. Grades 9–12 and adults; 1947–50; 4 scores: office vocabulary, office arithmetic, office checking, total; Richardson, Bellows, Henry & Co., Inc.; Science Research Associates, Inc. *

For additional information and reviews by Edward N. Hay and G. A. Satter, see 4:732.

[1850]

The Short Employment Tests. Applicants for clerical positions; 1951–56; George K. Bennett and Marjorie Gelink; Psychological Corporation. *

a) CA [CLERICAL].

b) N [NUMERICAL].

c) V [VERBAL].

For additional information and a review by P. L. Mellenbruch, see 5:854 (13 references).

[1851]

★Short Tests of Clerical Ability, Preliminary Edition. Applicants for office positions; 1959–60; 7 tests: Coding, Checking, Filing, Directions—Oral and Written, Arithmetic, Business Vocabulary, Language; Jean Maier; Science Research Associates, Inc. *

[1852]

★Survey of Clerical Skills (SOCS): Individual Placement Series (Area IV). Adults; 1959; 5 scores: spelling, office math, office terms, filing, grammar; J. H. Norman; the Author. *

[1853]

Survey of Working Speed and Accuracy. Grades 9–16 and adults; 1943–48; 4 scores: number checking, code translation, finger dexterity, counting; Floyd Ruch; California Test Bureau. *

For additional information and reviews by Edward N. Hay, Donald G. Paterson, and Erwin K. Taylor, see 3:631.

[1854]

Turse Clerical Aptitudes Test. Grades 8–12 and adults; 1955, c1953–55; 7 scores: verbal, number, written directions, learning ability, clerical speed, clerical aptitude, accuracy; Paul L. Turse; [Harcourt, Brace & World, Inc.]. *

For additional information and reviews by Robert A. Jones and Donald Spearritt, see 5:855 (1 reference).

INTERESTS

[1855]

★Analysis of Choices. Adults; 1948; 8 scores: clerical, mechanical, mathematics, physical science, biological science, persuasive, artistic, literary; Eugene J. Benge; Management Service Co. *

[1856]

Brainard Occupational Preference Inventory. Grades 8–12, adults; 1945–56; revision of *Specific Interest Inventory* ('32) by Paul P. Brainard and Frances G. Stewart; 6 scores: commercial, mechanical, professional, esthetic, scientific, personal service (girls), agriculture (boys); Paul P. Brainard and Ralph T. Brainard; Psychological Corporation. *

For additional information and a review by William C. Cottle, see 5:856 (2 references); for a review by Elmer D. Hinckley, see 4:737 (1 reference); for reviews by Edwin W. Davis and Herschel T. Manuel, see 3:634 (2 references); for reviews by Jack W. Dunlap and M. R. Trabue of the original edition, see 40:1675 (4 references); for a review by Everett B. Sackett, see 38:1176.

[1857]

★Burke Inventory of Vocational Development. Grades 9–16 and adults; 1958; Charles Burke; the Author. *

[1858]

★Career Finder. Grades 9–16 and adults; 1960; a short adaptation of the *Qualifications Record* (see 1885); 45 scores classified under 7 headings: arts (music, art, dramatics, dancing, graphic arts, crafts), biology (physiology, zoology, botany, foods, sports), computation (accounting, mathematics, drafting, purchasing, records, dexterity), literary (journalism, language, transcription, advertising, research), physical (tools, machinery, transportation, strength, hazards), social (management, instruction, public contacts, sales, consulting, religion, services, investigation, discipline), technology (chemistry, astronomy, electricity, mechanics, construction, geology, physics, aeronautics, standards); Keith Van Allyn; Personnel Research, Inc. *

[1859]

Cleeton Vocational Interest Inventory, Revised Edition. Grades 9–16 and adults; 1937–43; Glen U. Cleeton; McKnight & McKnight Publishing Co. *
a) [FORM FOR MEN.] 10 scores: biological sciences, specialized selling, physical sciences, social sciences, business administration, legal-literary, mechanical, finance, creative, agricultural.
b) [FORM FOR WOMEN.] 10 scores: office work, selling, natural sciences, social service, creative, grade school teacher, high school-college teacher, personal service, housekeeper-factory worker, homemaking-child care.
For additional information and reviews by Edward B. Greene, C. A. Oakley, and Arthur E. Traxler, see 3:635 (19 references, 1 excerpt); for reviews by Forrest A. Kingsbury and N. W. Morton, see 40:1682 (1 excerpt); for reviews by Albert S. Thompson, M. R. Trabue, and E. G. Williamson of an earlier edition, see 38:1181.

[1860]

★**College Planning Inventory, Senior College Edition.** High school seniors seeking counseling on choice of college; 1959; Franklyn Graff and Charles Burke; Charles Burke. *

[1861]

★**Curtis Interest Scale.** Grades 9–16 and adults; 1959; 10 scores (business, mechanics, applied arts, direct sales, production, science, entertainment, interpersonal, computation, farming) and 1 rating (desire for responsibility); James W. Curtis; Psychometric Affiliates. *

[1862]

Devon Interest Test. Ages 11–13; 1955; 2 scores: practical, academic; Stephen Wiseman and T. F. Fitzpatrick; Oliver & Boyd Ltd. *
For additional information and reviews by Arthur B. Royse and Alfred Yates, see 5:857 (3 references).

[1863]

★**Edmiston RO Inventory.** Grades 7–12; 1956–57; consistency of interests in 14 areas: social work-social improvement, social prestige, mechanical, scientific-technical-research, numerical-computational, art, music, journalism-literary, persuasive, clerical, business-economic, managerial authority and supervision, self-employment, total; R. W. Edmiston; the Author. *

[1864]

★**Fields of Occupational Interest.** High school students applying for admission to apprentice schools; 1948–54; reactions to specific occupational titles; 7 scores: production, trades, clerical, engineering, human relations, supervisory, total; W. H. Winkler; [Winkler Publications]. *

[1865]

*****Fowler-Parmenter Self-Scoring Interest Record.** Grades 9 and over; 1958–60; formerly called *G.C. Self-Scoring Interest Record;* 12 scores: outdoor, managerial, social service, verbal, operative, skilled mechanical, scientific, persuasive, clerical, artistic, numerical, musical; H. M. Fowler and M. D. Parmenter; Guidance Centre. *
For additional information concerning an earlier edition, see 5:858.

[1866]

★Geist Picture Interest Inventory. Grades 7–16 and adults; 1958–59; 11
interest scores (persuasive, clerical, mechanical, dramatic, musical, scientific,
outdoor, literary, computational, artistic, social service) and 8 motivation scores
(family, prestige, financial, intrinsic and personality, environmental, past experience, could not say, total); Harold Geist; Psychological Test Specialists. *

[1867]

Gregory Academic Interest Inventory. Grades 13–16; 1946; 28 scores: agriculture, architecture, biological sciences, business administration, chemistry,
civil engineering, commercial arts, electrical engineering, elementary education,
English, fine arts, geology, history, home economics, journalism, languages,
mathematics, mechanical engineering, military science, music, physics, physical
education, psychology, public service engineering, religion, secondary education,
sociology, speech; W. S. Gregory; Sheridan Supply Co. *
    For additional information and reviews by Paul S. Burnham, Lysle W. Croft,
and Herbert A. Toops, see 3:636 (1 reference).

[1868]

The Guilford-Shneidman-Zimmerman Interest Survey. Grades 9–16 and
adults; 1948; 18 scores: artistic (appreciative, expressive), linguistic (appreciative, expressive), scientific (investigatory, theoretical), mechanical (manipulative, designing), outdoor (natural, athletic), business-political (mercantile,
leadership), social activity (persuasive, gregarious), personal assistance (personal service, social welfare), office work (clerical, numerical); J. P. Guilford,
Edwin Shneidman, and Wayne S. Zimmerman; Sheridan Supply Co. *
    For additional information and reviews by George K. Bennett and Wilbur L.
Layton, see 4:739 (2 references).

[1869]

Henderson Analysis of Interest, [Second Edition]. Grades 9–16 and adults;
1950; occupational preferences in 14 areas: business service, clerical, accounting and statistics, persuasive, managerial, social science, physical science, biological science, engineering, art and music, teaching, writing, mechanical, manual; Robert W. Henderson; [William, Lynde & Williams]. *
    For additional information and reviews by Wilbur L. Layton and Donald E.
Super, see 4:740.

[1870]

*How Well Do You Know Your Interests. Grades 9–16, adults; 1957–58; 54
scores: numerical, clerical, retail selling, outside selling, selling real estate, one-
order selling, sales complaints, selling intangibles, buyer, labor management,
production supervision, business management, machine operation, repair and
construction, machine design, farm or ranch, gardening, hunting, adventure,
social service, teaching service, medical service, nursing service, applied chemistry, basic chemical problems, basic biological problems, basic physical problems,
basic psychological problems, philosophical, visual art appreciative, visual art
productive, visual art decorative, amusement appreciative, amusement productive, amusement managerial, literary appreciative, literary productive, musical
appreciative, musical performing, musical composing, sports appreciative, sports
participative, domestic service, unskilled labor, disciplinary, power seeking,
propaganda, self-aggrandizing, supervisory initiative, bargaining, arbitrative,

persuasive, disputatious, masculinity-femininity; Thomas N. Jenkins; Executive Analysis Corporation. *

For additional information and reviews by Jerome E. Doppelt and Henry S. Dyer, see 5:859.

[1871]

Interest Check List. Grades 9 and over; 1946–57; interviewing aid; interests related to 22 work areas: artistic, musical, literary, entertainment, public service, technical, managerial, computing, recording, clerical, public contact, cooking, child care, personal service, farming, marine, forestry, machine trades, crafts, observational, manipulative, elemental; United States Employment Service; United States Government Printing Office. *

For additional information, see 5:860; for reviews by Milton L. Blum and Howard R. Taylor of the original edition, see 4:741.

[1872]

Interest Questionnaire for High School Students, 1942 Edition. High school entrants; 1930–42; 3 curriculum preference scores: academic, commercial, technical; Oliver K. Garretson and Percival M. Symonds; Bureau of Publications. *

For additional information and a review by Lysle W. Croft, see 3:637 (6 references).

[1873]

Inventory of Vocational Interests: Acorn National Aptitude Tests. Grades 7–16 and adults; 1943–57; 5 scores: mechanical, academic, artistic, business and economic, farm-agricultural; Andrew Kobal, J. Wayne Wrightstone, and Karl R. Kunze; Acorn Publishing Co. *

For additional information, see 5:861; for reviews by Marion A. Bills, Edward S. Bordin, Harold D. Carter, and Patrick Slater, see 3:638.

[1874]

*****Kuder Preference Record—Occupational.** Grades 9–16 and adults; 1956–59; 43 scores: verification, county agricultural agent, farmer, forester, minister, newspaper editor, physician [revised], clinical psychologist, industrial psychologist, YMCA secretary, school superintendent, accountant, meteorologist, personnel manager, department store salesman, psychology professor, mechanical engineer, counseling psychologist, journalist, architect ['57], electrical engineer (revised), civil engineer, lawyer, retail clothier, insurance agent, dentist, veterinarian, industrial engineer, pediatrician, psychiatrist, radio station manager, interior decorator, high school counselor, high school science teacher, high school mathematics teacher, chemist, mining and metallurgical engineer, druggist, job printer ['58], bank cashier ('59), male librarian ('59), pharmaceutical salesman ('59), x-ray technician ('59); G. Frederic Kuder; Science Research Associates, Inc. *

For additional information and reviews by Edward S. Bordin and John W Gustad, see 5:862.

[1875]

Kuder Preference Record—Vocational. Grades 9–16 and adults; 1934–56; 2 forms; G. Frederic Kuder; Science Research Associates, Inc. *

a) FORM B. 1934–46; 9 or 10 scores: mechanical, computational, scientific, persuasive, artistic, literary, musical, social service, clerical, masculinity-femininity (optional).

b) FORM C. 1934–56; revision of Form B; 11 scores: same as for Form B plus outdoor, verification.

For additional information and reviews by Clifford P. Froehlich and John Pierce-Jones, see 5:863 (211 references); for reviews by Edward S. Bordin, Harold D. Carter, and H. M. Fowler, see 4:742 (146 references); for reviews by Ralph F. Berdie, E. G. Chambers, and Donald E. Super of an earlier edition, see 3:640 (60 references, 1 excerpt); for reviews by A. B. Crawford and Arthur E. Traxler of the original edition, see 40:1671 (2 references).

[1876]

Motivation Indicator. Grades 10–12; 1947; 14 scores: biological sciences, physical sciences, social sciences, creative writing, graphic arts, industrial arts, agriculture, clerical-verbal, clerical-computational, altruistic, promotional, administrative, commercial, creative initiative; G. Bernard Baldwin; Educational Test Bureau. *

For additional information and reviews by Norman Frederiksen and Arthur E. Traxler, see 3:641 (1 excerpt).

[1877]

★Occupational Interest Comparisons. High school; 1954; checklist of specific occupational titles; 5 scores: figures, ideas, artistic, human relations, trades and skills; W. H. Winkler; [Winkler Publications]. *

[1878]

Occupational Interest Inventory, 1956 Revision. Grades 7–16 and adults, 9–16 and adults; 1943–56; 10 scores grouped in 3 categories: fields of interests (personal-social, natural, mechanical, business, the arts, the sciences), types of interests (verbal, manipulative, computational), level of interests; Edwin A. Lee and Louis P. Thorpe; California Test Bureau. *

For additional information and reviews by Martin Katz and Wilbur L. Layton, see 5:864 (20 references); for a review by Arthur H. Brayfield of the original edition, see 4:743 (20 references); for reviews by Edward S. Bordin and Stanley G. Dulsky, see 3:643.

[1879]

★Occupational Interest Survey (With Pictures): Individual Placement Series (Area II). Adults; 1959; 9 scores: scientific, social service, literary, agricultural, business, mechanical, musical, clerical, artistic; J. H. Norman; the Author. *

[1880]

Occupational Interests: Self Analysis Scale. Applicants for employment; 1943; 4 scores: people, ideas, numbers, things; Eugene J. Benge; Management Service Co. *

For additional information and a review by Stanley G. Dulsky, see 3:644.

[1881]

★Occupational Satisfactions Inventory. High school and trade school; 1948; satisfactions and values seen in jobs being considered; W. H. Winkler; [Winkler Publications]. *

[1882]

★Office Occupational Interests of Women. High school; 1956; checklist of specific office job titles; 5 scores: office machines, filing, typing, record work, personnel work; W. H. Winkler; [Winkler Publications]. *

[1883]

★Pictorial Interest Inventory. Adult males, particularly poor readers and non-readers; 1959; 11 scores: clerical and sales, personal service, protective and custodial, farming, mechanical, building and maintenance, skilled-sedentary, vehicle operators, electrical workers, natural processors, assembly line workers; for research use only; Barron B. Scarborough; the Author. *

[1884]

Picture Interest Inventory. Grades 7 and over; 1958; 9 scores: interpersonal service, natural, mechanical, business, esthetic, scientific, verbal, computational, time perspective; Kurt P. Weingarten; California Test Bureau. *
For additional information, see 5:865.

[1885]

*Qualifications Record, 1960 Revision. Grades 9–16 and adults; 1958–60; includes *Job Qualification Inventory* ('47); 45 scores classified under 7 headings: arts (music, art, dramatics, dancing, graphic arts, crafts), biology (physiology, zoology, botany, foods, sports), computation (accounting, mathematics, drafting, purchasing, records, dexterity), literary (journalism, language, transcription, advertising, research), physical (tools, machinery, transportation, strength, hazards), social (management, instruction, public contacts, sales, consulting, religion, services, investigation, discipline), technology (chemistry, astronomy, electricity, mechanics, construction, geology, physics, aeronautics, standards); Keith Van Allyn; Personnel Research, Inc. *
For additional information concerning the earlier edition, see 5:866.

[1886]

Rothwell-Miller Interest Blank. Ages 13 and over; 1958; 12 scores: outdoor, mechanical, computational, scientific, personal contact, aesthetic, literary, musical, social service, clerical, practical, medical; Kenneth M. Miller and J. W. Rothwell; Australian Council for Educational Research. *
For additional information, see 5:867.

[1887]

*Strong Vocational Interest Blank for Men, Revised. Ages 17 and over; 1927–59; 60 scoring scales (50 occupations, 6 occupational group scales, and 4 nonvocational scales): group 1: group scale ('38), artist ('38), psychologist ('28–49) by P. H. Kriedt, architect ('38), physician ('38–52), psychiatrist ('52), osteopath ('47), dentist ('38), veterinarian ('49) by T. E. Hannum; group 2: group scale ('39), physicist ('52), chemist ('38), mathematician ('38), engineer ('38); group 3: production manager ('38); group 4: farmer ('38), carpenter ('38), printer ('38), mathematics-science teacher ('38), policeman ('38), forest service man ('38), army officer ('52), aviator ('40); group 5: group scale ('38), Y.M.C.A. physical director ('38), personnel manager ('38), physical therapist ('58), public administrator ('44), vocational counselor ('52) by Clements D. Brown, Y.M.C.A. secretary ('38), social science high school teacher ('38), business education teacher ('59) by Robert V. Bacon, city school superintendent ('38), minister ('38), social worker ('54); group 6: music performer ('54), music teacher ('54); group 7: C.P.A. owner ('38); group 8: group scale ('38), senior C.P.A. ('49), junior accountant ('38), office worker ('38), purchasing agent ('38), banker ('38), mortician ('46), pharmacist ('49) by Milton Schwebel, credit manager ('59); group 9: group scale ('38), sales manager ('38), real estate salesman ('38), life insurance salesman ('38); group

10: group scale ('38), advertising man ('38), lawyer ('38), author-journalist ('38); group 11: president of manufacturing concern ('38); nonvocational scales: occupational level ('39), masculinity-femininity ('38), specialization level ('52) by Milton G. Holmen, interest maturity ('41); Edward K. Strong, Jr.; Consulting Psychologists Press, Inc. *

For additional information, see 5:868 (153 references); for reviews by Edward S. Bordin and Elmer D. Hinckley, see 4:747 (98 references); see also 3:647 (104 references); for reviews by Harold D. Carter, John G. Darley, and N. W. Morton, see 40:1680 (71 references); for a review by John G. Darley of an earlier edition, see 38:1178; for excerpts from related book reviews, see 5:B115, 5:B414, 4:748, 3:648, 3:650, and 3:652.

[1888]

*Strong Vocational Interest Blank for Women, Revised. Ages 17 and over; 1933–59; 31 scoring scales (30 occupational scales and 1 nonvocational scale): artist ('46), author ('46), librarian ('46), English teacher ('46), social worker ('46–54), psychologist ('46), lawyer ('46), social science teacher ('46), Y.W.C.A. secretary ('46), life insurance saleswoman ('46), buyer ('46), housewife ('46), elementary teacher ('46) by Ralph Bedell, music performer ('54), music teacher ('54), office worker ('47), stenographer-secretary ('47), home economics teacher ('46), dietician ('46), college physical education teacher ('55) by Rosena M. Wilson, high school physical education teacher ('46) by Patricia Collins, occupational therapist ('46), nurse ('46), mathematics-science teacher ('46), dentist ('46), laboratory technician ('46), physician ('46), business education teacher ('48) by H. F. Koepke, engineer ('54), physical therapist ('58), femininity-masculinity ('47); Edward K. Strong, Jr.; Consulting Psychologists Press, Inc. *

For additional information, see 5:869 (19 references); for a review by Gwendolen Schneidler Dickson, see 3:649 (36 references); for a review by Ruth Strang of an earlier edition, see 40:1681 (9 references); for a review by John G. Darley, see 38:1179; for excerpts from related book reviews, see 3:650 and 3:652.

[1889]

Thurstone Interest Schedule. Grades 9–16 and adults; 1947; 10 scores: physical science, biological science, computational, business, executive, persuasive, linguistic, humanitarian, artistic, musical; L. L. Thurstone; Psychological Corporation. *

For additional information and reviews by Norman Frederiksen and Donald E. Super, see 4:745 (1 reference).

[1890]

The Vocational Apperception Test. College; 1949; Robert B. Ammons, Margaret N. Butler, and Sam A. Herzig; Psychological Test Specialists. *

a) [FORM FOR MEN.] Preferences in 8 areas: teacher, executive or office worker, doctor, lawyer, engineer, personnel or social worker, salesman, laboratory technician.

b) [FORM FOR WOMEN.] Preferences in 10 areas: laboratory technician, dietician, buyer, nurse, teacher, artist, secretary, social worker, mother, housewife.

For additional information and reviews by Benjamin Balinsky and William E. Henry, see 4:146 (1 reference, 1 excerpt).

[1891]

Vocational Interest Analyses: A Six-Fold Analytical Extension of the Occupational Interest Inventory. Grades 9–16 and adults; 1951; 6 scores in each of 6 areas; Edward C. Roeber, Gerald G. Perideaux, Edwin A. Lee, and Louis P. Thorpe; California Test Bureau. *

a) PERSONAL-SOCIAL ANALYSIS. 6 scores: domestic service, personal service, social service, teaching and related activities, law and law enforcement, health and medical service.

b) NATURAL ANALYSIS. 6 scores: general and crop farming, animal raising and care, garden and greenhouse care, fish-game-domestic fowl, lumbering and forestry, marine work.

c) MECHANICAL ANALYSIS. 6 scores: maintenance and repairing, machine operation and tending, construction, designing, bench work and bench crafts, processing.

d) BUSINESS ANALYSIS. 6 scores: clerical, shipping and distribution, bookkeeping and accounting, buying and selling, training and supervision, management and control.

e) THE ARTS ANALYSIS. 6 scores: art crafts, painting and drawing, decorating and landscaping, drama and radio, literary activities, music.

f) THE SCIENCES ANALYSIS. 6 scores: laboratory work, mineral-petroleum products, applied chemistry, chemical research, biological research, scientific engineering.

For additional information and a review by Wilbur L. Layton, see 5:870 (1 reference); for a review by Julian C. Stanley, see 4:746.

[1892]

★**Vocational Sentence Completion Blank, Experimental Edition.** High school and college; 1952–60; 28 scores: general self concern (problem, achievement, independence, satisfaction, material, obligation, effectiveness), general emphasis (intellectual, active, other people, recreational), specific preference area (outdoor, mechanical, computational, scientific, persuasive, artistic, literary, musical, social service, clerical, domestic, academic, negative academic), miscellaneous (other, negative, neutral, omit); Arthur A. Dole; distributed by University of Hawaii Bookstore. *

[1893]

★**WIPCO Vocational Interest Profile (VIP), Research Edition.** Ages 15 and over; 1960; formerly called *Psycan Vocational Interest Profile;* 9 scores: numerical, mechanical, scientific, clerical, persuasive, musical, literary, artistic, service; R. N. Smith and J. R. McIntosh; [Western Interprovincial Publishing Co.]. *

[1894]

★**William, Lynde & Williams Analysis of Interest.** Male adults; 1960; 8 scores: management, accounting, engineering, mechanical, sales, service, teaching, writing; R. W. Henderson; William, Lynde & Williams. *

[1895]

★**Your Educational Plans.** Grades 6–9, 9–12; 1958–60; for analysis of biographical data and environmental factors related to educational and vocational goals; Samuel A. Stouffer; Science Research Associates, Inc. *

MANUAL DEXTERITY

[1896]
★APT Manual Dexterity Test. Motor vehicle mechanics, mechanics' helpers, and truck drivers; 1960; distribution restricted to clients; Associated Personnel Technicians, Inc. *

[1897]
Benge HanDexterity Test. Adults; 1943; Eugene J. Benge; Management Service Co. *
For additional information and reviews by C. H. Lawshe, Jr. and Joseph E. Moore, see 3:656.

[1898]
Crawford Small Parts Dexterity Test. High school and adults; 1946–56; 2 scores: pins and collars, screws; John E. Crawford and Dorothea M. Crawford; Psychological Corporation. *
For additional information and a review by Neil D. Warren, see 5:871 (8 references); for a review by Raymond A. Katzell, see 4:752; for a review by Joseph E. Moore, see 3:667.

[1899]
Hand-Tool Dexterity Test. Industrial applicants; 1946; George K. Bennett; Psychological Corporation. *
For additional information and reviews by C. H. Lawshe, Jr. and Neil D. Warren, see 3:659 (2 references).

[1900]
Martin Peg Board (Finger Dexterity Test). High school and adults; 1947–51; 3 scores: right hand, left hand, both hands; Howard G. Martin; Martin Publishing Co. *
For additional information, see 4:749.

[1901]
Mellenbruch Curve-Block Series. Adults; 1946; originally called *Miami-Oxford Curve-Block Series;* P. L. Mellenbruch; the Author. *
For additional information and reviews by William R. Grove and Willard A. Kerr, see 3:662 (1 reference).

[1902]
Minnesota Manual Dexterity Test. Ages 13 and over; [pre-1931–37]; W. A. Ziegler; Marietta Apparatus Co. * For the revised edition entry, see 1903.

[1903]
Minnesota Rate of Manipulation Test, [1933 Edition]. Ages 13 and over; 1931–33; revision of *Minnesota Manual Dexterity Test* (see 1902); 2 scores: placing, turning; W. A. Ziegler; C. H. Stoelting Co. * For the revised edition entry, see 1904.

[1904]
*Minnesota Rate of Manipulation Test, [1946 Edition]. Adults; 1931–57; 5 scores: placing, turning, displacing, 1-hand turning and placing, 2-hand

turning and placing; Gilbert L. Betts and W. A. Ziegler; Educational Test Bureau. * For the earlier edition entry, see 1903; for an adaptation for the blind, see 1905.

For additional information and reviews by Edwin E. Ghiselli and John R. Kinzer, see 3:663 (23 references, 1 excerpt); for reviews by Lorene Teegarden and Morris S. Viteles (with Albert S. Thompson), see 40:1662 (4 references).

[1905]

★Motor Skills Tests Adapted to the Blind. Adults; 1944; adaptations of *Minnesota Rate of Manipulation Test, [1946 Edition]* (see 1904) and *Pennsylvania Bi-Manual Worksample* (see 1908); John R. Roberts and Mary K. Bauman; Educational Test Bureau. *

[1906]

O'Connor Finger Dexterity Test. Ages 14 and over; [1920–26]; Johnson O'Connor; C. H. Stoelting Co. *
For additional information and a review by Morris S. Viteles (with Albert S. Thompson), see 40:1659 (15 references).

[1907]

O'Connor Tweezer Dexterity Test. Ages 14 and over; [1920–28]; Johnson O'Connor; C. H. Stoelting Co. *
For additional information and a review by Morris S. Viteles (with Albert S. Thompson), see 40:1678 (13 references).

[1908]

Pennsylvania Bi-Manual Worksample. Ages 16 and over; 1943–45; 2 scores: assembly, disassembly; John R. Roberts; Educational Test Bureau. * For an adaptation for the blind, see 1905.
For additional information and reviews by Edwin E. Ghiselli, Thomas W. Harrell, Albert Gibson Packard, and Neil D. Warren, see 3:665 (3 references).

[1909]

★Purdue Hand Precision Test. Ages 17 and over; [1941]; 3 scores: attempts, correct responses, error time; [Joseph Tiffin]; Lafayette Instrument Co. *

[1910]

Purdue Pegboard. Grades 9–16 and adults; 1941–48; 5 scores: right hand, left hand, both hands, right plus left plus both hands, assembly; Purdue Research Foundation under the direction of Joseph Tiffin; Science Research Associates, Inc. *
For additional information and a review by Neil D. Warren, see 5:873 (11 references); see also 4:751 (12 references); for reviews by Edwin E. Ghiselli, Thomas W. Harrell, and Albert Gibson Packard, see 3:666 (3 references).

[1911]

Stromberg Dexterity Test. Trade school and adults; 1945–51; Eleroy L. Stromberg; Psychological Corporation. *
For additional information and a review by Julian C. Stanley, see 4:755 (1 reference).

MECHANICAL ABILITY

[1912]

A.C.E.R. Mechanical Comprehension Test. Ages 13.5 and over; 1942–53; Australian Council for Educational Research. *

For additional information and reviews by John R. Jennings and Haydn S. Williams, see 5:874 (2 references); for a review by D. W. McElwain, see 4:756.

[1913]

A.C.E.R. Mechanical Reasoning Test. Ages 14-9 and over; 1951–54; abbreviated adaptation of *A.C.E.R. Mechanical Comprehension Test* (see 1912); D. Spearritt, Research and Guidance Branch of the Queensland Department of Public Instruction, and the Australian Council for Educational Research; Australian Council for Educational Research. *

For additional information and reviews by John R. Jennings and Haydn S. Williams, see 5:875.

[1914]

Chriswell Structural Dexterity Test. Grades 8–9; 1953–54; M. Irving Chriswell; [Vocational Guidance Service]. *

For additional information and a review by A. Pemberton Johnson, see 5:876 (1 reference).

[1915]

[Cox Mechanical and Manual Tests.] Boys ages 10 and over, 11–14, 14 and over; 1928–34; 6 tests; J. W. Cox; D. Draycon. *

a) COX MECHANICAL TEST M. Ages 11–14, 14 and over.

b) MECHANICAL DIAGRAMS TEST. Ages 14 and over.

c) MECHANICAL EXPLANATION TEST I. Ages 14 and over.

d) COX EYEBOARD TEST NO. 2. Ages 10 and over.

e) COX NAILBOARD TEST. Ages 10 and over.

f) COX NAILSTICK TEST. Ages 10 and over.

For additional information and reviews by C. A. Oakley and Alec Rodger, see 40:1652–3 (4 references); for excerpts from related book reviews, see 40:B872.1 and 38:B336.

[1916]

★[Curtis Object Completion and Space Form Tests.] Applicants for mechanical and technical jobs; 1960–61; 2 tests; James W. Curtis; Psychometric Affiliates. *

a) OBJECT-COMPLETION TEST.

b) SPACE FORM TEST.

[1917]

Detroit Mechanical Aptitudes Examination, Revised. Grades 7–16; 1928–39; 12 scores: motor (circles, classification, total), visual imagery (disarranged pictures, sizes, pulleys, total), mechanical information (tool recognition, tool information, total), arithmetic, total; Harry J. Baker, Paul H. Voelker, and Alex C. Crockett; Public School Publishing Co. *

For additional information and reviews by Lloyd G. Humphreys and Dewey B. Stuit, see 3:668 (4 references); for a review by Irving Lorge, see 40:1656 (1 excerpt).

[1918]

★Flags: A Test of Space Thinking. Grades 9–16 and industrial employees; 1956–59; L. L. Thurstone and T. E. Jeffrey; Education-Industry Service. *

[1919]

Form Relations Group Test. Ages 14 and over; 1926–46; National Institute of Industrial Psychology. *
   For additional information and a review by A. T. Welford, see 4:757 (10 references).

[1920]

Group Test 80A. Ages 15 and over; 1943–51; spatial perception; National Institute of Industrial Psychology. *
   For additional information and reviews by E. G. Chambers and John Liggett, see 5:877.

[1921]

Group Test 81. Ages 14 and over; 1949; spatial perception; National Institute of Industrial Psychology. *
   For additional information and a review by E. G. Chambers, see 4:758 (5 references).

[1922]

MacQuarrie Test for Mechanical Ability. Grades 7 and over; 1925–43; 8 scores: tracing, tapping, dotting, copying, location, blocks, pursuit, total; T. W. MacQuarrie; California Test Bureau. *
   For additional information, see 4:759 (15 references); see also 4:760 (1 excerpt); for reviews by John R. Kinzer, C. H. Lawshe, Jr., and Alec Rodger, see 3:661 (43 references).

[1923]

Mechanical Aptitude Test: Acorn National Aptitude Tests. Grades 7–16 and adults; 1943–52; 5 scores: comprehension of mechanical tasks, use of tools and materials (verbal), matching tools and operations, use of tools and materials (non-verbal), total; Andrew Kobal, J. Wayne Wrightstone, and Karl R. Kunze; Acorn Publishing Co. *
   For additional information, see 5:878; for reviews by Reign H. Bittner, James M. Porter, Jr., and Alec Rodger, see 3:669.

[1924]

★Mechanical Information Questionnaire. Adults; 1944–57; 11 scores: automotive information, bench work, building construction, electrical, foundry practice, industrial engineering, maintenance, metal working, pipe fitting, woodworking, total; Eugene J. Benge; Management Service Co. *

[1925]

★Mechanical Knowledge Test. Adults; 1955; W. H. Winkler; Winkler Publications. *

[1926]

★Mechanical Movements: A Test of Mechanical Comprehension. Grades 9–16 and industrial employees; 1956–59; L. L. Thurstone and T. E. Jeffrey; Education-Industry Service. *

[1927]

Mellenbruch Mechanical Motivation Test. Grades 6–16 and adults; 1944–57; formerly called *Mellenbruch Mechanical Aptitude Test for Men and Women;* P. L. Mellenbruch; Psychometric Affiliates. *

For additional information and reviews by Arthur H. Brayfield and John B. Morris, see 5:879; for reviews by Lloyd G. Humphreys and C. A. Oakley of the original edition, see 3:670.

[1928]

Minnesota Assembly Test. Ages 11 and over; 1930–37; revision of *Stenquist Assembling Test* (see 1942) ; sometimes called *Minnesota Mechanical Assembly Test;* Donald G. Paterson, Richard M. Elliott, L. Dewey Anderson, Herbert A. Toops, and Edna Heidbreder; Marietta Apparatus Co. *

For additional information and a review by William R. Grove, see 3:671 (11 references).

[1929]

Minnesota Paper Form Board Test. Ages 11 and over; [1920–28]; D. G. Paterson and others; Marietta Apparatus Co. * For the revised edition entry, see 1939.

[1930]

Minnesota Spatial Relations Test. Ages 11 and over; 1930; revision of H. C. Link's *Spatial Relations Test* ('19) ; M. R. Trabue, Donald G. Paterson, Richard M. Elliott, L. Dewey Anderson, Herbert A. Toops, and Edna Heidbreder; Educational Test Bureau. *

For additional information and a review by Milton L. Blum, see 3:664 (18 references) ; for a review by Lorene Teegarden, see 40:1663 (10 references).

[1931]

★Moray House Space Tests. Ages 10 to 12-0, 12 to 14-6; 1951–54; Department of Education, University of Edinburgh; University of London Press Ltd. *
a) MORAY HOUSE SPACE TEST I. Ages 10 to 12-0; 1951.
b) MORAY HOUSE SPACE TEST (ADV.) I. Ages 12 to 14-6; 1953–54.

[1932]

N.I.I.P. Squares Test. Grades 9 and over; 1944–51; National Institute of Industrial Psychology; Australian Council for Educational Research. *

For additional information and a review by J. F. Clark, see 5:880 (9 references).

[1933]

O'Connor Wiggly Block. Ages 16 and over; 1928–51; Johnson O'Connor; C. H. Stoelting Co. *

[1934]

O'Rourke Mechanical Aptitude Test. Adults; 1939–57; L. J. O'Rourke; Psychological Institute. *

For additional information, see 5:882; for reviews by Jay L. Otis and George A. Satter, see 3:672 (8 references) ; for a review by Herbert A. Landry, see 40:1668.

[1935]

★Paper Puzzles: A Test of Space Relations. Grades 9–16 and industrial employees; 1956–59; L. L. Thurstone and T. E. Jeffrey; Education-Industry Service. *

[1936]

Prognostic Test of Mechanical Abilities. Grades 7–12 and adults; 1946–47; 6 scores: arithmetic computation, reading drawings and blueprints, identification and use of tools, spatial relationships, checking measurements, total; J. Wayne Wrightstone and Charles E. O'Toole; California Test Bureau. *
    For additional information and reviews by Willard A. Kerr and Douglas G. Schultz, see 4:761 (1 reference) ; see also 3:674 (1 excerpt).

[1937]

Purdue Mechanical Adaptability Test. Males ages 15 and over; 1945–50; C. H. Lawshe, Jr. and Joseph Tiffin; University Book Store. *
    For additional information, see 4:762 (6 references) ; for reviews by Jay L. Otis and Dewey B. Stuit, see 3:676.

[1938]

Purdue Mechanical Performance Test. Ages 17 and over; 1957; 4 scores: transfer boards, spatial relations, hub assemblies, total; Ernest J. McCormick and Robert L. Brown; distributed by Lafayette Instrument Co. *
    For additional information, see 5:883 (1 reference).

[1939]

Revised Minnesota Paper Form Board Test. Grades 9–16 and adults; 1930–48; original test by Donald G. Paterson, Richard M. Elliott, L. Dewey Anderson, Herbert A. Toops, and Edna Heidbreder; revision by Rensis Likert and William H. Quasha; Psychological Corporation. (Australian edition: ages 13.5 and over; 1943–55; test identical with American edition; manual by D. Spearritt; Australian Council for Educational Research.) * For the original edition entry, see 1929.
    For additional information and a review by D. W. McElwain, see 5:884 (29 references) ; for reviews by Clifford E. Jurgensen and Raymond A. Katzell, see 4:763 (38 references) ; for a review by Dewey B. Stuit, see 3:677 (48 references) ; for a review by Alec Rodger, see 40:1673 (9 references).

[1940]

SRA Mechanical Aptitudes. Grades 9–12 and adults; 1947–50; 4 scores: mechanical knowledge, space relations, shop arithmetic, total; Richardson, Bellows, Henry & Co., Inc.; Science Research Associates, Inc. *
    For additional information and reviews by Alec Rodger and Douglas G. Schultz, see 4:764.

[1941]

Spatial Tests 1, 2 and 3. Ages 11-0 to 13-11, 10-7 to 13-11, 10-0 to 11-11; 1950–59; published for the National Foundation for Educational Research in England and Wales; Newnes Educational Publishing Co. Ltd. *
 a) SPATIAL TEST 1. Ages 11-0 to 13-11; 1950; I. Macfarlane Smith.
 b) SPATIAL TEST 2. Ages 10-7 to 13-11; 1950–56; A. F. Watts, D. A. Pidgeon, and M. K. B. Richards.

c) SPATIAL TEST 3 (NEWCASTLE SPATIAL TEST). Ages 10-0 to 11-11; 1958–59; I. Macfarlane Smith and J. S. Lawes.

For additional information and reviews by E. G. Chambers and Charles T. Myers of *a* and *b*, see 5:885 (1 reference); for a review by E. A. Peel of *a*, see 4:753; for additional information concerning *c,* see 5:881.

[1942]

Stenquist Assembling Test. Grades 5–12 and adults; 1917–22; John L. Stenquist; C. H. Stoelting Co. * For the revised edition entry, see 1928.

For additional information and a review by William R. Grove, see 3:679 (10 references).

[1943]

Survey of Mechanical Insight. Grades 9–16 and adults; 1945–55; Daniel R. Miller; California Test Bureau. *

For additional information and a review by Arthur H. Brayfield, see 5:886 (3 references); for reviews by Reign H. Bittner, Jay L. Otis, and Shailer Peterson of the original edition, see 3:680.

[1944]

Survey of Object Visualization. Grades 9–16 and adults; 1945–55; Daniel R. Miller; California Test Bureau. *

For additional information and a review by William J. Micheels, see 5:887 (5 references); for reviews by Charles M. Harsh, Clifford E. Jurgensen, Shailer Peterson, and Patrick Slater of the original edition, see 3:681.

[1945]

Survey of Space Relations Ability. Grades 9–16 and adults; 1944–49; Harry W. Case and Floyd Ruch; California Test Bureau. *

For additional information and a review by D. W. McElwain, see 5:888 (4 references); for reviews by E. G. Chambers, Clifford E. Jurgensen, and James M. Porter, Jr., see 3:682.

[1946]

Tests of Mechanical Comprehension. Grades 9 and over; 1940–55; George K. Bennett, Dinah E. Fry, and William A. Owens; Psychological Corporation. *

a) FORM AA. Grades 9 and over; 1940–55.
b) FORM BB. Men in grades 13 and over; 1941–51.
c) FORM CC. Men in engineering schools; 1949.
d) FORM WI. Women in grades 9 and over; 1942–47.

For additional information, see 5:889 (46 references); for a review by N. W. Morton, see 4:766 (28 references); for reviews by Charles M. Harsh, Lloyd G. Humphreys, and George A. Satter, see 3:683 (19 references).

[1947]

Tool Knowledge Test. Ages 13 and over; 1951–54; D. Spearritt and Research and Guidance Branch of the Queensland Department of Public Instruction; Australian Council for Educational Research. *

For additional information and reviews by J. F. Clark and I. G. Meddleton, see 5:890.

[1948]

V.G.C. Object Visualization Indicator. High school; 1950; adaptation of Part H of the 1946–47 edition of the *General Aptitude Test Battery* (see 1376); distribution restricted to Canadian schools; Guidance Centre. *

For additional information, see 4:767.

[1949]

V.G.C. Space Relations Ability Indicator. High school; 1950; adaptation of Part F of the 1946–47 edition of *General Aptitude Test Battery* (see 1376); distribution restricted to Canadian schools; Guidance Centre. *

For additional information, see 4:768.

[1950]

The Vincent Mechanical Models Test A (Industrial). Ages 14 and over; 1936–46; D. F. Vincent; National Institute of Industrial Psychology. *

For additional information and a review by A. T. Welford, see 4:769 (7 references).

[1951]

★Weights and Pulleys: A Test of Intuitive Mechanics. Grades 9–16 and industrial employees; 1956–59; L. L. Thurstone and T. E. Jeffrey; Education-Industry Service. *

MISCELLANEOUS

[1952]

*Admission Test for Graduate Study in Business. Business graduate students; 1954–61; tests administered 4 times annually at centers established by the publisher; 3 scores: quantitative, verbal, total; Educational Testing Service. *

For additional information, see 5:910.

[1953]

*Business Judgment Test. Adults; 1953–59; social intelligence in work situations; Martin M. Bruce; the Author. *

For additional information and a review by Edward B. Greene, see 5:893 (2 references).

[1954]

Cancellation Test. Adults; 1946; perceptual speed; John R. Roberts; Educational Test Bureau. *

For additional information and a review by Herbert A. Tonne, see 5:894; for a review by Joseph E. King, see 3:684.

[1955]

★Conference Meeting Rating Scale. Conference leaders and participants; 1959; B. J. Speroff; Psychometric Affiliates. *

[1956]

★Dartnell Self-Administered Employee Opinion Unit. Industry; 1955–58; attitudes toward job; Central Surveys, Inc.; Dartnell Corporation. *
a) EMPLOYEE QUESTIONNAIRE.
b) SUPERVISOR'S QUESTIONNAIRE.

[1957]

★Diagnostic Counseling Form for Educational, Preventive, and Remedial Counseling. High school; 1944; work interests and personal problems; 4 problem scores: ability to learn, ability to get along with others, ability to appreciate and enjoy, total; W. H. Winkler; [Winkler Publications]. *

[1958]

★Employee Opinion Survey. Business and industry; 1956; distribution restricted to clients; opinions in 5 areas: management and the company, supervision, work conditions, pay and benefits, general; R. W. Henderson; William, Lynde & Williams. *

[1959]

★Five Factor Inventory. Employees in industry; 1958; morale; for research use only; 5 scores: organization and management, immediate supervision, material rewards, fellow employees, job satisfaction; distribution restricted to companies using the publisher's survey services; [Melany E. Baehr and Richard Renck]; Industrial Relations Center. *

[1960]

★The General Information Survey. Adult males; 1954–56; functional command of everyday, nonacademic knowledge; for research use only; Harrison G. Gough; the Author. *

[1961]

Guidance Summary Form for Use in Vocational and Educational Counseling. Adults; 1946; adaptation of Aids to the Vocational Interview; George K. Bennett and Charles E. Orbach; Psychological Corporation. *

For additional information and a review by Norman Frederiksen, see 3:446 (1 excerpt).

[1962]

★Labor Turnover Tests. Employees; 1944–[53]; a battery consisting of Test of Economic Information (see 1971) and the carelessness score from Interest Inventory (an abbreviated edition of Inventory of Interest and Temperament Areas, see 202); W. H. Winkler; Winkler Publications. *

[1963]

Mathematical and Technical Test. Ages 11 and over; 1948; 11 scores: completing pictures, copying models, calculations, completing the series, continuing patterns, filling up gaps, technical insight, figure series, geometrical figures, remembering drawings, total; J. Luning Prak; George G. Harrap & Co. Ltd. *

For additional information and reviews by Charles R. Langmuir and F. W. Warburton, see 4:779.

[1964]

★Observation Test. Right handed job applicants; 1949; perceptual speed; W. H. Winkler; [Winkler Publications]. *

[1965]

★The Organization Survey. Employees in industry; 1958–61; formerly called Organization Attitude Survey; 11 scores: work organization, work efficiency, administrative effectiveness, leadership practices, communication effectiveness, personnel development, pay and benefits, immediate supervision, work associates, job satisfaction, organization identification, reactions to the survey; modifications for government employees and teachers available for research use only; distribution restricted to companies using the publisher's survey services; [Richard Renck, Robert K. Burns, Melany E. Baehr, and Willard E. Erickson]; Industrial Relations Center. *

[1966]

Per-Flu-Dex Tests. College and industry; 1955; 7 tests; Frank J. Holmes; Psychometric Affiliates. *
a) PER-SYMB TEST. Symbol number substitution.
b) PER-VERB TEST. Letter perception and counting.
c) PER-NUMB TEST. Number counting and perception.
d) FLU-VERB TEST. Word completion and verbal fluency.
e) FLU-NUMB TEST. Arithmetic computation.
f) THE DEX-MAN SCALE. Manual speed of movement.
g) DEX-AIM TEST. Aiming accuracy and speed.
For additional information and reviews by Andrew L. Comrey and John W. French, see 5:901.

[1967]

★**Q-Sort Cards for Executive Position.** Industry; 1958; for rating personality requirements for executive positions; Robert N. McMurry; Dartnell Corporation. *

[1968]

SRA Employee Inventory. Employees; 1951–58; attitudes toward job; 16 scores: job demands, working conditions, pay, employee benefits, friendliness and cooperation of fellow employees, supervisor-employee relations, confidence in management, technical competence of supervision, effectiveness of administration, adequacy of communication, job security and work relations, status and recognition, identification with the company, opportunity for growth and advancement, total, reactions to the inventory; Robert K. Burns, L. L. Thurstone, David G. Moore, and Melany E. Baehr; Science Research Associates, Inc. *
For additional information and reviews by Erwin K. Taylor and Albert S. Thompson, see 5:905 (10 references).

[1969]

A Self-Rating Scale for Leadership Qualifications. Adults; 1942–48; E. J. Benge; [National Foremen's Institute, Inc.]. *
For additional information, see 5:906.

[1970]

The Tear Ballot for Industry: General Opinions. Employees in industry; 1944–48; job satisfaction; Willard A. Kerr; Psychometric Affiliates. *
For additional information and a review by Brent Baxter, see 4:783 (4 references).

[1971]

★**Test of Economic Information.** Adults; 1953–57; 5 scores: industrial information, recognition of superiority of U.S. standard of living, recognition of mutual dependency of people, recognition of unintentional aspects of human friction, willingness to accept everyday hardships and inconveniences; W. H. Winkler; [Winkler Publications]. *

[1972]

★[Tests A/9 and A/10.] Applicants for technical and apprentice jobs; [1955]; interest in scientific fields; 2 tests; National Institute for Personnel Research. *
a) TEST A/9: [TECHNICAL AND SCIENTIFIC KNOWLEDGE].
b) TEST A/10: [TECHNICAL READING COMPREHENSION].

[1973]

★Whisler Strategy Test. Business and industry; 1959, c1955–59; "intelligent action"; 5 scores: number circled (confidence), number attempted, number right (accuracy), net, plunger-risk avoider index; Laurence D. Whisler; Psychometric Affiliates. *

[1974]

★Work Information Inventory. Employees in industry; 1958; morale; Raymond E. Bernberg; Psychometric Affiliates. *

SELECTION AND RATING FORMS

[1975]

★APT Controlled Interview. Applicants for employment; [1945]–56; distribution restricted to clients; 19 ratings: job experience (2 ratings), work history, financial status (2 ratings), marital status, voice (3 ratings), appearance (4 ratings), health (2 ratings), family background, relations with the law, social history, total; Associated Personnel Technicians, Inc. *

[1976]

[Biography Forms]: Application-Interview Series. Industry; 1948–56; 5 forms: clerical, mechanical, sales, technical, supervisor; Joseph E. King; Industrial Psychology, Inc. *
For additional information, see 5:892.

[1977]

*Diagnostic Interviewer's Guide. Applicants for employment; 1935–42; E. F. Wonderlic and S. N. Stevens; E. F. Wonderlic. *
For additional information, see 3:685. (2 references).

[1978]

Employee Evaluation Form for Interviewers. Adults; 1943; Richard A. Fear and Byron Jordan; Psychological Corporation. *
For additional information and reviews by Douglas H. Fryer and C. H. Ruedisili, see 3:686 (2 excerpts).

[1979]

Employee Merit Report. Employees; 1949; also called *Comprehensive Plan for Rating Employees;* 13 ratings: quality of work, quantity of work, knowledge of work, dependability, attitude toward work, adaptability, cooperation, initiative, personality, judgment, supervision, safety, overall merit; Keith Van Allyn; [Personnel Research, Inc.]. *
For additional information, see 4:771.

[1980]

[Employee Rating and Development Forms.] Executive, industrial, office, and sales personnel; 1950–58; 8 forms; Robert N. McMurry; Dartnell Corporation. *

a) PATTERNED MERIT REVIEW—EXECUTIVE.
b) PATTERNED MERIT REVIEW FORM—PLANT AND OFFICE.
c) PATTERNED MERIT REVIEW—SALES.
d) PATTERNED MERIT REVIEW—TECHNICAL OFFICE, SPECIAL SKILLS.
e) PATTERNED EXIT INTERVIEW.
f) PERSONAL HISTORY REVIEW FORM.
g) PHYSICAL RECORD.
h) STATEMENT OF SUPERVISORY EXPECTANCIES.

For additional information, see 5:895; for reviews by Harry W. Karn and Floyd L. Ruch of *b* and *c,* see 4:781.

[1981]

[Executive, Industrial, and Sales Personnel Forms.] Applicants for executive, office, industrial, or sales positions; 1949–56; 17 forms; Robert N. McMurry; Dartnell Corporation. *
a) APPLICATION FOR EXECUTIVE POSITION.
b) PATTERNED INTERVIEW FORM—EXECUTIVE POSITION.
c) PATTERNED INTERVIEW FORM. Applicants for positions of supervisor, foreman, and engineer.
d) TELEPHONE CHECK ON EXECUTIVE APPLICANT.
e) SELECTION AND EVALUATION SUMMARY. Executive, industrial, and sales personnel.
f) POSITION ANALYSIS. Executive, industrial, and sales personnel.
g) APPLICATION FOR [INDUSTRIAL] POSITION.
h) APPLICATION FOR EMPLOYMENT. Industrial applicants.
i) APPLICATION FOR OFFICE POSITION.
j) PATTERNED INTERVIEW (SHORT FORM). Applicants for office and industrial positions.
k) TELEPHONE CHECK [WITH PREVIOUS EMPLOYERS]. Industrial applicants.
l) TELEPHONE CHECK WITH SCHOOLS. Industrial applicants.
m) APPLICATION FOR SALES POSITION.
n) PATTERNED INTERVIEW FORM—SALES POSITION.
o) TELEPHONE CHECK ON SALES APPLICANT.
p) SALES APPLICATION VERIFICATION.
q) HOME INTERVIEW REPORT FORM. Sales applicants.

For additional information, see 5:896; for a review by Floyd L. Ruch, see 4:773.

[1982]

Hiring Summary Worksheet. Industry; 1956; for use with the publisher's tests and biographical forms; Joseph E. King; Industrial Psychology, Inc. *
For additional information, see 5:898.

[1983]

★**[Job Description Forms.]** Industry; 1958–60; 3 forms; Psychological Research Services, Western Reserve University; distributed by Personnel Research Institute. *
a) JOB ANALYSIS FORM FOR THE STUDY OF ENGINEERING AND SCIENTIFIC POSITIONS. 1958.
b) INTERVIEW FORM FOR COLLECTION OF JOB DESCRIPTION DATA: CLERICAL, SUPERVISORY, AND ADMINISTRATIVE. 1960.
c) INTERVIEW FORM FOR COLLECTION OF JOB DESCRIPTION DATA: FACTORY JOBS. 1958.

[1984]

★Job Description Questionnaire. Employees; 1947–60; Personnel Institute, Inc. *

[1985]

Lawshe-Kephart Personnel Comparison System. For rating any aspect of employee performance by the paired comparison technique; 1946–48; C. H. Lawshe, Jr. and N. C. Kephart; Southworth's Extension Service. *

For additional information and a review by Reign H. Bittner, see 4:778 (1 reference).

[1986]

★The McQuaig Manpower Selection Series. Male applicants for office and sales positions; 1957; 4 parts; Jack H. McQuaig; McQuaig Institute of Executive Training. *
a) PART 1, THE MCQUAIG TELEPHONE REFERENCE CHECK LIST.
b) PART 2, THE MCQUAIG SCREENING INTERVIEW GUIDE.
c) PART 3, PERSONAL HISTORY AND EXPERIENCE RECORD.
d) PART 4, THE MCQUAIG OCCUPATIONAL TEST.

[1987]

Merit Rating Series. Industry; 1948–57; formerly called *Employee Evaluation Series;* 5 forms; Joseph E. King and Judith W. Wingert; Industrial Psychology, Inc. *
a) PERFORMANCE: CLERICAL. 1957.
b) PERFORMANCE: MECHANICAL. 1953.
c) PERFORMANCE: SALES. 1953.
d) PERFORMANCE: TECHNICAL. 1957.
e) PERFORMANCE: SUPERVISOR. 1953.

For additional information, see 5:900; for a review by Brent Baxter of the original series, see 4:770 (1 reference).

[1988]

[Occupational Adjustment Forms.] High school dropouts and graduates; 1941; Implementation Commission of the National Association of Secondary-School Principals; the Association. *
a) POST-SCHOOL INVENTORY.
b) FOLLOW-UP INTERVIEW SCHEDULE.
c) EMPLOYER INTERVIEW SCHEDULE.
d) FOLLOW-UP RECORD CARD.

[1989]

The Performance Record. Industry; 1955; form for recording behavior incidents; John C. Flanagan and Robert B. Miller; Science Research Associates, Inc. *

For additional information and reviews by Albert K. Kurtz and Albert S. Thompson, see 5:902 (1 reference).

[1990]

★[Performance Review Forms.] Employees, managers; 1960–61; 2 forms; Seymour Levy; Martin M. Bruce. *
a) COUNSELING INTERVIEW SUMMARY. Employees, managers; 1960; for summarizing a performance review interview.

b) MANAGERIAL PERFORMANCE REVIEW. Managers; 1961; ratings by supervisors preparatory to performance review interview.

[1991]

Personal Data Blank. Counselees of ages 15 and over; 1934–52; J. Gustav White; Consulting Psychologists Press, Inc. *

For additional information and a review by Arthur E. Traxler, see 5:903; for reviews by Edward S. Jones and Donald G. Paterson of an earlier edition, see 40:1669.

[1992]

★[**Personnel Interviewing Forms.**] Business and industry; 1956; Judd-Safian Associates; Martin M. Bruce. *
a) INITIAL INTERVIEW TABULATION.
b) PERSONAL HISTORY AUDIT.
c) DEPTH INTERVIEW PATTERN.
d) EMPLOYMENT REFERENCE INQUIRY.

SPECIFIC VOCATIONS

[1993]

Probst Rating System. Adults; 1928–47; 7 forms; J. B. Probst; Probst Rating System. *
a) PROBST SERVICE REPORT: FIRE DEPARTMENT FORM. Fire fighting personnel; 1932–47.
b) PROBST SERVICE REPORT: GENERAL FORM. Clerical workers, supervisors, salesmen, salesclerks, and personnel not covered by the other forms; 1928–45.
c) PROBST SERVICE REPORT: POLICE FORM. Police personnel, guards, and watchmen; 1932–48.
d) PROBST SERVICE REPORT: PROFESSIONAL FORM. Social service, library, medical, engineering, and other professions; 1932–46.
e) PROBST SERVICE REPORT: SKILLED LABOR FORM. Skilled trades, crafts, and special semiskilled workers; 1932–45.
f) PROBST SERVICE REPORT: LABOR FORM. Unskilled and semiskilled workers; 1932.
g) PROBST PERSONAL FITNESS REPORT: PERSONAL FITNESS FORM. Employees and applicants; 1936–45; formerly called *Probst Personality Report: Personality Form.*

For additional information and reviews by Milton M. Mandell and Dale Yoder, see 4:785 (2 references); for excerpts from related book reviews, see 4:786.

ACCOUNTING

[1994]

*****Accounting Orientation Test: High School Level.** Grades 10–12; 1953–60; 4 scores: vocabulary, arithmetic reasoning, accounting problems, total; Committee on Personnel Testing, American Institute of Certified Public Accountants. *
For additional information, see 5:907 (2 references).

[1995]

*****American Institute of Certified Public Accountants Testing Programs.** Grades 13–16 and accountants; 1946–60; 2 programs: College Accounting Testing Program (tests available 3 times annually) and Professional Accounting Testing Program (tests available to accountant employers at any time and also administered at regional testing centers) ; 3 tests; Committee on Personnel Testing, American Institute of Certified Public Accountants. *

a) ORIENTATION TEST. 3 scores: verbal, quantitative, total.

b) ACHIEVEMENT TEST: LEVELS I AND 2.

c) STRONG VOCATIONAL INTEREST BLANK FOR MEN, REVISED. See 1887; scored for 27 scales and plotted on an accountant's profile.

For additional information, see 5:911 (6 references) ; see also 4:787 (15 references).

DENTISTRY

[1996]

*Dental Aptitude Testing Program. Dental school applicants; 1946–60; tests administered 3 times annually at centers established by the publisher; 5 tests; Division of Educational Measurements, Council on Dental Education, American Dental Association; the Council. *

a) CARVING DEXTERITY TEST. 1946–60; Committee on Aptitude Testing.

b) COOPERATIVE SCHOOL AND COLLEGE ABILITY TESTS. See 743.

c) READING COMPREHENSION IN THE NATURAL SCIENCES. 1953–55; Committee on Aptitude Testing.

d) SPACE RELATIONS TEST: DIFFERENTIAL APTITUDE TESTS. See 1371.

e) SURVEY OF THE NATURAL SCIENCES. 1951–58; 5 scores: biology, chemistry, factual, application, total; Committee on Aptitude Testing.

For additional information, see 5:916 (6 references) ; see also 4:788 (2 references).

[1997]

*Dental Hygiene Aptitude Testing Program. Dental hygiene school applicants; 1947–59; tests administered 3 times annually at centers established by the American Dental Hygienists' Association; 4 tests; Psychological Corporation. *

a) STUDY-READING TEST. 1955.

b) DENTAL HYGIENE APTITUDE TESTING PROGRAM, PARTS I AND 2. 1947–57.

c) COLLEGE QUALIFICATION TESTS, TEST I. See 740.

d) THE PERSONAL PREFERENCE SCHEDULE. 1953–55; adaptation of *Edwards Personal Preference Schedule* (see 143) ; 6 scores: achievement, orderliness, persistence, congeniality, altruism, respectfulness.

For additional information, see 5:917.

ENGINEERING

[1998]

★AC Test of Creative Ability. Engineers and supervisors; 1953–60; 3 types of scores: quantity, uniqueness, quality; Richard H. Harris and A. L. Simberg; Education-Industry Service. *

[1999]

★Creativity Test. Applicants for engineering positions; 1960, c1957–60; 3 scores: fluency, flexibility, total; C. H. Lawshe and D. H. Harris; distributed by University Book Store. *

[2000]

Engineering Aide Test 50-A. Engineering aides; 1957; Public Personnel Association. *

For additional information, see 5:919.

[2001]

Engineering and Physical Science Aptitude Test. Grade 12 and technical school entrants; 1943–51; 7 scores: mathematics, formulation, physical science comprehension, arithmetic reasoning, verbal comprehension, mechanical comprehension, total; Bruce V. Moore, C. J. Lapp, Charles H. Griffin, and Henry Borow; Psychological Corporation. *

For additional information and a review by John W. French, see 4:810 (6 references); for reviews by Norman Frederiksen and Robert M. W. Travers, see 3:698.

[2002]

★**Engineering Interest Comparisons.** High school; 1949; checklist of specific engineering job titles; 5 scores: precision work, figures, production engineering, conference work, research; W. H. Winkler; [Winkler Publications]. *

[2003]

*****The Graduate Record Examinations Advanced Tests: Engineering.** Grades 16–17; 1939–60; Educational Testing Service. * For the testing program entry, see 1353.

For additional information, see 5:923. For a review of the testing program, see 5:601.

[2004]

Minnesota Engineering Analogies Test. Candidates for graduate school and industry; 1954–55; tests administered at licensed testing centers; Marvin D. Dunnette; Psychological Corporation. *

For additional information and reviews by A. Pemberton Johnson and William B. Schrader, see 5:933 (6 references).

[2005]

★**The Owens' Creativity Test for Machine Design.** Engineers and engineering students; 1960; 4 scores: power source apparatus designs (workable solutions, total solutions), applications of mechanisms, weighted total; William A. Owens; Iowa State University Press. *

[2006]

Pre-Engineering Ability Test. Engineering school entrants; 1951–52; an abbreviated adaptation of the *Pre-Engineering Inventory* ('43); Cooperative Test Division. *

For additional information and reviews by Jerome E. Doppelt and Dewey B. Stuit, see 4:812 (11 references).

[2007]

★**The Professional Employee Inventory: An Attitude Survey for Professional Personnel.** Scientists and engineers; 1959; 12 scores: job satisfaction, friendliness of associates, pay and benefits, immediate supervision, identification with company, supervisory practices, administrative effectiveness, work organization, adequacy of communications, opportunities for growth and advancement, relations with top management, reactions to the inventory; for research use only; distribution restricted to companies using the publisher's survey services; Industrial Relations Center. *

[2008]

Stanford Scientific Aptitude Test. Entrants to schools of engineering and science; 1929–30; D. L. Zyve; distributed by Consulting Psychologists Press, Inc. *

For additional information and reviews by Joseph E. Moore and Dewey B. Stuit, see 4:813 (4 references); for a review by A. B. Crawford, see 40:1676 (3 references).

LAW

[2009]

Iowa Legal Aptitude Test, 1946 Revision. Law school applicants; 1946–48; 8 scores: analogies, reasoning, opposites, relevancy, mixed relations, memory, information, total; Michael Adams, L. K. Funks, and D. B. Stuit; Bureau of Educational Research and Service. *

For additional information and a review by Alexander G. Wesman, see 4:814 (5 references).

[2010]

*Law School Admission Test. Law school entrants; 1948–61; test administered 4 times annually at centers established by the publisher; Educational Testing Service. *

For additional information, see 5:928 (7 references); for a review by Alexander G. Wesman of Form YLS2, see 4:815 (6 references).

MEDICINE

[2011]

Medical College Admission Test. Medical school applicants; 1946–56; test administered 2 times annually at centers established by the publisher; 4 scores: verbal, quantitative, modern society, science; Psychological Corporation. *

For additional information and a review by Alexander G. Wesman of forms previously published by Educational Testing Service, see 5:932 (4 references); for a review by Morey J. Wantman, see 4:817 (11 references).

[2012]

★Medical Preference Inventory, (Revised Edition). Medical school entrants; 1953–60; for research use only; Harrison G. Gough; the Author. *

[2013]

*Veterinary Aptitude Test. Veterinary school applicants; 1951–58; tests administered at centers established by the publisher; 3 booklets, 4 scores: total and the 3 scores listed below; Loyal C. Payne and William A. Owens; Psychological Corporation. *

a) PART 1 [READING COMPREHENSION].
b) PARTS 2 AND 3 [SCIENCE INFORMATION]. Part 2 formerly called *Veterinary Achievement Test;* part 3 is the stimulus material for part 4.
c) PART 4 [VERBAL MEMORY].
For additional information, see 5:957 (3 references).

MISCELLANEOUS

[2014]

★**Air Force Preference Inventory.** Adults; 1952; personal preferences; 3 scores: military officer effectiveness, intellectual aptitude, communality of interest; experimental form; Harrison G. Gough and Leslie H. Squire; Harrison G. Gough. *

[2015]

★**Aptitude Test E51 (Revision 3) for Electronic Data-Processing Programmers.** Applicants for computer programming positions; 1958–60; [Data Processing Systems & Sales], National Cash Register Co. *

[2016]

★**Chemical Operators Selection Test, Revised Edition.** Male high school students and applicants for positions of chemical operator; 1959, c1958; M. A. Storr, J. H. McPherson, P. A. Maschino, and R. G. Garner; Dow Chemical Co. *

[2017]

★**Correctional Officers' Interest Blank.** Applicants for jobs in penal institutions and correctional agencies; 1952–57; for research use only; Harrison G. Gough and F. L. Aumack; Harrison G. Gough. *

[2018]

★**The Diebold Personnel Tests.** Programmers and systems analysts for automatic data processing and computing installations; 1959; 5 tests; scoring by the publisher only; John Diebold & Associates, Inc. *
a) SYMBOLS BLOCK DIAGRAM TEST.
b) CODE INDEX TEST.
c) RELATIONS IN NUMBERS TEST.
d) CODE MATCHING TEST.
e) WORD SEQUENCE TEST.

[2019]

★**Educational Tests for New York Stock Exchange Member Organization Employees, 21st Edition.** Employees and employee applicants of investment and brokerage firms; 1939–61; new edition issued annually; New York Institute of Finance. *

[2020]

Firefighter Test. Firemen; 1954–58; Public Personnel Association. *
For additional information, see 5:921.

[2021]

P-L-S Journalism Test. High school and college; 1944; George H. Phillips, Harry Levinson, and H. E. Schrammel; Bureau of Educational Measurements. *
For additional information, see 3:149.

[2022]

Personnel Service Rating Report. Library personnel; 1948; Subcommittee on Service Ratings of the ALA Board on Personnel Administration; American Library Association. *
For additional information, see 5:939.

[2023]

Policeman Test. Policemen; 1953–57; Public Personnel Association. *
For additional information, see 5:940.

[2024]

★**The Potter-Nash Aptitude Test for Lumber Inspectors and Other General Personnel Who Handle Lumber.** Employees in woodworking industries; 1958; arithmetic; F. T. Potter and N. Nash; N. Nash. *

[2025]

Punched Card Machine Operator Aptitude Test. Prospective IBM punched card equipment operators; 1952–55; Walter J. McNamara; International Business Machines Corporation. *
For additional information, see 5:941.

[2025a]

★**Revised Programmer Aptitude Test.** Applicants for programming training on IBM electronic computers; 1955–59; 4 scores: number series, figure analogies, arithmetic reasoning, total; J. L. Hughes and W. J. McNamara; distributed by W. J. McNamara. *

[2026]

★**The Social Work Interest Inventory, Revised Edition.** Social welfare students and workers; 1953–57; for research use only; David W. Axelrod and Harrison G. Gough; Harrison G. Gough. *

[2027]

The Store Personnel Test. Food store employees; 1946–51; 2 scores: checking, problems; Harold G. Seashore and Charles E. Orbach; Psychological Corporation. *
For additional information and reviews by Raymond A. Katzell and John B. Morris, see 5:954 (1 reference).

NURSING

[2028]

*Achievement Tests in Nursing.** Nurses; 1952–61; 12 tests; Psychological Corporation. *
a) ANATOMY AND PHYSIOLOGY. 1953–60.
b) CHEMISTRY. 1954–58.
c) COMMUNICABLE DISEASES. 1953–61.
d) MEDICAL NURSING. 1952–61.
e) MICROBIOLOGY. 1952–61.
f) NUTRITION AND DIET THERAPY. 1952–58.
g) OBSTETRICAL NURSING. 1952–61.
h) PEDIATRIC NURSING. 1952–58.
i) PHARMACOLOGY. 1952–58.
j) PSYCHIATRIC NURSING. 1952–58.
k) PSYCHOLOGY AND SOCIOLOGY. 1958.
l) SURGICAL NURSING. 1952–58.
For additional information, see 5:908.

[2029]

Achievement Tests in Practical Nursing. Practical nursing students; 1957; 2 scores: medical and surgical nursing, nutrition-pediatric-obstetrical nursing; Psychological Corporation. *
For additional information, see 5:909.

[2030]

★**Entrance Examination for Schools of Nursing.** Nursing school applicants; 1938–60; tests administered at centers established by the publisher; 4 tests, 15 scores: scholastic aptitude (weighted total of verbal ability, numerical ability, science information, reading comprehension, and arithmetic reasoning scores from *a* and *b*) and 14 scores listed below; Psychological Corporation. *
a) POTTS-BENNETT TESTS, SECTION III. 1951; 2 scores: verbal ability, numerical ability; Edith Margaret Potts, George K. Bennett, and Alexander G. Wesman.
b) POTTS-BENNETT TESTS, SECTION IV. 1951; 5 scores: science information, arithmetic processes, general information, arithmetic reasoning, reading comprehension; Edith Margaret Potts and George K. Bennett.
c) TESTS OF MECHANICAL COMPREHENSION. See 1946.
d) THE PERSONAL PREFERENCE SCHEDULE FOR STUDENT NURSES. 1953–55; adaptation of *Edwards Personal Preference Schedule* (see 143); 6 scores: achievement, orderliness, persistence, congeniality, altruism, respectfulness.

[2031]

Entrance Examinations for Schools of Practical Nursing. Practical nursing school applicants; 1942–57; tests administered at regional centers established by the publisher; 3 tests; Psychological Corporation. *
a) ENTRANCE EXAMINATION FOR SCHOOLS OF PRACTICAL NURSING. 1957; 5 scores: verbal ability, numerical ability, academic ability, household information, arithmetic.
b) TESTS OF MECHANICAL COMPREHENSION. See 1946.
c) THE PERSONAL PREFERENCE SCHEDULE FOR STUDENT NURSES. 1953–55; adaptation of *Edwards Personal Preference Schedule* (see 143); 6 scores: achievement, orderliness, persistence, congeniality, altruism, respectfulness.
For additional information, see 5:920.

[2032]

George Washington University Series Nursing Tests. Prospective nurses; 1931–50; 5 tests; Thelma Hunt; Center for Psychological Service. *
a) APTITUDE TEST FOR NURSING. 1931–40.
b) ARITHMETIC TEST FOR PROSPECTIVE NURSES. 1940–49.
c) READING COMPREHENSION TEST FOR PROSPECTIVE NURSES. 1940.
d) GENERAL SCIENCE TEST FOR PROSPECTIVE NURSES. 1944.
e) INTEREST-PREFERENCE TEST FOR PROSPECTIVE NURSES. 1944.
For additional information, see 4:818 (2 references); see also 3:699 (6 references).

[2033]

***NLN Achievement Tests for Basic Professional Nursing Program.** Students in state-approved schools of professional nursing; 1943–61; 2 series; National League for Nursing, Inc. *
a) [REGULAR ACHIEVEMENT TESTS.] Undergraduates completing courses in the subjects specified; 1943–61; 12 tests.

1) *Anatomy and Physiology.* 1943–55.

2) *Chemistry.* 1943–55.

3) *Microbiology.* 1943–55.

4) *Nutrition and Diet Therapy.* 1946–57.

5) *Basic Pharmacology.* 1944–60; formerly called *Pharmacology and Therapeutics.*

6) *Medical-Surgical Nursing.* 1956.

7) *Communicable Disease Nursing.* 1946–55.

8) *Social Sciences in Nursing.* 1956.

9) *Public Health Nursing.* 1956.

10) *Obstetric Nursing.* 1945–61; 4 scores: ante-partal care, partal and post-partal care of mothers, care of newborn, total.

11) *Nursing of Children.* 1945–61; 4 scores: normal growth and development, pediatric nursing (psycho-social aspects, other aspects), total.

12) *Psychiatric Nursing.* 1945–59; 3 scores: psychiatric nursing practices, facts and principles, total.

b) [COMPREHENSIVE ACHIEVEMENT TESTS.] Seniors about to graduate; 1957–61; 4 tests.

1) *Pharmacology in Clinical Nursing (Facts and Principles and Their Application).* 1960.

2) *Natural Sciences in Nursing.* 1957; 3 scores: facts and principles (knowledge, application), total.

3) *Maternal and Child Health Nursing.* 1958; 3 scores: psychological aspects, non-psychological aspects, total.

4) *Disaster Nursing.* 1961; 3 scores: general nursing applied to disasters, facts and principles of disasters and disaster nursing, total.

For additional information, see 5:934 (1 reference).

[2034]

⋆**NLN Achievement Tests for Psychiatric Aides.** Hospital psychiatric aides and attendants; 1958; 2 tests; National League for Nursing, Inc. *

a) ELEMENTARY PSYCHIATRIC NURSING.

b) BASIC NURSING PROCEDURES AND ELEMENTARY NUTRITION. 3 scores: basic nursing procedures, elementary nutrition, total.

[2035]

***NLN Graduate Nurse Examination.** Registered professional nurses; 1945–60; formerly called *NLN Graduate Nurse Qualifying Examination;* tests administered at centers established by the NLN; National League for Nursing, Inc. *

a) NLN TEST OF ACADEMIC APTITUDE. Special printing of level 1 (for grades 12–14) of *Cooperative School and College Ability Tests* (see 743).

b) NLN READING COMPREHENSION TEST. Special printing of higher level (for grades 13–14) of *Reading Comprehension: Cooperative English Tests, [1960 Revision]* (see 1436).

c) [NURSING TESTS.] Earlier test called *Clinical Test;* 4 parts, 5 scores: total and 4 scores listed below.

1) *Medical-Surgical Nursing Section.*

2) *Psychiatric Nursing Section.*

3) *Maternal and Child Nursing Section.*

4) *Science Section (Selected Areas of the Natural Sciences and Applications).*

For additional information, see 5:935 (1 reference).

[2036]

NLN Practical Nurse Achievement Tests. Students in approved schools of practical nursing; 1950–58; 2 tests; National League for Nursing, Inc. *

a) PRACTICAL NURSE BASIC ACHIEVEMENT TEST. 1957–58; 4 scores: body structure and function, basic nursing procedures, nutrition and diet therapy, total.

b) PRACTICAL NURSE ACHIEVEMENT TEST. 1950–56; 3 scores: medical-surgical nursing, maternal-child nursing, total.

For additional information, see 5:936.

[2037]

NLN Pre-Admission and Classification Examination. Practical nursing school entrants; 1950–58; 2 tests, 8 scores: total and 7 scores listed below; National League for Nursing, Inc. *

a) GENERAL INFORMATION AND JUDGMENT TEST. 4 scores: science and health, general information, arithmetic, total.

b) VOCABULARY AND READING TEST. 3 scores: vocabulary, reading, total.

For additional information, see 5:937.

[2038]

*NLN Pre-Nursing and Guidance Examination. Applicants for admission to state-approved schools of professional nursing; 1941–61; tests administered at centers established by the NLN; 5 tests; National League for Nursing, Inc. *

a) NLN TEST OF ACADEMIC APTITUDE. Special printing of level 1 (for grades 12–14) of *Cooperative School and College Ability Tests* (see 743).

b) NLN READING COMPREHENSION TEST. Special printing of higher level (for grades 13–14) of *Reading Comprehension: Cooperative English Tests, [1960 Revision]* (see 1436).

c) NLN MATHEMATICS TEST. Abbreviated edition of an earlier form of *Cooperative Mathematics Tests for Grades 7, 8, and 9* (see 947).

d) NLN NATURAL SCIENCE ACHIEVEMENT TEST. Special printing of *Cooperative General Achievement Tests: Test 2, Natural Science* (see 1548).

e) NLN SOCIAL STUDIES ACHIEVEMENT TEST. Special printing of *Cooperative General Achievement Tests: Test 1, Social Studies* (see 1710).

For additional information, see 5:938 (2 references).

RESEARCH

[2039]

★Research Personnel Review Form. Research and engineering and scientific firms; 1959–60; for supervisor's evaluation of research personnel in preparation for a performance review interview; Morris I. Stein; Science Research Associates, Inc. *

[2040]

★Surveys of Research Administration and Environment. Research and engineering and scientific firms; 1959–60; 2 forms for gathering information and opinions on the company and its research activities; Morris I. Stein; Science Research Associates, Inc. *

a) STEIN RESEARCH ENVIRONMENT SURVEY. Research and technical personnel.

b) STEIN SURVEY FOR ADMINISTRATORS. Supervisors and administrators; also part of *Technical Personnel Recruiting Inventory* (see 2041).

[2041]

★Technical Personnel Recruiting Inventory. Research and engineering and scientific firms; 1959–60; 3 parts; Morris I. Stein; Science Research Associates, Inc. *

a) INDIVIDUAL QUALIFICATION FORM. For supervisor's description of an available research position.

b) PERSONAL DATA FORM FOR SCIENTIFIC, ENGINEERING, AND TECHNICAL PERSONNEL. Job applicants.

c) STEIN SURVEY FOR ADMINISTRATORS. For administrator's description of company's research environment; also part of *Surveys of Research Administration and Environment* (see 2040).

SELLING

[2042]

*Aptitude Index Selection Procedure. Prospective male ordinary life insurance agents; 1938–60; 2 tests; distribution restricted to home offices of member life insurance companies; Life Insurance Agency Management Association. *

a) BIOGRAPHICAL PROFILE. 1960; a preliminary screening test.

b) APTITUDE INDEX. 1938–60; 1 score combining an evaluation of life insurance information, personal background, interests, and attitudes.

For additional information concerning *b*, see 5:913 (1 reference); for reviews by Donald G. Paterson and Albert S. Thompson of an earlier form, see 4:825 (14 references); see also 40:1646 (5 references).

[2043]

*Aptitudes Associates Test of Sales Aptitude: A Test for Measuring Knowledge of Basic Principles of Selling. Applicants for sales positions; 1947–60; Martin M. Bruce; the Author. * For the revised edition, see 2061.

For additional information, see 5:914; for reviews by Milton E. Hahn and Donald G. Paterson, see 4:824 (1 reference).

[2044]

★Combination Inventory. Prospective debit life insurance salesmen; 1954; 5 parts: arithmetic, mental alertness (items in parts 1 and 2 selected from tests developed by the Life Office Management Association), vocational interest (items selected from *Strong Vocational Interest Blank for Men, Revised*), personality (social desirability), personal history (economic maturity); distribution restricted to home offices of member life insurance companies; Life Insurance Agency Management Association. *

[2045]

★The Dealer Inventory. Manufacturers' distributors; 1956–58; attitudes and opinions about company represented; 11 scores: company relations, administrative services, company products, product services, sales promotion, distribution system, pricing policies, credit policies, administrative ability of company representative, technical competence of the company representative, reactions to survey; distribution restricted to companies using the publisher's survey services; Richard Renck, George Y. Ogawa, David N. Larson, and Robert K. Burns; Industrial Relations Center. *

[2046]

Detroit Retail Selling Inventory. Candidates for training in retail selling; 1940, c1939; 5 scores: personality, intelligence, checking, arithmetic, total; Harry J. Baker and Paul H. Voelker; Public School Publishing Co. *

For additional information and reviews by Milton E. Hahn and Floyd L. Ruch, see 3:697 (2 excerpts).

[2047]

★**Diplomacy Test of Empathy.** Salesmen and sales managers; 1960; selling ability and persuasiveness; Willard A. Kerr; Psychometric Affiliates. *

[2048]

★**[Employee Rating Forms.]** Employees in sales organizations; 1946–57; supervisors' ratings in 3 areas: human factor, work history, developmental factor; Personnel Institute, Inc. *

a) EMPLOYEE RATING REPORT. General employees; 1950.

b) MANAGER RATING REPORT. 1946–57.

c) SALESMAN RATING REPORT. 1947.

[2049]

★**The Evaluation Record.** Prospective ordinary life insurance agency managers; 1955–58; combination of evaluation procedures yielding a composite score; distribution restricted to home offices of member life insurance companies; Life Insurance Agency Management Association. *

a) EXPERIENCE FORM.

b) STRONG VOCATIONAL INTEREST BLANK FOR MEN, REVISED. See 1887; scored for production manager only.

c) HOME OFFICE RATING CHART. Ratings of personal qualities by supervisors.

[2050]

Hall Salespower Inventory. Salesmen; 1946–57; 10 scores: background, intelligence, aggressiveness, dominance, sales temperament, sales interest, introversion-extroversion, motivation, emotional, total; Clifton W. Hall and Richard M. Page; Hall & Liles. *

For additional information, see 5:924.

[2051]

Hanes Sales Selection Inventory, Revised Edition. Insurance and printing salesmen; 1954–55; 3 scores: verbal, personality, drive; Bernard Hanes; Psychometric Affiliates. *

For additional information, see 5:925.

[2052]

Hiring Kit. Applicants for sales positions; 1944–48; formerly listed as *Bigelow Hiring Kit;* 8 parts; distribution restricted to clients; Edwin G. Flemming and Burton Bigelow; Edwin G. Flemming. *

a) PRELIMINARY EXPLORATORY INTERVIEW QUESTIONS. 1947.

b) RESULTS OF PRELIMINARY EXPLORATORY INTERVIEW. 1947.

c) PERSONAL HISTORY RECORD. 1944.

d) EVALUATION OF PERSONAL HISTORY RECORD. 1946.

e) QUESTIONS TO ASK PREVIOUS EMPLOYERS. 1947.
f) PATTERNED ANALYTICAL INTERVIEW: PART I, INTERVIEW GUIDE. 1947.
g) PATTERNED ANALYTICAL INTERVIEW: PART II, INTERVIEWER'S JUDGMENTS BLANK. 1947.
h) QUESTIONS FOR MEDICAL EXAMINER. 1947.
For additional information, see 4:826.

[2053]

★**How to Develop Sales Ability.** Salesmen; 1956; "initiative in the selling process"; W. H. Winkler; [Winkler Publications]. *

[2054]

*****Information Index.** Life insurance agents; 1951–59; life insurance information; distribution restricted to home offices of member life insurance companies; Life Insurance Agency Management Association. *
For additional information, see 5:927 (3 references).

[2055]

★**Interviewer's Impressions—Sales Applicants.** Adults; [1956]; [Eugene J. Benge]; Management Service Co. *

[2056]

LIAMA Inventory of Job Attitudes. Life insurance agents; 1956; job satisfaction in 17 areas; distribution restricted to home offices of member life insurance companies; Life Insurance Agency Management Association. *
For additional information, see 5:929.

[2057]

Measure of Consociative Tendency. Applicants for sales and supervisory positions; 1951; personal history blank; Doncaster G. Humm and Kathryn A. Humm; Humm Personnel Consultants. *
For additional information, see 5:931.

[2058]

*****Personnel Institute Hiring Kit.** Applicants for sales positions; 1954–59; Personnel Institute, Inc. *
a) PRELIMINARY SCREENING INTERVIEW. 1957.
b) PERSONAL HISTORY INVENTORY. 1957.
c) DIAGNOSTIC INTERVIEWER'S GUIDE. 1957.
d) PERSONAL OR TELEPHONE WORK REFERENCE CHECK. 1957–59; formerly called *Work Reference Investigation.*
e) SELECTOR TEST BATTERY. Applicants for routine selling jobs; 1955–56; 3 tests: *EM-AY Inventory* (reprint of Test 2 of *Otis Employment Tests*, Form A), *ESS-AY Inventory* (sales aptitude), and *The Personality Inventory* (see 246).
f) COMPREHENSIVE TEST BATTERY. Applicants for complex selling jobs; 1955–57; 6 tests: same as for *e* above plus *Vocabulary Inventory, Social Intelligence Test* (see 291), and *B-B-ESS Inventory* (business skills).
For additional information, see 5:904.

[2059]

★**Personnel Research Institute Area Interview-Long Form.** Applicants for sales positions; 1951; 14 ratings: work history, recent jobs, educational history, service record, family background, present domestic and economic situation, attitudes, reaction to present proposition, overall rating, appearance-manner-dress, physical energy and health, speech, judgment, persuasiveness; Personnel Research Institute. *

[2060]

★SRA Sales Attitudes Check List. Applicants for sales positions; 1960; extension of *Sales Personnel Description Form* (see 2065); Erwin K. Taylor and the Personnel Research & Development Corporation; Science Research Associates, Inc. *

[2061]

Sales Comprehension Test. Sales applicants; 1953–57; revision of *Aptitudes Associates Test of Sales Aptitude* (see 2043); Martin M. Bruce; the Author. *
    For additional information and a review by Raymond A. Katzell, see 5:947 (10 references); for reviews by Milton E. Hahn and Donald G. Paterson of the original edition, see 4:824 (1 reference).

[2062]

★Sales Employee Inventory. Outside salesmen; 1958; attitudes and opinions about company represented; 14 scores: the company, management, supervisory administrative skills, supervisory communication skills, company products, pricing and credit, customer service, advertising, sales training, work goals, job satisfaction, pay, benefits, reactions to the survey; distribution restricted to companies using the publisher's survey services; Richard Renck, George Y. Ogawa, and David N. Larson; Industrial Relations Center. *

[2063]

★Sales Method Index. Life insurance agents; 1948–60; continuous work-diary record of specific sales procedures and effectiveness for supervisory and self-analysis; distribution restricted to home offices of member life insurance companies; Life Insurance Agency Management Association. *

[2064]

Sales Motivation Inventory. Sales applicants; 1953; Martin M. Bruce; the Author. *
    For additional information and a review by S. Rains Wallace, see 5:948 (2 references).

[2065]

*Sales Personnel Description Form. Salesmen; 1953–60; forced-choice rating scale; Personnel Research Institute. *
    For additional information, see 5:949.

[2066]

Sales Situation Test. Prospective salesmen; 1951; Milton L. Rock; Aptitude Test Service. *
    For additional information, see 4:827 (1 reference).

[2067]

*Steward Basic Factors Inventory (1960 Edition). Applicants for sales and office positions; 1957–60; revision of *Steward Sales Aptitude Inventory;* originally called *Steward Vocational Fitness Inventory;* 12 scores: business knowledge (vocabulary, arithmetic, total), dominance, personal adjustment, occupational interests (clerical, artistic, supervisory, accounting, writing, selling, mechanical); Verne Steward; Verne Steward & Associates. *

For additional information concerning the earlier edition, see 5:953.

[2068]

Steward Life Insurance Knowledge Test. Applicants for life insurance agent or supervisory positions; 1952–56; 5 scores: arithmetic, vocabulary, principles, functions, total; Verne Steward; Verne Steward & Associates. *

For additional information, see 5:950.

[2069]

Steward Occupational Objectives Inventory, 1957 Edition. Applicants for supervisory positions in life insurance companies or agencies; 1956–57; formerly called *Steward Supervisory Personnel Inventory;* ratings in 8 areas: caliber level, life insurance knowledge, selling skills, leadership ability, supervisory skills, personal adjustment, survival on job, supplementary items; Verne Steward; Verne Steward & Associates. *

For additional information, see 5:951.

[2070]

*Steward Personal Background Inventory (1960 Revised Edition). Applicants for sales positions; 1949–60; revision of *Personal Inventory of Background Factors;* ratings in 7 areas: health, education, experience, financial status, activities, family status, miscellaneous; Verne Steward; Verne Steward & Associates. *

For additional information, see 5:952 (1 reference).

[2071]

★Steward Personnel Tests (Short Form), 1958 Edition. Applicants for sales and office positions; 1957–58; abbreviated version of *Steward Sales Aptitude Inventory;* 9 scores: business knowledge, arithmetic, occupational interests (clerical, artistic, supervisory, accounting, writing, selling, mechanical); Verne Steward; Verne Steward & Associates. *

[2072]

★[Steward Sales Personnel Analysis System.] Life insurance salesmen and agency supervisors; 1956–60; 4 tests and 3 rating forms; Verne Steward; Verne Steward & Associates. *

a) STEWARD BASIC FACTORS INVENTORY. See 2067.
b) STEWARD PERSONAL BACKGROUND INVENTORY. See 2070.
c) STEWARD OCCUPATIONAL OBJECTIVES INVENTORY. See 2069.
d) STEWARD LIFE INSURANCE KNOWLEDGE TEST. See 2068.
e) REPORT FORM A—MANAGER'S FINDINGS FOR THE AGENCY AS A WHOLE. 1956.
f) REPORT FORM B—MANAGER'S FINDINGS FOR EACH AGENT. 1956.
g) REPORT FORM C—MANAGER'S FINDINGS FOR EACH SUPERVISOR. 1956.

[2073]

Test for Ability to Sell: George Washington University Series. Grades 7–16 and adults; 1929–50; F. A. Moss, Herbert Wyle, William Loman, William Middleton, Thelma Hunt, Robert George, and William Schnell; Center for Psychological Service. *

For additional information, see 4:829; for a review by Floyd L. Ruch, see 3:705.

[2074]

★**Test of Sales Ability.** Applicants for sales positions; 1944-[55]; a battery consisting of *Inventory of Interest and Temperament Areas* (see 202), *Job Alertness Tests* (see 776), and (optionally) industrial information score from *Test of Economic Information* (see 1971); W. H. Winkler; Winkler Publications. *

[2075]

★**The Test of Sales Insight.** Applicants for sales positions; 1960; experimental form; Russell N. Cassel; the Author. *

[2076]

Test of Sales Judgment. Sales applicants; 1946; distribution restricted to business firms employing the consultant services of publisher; Edwin G. Flemming and Cecile W. Flemming; [Edwin G. Flemming]. *

For additional information, see 4:830.

[2077]

★**Word Check Forms.** Applicants for sales and managerial positions; 1952-60; a series of sentence completion and checklist forms yielding a "motivation profile" of 50 scores in 5 categories: wants (solving problems, making money, harmony-beauty, social values, authority power, enthuse), working media (people, ideas, numbers, things), pattern of behavior (forgives readily, cautious, reflective theoretical, yields to others, joins readily, usually calm, tries to mix, on the go, thickskinned, manually vigorous, resists restraint, seeks to excel, tends to take charge, reacts quickly, readiness to fight, showoff, humanitarian, aloof, daring, excited, masculinity-femininity), level of activity (physical assurance, mental assurance, objective drive, self starting tendency, scope of perception), occupational tie-in (welfare uplift, managerial supervisory, biological sciences, oral contact, musical, written contact, computational reports, business transactions, artistic activities, physical sciences, outdoor, clerical, natural resources, manipulative); distribution restricted to clients; V. J. Swanson; the Author. *

SKILLED TRADES

[2078]

The Fiesenheiser Test of Ability to Read Drawings. Trade school and adults; 1955; Elmer I. Fiesenheiser; Psychometric Affiliates. *

For additional information, see 5:897.

[2079]

Garage Mechanic Test. Automobile mechanics; 1956; P. L. Mellenbruch; Educational Test Bureau. *

For additional information, see 5:573.

[2080]

Purdue Blueprint Reading Test. Grades 9-12 and adults; 1942; Joseph Tiffin, H. F. Owen, and J. N. Arnold; Science Research Associates, Inc. *

For additional information, see 4:782.

[2081]

Purdue Industrial Training Classification Test. Grades 9-12 and adults; 1942; shop mathematics; C. H. Lawshe and A. C. Moutoux; [University Book Store]. *

For additional information and reviews by D. Welty Lefever and Charles I. Mosier, see 3:675 (2 references).

[2082]

Purdue Interview Aids. Applicants for industrial employment; 1943; 3 forms; C. H. Lawshe; distributed by University Book Store. *
a) CAN YOU READ A WORKING DRAWING?
b) CAN YOU READ A MICROMETER?
c) CAN YOU READ A SCALE?
For additional information and a review by William W. Waite, see 4:775.

[2083]

Purdue Test for Electricians. Grades 9–12 and adults; 1942; Joseph Tiffin, C. W. Caldwell, H. R. Goppert, H. G. McComb, and W. B. Hill; Science Research Associates, Inc. *
For additional information and a review by John W. French, see 3:701.

[2084]

Purdue Test for Machinists and Machine Operators. Grades 9–12 and adults; 1942–49; 6 scores: lathe, planer and shaper, grinder, milling machine, general bench operations, total; Joseph Tiffin, H. F. Owen, C. C. Stevason, H. G. McComb, and C. D. Hume; Science Research Associates, Inc. *
For additional information, see 4:816; for a review by William W. Waite, see 3:702.

[2085]

Purdue Trade Information Test for Sheetmetal Workers. Sheetmetal workers; 1958; Joseph Tiffin, B. R. Modisette, and Warren B. Griffin; University Book Store. *
For additional information, see 5:942.

[2086]

Purdue Trade Information Test in Carpentry. Vocational school and adults; 1952; Joseph Tiffin and Robert F. Mengelkoch; University Book Store. *
For additional information and a review by P. L. Mellenbruch, see 5:943 (1 reference).

[2087]

Purdue Trade Information Test in Engine Lathe Operation. Vocational school and adults; 1955; Robert Cochran and Joseph Tiffin; University Book Store. *
For additional information and a review by William J. Micheels, see 5:944.

[2088]

Purdue Trade Information Test in Welding, Revised Edition. Vocational school and adults; 1951–52; Joseph Tiffin and Warren B. Griffin; University Book Store. *
For additional information, see 5:945.

SUPERVISION

[2089]

A Chart for the Rating of a Foreman. Foremen; 1941–48; ratings by supervisors; R. D. Bundy; National Foremen's Institute, Inc. *
For additional information, see 5:915.

[2090]

How Supervise? Supervisors; 1943–48; Quentin W. File and H. H. Remmers; Psychological Corporation. *

For additional information, see 5:926 (18 references); for a review by Milton M. Mandell, see 4:774 (8 references); for reviews by D. Welty Lefever, Charles I. Mosier, and C. H. Ruedisili, see 3:687 (5 references).

[2091]

★**Leadership Opinion Questionnaire.** Supervisors and prospective supervisors; 1960; 2 scores: structure, consideration; Edwin A. Fleishman; Science Research Associates, Inc. *

[2092]

Managerial Scale for Enterprise Improvement. Supervisors; 1955; job satisfaction; Herbert A. Kaufman, Jr.; Psychometric Affiliates. *

For additional information and reviews by Brent Baxter and Edward B. Greene, see 5:930.

[2093]

★**Supervisory Aptitude Test.** Applicants for industrial supervisory positions; 1957; distribution restricted to clients; Ludwig Huttner; Stevens, Thurow & Associates Inc. *

[2094]

★**Supervisory Index.** Supervisors and prospective supervisors; 1960; 5 attitude scores: management, supervision, employees, human relations practices, total; Norman Gekoski and S. L. Schwartz; Science Research Associates, Inc. *

[2095]

★**Supervisory Inventory on Human Relations.** Supervisors and prospective supervisors; 1960; Donald L. Kirkpatrick and Earl Planty; Science Research Associates, Inc. *

[2096]

Supervisory Practices Test. Supervisors; 1957; Martin M. Bruce; the Author. *

For additional information and reviews by Clifford E. Jurgensen and Mary Ellen Oliverio, see 5:955 (1 reference).

[2097]

Test of Practical Judgment. Grades 9–16 and applicants for supervisory positions; 1942–50; Alfred J. Cardall; Science Research Associates, Inc. *

For additional information, see 4:784 (6 references); for reviews by Glen U. Cleeton and Howard R. Taylor, see 3:694.

[2098]

★**Test of Supervisory Ability.** Adults; 1944–[53]; a battery consisting of *Inventory of Interest and Temperament Areas* (see 202), *Knowledge of People Inventory* (see 208), and *Test of Ability to Understand Instructions: Job Alertness Tests* (see 776); W. H. Winkler; Winkler Publications. *

[2099]

★**WLW Supervisor Survey.** Supervisors; 1956–57; 2 scores: human relations attitudes, eager beaver behavior; R. W. Henderson; William, Lynde & Williams. *

TRANSPORTATION

[2100]

[American Transit Association Tests.] Transit operating personnel; 1941–51; *withdrawn pending revision;* Glen U. Cleeton, Merwyn A. Kraft, and Robert F. Royster; American Transit Association. *

a) STANDARD EXAMINATION FOR TRANSIT EMPLOYEES.
b) PERSONAL REACTION TEST FOR TRANSIT EMPLOYEES.
c) THE PLACEMENT INTERVIEW FOR TRANSIT EMPLOYEES.
d) A STANDARDIZED ROAD TEST FOR BUS OPERATORS.

    For additional information, see 5:912; for reviews by Harold G. Seashore, Morris S. Viteles, and J. V. Waits of *a, b,* and *c,* see 3:696 (1 reference).

[2101]

[Driver Selection Forms and Tests.] Truck drivers; 1943–55; Dartnell Corporation. *

a) EMPLOYMENT APPLICATION. 1946.
b) TELEPHONE CHECK. 1946–53.
c) DRIVER INTERVIEW. 1946.
d) PHYSICAL EXAMINATION RECORD. 1946–54.
e) SELECTION AND EVALUATION SUMMARY. 1950–55.
f) TRAFFIC AND DRIVING KNOWLEDGE FOR DRIVERS OF MOTOR TRUCKS. 1946–54; Amos E. Neyhart and Helen L. Neyhart. (Also distributed by Institute of Public Safety.)
g) ROAD TEST IN TRAFFIC FOR TESTING, SELECTING, RATING AND TRAINING TRUCK DRIVERS. 1943–46; 3 scores: specific driving skills, general driving habits and attitudes, total; Amos E. Neyhart. For the revised edition entry, see 2103.

    For additional information, see 5:918; for a review by S. Rains Wallace, Jr., see 4:789.

[2102]

Road Test Check List for Testing, Selecting, Rating, and Training Coach Operators. Bus drivers; 1958; 3–4 scores: general attitude and driving practices, specific driving errors, total, errors on an actual bus run (optional); Amos E. Neyhart; published jointly by American Automobile Association and Institute of Public Safety. *

    For additional information, see 5:946.

[2103]

*Road Test in Traffic for Testing, Selecting, Rating and Training Truck Drivers, [1955 Revision]. Truck drivers; 1943–55; 3 scores: specific skills, general habits and attitudes, total; Amos E. Neyhart; published jointly by American Automobile Association and Institute of Public Safety. *

    For additional information, see 4:790.

[2104]

Truck Driver Test 60-A. Drivers of light and medium trucks; 1957–58; Public Personnel Association. *

    For additional information, see 5:956.

OUT OF PRINT TESTS

ACHIEVEMENT BATTERIES

2105. *Comprehensive Achievement Tests for Oklahoma Eighth Grade*. For additional information, see 35:3.

2106. *Comprehensive Testing Program*. 4 tests: *Intelligence Test, Educational Background Questionnaire, Comprehensive Achievement Test, School Practices Questionnaire: A Test of the Curriculum*. For additional information and reviews by Richard Ledgerwood, W. J. Osburn, Ernest W. Tiegs, W. D. Commins, Verner M. Sims, Harriet M. Barthelmess [Morrison], and Hilda Taba, see 38:869 (2 references).

2107. *Cooperative General Achievement Test [Survey Series]*. 3 parts: *A Survey Test in the Social Studies, A Survey Test in the Natural Sciences, A Survey Test in Mathematics*. For additional information, see 38:870.

2108. *Entrance and Classification Examination for Teachers Colleges: Elementary Test, 1939 Edition*. For additional information, see 40:1185; see also 40:1280 (9 references).

2109. *Graduate Record Examination Profile Tests*. For additional information and a review by Max D. Engelhart, see 4:10 (5 references).

2110. *Graduate Record Examination Tests of General Education*. For additional information, see 4:11 (1 reference).

2111. *Harlow Achievement Tests for First and Second Grades*. For additional information, see 36:506.

2112. *Master Achievement Tests*. For additional information and a review by Clifford Woody, see 38:873.

2113. *Myers-Ruch High School Progress Test*. For additional information and reviews by Harl R. Douglass, August Dvorak, John M. Stalnaker, and Ernest W. Tiegs, see 40:1192.

2114. *North Carolina High School Senior Examination*. For additional information, see 35:14.

2115. *Public School Correlated Attainment Scales*. For additional information and reviews by C. W. Odell and Robert K. Speer, see 40:1196 (1 reference, 2 excerpts); for reviews by H. S. Conrad and H. E. Schrammel, see 38:877.

2116. *Unit Scales of Attainment*. For additional information and a review by D. Welty Lefever, see 40:1197 (2 references); for reviews by Herbert S. Conrad and Ethel L. Cornell, see 38:878. For reviews of subtests, see 40:1315, 40:1463, 40:1581, and 38:1115.

2117. *Wisconsin Composite Achievement Test*. For additional information and reviews by Ernest W. Tiegs and Maurice E. Troyer, see 3:22 (4 references).

BUSINESS EDUCATION

2118. *Business Backgrounds Test*. For additional information, see 40:1478 (1 reference, 1 excerpt).

2119. *General Clerical: Every Pupil Test*. For additional information, see 38:937.

2120. *Fundamentals Test: National Clerical Ability Tests*. For additional information, see 40:1484.

2121. *General Information Test: National Clerical Ability Tests*. For additional information, see 40:1485.

2122. *Thompson Business Practice Test.* For additional information and a review by Herbert A. Tonne, see 38:942.

BOOKKEEPING

2123. *Breidenbaugh Bookkeeping Tests: Division I, Single Proprietorship.* For additional information, see 40:1477 (1 excerpt).

2124. *Examination in Bookkeeping and Accounting.* For additional information and a review by Harvey A. Andruss, see 3:373.

MISCELLANEOUS

2125. *Clinton-LeMaster Commercial and Business Law Test.* For additional information, see 40:1479.

2126. *Examination in Commercial Correspondence—College Level.* For additional information and reviews by Orrel E. Little and Herbert A. Tonne, see 3:376.

2127. *Filing Test: United-NOMA Business Entrance Tests.* For additional information and reviews by Arnold E. Schneider and C. C. Upshall, see 3:379.

2128. *Qualifying Test for Ediphone Voice Writing.* For additional information, see 40:1488.

STENOGRAPHY

2129. *Dictating Machine Transcription Test: National Clerical Ability Tests.* For additional information, see 40:1482.

2130. *Examination in Gregg Shorthand.* For additional information and a review by Agnes E. Osborne, see 3:377.

2131. *Gregg Shorthand: Comprehensive Objective Tests in High School Subjects.* For additional information, see 35:129.

2132. *Hiett Stenography Test (Gregg).* For additional information and a review by Agnes E. Osborne, see 3:381.

2133. *Power-Achievement Tests in Gregg Shorthand.* For additional information, see 35:133.

2134. *SRA Dictation Skills.* For additional information and a review by Harold F. Rothe, see 4:454 (1 reference).

2135. *Stenography, Gregg: Every Pupil Scholarship Test.* For additional information, see 35:135.

TYPEWRITING

2136. *Examination in Typewriting.* For additional information and a review by E. G. Blackstone, see 3:378.

2137. *Grading Scales for Typewriting Tests.* For additional information, see 40:1486 (1 excerpt).

2138. *Kimberly-Clark Typing Ability Analysis.* For additional information, see 5:513 (2 references) ; for a review by E. G. Blackstone, see 3:383.

2139. *Typewriting II: Every Pupil Test.* For additional information, see 38:944.

CHARACTER AND PERSONALITY

NONPROJECTIVE

2140. *A-S Reaction Study: Revision for Business Use.* For additional information and a review by Doncaster G. Humm, see 40:1199 (4 references).

2141. *Attention Test: For the Measurement of Perseveration.* For additional information, see 35:86.

2142. [*Attitude Scales for Measuring the Influence of the Work Relief Program.*] 3 scales: *Attitude Toward Work Relief as a Solution to the Financial Depression. Atti-*

tude Toward Earning a Living, Attitude Toward Receiving Relief. For additional information, see 40:1203 (1 reference).

2143. *Attitudes Toward Child Behavior.* For additional information, see 40:1204 (2 references).

2144. *Babcock Test of Mental Deterioration.* For additional information and reviews by D. Russell Davis and Seymour G. Klebanoff, see 4:31 (10 references) ; see also 3:71 (21 references) and 40:1248 (16 references) ; for excerpts from related book reviews, see 3:72.

2145. [*The Baxter Group Test of Child Feeling.*] Revision of *Baxter Group Test of Child Personality* and *Baxter Individual Tests of Child Feelings;* 3 tests : *Child's Test: Baxter Group Story-Test of Child Feelings, The Baxter Test of Child Feelings, The Baxter Parent-Teacher Test of Child Feelings.* For additional information, see 4:32 (2 references)

2146. *Behavior Description, Experimental Form.* For additional information, see 38:898.

2147. *Behavior Maturity Blank.* For additional information, see 40:1209 (2 references).

2148. *Behavior Maturity Rating Scale for Nursery School Children.* For additional information, see 40:1210.

2149. *Beliefs About School Life: Test 4.6.* For additional information, see 40:1211.

2150. *Best Thing to Do: Northwestern University Citizenship Tests.* For additional information, see 35:87.

2151. *Brown Personality Inventory for Children.* For additional information, see 5:36 (10 references) ; for reviews by S. J. Beck and Carl R. Rogers, see 40:1240 (8 references).

2152. *Case Inventory, Third Edition.* For additional information and reviews by Harold E. Jones and E. G. Williamson, see 40:1214 (1 reference) ; for a review by Richard Ledgerwood, see 38:916.

2153. *Character and Inventory Chart.* For additional information, see 38:917 (1 excerpt).

2154. *Character and Personality Rating Scale.* For additional information and a review by Bessie Lee Gambrill, see 40:1215.

2155. *Controlled Association Test for the Indirect Measurement of Emotionalized Response Patterns.* For additional information, see 35:91 (1 reference).

2156. *The Cowan Adolescent Adjustment Analyzer.* For additional information, see 4:38 (1 reference) ; for reviews by Harold H. Abelson and William U. Snyder, see 3:30; for a review by Goodwin Watson of an earlier edition, see 40:1217 (3 references) ; for a review by Harold E. Jones, see 38:918.

2157. *Detroit Scale of Behavior Factors.* For additional information, see 3:32 (1 reference) ; for excerpts from related book reviews, see 3:33, 40:B835, 38:B306, and 36:B24.

2158. *Diagnosis and Treatment of Pupil Maladjustment.* 3 parts : *Pupil Adjustment Inventory, Case Study Record, Cumulative Pupil Adjustment Record.* For additional information and a review by Laurance F. Shaffer, see 3:34 (2 references).

2159. *Dunlap Academic Preference Blank.* For additional information and reviews by Lee J. Cronbach, W. C. Kvaraceus, and Edith I. M. Thomson, see 3:35 (6 references, 1 excerpt).

2160. *Environment Inventory for College and University Students.* For additional information and a review by E. G. Williamson, see 40:1218 (1 reference).

2161. *Ethical Judgment Test.* For additional information, see 35:93.

2162. *Euphorimeter.* For additional information, see 3:36 (2 references) ; for excerpts from related book reviews, see 3:37.

2163. *Experience Variables Record: A Clinical Revision.* For additional information, see 40:1219 (2 references).

2164. *Gardner Behavior Chart.* For additional information, see 4:44.

2165. *General Goals of Life Inventory: General Education Series.* For additional information and reviews by C. Robert Pace and Leona E. Tyler, see 4:45 (10 references).

2166. *Graphic Rating Scale on Four Desirable Traits.* For additional information, see 36:561.

2167. *How I Feel About It: Northwestern University Citizenship Tests.* For additional information, see 35:94.

2168. *Information Blank EA: A Questionnaire on Emotional Adjustment, Provisional Form.* For additional information and a review by Percival M. Symonds, see 3:50; for a review by Stanley G. Dulsky, see 40:1224.

2169. *Interaction Process Analysis.* For additional information and a review by Cecil A. Gibb, see 5:77 (10 references); for a review by Launor F. Carter, see 4:56 (3 references); for excerpts from related book reviews, see 4:57.

2170. *Interest Analysis, 1942 Revision.* For additional information and a review by Edward B. Greene, see 3:51.

2171. *Interest Index: General Education Series.* For additional information, see 4:58 (2 references); see also 40:1226 (4 references).

2172. *Interest Questionnaire: Games and Sports: Test 8.3.* For additional information, see 40:1227.

2173. *Interest-Values Inventory.* For additional information and reviews by E. Lowell Kelly and Paul E. Meehl, see 3:53 (5 references).

2174. *Interests and Activities: Tests 8.2b and 8.2c.* For additional information, see 40:1225 (7 references).

2175. *Inventory of Personal-Social Relationships: General Education Series.* For additional information and reviews by N. L. Gage and Theodore R. Sarbin, see 4:60 (2 references).

2176. *JNB Psychograph.* For additional information, see 3:56 (1 reference).

2177. *Jurgensen Classification Inventory.* For additional information and reviews by Robert G. Demaree (with Louis L. McQuitty) and William J. E. Crissy, see 4:63 (11 references).

2178. *Lewerenz-Steinmetz Orientation Test: Concerning Fundamental Aims of Education.* For additional information and reviews by Frederic L. Ayer and Roger T. Lennon, see 4:66 (3 references).

2179. *McCleery Scale of Adolescent Development.* For additional information and reviews by Eugene L. Gaier and John E. Horrocks, see 5:83 (1 reference).

2180. *The Minnesota Inventory of Social Attitudes.* For additional information and a review by Verner M. Sims, see 4:70 (12 references); for reviews by J. P. Guilford and George W. Hartmann, see 38:900.

2181. *Minnesota Personality Scale.* For additional information, see 5:87 (22 references); for reviews by Philip Eisenberg and John W. French, see 3:61 (9 references).

2182. *Minnesota Scale for the Survey of Opinions.* For additional information and reviews by H. H. Remmers and Goodwin Watson, see 38:901 (1 reference).

2183. *My Code: Northwestern University Citizenship Tests.* For additional information, see 35:96.

2184. *Nebraska Personality Inventory.* For additional information and reviews by John C. Flanagan and C. M. Louttit, see 38:922 (1 reference).

2185. *Occupational Personality Inventory.* For additional information, see 40:1232 (3 references).

2186. *Ohio Guidance Tests for Elementary Grades.* 5 tests: *Ohio Interest Inventory for the Intermediate Grades, Ohio Individual Summary Sheet for Committee Selections, Ohio Social Acceptance Scale for the Intermediate Grades, Ohio Recognition Scale for Intermediate Grades: Who's Who in My Group?, Ohio Thinking Checkup for Intermediate Grades.* For additional information and reviews by M. H. Elliott and John W. M. Rothney, see 3:63 (8 references).

2187. *P.Q. or Personality Quotient Test.* For additional information and reviews by Douglas Spencer and Simon H. Tulchin, see 40:1233 (5 references); for reviews by C. M. Louttit and Edmund G. Williamson, see 38:921.

2188. *P-S Experience Blank: Psycho-Somatic Inventory.* Now available, see 235b.

2189. *Parents Rating Scale.* For additional information, see 40:1235.

2190. *Personal Adaptability Test.* For additional information and a review by Harold Webster, see 5:91 (1 reference).

2191. *Personal Data Scale.* For additional information, see 38:1119.

2192. *Personal History Record.* For additional information, see 40:1236 (1 reference).

2193. *The Personal Preference Inventory: Student Form.* For additional information and reviews by E. Lowell Kelly and C. M. Louttit, see 4:76.

2194. *Personality-Maturity Test.* For additional information, see 36:564.

2195. *Personality Rating Chart for Preschool Children.* For additional information, see 40:1241 (1 reference).

2196. *Personality Rating Scale for Preschool Children.* For additional information, see 40:1242 (1 reference).

2197. *Personality Sketches.* For additional information and reviews by Henry E. Garrett and J. P. Guilford, see 38:925.

2198. *The Personality Survey.* For additional information and reviews by Douglas Courtney and John W. M. Rothney, see 4:79 (2 references).

2199. *Pressey Interest-Attitude Tests.* Revision of *Pressey X-O Tests.* For additional information and a review by Douglas Spencer, see 40:1243.1 (5 references).

2200. *Pupil Portraits.* For additional information and a review by Simon H. Tulchin, see 40:1244 (2 references).

2201. *Pupils Adjustment Inventory.* For additional information, see 35:102.

2202. *Radio Checklist.* For additional information, see 40:1245.

2203. *Reaman Personality Rating Chart.* For additional information, see 36:566.

2204. *Recreation Inquiry.* For additional information and reviews by Theodore F. Lentz and Louis Long, see 3:70 (2 references).

2205. *Scale for Developmental Age.* Now available, see 303b.

2206. *Scale for Evaluating the School Behavior of Children Ten to Fifteen.* For additional information, see 38:926 (1 reference, 1 excerpt).

2207. *Scale of Beliefs for Junior High School: Tests 4.4 and 4.5.* For additional information, see 40:1251 (1 reference).

2208. *Scale of Beliefs: Tests 4.21 and 4.31.* For additional information, see 40:1250 (7 references).

2209. *School Adjustment Questionnaire.* For additional information, see 36:568.

2210. *Selective Vocabulary Test.* For additional information and a review by James Maxwell, see 4:85 (2 references); for reviews by Jack W. Dunlap and Starke R. Hathaway, see 3:93.

2211. *Self-Appraisal Schedule.* For additional information, see 38:927 (1 reference).

2212. *Self-Comparison Inventory.* For additional information, see 35:105 (1 reference).

2213. *Social Attitude Scales.* For additional information and reviews by H. H. Remmers and Goodwin Watson, see 38:902.

2214. *Social Distance Scale, Seventh Experimental Edition.* For additional information and a review by Donald T. Campbell, see 4:88 (19 references).

2215. *Social Orientation.* For additional information and a review by Charles C. Peters, see 38:903.

2216. *Social Participation Scale, 1952 Edition.* For additional information, see 5:113.

2217. *Social Problems: Test 1.42.* For additional information, see 40:1254 (1 reference).

2218. *Student Questionnaire.* For additional information and a review by Simon H. Tulchin, see 3:98.

2219. *Study of Attitudes Toward the Administration of Justice.* For additional information, see 40:1255 (1 reference).

2220. *Survey of Attitudes and Beliefs.* For additional information and reviews by Donald T. Campbell and C. Robert Pace, see 5:116.

2221. *Teacher's Rating Scales for Pupil Adjustment.* For additional information and a review by Bessie Lee Gambrill, see 40:1256.

2222. *Tentative Check List for Determining Attitudes on Fifty Crucial Social, Economic, and Political Problems.* For additional information, see 40:1257.

2223. *Test of Social Attitudes.* For additional information, see 40:1260.

2224. *Tests of the Socially Competent Person.* For additional information and reviews by Alvin C. Eurich, Warren G. Findley, and Pedro T. Orata, see 40:1259 (1 reference); for reviews by Douglas E. Scates and Hilda Taba, see 38:1154.

2225. *Thurstone Personality Schedule: Clark Revision.* For additional information, see 35:107.

2226. [*Torgerson's Inventories and Record Forms.*] 6 forms: *Class Summary of Behavior Symptoms and Disabilities, Behavior Inventories, Home Environment Inventory, Speech Inventory, Developmental Inventory of Background Factors, Case Study Form.* For additional information and a review by Harold H. Abelson, see 3:105 (1 reference).

2227. *V.G.C. Personality Adjustment Indicator.* For additional information, see 3:106.

2228. *Walther Social Attitudes Test.* For additional information, see 40:1261.

2229. *Weitzman's Inventory of Social Behavior.* For additional information and reviews by Louis Long and Goodwin Watson, see 3:111 (3 references).

2230. *What Do You Think?* For additional information and a review by Ralph K. Watkins, see 40:1263 (3 references, 1 excerpt); for a review by Francis D. Curtis, see 38:1139.

2231. *What Kind of a Year Are You Having? A Series of Statements of Pupil Adjustment Attitudes.* For additional information, see 35:108.

2232. *What Should Our Schools Do? A Poll of Public Opinion on the School Program.* For additional information, see 40:1264 (1 excerpt).

2233. *What Would You Do? A Survey of Student Opinion.* For additional information, see 40:1265 (1 reference).

2234. *Willoughby Emotional Maturity Scale.* For additional information and a review by Lysle W. Croft, see 4:96 (7 references).

2235. *Winnetka Scale for Rating School Behavior and Attitudes.* For additional information and a review by Harriet M. Barthelmess [Morrison], see 38:929 (2 references).

2236. *The Wishing Well.* For additional information, see 4:98 (1 reference).

2237. *Work Preference Inventory.* For additional information, see 4:99; for reviews by Edwin W. Davis, John C. Flanagan, and Gilbert J. Rich, see 3:113.

2238. *Wrightstone Scale of Civic Beliefs.* For additional information and reviews by Stephen M. Corey and Harold Gulliksen, see 40:1266 (3 references).

2239. *Your Activities and Attitudes.* For additional information, see 4:100 (4 references, 1 excerpt); for excerpts from related book reviews, see 4:101.

PROJECTIVE

2240. *Animal Puzzles.* For additional information, see 38:1057.

2241. *Expressive Movement Chart.* For additional information, see 4:104 (2 references); for excerpts from a related book review, see 3:1245.

2242. *"F" [Fluency of Association] Test.* For additional information and reviews by J. M. Blackburn, P. E. Vernon, and Ll. Wynn Jones, see 40:1220 (10 references, 1 excerpt).

2243. *Plot-Completion Test.* For additional information and reviews by Robert C. Challman and Percival M. Symonds, see 4:116 (2 references).

ENGLISH

2244. *Cleveland English Composition and Grammar Test.* For additional information and a review by Frank P. De Lay, see 40:1269.

2245. *Davis-Schrammel Elementary English Test.* For additional information and reviews by Keith Goltry and Rachel Salisbury, see 40:1273.

2246. *Diagnostic Tests in English Composition.* Now available, see 420a.

2247. *"Dingwall" Test in English Usage.* For additional information and a review by Robert H. Thouless, see 3:124; for a review by Charles Fox, see 40:1275.

2248. *Elementary English Test: Every Pupil Scholarship Test.* For additional information, see 35:182.

2249. *English Classification Test for High Schools and Colleges.* For additional information, see 40:1277.

2250. *English Essentials Test.* For additional information, see 35:170.

2251. *English Grammar and Composition: Multiple-Purpose Objective Tests in High School Subjects.* For additional information, see 35:185.

2252. *English No. 4, Grammar and Style: Midland Attainment Tests.* For additional information, see 38:962.

2253. *English Placement Test.* For additional information and reviews by Roland L. Beck and Robert W. Howard, see 40:1278 (2 references).

2254. *English Placement Test for Iowa Universities and Colleges.* For additional information, see 38:958.

2255. *English Usage: Comprehensive Tests in High School Subjects.* For additional information, see 35:187.

2256. *Entrance and Classification Examination for Teachers Colleges: English Test.* For additional information, see 40:1280.

2257. *Examination in Business English—High-School Level.* For additional information and a review by Orrel E. Little, see 3:375.

2258. *Examination in English—College Level.* For additional information and a review by John S. Diekhoff, see 3:129.

2259. *Examination in English—High-School Level.* For additional information and reviews by Holland Roberts and Louis C. Zahner, see 3:130 (4 references).

2260. *Final Test in English: Comprehensive Objective Tests for Seventh-Grade Pupils in Texas.* For additional information, see 35:189.

2261. *Final Test in Fifth-Grade English: Comprehensive Objective Tests for Fifth-Grade Pupils in Texas.* For additional information, see 35:190.

2262. *Final Test in Sixth-Grade English: Comprehensive Objective Tests for Sixth-Grade Pupils in Texas.* For additional information, see 35:191.

2263. *First Year Grammar and Composition: Comprehensive Tests in High School Subjects.* For additional information, see 35:192 and 35:193.

2264. *Gregory Diagnostic Tests in Language.* For additional information and reviews by Keith Goltry and J. Paul Leonard, see 40:1282.

2265. *Iowa English Organization Test: Paragraph Organization in Reading and Comprehension.* For additional information, see 35:195.

2266. *Iowa Every-Pupil Test in English Correctness.* For additional information, see 38:965.

2267. *Language Arts Survey Test: Every Pupil Test.* For additional information, see 35:174.

2268. *Leonard Diagnostic Test in Punctuation and Capitalization.* For additional information and a review by Jean Hoard, see 40:1285 (2 references).

2269. *Los Angeles Diagnostic Tests: Language (A Test in Capitalization, Punctuation and Language Usage).* For additional information and a review by Gerald V. Lannholm, see 4:168.

2270. *Modern English Usage Test.* For additional information and a review by Holland Roberts, see 5:198; for a review by Walter N. Durost, see 4:170.

2271. *Pressey English Tests for Grades 5 to 8.* For additional information, see 40:1291 (2 excerpts).

2272. *SRA Language Skills.* For additional information, see 3:388c.

2273. *Second-Year Grammar and Composition: Comprehensive Tests in High School Subjects.* For additional information, see 35:201.

2274. *Shepherd English Test: The Clapp-Young Self-Marking Tests.* For additional information and a review by Ruth D. Churchill, see 3:136 (2 references).

2275. *Stanford Achievement Test [Language Arts].* For additional information, see 4:174 (1 reference).

2276. *Stanford Tests for Junior Colleges: Test in English.* For additional information, see 35:175.

2277. *Tools of Written English: State High School Tests for Indiana.* For additional information, see 4:177.

2278. *Wisconsin Language Usage Test.* For additional information, see 3:138.

COMPOSITION

2279. *College Entrance Examination Board Advanced Placement Examination: English Composition.* For additional information and a review by Robert C. Pooley of Form FBP, see 5:205.

2280. *Diagnostic Test of Letter-Writing Ability.* For additional information, see 40:1481 (1 excerpt).

2281. *Hudelson's Typical Composition Ability Scale.* For additional information and a review by Worth J. Osburn, see 4:179 (7 references).

2282. *Judging the Effectiveness of Written Composition: Test 3.8.* For additional information, see 40:1283 (1 reference).

2283. *Northamptonshire Composition Scale.* For additional information, see 35:169; for excerpts from related book reviews, see 38:B524 and 36:B284.

LITERATURE

2284. *Alphabetical List of 1000 Fiction Authors Classified by Subject and Maturity Level.* For additional information, see 40:1294 (1 reference).

2285. *American Literature: Manchester Semester-End Achievement Tests.* For additional information, see 36:655.

2286. *Analytical Scales of Attainment in Literature.* For additional information and reviews by Carleton C. Jones and Robert K. Speer, see 40:1295.

2287. *Check List of Novels.* For additional information and a review by John S. Diekhoff, see 4:183 (2 references).

2288. *Checklist of One Hundred Magazines.* For additional information, see 40:1297.

2289. *College Entrance Examination Board Advanced Placement Examination: Literature.* For additional information and a review by John S. Diekhoff of Form FBP, see 5:211.

2290. *Cooperative Literary Acquaintance Test.* For additional information, see 3:141 (1 reference); for reviews by Lou LaBrant and Edward S. Noyes, see 40:1298; for reviews by Carleton C. Jones and John H. Thompson, see 38:970.

2291. *Cooperative Literary Comprehension Test.* For additional information and reviews by Lou LaBrant and Edward A. Tenney, see 40:1299 (3 references); for reviews by Charles Swain Thomas and John H. Thompson, see 38:971.

2292. *Eaton Self-Correcting Literature Tests.* For additional information, see 35:214.

2293. *850-Tests with Keys.* For additional information, see 36:664.

2294. *English and American Literature: Every Pupil Scholarship Test.* For additional information, see 35:215.

2295. *English Classics: Multiple-Purpose Objective Tests in High School Subjects.* For additional information, see 35:216.

2296. *English Literature: Manchester Semester-End Achievement Tests.* For additional information, see 36:658.

2297. *English No. 5, Knowledge of Literature: Midland Attainment Tests.* For additional information, see 38:973.

2298. *English: Understanding and Appreciation of Poetry: State High School Tests for Indiana.* For additional information and a review by Chester W. Harris, see 3:143.

2299. *History of American Literature: Comprehensive Tests in High School Subjects.* For additional information, see 35:218.

2300. *History of English Literature: Comprehensive Tests in High School Subjects.* For additional information, see 35:219.

2301. *Interpretation of Literature Test: General Education Series.* For additional information and reviews by John S. Diekhoff and John M. Stalnaker, see 4:187.

2302. *Inventory of Satisfactions Found in Reading Fiction: General Education Series.* For additional information and a review by Holland Roberts, see 4:188 (2 references).

2303. *Iowa Every-Pupil Test in Reading Comprehension in Literature.* For additional information, see 38:975.

2304. *The Jones Book-A-Day Tests: For Checking Outside Reading of High School Pupils.* For additional information, see 4:189.

2305. *Literary Information Test: American Literature: Test 3.5.* For additional information, see 40:1288 (1 reference).

2306. *Literary Information Test: English Literature: Test 3.4.* For additional information, see 40:1289 (1 reference).

2307. *Literature Questionnaire: The Drama: Test 3.21.* For additional information, see 40:1302 (1 reference).

2308. *Literature Questionnaire: The Novel: Test 3.2a.* For additional information, see 40:1303 (1 reference).

2309. *Literature Test: Municipal Tests: National Achievement Tests.* For additional information, see 4:191.

2310. *Objective Tests for English Classics.* For additional information, see 36:666.

2311. *Questionnaire on Voluntary Reading: Test 3.31.* For additional information, see 40:1305 (1 reference).

2312. *Readings in English: Comprehensive Objective Tests in High School Subjects.* For additional information, see 35:222.

2313. *Stanford Achievement Test* [*Literature*]. For additional information and a review by Winifred L. Post, see 4:195.

2314. *Stanford Test of Comprehension of Literature.* For additional information and a review by J. Wayne Wrightstone, see 40:1306 (1 reference).

2315. *Tests for the Appreciation of Literature.* For additional information and a review by Ann L. Gebhardt, see 40:1307

2316. *Tests on English Classics.* For additional information, see 35:223.

SPEECH

2317. *Bryan-Wilke Scale for Rating Public Speeches.* For additional information, see 40:1308.

2318. *Guidance Questionnaire for Students of Speech.* For additional information, see 3:150 (4 references).

2319. *Oral English Observation Schedule.* For additional information, see 38:1094.

2320. *Speech Attitude Scale.* For additional information, see 3:151 (2 references).

2321. *Speech Experience Inventory.* For additional information, see 3:152 (2 references).

SPELLING

2322. *Buffalo Spelling Scale.* For additional information and reviews by John C. Almack and M. E. Broom, see 40:1310; for a review by Henry D. Rinsland, see 38:1158.

2323. *Final Test in Sixth-Grade Spelling: Comprehensive Objective Tests for Sixth-Grade Pupils in Texas.* For additional information, see 35:487.

2324. *Final Test in Spelling: Comprehensive Objective Tests for Fifth-Grade Pupils in Texas.* For additional information, see 35:485.

2325. *Final Test in Spelling: Comprehensive Objective Tests for Seventh-Grade Pupils in Texas.* For additional information, see 35:486.

2326. *High School Spelling Test.* For additional information and a review by Walter W. Cook, see 40:1312 (2 references).

2327. *The Morgan Spelling Test for Schools and Colleges.* Formerly called *Morgan Spelling Test for Business and Industry.* For additional information and a review by Harold H. Bixler, see 4:204.

2328. *Preliminary Spelling Test.* For additional information, see 35:488.

2329. *Standard Elementary Spelling Scale.* For additional information, see 40:1313.1.

2330. *Standard Self-Administering Spelling Test.* For additional information, see 36:859.

2331. *Unit Scales of Attainment in Spelling.* For additional information and reviews by John C. Almack and G. M. Wilson, see 40:1315 (1 reference). For reviews of the complete battery, see 40:1197 and 38:878.

VOCABULARY

2332. *Clinton General Vocabulary Test for High Schools and Colleges.* For additional information and a review by Harold H. Bixler, see 3:158.

2333. *Columbia Vocabulary Test.* For additional information and reviews by Verner M. Sims and Clifford Woody, see 3:159 (4 references).

2334. *English No. 2, Vocabulary: Midland Attainment Tests.* For additional information, see 38:980.

2335. *English Recognition Vocabulary Test.* For additional information and reviews by Paul S. Burnham and Edgar Dale, see 3:161 (12 references) ; see also 40:1319 (3 references).

2336. *High School Vocabulary Test.* For additional information and a review by Harold H. Bixler, see 3:162.

2337. *Kennon Test of Literary Vocabulary, 1941 Edition.* For additional information and a review by H. H. Remmers, see 3:165 (1 reference).

2338. *Vocabulary: Parr Skill-Ability Tests.* For additional information, see 40:1321.1.

2339. *Vocabulary Power Tests.* For additional information, see 40:1322.

FINE ARTS

2340. *Graduate Record Examinations Advanced Fine Arts Test.* For additional information, see 4:219.

ART

2341. *McAdory Art Test.* For additional information and reviews by Norman C. Meier and Edwin Ziegfeld, see 40:1325 (13 references).

2342. *Practical Drawing Ability Test: Gibson's Attainment Tests.* For additional information, see 38:1036.

2343. *Selective Art Aptitude Test, Second Edition.* For additional information and a review by Edwin Ziegfeld, see 3:173.

2344. *Seven Modern Paintings: Test 3.9.* For additional information, see 40:1328.

MUSIC

2345. *Conrad Instrument-Talent Test.* For additional information and a review by Herbert D. Wing, see 5:244.

2346. *Drake Musical Memory Test: A Test of Musical Talent.* For additional information and a review by William S. Larson, see 3:175 (2 references) ; for reviews by Paul R. Farnsworth and James L. Mursell, see 40:1330 (2 references) ; see also 38:1083 (1 excerpt).

2347. *Ear Tests in Harmony.* For additional information and a review by Jay W. Fay, see 38:1084.

2348. *Hillbrand Sight-Singing Test.* For additional information and a review by Alton O'Steen, see 40:1331 (1 reference).

2349. *McCauley Examination in Public School Music.* For additional information and a review by Alton O'Steen, see 40:1335.

2350. [*Measure of Singing and Rhythmic Development of Preschool Children.*] For additional information, see 36:786.

2351. *Musical Achievement Test.* For additional information and a review by Raleigh M. Drake, see 40:1336.

2352. *Musical Appreciation Ability Test: Gibson's Attainment Tests.* For additional information, see 38:1086.

2353. *Providence Inventory Test in Music.* For additional information and reviews by William S. Larson and Clara J. McCauley, see 40:1337.

FOREIGN LANGUAGES

2354. *Language Aptitude Test: George Washington University Series.* For additional information and a review by H. E. Brogden, see 3:179.

FRENCH

2355. *American Council Alpha French Test.* For additional information and reviews by C. E. Ficken and Warren S. Holmes, see 40:1342 (9 references).

2356. *American Council Alpha French Test: Aural Comprehension.* For additional information and a review by Nelson Brooks, see 40:1343 (3 references).

2357. *American Council French Grammar Test.* For additional information and reviews by Harry Heller and Charles Holzwarth, see 40:1345 (5 references).

2358. *American Council on Education French Reading Test.* For additional information and a review by Charles Holzwarth, see 40:1346 (1 reference); for a review by Nelson Brooks, see 38:984.

2359. *Columbia Research Bureau Aural French Test.* For additional information and a review by Clarence E. Turner, see 40:1347 (1 reference).

2360. *Columbia Research Bureau French Test.* For additional information and reviews by Joseph F. Jackson and Laura B. Johnson, see 40:1348 (3 references).

2361. *Cooperative Advanced French Reading Test: Experimental Edition.* For additional information, see 35:230.

2362. *Cooperative French Test: Lower and Higher Levels.* For additional information and a review by Elton Hocking, see 4:238 (3 references); for reviews by John H. Meyer and Roland Vinette, see 3:182; for reviews by Joseph F. Jackson and Clarence E. Turner of Part 1, *Cooperative French Comprehension Test,* see 3:180.

2363. *Examination in French Grammar.* For additional information and a review by Nelson Brooks, see 3:183.

2364. *Examination in French Reading Comprehension.* For additional information and reviews by Joseph F. Jackson and Clarence E. Turner, see 3:184.

2365. *Examination in French Vocabulary.* For additional information and a review by Nelson Brooks, see 3:185.

2366. *First and Second Year French: Every Pupil Test.* For additional information, see 35:233.

2367. *First Year French: Multiple-Purpose Objective Tests in High School Subjects.* For additional information, see 35:234.

2368. *First Year French: State High School Tests for Indiana.* For additional information, see 38:987.

2369. *French Grammar Test: Dominion Tests.* For additional information and a review by John H. Meyer, see 3:186

2370. *French Life and Culture Test.* For additional information and reviews by Bateman Edwards and Clarence E. Turner, see 40:1351 (1 reference).

2371. *French Reading Test: Dominion Tests.* For additional information and a review by Geraldine Spaulding, see 3:187.

2372. *French Vocabulary Test: Dominion Tests.* For additional information and a review by Roland Vinette, see 3:188.

2373. *Miller-Davis French Test.* For additional information and reviews by Walter V. Kaulfers and James B. Tharp, see 40:1355 (1 reference).

2374. *Second Year French: Every Pupil Scholarship Test.* For additional information, see 35:238.

2375. *Second Year French: State High School Tests for Indiana.* For additional information, see 38:988.

2376. *A Standardised French Grammar Test.* For additional information and reviews by Nelson Brooks and Donald G. Burns, see 4:242 (1 reference).

2377. *A Standardised French Vocabulary Test.* For additional information and reviews by Nelson Brooks and Donald G. Burns, see 4:243 (1 reference).

GERMAN

2378. *American Council Alpha German Test.* For additional information and a review by C. H. Handschin, see 40:1357 (3 references).

2379. *American Council on Education German Reading Test.* For additional information, see 40:1358; for a review by Curtis C. D. Vail, see 38:999.

2380. *Columbia Research Bureau German Test.* For additional information and a review by Harold B. Dunkel, see 40:1359 (1 reference).

2381. *Cooperative German Test: Advanced Form.* For additional information and a review by Herbert Schueler, see 4:245 (3 references); for a review by Harold B. Dunkel, see 3:190; for a review by C. H. Handschin, see 40:1360 (4 references); for a review by Curtis C. D. Vail, see 38:1000.

2382. *Cooperative German Test, [Elementary Form].* For additional information, see 40:1361; for a review by Curtis C. D. Vail, see 38:1001.

2383. *Examination in German Grammar—Lower Level.* For additional information and a review by Herbert Schueler, see 3:191.

2384. *Examination in German Reading Comprehension—Lower Level.* For additional information and a review by Herbert Schueler, see 3:192.

2385. *Examination in German Vocabulary—Lower Level.* For additional information and a review by Herbert Schueler, see 3:193.

2386. *First Year German: Every Pupil Scholarship Test.* For additional information, see 35:268.

2387. *First Year German: State High School Tests for Indiana.* For additional information, see 36:698.

2388. *Graduate Record Examinations Advanced German Test.* For additional information, see 4:247.

2389. *Second Year German: State High School Tests for Indiana.* For additional information, see 36:699.

HEBREW

2390. *Group Test in Siddur Reading.* For additional information, see 3:195.

2391. *Hebrew Aptitude Test.* For additional information, see 3:196 (1 reference).

2392. *Hebrew Intermediate Test.* For additional information, see 3:197.

2393. *Hebrew Primary Test.* For additional information, see 3:198.

ITALIAN

2394. *Cooperative Italian Test.* For additional information and a review by Elton Hocking, see 3:199.

2395. *Examination in Italian Grammar—Lower Level.* For additional information, see 3:200.

2396. *Examination in Italian Reading Comprehension—Lower Level.* For additional information, see 3:201.

2397. *Examination in Italian Vocabulary—Lower Level.* For additional information, see 3:202.

LATIN

2398. *Cooperative Latin Test: Lower and Higher Levels.* For additional information and a review by Konrad Gries, see 4:251 (3 references); for a review by C. W. Odell, see 3:205; for a review by Hazel M. Toliver of Part 1, *Cooperative Latin Test,* see 3:203.

2399. *First-Year Latin: Multiple-Purpose Objective Tests in High School Subjects.* For additional information, see 35:372.

2400. *Godsey Latin Composition Test.* For additional information and a review by Konrad Gries, see 4:253 (2 references).

2401. *Hutchinson Latin Grammar Scale.* For additional information and a review by S. D. Atkins, see 40:1367 (2 references).

2402. *Iowa Every-Pupil Test in Latin Reading Comprehension.* For additional information, see 38:1069.

2403. *Second Year Latin: Multiple-Purpose Objective Tests in High School Subjects.* For additional information, see 35:376.

2404. *White Latin Test.* For additional information and a review by Konrad Gries, see 4:258 (1 reference).

SPANISH

2405. *American Council Alpha Spanish Test.* For additional information and reviews by Lawrence Andrus and Christian O. Arndt, see 40:1371 (4 references).

2406. *Columbia Research Bureau Spanish Test.* For additional information and reviews by James C. Babcock and Harry J. Russell, see 40:1372 (7 references).

2407. *Cooperative Spanish Reading Test: Experimental Edition.* For additional information, see 35:473.

2408. *Cooperative Spanish Test: Lower and Higher Levels.* For additional information and a review by James B. Tharp, see 4:260 (3 references).

2409. *Examination in Spanish Grammar—Lower Level.* For additional information and a review by Frederick B. Agard, see 3:208.

2410. *Examination in Spanish Reading Comprehension—Lower Level.* For additional information and a review by Harry J. Russell, see 3:209.

2411. *Examination in Spanish Vocabulary—Lower Level.* For additional information, see 3:210.

2412. *First and Second Year Spanish: Every Pupil Test.* For additional information, see 35:477.

2413. *First Course in Spanish: Comprehensive Tests in High School Subjects.* For additional information, see 35:476.

2414. *First Year Spanish: Every Pupil Scholarship Test.* For additional information, see 35:478.

2415. *First Year Spanish: Multiple-Purpose Objective Tests in High School Subjects.* For additional information, see 35:479.

2416. *Second Course in Spanish: Comprehensive Tests in High School Subjects.* For additional information, see 35:480.

2417. *Second Year Spanish: Every Pupil Scholarship Test.* For additional information, see 35:481.

2418. *Second Year Spanish: Multiple-Purpose Objective Tests in High School Subjects.* For additional information, see 35:482.

2419. *Spanish Life and Culture.* For additional information and a review by James C. Babcock, see 40:1375; for a review by Walter V. Kaulfers, see 38:1157.

2420. *The Stanford Spanish Tests.* For additional information and a review by James B. Tharp, see 4:266.

INTELLIGENCE

GROUP

2420a. *A.C.E.R. Intermediate Test C.* Formerly called *A.C.E.R. General Test C.* For additional information and a review by James Lumsden, see 5:298 (2 references).

2421. *A.C.E.R. Non-Verbal Test.* For additional information and a review by F. J. Schonell, see 4:272 (2 references).

2422. *A.C.E.R. Test L.* For additional information, see 4:273.

2423. *Akron Classification Test.* For additional information and a review by Erwin K. Taylor, see 4:276.

2424. *The Army Alpha Examination: First Nebraska Revision.* For additional information and a review by Robert G. Demaree (with Louis L. McQuitty), see 4:279 (1 reference); for a review by W. D. Commins, see 38:1039 (1 reference); see also 3:220 (77 references for *Army Group Examination Alpha* and revisions).

2425. *Auditory Scale for Group Measurement of General Mental Ability.* For additional information, see 38:1041.

2426. *Bregman Language Completion Scale.* For additional information, see 35:334.

2427. *Bristol Group Reasoning Tests.* For additional information and reviews by Charles Fox and Percival Smith, see 40:1381 (1 reference).

2428. *The Business Test.* For additional information and reviews by Louis C. Nanassy and James H. Ricks, Jr., see 5:311.

2429. *Carnegie Mental Ability Tests.* For additional information and reviews by W. D. Commins and Robert L. Thorndike, see 3:224 (3 references).

2430. *College Transfer Test.* Formerly called *College Ability Test.* For additional information, see 4:286 (1 reference).

2431. *Culture-Free Test.* For additional information and a review by Raleigh M. Drake, see 4:287; for reviews by L. S. Penrose, Walter C. Shipley, and David Wechsler, see 3:228 (4 references).

2432. *Fiji Test of General Ability.* For additional information, see 40:1395 (2 references).

2433. *General Intelligence Test for Africans.* For additional information, see 40:1396 (4 references).

2434. *Gibson's Intelligence Tests.* For additional information, see 38:1045.

2435. *Glick-Germany Scholastic Aptitude Test.* For additional information, see 40:1186.

2436. *Group Selective Test No. 1.* For additional information and a review by T. R. Miles, see 5:337.

2437. *Information Sheet.* For additional information, see 35:337.

2438. *Mental Alertness Test: George Washington University Series, Revised Form.* For additional information and a review by J. P. Guilford, see 3:238.

2439. *Moray House Test 11a.* For additional information, see 35:342.

2440. *Multi-Mental Scale.* For additional information and a review by D. A. Worcester, see 3:242 (8 references).

2441. *Northox Group Intelligence Test.* For additional information and a review by E. Patricia Hunt, see 40:1410; see also 38:1050 (1 excerpt).

2442. *The Peel Group Tests of Practical Ability.* For additional information and a review by George Westby of the first edition, see 4:313 (2 references).

2443. *Perception of Relations Scales.* For additional information and a review by Charles D. Flory, see 3:251.

2444. *Personnel Classification Test [Henderson].* For additional information and reviews by Brent Baxter and John C. Flanagan, see 3:252.

2445. *Pintner Non-Language Primary Mental Test.* For additional information and reviews by Psyche Cattell and Carroll A. Whitmer, see 3:256 (6 references).

2446. *Psychological Examination.* For additional information, see 40:1418.

2447. *Revised Alpha Examination, Form 5.* For additional information and a review by Dael Wolfle, see 4:315 (4 references); see also 3:220 (75 references for *Army Group Examination Alpha* and revisions).

2448. *Revised Alpha Examination Form 6, Short Form.* For additional information and reviews by Edwin R. Henry and Dael Wolfle, see 4:316 (1 reference).

2449. *Revision of Army Alpha Examination.* For additional information and reviews by Edward E. Cureton and Edwin R. Henry, see 4:317 (3 references).

2450. *The Scholarship Qualifying Test.* For additional information and reviews by Lee J. Cronbach and Roger T. Lennon, see 5:379.

2451. *Scottish Council for Research in Education 1932 Mental Survey Test.* For additional information, see 35:350 (1 reference).

2452. *Scovill Classification Test.* For additional information and reviews by Robert G. Bernreuter and Edward E. Cureton, see 4:320 (1 reference).

2453. *Test of Mental Capacity.* For additional information, see 35:353.

2454. *Thorndike Intelligence Examination for College Entrance.* For additional information, see 35:354.

2455. *Unit Scales of Aptitude.* For additional information and a review by Herschel T. Manuel, see 40:1428.

2456. *V.G.C. Intelligence Indicator.* For additional information and a review by George A. Ferguson, see 4:327.

2457. *Verbal Intelligence Test.* Formerly called *Verbal Intelligence Test for Business Executives.* For additional information and a review by John P. Foley, Jr., see 5:395; for a review by William B. Schrader, see 4:329.

2458. *Willis-Smith Advanced Mental Test.* For additional information and reviews by Harold H. Bixler and F. T. Tyler, see 3:268.

INDIVIDUAL

2459. *California First-Year Mental Scale.* For additional information and a review by Florence L. Goodenough, see 40:1382 (1 reference).

2460. *California Preschool Mental Scale.* For additional information and reviews by B. M. Castner and Florence L. Goodenough, see 40:1383 (1 reference).

2461. *Cornell-Coxe Performance Ability Scale.* For additional information and reviews by Francis N. Maxfield and Carroll A. Whitmer, see 40:1388 (3 references); for excerpts from related book reviews, see 38:B335 and 36:B77.

2462. *Curtis Classification Form.* For additional information and a review by Harold G. Seashore, see 4:338.

2463. *Dearborn Formboard 3.* For additional information and a review by Grace H. Kent, see 40:1391 (8 references).

2464. *Dearborn-Anderson Formboards 2 and 2b.* For additional information and a review by Grace H. Kent, see 40:1390 (4 references).

2465. *Ferguson Formboards.* For additional information and a review by Grace H. Kent, see 40:1394 (12 references).

2466. *Herring Revision of the Binet-Simon Tests.* For additional information and a review by Andrew W. Brown, see 40:1399 (13 references).

2467. *Kent-Shakow Formboard.* 2 models: Industrial Model (also called *Kent-Shakow Spatial Relations Test*), Clinical Model. For additional information and a review by Milton L. Blum, see 3:660 (11 references); for a review by Lorene Teegarden, see 40:1401 (9 references).

2468. *Leiter-Partington Adult Performance Scale.* For additional information and reviews by Harold A. Delp and Herschel Manuel, see 4:350 (4 references, 1 excerpt).

2469. *Linfert-Hierholzer Scale for Measuring the Mental Development of Infants During the First Year of Life.* For additional information and a review by Nancy Bayley, see 3:285 (6 references).

2470. *Modification of the Kent-Shakow Formboard.* For additional information, see 40:1408 (3 references).

2471. *Non-Verbal Perception Scale.* For additional information, see 35:361.

2472. *Pintner-Paterson Scale of Performance Tests.* For additional information and a review by Francis N. Maxfield, see 38:1061 (1 reference).

2473. *Stencil Design Test II.* For additional information and a review by Benjamin Balinsky, see 4:359 (4 references); for a review by James M. Anderson, see 3:295.

2474. *Van Alstyne Picture Vocabulary Test for Pre-school Children.* For additional information and a review by Ruth W. Washburn, see 3:296 (1 reference).

MATHEMATICS

2475. *Cooperative College Mathematics Test for First-Year Courses.* For additional information and reviews by Albert A. Bennett and Nathan Morrison, see 3:304.

2476. *Cooperative General Mathematics Test for College Students.* For additional information and a review by Tomlinson Fort, see 40:1431; for a review by M. W. Richardson, see 38:1071.

2477. *Cooperative Test in Secondary School Mathematics: Higher Level.* For additional information and a review by E. H. C. Hildebrandt, see 3:303.

2478. *Foust-Schorling Test of Functional Thinking in Mathematics.* For additional information and reviews by William Betz and M. L. Hartung, see 3:306 (1 reference, 2 excerpts).

2479. *General High School Mathematics: Manchester Semester-End Achievement Tests.* For additional information, see 35:381.

2480. *Mathematics Test: Ohio Senior Survey Tests.* For additional information and a review by William G. Mollenkopf, see 3:313.

2481. *Problems in Quantitative Thinking.* For additional information, see 38:1077.

2482. *Solution of Mathematical Problems.* For additional information, see 38:1078.

2483. *Survey Test in Mathematics:Cooperative General Achievement Test,* [*Survey Series*], *Part 3.* For additional information and a review by Paul R. Rider, see 40:1434; for reviews by Arnold Dresden, Palmer O. Johnson, M. W. Richardson, and S. S. Wilks, see 38:870.

ALGEBRA

2484. *Algebra Prognosis Test.* For additional information and reviews by Paul J. Blommers and William G. Mollenkopf, see 4:383.

2485. *Columbia Research Bureau Algebra Test.* For additional information and a review by Stanley Clark, see 4:386; for reviews by L. B. Kinney and S. S. Wilks, see 40:1436 (1 reference).

2486. *Cooperative Mathematics Test for College Students: Comprehensive Examination in College Algebra.* For additional information and reviews by Albert A. Bennett and Paul R. Rider, see 40:1440 (1 reference); for reviews by Arnold Dresden, Marion W. Richardson, and Henry L. Rietz, see 38:882.

2487. *Examination in College Algebra.* For additional information and reviews by Albert A. Bennett and Edmund P. Churchill, see 3:323 (1 reference).

2488. *Examination in Elementary Algebra—High-School Level.* For additional information and reviews by Richard M. Drake and John A. Long, see 3:324.

2489. *Examination in Second-Year Algebra—High-School Level.* For additional information and reviews by L. B. Plumlee and Daniel W. Snader, see 3:325.

2490. *First Year Algebra: Comprehensive Tests in High School Subjects.* For additional information, see 35:29.

2491. *First-Year Algebra: Multiple-Purpose Objective Tests in High School Subjects.* For additional information, see 35:30.

2492. *Iowa Every-Pupil Test in Ninth Year Algebra.* For additional information and a review by John R. Clark, see 40:1442.

2493. *Second Course in Algebra: Comprehensive Tests in High School Subjects.* For additional information, see 35:35.

2494. *Survey Test in Elementary Algebra.* For additional information and reviews by John A. Long and Daniel W. Snader, see 3:328.

2495. *Wisconsin Algebra Test.* For additional information, see 3:330.

ARITHMETIC

2496. *Arithmetic: Midland Attainment Tests.* For additional information and a review by Fred J. Schonell, see 40:1448.

2497. *Arithmetical Reasoning Test.* For additional information and a review by William L. Schaaf, see 4:407.

2498. *Business Arithmetic: Every Pupil Scholarship Test.* For additional information, see 36:582.

2499. *Chicago Arithmetic Readiness Test.* For additional information and a review by Foster E. Grossnickle, see 3:337 (1 reference).

2500. *Chicago Arithmetic Survey Tests.* For additional information and reviews by William A. Brownell and Foster E. Grossnickle, see 3:338; see also 40:1453 (1 excerpt).

2501. *Compass Diagnostic Tests in Arithmetic.* For additional information and reviews by William A. Brownell and Foster E. Grossnickle, see 40:1454.

2502. *Compass Survey Tests in Arithmetic.* For additional information and a review by William A. Brownell, see 40:1455.

2503. *Cooperative Commercial Arithmetic Test.* For additional information and a review by Bertram Epstein, see 4:449.

2504. *Courtis Standard Research Tests: Arithmetic.* For additional information, see 35:42.

2505. *Dearborn Arithmetic Test: Arithmetic Fundamentals.* For additional information, see 35:43.

2506. *Diagnostic Test in Arithmetic Reasoning: The Harlow Objective Tests.* For additional information, see 36:534.

2507. *Diagnostic Test in Decimals.* For additional information, see 35:44.

2508. *Diagnostic Test in Fractions.* For additional information, see 35:45.

2509. *Diagnostic Test in Percentage.* For additional information, see 35:46.

2510. *Diagnostic Test in Practical Measurements.* For additional information, see 35:47.

2511. *Diagnostic Test of Whole Numbers.* For additional information, see 35:48.

2512. *Eighth Grade Arithmetic: Comprehensive Objective Tests in Elementary Subjects.* For additional information, see 35:49.

2513. *Examination in Advanced Arithmetic—High-School Level.* For additional information and reviews by Monica M. Hoye and F. Lynwood Wren, see 3:343.

2514. *Examination in Business Arithmetic.* For additional information, see 3:374.

2515. *Final Test in Arithmetic: Comprehensive Objective Tests for Seventh-Grade Pupils in Texas.* For additional information, see 35:50.

2516. *Final Test in Fifth-Grade Arithmetic: Comprehensive Objective Tests for Fifth-Grade Pupils in Texas.* For additional information, see 35:51.

2517. *Final Test in Sixth-Grade Arithmetic: Comprehensive Objective Tests for Sixth-Grade Pupils in Texas.* For additional information, see 35:52.

2518. *Grossnickle Test of Concepts Found in Social Uses of Arithmetic.* For additional information, see 36:535 (1 reference).

2519. *Hildreth Arithmetic Achievement Tests.* For additional information and reviews by William A. Brownell and Leo J. Brueckner, see 38:890.

2520. *Lazerte Diagnostic Problem-Solving Test in Arithmetic.* For additional information, see 35:55.

2521. *Phonograph Record Tests in Arithmetic.* For additional information, see 35:57.

2522. *Renfrow Survey Tests of Mathematical Skills and Concepts.* For additional information and a review by C. L. Thiele, see 3:349.

2523. *Retail Arithmetic Worksample.* For additional information and a review by William J. E. Crissy, see 4:418 (1 reference).

2524. *Sangren-Reidy Survey Tests in Arithmetic.* For additional information and reviews by Leo J. Brueckner and C. L. Thiele, see 40:1460.

2525. *Scale of Problems in Commercial Arithmetic.* For additional information, see 40:1489 (3 references, 1 excerpt).

2526. *Seventh Grade Arithmetic: Comprehensive Objective Tests in Elementary Subjects.* For additional information, see 35:61.

2527. *Speed Addition Test.* For additional information, see 38:1081.

2528. *Test in Fundamental Processes in Arithmetic.* For additional information, see 38:894.

2529. *Test on Arithmetic Meanings and Vocabulary.* For additional information and a review by Foster E. Grossnickle, see 3:353.

2530. *Unit Scales of Attainment in Arithmetic.* For additional information and reviews by W. J. Osburn and Peter L. Spencer, see 40:1463. For reviews of the complete battery, see 40:1197 and 38:878.

2531. *Wisconsin Inventory Tests in Arithmetic.* For additional information and a review by Leo J. Brueckner, see 40:1464.

2532. *Woody-McCall Mixed Fundamentals in Arithmetic.* For additional information and a review by William A. Brownell, see 4:421.

CALCULUS

2533. *Examination in Calculus II—Integral Calculus (Following Initial Course Containing No Integration).* For additional information and a review by John F. Randolph, see 3:355 (1 reference).

2534. *Examination in Differential Calculus.* For additional information, see 3:354 (1 reference).

GEOMETRY

2535. *Columbia Research Bureau Plane Geometry Test.* For additional information and a review by Cyril J. Hoyt (with Theodore E. Kellogg), see 4:422 (1 reference); for reviews by W. Elmer Lancaster and J. H. Minnick, see 40:1466.

2536. *Examination in Analytic Geometry.* For additional information and a review by C. O. Oakley, see 3:358 (1 reference).

2537. *Examination in Plane Geometry—High-School Level.* For additional information and a review by Hale C. Pickett, see 3:359.

2538. *Iowa Every-Pupil Test in Plane Geometry.* For additional information and a review by J. H. Blackhurst, see 38:994.

2539. *Nelson-Richardson Plane Geometry Readiness Test.* For additional information, see 38:995.

2540. *Orleans Plane Geometry Achievement Test.* For additional information and a review by Harold P. Fawcett, see 3:361.

2541. *Plane Geometry: Comprehensive Tests in High School Subjects.* For additional information, see 35:258.

2542. *Solid Geometry: Comprehensive Objective Tests in High School Subjects.* For additional information, see 35:262.

2543. *Survey Test in Plane Geometry.* For additional information and a review by Harold P. Fawcett, see 4:436.

2544. *The Van Dyke Solid Geometry Test.* For additional information, see 4:437.

2545. *Wisconsin Geometry Test.* For additional information, see 3:362.

TRIGONOMETRY

2546. *Examination in Plane Trigonometry.* For additional information, see 3:364 (1 reference).

MISCELLANEOUS

2547. *Hoffman Bilingual Schedule.* For additional information, see 35:227 (1 reference).

2548. *Sign-Search Test.* For additional information, see 38:1080.

AGRICULTURE

2549. *Clinton-Walker General Farm Mechanics Test.* For additional information, see 40:1475.

2550. *Final Test in Agriculture: Comprehensive Objective Tests for Seventh-Grade Pupils in Texas.* For additional information, see 35:23.

2551. *Graduate Record Examinations Advanced Agriculture Test.* For additional information, see 4:442.

COMPUTATIONAL AND SCORING DEVICES

2552. *Age and Quotient Slide Rule.* For additional information, see 35:139.

2553. *The Delp I.Q. Computer.* For additional information, see 4:465 (1 excerpt).

2554. *Morgan IQ Calculator.* For additional information, see 40:1493 (1 excerpt).

2555. *The Multiscore Profile Form and Scoring Codes.* For additional information, see 4:467.

2556. *Plumb IQ Slide Rule for Use With the Wechsler-Bellevue Intelligence Scale.* For additional information, see 4:362 (1 excerpt).

2557. *SRA Self-Scorer.* For additional information and reviews by James M. Anderson and Arthur E. Traxler, see 4:468 (4 references).

2558. *Score Transmuter.* For additional information, see 36:616.

2559. *Thurstone Scoring Board.* For additional information, see 3:398.

2560. *Winnetka Chart Form.* For additional information, see 36:618.

DRIVING AND SAFETY EDUCATION

2561. *Auto and Highway Safety Test.* For additional information and a review by Harry R. DeSilva, see 40:1521.

2562. *General Achievement Test in Fire Safety: National Fire Prevention Tests.* For additional information, see 4:523.

2563. *General First-Aid Test for Senior-High-School Students: National Safety Education Tests.* For additional information, see 40:1522.

2564. *General Safety Education Test for Junior-High-School Pupils: National Safety Education Tests.* For additional information, see 40:1523.

2565. *Home Safety Test for High-School Students and Adults: National Safety Education Tests.* For additional information, see 40:1524.

2566. *An Instructional Test in Safety.* For additional information, see 3:457.

2567. *Judgment Test on Safe Driving Practices.* For additional information and a review by Harry R. DeSilva, see 40:1525 (2 excerpts).

2568. *National Bicycle Tests.* For additional information, see 40:1526.

2569. *National Safe Drivers Tests.* For additional information, see 35:436.

EDUCATION

2570. *Attitude Toward Student Ratings of Instruction.* For additional information, see 5:532.

2571. *Barr-Harris Teacher's Performance Record.* For additional information, see 4:793.

2572. *Brown Rating Profile for Student Teachers and Teachers of Physical Education.* For additional information, see 40:1494.

2573. *Clinton-Castle Self-Rating Scale for County School Superintendents.* For additional information, see 40:1495.

2574. *College Efficiency-of-Instruction Index.* For additional information, see 40:1496 (1 reference).

2575. *Comprehensive Examination in Education.* For additional information, see 35:159.

2576. *Comprehensive Examination in Secondary Education.* For additional information, see 38:953.

2577. *Cooperative Professional Education Test.* For additional information, see 35:160.

2578. *Coxe-Orleans Prognosis Test of Teaching Ability.* For additional information and reviews by Harl R. Douglass and David G. Ryans, see 3:399 (5 references).

2579. *Exceptional Teacher Service Record.* For additional information and reviews by Leo J. Brueckner and Edwin Wandt, see 4:796.

2580. *How Teach and Learn in College? Experimental Edition.* For additional information and a review by Dean A. Worcester, see 4:800 (4 references).

2581. *Morrison Rating Scale Profile for Teachers.* For additional information and a review by Leo J. Brueckner, see 38:955.

2582. *Principles of Organization and Management in Secondary Education.* For additional information, see 35:162.

2583. *Rating Instrument for the Evaluation of Student Reactions.* For additional information, see 40:1497 (2 references); for excerpts from related book reviews, see 40:B854, 40:B855, and 38:B323.

2584. *Rating Instrument for the Evaluation of the Reactions of College Students.* For additional information, see 40:1498 (2 references); for excerpts from related book reviews, see 40:B854, 40:B855, and 38:B323.

2585. *Scale for Measuring Attitude Toward Teaching.* For additional information, see 35:70.

2586. *Scale for Rating Effective Teacher Behavior.* For additional information and reviews by Leo J. Brueckner and Edwin Wandt, see 4:804 (1 reference).

2587. *Standardized Examination on Principles of Secondary Education.* For additional information, see 35:165.

2588. *Stanford Educational Aptitudes Test.* For additional information and reviews by A. S. Barr and David G. Ryans, see 3:404 (4 references).

2589. *Teachers' Judgment in Child Discipline Test.* For additional information, see 35:166.

2590. *Teachers' Professional Judgment Test.* For additional information, see 35:167.

2591. *Test on Controversial Issues in Higher Education: Revised Edition.* For additional information, see 35:168 (1 reference).

2592. *Toothman Test in Elementary Educational Psychology.* For additional information and a review by V. A. C. Henmon, see 38:956.

ETIQUETTE

2593. *The Best Thing to Do: A Test of Knowledge of Social Standards.* For additional information and a review by Helen Shacter, see 4:471.

2594. *Right Conduct Test.* For additional information, see 36:834.

2595. *Test of Etiquette: George Washington University Series.* For additional information and a review by James H. Ricks, Jr., see 4:473.

2596. *Test of Knowledge of Social Usage.* For additional information and a review by Hilda Taba, see 4:474 (1 reference).

HANDWRITING

2597. *The Thorndike Scale for Handwriting of Children.* For additional information and a review by Stuart A. Courtis, see 4:477 (4 references).

HEALTH AND PHYSICAL EDUCATION

2598. *ACH Index of Nutritional Status.* For additional information, see 38:1002 (1 reference, 1 excerpt).

2599. *Achievement Scales in Physical Education Activities for Boys and Girls in Elementary and Junior High Schools.* For additional information, see 38:1003.

2600. *Achievement Scales in Physical Education Activities for College Men.* For additional information, see 38:1004.

2601. *Final Test in Fifth-Grade Hygiene and Health: Comprehensive Tests for Fifth-Grade Pupils in Texas.* For additional information, see 35:273.

2602. *Final Test in Physiology: Comprehensive Objective Tests for Seventh-Grade Pupils in Texas.* For additional information, see 35:274.

2603. *Final Test in Sixth-Grade Physiology: Comprehensive Objective Tests for Sixth-Grade Pupils in Texas.* For additional information, see 35:275.

2604. [*French Tests for Professional Courses in Knowledge of Sports*]: *Physical Education Major Examinations.* For additional information and a review by H. Harrison Clarke, see 4:480 (2 references).

2605. *Gates-Strang Health Knowledge Tests.* For additional information and a review by Paul E. Kambly, see 4:481 (2 references) ; see also 3:419 (1 excerpt) ; for reviews by Frederick Rand Rogers and A. H. Turney, see 40:1500 (1 excerpt).

2606. *Health Awareness Test.* For additional information and a review by R. Lenox Criswell, see 40:1501 (1 reference, 1 excerpt) ; for a review by Austin H. Turney, see 38:1006.

2607. *Health Inventories.* For additional information and a review by Benjamin Shimberg, see 4:484 (1 reference).

2608. *Health Knowledge and Attitude: Every Pupil Scholarship Test.* For additional information, see 36:704.

2609. *Health Knowledge Test.* For additional information, see 36:705.

2610. *Personal Health Inventory.* For additional information and a review by Willard W. Patty, see 4:487.

2611. *Physical Education Achievement Scales for Boys in Secondary Schools.* For additional information, see 38:B338 (1 excerpt) ; see also 36:707 (1 reference) and 36:B79 (4 excerpts).

2612. *Physical Examination Record.* For additional information, see 40:1504 (1 reference).

2613. *Physiology: Every Pupil Scholarship Test.* For additional information, see 35:278.

HOME ECONOMICS

2614. *Cooperative Test in Foods and Nutrition.* For additional information and a review by Robert L. Ebel, see 4:491 (1 reference).

2615. *Cooperative Test in Home Management.* For additional information, see 4:492 (1 reference).

2616. *Cooperative Test in Household Equipment.* For additional information and reviews by Faith Madden and Victor H. Noll, see 4:493 (1 reference).

2617. *Cooperative Test in Textiles and Clothing.* For additional information, see 4:494 (1 reference).

2618. *Engle-Stenquist Home Economics Test.* For additional information and reviews by Clara M. Brown [Arny] and Hester Chadderdon, see 40:1505.

2619. *Frear-Coxe Clothing Test.* For additional information and reviews by Laura B. Hadley and Esther F. Segner, see 40:1507.

2620. *General Home Economics: State High School Tests for Indiana.* For additional information and a review by Clara M. Brown [Arny], see 38:1030.

2621. *Graduate Record Examinations Advanced Home Economics Test.* For additional information, see 4:497.

2622. *Home Economics—Foods: Multiple-Purpose Objective Tests in High School Subjects.* For additional information, see 35:327.

2623. *Information Test on Foods: Illinois Food Test.* For additional information and reviews by Norma A. Albright and Clara M. Brown [Arny], see 40:1508 (1 reference).

2624. *Minnesota Food Score Cards, Revised Edition.* For additional information, see 3:439.

2625. *Minnesota House Design and House Furnishing Test.* For additional information and a review by Ray Faulkner, see 38:1031 (1 reference).

2626. *Nutrition Information.* For additional information, see 4:502.

2627. *Scale for Evaluating Student-Efficiency in the Home Economics Laboratory.* For additional information, see 36:748.

2628. *Tests in Comprehension of Patterns.* For additional information and reviews by Laura B. Hadley and Berenice Mallory, see 40:1510.

INDUSTRIAL ARTS

2629. *Achievement Test in Mechanical Drawing.* For additional information and a review by Verne C. Fryklund, see 40:1512 (1 reference).

2630. *Achievement Test in Printing.* For additional information, see 35:329 (1 reference).

2631. *Drawing Aptitude Test.* For additional information, see 40:1512.1.

2632. *Examination in Mechanical Drawing.* For additional information, see 3:440.

2633. *Mechanical Drawing Performance Test.* For additional information and a review by Emanuel E. Ericson, see 40:1514 (1 reference) ; see also 38:1034 (1 excerpt).

2634. *Mechanical Drawing Tests.* For additional information and a review by Emanuel E. Ericson, see 40:1515.

2635. *Newkirk-Stoddard Home Mechanics Test.* For additional information and a review by Arthur B. Mays, see 40:1516 (1 reference).

2636. *Ninth Grade Industrial Arts: Manchester Semester-End Achievement Tests.* For additional information, see 36:752.

2637. *Practical Arts: Every Pupil Test.* For additional information, see 38:1035.

2638. *Standard Test in Fundamental Mechanical Drawing.* For additional information and a review by Verne C. Fryklund, see 40:1517.

PSYCHOLOGY

2639. *Comprehensive Examination in Psychology.* For additional information and a review by Edith M. Huddleston, see 4:507.

2640. *Examination in Elementary Psychology—College Level.* For additional information, see 3:401.

RECORD AND REPORT FORMS

2641. *The Cassel Developmental Record.* Now available, see 1303a.

2642. *Comprehensive Individual History Record Form for Infancy Through High School.* For additional information and reviews by Charles D. Flory and Chauncey M. Louttit, see 38:1116.

2643. *Diagnostic Child Study Record.* For additional information and reviews by Charles D. Flory, Chauncey M. Louttit, and J. W. M. Rothney, see 38:1117 (2 references).

2644. *Hamilton Cumulative Record Folder, Revised Edition.* For additional information, see 3:447.

2645. *Home Information Blank.* For additional information, see 35:429.

2646. *Indiana Psychodiagnostic Blank, Fourth Edition.* For additional information, see 40:1518 (3 references).

2647. *[Personnel Record Form.]* For additional information and a review by Charles D. Flory, see 38:1120.

2648. *Profile Chart for Individual Diagnosis.* For additional information, see 38:1121.

2649. *[Pupils' Record Cards.]* For additional information, see 40:1519 (1 reference).

2650. *Supplementary Entrance Interview Schedule.* For additional information, see 38:1122.

2651. *Winnetka Academic Analysis Chart.* For additional information, see 36:817.

RELIGIOUS EDUCATION

2652. *Attitude Toward the Bible.* For additional information, see 35:66 (1 reference).

2653. *Hebrew School Attitude Test.* For additional information, see 3:452a.

2654. *Jewish Home Environment Test.* For additional information, see 3:453.

2655. *Jewish Information Test.* For additional information, see 4:518.

2656. *Opinion Survey.* For additional information, see 4:519.

2657. *Religion Essentials Test.* For additional information, see 3:455 (2 references).

2658. *Uniform Achievement Tests.* For additional information, see 5:278.

READING

2659. *Basic Reading Tests.* For additional information, see 38:1096.

2660. *"Brighton" Reading Tests.* For additional information and a review by Frederick B. Davis, see 40:1529.

2661. *Chicago Reading Tests.* For additional information, see 3:478 (1 reference, 1 excerpt) ; for reviews by Robert Lawrence McCaul and W. J. Osburn, see 40:1531.

2662. *DeVault Primary Reading Test.* For additional information and a review by Alice N. Jameson, see 3:479.

2663. *English No. 1, Reading Comprehension: Midland Attainment Tests.* For additional information, see 38:1101.

2664. *Final Test in Fifth-Grade Reading: Comprehensive Objective Tests for Fifth-Grade Pupils in Texas.* For additional information, see 35:403.

2665. *Final Test in Reading: Comprehensive Objective Tests for Seventh-Grade Pupils in Texas.* For additional information, see 35:404.

2666. *Garrison First Year Reading Test.* For additional information and a review by Ruth Lowes, see 3:483 (2 references).

2667. *Garvey Primary Reading Test.* For additional information, see 4:533.

2668. *Haggerty Reading Examination.* For additional information and a review by William S. Gray, see 4:535 (5 references).

2669. *Ingraham-Clark Diagnostic Reading Tests.* For additional information and a review by Katherine G. Keneally, see 4:538.

2670. *Los Angeles Primary Reading Test.* For additional information and a review by Nila Banton Smith, see 4:542 (1 reference).

2671. *Lothian English Tests: Vocabulary and Comprehension.* For additional information, see 35:411.

2672. *Manwiller Word Recognition Test.* For additional information, see 35:412.

2673. *Mount Holyoke College Reading Test.* For additional information, see 35:416.

2674. *Shank Tests of Reading Comprehension.* For additional information and a review by William D. Sheldon, see 4:553; for a review by James R. Hobson, see 40:1567 (3 references).

2675. *Thorndike-Lorge Reading Test.* For additional information and a review by Ivan A. Booker, see 4:558 (1 reference) ; for a review by Robert L. McCaul, see 3:506 (1 excerpt).

2676. *Unit Scales of Attainment in Reading.* For additional information and reviews by Ivan A. Booker and J. Wayne Wrightstone, see 40:1581; for a review by Joseph C. Dewey, see 38:1115. For reviews of the complete battery, see 40:1197 and 38:878.

2677. *Whipple's High-School and College Reading Test.* For additional information and a review by Frederick B. Davis, see 3:507 (3 references).

2678. *Ypsilanti Reading Test.* For additional information, see 40:1583.1.

MISCELLANEOUS

2679. *Hildreth Diagnostic Reading Record.* For additional information, see 40:1541.

2680. *Instructional Reading Tests for the Intermediate Grades.* For additional information, see 40:1543.

2681. *Inventory of Reading Experiences.* For additional information and a review by Albert J. Harris, see 3:511 (2 references).

2682. *Phillips-Woody Group Tests for Reversals.* For additional information, see 35:417.

2683. *Poley Precis Test: A Test by Paragraph Summaries of Reading Comprehension.* For additional information and a review by Edward A. Tenney, see 40:1561.

2684. *Record for Reading Diagnosis.* For additional information and a review by Carolyn M. Welch, see 3:512.

2685. *SRA Achievement Series: Language Perception.* For additional information, see 5:668.

ORAL

2686. *Articulation Test With Reading Disability Feature.* For additional information and a review by Irving H. Anderson, see 38:1095.

2687. *Jenkins Oral Reading Test: Individualized Oral Diagnostic Test for Children With Serious Reading Difficulties.* For additional information and reviews by Guy L. Bond, David Kopel, and Clarence R. Stone, see 40:1548.

2688. *Kindergarten-Primary Articulation Test.* For additional information and a review by Irving H. Anderson, see 38:1104.

READINESS

2689. *Stevens Reading Readiness Test.* For additional information and reviews by Irving H. Anderson and Marion Monroe Cox, see 3:521.

SPECIAL FIELDS

2690. *Mathematics, Biology, Physical Science [Reading Test]: Booklet No. 2.* For additional information, see 40:1550.

2691. *Reading Scales in History.* For additional information and reviews by Paul Blommers and Albert J. Harris, see 3:530.

2692. *Reading Scales in Literature.* For additional information, see 3:531.

2693. *Reading Scales in Science.* For additional information and a review by Ivan A. Booker, see 3:532.

2694. *Southeastern Problems and Prospects, Social Studies and English [Reading Test]: Booklet No. 1.* For additional information, see 40:1569.

SPEED

2695. *Michigan Speed of Reading Test.* For additional information and a review by Eason Monroe, see 3:523 (1 reference); see also 40:1553 (2 references); for reviews by Richard Ledgerwood and M. R. Trabue, see 38:1171.

2696. *Reading Speed Test: National Achievement Test.* For additional information and a review by Eason Monroe, see 3:525.

STUDY SKILLS

2697. *Analysis of Controversial Writing: Test 5.31.* For additional information, see 40:1527.

2698. *Applied Reading for Junior-Senior High School: Every Pupil Test.* For additional information and a review by Ivan A. Booker, see 3:534.

2699. *Attitudes and Skills in the Use of References: Every Pupil Test.* For additional information, see 35:490.

2700. *Critical Classification of Magazines and Newspapers.* For additional information, see 38:1163.

2701. *Critical-Mindedness in the Reading of Fiction: Test 3.7.* For additional information, see 40:1530 (1 reference).

2702. *Information Concerning Library Processes.* For additional information, see 38:1164.

2703. *Interpretation of Data Test: General Education Series.* For additional information and reviews by J. Raymond Gerberich and Victor H. Noll, see 4:581 (5 references); for a review by J. Wayne Wrightstone, see 3:535 (4 references); see also 40:1544 (9 references).

2704. *Interpretation of Data: Test 2.71.* For additional information, see 40:1545 (4 references).

2705. *Library Test for Junior High Schools.* For additional information and reviews by Robert A. Davis and Ethel M. Feagley, see 3:536.

2706. *Logical Reasoning Test: General Education Series.* For additional information and a review by Robert L. Ebel, see 4:582 (1 reference); see also 40:1528 (4 references).

2707. *Nature of Proof: Test 5.22.* For additional information, see 40:1556 (3 references).

2708. *Parr Skill-Ability Tests.* For additional information, see 40:1559.1.

2709. *Reading and Construction of Tables and Graphs.* For additional information, see 38:1165.

2710. *Student Skills Inventory, Experimental Edition.* For additional information, see 40:1573 (1 reference).

2711. *Study Outline Test.* For additional information and a review by Harriet Barthelmess Morrison, see 40:1575 (1 reference).

2712. *Test on the Use of Books and Libraries: General Education Series.* For additional information and reviews by Henry D. Rinsland and Louis Shores, see 4:585 (1 reference).

2713. *The Use of Library and Study Materials.* For additional information and a review by Robert Murray Bear, see 4:586 (1 reference); for a review by Ethel M. Feagley, see 3:543.

2714. *Young-Estabrooks Scale for Measuring Studiousness by Means of the Strong Vocational Interest Blank for Men.* For additional information and a review by Edmund G. Williamson, see 38:904 (4 references).

SCIENCE

2715. *Analytical Scales of Attainment in Elementary Science.* For additional information and reviews by Francis D. Curtis and Victor H. Noll, see 40:1598; see also 38:1123 (1 excerpt).

2716-7. *Application of Principles in Science: Test 1.3b.* For additional information, see 40:1599 (2 references).

2718. *Cooperative General Science Test for College Students.* For additional information, see 38:1126.

2719. *Examination in General Science—High-School Level.* For additional information and reviews by Hans C. Gordon and Victor H. Noll, see 3:573.

2720. *Examination in Senior Science—High-School Level.* For additional information and a review by Richard H. Jordan, see 3:574.

2721. *General Science: Comprehensive Objective Tests in High School Subjects.* For additional information, see 35:445 and 35:446.

2722. *General Science Test: Gibson's Attainment Tests.* For additional information, see 38:1129.

2723. *Iowa Every-Pupil Test in General Science.* For additional information and a review by Edward E. Cureton, see 38:1131.

2724. *Science Applications Test: Gibson's Attainment Tests.* For additional information, see 38:1132.

2725. *Science Information Test.* Also called *Calvert Science Information Test.* For additional information and reviews by Hans C. Gordon and G. W. Hunter, see 40:1603.

2726. *Survey Test in the Natural Sciences: Cooperative General Achievement Test,* [*Survey Series*], *Part 2.* For additional information, see 40:1604; for a review by Palmer O. Johnson, see 38:870.

2727. *Test of Application of Principles in General Science: General Education Series.* For additional information and a review by R. Will Burnett, see 4:629 (3 references).

2728. *Test of Application of Principles in Physical Science: General Education Series.* For additional information and a review by Palmer O. Johnson, see 4:594 (3 references).

2729. *Wisconsin General Science Test.* For additional information, see 3:577.

BIOLOGY

2730. *Application of Principles in Biological Science: Test 1.33A.* For additional information, see 40:1584 (2 references).

2731. *Biology: Multiple-Purpose Objective Tests in High School Subjects.* For additional information, see 35:75.

2732. *Cooperative Botany Test: Provisional Form 1936.* For additional information and a review by F. C. Jean, see 38:908.

2733. *Cooperative College Biology Test.* For additional information and reviews by Clarence H. Nelson and Joseph J. Schwab, see 3:551.

2734. *Cooperative Zoology Test: Provisional Form 1936.* For additional information and a review by Dael L. Wolfle, see 38:909.

2735. *Examination in Biology—College Level.* For additional information and a review by C. W. Horton, see 3:552.

2736. *Examination in Biology—High-School Level.* For additional information and reviews by C. W. Horton and Richard H. Jordan, see 3:553 (1 reference).

2737. *Examination in Botany—College Level.* For additional information and reviews by C. W. Horton and Clarence H. Nelson, see 3:554.

2738. *Hanes-Benz Biology Test.* For additional information and a review by Clark W. Horton, see 40:1586 (1 reference).

2739. *Iowa Every-Pupil Test in Biology.* For additional information and a review by George W. Hunter, see 38:910.

2740. *Presson Biology Test.* For additional information and reviews by Thomas F. Morrison and Dael L. Wolfle, see 40:1587 (2 references).

2741. *Ruch-Cossmann Biology Test.* For additional information and reviews by Thomas F. Morrison and Dael L. Wolfle, see 40:1588 (3 references).

2742. *Test of Application of Principles of Biology: General Education Series.* For additional information and reviews by Clark W. Horton and Clarence H. Nelson, see 4:606 (4 references).

2743. *Wisconsin Biology Test.* For additional information, see 3:555.

CHEMISTRY

2744. *Chemistry: Comprehensive Tests in High School Subjects.* For additional information, see 35:109.

2745. *Chemistry: Multiple-Purpose Objective Tests in High School Subjects.* For additional information, see 35:112.

2746. *Clinton-Osborn-Ware General Chemistry Test.* For additional information, see 40:1590.

2747. *Columbia Research Bureau Chemistry Test.* For additional information and a review by Max D. Engelhart, see 40:1591.

2748. *Cooperative Chemistry Test: Provisional Form.* For additional information and a review by Max D. Engelhart, see 38:933.

2749. *Examination in Chemistry—High-School Level.* For additional information and a review by Victor H. Noll, see 3:564 (1 reference).

2750. *Examination in General Chemistry—College Level.* For additional information and reviews by John H. Daugherty and Florence E. Hooper, see 3:565 (1 reference).

2751. *Glenn-Welton Chemistry Achievement Test.* For additional information and reviews by Max D. Engelhart, Victor H. Noll, and Eugene A. Waters, see 40:1596 (1 excerpt) ; see also 38:934 (1 excerpt).

2752. *Intermediate Chemistry Test.* For additional information, see 40:1597.

2753. *Wisconsin Achievement Tests: Chemistry.* For additional information and a review by Victor H. Noll, see 3:569.

MISCELLANEOUS

2754. *Cause and Effect Relationship Test in Science: Scientific Attitudes, Test 2.* For additional information and a review by Louis M. Heil, see 40:1600.

2755. *Common Science Vocabulary.* For additional information, see 38:1124.

2756. *Cooperative Geology Test.* For additional information, see 3:579.

2757. *Examination in Astronomy—College Level.* For additional information, see 3:578.

2758. *Examination in Meteorology—High-School Level.* For additional information, see 3:580.

2759. *The New Air World.* For additional information, see 4:632.

2760. *Scientific Attitudes.* For additional information, see 38:1135.

2761. *Scientific Methods: Test 1, Controlled Experimentation Test in Science.* For additional information, see 38:1136.

2762. *Scientific Thinking: Every Pupil Test.* For additional information and a review by Victor H. Noll, see 38:1137.

2763. *Steps in Problem Solving.* For additional information, see 38:1138.

PHYSICS

2764. *Application of Principles in Physical Science: Test 1.34.* For additional information, see 40:1606 (2 references).

2765. *Columbia Research Bureau Physics Test.* For additional information and a review by Eugene A. Waters, see 40:1607 (1 reference).

2766. *Cooperative Physics Tests for College Students.* For additional information and a review by Edgar P. Slack, see 3:582 (1 reference) ; for a review by Alan T. Waterman, see 40:1609 (4 references) ; for a review by Paul A. Northrop, see 38:1089.

2767. *Examination in Electricity and Magnetism—College Level.* For additional information, see 3:583.

2768. *Examination in Electron Tubes and Circuits.* For additional information, see 3:584.

2769. *Examination in Physics—College Level.* For additional information, see 3:586.

2770. *Examination in Physics—High-School Level.* For additional information and reviews by G. P. Cahoon and Palmer O. Johnson, see 3:585.

2771. *High School Physics: Comprehensive Tests in High School Subjects.* For additional information, see 35:389.

2772. *Hurd Test in High School Physics.* For additional information and reviews by Andrew Longacre and Paul A. Northrop, see 40:1611.

2773. *Iowa Every-Pupil Test in Physics.* For additional information and reviews by Ernest E. Bayles and Archer W. Hurd, see 38:1091.

2774. *Physics: Multiple-Purpose Objective Tests in High School Subjects.* For additional information, see 35:393.

2775. *Torgerson-Rich-Ranney Tests in High School Physics.* For additional information and reviews by Palmer O. Johnson and Paul A. Northrop, see 40:1612.

2776. *Wisconsin Physics Test.* For additional information, see 3:589 (1 reference); for a review by Louis M. Heil, see 40:1613.

SENSORY-MOTOR

2777. *Ambigraph Laterality Test.* For additional information, see 36:782.

HEARING

2778. *ADC Audiometers.* For additional information, see 5:762.

2779. *Tests for the Hearing of Speech by Deaf People.* For additional information, see 40:1526.1 (1 reference, 3 excerpts).

2780. *Western Electric Audiometer.* For additional information, see 3:475 (9 references).

MOTOR

2781. *Brace Scale of Motor Ability.* For additional information and a review by Anna S. Espenschade, see 5:766 (17 references)

2782. *V.D.L. Psychomotor Scale for the Measurement of Manual Ability.* Revision of *Un Profil Psychomoteur* and *Manual Ability Test Series (Psycho-Motor Profile).* 2 tests: *Psychomotor Tests for Children, Psychomotor Tests for Adults.* For additional information and reviews by Anna Espenschade and William Sloan, see 4:653 (1 reference).

VISION

2783. *Dvorine Color Discrimination Screening Test.* For additional information, see 3:461a (1 reference).

2784. *Glenn Colorule.* For additional information, see 4:658 (1 reference).

2785. *The Master Opthalmograph.* For additional information and a review by Miles A. Tinker, see 4:660 (8 references); see also 3:470 (15 references); for a review by G. T. Buswell of an earlier model, see 40:1559 (2 references, 2 excerpts); for reviews by Stella S. Center, David Kopel, Marion Monroe [Cox], Joseph Tiffin, and Miles A. Tinker, see 38:1108 (1 excerpt).

2786. *Tests for Color-Blindness, Visual Acuity, and Astigmatism.* For additional information, see 36:783.

SOCIAL STUDIES

2787. *Beard-Erbe Social Science Tests.* For additional information and a review by Kenneth E. Gell, see 40:1614; for a review by Edgar B. Wesley, see 38:1144.

2788. *Cooperative Test of Social Studies Abilities.* For additional information and a review by Roy A. Price, see 40:1615; for a review by Howard R. Anderson, see 38:1146.

2789. *Historical Development and Cultural Change.* For additional information, see 38:1147.

2790. *Illinois Teachers College Cooperative Social Science Test.* For additional information and a review by Harry D. Berg, see 3:593.

2791. *Kansas Social Studies Unit Test.* For additional information, see 35:463.

2792. *Kelty-Moore Test of Concepts in the Social Studies.* For additional information, see 35:464 (1 reference).

2793. *Melbo Social Science Survey Test.* For additional information and reviews by Howard R. Anderson and R. M. Tryon, see 40:1616 (2 references) ; for a review by Alvin C. Eurich, see 38:1150.

2793a. *Social-Knowledge Tests, Upper and Lower Social Stratas.* For additional information, see 36:845.

2794. *Social Situation Interview.* For additional information, see 38:1152.

2795. *Social Studies Unit Test: Every Pupil Scholarship Test.* For additional information, see 36:847.

2796. *Survey Test in the Social Studies: Cooperative General Achievement Test, [Survey Series], Part 1.* For additional information and a review by Hilda Taba, see 40:1618; for a review by Harold Gulliksen, see 38:870.

2797. *Test of Critical Thinking in the Social Studies: Elementary School Series.* For additional information and reviews by Warren G. Findley, Pedro T. Orata, and G. M. Ruch, see 40:1619 (1 excerpt).

2798. *Wesley Test in Social Terms.* For additional information and a review by Howard R. Anderson, see 40:1622 (3 references).

CONTEMPORARY AFFAIRS

2799. *Contemporary Problems.* For additional information and a review by Harry D. Berg, see 5:832.

2800. *Contemporary World Problems: Every Pupil Scholarship Test.* For additional information, see 36:619.

2801. *Cooperative Contemporary Affairs Test for College Students.* For additional information and reviews by Benjamin S. Bloom and John V. McQuitty, see 4:4 (4 references) ; for a review by H. T. Morse, see 3:2 (12 references) ; for a review by Ralph W. Tyler, see 40:1182 (5 references) ; for a review by Paul M. Limbert, see 38:948.

2802. *Cooperative Contemporary Affairs Test for High School Classes.* Formerly called *Cooperative Current Public Affairs Test for High School Classes.* For additional information and reviews by John M. Stalnaker and R. M. Tryon, see 40:1183; for reviews by Howard R. Anderson and J. Wayne Wrightstone, see 38:950.

2803. *Cooperative Current Literature and Arts Test for High School Classes.* For additional information and reviews by Walter Barnes and H. H. Giles, see 38:949.

2804. *Cooperative Test on Recent Social and Scientific Developments.* For additional information and a review by Roger T. Lennon, see 4:7 (2 references) ; for reviews by Ernest W. Tiegs, Ralph W. Tyler, and Edgar B. Wesley, see 3:5.

2805. *Iowa Every-Pupil Test in Understanding of Contemporary Affairs.* For additional information and a review by Alvin C. Eurich, see 38:951.

ECONOMICS

2806. *Cooperative Economics Test.* For additional information, see 3:597; for a review by Edgar B. Wesley, see 40:1624.

2807. *Economics: Comprehensive Objective Tests in High School Subjects.* For additional information, see 35:153.

2808. *Economics: Every Pupil Scholarship Test.* For additional information, see 35:154.

2809. *Iowa Every-Pupil Test in Economics.* For additional information, see 38:1148.

2810. *Money and Banking: Every Pupil Scholarship Test.* For additional information, see 35:157.

2811. *20th Century Test for Economics.* For additional information, see 4:671.

GEOGRAPHY

2812. *Analytical Scales of Attainment in Geography*. For additional information and a review by Ernest C. Witham, see 40:1625.

2813. *Final Test in Fifth-Grade Geography: Comprehensive Objective Tests for Fifth-Grade Pupils in Texas*. For additional information, see 35:242.

2814. *Final Test in Geography: Comprehensive Objective Tests for Seventh-Grade Pupils in Texas*. For additional information, see 35:243.

2815. *Final Test in Geography: Comprehensive Objective Tests for Sixth-Grade Pupils in Texas*. For additional information, see 35:244.

2816. *Fourth Grade Geography Test*. Also called *National Council of Geography Teachers Geography Test*. For additional information and reviews by Elaine Forsyth [Cook] and Agatha Townsend, see 3:599 (1 reference).

2817. *Geography Ability Test: Gibson's Attainment Tests*. For additional information, see 38:990.

2818. *Industrial and Commercial Geography: Comprehensive Objective Tests in High School Subjects*. For additional information, see 35:247.

2819. *Industrial Geography: Every Pupil Scholarship Test*. For additional information, see 35:248.

2820. *Industrial Geography: Multiple-Purpose Objective Tests in High School Subjects*. For additional information, see 35:249.

2821. *Modern Geography and Allied Social Studies*. For additional information and reviews by Edith M. Huddleston and Edwin H. Reeder, see 4:678.

2822. *Physical Geography: Multiple-Purpose Objective Tests in High School Subjects*. For additional information, see 35:250.

2823. *Physiography Test*. For additional information, see 35:251.

2824. *Wiedefeld-Walther Geography Test*. For additional information and a review by Marguerite Uttley, see 3:602; for reviews by Anna Parsek and Marie E. Trost, see 40:1626.

2825. *World Geography Test: Dominion Tests*. For additional information and a review by Edwin H. Reeder, see 3:603.

HISTORY

2826. *American Council European History Test*. For additional information and a review by S. P. McCutchen, see 40:1628.

2827. *American History: Comprehensive Tests in High School Subjects*. For additional information, see 35:281.

2828. *American History: Multiple-Purpose Objective Tests in High School Subjects*. For additional information, see 35:284.

2829. *American History Test for Catholic Elementary Schools*. For additional information, see 35:285.

2830. *Analytical Scales of Attainment in American History*. For additional information and reviews by Wilbur F. Murra and Margaret Willis, see 40:1631.

2831. *Ancient and Medieval History: Comprehensive Tests in High School Subjects*. For additional information, see 35:287.

2832. *Ancient and Medieval History: Every Pupil Scholarship Test*. For additional information, see 35:288.

2833. *Ancient and Medieval History: Multiple-Purpose Objective Tests in High School Subjects*. For additional information, see 35:289.

2834. *Bowman United States History Test*. For additional information and a review by W. C. McCall (with Grace Graham), see 40:1632.

2835. *Canadian History Test*. For additional information, see 35:290.

2836. *Cooperative English History Test*. For additional information, see 35:294 (1 reference).

2837. *Cooperative Medieval History Test*. For additional information, see 35:295 (1 reference).

2838. *Ely-King Interpretation Tests in American History.* For additional information and reviews by Clinton C. Conrad and Edgar B. Wesley, see 40:1637.

2839. *English History: Comprehensive Objective Tests in High School Subjects.* For additional information, see 35:298.

2840. *Every-Pupil Test in United States History: South Carolina Every-Pupil Testing Program.* For additional information, see 36:716.

2841. *Examination in American History.* For additional information and a review by Howard R. Anderson, see 3:607 (1 reference).

2842. *Examination in Modern European History.* For additional information and a review by Frederick H. Stutz, see 3:608.

2843. *Examination in World History—High-School Level.* For additional information and reviews by Dorothy C. Adkins and Wallace W. Taylor, see 3:609.

2844. *Exercises in the Use of Historical Evidence.* For additional information, see 35:301 (1 reference).

2845. *Final Test in Fifth-Grade United States History: Comprehensive Objective Tests for Fifth-Grade Pupils in Texas.* For additional information, see 35:302.

2846. *Final Test in Texas History: Comprehensive Objective Tests for Sixth-Grade Pupils in Texas.* For additional information, see 35:303.

2847. *Final Test in United States History: Comprehensive Objective Tests for Seventh-Grade Pupils in Texas.* For additional information, see 35:304.

2848. *High School American History: Every Pupil Scholarship Test.* For additional information, see 35:305.

2849. *Information Tests in American History.* For additional information and a review by Roy A. Price, see 40:1638.

2850. *Iowa Every-Pupil Test in United States History.* For additional information, see 38:1020.

2851. *Iowa Every-Pupil Test in World History.* For additional information, see 38:1021.

2852. *Kniss World History Test.* For additional information and reviews by Dorothy C. Adkins and Wallace W. Taylor, see 3:612 (2 references, 2 excerpts).

2853. *Medieval History: Every Pupil Test.* For additional information, see 38:1022.

2854. *Modern European History: Comprehensive Tests in High School Subjects.* For additional information, see 35:308 and 35:310.

2855. *Modern European History: Every Pupil Scholarship Test.* For additional information, see 35:309.

2856. *Modern European History: Multiple-Purpose Objective Tests in High School Subjects.* For additional information, see 35:311.

2857. *Modern History: Every Pupil Test.* For additional information, see 38:1023.

2858. *Survey Test in United States History.* For additional information, see 3:613 (16 references).

2859. *Test of Factual Relations in American History.* For additional information and a review by Robert E. Keohane, see 40:1642 (1 reference); for a review by Wilbur F. Murra, see 38:1024.

2860. *Wisconsin American History Test.* For additional information, see 38:1025.

2861. *World History: Comprehensive Objective Tests in High School Subjects.* For additional information, see 35:316.

2862. *World History: Multiple-Purpose Objective Tests in High School Subjects.* For additional information, see 35:319.

POLITICAL SCIENCE

2863. *American Government and Civics: Comprehensive Tests in High School Subjects.* For additional information, see 35:454.

2864. *Attitude Toward Politicians Scale.* For additional information and a review by Donald T. Campbell, see 5:829.

2865. *Civics: Every Pupil Test.* For additional information, see 38:1145.

2866. *Community Civics: Comprehensive Tests in High School Subjects.* For additional information, see 35:456.

2867. *Cooperative Community Affairs Test.* For additional information and reviews by W. H. Cartwright, J. R. Gerberich, and Lavone A. Hanna, see 3:591 (1 reference).

2868. *Elementary Civics: Every Pupil Scholarship Test.* For additional information, see 36:840.

2869. *Examination in Civics.* For additional information and a review by Roy A. Price, see 3:616 (1 reference).

2870. *Examination in Problems of Democracy—High-School Level.* For additional information and a review by Lavone A. Hanna, see 3:617 (2 references).

2871. *Final Test in Civics: Comprehensive Objective Tests for Seventh-Grade Pupils in Texas.* For additional information, see 35:461.

2872. *General Knowledge Test of Local, State, and National Government.* For additional information and a review by Wayne A. Frederick, see 5:834

2873. *Iowa Every-Pupil Test in American Government.* For additional information, see 38:1019.

2874. *Mordy-Schrammel Constitution Test.* For additional information and a review by W. H. Cartwright, see 3:618.

2875. *Mordy-Schrammel Elementary Civics Test.* For additional information and a review by C. Robert Pace, see 3:619.

2876. *Newspaper Reading Survey: What Do You Read?* For additional information and reviews by Frederick H. Stutz and M. J. Wantman, see 5:837.

2877. *Ninth Grade Civics: Manchester Semester-End Achievement Tests.* For additional information, see 36:843.

2878. *Principles of American Citizenship Test.* For additional information and reviews by Howard R. Anderson and M. J. Wantman, see 5:841 (1 reference).

2879. *Problems in Democracy: Comprehensive Objective Tests in High School Subjects.* For additional information, see 35:466.

2880. *Wesley Test in Political Terms.* For additional information and a review by Howard R. Anderson, see 40:1621 (1 reference).

SOCIOLOGY

2881. *Black-Schrammel Sociology Test.* For additional information, see 4:708.

VOCATIONS

CLERICAL

2882. *Number Comparison Test.* For additional information, see 35:496.

2883. *Speed Tabulation Test.* For additional information, see 38:1082.

2884. *V.G.C. Clerical Indicator.* For additional information and a review by George A. Ferguson, see 4:735.

INTERESTS

2885. *ABC Occupational Inventory.* For additional information, see 4:736.

2886. *Basic Interest Questionnaire: For Selecting Your Vocation or Avocation.* For additional information, see 3:633 (1 excerpt).

2887. *Career Incentive and Progress Blank.* For additional information, see 40:1648.

2888. *Edmiston Inventory of Interest.* For additional information and a review by Arthur E. Traxler, see 4:738 (1 reference).

2889. *Job Qualification Inventory.* For additional information and reviews by Ralph F. Berdie and Stanley G. Dulsky, see 3:639 (5 references, 2 excerpts).

2890. *Occupational Interest Blank.* For additional information and reviews by Stanley G. Dulsky and J. B. Miner, see 40:1666; for reviews by W. V. Bingham and M. R. Trabue, see 38:1174.

2891. *Occupational Interest Blank for Women.* For additional information and reviews by Gwendolen Schneidler Dickson and Frances Oralind Triggs, see 3:642 (6 references).

2892. *Pattern Similarity Quotient.* For additional information, see 36:866.

2893. *Primary Business Interests Test.* For additional information and **reviews by**

George K. Bennett, Glen U. Cleeton, and George A. Ferguson, see 3:645 (2 references).

2894. *Self-Administering Vocational Interest Locator With Work Interest Picture.* For additional information and a review by Donald E. Super, see 4:744.

2895. *Vocational Interest Schedule.* For additional information and a review by Donald E. Super, see 3:653 (8 references) ; for a review by J. B. Miner, see 40:1683 (4 references) ; for reviews by Harold D. Carter and N. W. Morton, see 38:1180.

2896. *A Vocational Interest Test for College Women.* For additional information and a review by Frances Oralind Triggs, see 3:654 (2 references).

2897. *Vocational Inventory.* For additional information and reviews by Edward S. Bordin, Harold D. Carter, and Donald E. Super, see 3:655 (4 references, 1 excerpt).

MANUAL DEXTERITY

2898. *Benge Two Hand Coordination Test.* For additional information and a review by Milton L. Blum, see 3:657.

MECHANICAL ABILITY

2899. *College Entrance Examination Board Special Aptitude Test in Spatial Relations.* For additional information and a review by Robert L. Thorndike, see 4:808.

2900. *Crawford Spatial Relations Test.* For additional information and a review by William R. Grove, see 3:658 (7 references).

2901. *Dynamicube Test of Power to Visualize.* For additional information, see 38:1167.

2902. *Girls' Mechanical Assembly Test, Abridged Form.* For additional information and a review by Richard Ledgerwood, see 38:1032 (2 references).

2903. *Mutilated Cubes Test of Power to Visualize.* For additional information, see 38:1173.

2904. *Perceptual Mechanics Test.* For additional information and a review by Charles M. Harsh, see 3:673.

2905. *Staticube Test of Power to Visualize.* For additional information, see 38:1177.

2906. *Stenquist Mechanical Aptitude Test.* For additional information and a review by James M. Porter, Jr., see 3:678 (18 references).

MISCELLANEOUS

2907. *Adjusted Graphic Analysis Chart.* For additional information, see 40:1644 (1 reference).

2908. *Aids to Self-Analysis and Vocational Planning Inventory.* For additional information, see 40:1645 (1 reference).

2909. *Check List for Self-Guidance in Choosing an Occupation.* For additional information, see 40:1649.

2910. *Check List of Occupations.* For additional information, see 40:1650.

2911. *Diagnostic Scale for Measuring Apprentices' Attitudes.* For additional information, see 36:864 (3 references).

2912. *Entrance Questionnaire and Experience Record.* For additional information, see 40:1658 (1 reference).

2913. *Guidance Questionnaire.* For additional information, see 40:1659.1.

2914. *Identical Forms.* For additional information, see 5:899.

2915. *Individual Guidance Record.* For additional information, see 40:1660 (1 reference).

2916. *Information Blank: For Obtaining Data About Vocational Plans and Problems of High School Students.* For additional information, see 38:1169.

2917. *Job Satisfaction Inquiry Blank No. 10.* For additional information, see 36:868.

2918. *Kahn Career Orientation Questionnaire: A Preliminary to Vocational or Educational Counseling, Student Form.* For additional information and a review by Arthur E. Traxler, see 4:777.

2919. *Kefauver-Hand Guidance Tests and Inventories.* 8 tests: *Educational Guidance Test, Health Guidance Test, Inventory of Student Plans, Inventory of Student Self-*

Ratings, Recreational Guidance Test, Student-Judgment Guidance Test, Vocational Guidance Test. For additional information and a review by E. G. Williamson, see 40:1661; for reviews by Harold D. Carter, Gwendolen Schneidler, and M. R. Trabue, see 38:1170 (2 excerpts).

2920. *Michigan Adult Profile.* 4 tests: *Michigan Occupational Preference Check List, Michigan Vocabulary Profile* (see 572), *Michigan Nonverbal Series, Michigan Speed of Reading.* For additional information and reviews by Richard Ledgerwood, M. R. Trabue, John G. Darley, John M. Stalnaker, and Arthur E. Traxler, see 38:1171.

2921. *Miles Career Evaluation Inventory.* For additional information, see 4:780 (1 reference).

2922. *Minnesota Occupational Rating Scales and Counseling Profile.* For additional information and a review by M. H. Elliott, see 3:689 (5 references).

2923. *Occupational Analysis Form.* For additional information, see 40:1665.1.

2924. *Occupational Orientation Inquiry.* For additional information and reviews by John Gray Peatman and C. Gilbert Wrenn, see 40:1667 (1 reference).

2925. *Survey of Company Morale: Job Satisfaction Blank No. 12.* For additional information and a review by William W. Waite, see 3:693 (1 reference).

2926. *Vocational Guidance Questionnaire.* For additional information, see 40:1679.1.

SELECTION AND RATING FORMS

2927. *Aids to the Vocational Interview: Record Form B.* For additional information, see 35:493.

2928. [*Employee Selection Forms.*] 4 forms: *Application for Employment, Application for Sales Position, Telephone Check With Previous Employers, Standardized Selection Interview (Short Form).* For additional information, see 4:772.

2929. *Interview Rating Scale for Prospective Employees.* For additional information and reviews by Jay L. Otis and S. Rains Wallace, Jr., see 4:776.

2930. *Rating Form for Use of Interviewers and Oral Examiners.* For additional information and a review by Douglas H. Fryer, see 3:691 (2 references); for a review by Ruth Strang, see 40:1672.

SPECIFIC VOCATIONS

ENGINEERING

2931. *College Entrance Examination Board Test in Pre-Engineering Science Comprehension.* For additional information, see 4:809.

2932. *Examination in Advanced Engineering Electronics.* For additional information, see 3:407.

2933. *Examination in Advanced Radio Engineering—College Level.* For additional information, see 3:414.

2934. *Examination in Diesel Engineering.* For additional information, see 3:408.

2935. *Examination in Engineering Drawing.* For additional information, see 3:409.

2936. *Examination in Engineering Electronics.* For additional information, see 3:410.

2937. *Examination in Engineering Mechanics.* For additional information, see 3:411.

2938. *Examination in Fluid Mechanics.* For additional information, see 3:412.

2939. *Examination in Machine Design.* For additional information, see 3:413.

2940. *Examination in Strength of Materials.* For additional information, see 3:415.

2941. *Examination in Surveying.* For additional information, see 3:416.

2942. *Placement Examination in General Engineering Drawing, Revised Edition.* For additional information, see 38:1175.

MISCELLANEOUS

2943. *Leahy-Fenlason Rating Scale for Social Case Workers.* For additional information, see 35:494.

2944. *Mooseheart Graphic Rating Scale for Housemothers and Housefathers.* For additional information, see 38:1172.

NURSING

2945. *The Gordon-Douglass Fraction Test for Beginning Students of Nursing.* For additional information, see 38:1168 (1 excerpt).

SELLING

2946. *Personal History.* For additional information, see 40:1670 (5 references).

2947. *Sales Questionnaire.* For additional information and a review by Robert G. Bernreuter, see 3:703 (1 reference).

2948. *Steward Selection System.* Revision of *Composite Inventory and Examination;* 3 parts: *Personal Inventory of Basic Factors, Personal Inventory of Background Factors, Guide to Employment Decision: For Sales Personnel Only.* For additional information and reviews by Donald G. Paterson and Albert S. Thompson, see 4:828 (2 references) ; for reviews by Milton E. Hahn and Floyd L. Ruch, see 3:704 (2 references) ; see also 40:1651 (3 references).

TECHNICAL RECOMMENDATIONS FOR PSYCHOLOGICAL TESTS AND DIAGNOSTIC TECHNIQUES *

FOREWORD

This statement has been endorsed by the respective governing bodies of the American Psychological Association, the American Educational Research Association, and the National Council on Measurements Used in Education. The original drafts were developed in the APA Committee on Test Standards, whose members were Edward S. Bordin, R. C. Challman, H. S. Conrad, Lloyd G. Humphreys, Paul E. Meehl, Donald E. Super, and Lee J. Cronbach, chairman. The work was modified and extended in cooperation with the AERA committee (Jacob S. Orleans, chairman, Saul B. Sells, and J. R. Gerberich) together with three liaison members (Conrad, Cronbach, and Super) and the NCMUE committee, whose successive chairmen have been Gerberich, Henry Rinsland, and Robert L. Ebel. An extension of the recommendations to cover additional problems related to achievement tests is in preparation.

The statements presented here were submitted for criticism by specialists in test construction and use, including test publishers, and a preliminary version was published in the *American Psychologist* (*Amer. Psychologist*, 1952, 7, 461–475) for wider examination. The present statement is the result of successive revisions.

DEVELOPMENT AND SCOPE OF THE RECOMMENDATIONS

Psychological and educational tests are used in arriving at decisions which may have great influence on the ultimate welfare of the persons tested, and of the community. Test users, therefore, wish to apply high standards of professional judgment in selecting and interpreting tests, and test producers wish to produce tests which can be of the greatest possible service. The test producer, in particular, has the task of providing sufficient information about each test so that users will know what reliance can safely be placed on it.

Professional workers agree that test manuals and associated aids to test usage should be made complete, comprehensible, and unambiguous, and for this reason there have always been informal "test standards." Publishers and authors of tests have adopted standards for themselves, and standards

* Prepared by a joint committee of the American Psychological Association, the American Educational Research Association, and the National Council on Measurements Used in Education. Reprinted with permission from *Psychological Bulletin*, Vol. 51, No. 2, Part 2, March 1954.

have been stated in textbooks and other publications. Through application of these standards, tests have attained a high degree of quality and usefulness.

Until this time, however, there has been no statement representing a consensus as to what information is most helpful to the test consumer. In the absence of such a guide, it is inevitable that some tests appear with less adequate supporting information than others of the same type, and that facts about a test which some users regard as indispensable have not been reported because they seemed relatively unimportant to the test producer. This report is the outcome of an attempt to survey the possible types of information that test producers might make available, to weigh the importance of these, and to make recommendations regarding test preparation and publication.

Improvement of testing has long been a concern of professional workers. In 1906, an APA committee, with Angell as chairman, was appointed to act as a general control committee on the subject of measurements. The purpose of their work was to standardize testing techniques, whereas the present effort is concerned with standards of reporting information about tests.

In a developing field, it is necessary to make sure that standardizing efforts do not stifle growth. The words of the earlier committee are appropriate today:

> The efforts of a standardizing committee are likely to be regarded with disfavor and apprehension in many quarters, on the ground that the time is not yet ripe for stereotyping either the test material or the procedure. It may be felt that what is called for, in the present immature condition of individual psychology, is rather the free invention and the appearance of as many variants as possible. Let very many tests be tried, each new investigator introducing his own modification; and then, the worthless will gradually be eliminated and the fittest will survive.

Issuing specifications for tests could indeed discourage the development of new types of tests. So many different sorts of tests are needed in present psychological practice that limiting the kind or the specifications would not be sound procedure. Appropriate standardization of tests and manuals, however, need not interfere with innovation. The recommendations presented here are intended to assist test producers to bring out a wide variety of tests that will be suitable for all the different purposes for which tests should be used and to make those tests as valuable as possible.

INFORMATION STANDARDS AS GUIDES

The essential principle that sets the tone for this document is that a test manual should carry information sufficient to enable any qualified user to make sound judgments regarding the usefulness and interpretation of the test. This means that certain research is required prior to release of a test for general use by psychologists or school personnel. The results must be reported or summarized in the manual, and the manual must help the reader to interpret these results.

A manual is to be judged not merely by its literal truthfulness, but by the impression it leaves with the reader. If the typical professional user is likely to obtain an inaccurate impression of the test from the manual, the manual is poorly written. Ideally, manuals would be tested in the field by comparing the typical reader's conclusions with the judgment of experts regarding the test. In the absence of such trials, our recommendations are intended to apply to the spirit and tone of the manual as well as its literal statements.

A manual must often communicate information to many different groups. Many tests are used by classroom teachers or psychometrists with very limited training in testing. These users will not follow technical discussion or statistical information. At the other extreme of the group of readers, the available information about any test should be sufficiently complete for specialists in the area to judge the technical adequacy of the test. Sometimes the more technical information can be presented in a supplementary handbook, but it is most important that there be made available to the person concerned with the test a sound basis for whatever judgments his duties require.

The setting of numerical specifications has been avoided, even though it would have been tempting to say, for instance, that a validity coefficient ought to reach .50 before a test of Type A is ready for use or that a test of Type B should always have a reliability of .90 before it is used for the measurement of individual subjects. There are different problems in different situations, depending, for instance, on whether clinical analysis or personnel selection is involved, or whether preliminary or final decisions are being made. It is not appropriate to call for a particular level of validity and reliability, or to otherwise specify the nature of the test. It *is* appropriate to ask that the manual give the information necessary for the user to decide whether the accuracy, relevance, or standardization of the test makes it suitable for his purposes. These recommendations, then, suggest standards of *test description and reporting* without stating minimum statistical specifications.

The aim of the present standards is partly to make the requirements as to information accompanying published tests explicit and conveniently available. In arriving at those requirements, it has been necessary to judge what is presently the reasonable degree of compromise between pressures of cost and time, on the one hand, and the ideal, on the other. The test producer ordinarily spends large sums of money in developing and standardizing a test. Insofar as these recommendations indicate the sort of information that would be most valuable to the people who use tests, test authors and publishers can then direct their funds to gathering and reporting those data. Validation on job criteria, for example, is essential before a vocational interest inventory can be used practically, but only a desirable addition for a values inventory, and irrelevant for an inventory designed to diagnose mental disorders. The recommendations therefore attempt to state what type of studies should be completed before a test is ready for release to the profession for operational use. The recommendations attempt to describe standards which are already reached by our better tests.

TESTS TO WHICH THESE RECOMMENDATIONS APPLY

These recommendations cover not only tests as narrowly defined, but also most published devices for diagnosis and evaluation. The recommendations apply to interest inventories, personality inventories, projective instruments and related clinical techniques, tests of aptitude or ability, and achievement tests. The same general types of information are needed for all these varieties of tests. General recommendations have been prepared with all these techniques and instruments in mind. Since each type of test presents certain special requirements, additional comments have been made to indicate specific applications of the recommendations to particular techniques. Many principles of specific importance in measurement of achievement remain to be worked out in a subsequent statement.

Tests can be arranged according to degree of development. The highest degree of development is needed for tests distributed for use in practical situations where the user is unlikely to validate the tests for himself. Such a user must assume that the test does measure what it is presumed to measure on the basis of its title and manual. For instance, if a clerical aptitude measure is used in vocational guidance under the assumption that this will predict success in office jobs, there is very little possibility that the counselor could himself validate the test for the wide range of office jobs to which his clients might go.

At the other extreme of the continuum are tests in the very beginning stages of their development. At this point, perhaps the investigator is not sure whether his test is measuring any useful variable. Sometimes, because the theory for interpreting the test is undeveloped, the author restricts use of the test to situations where he himself knows the persons who will use the test, can personally caution them as to its limitations, and is using the research from these trials as a way of improving the test.

Between these tests which are so to speak embryonic, and the tests which are released for practical application without local validation, are tests released for somewhat restricted use. There are many tests which have been examined sufficiently to indicate that they will probably be useful tools for psychologists, but which are released with the expectation that the user will conduct validation studies against performance criteria, or will verify suggested clinical interpretations by studying the subsequent behavior of persons in treatment. Examples are certain tests of spatial ability, and some inventories measuring such traits as introversion.

The present recommendations apply to devices which are distributed for use as a basis for practical judgments rather than solely for research. Most tests which are made available for use in schools, clinics, and industry are of this practical nature. Tests released for operational use should be prepared with the greatest care. They should be released to the general user only after their developer has gathered information which will permit the user to know for what use the test can be trusted. These statements regarding recommended information apply with especial force to tests distributed to users who have only that information about the test which is provided in the manual and other accessories. In the preparation of the recommendations, no attention was paid to tests which are privately distributed and circulated only to specially trained users. The recommendations also do not apply to tests presented in journal articles unless the article is intended to fulfill the functions of a manual.

A brief discussion of problems of projective techniques is needed here because of the opinion occasionally voiced that these devices are so unlike other testing procedures that they cannot be judged according to the same standards.

Many users of projective devices aim at idiographic analysis of an individual. Since this kind of analytical thinking places heavy reliance on the creative, artistic activity of the clinician, not all of this process can be covered in test standards. Thus, the recommendations herein presented are necessarily of a psychometric nature and should not be interpreted as meaning that projective techniques are intended primarily for such use. Nevertheless, proposals for arriving at such unique idiographic interpretations are almost always partially based upon some nomothetic premises, e.g., that a Rorschach determinant tends to correlate with a specified internal factor. There is no justification for failure to apply the usual standards in connection with these premises. Therefore, although these devices present unusual problems, the user of projective techniques requires much of the same information that is needed by users of other tests.

Even though the data from projective tests are more often qualitative than quantitative, these devices should be accompanied by appropriate evidence on validity, reliability, and so on. A projective test author need not identify his test's validity by correlating it with any simple criterion. But if he goes so far as to make any generalization about what "most people see" or what "schizophrenics rarely do," he is making an out-and-out statistical claim and should be held to the usual rules for backing it up. Obviously, when quantitative information is asked for in the recommendations, it is expected to apply where a quantitative kind of claim has been made. If a projective test makes no such claim, a recommendation would not be meaningful for it.

On the other hand, clinicians sometimes forget that the words "more," "usual," "typical," and the like are *quantity* words. Any textual discourse containing such words, or any verbal statement describing a correspondence between test performance and personality structure is making a quantitative claim. The only difference between such a verbal statement and a statistical table is the relative exactness of the latter. For this reason, many of the recommendations apply to aspects of projective instruments for which verbal rather than numerical interpretations are suggested.

The general topics to be covered in the recommendations are Dissemination of Information, Interpretation, Validity, Reliability, Administration, and Scales and Norms.

Many comments have been made to amplify and illustrate the recommendations. Tests mentioned in the comments have not been singled out as being particularly good or poor tests. The tests used for illustrative purposes were chosen because they are widely known, except where some less prominent test provides an unusually clear illustration of the point under discussion. These references to tests are not intended as critical evaluations of the test as a whole and should not be quoted or referred to in test advertising.

THREE LEVELS OF RECOMMENDATIONS

Manuals can never give all the information that might be desirable, because of economic limitations. At the same time, restricting this statement of recommendations to essential information might tend to discourage reporting of additional information. To avoid this, recommendations are grouped in three levels: ESSENTIAL, VERY DESIRABLE, and DESIRABLE. Each proposed requirement is judged in the light of its importance and the feasibility of attaining it.

The statements listed as ESSENTIAL are intended to be the consensus of present-day thinking as to what is normally required for operational use of a test. Any test presents some unique problems, and it is undesirable that standards should bind the producer of a novel test to an inappropriate procedure or form of reporting. The ESSENTIAL standards indicate what information will be genuinely needed for most tests in their usual applications. When a test producer fails to satisfy this need, he should do so only as a considered judgment. In any single test, there will be very few ESSENTIAL standards which do not apply.

If some type of ESSENTIAL information is not available on a given test, it is important to help the reader recognize that the research on the test is incomplete in this respect. A test manual can satisfy all the ESSENTIAL standards by clear statements of what research has and has not been done and by avoidance of misleading statements. It will not be necessary to perform much additional research to satisfy the standards, but only to discuss the test so that the reader fully understands what is known (and unknown) about it.

The category VERY DESIRABLE is used to draw attention to types of information which contribute greatly to the user's understanding of the test. They have not been listed as ESSENTIAL for various reasons. For example, if it is very difficult to acquire information (e.g., long-term follow-up), it cannot always be expected to accompany the test. At times a closely reasoned minority opinion regards a type of information as unimportant. Such information is still very desirable, since many users wish it, but it is not classed as ESSENTIAL so long as its usefulness is debated.

The category DESIRABLE includes information which would be helpful, but less so than the ESSENTIAL and VERY DESIRABLE information. Test users welcome any information of this type the producer offers.

When a test is widely used, the producer has a greater responsibility for investigating it thoroughly and providing more extensive reports. The larger sale of such tests makes such research financially possible. Therefore the producer of a popular test can add more of the VERY DESIRABLE and DESIRABLE information in subsequent editions of the manual. For tests having limited sale, it is unreasonable to expect that as much of these two categories of information will be furnished. In making such facts available, the producer performs a service beyond the level that can reasonably be anticipated for most tests at this time.

THE AUDIENCE FOR THESE RECOMMENDATIONS

These recommendations are intended to guide test development and reporting. A good deal of the information to be reported about tests is technical, and therefore the wording of the recommendations is of necessity technical. They should be meaningful to readers who have had a minimum of one substantial course in tests and measurements.

One audience for the recommendations is the authors and publishers who are responsible for test development. The recommendations should also aid the thinking of test users working either in psychology or education. It is not expected that the classroom teacher who has not had a course in tests and measurements will himself use this report. The report should, however, be helpful to directors of research, school psychologists, counselors, supervisors, and administrators who select tests to use for various school purposes.

As an aid to test development, the recommendations provide a kind of check list of factors to consider in designing standardization and validation studies. Test authors should refer to them in deciding what studies to perform on their tests and how to report them in their manuals. Test publishers will be able to use them in planning revision of their present tests. In considering proposed manuals, publishers can suggest to authors the types of information which need to be gathered in order to make the manual as serviceable as it should be. Because of the ease with which such claims could be misinterpreted, it would not be appropriate to state in a test manual that it "satisfies" or "follows" these Technical Recommendations. There would be no such objection to a statement that an author had "attempted to take into account or considered" these recommendations in preparing the manual.

Almost any test can be useful for some functions and in some situations. But even the best test can have damaging consequences if used inappropriately. Therefore, ultimate responsibility for improvement of testing rests on the shoulders of test users. These recommendations should serve to extend the professional training of these users so that they will make better use of the information about tests and the tests themselves. The recommendations draw attention to recent developments in thinking about tests and test analysis. The report should serve as a reminder regarding features to be considered in choosing tests for a particular program.

Professional thinking about tests is much influenced by test reviews, textbooks on testing, and courses in measurement. These recommendations may be helpful in improving such aids, for instance, by suggesting features especially significant to examine in a test review. The recommendations can be a teaching aid in measurement courses. It is important to note that publication of superior information about tests by no means guarantees that tests will be used well. The continual improvement of courses which prepare test users and of leadership in all institutions using tests is a responsibility in which everyone must share.

REVISION AND EXTENSION

For many reasons, it will be necessary to revise the recommendations periodically. Despite the care with which the standards have been developed, experience will no doubt reveal that some of our judgments would benefit from further examination. New tests will present problems not considered in the present work. The improvement of statistical techniques and psychometric theory will yield better bases for test analysis. The efforts of test producers will lead to continued improvement in tests, and as this continues it will be possible to raise the standards so that the test user will have ever better information about his tools.

The recommendations here presented are intended to be used without reference to any enforcement machinery. The statement will be used by individual members of the professions to improve their own work.

THE RECOMMENDATIONS
A. DISSEMINATION OF INFORMATION

The test user needs information to help him select the test which is most adequate for a given purpose. He must rely in large part on the test producer for such data. The practices in furnishing the needed information have varied. In the case of some tests, the user has had access to virtually nothing beyond directions for administering and scoring the test, and norms of uncertain origin. On the other hand, other tests have manuals which furnish extensive data on the development of the test, its validity and reliability, the origin of the norms, the kinds of interpretations which are appropriate, and the uses for which it can be employed. The diversity of practice in making information about tests available suggests the need for standards for the dissemination of information.

A1. When a test is published for operational use, it should be accompanied by a manual which takes cognizance of the detailed recommendations in this report. ESSENTIAL

Comment: Sometimes information needed to support interpretations suggested in the manual cannot be presented at the time the manual is published. The manual satisfies the intent of recommendation A1 if it points out the absence and importance of this information.

It should be recognized that a recommendation may not apply to a particular test. The manual writer "takes cognizance of" the recommendation if he examines it with care to make certain whether it has implications for his test. It is not proper to ignore a recommendation merely because the recommendation, while applicable to claims made for the test, is difficult to meet or has ordinarily not been met by similar tests.

A1.1 Some form of manual, presenting at least minimum information, should be given or sold to all purchasers of the test. ESSENTIAL

A1.2 Where the information is too extensive to be fully reported in such a manual, the manual should summarize the ESSENTIAL information and indicate where further details may be found. ESSENTIAL

Comment: The Differential Aptitude Tests provide an extensive manual, and also make further research data available through the American Documentation Institute. A great deal of the information about the Stanford-Binet is included in a book which all users must have. The Strong Vocational Interest Blank has been the subject of unusually thorough research which is reported in a technical book; a brief version of the ESSENTIAL information is given in a manual sold with the blanks.

For many projective techniques, such as the Rorschach and TAT, publications by persons other than the test author fulfill many functions of a manual. Insofar as a book about a technique fulfills the functions of a manual, the author has the same responsibility in preparing it as does the original author of the test.

A1.3 If information about the test is provided in a separate publication, any such publication should meet the same standards of accuracy as apply to the manual. ESSENTIAL

Comment: A report in a professional journal, for instance, on the validity of an instrument should meet the same standards of completeness and freedom from misleading impressions as a report in the manual. Recommendation A1.3 applies also to advertising literature.

A2. The manual should be up-to-date. It should be revised at appropriate intervals. ESSENTIAL

Comment: As criteria change, the predictive validity of a test may be altered. Also, the norms may require revision. Thus, a change in school objectives which places increased emphasis on problem solving in algebra, rather than on factoring and other mechanics, could appreciably affect the validity of an algebra aptitude test. It would also alter the norms for an algebra achievement test.

A2.1 When new information emerges, from investigations by the test author or others, which indicates that some facts and recommendations presented in the manual are substantially incorrect, a revised manual should be issued at the earliest feasible date. ESSENTIAL

Comment: A revised manual for the Army Beta which arose out of World War I was issued in 1946. In contrast, although extensive published research points out the need for altering statements made in the manual of the Bernreuter Personality Inventory, no revised edition of that manual has been prepared. Likewise, the 1943 manual for the TAT has not been revised despite extensive development in the field since that date.

A2.2 When a test is revised or a new form is prepared, the manual should be thoroughly revised to take changes in the test into account. ESSENTIAL

Comment: The Wechsler-Bellevue Scale was modified in several respects in the third edition of the manual. For example, the directions and scoring procedure were altered. The norms should have been reviewed or redetermined. Instead, the earlier tables for converting scores to IQ were carried over, without change, to the new edition.

A2.21 When a short form of a test is prepared by reducing the number of items or organizing a portion of the test into a separate form, new evidence should be obtained and reported for that new form of the test. VERY DESIRABLE

Comment: This is especially important for inventories, where placing items in a new context might alter the person's responses. For example, the MMPI properly retains some items which were not scored in any key, because removing those items might alter the discriminating power of the items which were scored.

A2.22 When a short form is prepared from a test, the manual should present the correlation between the long and short forms, separately administered. DESIRABLE

A2.3 The copyright date of the manual or the date of the latest revision should be clearly indicated. ESSENTIAL

B. INTERPRETATION

In interpreting tests, the user always is responsible for making inferences as to the meaning and legitimate uses of test results. In making such judgments, he is dependent upon the available data about the test.

The degree to which a test manual can be expected to prepare the user for accurate interpretation and effective use of the test varies with the type of test and the purpose for which it is used. For any test, it is sometimes necessary to make judgments which have not been substantiated by the published evidence. Thus the vocational counselor cannot expect to have regression equations available for predictions he must make from test scores, and the clinician must interpret a personality inventory on the basis of general data and theory because research on any one instrument is incomplete. The manual of a projective test cannot fully prepare the user for interpretation. Test users should be wary of interpreting projective test results without supervised training with that device and instruction in the clinical concepts and data which are part of its background.

This problem of accuracy is not the only consideration related to test interpretation. An equally important concern is the examinee's reactions to interpretations of his test scores, if the interpretation is made to him. Many educational and clinical uses of tests require reporting the interpretations to the person tested. The teacher who interprets the results of academic achievement tests affects the student's self concept and future learning. The clinician, in making interpretations which bear upon the client's areas of conflict, may unwittingly intensify those conflicts.

B1. Insofar as possible, the test, the manual, record forms, and other accompanying material should assist users to make correct interpretations of the test results. ESSENTIAL

B1.1 Names given to tests, and to scores within tests, should be chosen to minimize the risk of misinterpretation by test purchasers and subjects. ESSENTIAL

Comment: The Army General Classification Test, the Blacky Test, and the Draw-A-Person Test are examples of names based on the content or process involved in the test which carry no unwarranted suggestions as to characteristics measured. Such names as "culture-free test," "primary abilities test," "measure of mental growth," and "temperament test" are likely to suggest interpretations going beyond the demonstrable meaning of test scores.

Names designed to disguise the purpose of a test from a subject may properly be used. In such a case, the manual should contain in an early and conspicuous place an explanation of the reason for choosing this name and a statement of what in fact the test is supposed to measure.

B1.1 and subordinate recommendations can be followed in developing new tests, but it will rarely be feasible to rename established tests, even when this would be desirable.

B1.11 Interest and personality indices based on the self-report principle should be called "inventories," "questionnaires," or the like, rather than "tests." ESSENTIAL

B1.2 The manual or other accompanying material should describe the process by which interpretations are to be derived from test scores. VERY DESIRABLE

Comment: The manual need not include such information as all professionally qualified users may be expected to have. The original manual for the Differential Aptitude Tests presented a few profiles and gave an interpretation and a too brief case summary for each one. Later, more extensive case reports were reported in Counseling from Profiles, a supplementary booklet on the test, and the sketchy profiles were removed from the manual. The case reports avoid oversimplification and emphasize the possible influence of nontest data on test interpretation.

The Atlas for the MMPI makes available for study examples of a variety of complex personality profiles. Few other personality inventories are supplemented by such materials as aids in their interpretation.

B1.21 The manual should draw the user's attention to data other than the test scores which need to be taken into account in interpreting the test. VERY DESIRABLE

Comment: For example, Murray's TAT manual states that "the psychologist should know the following basic facts: the sex and age of the subject, whether his parents are dead or separated, the ages and sexes of his siblings, his vocational and his marital status."

B1.22 When case studies are used as illustrations for the interpretations of test scores, the examples presented should include some relatively complicated cases whose interpretation is not clear-cut. VERY DESIRABLE

B1.23 Where a certain misinterpretation of a given test is known to be frequently made (or can reasonably be anticipated in the case of a new test), the manual should draw attention to this error and warn against it. ESSENTIAL

Comment: Since the Terman-McNemar Test of Mental Ability reports scores in terms of a deviation IQ rather than a ratio IQ, it discusses at some length the fact that deviation IQ's do not have the same properties as ratio IQ's. Complete avoidance of the term IQ for deviation scores would be a more certain way to avoid confusion.

Another common misconception is that intelligence tests are measures of inherent native ability alone; it would be desirable for manuals of such tests to caution against this interpretation.

Manuals for interest measures should make clear, and urge counselors to stress to the client, the fact that interest does not imply ability and is only one factor to be considered in choosing among occupations. A desirable caution of this type is found in the Lee-Thorpe Occupational Interest Inventory.

B2. The test manual should state explicitly the purposes and applications for which the test is recommended. ESSENTIAL

B2.1 If a test is intended for research use only, and is not distributed for operational use, that fact should be prominently stated in the accompanying materials. ESSENTIAL

Comment: If, for example, an investigator plans to release tests developed by factor analysis for research use, it would be appropriate to print "distributed for research use only" on the test package or cover of the booklet of directions. This would serve to caution against premature use of the tests in guidance.

B3. The test manual should indicate the professional qualifications required to administer and interpret the test properly. ESSENTIAL

B3.1 Where a test is recommended for a variety of purposes or types of inference, the manual should indicate the amount of training required for each use. ESSENTIAL

Comment: One suggested categorization of tests approved by the APA is as follows: [1]

Level A. Tests or aids which can adequately be administered, scored, and interpreted with the aid of the manual and a general orientation to the kind of organization in which one is working. (E.g., achievement or proficiency tests.)

Level B. Tests or aids which require some technical knowledge of test construction and use, and of supporting psychological and educational subjects such as statistics, individual differences, and psychology of adjustment, personnel psychology, and guidance. (E.g., aptitude tests, adjustment inventories with normal populations.)

Level C. Tests and aids which require substantial understanding of testing and supporting psychological subjects, together with supervised experience in the use of these devices. (E.g., projective tests, individual mental tests.)

The manual might identify a test according to one of the foregoing levels, or might employ some form of statement more suitable for that test. Regarding a particular industrial personnel test, the manual might say: "This test can be administered and scored by an intelligent clerical employee, but decisions regarding hiring and related interpretations should be made only by a psychologist or personnel manager who has studied fundamental statistics including correlation. Only a vocational counselor with specialized graduate training should use the test for vocational guidance."

[1] APA Code of Standards for Test Distribution, *American Psychologist*, November, 1950. This statement also includes descriptions of general levels of training which correspond to the three levels of tests.

B3.11 The manual should not imply that the test is "self-interpreting," or that it may be interpreted by a person lacking proper training. ESSENTIAL

B3.12 The manual should point out the counseling responsibilities assumed when a tester communicates interpretations about ability or personality traits to the person tested. ESSENTIAL

Comment: While examinees may properly score their own interest inventories and examine their own profiles, the manual for the Kuder Preference Record properly recommends that they should make interpretations and future plans only with professional help in individual or group counseling situations.

B3.2 The manual should draw attention to references dealing with the test in question with which the user should become familiar before attempting to interpret the test. The statement should avoid the implication that this constitutes the only training needed, if other training is required. VERY DESIRABLE

B.4 When a test is issued in revised form, the nature and extent of any revision, and the comparability of data for the revised and the old test should be explicitly stated. ESSENTIAL

Comment: An example of desirable practice is found in the manual for the revised edition of the Study of Values.

B5. Statements in the manual reporting relationships are by implication quantitative, and should be stated as precisely as the data permit. If data to support such a statement have not been collected, that fact should be made clear. ESSENTIAL

Comment: Writers sometimes say, for example, "Spatial ability is required for architectural engineering" or, "Bizarre responses often indicate schizophrenic tendencies." Such statements need to be made more definite. In what proportion of cases giving bizarre responses does schizophrenia develop? How much does architectural success depend upon spatial ability? Numerical data would provide the needed answer.

B5.1 When the term "significant" is employed, the manual should make clear whether statistical or practical significance is meant, and the practical significance of statistically reliable differences should be evaluated. ESSENTIAL

B5.2 The manual should clearly differentiate between an interpretation justified regarding a group taken as a whole, and the application of such an interpretation to each individual within the group. ESSENTIAL

Comment: For example, if the standard error of measurement is five points, this statement should not be presented so as to imply that the obtained score for any one individual is within five points of his true score. For a single pupil, the difference between the obtained and true score might be very much larger.

C. VALIDITY

Validity information indicates to the test user the degree to which the test is capable of achieving certain aims. Tests are used for several types of judgment, and for each type of judgment, a somewhat different type of validation is involved. We may distinguish four aims of testing:

a) The test user wishes to determine how an individual would perform at present in a given universe of situations of which the test situation constitutes a sample.

b) The test user wishes to predict an individual's future performance (on the test or on some external variable).

c) The test user wishes to estimate an individual's present status on some variable external to the test.

d) The test user wishes to infer the degree to which the individual possesses some trait or quality (construct) presumed to be reflected in the test performance.

Thus, a vocabulary test might be used simply as a measure of present vocabulary, as a predictor of college success, as a means of discriminating schizophrenics from organics, or as a means of making inferences about "intellectual capacity."

Four Types of Validity

To determine how suitable a test is for each of these uses, it is necessary to gather the appropriate sort of validity information. These four aspects of validity may be named content validity, predictive validity, concurrent validity, and construct validity.

a) Content validity is evaluated by showing how well the content of the test samples the class of situations or subject matter about which conclusions are to be drawn. Content validity is especially important in the case of achievement and proficiency measures.

In most classes of situations measured by tests, quantitative evidence of content validity is not feasible. However, the test producer should indicate the basis for claiming adequacy of sampling or representativeness of the test content in relation to the universe of items adopted for reference.

b) Predictive validity is evaluated by showing how well predictions made from the test are confirmed by evidence gathered at some subsequent time. The most common means of checking predictive validity is correlating test scores with a subsequent criterion measure. Predictive uses of tests include long-range prediction of intelligence measures, prediction of vocational success, and prediction of reaction to therapy.

c) Concurrent validity is evaluated by showing how well test scores correspond to measures of concurrent criterion performance or status. Studies which determine whether a test discriminates between presently identifiable groups are concerned with concurrent validity. Concurrent validity and predictive validity are quite similar save for the time at which the criterion is obtained. Among the problems for which concurrent validation is used are the validation of psychiatric screening instruments against estimates of adjustment made in a psychiatric interview, differentiation of vocational groups, and classification of patients. It should be noted that a test having concurrent validity may not have predictive validity.

d) Construct validity is evaluated by investigating what psychological qualities a test measures, i.e., by demonstrating that certain explanatory constructs account to some degree for performance on the test. To examine construct validity requires both logical and empirical attack. Essentially, in studies of construct validity we are validating the theory underlying the test. The validation procedure involves two steps. First, the investigator inquires: From this theory, what predictions would we make regarding the variation of scores from person to person or occasion to occasion? Second, he gathers data to confirm these predictions.

There are various specific procedures for gathering data on construct validity. If it is supposed that form perception on the Rorschach test indicates probable ability to resist stress, this supposition may be validated by placing individuals in an experimental stress situation and observing whether behavior corresponds to prediction. Another much simpler procedure for investigating what a test measures is to correlate it with other measures; we would expect a valid test of numerical reasoning, for example, to be substantially correlated with other numerical tests, but not to be correlated with a clerical perception test. Factor analysis is another way of organizing data about construct validity.

We can distinguish among the four types of validity by noting that each involves a different emphasis on the criterion. In predictive or concurrent validity, the criterion behavior is of concern to the tester, and he may have no concern whatsoever with the type of behavior exhibited in the test. (An employer does not care if a worker can manipulate blocks, but the score on the block test may predict something he cares about.) Content validity is studied when the tester *is* concerned with the type of behavior involved in the test performance. Indeed, if the test is a work sample, the behavior represented in the test may be an end in itself. Construct validity is ordinarily studied when the tester has no definitive criterion measure of the quality with which he is concerned, and must use indirect measures to validate the theory. Here the trait or quality underlying the test is of central importance, rather than either the test behavior or the scores on the criteria.

It is ordinarily necessary to evaluate construct validity by integrating evidence from many different sources. The problem of construct validation becomes especially acute in the clinical field since for many of the constructs dealt with it is not a question of finding an imperfect criterion but of finding any criterion at all. The psychologist interested in construct validity for clinical devices is concerned with making an estimate of a hypothetical internal process, factor, system, structure, or state and cannot expect to find a clear unitary behavioral criterion. Concern for validity is in no way a challenge to the dictum that prediction of behavior is the final test of any theoretical construction. But it is necessary to understand that *behavior-relevance* in a construct is not logically the same as *behavior-equivalence*. It is one thing to insist that in order to be admissible, a complex psychological construct must have some relevance to behavioral indicators; it is quite another thing to require that any admissible psychological construct must be *equivalent to* any direct operational behavior measure. Any position that cuts the test inference off from all possible nontest sources of confirmation appears to be an unreasonable one. If the test is to be interpreted in terms of internal constructs, there must be some facts, quantitative or not, that would argue for the existence of the particular internal system postulated. An attempt to identify any one criterion measure or any composite as *the* criterion aimed at is, however, usually unwarranted.

This viewpoint, while fraught with grave dangers and sometimes misused, is nevertheless methodologically sound. The clinician interested in construct validity has in mind an admittedly incomplete construct, the evidence for which is to be found roughly in such-and-such behavioral domains. The vagueness of the construct is an inevitable consequence of the incompleteness of current psychological theory, and cannot be rectified faster than theory grows and is confirmed. At a given stage of theoretical development, the only kind of prediction that can be made may be that certain correlations should be positive, or that patients who fail to conform to a group trend should be expected with considerable frequency to exhibit such-and-such an additional feature, or the like. It is clear that these deductions do involve behavioral prediction. They require the test-constructs to be behaviorally relevant. But they still do not necessarily *identify* any of the test-inferred constructs or variables with any criterion measures. A clinician may say, "I expect to find cases of psychosomatic ulcer showing large discrepancies between latent n Succorance as inferred from TAT stories and manifest n Succorance as revealed by the score on a questionnaire." Such a declaration leads to an empirical test.

The correlation or measure of discrimination obtained in studying construct validity is not to be taken as the "validity coefficient," in the same sense that prediction of washouts during flight training is *the* validity coefficient for the battery employed. Studies of many such predictions, possibly involving quite independent components of theory, will in the mass confirm or disconfirm the claims made.

One tends to ask regarding construct validity just what *is* being validated —the test or the underlying hypothesis? The answer is, *both,* simultaneously. If one predicts an empirical relation by supposing a certain personality organization, the verification of this prediction tends to confirm both the component suppositions that gave rise to it. True, there might be plausible alternative hypotheses, but this is always the case in science. The more alternatives there are, the more cumulated evidence is needed to justify confidence in the particular test-hypothesis pair. A further characteristic of this type of validity inference is that the construct itself undergoes modification as evidence accumulates. We do not merely alter our confidence in the correctness of the construct, or in the estimates of its magnitudes, but we actually reformulate or clarify our characterization of its nature on the basis of new data.

It must be kept in mind that these four aspects of validity are not all discrete and that a complete presentation about a test may involve information about all types of validity. A first step in the preparation of a predictive instrument may be to consider what constructs or predictive dimensions are likely to give the best prediction. Examining content validity may also be an early step in producing a test whose predictive validity is ultimately of major concern. Even after satisfactory predictive validity has been established, information relative to construct validity may make the test more useful. To analyze construct validity, our total background of knowledge regarding validity would be brought to bear.

Application of the Concepts to Ability Tests

Several examples of the application of these principles to intelligence tests should clarify the concepts involved. Correlations between an intelligence test used to select university students and later academic success are predictive validities. Such correlations will typically vary in size from those with criteria of proficiency in art or music at the lower end to those with grades in science at the upper end. If the test is used to predict an art criterion, then the correlation obtained, even though low, is the predictive validity of the test. Even if validities of intelligence tests are corrected for attenuation, a value substantially less than unity is the usual result. This is not interpreted, when predictive validity is at issue, that the criterion is an imperfect index of intelligence. Rather the test is regarded as an imperfect index of the criterion.

Relationships of subscores on an intelligence test to membership in various clinical groups are an example of evidence concerning concurrent validity. Again, low or imperfect validities are interpreted as due to inadequacies in the test as a discriminating device. A test is likely to be developed for making discriminations if it is difficult to measure status on a criterion directly. If the direct measurement of the criterion is expensive, dangerous, or highly unreliable, tests having concurrent validity are needed to assess status on the criterion indirectly.

Content validity is indicated by a description of the universe of items from which selection was made, including a description of the selection process. The universe of items in intelligence test construction is usually defined by the types of items used originally by Binet. Judges' ratings of appropriateness of items are frequently involved. Content validity is ordinarily of little direct interest to the user of intelligence tests. The distinction between verbal and nonverbal tests of intelligence is, however, based on content analysis.

Construct validity may be judged from all of the information ordinarily subsumed under the preceding categories. Certain types of information, however, are employed here alone. Examples are as follows: correlations with other tests of intelligence, correlations with ratings of intelligence, factor analyses, nature-nurture studies, and studies of the effects of practice upon test scores. All relate to the problem of the meaning of the concept of intelligence. From this point of view a low correlation of the test with athletic ability may be just as important and encouraging as a high correlation with reading comprehension. This reverses the earlier emphasis from the viewpoint of concurrent or predictive validity, where a low correlation indicated weakness in the test.

Information concerning construct validity is of help to the theorist in formulating hypotheses concerning individual differences and to the test constructor in improving intelligence tests. For the practical test user this information is most frequently used to generalize beyond established predictive and concurrent validities. The careful verification of theory should serve to reduce the errors of extrapolation, but does not reduce the necessity of objective check upon extrapolations whenever possible.

Application of the Concepts to Personality Inventories

Evidence of the predictive validity of personality questionnaires provides the basis for their use for screening. One of the screening uses is to identify persons who will become maladjusted (as in the armed services). If personality instruments are used as a basis for predicting vocational or educational achievement, this inference also rests upon *predictive* validity.

Evidence of *concurrent* validity supports the use of personality questionnaires for screening and diagnostic purposes. An example is the use of check lists to determine which students are presently most in need of counseling.

Interpretation of responses as self-description (e.g., by judging conservatism from responses to a group of statements) represents one kind of assumption of *content* validity in the context of personality inventories.

Construct validity is involved when the personality inventory is used to ascertain the personality traits or structure of the individual.

Predictive or concurrent validation of personality questionnaires can depend upon fairly clear-cut operational criteria, e.g., reporting for sick call, membership in one occupational group as compared to another, psychiatric classifications. On the other hand, in validation of conceptual inferences, problems arise because of the lack of a simple relationship between personality traits and overt behavior. The "retiring" person may not actually behave in an unsociable manner, but the social activities in which he engages may be less satisfying to him, and participating in them may result in emotional stress which manifests itself in tics or other psychosomatic symptoms. This type of validity will not be judged by the size of any given relationship between a score and one criterion, but by the pattern of relationships which have been demonstrated to hold between a score and a number of different kinds of behavior criteria.

Application of the Concepts to Interest Inventories

Most interest inventories are used for predictive purposes. In counseling, scores are discussed in the context of a consideration of educational or vocational plans of the client. Even if the counselor makes very restricted interpretations (e.g., "the number of preferences for mechanical activities you reported is exceeded by only 5 per cent of high school seniors"), the context in which this discussion occurs implies that this information has some direct bearing on future performance. The test is really interpreted as indicating something about the client's probable success, satisfaction, or continuity in some activity.

Description of the individual is a second use of interest inventories. Interests are described in terms of categories or traits. In some devices, the description of interests involves such broad categories as to be essentially a description of generalized personality traits. This involves content validity, and often construct validity.

Different inferences must be supported by different types of evidence. In general, since counseling involves consideration of a very large number of vocations, it is not expected that every judgment for which an interest inventory is used will be validated by direct empirical evidence. Clients wish to consider very many occupations and activities. It is not possible to perform empirical studies with respect to all these, and reasonable tentative inferences may often be made in the absence of evidence from empirical studies. Knowledge from internal analysis of the inventory, job descriptions, and other sources may permit interpretations that will assist the client. Such extrapolations should be made tentatively, however. Extrapolation is found in the use of the Strong Blank to describe such traits as "interest in social uplift occupations," and in the use of Kuder scores to describe interest in vocations for which validity has not been tested.

Application of the Concepts to Projective Techniques and Related Clinical Methods

Predictive, concurrent, and construct validity all have pertinence to projective techniques although construct validity greatly overshadows the other two kinds. The prediction of a specific act of behavior is rarely made on the basis of projective instruments. Even the prediction of less specific behavior, such as "ability to profit from psychotherapy" is seldom made on the basis of projective techniques alone; in fact, there are a number of workers in this field who take the position that such an attempt should never be made.

Concurrent validity may be desired in projective techniques and clinical use of ability tests since they are used in making diagnostic classifications.

C1. When validity is reported, the manual should indicate clearly what type of validity is referred to. The unqualified term "validity" should be avoided unless its meaning is clear from the context. ES-SENTIAL

Comment: The manual should make clear what type of inference the validation study reports. No manual should report that "this test is valid." In the past, evidence that is not appropriately termed evidence of validity has been presented in the manual under that heading. For example, the "validity" report of the Thurstone Interest Schedule deals solely with item-test correlations. The discussion of item-test correlations in the manual of the Heston Personal Adjustment Inventory illustrates how such data may be used in reporting test validity without risk of misleading readers.

It is not desirable for the manual to state that any one type of evidence is the only possible sort of validity evidence. The following statement made regarding the Ohio Penal Classification Test is misleading: "The only criterion which establishes an intelligence test as valid is that labelled 'expert judgment' or 'expert agreement.'"

C2. The manual should report the validity of each type of inference for which a test is recommended. If validity of some recommended interpretation has not been tested, that fact should be made clear. ESSENTIAL

Comment: In a test used for guidance it is obviously impossible to present predictive validities for all possible criteria in which a counselor might be interested. The manual should make clear to the test user the nature and extent of the extrapolations suggested by the author of the test, or forced upon him by the problem confronting him. Enough information is available concerning intelligence tests, for example, that the limits of generalization can be fairly accurately gauged. Less is known about tests of spatial ability and they cannot be readily applied as predictors for criteria for which validity studies have not been made. Hazardous extrapolation is likewise involved when tests are suggested as predictors of jobs solely on the basis of job analysis information.

C2.1 The manual should indicate which, if any, of the interpretations usually attempted for tests such as the one under discussion have not been substantiated or are based merely on clinical impressions. ESSENTIAL

Comment: An example of a highly desirable practice is the warning to readers in the manual of the Purdue Pegboard: "Generalizations concerning the validity of any test should be made with great caution, and this is particularly true of dexterity tests. As Seashore has reported, motor skills are quite specific and ordinarily not highly correlated with each other. This situation perhaps accounts for the fact that a given dexterity test may have a rather satisfactory validity for certain manipulative jobs and yet be unsuitable for other manipulative jobs which might seem to be very similar. It is therefore highly desirable to conduct a study of the validity of the several Pegboard tests among employees on specific jobs for which the use of the test is contemplated, rather than attempt to generalize from available validity studies."

C2.11 If the manual for an inventory suggests that the user consult specific items as a basis for personality assessment, it should either present validation data for this use or call attention to their absence. The manual should also warn of the wide margins of error inherent in such interpretative procedures. ESSENTIAL

C2.12 Validity of self-report as a description of the person's behavior can be demonstrated only by comparing responses on single items to observed behavior. In the absence of such evidence, the manual should warn the reader that such references are subject to extreme error and should be used only to direct further inquiry, as in a counseling interview. ESSENTIAL

Comment: If two investigators using similar criteria obtain very different predictive validities for a test, a presentation of both sets of facts in the test manual is in order. If a test of mechanical comprehension is validated against a clerical criterion, on the other hand, there is probably no value in reviewing these data in the manual. Badly controlled or badly analyzed studies need not be reported in the manual.

Validation samples are frequently small, with large standard errors of resulting coefficients. The only way in which large samples can be built is to pool results from several comparable studies. The cumulation of validating studies serves to set the limits on generalization, by demonstrating whether a test applies equally well in a variety of situations. Desirable practice is illustrated by the summary of validation studies provided in the 1946 manual for the Minnesota Clerical Test.

Content Validity

C3. **Findings based on logical analysis should be carefully distinguished from conclusions established by correlation of test behavior with criterion behavior.** ESSENTIAL

Comment: Content validity may be established by demonstrating that a test samples a particular area. The user cannot judge, from this alone, how well the test permits drawing conclusions about any form of behavior other than the test behavior. For instance, it is reported that an occupational interest in inventory inquires about a sample of items, chosen to represent vocational areas according to their frequency of occurrence. This is important information about the content validity of the interest scores, but it does not alone establish whether the student's scores predict how well he will be satisfied in a given type of job.

C4. If a test performance is to be interpreted as a sample of performance in some universe of situations, the manual should indicate clearly what universe is represented and how adequate the sampling is. ESSENTIAL

C4.1 The universe of content should be defined in terms of the sources from which items were drawn, or the content criteria used to include and exclude items. ESSENTIAL

Comment: For example, the manual for the Lee-Thorpe Occupational Interest Inventory describes the method used in devising items from the definitions in the Dictionary of Occupational Titles.

C4.2 The method of sampling items within the universe should be described. ESSENTIAL

Comment: R. H. Seashore prepared a vocabulary test, defining his universe as all words in a certain unabridged dictionary, and sampled according to a definite plan.

C4.3 If items are regarded as a sample from a universe, a coefficient of internal consistency should be reported for each descriptive score, to demonstrate the extent to which the score is saturated with common factors. ESSENTIAL

Comment: The present Lee-Thorpe manual does not report the internal consistency of its scales. See additional recommendations D5–D6 regarding internal consistency studies.

C4.4 If test performance is to be interpreted as a sample of performance in some universe of situations, and if the test is administered with a time limit, evidence should be presented concerning the effect of speed on test scores. ESSENTIAL

Comment: The most satisfactory evidence would be the correlation of one form, given with the usual time limit, against another form given with unlimited time. This could be compared to the form-form coefficient with time limits on both forms. Other simpler information about degree of speeding should be given when this correlational study is impractical.

C4.5 The date at which any study of the adequacy of sampling was made should be reported, and also the date of any sources of items. ESSENTIAL

Comment: In achievement testing, it is frequently the practice to select items by a careful sampling from textbooks to identify significant topics. Textbooks and courses of study change, however, and the test which was once an excellent sample becomes obsolete. Therefore the manual should report some such statement as the median copyright date of the textbooks studied, or the date at which the experts agreed that the items were representative. In another field, the Mooney Problem Checklist lists problems which are common to students, on which each individual is to check those which concern him. The Mooney manual properly reports the date when the list was collected. After this list has been used for many years, it will be valuable to conduct a further study to determine whether student problems have changed significantly, and, if so, to change the test and manual accordingly.

Predictive Validity

C5. When predictive validity is determined by statistical analysis, the analysis should be reported in a form from which the reader can determine confidence limits of estimates regarding individuals, or the probability of misclassification of the individual on the criterion. ESSENTIAL

C5.1 Statistical procedures which are well known and readily interpreted should be used in reporting validity whenever they are appropriate to the data under examination. Any uncommon statistical techniques should be explained. ESSENTIAL

C5.11 Reports of statistical validation studies should ordinarily be expressed by: (*a*) correlation coefficients of familiar types; (*b*) description of the efficiency with which the test separates groups, indicating amount of misclassification or overlapping; or (*c*) expectancy tables. ESSENTIAL

Comment: Reports of differences between means of groups, or critical ratios, are by themselves inadequate information regarding predictive validity. If a sample is large, high critical ratios may be found even when classification is very inaccurate.

In general, since manuals are directed to readers who have limited statistical knowledge, every effort should be made to communicate validity information clearly. An example of unwise use of a novel statistical method is found in the manual for the Ohio Penal Classification Test. Ten cases were chosen, separated at five-point intervals along the OPCT IQ scale. The IQ's were then correlated with Wechsler IQ's, yielding a rank correlation of .93. This correlation is greater than would be obtained for any sample not artificially spread along the scale. While unusual statistical procedures should be used for special problems, they should not be used where standard methods are equally or more efficient for evaluating the data. They certainly should be presented so that they will not mislead the typical user of the manual.

When a test is recommended for the purpose of dividing patients among discrete categories, correlational measures of association should be supplemented by percentage figures on misclassification, i.e., "false positives" and "false negatives." When validation involves comparison of men in an occupation with men-in-general, the comparison should be presented in such a way as to make clear the degree to which the occupational group overlaps the general group.

C5.2 An over-all validity coefficient should be supplemented with evidence as to the validity of the test at different points along the range, unless the author reports that the validity is essentially constant throughout. VERY DESIRABLE

Comment: This might be reported by giving the standard error of estimate at various test score levels, or by indicating the proportion of hits, misses, and false positives at various cutting scores. The Metropolitan Reading Readiness Test reports the number of failures in primary reading expected at each level of test score.

C5.3 Test manuals should not report coefficients corrected for unreliability of the test as estimates of predictive validity. ESSENTIAL

Comment: Corrections for attenuation are very much open to misinterpretation, and if misinterpreted give an unjustifiably favorable picture of the validity of the test. The hazard is illustrated in the manual for the Heston Personal Adjustment Inventory. Heston reports correlations between inventory scores and criterion ratings, and also reports the correlations augmented to correct for attenuation. He then applies significance tests to the augmented correlations rather than to the raw correlations only. Further, he comments that the augmented correlations "are as high as those often secured between college aptitude tests and college grades." This comparison is improper, since Heston is comparing his augmented coefficients with uncorrected coefficients for ability tests.

C5.31 If such coefficients are reported for the special purpose of studying construct validity, the uncorrected coefficients must be reported also and the proper interpretation of the corrected coefficients must be discussed. ESSENTIAL

C6. All measures of criteria should be described accurately and in detail. The manual should evaluate the adequacy of the criterion. It should draw attention to significant aspects of performance which the criterion measure does not reflect and to the irrelevant factors which it may reflect. ESSENTIAL

Comment: Desirable practices are illustrated in the manual of the General Clerical Test, where validity is reported in three specific studies. The nature of the criterion, and the nature of the work done by the employees tested is described. Limitations on the data are mentioned, and stress is placed on the necessity of making comparable studies with local criteria in any new situation where the test is to be applied.

For specific types of criteria, particular cautions in description are needed to avoid misconceptions or ambiguities. Some of these are listed in the recommendations which follow.

C6.1 When validity of a test is measured by agreement with psychiatric diagnoses, the diagnostic terms should be specific and the categories clearly described. VERY DESIRABLE

Comment: "Paranoid schizophrenia, chronic" is preferable as a category to "schizophrenia." Since the types of patients included in specific diagnostic classifications vary to some extent depending on the point of view of the psychiatrists, a description of each diagnostic category used in the validity study should be presented. An example of good practice is found in Rapaport's *Diagnostic Psychological Testing* where each diagnostic group is summarily described in terms of characteristics judged by the psychiatrists to be basic.

C6.11 If the individual usage given to a vague or variable clinical term by the validating psychiatrist is not known, this fact should be clearly stated and the reader warned that other raters or measuring devices might not agree with the criterion. VERY DESIRABLE

C6.12 When validity of a clinical test is indicated by agreement with psychiatric judgment, the training, experience, and professional status (e.g., diplomate) of the psychiatrist should be stated. VERY DESIRABLE

C6.13 When validity of a clinical test is indicated by agreement with psychiatric judgment, the amount and character of the patient contacts upon which the judgment is based should be stated. ESSENTIAL

C6.2 When validity of an aptitude test is determined for predicting performance in an occupation, the occupation should be accurately defined. The test user should be given a clear understanding as to what duties are performed by workers in that occupation. ESSENTIAL

C6.21 Where a wide range of duties is subsumed under a given occupational label, the test user should be warned against assuming that only one pattern of interests or abilities can be satisfied in the occupation. VERY DESIRABLE

C6.3 When validity of an aptitude or interest test for predicting performance in a course or curriculum is reported, the character of the course or curriculum should be clearly defined. The test user should be given a clear understanding as to what types of performance are required in the course. ESSENTIAL

C6.4 When predictive validity of an interest test is reported, the manual should state whether the criterion indicates satisfaction, success, or merely continuance in the activity under examination. ESSENTIAL

Comment: When validation data compare men in an occupation to men-in-general, the manual should point out the limitations of presence in an occupation as a sign of success.

C6.5 The time elapsing between the test and determination of the criterion should be reported. ESSENTIAL

C6.51 If a test is recommended for long-term predictions, but data from longitudinal studies are not presented, the manual should emphasize that predictions of this sort have uncertain validity. ESSENTIAL

C7. The reliability of the criterion should be reported if it can be determined. If such evidence is not available, the author should discuss the probable reliability as judged from indirect evidence. VERY DESIRABLE

Comment: When validity is measured by agreement of the test with psychiatric judgment, for example, statistical evaluation of the agreement among judges should be reported.

C7.1 If validity coefficients are corrected for unreliability *of the criterion,* both corrected and uncorrected coefficients should be reported and properly interpreted. ESSENTIAL

C8. The date when validation data were gathered should be reported. ESSENTIAL

C8.1 If the criterion, the conditions of work, the type of person likely to be tested, or the meaning of the test items is suspected of changing materially with the passage of time, the validity of the test should be rechecked periodically and the results reported in subsequent editions of the manual. VERY DESIRABLE

Comment: Criterion data for the Psychologist scale of the Strong Vocational Interest Blank were gathered in 1927. Subsequent research showed that these psychologists were no longer representative of the field. The current manual reports the date (1948) of the validating studies for the revised key.

C9. The criterion score of a person should be determined independently of his test score. The manual should describe precautions taken to avoid contamination of the criterion or should warn the reader of any possible contamination. ESSENTIAL

C9.1 When the criterion consists of a rating, grade, or classification assigned by an employer, teacher, psychiatrist, etc., the manual must state whether the test data were available to the rater or were capable of influencing his judgment in any way, e.g., indirectly through other reports of the psychologist. ESSENTIAL

C9.11 If the test data could have influenced the criterion rating, this fact should be emphasized and the user warned that the reported validities are thus contaminated and are likely to be spuriously raised. ESSENTIAL

C10. Test scores to be used in validation should be determined independently of criterion scores. ESSENTIAL

Comment: In any test where knowledge about the subject may influence test administration or scoring, for instance in individual intelligence tests or projective techniques, the test administrator should possess no knowledge of the behavior of the subject outside the test situation. The manual should discuss the extent to which contamination of this type is possible unless it is obvious from the character of the test that no such contamination could occur. Recommendation C11 below refers to a special kind of contamination frequently found in studies of objective tests.

C11. When items are selected or a scoring key is established empirically on the basis of evidence gathered on a particular sample, the manual should not report validity coefficients computed on this sample, or on a group which includes any of this sample. The reported validity coefficients should be based on a cross-validation sample. ESSENTIAL

C11.1 If the manual recommends certain regression weights, any validity reported for the composite should be based on a cross-validation sample. VERY DESIRABLE

Comment: A possible exception to recommendation C11.1 is that a cross-validation sample would not be required if an appropriate correction for shrinkage could be applied to data from the original sample. Corrections available at present are not adequate for this purpose.

C12. If the manual recommends that interpretation be based on the test profile, evidence should be provided that the shape of the profile is a valid predictor. VERY DESIRABLE

Comment: One suitable method, for example, is to tabulate test profiles having the same two highest scores, to show what proportion of these persons are successful or unsuccessful, and to compare the discriminating ability of these combined scores with that of a single score.

C12.1 If the interpretation emphasizes complex nuances of the profile pattern which cannot be fully specified and depend upon the clinical experiences of the user, evidence, specifying the training and experience of the clinicians, should be presented to show how much increase in accuracy over more simplified interpretations is gained. ESSENTIAL

C12.2 If the matching method is used to establish validity for the test report as a whole, the manual should point out that this analysis does not establish the validity of the component variables. ESSENTIAL

C13. The validation sample should be described sufficiently for the user to know whether the persons he tests may properly be regarded as represented by the sample on which validation was based. ESSENTIAL

C13.1 The user should be warned against assuming validity when the test is applied to persons unlike those in the validating sample. ESSENTIAL

C13.2 Appropriate measures of central tendency and variability of test scores for the validation sample should be reported. ESSENTIAL

C13.3 The number of cases in the validation sample should be reported. The group should be described in terms of those variables known to be related to the quality tested: these will normally include age, sex, socioeconomic status, and level of education. Any selective factor which restricts or enlarges the variability of the sample should be indicated. ESSENTIAL

Comment: In tests validated on patients, the diagnoses of the patients would usually be important to report. The severity or obviousness of the diagnosed condition should be stated when feasible. In tests for industrial use or vocational guidance, occupation and experience of the validation sample should be described.

C13.4 If the validation sample is made up merely of "available records," this fact should be stated. The test user should be warned that the group is not a systematic sample of any specifiable population. ESSENTIAL

C13.5 A sample made up of "available records" should be discussed in some detail as to probable selective factors and their presumed influence on test variables. VERY DESIRABLE

C13.6 If validation is demonstrated by comparing groups which differ on the criterion, the manual should report whether and how much the groups differ on other relevant variables. ESSENTIAL

Comment: Groups which differ on a criterion may also differ in other respects, so that the test may be discriminating on a quality other than that intended. Score differences between types of patients, for instance, may reflect differences in age, education, or length of time in hospital, unless these factors are controlled.

C14. The author should base validation studies on samples comparable, in terms of selection of cases and conditions of testing, to the groups to whom the manual recommends that the test be applied. VERY DESIRABLE

C14.1 If the test score distribution of the validation sample is markedly different from the distribution of the group with whom the test is ordinarily to be used, coefficients or other measures of discrimination should be corrected to the value estimated for the group to whom the test is to be given. ESSENTIAL

Comment: A biserial correlation between a scholastic aptitude test and college success, where the persons distinguished are dropouts and honor students, will be much higher than a coefficient based on all entering students. The test will normally be applied to the latter group, and the validity coefficient should emphasize the power of the test in that group. A correction to raise the validity coefficient may likewise be needed when a test is validated on a group of selected employees. It is always preferable, however, to gather criterion data for an unselected group.

C14.2 In reporting coefficients corrected for range, the manual should report the original coefficient, and the distribution characteristics used in making the correction and the formula employed in making the correction. ESSENTIAL

C14.3 Validation of tests intended for use in guidance should generally be based upon subjects tested at the time when they are making educational or vocational choices. VERY DESIRABLE

Comment: Strong standardized his Vocational Interest Blank on men who were currently employed in the occupation in question. The ability of these scales to differentiate between occupational groups did not, in and of itself, warrant using the inventory in the counseling of high school or college students. Strong obtained better evidence by administering the inventory to students and ascertaining the nature of their later employment, thus establishing the relationship between preoccupational score and later occupation.

C14.4 If a test is presented as being useful in the differential diagnosis of patients, it should include evidence of the test's ability to separate diagnostic groups from one another. Emphasis should be placed on this rather than on the differentiation of diagnosed abnormal cases from the normal population. ESSENTIAL

C15. **If the validity of the test can reasonably be expected to be different in subgroups which can be identified when the test is given, the manual should report the validity for each group separately or should report that no difference was found.** VERY DESIRABLE

C15.1 Occupational predictions by means of interest tests should be validated within a group all of whom have the same stated vocational aim. DESIRABLE

Comment: An interest inventory is an attempt to obtain more accurate and complete information than would be obtained by a simple question such as "List your preferred occupation." Whether the inventory yields useful information can be demonstrated only by showing that, among persons who give the same answer to this simple question, the test makes valid discriminations. It is important to move in the direction of reporting whether *among students stating a preference for engineering* (for example), those who earn high scores do differ on the criterion from those who earn lower scores.

C15.2 Validity of predictions from interest tests should be estimated separately at different levels of mental ability. DESIRABLE

C16. Reports of validation studies should describe any conditions likely to affect the motivation of subjects for taking the test. ESSENTIAL

Comment: If an ability test is to be used for employee selection, it should be validated using subjects who are candidates for employment and are therefore motivated to perform well. Under some testing conditions, a subject might try to "fake" his self-report of interests or personality; the controls used to discourage such faking should be reported.

Concurrent Validity

All recommendations listed under predictive validity also apply to reports of concurrent validity, with the exception of C5.

C17. Reports of concurrent validity should be so described that the reader will not regard them as establishing predictive validity. ESSENTIAL

Comment: The Minnesota Teacher Attitude Inventory is validated against contemporary teaching performance. This is reported under the general heading of "validity," and use of the test for selecting teachers or teacher-training candidates is recommended. The manual should point out that there have so far been no studies measuring entering students and observing them later on the job.

C17.1 For occupational tests where there are no longitudinal studies following subjects from the time of testing to the point where criterion information is available, validation data obtained by testing samples of employed persons should be presented. VERY DESIRABLE

Comment: One such method of preliminary validation is to compare the distribution of scores for men in an occupation with those for men-in-general.

C17.11 If data from employed persons are used, evidence as to the effects of experience on interest inventory scores should be presented. ESSENTIAL

Construct Validity

Recommendations C3–C16 and D5 apply to some reports of construct validity.

C18. The manual should report all available information which will assist the user in determining what psychological attributes account for variance in test scores. ESSENTIAL

C18.1 The manual should report correlations between the test and other tests which are better understood. VERY DESIRABLE

Comment: It is desirable, for instance, to know the correlation of an "art aptitude" test for college freshmen with measures of general or verbal ability, and also with measures of skill in drawing. The interpretation of test scores would differ, depending on whether these correlations are high or low. On the other hand, it is clearly impractical to ask that the test author correlate his test with all prominent tests. It is especially valuable to know correlations of this test with other measures likely to be used in making decisions about the person tested.

C18.2 The manual should report the correlations of the test with other previously published and generally accepted measures of the same attributes. VERY DESIRABLE

Comment: When a test is advanced as a measure of "general adjustment," its correlation with one or more other such measures should be reported. Similarly, if a test is advanced as a measure of "mechanical interest" or "introversion," its correlations with other measures of these traits should be reported. The user can infer, from the size of such correlations, whether generalizations established on the older test can be expected to hold for the new one. Practical limitations will prevent the author from correlating his test with all competing tests. An example of good practice is the report, in the Thurstone Interest Schedule, of correlations with corresponding Kuder scores.

C18.3 If a test given with a time limit is to be interpreted as measuring a hypothetical psychological attribute, evidence should be presented concerning the effect of speed on test scores and on the correlation of scores with other variables. VERY DESIRABLE

C18.4 If a test has been included in factorial studies which indicate the proportion of the test variance attributable to widely known reference factors, such information should be presented in the manual. DESIRABLE

C19. The manual for a test which is used primarily to assess postulated attributes of the individual should outline the theory on which the test is based and organize whatever partial validity data there are to show in what way they support the theory. VERY DESIRABLE

D. RELIABILITY

Reliability is a generic term referring to many types of evidence. The several types of reliability coefficient do not answer the same questions and should be carefully distinguished. We shall refer to a measure based on internal analysis of data obtained on a single trial of a test as a *coefficient of internal consistency.* The most prominent of these are the analysis of variance method (Kuder-Richardson, Hoyt) and the split-half method. A correlation between scores from two forms given at essentially the same time we shall refer to as a *coefficient of equivalence.* The correlation between test and retest, with an intervening period of time, is a *coefficient of stability.* Such a coefficient is also obtained when two forms of the test are given with an intervening period of time.

Comment on projective tests: It is generally recognized that projective tests present even more than the usual difficulties in assessing reliability. It is not always clearly appropriate to demand internal consistency or stability and as yet equivalent forms for the most part do not exist. It seems reasonable, however, to require an assessment of stability for such instruments even though it is recognized in some instances that a low retest stability over a substantial period merely reflects true trait fluctuation and hence indicates good validity. Clinical practice rarely presumes that inferences from projective tests are to be applied on the very day the test is given. Realistically, we must recognize that pragmatic decisions are being made from test data which are meaningful only in terms of at least days, and usually weeks or months, of therapy and other procedures following the test administration. If a certain test result is empirically found to be highly unstable from day to day, this evidence casts doubt upon the utility of the test for most purposes even if that fluctuation might be explained by hypothesis of trait inconstancy.

This reasoning applies strictly only to the inferred dimensions, and not necessarily to the directly scored dimensions. If a personality variable is estimated from a complex of several test variables, and in such a way that rather different combinations of the test variables can lead to the same value of the estimate, it is the temporal stability of the *estimate* which is subjected to the preceding requirement. But the burden of proof lies clearly upon the test manual. If component scores are unstable, it is then necessary to gather evidence regarding the degree to which estimates of the underlying personality dimension are stable during the interval for which they are intended to be used.

D1. The test manual should report such evidence of reliability as would permit the reader to judge whether scores are sufficiently dependable for the recommended uses of the test. If any of the necessary evidence has not been collected, the absence of such information should be noted. ESSENTIAL

D1.1 Recommendation D1 applies to every score, subscore, or combination of scores whose interpretation is suggested. ESSENTIAL

D1.2 If differences between scores are to be interpreted or if the plotting of a profile is suggested, the manual should report the reliability of differences between scores. ESSENTIAL

D1.21 If reliability of differences between an individual's scores is low, the manual should caution the user against interpreting profiles or score differences except as a source of preliminary information to be verified. ESSENTIAL

Comment: The California Test of Mental Maturity reports reliability coefficients for the main scores and for scores on the major sections. Each section is further divided, the Spatial subtests, for example, including a group of items on Manipulation of Areas. By listing scores for such subsections on the profile sheet, the authors indirectly encourage interpretation of them. While supplementary material on the test mentions the low reliability of the subsections, the manual does not. It would be sounder practice to plot only those scores whose reliability is determined and reported in the manual.

The Watson-Glaser Critical Thinking Appraisal suggests that study of pupil performance on various types of items may enrich the interpretation. The manual adds this desirable caution:

"For a relatively small number of items such indices and special scores would not have high statistical reliability, and hence attention should be paid only to extreme deviates. For this reason norms for these special scores are not given and they are suggested only as an aid in helping students."

This paragraph illustrates how a manual may conform to the spirit of the Technical Recommendations even when some form of data is not provided in the manual. The statement would be improved if it were worded "such indices are probably unreliable" in the place of the present correct but euphemistic phrasing.

D1.3 One or more measures of reliability should be reported even when tests are recommended solely for empirical prediction of criteria. DESIRABLE

Comment: The E.R.C. Stenographic Aptitude Test reports validity coefficients without also giving an estimate of reliability. For certain judgments such as the potential effect of lengthening the test information about reliability is required and should be available to the user.

D1.4 In connection with reliability measures, the manual should report whether the error of measurement varies at different score levels. If there is significant change in the error of measurement from level to level, this fact should be properly interpreted. VERY DESIRABLE

Comment: Terman and Merrill point out that differences in IQ from Form L to Form M of the Revised Stanford-Binet Scale are much larger for IQ's above 100 than for low IQ's.

The California Test of Personality intentionally yields markedly skewed scores. This lowers the reliability coefficients from the value that might be attained with a normal distribution of raw scores, but reduces the error of identifying the most maladjusted cases. Here the most appropriate information on reliability would be the expected variation of percentile scores from trial to trial, reported separately for low and high scores.

D1.5 Reports of reliability studies should ordinarily be expressed in terms of: (*a*) the product-moment correlation coefficient; (*b*) another standard measure of relationship suitable to categorical judgments; or (*c*) the standard error of measurement. ESSENTIAL

Comment: Chi square is not an adequate index of reliability for categorical judgments, since it reflects level of significance rather than magnitude of relationship.

D2. The manual should avoid any implication that reliability measures demonstrate the predictive or concurrent validity of the test. ESSENTIAL

Comment: Properly interpreted reliability coefficients may support analysis of content or construct validity.

D3. In reports of reliability, procedures and sample should be described sufficiently for the reader to judge whether the evidence applies to the persons and problem with which he is concerned. ESSENTIAL

D3.1 Evidence of reliability should be obtained under conditions like those in which the author recommends that the test be used. VERY DESIRABLE

Comment: The maturity of the group, the variation in the group, and the attitude of the group toward the test should represent normal conditions of test use. For example, the reliability of a test to be used in selecting employees should be determined by testing applications for positions rather than by testing college students, or workers already employed.

D3.2 The reliability sample should be described in terms of any selective factors related to the variable being measured, usually including age, sex, and educational level. Number of cases of each type should be reported. ESSENTIAL

D3.3 Appropriate measures of central tendency and variability of the test scores of the reliability sample should be reported. ESSENTIAL

D3.31 If reliability coefficients are corrected for restriction of range, the nature of the correction should be made clear. The manual should also report the uncorrected coefficient, together with the standard deviation of the group tested and the standard deviation assumed for the corrected sample. In discussing such coefficients, emphasis should be placed on the one which refers to the degree of variation within which discrimination is normally required. ESSENTIAL

D3.4 When a test is ordinarily required to make discriminations within a subclass of the total reliability sample, the reliability within each class should be investigated separately. If the coefficients differ, each separate coefficient should be reported. VERY DESIRABLE

Comment: The Mechanical Reasoning section of the Differential Aptitude Tests has different reliability for boys and girls. The manual reports the reliability for each sex and grade.

D3.5 The manual should not imply that if some method had been used to determine reliability other than the one actually used, an appreciably higher coefficient would have been obtained. ESSENTIAL

Equivalence of Forms

D4. If two forms of a test are made available, with both forms intended for possible use with the same subjects, the correlation between forms and information as to the equivalence of scores on the two forms should be reported. If the necessary evidence is not provided, the manual should warn the reader against assuming comparability. ESSENTIAL

D4.1 Where two trials of a test are correlated to determine equivalence, the time between testings should be stated. ESSENTIAL (see also D7)

D4.2 Where the content of the test items can be described meaningfully, a comparative analysis of the forms is desirable to show how similar they are. DESIRABLE

Internal Consistency

D5. If the manual suggests that a score is a measure of a generalized, homogeneous trait, evidence of internal consistency should be reported. ESSENTIAL

Comment: Internal consistency is important if items are viewed as a sample from a relatively homogeneous universe, as in a test of addition with integers, or a test presumed to measure introversion. In a test which is regarded as a collection of diverse items, such as the Mooney Checklist, internal consistency is a minor consideration.

D5.1 When a test consists of separately scored parts or sections, the correlation between the parts or sections should be reported. ESSENTIAL

Comment: Whether it is desirable or undesirable to have high subtest correlations depends on the nature and purpose of the test. Information on homogeneity or internal consistency may be relevant to the construct validity of the test.

D5.11 If the manual reports the correlation between a subtest and a total score, it should point out that part of this correlation is an artifact. ESSENTIAL

Comment: Desirable practice is illustrated in the 1953 manual for the California Test of Personality.

D6. Coefficients of internal consistency should be determined by the split-half method or methods of the Kuder-Richardson type, if these can properly be used on the data under examination. Any other measure of internal consistency which the author wishes to report in addition should be carefully explained. ESSENTIAL

Comment: There will no doubt be unusual circumstances where special coefficients give added information. There are grave dangers of giving unwarranted impressions, however, as is illustrated in the case of the Brainard Occupational Preference Inventory. This test yields a set of scores which are interpreted as a profile. The manual reports no information on the reliability of these scores, but does report a "total reliability" based on a formula by Ghiselli. This reliability seems not to correspond to any score actually interpreted, and what it indicates about the value of this particular test is unclear without more discussion than the manual provides.

The original Kuder-Richardson formulas apply to a restricted case. Of those formulas, the one known as Number 20 is most satisfactory. A formula given by Hoyt, and others, has the same meaning but is more general in application.

Guttman has also suggested a "reproducibility" formula which relates to internal consistency. This index presents such special problems that it seems to have little suitability for test manuals.

D6.1 For time-limit tests, split-half or analysis of variance coefficients should never be reported unless: (*a*) the manual also reports evidence that speed of work has negligible influence on scores; or (*b*) the coefficient is based on the correlation between parts administered under separate time limits. ESSENTIAL

Comment: Evidence of accuracy of measurement for highly speeded tests is properly obtained by retesting or testing with independent equivalent forms. If better evidence is not available, it is appropriate to use lower-bound formulas designed for estimating the internal consistency of speeded tests to determine the minimum coefficient.

D6.2 If several questions within a test are experimentally linked so that the reaction to one question influences the reaction to another, the entire group should be treated as an "item" in applying the split-half or analysis of variance methods. ESSENTIAL

Comment: In a reading test, several questions about the same paragraph are ordinarily experimentally dependent. All of these questions should be placed in the same half-test in using the split-half method. In the Kuder-Richardson method, the score on the group of questions should be treated as an "item" score.

D6.3 If a test can be divided into sets of items of different content, internal consistency should be determined by procedures designed for such tests. VERY DESIRABLE

Comment: One such procedure is the division of the test into "parallel" rather than random half-tests. Another procedure is to apply the Jackson-Ferguson "battery reliability" formula.

Stability

D7. The manual should indicate what degree of stability of scores may be expected if a test is repeated after time has elapsed. If such evidence is not presented, the absence of information regarding stability should be noted. ESSENTIAL

Comment: Most educational and psychological tests measure qualities which are presumed to be stable for some time, unless training or specified experiences intervene. Stability is not always desirable. A measure of interests in childhood and adolescence which is highly stable would not be sensitive to developmental changes.

D7.1 Stability of scores should be determined by administering the test to the same group at different times. The manual should report changes in mean score as well as the correlation between the two sets of scores. ESSENTIAL

D7.11 If a test result is reported in terms of pass-fail or some other categorical classification, stability should be reported in terms of proportion of altered classifications on retest. VERY DESIRABLE

D7.12 In determining stability of scores by repeated testing, other precautions such as giving alternate forms of the test should be used to minimize recall of specific answers, especially if the time-interval is not long enough to assure forgetting. VERY DESIRABLE

D7.13 In reporting a coefficient of stability, the manual should describe the experience or education of the group between testings, if this would be expected to affect test scores. ESSENTIAL

D7.2 For tests of interest and ability intended for use prior to adulthood, the coefficient of stability should correlate scores obtained at one particular age with scores at some later significant age. Coefficients should be reported separately for different ages at first test and for different periods of intervening time. ESSENTIAL

E. ADMINISTRATION AND SCORING

E1. The directions for administration should be presented with sufficient clarity that the test user can duplicate the administrative

conditions under which the norms and data on reliability and validity were obtained. ESSENTIAL

E1.1 The published directions should be complete enough so that people tested will understand the task in the way the author intended. ESSENTIAL

Comment: If, for example, in a personality inventory, it is intended that subjects give the first response that occurs to them, this should be made clear in the directions for administration. Directions for interest inventories should specify whether the person is to mark what he would ideally like to do, or whether he is also to consider the probability that he would have the opportunity and ability to do them. Likewise, the directions should specify whether the person is to mark those things he would wish to do or does occasionally, or only those things he would like to do or does regularly.

E1.2 If expansion or elaboration of instructions, giving of hints, etc., is permitted, the conditions for it should be clearly stated either in the form of general rules or by giving numerous examples, or both. VERY DESIRABLE

E1.21 If the examiner is allowed freedom and judgment in elaborating instructions or giving samples, empirical data should be presented regarding the effect of variation in examiner procedures upon scores. If empirical data on the effect of variation in examiner procedure are not available, this fact should be explicitly stated and the user warned that the effects of such variation are unknown. ESSENTIAL

E1.3 If the test under consideration is of a type where previous experience demonstrates that subjects are likely to present an unrealistic picture of themselves, the manual should give evidence regarding the extent to which such distortion may affect scores. ESSENTIAL

Comment: Such evidence is ordinarily to be provided by measuring the shift of scores when the test is administered in different situations (e.g., pre-employment and postemployment) or with instructions intended to induce different sets. This problem is especially acute for personality and interest inventories and projective techniques.

E1.31 If the test is provided with a verification key or key to correct for inappropriate test-taking attitudes, evidence that this key performs its function should be provided. ESSENTIAL

E2. **Where subjective processes enter into the scoring of the test, evidence on degree of agreement between independent scorings should be presented. If such evidence is not provided, the manual should draw attention to scorer error as a possible source of error of measurement.**

Comment: With projective tests, the role of interscorer agreement in the actual *classification* of raw response data is more crucial than in the case of a test where an "error in scoring" means a clerical error or something close to that. Interscorer agreement is not a demonstration of reliability in the usual sense, or a substitute for it. Interscorer agreement deals solely with the objectivity of classifying the behavior sampled from subjects, and is, therefore, directed at a condition on the part of the judge's behavior that is *necessary* for "reliability." Interscorer consistency is obviously not a *sufficient* condition, since it cannot possibly give information regarding the adequacy of that behavior *as* a sample from the subject.

E2.1 The bases for scoring and the procedure for training the scorers should be presented in sufficient detail to permit other scorers to reach the degree of agreement reported in studies of scorer agreement given in the manual. VERY DESIRABLE

Comment: One desirable practice is to present a list of the commoner responses or response categories with their scoring indicated.

E2.11 If persons having various degrees of supervised training are expected to score the test, studies of the interscorer agreement at each skill level should be presented. DESIRABLE

E2.2 If reliability of scoring is low, the manual should caution the user against interpreting combinations of such scores. ESSENTIAL

Comment: Combinations such as ratios generally will be even less reliable than the component scores.

F. SCALES AND NORMS

F1. Scales used for reporting scores should be such as to increase the likelihood of accurate interpretation and emphasis by test interpreter and subject. ESSENTIAL

Comment: Scales in which test scores are reported are extremely varied. Raw scores are used. Relative scores are used. Scales purporting to represent equal intervals with respect to some external dimension (such as age) are used. And so on. It is unwise to discourage the development of new scaling methods by insisting on one form of reporting. On the other hand, many different systems are now used which have no logical advantage, one over the other. Recommendations below that the number of systems now used be reduced to a few with which testers can become familiar, are not intended to discourage the use of unique scales for special problems. Suggestions as to preferable scales for general reporting are not intended to restrict use of other scales in research studies.

F2. Where there is no compelling advantage to be obtained by reporting scores in some other form, the manual should suggest reporting scores in terms of percentile equivalents or standard scores. VERY DESIRABLE

Comment: Professional opinion is divided on the question whether mental test scores should be reported in terms of some theoretical growth scale, such as the intelligence quotient or the Heinis index. Thus, a test developer who has rationale for such scales as these should use them if he regards them as especially adequate.

On the other hand, there is no theoretical justification for scoring mental tests in terms of an "IQ" which is not derived in terms of the theory underlying the Binet IQ and which has different statistical properties than the IQ does. Standard or percentile scores would be preferable to arbitrarily defined IQ scales such as are used in the Otis Gamma and Wechsler-Bellevue tests.

Strong recommends that Vocational Interest Blank scores be converted into letter grades where "A" indicates that at least two-thirds of the criterion group equaled or exceeded a given score, etc. He bases this recommendation on the ground that finer score discriminations would lead only to unwarranted attempts at finer interpretative discrimination.

F2.1 If grade norms are provided, tables for converting scores to percentiles (or standard scores) within each grade should also be provided. ESSENTIAL

Comment: At the high school level, norms within courses (e.g., second year Spanish) may be more appropriate than norms within grades.

F3. **Standard scores obtained by transforming scores so that they have a normal distribution and a fixed mean and standard deviation should in general be used in preference to other derived scores. For some tests, there may be a substantial reason to choose some other type of derived score.** VERY DESIRABLE

F3.1 If a two-digit standard score system is used, the mean of that system should be 50 and the standard deviation 10. DESIRABLE

F3.2 If a one-digit standard score system is used, the mean of the system should be 5 and the standard deviation 2 (as in stanines). DESIRABLE

Comment: The foregoing are proposed as ways of standardizing practice among test developers. It is expected that institutions with established systems, such as the College Board Scale, with mean at 500, will often retain them as suited to their purposes.

F3.3 Where percentile scores are to be plotted on a profile sheet, the profile sheet should be based on the normal probability scale. VERY DESIRABLE

F4. **Local norms are more important for many uses of tests than published norms. In such cases the manual should suggest appropriate emphasis on local norms.** VERY DESIRABLE

Comment: The Cooperative Dictionary Test manual precedes its presentation of norms with a discussion urging schools to prepare local norms and explaining their advantages over the published norms with respect to this test. Many achievement tests, clinical tests, and tests used for vocational guidance might well present a similar statement.

F5. **Except where the primary use of a test is to compare individuals with their own local group, norms should be published at the time of release of the test for operational use.** ESSENTIAL

Comment: The Thurstone Interest Schedule provides a profile of 20 raw scores. Because each field is based on the same number of items, norms are said to be unnecessary. Yet a change of items in any group would make that category more or less preferred. Hence, to know whether a high score reflects this individual's interests, or only that these items are popular with everyone, the user must consult a set of norms. Judgment in terms of raw scores could be made only if by some unusual method it could be demonstrated that the items in each category are a representative sample of that field.

F5.1 Even though a test is used primarily with local norms, the manual should give some norms to aid the interpreter who lacks local norms. DESIRABLE

F6. Norms should report the distribution of scores in an appropriate reference group or groups. ESSENTIAL

F6.1 Unless they can be readily inferred from the table of norms, measures of central tendency and variability of each distribution should be given. ESSENTIAL

F6.2 If the distribution in the norm group is not essentially normal, some form of percentile table should be provided. ESSENTIAL

F6.3 In addition to norms, tables showing what expectation a person with a given test score has of attaining or exceeding some relevant criterion score should be given where possible. Conversion tables translating test scores into proficiency levels should be given when proficiency can be described on a meaningful absolute scale. DESIRABLE

F7. Norms should refer to defined and clearly described populations. These populations should be the groups to whom users of the test will ordinarily wish to compare the persons tested. ESSENTIAL

Comment: Intelligence tests designed for use with elementary school children might well present norms by grade-groups as well as by chronological age-groups.

For occupational inventories, norms based on men who have entered specific occupations should be developed, except where cutting scores or regression formulas are provided for predicting occupational criteria.

The manual should point out that a person who has a high degree of interest in a curriculum or occupation, when compared to men-in-general, will generally have a much lower degree of interest when compared with persons actually engaged in that field.

Thus a *high* percentile score on the Kuder mechanical scale, in which the examinee is compared with men-in-general, may be equivalent to a *low* percentile when the examinee is compared with auto mechanics.

F7.1 The manual should report the method of sampling within the population, and should discuss any probable bias within the sample. ESSENTIAL

F7.11 Norms should be based on a well-planned sample rather than on data collected primarily on the basis of availability. VERY DESIRABLE

Comment: Occupational and educational test norms have often been based on scattered groups of test papers, and authors sometimes request that all users mail in results for use in subsequent reports of norms. Distributions so obtained will contain unknown biases. Hence, the methods for obtaining the samples should be clearly described, as in Strong's manual, and whenever possible, samples should be stratified to remove some of the bias. Planned samples will give more dependable norms, however, since stratification cannot remove all sampling error.

F7.2 The number of cases on which the norms are based should be reported. ESSENTIAL

F7.21 If the sample on which norms are based is small or otherwise undependable, the user should be explicitly cautioned regarding this. ESSENTIAL

Comment: In addition to general high school and college norms based on substantial samples, medians and ranges in small, special groups are reported for the Watson-Glaser Critical Thinking Appraisal. Since these samples vary from 10 cases to 65 cases, the ranges and medians are highly unstable. This manual should report quartiles in preference to ranges because quartiles are more stable. This manual should warn the reader as to the fallibility of estimates from these special samples.

F7.3 The manual should report whether scores differ for groups differing on age, sex, amount of training, and other equally important variables. ESSENTIAL

F7.31 If appreciable differences between groups exist, and if a person would ordinarily be compared with a subgroup rather than with a random sample of persons, then separate norm tables should be provided in the manual for each group. ESSENTIAL

Comment: An example of unusually excellent practice is the norms for the Minnesota Teacher Attitude Inventory. Here norms are based on teachers separated by levels of experience, amount of training, and type of position. The teachers were obtained by a planned sample. The manual discusses differences between sex groups but does not present separate norms, as the decision to employ a particular man teacher rather than a woman would be based on the raw score of each, rather than upon their standings within their sex group.

Norms for interest inventories should be prepared separately for student examinees having different levels of general academic ability unless there is evidence that scores have no relation to ability.

F7.32 When the total amount of scorable behavior is allowed by the task to vary, separate norms on the various scored variables should be presented for different levels of total response. VERY DESIRABLE

F7.33 If the standardizing sample is too small to permit calculation of separate norms on scored variables at different levels of total response, the correlation of each of these with response level must be presented. ESSENTIAL

F7.34 If correlation data suggest that the dependence of scores on total responsiveness is nonlinear, this should be explicitly stated and the user warned that linear corrections, prorating, or computing of percentages are inappropriate procedures. ESSENTIAL

F7.35 If data are insufficient to determine the nature of the dependence of the several scores upon responsivity (such as linearity, array scatter), this lack of information should be explicitly mentioned and the possible dangers in interpretation should be stressed. ESSENTIAL

F7.4 If conditions affecting test scores are expected to change as time elapses, periodic review of norms is required. VERY DESIRABLE

F7.5 Some profile sheets record, side by side, scores from tests so standardized that different scores compare the person to different norm groups. Profiles of this type should be recommended for use only where tests are intended to assess or predict the person's standing in different situations, where he competes with the different groups. Where such mixed scales are compared, the fact that the norm groups differ should be made clear on the profile sheet. VERY DESIRABLE

F7.6 The description of the norm group should be sufficiently complete so that the user can judge whether his case falls within the population represented by the norm group. The description should include number of cases, classified by relevant variables such as age, sex, educational status, etc. ESSENTIAL

F7.7 The conditions under which normative data were obtained should be reported. The conditions of testing, including the purpose of the subjects in taking the test, should be reported. ESSENTIAL

Comment: Some tests are standardized on job applicant groups, others on groups which have requested vocational guidance, and still others on groups which realized they were "guinea pigs." Motivation for taking tests, test-taking attitudes, abilities, and personality characteristics possibly differ on all of these groups.

TECHNICAL RECOMMENDATIONS
FOR ACHIEVEMENT TESTS *

FOREWORD

The Technical Recommendations presented in this report are intended as standards of professional practice in achievement testing for the guidance both of test producers and test users. It is expected that the recommendations will influence authors and publishers of achievement tests in developing and reporting relevant information. Test users will find the recommendations helpful in evaluating tests for their particular purposes.

This statement was prepared initially by a committee consisting of Robert L. Ebel, Saul B. Sells, and Jacob S. Orleans, chairman, for the Committees on Test Standards of the American Educational Research Association and the National Council on Measurements Used in Education. It was reviewed by the remaining members of the two committees and a number of other specialists in achievement testing. The present statement is a revision made in the light of their suggestions and recommendations.

The Committee profited materially from the work done previously by the Committee on Test Standards of the American Psychological Association, which under the chairmanship of Lee J. Cronbach, produced *Technical Recommendations for Psychological Tests and Diagnostic Techniques* which appeared as a supplement to the March 1954 issue of the *Psychological Bulletin*. This document has been formally adopted by the American Psychological Association, the American Educational Research Association, and the National Council on Measurements Used in Education. Copies of the APA report may be purchased from the American Psychological Association.

As far as possible the form and text of the APA document have been retained in the present report. This will facilitate cross reference. In many respects this statement is an adaptation of the recommendations for psychological tests and diagnostic technics to the problems of achievement tests. However, extensive changes have been made in this draft, both in specific recommendations and in the explanatory comments. Many recommendations applicable primarily to certain specialized instruments, such as personality inventories or projective technics, but having little relevance to achievement tests, have been dropped. Some other alterations have been made to fit recommendations more closely to the problems of achievement

* Prepared by a joint committee of the American Educational Research Association and the National Council on Measurements Used in Education. Originally published in January 1955 by the American Educational Research Association. Reprinted with permission.

testing; these modifications do not imply any necessity for change in the recommendations for psychological tests. A number of new recommendations have been added, on points not considered in the previous report. The text was completed in June 1954. We gratefully acknowledge the American Psychological Association's permission to use materials from its report.

Upon recommendation of its Committee on Psychological Tests the American Psychological Association has officially endorsed the present statement of standards.

Jacob S. Orleans, *Chairman*
Committee on Test Standards, AERA
Robert L. Ebel, *Chairman*
Committee on Test Standards, NCMUE

DEVELOPMENT AND SCOPE OF THE RECOMMENDATIONS

Textbooks on educational measurement have for decades served as guides for test producers thru their discussions of standards of validity, reliability, and other aspects of test construction. The need for such standards derives from the strategic influence of test scores on important decisions affecting individuals, and on educational viewpoints and practices. The test user needs information in order to satisfy himself that the test meets his particular requirements. The test producer, consequently, has the responsibility of furnishing information to the test user concerning pertinent characteristics of the test.

The informal standards stated in textbooks and test manuals have undoubtedly had a salutary effect on the preparation and use of tests. However, until the preparation of this document, and the *Technical Recommendations for Psychological Tests and Diagnostic Techniques,* there was no statement by a professional body which could be regarded as a *standard* of approved practice for the guidance of both users and producers of tests. The intent of this document is to specify what essential information should usually accompany a test in order to enable users to evaluate it properly.

Issuing specifications for tests could indeed discourage the development of new types of tests. So many different sorts of tests are needed in present educational practice that limiting the kind thru specifications would not be sound procedure. New types of tests are needed to keep up with changes in educational theory and practice. Particularly in the elementary grades, there is a trend in the direction of more functional educational processes. This trend makes it all the more important that types of achievement tests be developed that are appropriate to the new programs. Therefore, it is essential that the present recommendations serve to stimulate the creation of new tests rather than to hinder their development. Appropriate standardization of tests and manuals, however, need not interfere with innovation. The recommendations presented here are intended to assist test producers to bring out a wide variety of tests that will be suitable for all the different purposes for which tests should be used and to make those tests as valuable as possible.

INFORMATION STANDARDS AS GUIDES

The essential principle that sets the tone for this document is that a test manual should furnish sufficient information to enable any qualified user to make sound judgments regarding the usefulness of tests and the interpretation of test data. This means that certain research is required prior to release of a test for general use by school personnel and psychologists. The results should be reported or summarized in the manual, and the manual should help the reader to interpret and apply these results.

A manual is to be judged not merely by its literal truthfulness, but by the impression it leaves with the reader. If the professional user is likely to obtain an untrue impression of the test from the manual, the manual is inappropriately written. Ideally, manuals should be pretested in the field by comparing the typical reader's conclusions with the judgments of experts regarding the tests. In the absence of such trials, these recommendations are intended to apply to the *spirit* and *tone* of the manual as well as to its literal statements.

A manual must often communicate information to different groups of users. At one extreme are many classroom teachers, counselors, school supervisors and administrators, and psychometricians with limited training in testing. Such users frequently will not follow technical discussions or presentations of statistical information. At the other extreme are the measurement specialists. The information available about any test should be sufficiently complete for specialists in the area to judge the technical adequacy of the test. It is most important that there be made available to each person concerned with the test a sound basis for whatever judgments his functions require.

The setting of numerical specifications has been avoided even tho it would have been tempting to say, for instance, that a validity coefficient ought to reach .50 before a test of a certain type is ready for use, or that a test of another type should always have a reliability of .90 before it is used for decisions concerning individual subjects. There are different problems in different situations depending, for instance, on whether decisions are to be made concerning an individual or a group, or on the nature of the decision. It is not appropriate to call for a particular level of validity and reliability, or to otherwise specify the nature of the test. It *is* appropriate to ask that the manual give information so that the user can decide whether the accuracy, relevance, or standardization of the test makes it suitable for his purposes. *These recommendations, then, suggest standards of test description and reporting without stating minimum statistical specifications.*

In arriving at those recommendations, it has been necessary to judge what is presently the reasonable degree of compromise between pressures of cost and time on the one hand, and ideal standards on the other. The test producer ordinarily spends large sums of money in developing and standardizing an achievement test. So far as these recommendations indicate the sort of information that would be most valuable to the people who use tests, test authors and publishers can then direct their funds to gathering and reporting these data. The recommendations, therefore, attempt to state what types of studies should be completed before a test is ready for release to the profession for operational use. The recommendations attempt to describe standards which are already reached by our better tests.

TESTS TO WHICH THESE RECOMMENDATIONS APPLY

These recommendations cover tests of educational outcomes which are used for purposes of measuring individual performance and indirectly for evaluating educational programs, procedures, and personnel. They are intended primarily for published tests of knowledge, skills, and cognitive process, but they also provide recommendations for the measurement of such other educational outcomes as attitudes, interests, understandings, and appreciations.

The general topics to be covered in the recommendations are dissemination of information, interpretation, validity, reliability, administration, and scales and norms.

Many comments have been included for the purpose of amplifying and illustrating the recommendations. Tests mentioned in the comments have not been singled out as being particularly good or poor tests, but only to illustrate certain points.

THREE LEVELS OF RECOMMENDATIONS

Manuals can probably never give all the information that might be desirable. At the same time, restricting this statement of recommendations only to essential information might tend to discourage reporting of desirable additional information. To avoid this, recommendations are designated at three levels: ESSENTIAL, VERY DESIRABLE, and DESIRABLE. Each proposed requirement is judged in the light of its importance and the feasibility of attaining it.

The statements listed as ESSENTIAL are intended to represent the consensus of presentday thinking as to what is normally required for operational use of a test. Almost every test presents some unique problems, and it is undesirable that standards should bind the producer of a novel test to an inappropriate procedure or form of reporting. The ESSENTIAL standards indicate what information is genuinely needed for most tests in their usual applications. When a test producer fails to satisfy this need, he should do so only as a considered judgment. There will be very few ESSENTIAL standards which do not apply to any single test.

If some type of ESSENTIAL information is not available for a given test, it is important for the test producer to help the reader recognize that the research on the test is incomplete in this respect. *A test manual can satisfy all the ESSENTIAL standards by clear statements of what research has and has not been done, and by avoidance of misleading statements.* It will not be necessary to perform much additional research to satisfy the standards, provided the information about the test is so presented that the reader can fully understand both what is known and what is unknown about it.

The category VERY DESIRABLE is used to draw attention to types of information which contribute greatly to the user's understanding of the test. These are not labeled as essential because, for instance, of the time it would take to gather the necessary data.

The category DESIRABLE includes information which would be helpful, but less so than the ESSENTIAL and VERY DESIRABLE information. Test users welcome any information of this type which the producer offers.

When a test is widely used, the producer has a greater responsibility for investigating it thoroly and providing more extensive reports. The larger sale of such tests makes more research financially possible. Therefore, the producer of a popular test can add more of the VERY DESIRABLE and DESIRABLE information in subsequent editions of the manual. For tests having limited sale, it is unreasonable to expect that as much of these two categories of information will be furnished. In making such facts available, the producer performs a service beyond the level that can reasonably be anticipated for most tests at this time.

THE AUDIENCE FOR THESE RECOMMENDATIONS

One audience for these recommendations is the authors and publishers who are responsible for test development. The recommendations should also aid the thinking of test users. A good deal of the information to be reported about tests is technical, and, therefore, the wording of the recommendations is of necessity technical. It is not expected that the classroom teacher who has had at least one substantial course in tests and measurements will himself make extensive use of this report. The report should, however, be helpful to directors of research, school psychologists, counselors, supervisors, and administrators who select and use tests for various school purposes.

As an aid to test development, the recommendations may be regarded as a kind of checklist of factors to consider in the selection of test content, test construction, and in designing standardization and validation studies. Test authors should refer to them in deciding what studies to perform on their tests and how to report them in their manuals. Test publishers should use them in planning revision of their present tests. In considering proposed manuals, publishers can suggest to authors the types of information which need to be gathered in order to make the manual as serviceable as it should be. Because of the ease with which such claims could be misinterpreted, *it would not be appropriate to state in a test manual that it "satisfies" or "follows" these technical recommendations.* There would be no objection to a statement that an author had attempted to take these recommendations into account in preparing the manual.

It is important to note that publication of superior information about tests by no means guarantees that tests will be used well. Ultimate responsibility for improvement of testing rests on the shoulders of test users. The continual improvement of courses which prepare test users, and of professional leadership in all institutions using tests, is a responsibility in which all concerned must share.

REVISION AND EXTENSION

For many reasons it will be necessary to revise the standards periodically. Despite the care with which these standards have been developed, experience will no doubt reveal that some of the present judgments would benefit from further examination. New tests will present problems not considered in the present work. The improvement of statistical technics and psychometric theory will yield better bases for test analysis. The efforts of test producers will lead to continued improvement in tests, and, as this continues, it will be possible to raise the standards so that the test user will have even better information about his tools.

THE RECOMMENDATIONS

The test user needs information to help him select the test which is most adequate for a given purpose. He must rely in large part on the test producer for such data. The practices in furnishing the needed information have varied. In the case of some tests, the user has had access to virtually nothing beyond directions for administering and scoring the test and norms of uncertain origin. On the other hand, other tests have manuals which furnish extensive data on the development of the test, the basis for the selection of test items, the validity and reliability of the test, the origin of the norms, the kinds of interpretations which are appropriate, and the uses for which they can be employed.

A. DISSEMINATION OF INFORMATION

The diversity of practice in making information about tests available suggests the need for standards for the dissemination of information.

A1. When a test is published for operational use, it should be accompanied by a manual which takes cognizance of the recommendations in this report. ESSENTIAL

Comment: It should be recognized that a particular recommendation may not apply to a particular test. The manual writer "takes cognizance of" the recommendation if he examines it with care to ascertain whether it has implications for his test. It is not proper to ignore a recommendation merely because the recommendation, while applicable to claims made for the test, is difficult to meet or has ordinarily not been met by preceding tests.

A1.1 Some form of manual, presenting at least minimum information, should be given or sold to all purchasers of the test. ESSENTIAL

A1.2 Where the information is too extensive to be fully reported in such a manual, the manual should summarize the essential information and indicate where further details may be found. ESSENTIAL

Comment: **Several test publishers have followed the practice of dis-**

tributing periodic bulletins, loose-leaf reports, or annual supplements to their users. Such publications may be used as mediums for referring to or presenting essential additional information during interim periods between revisions of manuals.

A1.3 If information about the test is provided in a separate publication, any such publication should meet the same standards of accuracy as apply to the manual. ESSENTIAL

Comment: For example, a report in a professional journal on the validity of an instrument should meet the same standards of completeness and freedom from misleading impressions as a report in the manual. The author or publishers of a test cannot, of course, be held responsible for professional publication by other persons who choose to use the test and report on it. This recommendation applies also to advertising literature.

A2. The test and supporting data in the manual should be up to date for the purposes for which they are sold. Revisions should be made when required, and information identifying dates of issue, copyright, and revision should be clearly displayed. ESSENTIAL

Comment: Changes in instructional content or emphasis may cause some tests to become obsolete. Norms published at one time may require change at a later time as a result of trends in curriculum organization, promotional policy, or population. New information published or available about a test may indicate a need for revision of the test, the manual, or both. When such discrepancies exist, revisions are indicated. On the other hand, the mere passage of time may not be a sufficient requirement for revision of a test or a manual if the date of issue is displayed and the scope, content, and norms are appropriate to current uses of the instrument.

A2.1 When dependable information emerges from subsequent investigations by the author or others, which indicates that some statements made in the manual are no longer correct, a revised manual should be issued at the earliest feasible date. ESSENTIAL

A2.2 When a test is revised or a new form is prepared, the manual should be appropriately revised to take changes in the test into account. ESSENTIAL

B. INTERPRETATION

In interpreting test results, the user always is responsible for making inferences as to the meaning and legitimate uses of scores. In making such judgments, he is dependent upon the nature of the content of the test and the available data about the test.

The degree to which a test manual can be expected to prepare the user for accurate interpretation and effective use of the test results varies with the purpose for which it is used. Manuals of achievement tests should be expected to present basic information needed for sound interpretation of test scores. It is usually necessary to make judgments which depend on considerations other than the data furnished in the manual of any achievement test. Thus, the quality of instruction in a given school or community can be assessed by achievement test results, only if the other characteristics of the pupil population which influence their achievement are also taken into account.

B1. So far as possible, the test, the manual, record forms, and other accompanying material should assist users to make correct interpretations of the test results. ESSENTIAL

B1.1 Names given to tests, and to scores within tests, should be chosen to describe them as definitively as possible to test users and examinees. ESSENTIAL

Comment: The name of an achievement test should be descriptive of the aspect of achievement which the test purports to measure. When a subject-matter area or curriculum field covers many objectives, the name of the test and the discussion in the manual should make clear what objectives the test is intended to measure. Thus, a test of high-school chemistry might deal with knowledge of basic facts and processes, with ability to read new scientific material, or ability to solve chemical problems. Such a title as *Test of Essentials in Chemistry* would not make clear the limited scope of the test. A more definitive title should be prepared. The title of the Dimond-Pflieger Problems of Democracy Test leads one to expect that the items in it would deal principally and directly with the recognition, analysis, and solution of problems in public finance, civil liberties, national defense, intelligent voting, and the like. However, the items in the test are largely informational rather than problematic. This emphasis perhaps reflects the type of content of many courses called "Problems of Democracy." It would be more desirable if both courses and tests were truer to the title they carry.

B1.2 The manual or other accompanying material should describe the processes by which interpretations are to be derived from test scores. VERY DESIRABLE

Comment: The manual need not include such information as all professionally qualified users may be expected to have. It should report the rationales and procedures specifically designed for or adapted to the interpretation of the test it accompanies. For example, the Iowa Tests for Educational Development provide, in separate manuals for school administrators, for teachers, and for students, guides for the interpretation and uses of test results, making reference to data other than test scores which should be taken into account.

B1.3 Where a certain kind of misinterpretation is known to be frequently made (or can reasonably be anticipated), the manual should draw attention to this error and warn against it. ESSENTIAL

Comment: For many classroom uses and for classroom work, national norms may be inappropriate or insufficient for a particular group or community. Achievement test manuals by adequately describing the applicability of their norms and by providing guidance in the development of local norms to supplement the more general norms, can contribute to the reduction of incorrect interpretation of their test scores.

B2. The test manual should state explicitly the purposes and applications for which the test is recommended. ESSENTIAL

B3. When the administering and interpreting of a test requires professional qualifications beyond those of the usual classroom teacher, this fact should be clearly indicated in the manual. ESSENTIAL

Comment: Where profile or percentile charts are made available, the tendency to plot individual graphs is thereby encouraged. The proper interpretation of such individual reports should be presented as a matter of grave concern. The National Achievement Tests for Secondary Schools, by Speer and Smith, makes use of efficiency norms, in which an individual's achievement gain or loss in relation to expectancy on the basis of IQ can be computed. The manual does not point out variations to be expected in IQ's derived from different tests, nor does it indicate the variation in achievement levels among schools and communities. The limitations of this concept and procedure and the possible harmful effects of false knowledge based on it are not discussed.

B4. When a test is issued in revised form, the nature and extent of any revision, and the comparability of data for the revised and the old test should be explicitly stated. ESSENTIAL

Comment: To insure that the revision can be distinguished readily from previous editions, it is desirable that the date and number of the revision be indicated in the title or subtitle of the revised form.

B5. Statements in the manual reporting relationships are by implication quantitative, and should be stated as precisely as the data permit. If data to support such a statement have not been collected, that fact should be made clear. ESSENTIAL

Comment: The manual for the National Achievement Tests for Secondary Schools, by Speer and Smith, states that its norms "were checked against returns of thousands of additional pupils and were found to be accurate." This is a quantitative statement regarding both size of validation sample and level of significance of results and requires more explicit reporting to avoid misleading implications.

B5.1 When the term *significant* is employed, the manual should make clear whether statistical or practical significance is meant, and the practical significance of statistically reliable differences should be evaluated. ESSENTIAL

B5.2 The manual should clearly differentiate between an interpretation justified for a group taken as a whole, and the application of such an interpretation to each individual within the group. ESSENTIAL

Comment: For example, if the standard error of measurement is five points, this statement should not be presented so as to imply that the obtained score for any one individual is within five points of his true score. For a single pupil, the difference between the obtained and the true score might be very much larger.

B6. If a test manual presents guides or procedures, or suggests reporting of test results to the persons tested, it should point out relevant background facts concerning the individual which should be considered, as well as the possible effects on the individual of the information so reported. VERY DESIRABLE

C. VALIDITY

Validity information indicates the degree to which the test is capable of accomplishing certain aims. Tests are used for several types of judgment, and for each type of judgment a somewhat different type of validating evidence is required.

Four Types of Validity

Four types of validity have been distinguished, namely, content validity, concurrent validity, predictive validity, and construct validity.

a) *Content validity* is concerned with the sampling of a specified universe of content.

b) *Concurrent validity* is concerned with the relation of test scores to an accepted contemporary criterion of performance on the variable which the test is intended to measure.

c) *Predictive validity* is concerned with the relation of test scores to measures on a criterion based on performance at some later time.

d) *Construct validity.* More indirect validating procedures, which we refer to under the name *construct validation,* are invoked when the preceding three methods are insufficient to indicate the degree to which the test measures what it is intended to measure.

We can illustrate these concepts by examining various ways in which a test of interpretative reading in science might be employed. A science teacher may wish to determine the proficiency of his students with respect to this teaching objective. Interpreting the test for this purpose requires information on *content validity:* Does the test present the types of situations to which the teacher is trying to teach students to respond?

The teacher would examine the evidence furnished by the producer of the test specifying the universe from which reading selections were sampled, and he would examine the types of questions included in the test. The teacher might be interested in knowing either whether the paragraphs and questions asked are representative of the reading materials his students have been studying, or whether they are representative of the science reading materials encountered in adult activities.

The teacher may also be interested in using the objective test to replace the much more time consuming and difficult method he now employs to evaluate the achievements of the students in a particular course. A decision as to whether this test is a satisfactory substitute requires evidence of *concurrent validity*. If the teacher, for instance, is satisfied that the students' ability to make critical interpretations and applications in free response to a paragraph is a good measure of the objective, he may inquire whether ability to select the best of several interpretations offered in a multiple-choice test measures the same ability.

The guidance counselor may have occasion to consult the same test scores for the purpose of advising students concerning election of a science course in college. Such use of test scores involves prediction of later performance and, hence, depends on *predictive validity*. The counselor would need to know how accurately scores on this test predict achievement in college science courses. He would consult the evidence concerning the correlation of the test scores with measures of achievement in college science courses accepted as criteria for the purpose.

It may be noted that concurrent validity refers to the relation between test scores and criterion scores which can be obtained at the same time, while predictive validity refers to the relation between test scores and criterion scores which cannot be secured until some time later. The former answers the question, "With what degree of accuracy can the test scores replace the scores on an existing criterion?" The latter answers the question, "With what degree of accuracy can the test scores estimate the scores on the criterion that the test subjects would achieve some time later?"

For any of the three purposes described above, the specified types of evidence of validity may not be available, either because the universe of content cannot adequately be specified or because an acceptable criterion is not available. In such cases the test user must judge the validity of the test for his purpose on the basis of such evidence as the test producer presents. The use of logical inferences from experimental evidence or other information relevant to any aspect of test validity has been termed *construct validity*.

Construct validity is highly important in achievement testing. In the first place, universes of content, while relatively easy to specify in the traditional school subjects, nevertheless are very difficult to specify in many important areas such as study skills, attitudes, interests, understandings, and appreciations. Second, altho in some cases criteria for concurrent validity can be obtained, as in the example above, this is not generally the case. In fact, for the purposes of most educational achievement tests, no suitable concurrent criterion of performance has usually been available to determine validity in terms of a correlation coefficient or other quantitative objective measure. Such criterion data as teachers' ratings, course grades, or teacher-constructed examination grades are generally inadequate for this purpose and frequently inferior to the tests for which they are to be used. The same considerations apply to predictive validity in many situations.

The most typical example of construct validity applied to an achievement test in a traditional subject in which the universe of content is accepted, but a suitable (concurrent) criterion is not available, is the procedure by means of which the discrimination of the test scores is measured between successive grades in a sequence of courses. The information obtained by this means permits the logical inference that those grade groups in the sequence which have received more instruction attain a higher level of achievement. The same or experimentally similar approaches may be followed to adduce information bearing on construct validity for any use of a test. Content, concurrent, and predictive validity may be thought of as specialized aspects of construct validity.

In the earlier days of educational measurements this second consideration was commonly referred to as the "statistical validity" of the test. That label was neither descriptive nor meaningful. The terms *concurrent* and *construct* validity are recommended as more understandable concepts.

The use of construct validity in achievement testing may also be clarified by an illustration with a test of study habit skills, that is, a test not in a traditional subject. What evidence might be presented to support the claim that such a test is valid? For a given group of students predictive evidence of expected achievement status at the end of the year in a given course is available. The predictions are based on both a prognosis test in the subject and a general scholastic aptitude test. The correlation between scores on these two tests and final achievement status for similar groups in the past has been above .70. From among the several hundred students in the group, 30 are chosen who after the middle of the year are far above their predicted achievement status. Another 30 are chosen who at that time are far below their predicted achievement status.

It is hypothesized that differences in study habit skills are in large measure responsible for the fact that the first group of students are doing much better than is expected of them and that the second group are doing much less well than is expected of them. If this hypothesis is sound, the items on the study skills test and the test as a whole should discriminate significantly between the two groups. The selection of the items to remain in the test would then be based on the degree to which they discriminate between the two groups provided other variables, such as home background and academic preparation, are controlled. The validity of the test in its final form would be determined by its ability to discriminate between two other groups similarly chosen.

The evidence for validity presented in this instance is clearly evidence of construct validity. It is by the very nature of the case inferential rather than conclusive. The acceptance of this evidence by a prospective user of the test would depend on his acceptance of the hypothesis stated above, on the method employed to secure and analyze the data, and on the degree to which the items discriminated between the groups who are presumed to differ in study habits.

It may be advisable to point out that for instructional uses of achievement tests (diagnosis and analysis of achievement, planning of remedial work, and determination of supervisory needs of the teacher) content validity is important. For administrative uses of test scores (classification of pupils, promotion, and school records of achievement) it is only the concurrent and construct validity that are important. It is the measure of the accuracy of the inferences which determine administrative decisions. In such cases content validity is important primarily as it lends logical support to concurrent or construct validity.

General Recommendations

C1. The manual should report the validity of each type of inference for which a test is recommended. If validity of some recommended interpretation has not been tested, that fact should be made clear. ESSENTIAL

Comment: For guidance uses of a test it is obviously impossible to present predictive validities for all possible criteria in which a counselor may be interested. The manual should make clear to the test user the nature and extent of the extrapolations suggested by the test author or forced upon him by the problem confronting him.

C2. When validity is reported, the manual should indicate clearly what type of validity is referred to. The unqualified term "validity" should be avoided unless its meaning is clear from the context. ES-SENTIAL

Comment: It is not desirable for the manual to encourage the use of inappropriate methods of judging validity. Thus, the manual for the school administrator of the Iowa Tests of Educational Development states that "there is no better way to judge the validity of these tests than to put yourself in the student's place and take the test yourself. In this way, decide for yourself what the tests really measure. . . . There is no adequate statistical substitute for a common sense evaluation of this kind." Altho the actual taking of the test may be of marked assistance in evaluating it, this procedure cannot take the place of evidence concerning each type of validity.

C2.1 Limitations concerning the uses of subtest scores, profiles, and diagnostic uses should be made explicit. ESSENTIAL

C2.2 Item-test correlations should not be presented as evidence of validity, except possibly in connection with a closely reasoned argument regarding construct validity. ESSENTIAL

Comment: In a test used for diagnosis of individual learning problems, for planning or evaluating remedial instruction, or for educational guidance, both the content validity and the concurrent or construct validity of the subtests are important. The validity of a profile for diagnostic use needs to be considered as a separate problem, not inferred from the validities of the separate scores.

C2.3 As competent studies of the validity of the test are reported by investigators independent of the test authors, such evidence should be taken into account in the discussion of validity in subsequent editions of the manual or in supplementary reports. ESSENTIAL

C3. The manual should indicate which, if any, of the interpretations of test scores usually attempted for achievement tests of this type have not been substantiated. ESSENTIAL

Content Validity

Even the better educational achievement tests have couched their claims for content validity in rather general terms. A common statement in the test manual is that the selection of test items is based on an analysis of widely used textbooks in the subject or of a sampling of courses of study. Ordinarily the user would need to make analyses of the content himself to determine the content validity of the test, unless he were willing to accept the producer's contention that it possesses a high degree of content validity, or assumes that the method employed is bound to achieve content validity. The following standards indicate the kind of detailed information which the producer should furnish the test user in support of claims of content validity.

C4. If a test performance is to be interpreted as a sample of per-

formance in some universe of situations, the manual should indicate clearly what universe is represented and how adequate the sampling is. ESSENTIAL

Comment: The examiner's manual for the Iowa High School Content Examination contains the statement, "Its first claim to validity is that the items in the test were carefully selected to measure the important facts and concepts in the four specified fields." It would be more valuable to the user if it also presented a listing of the areas of content covered within each of the four fields. The manual for the Tate Economic Geography Test states: "The content of this test is based on the common content of several recent text books and courses of study. The items were carefully selected and checked by teachers and supervisors and test specialists. Studies of student responses on trial editions of the test were also made and utilized." This statement indicates only how the author attempted to achieve content validity. It would help the test user, if without having to tabulate and classify the test items himself, he were informed of the categories of content covered by the test, and the number in each category with evidence of how adequately they sample the important aspects of economic geography content.

C4.1 The universe of content should be defined in terms of the sources of subjectmatter and other content criteria used to include and exclude items. ESSENTIAL

C4.2 The method of sampling items within the universe should be described. ESSENTIAL

Comment: One of the best aids to sampling is a table of specifications of behaviors and content to be measured.

C4.3 If items are regarded as a sample from a universe, a coefficient of internal consistency should be reported for each descriptive score. VERY DESIRABLE

C4.4 If experts are asked to judge whether items are an appropriate sample of a universe or are correctly scored, the number of experts, the facts regarding their relevant professional experience and qualifications, the details of the judging process, and the data on independent agreement among them in judging should be reported. ESSENTIAL

C4.5 The date at which any study of the adequacy of sampling was made should be reported, and also the date of any source of items. VERY DESIRABLE

Comment: If curriculum bulletins are used as a basis for sampling items, the source, date of adoption, and other identifying data for each should be reported.

C4.6 If test performance is to be interpreted as a sample of performance in some universe of situations, and if the test is administered with a time limit, evidence should be presented concerning the effect of speed on test scores. ESSENTIAL

Comment: The most satisfactory evidence would be the correlation of one form, given with the usual time limit, against another form given with unlimited time. This could be compared with form-form coefficient with time limits on both forms. Other simpler information about effect of degree of speeding should be given when this correlational study is impractical.

Concurrent Validity

C5.When concurrent validity is determined by statistical analysis, the analysis should be reported in a form from which the reader can determine confidence limits of estimates regarding individuals, or the probability of misclassification of the individual on the criterion. ESSENTIAL

C5.1 Statistical procedures which are well known and readily interpreted should be used in reporting validity whenever they are appropriate to the data under examination. Any uncommon statistical technics should be explained. ESSENTIAL

C5.11 Reports of statistical validation studies should ordinarily be expressed by (*a*) correlation coefficients of familiar types; or (*b*) description of the efficiency with which the test separates groups, indicating amount of misclassification or overlapping. ESSENTIAL

Comment: Reports of differences between means of groups, or critical ratios, are by themselves inadequate information regarding predictive validity. If a sample is large, high critical ratios may be found even when classification is very inadequate.

C5.2 An over-all validity coefficient should be supplemented with evidence as to the validity of the test at different intervals along the range, unless the author reports that the validity is essentially constant thruout. DESIRABLE

Comment: This might be reported by giving the standard error of estimate at various test score levels, or by indicating the proportion of hits, misses, and false positives at various cutting scores. The Metropolitan Reading Readiness Test reports the number of failures in primary reading expected at each level of test score.

C5.3 Test manuals should not report validity coefficients corrected for unreliability of the test. ESSENTIAL

Comment: Corrections for attenuation are very much open to misinterpretation and, if misinterpreted, they give an unjustifiably favorable picture of the validity of the test.

C6. All measures of criteria should be described accurately. The manual should evaluate the adequacy of the criterion. It should draw attention to significant aspects of performance which the criterion measure does not reflect and to the irrelevant factors which it may reflect. ESSENTIAL

Comment: Desirable practices are illustrated in the manual of the General Clerical Test, where validity is reported in three specific studies. The nature of the criterion and the nature of the work done by the employees tested is described. Limitations on the data are mentioned, and stress is placed on the necessity of making comparable studies with local criteria in any new situation where the test is to be applied.

The specification of the criterion should include a description of the populations tested, and furnish information on age, grade, sex, intellectual level, type of educational program, type of community, and dates of testing.

C6.1 The correlation between scores on the test and "criterion" measures whose validity is uncertain or known to be inferior to that of the test scores should not be reported as a validity coefficient. ESSENTIAL

C7. The reliability of the criterion should be reported if it can be determined. If such evidence is not available, the author should emphasize this fact and discuss the probable limits of reliability as judged from indirect evidence. ESSENTIAL

C7.1 If validity coefficients are corrected for unreliability of the *criterion,* both corrected and uncorrected coefficients should be reported and properly interpreted. ESSENTIAL

C8. The date when validation data were gathered should be reported. ESSENTIAL

C8.1 If the criterion, the conditions of work, the type of person likely to be tested, or the meaning of the test items is suspected of changing materially with the passage of time, the validity of the test should be rechecked periodically and the results reported in subsequent editions of the manual. VERY DESIRABLE

C9. The criterion score of a person should be determined independently of his test score. The manual should describe precautions taken to avoid contamination of the criterion or it should warn the reader of any possible contamination. ESSENTIAL

Comment: To avoid possible bias thru knowledge about subjects which may influence administration or scoring of the predictor tests, the test administrator and scorers should possess no knowledge of the behavior of the subjects outside the test situation. The manual should discuss the extent to which contamination of this type is possible unless it is obvious from the character of the test that no such contamination could occur.

C9.1 If the test data could have influenced the criterion rating, this fact should be emphasized and the user warned that the reported validities are thus contaminated and are likely to be spuriously high. ESSENTIAL

C10. When items are selected empirically on the basis of evidence gathered on a particular sample, the manual should not report validity coefficients computed on this sample or on a group which includes any of this sample. The reported validity coefficients should be based on a cross-validation sample. ESSENTIAL

C11. If the manual recommends that diagnostic interpretation be based on the test profile, evidence should be provided that the profile patterns used are valid discriminators. VERY DESIRABLE

Comment: One suitable method, for example, is to tabulate similar test profiles having the same scores, to show what proportion of persons in each profile group have the same strengths and weaknesses, and to compare the discriminating ability of these patterns of scores with that of a combined score.

C12. The validation sample should be described sufficiently for the user to know whether the persons he tests may properly be regarded as represented by the sample on which validation was based. ESSENTIAL

C12.1 Appropriate measures of central tendency and variability of test scores for the validation sample should be reported. ESSENTIAL

C12.2 The number of cases in the validation sample should be reported. The group should be described in terms of those variables known to be related to the quality tested. These will normally include age, sex, socioeconomic status, and level of education. Any selective factor which restricts or enlarges the variability of the sample should be indicated. ESSENTIAL

C12.3 If the validation sample is made up merely of "available cases," this fact should be stated. The test user should be warned that the group is not a systematic sample of any specifiable population. ESSENTIAL

C12.4 If validation is demonstrated by comparing groups which differ on the criterion, the manual should report whether and how much the groups differ on other related variables. ESSENTIAL

C13. The author should base validation studies on samples comparable, in terms of selection of cases and conditions of testing, to the groups to whom the manual recommends that the test be applied. ESSENTIAL

C13.1 If the manual reports coefficients corrected for range, the original coefficients, the distribution characteristics used in making the correction, and the formula employed in making the correction should be reported. ESSENTIAL

C14. If the validity of the test can reasonably be expected to be different in subgroups which can be identified when the test is given, the manual should report the validity for each group separately or should report that no difference was found. VERY DESIRABLE

C15. Reports of concurrent validity should be so described that the reader will not regard them as establishing predictive validity. ESSENTIAL

Predictive Validity

An achievement test employed for predictive purposes should satisfy the recommendations concerning predictive validity in *Technical Recommendations for Psychological Tests and Diagnostic Techniques* (Supplement to *Psychological Bulletin,* March 1954).

Construct Validity

As indicated above, construct validity is particularly important in cases, such as usually prevail in relation to educational achievement tests, where a suitable independent criterion is not available. Validation of achievement tests by demonstration of their discrimination among selected reference criterion groups is, in effect, construct validity. Such discrimination provides evidence to validate both the theory on which an achievement test is based and the test scores themselves. Evidence of discriminating power in conjunction with content validity is sufficient for most achievement tests organized around content subjectmatter. The remaining recommendations under Construct Validity are significant for newer types of achievement tests which attempt to measure such constructs as understandings, attitudes, interests, appreciations, and study habits or skills. These educational outcomes for the most part do not represent identifiable universes of content, but are more like psychological traits or qualities.

C16. The manual should report all available information which will assist the user in determining what attributes (such as understandings, attitudes, interests, appreciations, and study habits or skills) account for variance in test scores. ESSENTIAL

C16.1 The manual should report correlations between the test or subtest and other tests which are better understood. VERY DESIRABLE

C16.2 If a test has been included in factorial studies which indicate the proportion of test variance attributable to widely known reference factors, such information should be presented in the manual. DESIRABLE

C17. The manual for a test which is used primarily to assess postulated attributes of the individual should outline the theory on which the test is based and organize whatever partial validity data there are to show in what way they support the theory. VERY DESIRABLE

C18. When a test consists of separately scored parts or sections, the correlation between each pair of parts or sections should be reported. ESSENTIAL

Comment: Whether it is desirable or undesirable to have high subtest correlations depends on the nature and purpose of the test. Information on homogeneity or internal consistency of subtest may be relevant to the construct validity of the test.

D. RELIABILITY

Reliability is a generic term referring to many types of evidence. The several types of reliability coefficient do not answer the same questions and should be carefully distinguished. We shall refer to a measure based on internal analysis of data obtained on a single trial of a test as a *coefficient of internal consistency*. The most prominent of these are the analysis of variance method (Kuder-Richardson, Hoyt) and the split-half method. A correlation between scores from two forms given at essentially the same time we shall refer to as a coefficient of equivalence. The correlation between test and retest, with an intervening period of time, is a coefficient of stability. Such a coefficient is also obtained when two equivalent forms of the test are given with an intervening period of time.

General Recommendations

D1. The test manual should report such evidence of reliability as would permit the reader to judge whether scores are sufficiently dependable for the recommended uses of the test. If any of the necessary evidence has not been collected, the absence of such information should be noted. ESSENTIAL

Comment: The manual for the Cooperative Inter-American Reading Tests presents interpretations of hypothetical reliability measures, both correlation coefficients and probable error of a pupil's score. Since no reliability data for the tests were presented, such explicit interpretations might be misleading and should have been omitted.

D1.1 Recommendation D1 applies to every score, subscore, or combination of scores whose interpretation is suggested. ESSENTIAL

Comment: It is particularly important to assess the reliability of scores which are to be recorded on permanent or cumulative pupil record cards. Part scores and subtest scores may be too unreliable to justify recording on such records. Reported reliability data for such scores should assist the user in making an appropriate decision.

D1.2 If differences between subtest scores are to be interpreted or if the plotting of a profile is suggested, the manual should report the reliability of these differences between scores. ESSENTIAL

D1.21 If the reliability of differences among subtest scores is low, the manual should caution the user against interpretations which assume reliable score differences. ESSENTIAL

Comment: The Watson-Glaser Critical Thinking Appraisal suggests that study of pupil performance on various types of items may enrich the interpretation. The manual adds this desirable caution: "For a relatively small number of items such indices and special scores would not have high statistical reliability, and hence attention should be paid only to extreme deviates. For this reason norms for these special scores are not given and they are suggested only as an aid in helping students."

This paragraph illustrates how a manual may conform to the spirit of the *Technical Recommendations* even when some form of data is not furnished in the manual. The statement would be improved if it were worded "such indices are probably unreliable" in the place of the present correct but euphemistic phrasing.

D1.3 The manual should report whether the error of measurement varies at different score levels. If there is significant change in the error of measurement from level to level, this fact should be properly interpreted. VERY DESIRABLE

Comment: In wide-range tests it is possible for the reliability of scores to vary over different portions of the score range. To report a single error of measurement may result in erroneous interpretations which may be serious for score levels for which the error of measurement is much larger than that reported.

D1.4 Reports of reliability studies should ordinarily be expressed in terms of the product-moment correlation coefficient. ESSENTIAL

Comment: The standard error of measurement is a useful adjunct in interpreting reliability coefficients, but it is not an alternative to them. Two tests, totally different in reliability, may have identical standard errors of measurement.

D2. The manual should avoid any implication that validity can be estimated on the basis of reliability measures alone. ESSENTIAL

Comment: Reliability is a necessary, but not a sufficient, condition for validity. For those types of validity—predictive, concurrent, and sometimes construct—which permit or require correlational evidence, it is not essential that supporting evidence of reliability be furnished. But for content validity and some kinds of construct validity, it is essential that descriptive analyses of the content or construct be supplemented by reliability coefficients.

D3. In reports of reliability, procedures and samples should be described sufficiently for the reader to judge whether the evidence applies to the persons and problems with which he is concerned. ES-SENTIAL

D3.1 Evidence of reliability should be obtained under conditions like those in which the author recommends that the test be used. VERY DESIRABLE

Comment: The maturity of the group, the variation in the group, and the attitude of the group toward the test should represent normal conditions of test use. If test scores are to be used over a range of ages, grades, and for both sexes, the reliability of the test should be determined by testing such groups.

D3.2 The reliability sample should be described in terms of any selective factors related to the variable being measured, usually including age, sex, and educational level. Number of cases of each type should be reported. ESSENTIAL

D3.3 Appropriate measures of central tendency and variability of the test scores of the reliability sample should be reported. ESSENTIAL

D3.31 If reliability coefficients are corrected for restriction of range, the nature of the correction should be made clear. The manual should also report the uncorrected coefficient, together with the standard deviation of the group tested and the standard deviation assumed for the corrected sample. In discussing such coefficients, emphasis should be placed on the one which refers to the degree of variation within which discrimination is normally required. ESSENTIAL

D3.4 When a test is ordinarily required to make discriminations within a single grade or other subclass of the total reliability sample, the reliability should be reported by a single grade or subclass, rather than for the sample as a whole. ESSENTIAL

Comment: The reliability coefficient reported for a single grade should be the median—or other proper statistical average—of the coefficients for that grade in a fair sample of different school systems. This is necessary in order to protect against possible bias. It is also desirable to present the full distribution of the coefficients obtained for each grade.

D3.5 If the manual implies that the use of some method other than the one actually used to determine reliability would have resulted in an appreciably higher coefficient, it should indicate specifically what other method might have been used and how much higher the coefficient could be expected to be with the use of that method. Evidence supporting this predicted increase in reliability should be presented. ESSENTIAL

Equivalence of Forms

D4. If two forms of a test are made available, with both forms intended for possible use with the same subjects, the correlation between forms and information as to the equivalence of scores on the two forms should be reported. If the necessary evidence is not provided, the manual should warn the reader against assuming comparability. ESSENTIAL

D4.1 Where the content of the test items can be described meaningfully, a comparative analysis of the forms should be furnished to show how similar they are. ESSENTIAL

Comment: The forms should be matched on the basis of item categories, not on the basis of individual items. These categories should cover all content relevant to the test. The two forms should represent different samples of items within each category. Artificially close similarity between forms, which could be attained by matching item for item, is not desirable because it hides real errors of measurement associated with content sampling.

Internal Consistency

D5. Evidence of internal consistency should be reported for any test or subtest unless correlation with an equivalent form is reported. ESSENTIAL

D6. Coefficients of internal consistency should be determined by the split-half method or methods of the Kuder-Richardson type, if these can properly be used on the data under examination. Any other measure of internal consistency which the author wishes to report in addition should be explained. ESSENTIAL

D6.1 For time-limit tests, split-half or analysis-of-variance coefficients should never be reported unless (*a*) the manual also reports evidence that speed of work has negligible influence on scores, (*b*) the coefficient is based on the correlation between parts administered under separate time limits, or (*c*) special experimental and computational procedures which rule out the influence of speed of work have been employed. ESSENTIAL

Comment: Evidence of accuracy of measurement for highly speeded tests is properly obtained by retesting or testing with independent equivalent forms. If better evidence is not available, it is appropriate to use lower-bound formulas designed for estimating the internal consistency of speeded tests to determine the minimum coefficient.

D6.2 If several questions within a test are so linked by content that the reaction to one question influences the reaction to another, the entire group should be treated as an "item" in applying the split-half or analysis-of-variance methods. ESSENTIAL

D6.3 If a test can be divided into sets of items of different content, internal consistency should be determined by procedures designed for such tests. VERY DESIRABLE

Comment: After the internal consistencies of the sets of items have been determined separately, as well as their intercorrelations, the Jackson-Ferguson "battery reliability" formula may be applied.

Stability

D7. The manual should indicate what degree of stability of scores may be expected if a test is repeated after time has elapsed. DESIRABLE

D7.1 When stability of scores is determined by administering the test to the same group at different times, the manual should report changes in mean score as well as the correlation between the two sets of scores. ES-SENTIAL

D7.11 In determining stability of scores by repeated testing, other precautions, such as giving alternate forms of the test, should be used to minimize recall of specific answers, especially if the time interval is not long enough to assure forgetting. DESIRABLE

E. ADMINISTRATION AND SCORING

E1. The directions for administration should be presented with sufficient clarity that the test user can duplicate the administrative conditions under which the norms and data on reliability and validity were obtained. ESSENTIAL

E1.1 The published directions should be complete enough so that people tested will understand the task in the way the author intended. ESSENTIAL

E1.2 If expansion or elaboration of instructions, giving of hints, etc., is permitted, the conditions for them should be clearly stated either in the form of general rules or by giving numerous examples or both. ESSENTIAL

Comment: The manual should specify how much freedom the examiner has to deviate from printed directions for test administration. It should point out critical matters, such as time limits and instructions on guessing, and it should explain the meaning of test questions which might reduce the validity of scores or norms.

E2. Where subjective processes enter into the scoring of the test, evidence on degree of agreement between independent scoring under operational conditions should be presented. If such evidence is not provided, the manual should draw attention to scoring variations as a possible source of errors of measurement. ESSENTIAL

E2.1 The bases for scoring and the procedure for training the scorers should be presented in sufficient detail to permit other scorers to reach the degree of agreement reported in studies of scorer agreement given in the manual. VERY DESIRABLE

Comment: Subjectivity enters, for example, in the scoring of completion tests, in the scoring of such performances as oral reading, and in the scoring of certain products such as handwriting, shorthand, and composition.

F. SCALES AND NORMS

F1. Scales used for reporting scores should be those which have been shown to increase the likelihood of accurate interpretation and emphasis by test interpreter and subject. ESSENTIAL

Comment: Scales in which test scores are reported are extremely varied. Raw scores are used. Relative scores are used. Scales purporting to represent equal intervals with respect to some external dimension (such as age) are used; and so on. It is unwise to discourage the development of new scaling methods by insisting on one form of reporting. On the other hand, many different systems are now used which have no logical advantage, one over the other. Recommendations that the number of systems now used be reduced to a few with which testers can become familiar are not intended to discourage the use of unique scales for special problems. Suggestions as to preferable scales for general reporting are not intended to restrict use of other scales in research studies.

F1.1 Norms on subtests or groups of test items should be reported only if data on the reliability of such subtests or groups of items are also reported. ESSENTIAL

Comment: The test user is justified in assuming that, when norms are given for a part of a test, the author implies the usefulness of them for interpreting pupil achievement. The reliability of such scores should be reported to support such uses.

F2. Where there is no compelling advantage to be obtained by reporting scores in some other form, the manual should report scores for defined groups in terms of percentile equivalents or normalized scores for defined groups. VERY DESIRABLE

F2.1 If grade norms are provided, tables for converting scores to percentiles (or standard scores) within each grade should also be provided. ESSENTIAL

Comment: At the high-school level, norms within courses, e.g., second-year Spanish, may be more appropriate than norms within grades.

F3. If scales are revised, new forms added, or other changes made, the revised manual should provide tables of equivalence between the new and the old. This is particularly important in cases where data are recorded on cumulative records. ESSENTIAL

F4. Standard scores obtained by transforming scores so that they have a normal distribution and a fixed mean and a standard deviation should in general be used in preference to other derived scores. However, for some tests there may be a substantial reason to choose some other type of derived score. Such reason should be stated in the manual. VERY DESIRABLE

Comment: Sometimes it is appropriate to adopt a special standard score scale in order to serve a particular purpose. For example, raw scores for tests in the Evaluation and Adjustment Series are converted to standard scores whose mean and standard deviation are those of the Terman-Mc-Nemar IQ's of the students in the standardizing sample for each test. This procedure is used to eliminate the effect of differences in the level and spread of ability in the various standardizing samples on the level and spread of standard scores for different tests in the series. The most widely used conventions are as follows: for a two-digit standard score, a mean of 50 and standard deviation of 10; for a one-digit standard score, a mean of 5 and a standard deviation of 2 (as in Stanines). The foregoing are proposed as ways of standardizing practice among test developers. It is expected that institutions with established systems, such as the College Board Scale, with a mean at 500, will continue to retain them as suited to their purposes.

F4.1 Where percentile scores are to be plotted on a profile sheet, the profile sheet should ordinarily be based on the normal probability scale. VERY DESIRABLE

F5. The manual should suggest appropriate emphasis on local norms. VERY DESIRABLE

Comment: Local norms furnish types of information different from that furnished by regional or national norms. They are more important for many uses of tests than are published norms. The Cooperative Dictionary Test manual precedes its presentation of norms with a discussion urging schools to prepare local norms and explaining their advantages over the published norms with respect to this test. Many achievement tests, clinical tests, and tests used for vocational guidance might well present a similar statement.

F6. Except where the primary use of a test is to compare individuals with their own local groups, or in the rare situation where preliminary standardization is not feasible, norms should be published at the time of release of the test for operational use. ESSENTIAL

Comment: Certain types of current events tests might illustrate a situation in which preliminary standardization is not feasible, but even in this area such a situation will rarely occur justifiably.

F7. Norms should report measures which will permit as sound interpretation as could be made from complete distributions. ESSENTIAL

F7.1 Unless these can readily be inferred from the table of norms, measures of central tendency and variability of each distribution should be given. ESSENTIAL

F7.2 When skewness is considerable or there are other important abnormalities in the standardization distribution, this fact should be called to the reader's attention. If complete distributions are not given, the areas beyond and between the common sigma points or a percentile table should be given. ESSENTIAL

F7.3 Conversion tables translating test scores into proficiency levels should be given when proficiency can be described on a meaningful absolute scale. VERY DESIRABLE

F8. The manual should describe the procedures followed in developing the test norms. ESSENTIAL

Comment: Such description should include the detailed method of deriving the norms, the bases for extrapolation of the norms, if any, the methods used to assure comparability of levels and of alternate forms, and the methods used to determine the comparability of revised and earlier forms.

F8.1 Norms should refer to defined populations which should be the groups to whom users of the test will ordinarily wish to compare the persons tested. ESSENTIAL

Comment: Tests designed for use with elementary-school children might well present norms by chronological age groups as well as by grade groups. Model age-grade groups are especially useful for reference, independent of local promotional policy.

F8.2 Norms should be based on a well-planned sample rather than on data collected primarily on the basis of availability. Where data are used on an "availability" basis of selection, information concerning their representativeness or possible bias should be reported. ESSENTIAL

F8.3 The manual should report the method of sampling within the population and should discuss any probable bias within the sample. ESSENTIAL

F8.4 If appreciable differences between groups exist, and if a person would ordinarily be compared with a subgroup rather than with a random sample of persons, separate norm tables should be provided in the manual for each group. ESSENTIAL

F8.5 Since conditions affecting test scores may be expected to change as time elapses, periodic review of norms is required. ESSENTIAL

F8.6 The description of the norm group should be sufficiently complete so that the user can judge whether his case falls within the population represented by the norm group. The description should include number of cases, classified by relevant variables such as age, sex, educational status, etc. ESSENTIAL

F8.7 The time and conditions under which normative data were obtained should be reported. The conditions of testing, including the purpose of the subjects in taking the test, should be reported. ESSENTIAL

F8.8 Norms for the several forms of a test should be based on data, not inferred, for instance, from parallelism of construction of the forms. ESSENTIAL

PUBLISHERS DIRECTORY
AND INDEX *

★ACORN Publishing Co., Rockville Centre, Long Island, N.Y.: 29-30, 43, 213, 408, 432-3, 509, 557, 582, 717-8, 960, 985, 1000, 1033-4, 1118, 1128, 1133, 1230, 1233, 1235, 1238, 1342, 1358, 1412, 1432, 1437-8, 1441, 1493, 1531, 1554, 1560, 1590, 1618, 1636, 1706, 1713, 1724-5, 1747-8, 1758, 1793, 1831, 1873, 1923; *out of print,* 2309, 2696

Addison-Wesley Publishing Co., Inc.: *out of print,* 2169

Administrative Research Associates, P.O. Box 1160, Chicago 90, Ill.: 1201, 1212

Allied Publishers, Inc., 645 Southeast Ankeny St., Portland 14, Ore.: 68

Ambco, Inc., 1222 West Washington Blvd., Los Angeles 7, Calif.: 1655-6

American Association for Health, Physical Education, and Recreation, 1201 16th St., N.W., Washington 6, D.C.: 1222

American Association for Jewish Education, 101 Fifth Ave., New York 3, N.Y.: 661

American Automobile Association, 1712 G St., N.W., Washington 6, D.C.: 1162, 1164-5, 1171, 2102-3

American Book Co.: *out of print,* 2347

American Chemical Society. See Examinations Committee, Division of Chemical Education, American Chemical Society.

American Council on Education, 1785 Massachusetts Ave., N.W., Washington 6, D.C.: 249, 1301. See also Veterans' Testing Service.

American Dental Association. See Council on Dental Education, American Dental Association.

American Education Press, Inc.: *out of print,* 2112

American Film Registry, Division of Robert H. Redfield, Inc., 1020 South Wabash Ave., Chicago 5, Ill.: 1139

American Foundation for the Blind, Inc., 15 West 16th St., New York 11, N.Y.: 220

American Guidance Service, Inc., 720 Washington Ave., S.E., Minneapolis 14, Minn.: 785, 905, 988, 1300, 1473, 1486

American Institute of Certified Public Accountants. See Committee on Personnel Testing, American Institute of Certified Public Accountants.

American Language Center, American University. See American University Language Center.

American Library Association, Publishing Department, 50 East Huron St., Chicago 11, Ill.: 2022

American Optical Co., Vision Park, Southbridge, Mass.: 1678-80; *out of print,* 2785

American Orthopsychiatric Association, Inc., 1790 Broadway, New York 19, N.Y.: 327

American Public Health Association, Inc.: *out of print,* 2598

American Transit Association, 355 Lexington Ave., New York 17, N.Y.: 2100

American University Language Center, Washington 16, D.C.: 623, 625, 629

Ann Arbor Press: *out of print,* 2575

Applezweig (Mortimer H.), Southern Illinois University, Carbondale, Ill.: 114, 239

Aptitude Associates, Merrifield, Va.: 160, 969, 1039; *out of print,* 2270, 2327, 2457, 2929

Aptitude Test Service, Box 239, Swarthmore, Pa.: 82, 92, 1839, 2066; *out of print,* 2428

Associated Personnel Technicians, Inc., 118 South Main St., Wichita 2, Kan.: 67, 715, 1819, 1896, 1975

Associated Publishers, 363 State St., Los Altos, Calif.: 130

Association of Georgia Colleges: *out of print,* 2690, 2694

Association Press, 291 Broadway, New York 7, N.Y.: 306; *out of print,* 2213

Atlantic Refining Co., 260 South Broad St., Philadelphia 1, Pa.: 73

Audiometer Sales Corporation: *out of print,* 2778

Audivox, Inc.: *out of print,* 2780

★Australian Council for Educational Research, 369 Lonsdale St., Melbourne C.1, Victoria, Australia: 75, 342, 398, 531-2, 560, 631, 706-14, 721, 754, 775, 818, 831, 992, 1014, 1016, 1058, 1151,

* References are to test entry numbers, not to page numbers. Stars indicate publishers issuing catalogs—as distinct from price lists—devoted entirely or in large part to tests. The words "out of print" precede references to out of print tests. Addressees are not included for publishers represented only by out of print tests.

1387-8, 1436, 1471, 1495, 1799, 1829-9, 1886, 1912-3, 1932, 1939, 1947; *out of print,* 2420a, 2421-2, 2752. See also Distributors Directory.

Avent (Joseph E.) : *out of print,* 2349

BADGER Tests Co., Ltd., Liverpool House, 15-17 Eldon St., London E.C. 2, England: 360-1

Baird (A. H.), Instrument Maker, 33-39 Lothian St., Edinburgh 1, Scotland: 906

Baisden (Joyce B.), 14460 Dunbar Place, Sherman Oaks, Calif.: 394

Banks Upshaw & Co., 703 Browder St., Dallas 1, Tex.: 692

Barnes (A. S.) & Co.: *out of print,* 2599, 2611, 2781

Bausch & Lomb Inc., Rochester 2, N.Y.: 1697-8

Baxter Foundation for Research in Education, Inc.: *out of print,* 2145. (No reply has been received to inquiries sent to this publisher in 1961.—Editor)

Bealls (J. & P.) Ltd., Gallowgate, Newcastle Upon Tyne, England: 377

Beaver Country Day School: *out of print,* 2146

Beecher (Dwight E.) : *out of print,* 2579, 2586

Benton Review Publishing Co., Inc., Fowler, Ind.: 479-80, 1012, 1130, 1593, 1650, 1780-1, 1814; *out of print,* 2811

Bernberg (Raymond E.), West Coast Missile and Surface Radar Division, Radio Corporation of America, 8500 Balboa Blvd., Van Nuys, Calif.: 242

Better Reading Program, Inc., 230 East Ohio St., Chicago 11, Ill.: 1475

Betts (G. L.), 1035 Reed Ave., Reedley, Calif.: 214, 801

Bigelow (Burton) Organization. See Edwin G. Flemming.

Blackwell Scientific Publications, Ltd., 24-25 Broad St., Oxford, England: 362

Blumenthal (Sidney) & Co., Inc.: *out of print,* 2784. (No reply has been received to inquiries sent to this publisher in 1961.—Editor)

Bobbs-Merrill Co., Inc., 1720 East 38th St., Indianapolis 6, Ind.: 191, 723a, 733. See also C. A. Gregory Co.; and Public School Publishing Co.

Bogardus (Emory S.) : *out of print,* 2214

Book-A-Day Series: *out of print,* 2304. (No reply has been received to inquiries sent to this publisher in 1961. —Editor)

Book Society of Canada Ltd., 4386 Sheppard Ave., Agincourt, Ontario, Canada: 1506

Borgatta (Edgar F.), University of Wisconsin, Madison 6, Wis.: 364

Briggs (Peter F.), University of Minnesota, Minneapolis 14, Minn.: 217

Brigham Young University. See University Press, Brigham Young University.

Brooks (A. M.) Co. See Ambco, Inc.

Brown (Margaret) : *out of print,* 2572

★Bruce (Martin M.), 71 Hanson Lane, New Rochelle, N.Y.: 108, 254, 307, 561, 936, 1141, 1953, 1990, 1992, 2043, 2061, 2064, 2096

Bruce Publishing Co., 400 North Broadway, Milwaukee 1, Wis.: 491, 1332; *out of print,* 2633-4

Bryan (Roy C.) : *out of print,* 2583-4

Brye (Edvin), 7914 South Oglesby Ave., Chicago 17, Ill.: 1150

Burdock (E. I.), Biometrics Research, State of New York Department of Mental Hygiene, 722 West 168th St., New York 32, N.Y.: 116

Bureau of Cooperative Research and Field Service, Indiana University. See Indiana University Bookstore.

★Bureau of Educational Measurements, Kansas State Teachers College, Emporia, Kan.: 13, 50, 52, 54, 63-4, 66, 71, 88, 94, 127, 280, 322, 402, 423, 441, 485, 488, 494, 497, 508, 536, 541, 550, 553, 570, 576, 579, 596, 610, 638, 649, 654, 665, 669, 671-3, 682, 695-6, 699, 726-7, 737, 846, 940, 952, 961, 973, 989, 996, 1002, 1023, 1060, 1064-5, 1079, 1085, 1102, 1113, 1121, 1134, 1143, 1181, 1213, 1215, 1224, 1228-9, 1239, 1249, 1256, 1258, 1261, 1269, 1278, 1280, 1282, 1297, 1299, 1327, 1335, 1351, 1404, 1406, 1414, 1429, 1520, 1553, 1555, 1565, 1578, 1595, 1605, 1623, 1635, 1641, 1708, 1720-1, 1730, 1739, 1744-5, 1749, 1751-3, 1760, 1770, 1772-6, 1785, 1788, 1797, 1800, 1806-7, 1817-8, 2021; *out of print,* 2132, 2135, 2156, 2245, 2248, 2294, 2370, 2373-4, 2386, 2414, 2417, 2419, 2498, 2608, 2613, 2635, 2791, 2795, 2800, 2808, 2810, 2819, 2832, 2848, 2855, 2868, 2874-5, 2881

Bureau of Educational Reference and Research, University of Michigan: *out of print,* 2682, 2891

Bureau of Educational Research, University of North Carolina: *out of print,* 2114

★Bureau of Educational Research and Service, State University of Iowa, Iowa City, Iowa: 23, 442, 444-6, 448, 517, 521, 529, 539-40, 546, 593, 605-6, 615, 646, 684, 694, 957-8, 1004, 1006, 1109-10, 1354, 1567, 1620-1, 1638-9, 2009; *out of print,* 2265-6, 2303, 2402, 2492, 2538, 2723, 2739, 2773, 2805, 2809, 2850-1, 2873

Bureau of Personnel Research, Inc. See Personnel Research, Inc.

★Bureau of Publications, Teachers College, Columbia University, New York 27, N.Y.: 28, 243, 384, 537, 614, 803, 1184, 1211, 1407-10, 1470, 1476, 1495, 1527, 1872; *out of print,* 2152, 2154,

2173, 2200, 2218, 2222, 2224, 2230-2, 2337, 2341, 2351, 2356, 2440, 2445, 2454, 2519, 2532, 2547, 2596-7, 2605-6, 2675, 2772, 2797
Bureau of Tests, 1108 North Sycamore St., North Manchester, Ind.: 62, 86, 422, 459, 472, 475, 670, 683, 997, 1010, 1046, 1116, 1126, 1135, 1173, 1236, 1273, 1276, 1355, 1582, 1617, 1645, 1738, 1787, 1791, 1815; *out of print,* 2285, 2296, 2479, 2636, 2877
Burgess Cellulose Co. See Grade-O-Mat Division, Burgess Cellulose Co.
Burke (Charles), Box 494, Westport, Conn.: 1857, 1860
Butler (Edward), 1355 Hunter Ave., Columbus 1, Ohio: 212

C.P.S. Co., P.O. Box 83, Larchmont, N.Y.: 329, 388
★California Test Bureau, Del Monte Research Park, Monterey, Calif.: 4-7, 115, 119, 124, 204, 222, 382, 405-6, 473, 476, 559, 594, 597, 608, 729-32, 757, 858, 976, 1011, 1043-4, 1054, 1067-9, 1076, 1091, 1111, 1146, 1234, 1344, 1368, 1381, 1394-5, 1418-9, 1455, 1498, 1522, 1575-6, 1594, 1654, 1750, 1784, 1824, 1853, 1878, 1884, 1891, 1922, 1936, 1943-5; *out of print,* 2178, 2269, 2662, 2667, 2669-70, 2705, 2725, 2838
Campus Stores, State University of Iowa, Iowa City, Iowa: 326
Carlile (A. B.), 330 West 44th St., Indianapolis 8, Ind.: 247, 318
Carlisle (A.) & Co., 645 Harrison St., San Francisco 7, Calif.: 1303
Casanova (Teobaldo): *out of print,* 2558
Cassel (Russell N.), 501 North Poppy St., Lompoc, Calif.: 128, 214, 1303a, 2075
Catholic University of America. See Program of Affiliation, Catholic University of America.
Catholic University of America Press, 620 Michigan Ave., N.E., Washington 17, D.C.: 303b; *out of print,* 2469
★Center for Psychological Service, 1835 Eye St., N.W., Washington 6, D.C.: 198, 291, 1183, 1208, 2032, 2073; *out of print,* 2354, 2438, 2595
Center for Research in Child Development, Catholic University of America. See Catholic University of America Press.
Center for Safety Education, New York University, New York 3, N.Y.: 1163, 1166-7, 1169, 1174-5; *out of print,* 2562-5, 2568
Century School Crafts, 723 Sixth St., N.E., Faribault, Minn.: 1214
Central Institute for the Deaf, 818 South Kingshighway, St. Louis 10, Mo.: 908
Cerebral Palsy Review, Institute of Logopedics, Inc., 2400 Jardine Drive, Wichita 19, Kan.: 524a

Chandler Publishing Co., 660 Market St., San Francisco 4, Calif.: 565a
Chapple (E. D.) Co., Inc., Noroton, Conn.: 197
Character Research Association, 5937 Enright Ave., St. Louis 12, Mo.: 122, 1206
Chatto & Windus Ltd., 40-42 William IV St., London W.C.2, England: 1452
Child Development Laboratories, University of Michigan, Ann Arbor, Mich.: 105
Child Development Publications of the Society for Research in Child Development, Inc., Purdue University, Lafayette, Ind.: 357
Chronicle Guidance Publications, Inc., Moravia, N.Y.: 1310
Civil Service Assembly. See Public Personnel Association.
Clarke, Irwin & Co., Ltd.: *out of print,* 2203, 2520. See also Distributors Directory.
Clarke (Walter V.) Associates, Inc., 324 Waterman Ave., East Providence 14, R.I.: 101
College Entrance Examination Board, 425 West 117th St., New York 27, N.Y.: 409, 480a, 481, 632-4, 651-3, 659-60, 662-3, 666-7, 685, 687-9, 738, 828, 941-3, 1345-6, 1586-7, 1612-3, 1629-31, 1709, 1761-2; *out of print,* 2279, 2289, 2430, 2450, 2899, 2931
College of Home Economics, Pennsylvania State University, University Park, Pa.: 1266
Color Institute, P.O. Box 185, Belmont 78, Mass.: 330
Colorado State College of Education: *out of print,* 2191
Columbia University. See Bureau of Publications; and Institute of Psychological Research; *out of print,* see also Institute of School Experimentation.
Committee on Diagnostic Reading Tests, Inc., Mountain Home, N.C.: 1403
Committee on Personnel Testing, American Institute of Certified Public Accountants, 21 Audubon Ave., New York 32, N.Y.: 1994-5
Committee on Publications, Harvard Graduate School of Education: *out of print,* 2233
Committee on State-Wide Placement, Iowa Colleges Conference on English, Iowa State University: *out of print,* 2254
Concordia Publishing House, 3558 South Jefferson Ave., St. Louis 18, Mo.: 258, 1323, 1333, 1334
★Consulting Psychologists Press, Inc., 577 College Ave., Palo Alto, Calif.: 103, 123, 131, 180, 182, 246, 278, 282, 292, 294, 305, 319, 724, 1290a, 1481, 1537, 1542, 1887-8, 1991, 2008
Cooper Union for the Advancement of

Science and Art, Cooper Square, New York 3, N.Y.: 587

Cooperative Book Store. See O.S.C. Cooperative Association.

Cooperative Bureau of Educational Research: *out of print*, 2319, 2481, 2482, 2528, 2648, 2650, 2700, 2702, 2709, 2755, 2763, 2789, 2794

Cooperative Intercollegiate Examination Program, 22 East 54th St., New York 22, N.Y.: 1348

Cooperative Psychological Test Distributors, 2366 University Station, Gainesville, Fla.: 100

★Cooperative Test Division, Educational Testing Service, Princeton, N.J.: 8-9, 39, 413-4, 424, 482-3, 493, 563, 635-6, 668, 690, 722-3, 743, 944-7, 974, 990-1, 1103-4, 1132, 1218, 1284, 1359, 1436, 1449, 1523, 1548-50, 1573, 1588, 1614, 1632, 1649, 1710-1, 1719, 1763-6, 1801, 2006; *out of print*, 2107, 2165, 2171, 2175, 2287, 2290-1, 2301-2, 2358, 2361-2, 2379, 2381-2, 2394, 2398, 2407-8, 2475-7, 2483, 2486, 2503, 2577, 2607, 2614-7, 2624, 2718, 2726, 2732-4, 2748, 2756, 2766, 2788, 2796, 2801-4, 2806, 2836-7, 2867

Cornell University Medical College, c/o Keeve Brodman, Cornell-New York Hospital Center, Room F636, 525 East 68th St., New York 21, N.Y.: 136, 1227

Cottrell (D. P.): *out of print*, 2591

Council on Dental Education, American Dental Association, 222 East Superior St., Chicago 11, Ill.: 1996

Courtis Standard Research Tests: *out of print*, 2504

Cowell (Charles C.), Department of Physical Education for Men, Purdue University, Lafayette, Ind.: 138-9

Crabtree (Margaret), 10133 Bassoon, Houston 25, Tex.: 524

Crowley, Milner & Co.: *out of print*, 2523

Curriculum Bulletin, School of Education, University of Oregon, Eugene, Ore.: 150, 484, 522, 1540, 1628

DANE (M. W. A.): *out of print*, 2916

Dartnell Corporation, 4660 Ravenswood Ave., Chicago 40, Ill.: 1956, 1967, 1980-1, 2101

Data Processing Systems & Sales Department, National Cash Register Co., Dayton 9, Ohio: 2015

Davis (F. A.) Co.: *out of print*, 2507-11

Degering (Ed. F.), 26 Robinhood Road, Natick, Mass.: 1616

Dembar Publications, Inc.: *out of print*, 2571

Dent (J. M.) & Sons (Canada) Ltd., 100 Scarsdale Road, Don Mills, Ontario, Canada: 637, 1178

DePalma (Nicholas), Davidson County Hospital, Nashville 8, Tenn.: 373

Department of Education, Archdiocese of Milwaukee: *out of print*, 2913, 2926

Department of Educational Research, Ontario College of Education, University of Toronto, 371 Bloor St., West, Toronto 5, Ontario, Canada: 17-8, 575, 770, 834, 1032, 1055, 1061, 1077, 1092, 1149, 1349, 1390, 1488, 1496; *out of print*, 2369, 2371-2, 2823, 2825, 2835

Department of Physical Education for Women, State University of Iowa, Iowa City, Iowa: 1253; *out of print*, 2604

Department of Psychiatry, School of Medicine, University of Maryland, Baltimore, Md.: 369

Department of Psychological Testing, DePaul University, 25 East Jackson Blvd., Chicago 4, Ill.: 1397

Department of Public Services, General Mills, Inc.: *out of print*, 2626

DePaul University. See Department of Psychological Testing, DePaul University.

Devereaux Foundation, Devon, Pa.: 373

Diebold (John) & Associates, Inc., 40 Wall St., New York 5, N.Y.: 2018

Division of Educational Reference, Purdue University: *in print*, see University Book Store; *out of print*, 2368, 2585, 2627, 2911

Division of Psychiatry, Medical School, University of Minnesota, Minneapolis, Minn.: 263

Division of Research, Northwestern University: *in print*, see Garrett Biblical Institute; *out of print*, 2150, 2167, 2183

Dominion (Joseph): *out of print*, 2460

Dow Chemical Co., Midland Division, Midland, Mich.: 2016

Draycon (D.), Wentsland House, Pontypool, Monmouth, England: 1915

Drew (H. & W. B.) Co., Jacksonville 1, Fla.: 1305

Dunford (R. E.): *out of print*, 2907

EDISON (Thomas A.) Industries: *out of print*, 2128

Edmiston (R. W.), Miami University, Oxford, Ohio: 1524, 1668, 1863; *out of print*, 2888

Education-Industry Service, 1225 East 60th St., Chicago 37, Ill.: 145a, 303a, 919a, 924a, 931a, 1918, 1926, 1935, 1951, 1998

Educational Books, 19 Park Ave., Lower Hutt, New Zealand: 818, 1015, 1389, 1489, 1500. See also Distributors Directory.

Educational Development Laboratories, Inc., 75 Prospect St., Huntington, N.Y.: 1477, 1482

Educational Division, Reader's Digest Services, Inc., Pleasantville, N.Y.: 573

Educational Records Bureau, 21 Audubon Ave., New York 32, N.Y.: 543, 777, 949, 1041, 1386, 1539, 1589, 1615, 1633

Educational Services, 1730 Eye St., N.W., Washington 6, D.C.: 619

★Educational Test Bureau, 720 Washington Ave., S.E., Minneapolis, Minn.: 10, 49, 56, 87, 240, 313-4, 415, 438, 449, 452, 490, 535, 602, 642, 656, 677, 702, 774, 899, 911, 950, 953, 980, 995, 1019, 1042, 1049, 1117, 1127, 1136, 1154, 1188, 1275, 1316, 1319, 1357, 1379, 1396, 1426, 1466, 1499, 1515, 1530, 1551, 1563, 1583, 1609, 1646, 1670, 1722-3, 1741, 1743, 1767, 1782-3, 1832, 1876, 1904-5, 1908, 1930, 1954, 2079; *out of print*, 48, 55, 426, 641, 655, 676, 701, 954, 979, 994, 1115, 1125, 1341, 1562, 1581, 1608, 1644, 1714, 1742, 1756, 1777, 2116, 2286, 2331, 2443, 2455, 2471, 2494, 2530, 2543, 2676, 2691-3, 2715, 2812, 2830, 2849, 2859, 2897

★Educational Testing Service, Princeton, N.J.: 15, 38, 46, 118, 169, 226, 230, 271, 409, 480a, 481, 498-9, 504, 523, 585-6, 600, 607, 617, 620, 632-4, 644-5, 648, 651-3, 658-60, 662-4, 666-7, 685-9, 693, 698, 705, 738, 764, 828, 851, 941-3, 956, 965-6, 1186, 1192, 1202, 1205, 1244-5, 1268, 1277, 1279, 1293-4, 1296, 1345-6, 1348, 1353, 1360, 1546-7, 1568, 1577, 1586-7, 1591, 1612-3, 1619, 1626-7, 1629-31, 1637, 1709, 1726-7, 1737, 1761-2, 1771, 1804, 1816, 1952, 2003, 2010; *out of print*, 2109-10, 2279, 2289, 2340, 2388, 2430, 2450, 2551, 2621, 2899, 2931. See also Cooperative Test Division.

Educators Publishing Co., 97 Hodge Ave., Buffalo 22, N.Y.: 1209

Edwards Brothers, Inc.: *out of print*, 2201, 2425, 2518

8CRT, Box 31, Gracie Station, New York 28, N.Y.: 336

Employers' Tests and Services Associates, 120 Detzel Place, Cincinnati 19, Ohio: 1182, 1821

English Language Institute, University of Michigan, Ann Arbor, Mich.: 621, 624, 626-8

Essay Press, P.O. Box 5, Planetarium Station, New York 24, N.Y.: 1478

Evaluation Division, Bureau of Educational Research, Ohio State University: *out of print*, 2236

Evaluation in the Eight Year Study, Progressive Education Association: *out of print*, 2149, 2172, 2174, 2202, 2207-8, 2217, 2282, 2284, 2288, 2305-8, 2311, 2344, 2697, 2701, 2703-4, 2706-7, 2712, 2716-7, 2727-8, 2730, 2742, 2764

Evans Brothers Ltd.: *out of print*, 2649

★Examinations Committee, Division of Chemical Education, American Chemical Society, University of South Florida, Tampa, Fla.: 1596-1603, 1624

Executive Analysis Corporation, 76

Beaver St., New York 5, N.Y.: 183, 1870

Expression Co., Magnolia, Mass.: 527-8, 1664

Extra-Curricular Publishing Co.: *out of print*, 2576

FAMILY Life Publications, Inc., P.O. Box 6725, College Station, Durham, N.C.: 290, 1285-6, 1289-91

Federation of Societies for Paint Technology, 121 South Broad St., Philadelphia 7, Pa.: 1692

Fels Research Institute, Antioch College, Yellow Springs, Ohio: 158

Fetler (Daniel), School of Commerce, Accounts, and Finance, New York University, Washington Square, New York 3, N.Y.: 300

Fischer (Carl), Inc., 56-62 Cooper Square, New York 3, N.Y.: 601, 603

Flemming (Edwin G.), 100 Fifth Ave., New York 11, N.Y.: 2052, 2076

Follett's Michigan Book Store, Inc., 322 South State St., Ann Arbor, Mich.: 621, 624, 626-8

Freeman Technical Associates, 1206 Benjamin Franklin Drive, Sarasota, Fla.: 1689-91

Fritz (Martin F.), Iowa State University, Ames, Iowa: 257

GALLAGHER (Ralph), 613 North Mountain Ave., Bound Brook, N.J.: 170

Galloway (June P.), Woman's College, University of North Carolina, Greensboro, N.C.: 1223

Galton Laboratory, University College, Gower St., London W.C.1, England: 819

Garrard Press, 510-524 North Hickory St., Champaign, Ill.: 1463; *out of print*, 2137

Garrett Biblical Institute, Northwestern University, Evanston, Ill.: 1325-6

General Mills, Inc. See Department of Public Services, General Mills, Inc.

★Gibson (Robert) & Sons (Glasgow), Ltd., 45 Queen St., Glasgow, Scotland: 137, 418-9, 542, 744-5, 779-80, 811, 838, 1050-1, 1066, 1416; *out of print*, 2342, 2352, 2434, 2554, 2722, 2724, 2817

Ginn & Co., Statler Bldg., Park Square, Boston 17, Mass.: 567, 571

Gough (Harrison G.), Institute of Personality Assessment and Research, University of California, Berkeley 4, Calif.: 102, 251, 562, 1298, 1337, 1960, 2012, 2014, 2017, 2026

Government Printer, Colony of Fiji: *out of print*, 2432

Government Printer, Kenya Colony: *out of print*, 2433

Holst Printing Co.: *out of print,* 2787
Holt, Rinehart & Winston, Inc., 1010 Arch St., Philadelphia 7, Pa.: 1080
★Houghton Mifflin Co., 2 Park St., Boston 7, Mass.: 22, 24, 99, 266, 299, 404, 407, 457-8, 467, 771-2, 787, 902, 909-10, 1038, 1045, 1189, 1424-5, 1427, 1431, 1450, 1474, 1497, 1502, 1544; *out of print,* 2244, 2274, 2316, 2429, 2553, 2680
★Huber (Hans), Marktgasse 9, Berne, Switzerland: 373, 385, 396. See also Distributors Directory.
Human Engineering Laboratory. See Johnson O'Connor Research Foundation Inc.
Humm Personnel Consultants, P.O. Box 15433 Del Valle Station, Los Angeles 15, Calif.: 185, 2057

INDIANA University. See Psychology Department, Indiana University.
Indiana University Bookstore, Memorial Union Bldg., Bloomington, Ind.: 1240
Industrial Psychological Laboratory, Box 718, Sparta, N.J.: 1682
Industrial Relations Center, University of Chicago, 1225 East 60th St., Chicago 37, Ill.: 1959, 1965, 2007, 2045, 2062. See also Education-Industry Service.
★Industrial Psychology, Inc., 515 Madison Ave., New York 22, N.Y.: 189, 194, 289, 1367, 1976, 1982, 1987
Inor Publishing Co.: *out of print,* 2582. (No reply has been received to inquiries sent to this publisher in 1961.—Editor)
★Institut de Recherches psychologiques, 10314 St. Lawrence Blvd., Montreal 12, Quebec, Canada: 308. See also Distributors Directory.
Institut pédagogique Saint-Georges, 2101 Maplewood Ave., Montreal 26, Quebec, Canada: 303. See also Distributors Directory.
★Institute for Personality and Ability Testing, 1602 Coronado Drive, Champaign, Ill.: 187-94, 228, 231, 234-5, 279, 289, 733
Institute of Applied Art Ltd.: *out of print,* 2336, 2458
Institute of Living, 200 Retreat Ave., Hartford 2, Conn.: 371
Institute of Psychological Research [Canada]. See Institut de Recherches psychologiques.
Institute of Psychological Research, Teachers College, Columbia University, New York 27, N.Y.: 581
Institute of Public Safety, Pennsylvania State University, University Park, Pa.: 1171, 2101-3
Institute of School Experimentation, Teachers College, Columbia University: *out of print:* 2141, 2155
International Business Machines Corporation, 112 East Post Road, White Plains, N.Y.: 1153, 2025

International Textbook Co.: *out of print,* 2343
Interstate Printers & Publishers, Inc., Jackson at Van Buren, Danville, Ill.: 1199
Iowa State University. See Committee on State-Wide Placement, Iowa Colleges Conference on English, Iowa State University.
Iowa State University Press, Ames, Iowa: 1168, 1172, 1271, 2005

JEWISH Education Committee of New York, Inc., 426 West 58th St., New York 19, N.Y.: *in print,* see Jewish Education Committee Press; *out of print,* 2390-3, 2653-6, 2658
Jewish Education Committee Press, 426 West 58th St., New York 19, N.Y.: 1322
Joël (Walther): *out of print,* 2148, 2189
Johns Hopkins Press, Baltimore 18, Md.: 592
Joint Committee on Tests. See United Business Education Association.
Joint Council on Economic Education, 2 West 46th St., New York 36, N.Y.: 1740
Jones Teaching Aids, 3442 Avenue C, Council Bluffs, Iowa: 205
Journal of Clinical Psychology, 5 Pearl St., Brandon, Vt.: 351
Jung (C. G.) Educational Center, 5 Chelsea Place, Houston 6, Tex.: 376
Jurgensen (Clifford E.): *out of print,* 2138, 2177

KANSAS State Teachers College. See Bureau of Educational Measurements.
Kentucky Cooperative Counseling and Testing Service, University of Kentucky, Lexington, Ky.: 781
Kessler (Sydney), 4849 Van Nuys Blvd., Suite 211, Sherman Oaks, Calif.: 207, 359
Keystone View Co., Meadville, Pa.: 1652, 1693-4, 1700
Kilander (H. Frederick), 33 Colonial Terrace, East Orange, N.J.: 1242, 1248, 1274, 1288
Knauber (Alma Jordan), 9871 Lorelei Drive, Cincinnati 31, Ohio: 590-1
Krout (Maurice H.). See Johanna Krout Tabin.

LA RUE Printing Co., 906 Baltimore Ave., Kansas City 6, Mo.: 245
Lafayette Instrument Co., North 26th St. and 52 By-Pass, Lafayette, Ind.: 926, 1674, 1676, 1909, 1938
Laidlaw Brothers: *out of print,* 2106
Landis (R. H.): *out of print,* 2630
Language Research Associates, 950 East 59th St., Box 95, Chicago 37, Ill.: 1657

Lea & Febiger: *out of print, 2600*

Leach (Richard H.), Duke University, Durham, N.C.: 1803

Leonard (Hal) Music, Inc., 64 East Second St., Winona, Minn.: 612

Lewis (H. K.) & Co. Ltd., 136 Gower St., London W.C.1., England: 331, 793, 831, 883, 1703; *out of print, 2779*

Life Insurance Agency Management Association, 170 Sigourney St., Hartford 5, Conn.: 2042, 2044, 2049, 2054, 2056, 2063; *out of print, 2946*

Liverant (Shephard), Ohio State University, Columbus 10, Ohio: 162

Livingstone (E. & S.) Ltd., 15-17 Teviot Place, Edinburgh 1, Scotland: 1315

Lockwood (Crosby) & Son Ltd., 26 Old Brompton Road, London S.W.7, England: 759

Logos Press, Box 273, Cooper Station, New York 3, N.Y.: 366

Long's College Book Co., 1836 North High St., Columbus 1, Ohio: 1696, 1704

Loyola University Press, 3441 North Ashland Ave., Chicago 13, Ill.: 1324, 1328-9; *out of print, 2657*

Lufburrow (N. A.): *out of print, 2885, 2887, 2894*

Lynchburg State Colony. See Steward's Office, Lynchburg State Colony.

Lyons & Carnahan, 223-225 South Main St., Wilkes-Barre, Pa.: 465-6, 1401, 1479; *out of print, 2330*

MACDONALD (Edward): *out of print, 2612*

McFarland (Ross A.), School of Public Health, Harvard University, 1 Shattuck St., Boston 15, Mass.: 235b

McGraw-Hill Book Co., Inc., 330 West 42nd St., New York 36, N.Y.: 109

McHale (Kathryn): *out of print, 2896*

McIntosh (Thelma A.), University of Hawaii, Honolulu 14, Hawaii: 1194

McKnight & McKnight Publishing Co., Bloomington, Ill.: 1216, 1827, 1859; *out of print, 2567, 2631, 2790, 2816, 2923*

Macmillan & Co. Ltd., St. Martin's St., London W.C.2, England: 1487

Macmillan Co.: *out of print, 2157, 2162*

McNamara (W. J.), Applied Personnel Research, International Business Machines Corporation, 590 Madison Ave., New York 22, N.Y.: 2025a

McQuaig Institute of Executive Training, Suite 1739, Hotel Statler-Hilton, Buffalo 2, N.Y.: 1986

Maico Electronics, Inc., 21 North Third St., Minneapolis 1, Minn.: 1659-60

Maller (J. B.): *out of print, 2161, 2197, 2215*

Management Research Associates, 185 North Wabash Ave., Chicago 1, Ill.: 1158, 1203

★Management Service Co., Spruce and College Sts., Asheville, N.C.: 79, 580, 728, 861, 1833, 1855, 1880, 1897, 1924, 2055; *out of print, 2170, 2898, 2904, 2947*

Marietta Apparatus Co., 118 Maple St., Marietta, Ohio: 1674, 1676, 1902, 1928-9

Martin (Owen) Pty. Ltd., Gardner Ave., French's Forest, New South Wales, Australia: 1088

Martin Publishing Co., Box 1012, San Diego 12, Calif.: 1840, 1900

Mason (Clarence E.), Jr., Philadelphia College of Bible, 1800 Arch St., Philadelphia 3, Pa.: 1331

Massachusetts Department of Public Health, Division of Maternal and Child Health Services, 88 Broad St., Boston 10, Mass.: 1661

Measurement Research Center, Inc., P.O. Box 30, Iowa City, Iowa: 1157

Meed Scientific Apparatus Co.: *out of print, 2782.* (No reply has been received to inquiries sent to this publisher in 1961.—Editor)

Mellenbruch (P. L.), University of Kentucky, Lexington, Ky.: 1901

Mellon (Mary Conover) Foundation, Vassar College, Poughkeepsie, N.Y.: 312

Merrill (Charles E.) Books, Inc., 1300 Alum Creek Drive, Columbus 16, Ohio: 1180

Merrill-Palmer Institute, 71 East Ferry Ave., Detroit 2, Mich.: 1287, 1312; *out of print, 2195-6, 2350*

Methuen & Co. Ltd., 36 Essex St., Strand, London W.C.2, England: 386, 809, 892

Michael (R. E.): *out of print, 2166*

Miles (Mrs. Lester F.): *out of print, 2921.*

Mills Center, Inc., 1512 East Broward Blvd., Ft. Lauderdale, Fla.: 1472

Mills Music, Inc., 1619 Broadway, New York 19, N.Y.: 604; *out of print, 2345*

Missouri Educational Test Co.: *out of print, 2901, 2903, 2905, 2942*

Modern Language Association of America, 6 Washington Square, North, New York, N.Y.: 617, 648, 658, 664, 686, 698

Moore (B. V.), University of Miami, Coral Gables 46, Fla.: 1028

Moore (Joseph E.) & Associates, 4406 Jett Road, N.W., Atlanta 5, Ga.: 1653

Mooseheart Laboratory for Child Research, Mooseheart, Ill.: 323

Morningside College, Sioux City 6, Iowa: 1195

Morrison (James H.), 6415 West 83rd St., Overland Park, Kan.: 304

Mount Holyoke College. See Psychological Laboratory, Mount Holyoke College.

Munsell Color Co., Inc., 2441 North Calvert St., Baltimore 18, Md.: 1681, 1688

NEA SERVICE, Inc., 1200 West Third St., Cleveland 13, Ohio: 1251

Nash (N.), Great Eastern Lumber Co.,

Inc., 2315 Broadway, New York 24, N.Y.: 2024

National Association of Secondary-School Principals, 1201 16th St., N.W., Washington 6, D.C.: 248, 1304, 1311, 1314, 1318, 1988

National Bureau of Casualty and Surety Underwriters: *out of print,* 2569

National Bureau of Educational and Social Research, Department of Education, Arts and Science, Pretoria, Union of South Africa: 104, 800, 802, 1052, 1073, 1370, 1451, 1825

National Cash Register Co. See Data Processing Systems & Sales Department, National Cash Register Co.

National Council of Teachers of English, 508 South Sixth St., Champaign, Ill.: 1464

National Foremen's Institute, Inc., 100 Garfield Ave., New London, Conn.: 1969, 2089

★National Foundation for Educational Research in England and Wales, 79 Wimpole St., London W.1, England: 142, 337, 429, 431, 434-5, 613, 761, 795, 804, 825, 830, 850, 863, 867, 869-70, 876, 886, 904, 931, 967-8, 1027, 1035, 1063, 1095, 1372, 1448, 1667, 1701, 1834, 1941. See also Distributors Directory.

National Institute for Personnel Research, South African Council for Scientific and Industrial Research, P.O. Box 10319, Johannesburg, Union of South Africa: 236, 450-1, 762, 791-2, 913, 1037, 1048, 1093-4, 1382-3, 1822, 1972. See also Distributors Directory.

National Institute of Industrial Psychology, 14 Welbeck St., London W.1, England: 765-9, 1837-8, 1919-21, 1950

National Institute of Vocational Research. See Personnel Research, Inc.

National League for Nursing, Inc., 10 Columbus Circle, New York 19, N.Y.: 2033-8

National Office Management Association. See United Business Education Association.

National Safety Council, 425 North Michigan Ave., Chicago 11, Ill.: 1162a

National Science Foundation, Washington 25, D.C.: 1360

Nelson (S. F.): *out of print,* 2539

Nelson (Thomas) & Sons Ltd.: *out of print,* 2442

Netherlands Institute of Industrial Psychology, Utrecht, Holland: 341

New York Institute of Finance, 37 Wall St., New York 5, N.Y.: 2019

New York Times, College and School Service, 229 West 43rd St., New York 36, N.Y.: 1732-3

New York University. See Center for Safety Education; *out of print,* see also Psychological Laboratory, New York University.

New Zealand Council for Educational Research, Southern Cross Bldg., 22 Brandon St., Wellington C.1, New Zealand: 818, 1015, 1389, 1489, 1500

Newnes Educational Publishing Co. Ltd., Tower House, 8-11 Southampton St., Strand, London W.C.2, England: 429, 431, 434-5, 761, 804, 825, 830, 850, 867, 869-70, 967-8, 1027, 1035, 1063, 1095, 1448, 1834, 1941

Newsweek Educational Division, 444 Madison Ave., New York 22, N.Y.: 1734-5

Nijhoff (Martinus), P.O. Box 269, The Hague, Holland: 341

Nilsson (Sven G.): *out of print,* 2467

Norman (J. H.), 3354 Glenhaven St., Dallas, Tex.: 77, 97, 301, 716, 820, 1435, 1823, 1852, 1879

Northwestern University. See Garrett Biblical Institute; *out of print,* see also Division of Research, Northwestern University; and Northwestern University Psycho-Educational Clinic.

Northwestern University Psycho-Educational Clinic: *out of print,* 2643

O.S.C. COOPERATIVE Association: *out of print,* 2125, 2332, 2338, 2549, 2573-4, 2708, 2746

O'Connor (Johnson) Research Foundation Inc., 11 East 62nd St., New York 21, N.Y.: 569

Odell's Instrument Service, 925 Massachusetts St., Lawrence, Mass.: 611

Ohio College Association, Ohio State University, Columbus, Ohio: 235a, 808, 1538

★Ohio Scholarship Tests, State Department of Education, 751 Northwest Blvd., Columbus 15, Ohio: 11, 14, 57-9, 76, 93, 425, 427, 430, 437, 486, 500, 551, 640, 643, 674-5, 678, 700, 703, 963-4, 981-2, 903, 998-9, 1024, 1106, 1114, 1119, 1232, 1352, 1362-3, 1405, 1411, 1430, 1457, 1517, 1534, 1552, 1556-8, 1579-80, 1584, 1606-7, 1610, 1642-3, 1647, 1717-8, 1729, 1746, 1754-5, 1757, 1779, 1789-90, 1792, 1796; *out of print,* 2119, 2139, 2186, 2267, 2366, 2412, 2480, 2637, 2698-9, 2762, 2853, 2857, 2865

Ohio State University. See Ohio College Association; and Publication Office, Ohio State University; *out of print,* see also Evaluation Division, Bureau of Educational Research.

Ohio State University Press. See Publication Office, Ohio State University.

★Oliver & Boyd Ltd., Tweeddale Court, 14 High St., Edinburgh 1, Scotland: 471, 538, 758, 789, 835, 906, 1056-7, 1059, 1084, 1160, 1446, 1862

PACIFIC Books: *out of print,* 2193

Page (Horace A.), Temple University, Philadelphia 22, Pa.: 156

1795, 1798, 1808-9, 1836, 1917, 2046; *out of print*, 2115, 2123, 2151, 2153, 2190, 2198, 2271, 2281, 2315, 2322, 2346, 2401, 2473, 2524-5, 2531, 2619, 2623, 2628-9, 2638, 2677, 2683, 2711, 2793, 2829, 2834, 2944

Publication Office, Ohio State University, 242 West 18th Ave., Columbus 10, Ohio: 260-1, 1193, 1512

Purdue University. See Child Development Publications of the Society for Research in Child Development, Inc.; State High School Testing Service for Indiana; TV Program Research Unit; and University Book Store; *out of print*, see also Division of Educational Reference.

QUADRANGLE Books, Inc., 119 West Lake St., Chicago 1, Ill.: 367

RANDOLPH School Supply Co., 708 South Fifth St., Champaign, Ill.: 526, 1321

Reader's Digest Services, Inc. See Educational Division, Reader's Digest Services, Inc.

Reading and Study Skills Center, Inc., 15 Washington Place, New York 3, N.Y.: 1469

Reading Laboratory and Clinic, University of Florida, Gainesville, Fla.: 353, 538a, 552, 1541a

Redfield (Robert H.), Inc. See American Film Registry.

Reiterman (William F.), Jr., 424 High St., Moorestown, N.J.: 255

Research Center for Group Dynamics, University of Michigan, Ann Arbor, Mich.: 346

Research Foundation, University of Toledo, Toledo 6, Ohio: 1625

Revere Copper & Brass Inc., General Industrial Relations Department, Rome, N.Y.: 1170

Rice (Ralph R.): *out of print*, 2280

Ridge Manor Publishing Co., Ridge Manor, Fla.: 421, 495-6, 512-3, 1098-9, 1810

Rinehart & Co., 232 Madison Ave., New York 16, N.Y.: 153

Rosenzweig (Saul), 8029 Washington St., St. Louis 33, Mo.: 374

Rowland & Co., P.O. Box 61, Haddonfield, N.J.: 788

Rulon (Philip J.), Harvard Graduate School of Education, 13 Kirkland St., Cambridge 38, Mass.: 112

Ryerson Press, 299 Queen St., West, Toronto 2B, Ontario, Canada: 878, 903, 962. See also Distributors Directory.

ST. MARTIN'S Press, Inc., 175 Fifth Ave., New York 10, N.Y.: 1487

Sallak (V. J.), Buffalo and Erie County Tuberculosis and Health Association,

766 Ellicott St., Buffalo 3, N.Y.: 1247

Scandinavian Test Publishing Co. See Skandinaviska Testförlaget AB.

Scarborough (Barron B.), Florida State University, Tallahassee, Fla.: 1883

Scherer (Isidor W.), P.O. Box 95, Florence, Mass.: 233

Schlesser (George E.), Colgate University, Hamilton, N.Y.: 1204

★Scholastic Testing Service, Inc., 3774 West Devon Ave., Chicago 45, Ill.: 37, 470, 773, 844, 1083, 1402, 1445, 1505, 1712

School Administrator's Service, 2335 Winnemac Ave., Chicago 25, Ill.: 1317

Schubert (Herman J. P.), 500 Klein Road, Buffalo 21, N.Y.: 333, 847; *out of print*, 2437, 2882

Sci-Art Publishers, 6 Sacramento St., Cambridge 38, Mass.: 286, 741, 837, 848

★Science Research Associates, Inc., 259 East Erie St., Chicago 11, Ill.: 1, 25, 31-2, 35-6, 70, 89-90, 120, 209, 237-8, 269, 274-6, 309, 320, 332, 365, 447, 469, 506, 568, 598, 719, 725, 739, 808, 833, 839-43, 865, 959, 1040, 1082, 1097, 1200, 1375, 1384, 1403, 1442-3, 1510-1, 1526, 1532, 1564, 1715, 1849, 1851, 1874-5, 1895, 1910, 1940, 1968, 1989, 2039-41, 2060, 2080, 2083-4, 2091, 2094-5, 2097; *out of print*, 2134, 2220, 2239, 2272, 2462, 2497, 2557, 2685, 2893, 2908, 2912, 2914-5, 2922, 2928

Science Service, Inc., 1719 N St., N.W., Washington 6, D.C.: 1571-2

Scientific Publishing Co., 2328 Eutaw Place, Baltimore 17, Md.: 1683-4; *out of print*, 2783

Scott, Foresman & Co., 433 East Erie St., Chicago 11, Ill.: 1086; *out of print*, 2339, 2501-2, 2529, 2659

Scribner's (Charles) Sons: *out of print*, 2792, 2798, 2844, 2880

Seashore (Robert H.): *out of print*, 2335

Sexology Corporation, 154 West 14th St., New York 11, N.Y.: 1292

Sheppard and Enoch Pratt Hospital: *out of print*, 2163

★Sheridan Supply Co., P.O. Box 837, Beverly Hills, Calif.: 140, 151, 171-6, 199, 201, 852, 891, 916, 919-20, 932, 1377, 1529, 1867-8; *out of print*, 2184, 2229, 2424

Sherman (I.): *out of print*, 2686, 2688

Shipley (Mrs. Walter C.), 22 Howard St., Norton, Mass.: 288

Shumaker (L. K.): *out of print*, 2253

Silliman (Henrietta), Toulon, Ill.: 501

Skandinaviska Testförlaget AB, Oxenstiernsgatan 17, Stockholm NO, Sweden: 1504, 1675. See also Distributors Directory.

Smith (Turner E.) & Co., 441 West Peachtree St., N.E., Atlanta 8, Ga.: 410-1, 454, 487, 507, 515, 518-20, 547, 1528; *out of print*, 2326, 2329, 2858

Sonotone Corporation, Elmsford, N.Y.: 1666

South African Council for Scientific and Industrial Research. See National Institute for Personnel Research.

South Carolina Every-Pupil Testing Service: *out of print,* 2840

Southworth's Extension Service, 308-320½ State St., West Lafayette, Ind.: 1985

Spache (George). See Reading Laboratory and Clinic.

Spastic Aid Council, Inc., 1850 Boyer Ave., Seattle 2, Wash.: 881

Specialty Case Manufacturing Co., 977 Vernon Road, Philadelphia 50, Pa.: 1376

Springer Publishing Co., Inc., 44 East 23rd St., New York 10, N.Y.: 393

Stanford University Press, Stanford, Calif.: 1225-6, 1237, 1243, 1252; *out of print,* 2234, 2276, 2314, 2420, 2588, 2593, 2610, 2681, 2714. See also Consulting Psychologists Press, Inc.

Staples Press Ltd., 29 Great Portland St., Oxford-Circus, London W.1, England: 3

Starr (Anna Spiesman), 126 Montgomery St., Highland Park, N.J.: 933

State High School Testing Service for Indiana, Purdue University, Lafayette, Ind.: 61, 78, 96, 455, 639, 679, 691, 983, 1001, 1025, 1047, 1120, 1129, 1137, 1144-5, 1231, 1254-5, 1257, 1259-60, 1262-5, 1267, 1270, 1281, 1366, 1433, 1561, 1585, 1611, 1648, 1736, 1759, 1794, 1805, 1812-3; *out of print,* 2277, 2298, 2375, 2387, 2389, 2620

State University of Iowa. See Bureau of Educational Research and Service; Campus Stores; and Department of Physical Education for Women.

Steck Co., Austin 1, Tex.: 16, 21, 533, 862, 1013, 1022, 1210, 1302, 1320, 1503, 1541; *out of print,* 2168, 2561, 2566, 2713, 2759

Stevens, Thurow & Associates Inc., 105 West Adams St., Chicago 3, Ill.: 2093

Stevenson, Jordan & Harrison, Inc., Personnel Services Department, 205 West Wacker Drive, Chicago 6, Ill.: 148

★Steward (Verne) & Associates, 14828 Mar Vista St., Whittier, Calif.: 2067-72; *out of print,* 2948

Steward's Office, Lynchburg State Colony: *out of print,* 2176

★Stoelting (C. H.) Co., 424 North Homan Ave., Chicago 24, Ill.: 113, 133, 343, 358, 397, 589, 849, 877, 895-8, 904, 907, 918, 921-5, 927-30, 934, 938, 1465, 1669, 1671, 1673-4, 1676, 1686, 1705, 1903, 1906-7, 1933, 1942; *out of print,* 2144, 2192, 2211, 2318, 2320-1, 2459, 2461, 2463, 2465, 2467, 2472, 2559, 2589-90, 2902

Stogdill (Ralph M.), 3658 Olentagy Blvd., Columbus 14, Ohio: 111; *out of print,* 2143

Sumner (F. C.): *out of print,* 2219

Sunday School Board of the Southern Baptist Convention, 127 Ninth Ave., North, Nashville 3, Tenn.: 1330

Surveys, Inc. See personnel Research, Inc.

Swanson (V. J.), P.O. Box 365, Lake Delton, Wis.: 2077

Swets & Zeitlinger, Keizersgracht 471 and 487, Amsterdam-C, Holland: 379, 901. See also Distributors Directory.

Syracuse University. See Psychological Research Center.

TV PROGRAM Research Unit, Audio-Visual Center, Memorial Center, Purdue University, Lafayette, Ind.: 1196

Tabin (Johanna Krout), 162 Park Ave., Glencoe, Ill.: 200, 241, 383

Tavistock Publications, 11 New Fetter Lane, London E.C.4, England: 367

Teachers College Personnel Association: *out of print,* 2108, 2256, 2446

Technisonic Studios, Inc., 1201 Brentwood Blvd., St. Louis 17, Mo.: 1658, 1665

Test Developments, Box 8306, Denver, Colo.: 381

Testscor, 2309 Snelling Ave., Minneapolis 4, Minn.: 1152

Tharp (James B.), 143 Brighton Road, Columbus 2, Ohio: 647, 657, 697

Thomas (Charles C), Publisher, 327 East Lawrence Ave., Springfield, Ill.: 362

Time, Inc., Education Department, P.O. Box 1961, Radio City Station, New York 19, N.Y.: 1731

Titmus Optical Co., Inc., Petersburg, Va.: 1702

Torgerson (T. L.): *out of print,* 2226

UNITED Business Education Association, 1201 16th St., N.W., Washington 6, D.C.: 47, 51, 53, 60, 65, 81, 95, 98; *out of print,* 2120-1, 2127, 2129

United States Employment Service, Washington 25, D.C.: 1376, 1385

United States Government Printing Office, Washington 25, D.C.: 1871

★University Book Store, 360 State St., West Lafayette, Ind.: 178, 267-8, 574, 971-2, 1187, 1197-8, 1365, 1434, 1569, 1848, 1937, 1999, 2081-2, 2085-8

University Counseling Center, University of Maryland, College Park, Md.: 264

University Extension Division, University of Nebraska: *out of print,* 2249

University of Birmingham Institute of Education, 5 Great Charles St., Birmingham 3, England: 915

University of Chicago. See Industrial Relations Center.

University of Chicago Press, 5750 Ellis Ave., Chicago 37, Ill.: 250; *out of print,* 2221, 2652

University of Denver Bookstores, 1445 Cleveland Place, Denver 2, Colo.: 285
University of Detroit Bookstore, Detroit 21, Mich.: 344
University of Florida Press: *out of print,* 2142
University of Hawaii Bookstore, Honolulu 14, Hawaii: 1892
University of Kentucky. See Kentucky Cooperative Counseling and Testing Service.
★University of London Press Ltd., Little Paul's House, Warwick Square, London E.C.4, England: 40, 121, 219, 399, 428, 436, 456, 555, 746, 760, 778, 790, 797-8, 805, 845, 866, 871, 873-4, 955, 978, 1026, 1031, 1036, 1071, 1074, 1100, 1105, 1356, 1361, 1374, 1420, 1440, 1480, 1484, 1545, 1931; *out of print,* 2242, 2247, 2252, 2297, 2334, 2376-7, 2427, 2436, 2439, 2451, 2496, 2660, 2663
University of Maryland. See Department of Psychiatry, School of Medicine; and University Counseling Center.
University of Michigan. See Child Development Laboratories; English Language Institute; and Research Center for Group Dynamics; *out of print, see also* Bureau of Educational Reference and Research.
University of Minnesota. See Division of Psychiatry, Medical School, University of Minnesota.
University of Minnesota Press, Minneapolis 14, Minn.: 186, 225, 595, 1272, 1338, 1340, 1422, 1516, 1518; *out of print,* 2182, 2216, 2625, 2943, 2945
University of Natal Press, P.O. Box 375, Pietermaritzburg, Union of South Africa: 391
University of Nebraska. See University Extension Division, University of Nebraska.
University of Nebraska Press, Lincoln 8, Neb.: 1179; *out of print,* 2179
University of North Carolina. See Bureau of Educational Research, University of North Carolina.
University of Oregon. See Curriculum Bulletin.
University of Pittsburgh Project Talent Office, 1808 Adams Mill Road, N.W., Washington 9, D.C.: 1364
University of Queensland Press, George St., Brisbane, Queensland, Australia: 1622, 1640
University of Saskatchewan Bookstore, Saskatoon, Saskatchewan, Canada: 786
University of Toledo. See Research Foundation, University of Toledo.
University Press, Brigham Young University, Provo, Utah: 525
University Printing Co., Inc.: *out of print,* 2250

VALENTINE (C. W.), The White House, Wythall, Birmingham, England: 270
Van Allyn Institute. See Personnel Research, Inc.
Vassar College. See Mary Conover Mellon Foundation.
Veenker (C. H.), Department of Physical Education for Men, Purdue University, Lafayette, Ind.: 1250
Veterans Administration, Vermont and H Sts., N.W., Washington 25, D.C.: 229
Veterans' Testing Service, American Council on Education, 1785 Massachusetts Ave., N.W., Washington 6, D.C.: 44, 417, 505, 951, 1508-9; *out of print,* 2124, 2126, 2130, 2136, 2257-9, 2363-5, 2383-5, 2395-7, 2409-11, 1487-9, 2513-4, 2533-4, 2536-7, 2546, 2632, 2640, 2719-20, 2735-7, 2749-50, 2757-8, 2767-70, 2841-3, 2869-70, 2932-41
Vicon Instrument Co., P.O. Box 2742, Colorado Springs, Colo.: 1662-3
Vocational Guidance Service, 95 Portland St., Buffalo, N.Y.: 1914
Volta Bureau, 1537 35th St., N.W., Washington 7, D.C.: 908

WAGNER (Mazie Earle), 500 Klein Road, Buffalo 21, N.Y.: 1393
Walch (J. Weston), Publisher, Box 1075, Portland, Me.: 460, 502-3, 516; *out of print,* 2293, 2310
Walther (E. Curt): *out of print,* 2228
Warwick Products Co., 7909 Rockside Road, Cleveland 31, Ohio: 1376
Washington Publications, 3915 Military Road, N.W., Washington 15, D.C.: 622
Washington Square Reading Center. See Reading and Study Skills Center.
Washington State University, Department of Rural Sociology, Pullman, Wash.: 297
Webb-Duncan Publishing Co., Inc.: *out of print,* 2251, 2295, 2367, 2399, 2403, 2415, 2418, 2453, 2491, 2622, 2731, 2745, 2774, 2820, 2822, 2828, 2833, 2856, 2862
Webster Publishing Co., 1154 Reco Ave., St. Louis 26, Mo.: 1454, 1494, 1507; *out of print,* 2160, 2581, 2684
Welch Allyn, Inc., Skaneateles Falls, N.Y.: 1695
Western Electric Co.: *out of print,* 2780
Western Interprovincial Publishing Co., P.O. Box 251, Station A, Vancouver, British Columbia, Canada: 1893
★Western Psychological Services, Box 775, Beverly Hills, Calif.: 106, 125-6, 167, 181, 209a, 215-6, 218, 227a, 244, 252, 265, 287, 315, 325, 338-40, 348, 370, 373, 378, 937, 1096, 1684; *out of print,* 2555
Western Reserve University. See Personnel Research Institute.

Wheaton (A.) & Co., Ltd., 143 Fore St., Exeter, England: 799

Wilcox (Paul H.) : *out of print,* 2164

William, Lynde & Williams, 113 East Washington St., Painesville, Ohio: 316, 321, 821, 1869, 1894, 1958, 2099

Winkler Publications, 15095 Tracey St., Detroit 27, Mich.: 146, 195, 202, 208, 262, 776, 1138, 1140, 1142, 1176, 1519, 1864, 1877, 1881-2, 1925, 1957, 1962, 1964, 1971, 2002, 2053, 2074, 2098

Winnetka Educational Press: *out of print,* 2235, 2560, 2651

Winston (John C.) Co. See Holt, Rinehart & Winston, Inc.

Winter Haven Lions Research Foundation, Inc., P.O. Box 1045, Winter Haven, Fla.: 1699

Witkin (Herman A.), State University College of Medicine, 450 Clarkson Ave., Brooklyn 3, N.Y.: 145

Wold (Olga) : *out of print,* 2209

Wolters (J. B.), Groningen, Holland: 901. See also Distributors Directory.

Wonderlic (E. F.), P.O. Box 7, Northfield, Ill.: 875, 1977

Woodruff (Asahel D.), 1457 Cherry Lane, Provo, Utah: 298

World Book Co. See Harcourt, Brace & World, Inc.

YOUTH Character Research Institute, 3706 East Fifth St., Tucson, Ariz.: 310

ZANER-BLOSER Co., 612 North Park St., Columbus 15, Ohio: 1219, 1221

DISTRIBUTORS DIRECTORY
AND INDEX *

ARGENTINA

Librería Paidós, Cabildo 2454, Buenos Aires, Argentina.
a) C.P.S. Co.: *adapted*, 329.
b) Institute for Personality and Ability Testing.
c) Psychological Corporation.

AUSTRALIA

Australasian Publishing Co. Pty. Ltd., Bradbury House, 55 York St., Sydney, New South Wales, Australia.
a) George G. Harrap & Co. Ltd.
Australian Council for Educational Research, 369 Lonsdale St., Melbourne C.1, Victoria, Australia.
a) American Optical Co.: 1678.
b) American Orthopsychiatric Association, Inc.: 327a.
c) Association Press: 306.
d) Bureau of Publications: 384, 537, 1470; *adapted*, 1495.
e) C.P.S. Co.: 329.
f) Chatto & Windus Ltd.: 1452.
g) Cooperative Test Division: *adapted*, 1436.
h) Department of Educational Research, Ontario College of Education, University of Toronto: 1488; *adapted*, 770.
i) Educational Test Bureau: 314, 1466.
j) Robert Gibson & Sons (Glasgow), Ltd.: 779.
k) Harcourt, Brace & World, Inc.: *adapted*, 818.
l) Harvard University Press: 387.
m) Houghton Mifflin Co.: 99, 299, 909.
n) Hans Huber: 373a, 373f, 385.

o) Institute for Personality and Ability Testing: 187-9, 191, 194, 289.
p) H. K. Lewis & Co. Ltd.: 331, 831b, 1703; *adapted*, 793, 831a, 831c.
q) National Foundation for Educational Research in England and Wales: 337, 613, 1667; *adapted*, 804a.
r) Oliver & Boyd Ltd.: 471, 538, 758, 1056-7, 1059, 1084, 1446.
s) Psychological Corporation: 135, 163, 224, 324, 328, 363, 389, 609, 907, 912-4, 939, 2090; *adapted*, 1939.
t) Public School Publishing Co.: 1053.
u) Saul Rosenzweig: 374.
v) Science Research Associates, Inc.: 269, 365, 1874-5.
w) Tavistock Publications: 367.
x) Test Developments.
y) University of Birmingham Institute of Education: 915.
z) University of London Press Ltd.: 121, 219.
aa) Western Psychological Services: 378.
Birchall (A. W.) & Sons Pty. Ltd., 118-20 Brisbane St., Launceston, Tasmania, Australia.
a) Oliver & Boyd Ltd.: 538, 1084, 1446.
Carroll's Pty. Ltd., 566 Hay St., Perth, Western Australia.
a) Oliver & Boyd Ltd.
Rigby Ltd., 22 James Place, Adelaide, South Australia.
a) Oliver & Boyd Ltd.

BELGIUM

Editest, S.P.R.L., 94 rue Général Capiaumont, Brussels 4, Belgium.

* The Distributors Directory includes individuals and organizations who act as agents for or stock tests of English-language test publishers in other countries, or who publish or distribute a major adaptation of one or more English-language tests originating outside of their country. It is not exhaustive and it does not include United States distributors of foreign tests since this information is given in the text within the entry for each test of foreign origin which is stocked or published by a United States publisher. References are to test entry numbers, not to page numbers. The references may be interpreted thus: "ABC Co.: 29, 176" indicates that the distributor carries quantity stocks of tests 29 and 176 of the ABC Co.; "ABC Co.: 29; *adapted*, 241" indicates that the distributor stocks test 29 of the ABC Co. and also publishes or distributes a translation, restandardization, or substantial revision for foreign use of test 241, which was originally published or distributed by the ABC Co.; "ABC Co." without references to test entry numbers indicates that the distributor acts as agent for the ABC Co. but does not stock any tests of the company in quantity, importing them only upon order. Tests which are published for use in other countries with only minor changes, such as in spelling or wording, are treated here as stocked rather than adapted tests. Numbers beyond 2104 refer to tests which are out of print in their originally published form. The addresses of publishers represented will be found in the Publishers Directory.

a) Badger Tests Co., Ltd: 361.
b) Martin M. Bruce.
c) Bureau of Educational Research and Service: 593.
d) California Test Bureau.
e) Educational Test Bureau: 774, 1670.
f) Harcourt, Brace & World, Inc.: 882.
g) Institute for Personality and Ability Testing: 733; *adapted,* 289.
h) Psychological Corporation: 163, 328, 363, 836, 912, 1371, 1677, 1946.
i) Science Research Associates, Inc.: 840, 1384.
j) Stanford University Press: *adapted,* 2008.
k) C. H. Stoelting Co.: 397.

BRAZIL

Centro de Psicologia Aplicada, Rua Senador Dantas, 118-9 Andar, Rio de Janeiro, Brazil.
a) Psychological Corporation.

CANADA

Clarke, Irwin & Co. Ltd., Clarwin House, 791 St. Clair Ave., West, Toronto 10, Ontario, Canada.
a) Chatto & Windus Ltd.
b) George G. Harrap & Co. Ltd.
c) Oliver & Boyd Ltd.: 471, 538, 1057, 1084, 1446.
d) University of London Press Ltd.
e) A. Wheaton & Co. Ltd.
Guidance Centre, Ontario College of Education, University of Toronto, 371 Bloor St., West, Toronto 5, Ontario, Canada.
a) Acorn Publishing Co.: 717-8, 1831, 1873.
b) American Institute of Certified Public Accountants: 1994.
c) Association Press: 306.
d) Bobbs-Merrill Co., Inc.
e) Bureau of Educational Research and Service: 593.
f) Bureau of Publications: 28, 243, 384, 803, 1407-10, 1495, 1527.
g) Center for Psychological Service: 198, 291, 2073.
h) Consulting Psychologists Press, Inc.: 103, 131, 246, 278, 1537.
i) Educational Test Bureau: 1396, 1466, 1499, 1515, 1904, 1908, 1930.
j) C. A. Gregory Co.
k) Harcourt, Brace & World, Inc.: 26, 41, 84, 107, 117, 164-5, 179, 317, 545, 572, 750-1, 763, 815-8, 826-7, 860, 882, 884, 975, 1062, 1147, 1283, 1413, 1415, 1467, 1483, 1500, 1535, 1543, 1570, 1634, 1685, 1854.
l) Houghton Mifflin Co.: 24, 299, 787, 909-10, 1424-5, 1427, 1502.

m) Institute for Personality and Ability Testing: 191, 733.
n) McKnight & McKnight Publishing Co.: 1859.
o) Marietta Apparatus Co.: 1928.
p) Psychological Corporation: 45, 74, 80, 143, 223, 227, 583, 588, 599, 609, 618, 735, 740, 824, 836, 872, 912-4, 1371, 1380, 1398, 1521, 1687, 1841, 1847, 1850, 1856, 1889, 1898-9, 1911, 1939, 1946, 2001, 2090.
q) Psychological Institute: 1844, 1934.
r) Psychological Services, Inc.
s) Public School Publishing Co.: 534, 544, 1459-60, 1491, 1836, 1917, 2046.
t) C. H. Stoelting Co.
u) University Book Store: 971, 1848, 1937.
Institut de Recherches psychologiques, 10314 St. Lawrence Blvd., Montreal 12, Quebec, Canada.
a) Martin M. Bruce.
b) Bureau of Educational Research and Service: *adapted,* 593.
c) Bureau of Publications.
d) Center for Psychological Service.
e) Consulting Psychologists Press, Inc.: *adapted,* 1887.
f) Editest, S.P.R.L.
g) Educational Test Bureau.
h) Harcourt, Brace & World, Inc.: *adapted,* 164.
i) Harvard University Press.
j) Houghton Mifflin Co.: *adapted,* 910.
k) Institute for Personality and Ability Testing.
l) Journal of Clinical Psychology.
m) Martinus Nijhoff.
n) Psychological Corporation: 836, 1939, 1946; *adapted,* 1371, 1939.
o) Stanford University Press.
p) Western Psychological Services.
Institut pedagogique Saint-Georges, 2101 Maplewood Ave., Montreal 26, Quebec, Canada.
a) Houghton Mifflin Co.: *adapted,* 771.
Les Presses Universitaires Laval, 26, rue Ste-Famille, Quebec 4, Canada.
a) Psychological Corporation: *adapted,* 1889.
b) Science Research Associates, Inc.: *adapted,* 1875.
PSYCAN Psychological Services of Canada Ltd., P.O. Box 251, Station A, Vancouver, British Columbia, Canada. All tests, except apparatus tests, of the following publishers are stocked.
a) Acorn Publishing Co.
b) American Guidance Service, Inc.
c) Bobbs-Merrill Co., Inc.
d) Martin M. Bruce.
e) Bureau of Publications.
f) California Test Bureau.
g) Cooperative Test Division.
h) Educational Test Bureau.

i) C. A. Gregory Co.
j) Harcourt, Brace & World, Inc.
k) Houghton Mifflin Co.
l) Institute for Personality and Ability Testing.
m) Marietta Apparatus Co.
n) Psychological Corporation.
o) Psychological Services, Inc.
p) Public School Publishing Co.
q) Science Research Associates, Inc.
r) C. H. Stoelting Co.
Ryerson Press, 299 Queen St., West, Toronto 2B, Ontario, Canada.
a) Lyons & Carnahan.
b) Steck Co.
University of Ottawa, 1, rue Stewart, Ottawa 2, Ontario, Canada.
a) Consulting Psychologists Press, Inc.: *adapted,* 103, 246.
b) Harcourt, Brace & World, Inc.: *adapted,* 818, 2906.
c) Houghton Mifflin Co.: *adapted,* 299.
d) Psychological Corporation: *adapted,* 913.
e) Public School Publishing Co.: *adapted,* 2151.
f) E. F. Wonderlic: *adapted,* 875.

COLOMBIA

Psicologia Industrial de Colombia, Carrera 8a, 13-61, Office 603, Bogota, Colombia.
a) Industrial Psychology, Inc.

DENMARK

Adam (Raymond P.), William Collins Sons & Co. Ltd., 13 Bakketoppen, Virum, Copenhagen, Denmark.
a) Oliver & Boyd Ltd.

ENGLAND

Harrap (George G.) & Co. Ltd., 182 High Holborn, London W.C.1, England.
a) Harcourt, Brace & World, Inc.: 816, 818; *adapted,* 815, 816a.
b) Houghton Mifflin Co.: 909; *adapted,* 910.
Methuen & Co. Ltd., 36 Essex St., Strand, London W.C. 2, England.
a) Hans Huber: 373n.
National Foundation for Educational Research in England and Wales, 79 Wimpole St., London W.1., England.
a) American Orthopsychiatric Association, Inc.: 327a.
b) Association Press: 306.
c) Australian Council for Educational Research: 1829, 1912-3, 1947.
d) Martin M. Bruce.

e) Bureau of Educational Research and Service: 593.
f) Bureau of Publications: 384, 1407-10, 1495.
g) C.P.S. Co.: 329.
h) California Test Bureau.
i) Center for Psychological Service: 291.
j) Consulting Psychologists Press, Inc.: 103, 246, 1537, 1887-8.
k) Educational Test Bureau: 314.
l) Harcourt, Brace & World, Inc.: 373j, 763, 882, 1413, 1467, 1500.
m) Harvard University Press: 387.
n) Houghton Mifflin Co.: 299.
o) Hans Huber: 373f, 373i.
p) Institute for Personality and Ability Testing.
q) Psychological Corporation: 80, 135, 143, 152, 163, 224, 227, 328, 363, 373c, 373d, 375, 735, 740, 742, 824, 877b, 894, 912-4, 917, 939, 1191, 1371, 1651, 1677, 1841, 1847, 1850, 1856, 1889, 1899, 1939, 1946, 2001, 2090.
r) Saul Rosenzweig: 374.
s) Science Research Associates, Inc.: 209, 1874-5.
t) C. H. Stoelting Co.

FRANCE

Centre de Psychologie Appliquée, Square Jovenet, Paris 16, France.
a) Australian Council for Educational Research.
b) Badger Tests Co. Ltd.: 361.
c) C.P.S. Co.: *adapted,* 329.
d) Educational Test Bureau: 314.
e) Harcourt, Brace & World, Inc.: 763, 882.
f) Institute for Personality and Ability Testing: 193; *adapted,* 289, 733.
g) H. K. Lewis & Co. Ltd.: 1703.
h) Psychological Corporation: 163, 328, 363, 599, 609, 913, 1677.
i) Saul Rosenzweig: *adapted,* 374.
j) Science Research Associates, Inc.
k) C. H. Stoelting Co.: 898.

GUATEMALA

American School, Apartado Postal 83, Guatemala, C. A.
a) Harcourt, Brace & World, Inc.

HOLLAND

Swets & Zeitlinger, Keizersgracht 471 & 487, Amsterdam-C, Holland.
a) Badger Tests Co. Ltd.: 361.
b) Bobbs-Merrill Co., Inc.
c) C.P.S. Co.
d) Center for Psychological Service.

e) Consulting Psychologists Press, Inc.
f) Crosby Lockwood & Son Ltd.: 759.
g) Educational Test Bureau.
h) Houghton Mifflin Co.
i) Institute for Personality and Ability
Testing.
j) Psychological Corporation: 1371.
k) Science Research Associates, Inc.
l) Western Psychological Services.
Twents Instituut voor Bedryfspsychol-
ogie, Grundel Laan 18, Hengelo (o),
Holland.
a) Industrial Psychology, Inc.
Wolters (J. B.), Groningen, Holland.
a) Harcourt, Brace & World, Inc.

INDIA

Blackie & Son Ltd., 103-5 Fort St., P.O.
Box 21, Fort, Bombay 1, India.
a) Oliver & Boyd Ltd.
Manasayan, 32 Faiz Bazar, Delhi 7, India.
a) American Orthopsychiatric Association, Inc.: 327a.
b) C.P.S. Co.: *adapted, 329.*
c) Harvard University Press: 387.
d) Houghton Mifflin Co.: 99, 299.
e) Hans Huber: 373f, 385.
f) H. K. Lewis & Co. Ltd.: 831.
g) Martinus Nijhoff: 341.
h) Psychological Corporation: 74, 152,
223-4, 227, 324, 328, 375, 389, 588, 740,
742, 836, 894, 907b, 935, 939, 1191, 1371,
1380, 1847, 1850, 1856, 1889, 1939, 1946,
1961, 1978, 2001, 2090.
i) Psychological Test Specialists: 221,
352, 832, 887, 1866.
j) Saul Rosenzweig: *adapted,* 374.
k) Science Research Associates, Inc.:
365, 1375.
l) Western Psychological Services:
338, 348, 370, 373h.
Oxford University Press, Oxford House,
Apollo Bunder, Bombay 1, India.
a) George G. Harrap & Co. Ltd.

INDONESIA

Moore (Donald) Ltd., c/o N. V. Gunung
Agung, Kwitang 13, Djakarta, Indo-
nesia.
a) Chatto & Windus Ltd.
b) J. M. Dent & Sons Ltd.
c) George G. Harrap & Co. Ltd.
d) Crosby Lockwood & Son Ltd.
e) Staples Press Ltd.
f) Tavistock Publications.

ITALY

Instituto Superiore di Pedagogia, P. Conti
Rebaudengo, 22, Turin, Italy.

a) Harcourt, Brace & World, Inc.
Organizzazioni Speciali, Via Torta N. 14,
Firenze, Italy.
a) American Orthopsychiatric Association, Inc.: *adapted,* 327a.
b) Association Press: *adapted,* 306.
c) Bureau of Publications.
d) C.P.S. Co.: *adapted,* 329.
e) Consulting Psychologists Press,
Inc.: *adapted,* 103, 123, 246.
f) Educational Test Bureau: *adapted,*
314, 1904, 1908, 1930.
g) Grune & Stratton, Inc.
h) Harcourt, Brace & World, Inc.:
adapted, 373j, 747.
i) Harvard University Press: *adapted,*
387.
j) Houghton Mifflin Co.: *adapted,* 299,
909.
k) Institute for Personality and Ability
Testing: *adapted,* 187, 193, 289, 733.
l) Journal of Clinical Psychology:
adapted, 351.
m) Alma Jordan Knauber: *adapted,*
590.
n) H. K. Lewis & Co. Ltd.: *adapted,*
831.
o) Ross A. McFarland: *adapted,* 235b.
p) National Foundation for Educational Research in England and Wales:
adapted, 876.
q) National Institute of Industrial Psychology: *adapted,* 767-9, 1920.
r) Psychological Corporation: *adapted,*
143, 163, 224, 324, 363, 824c, 894, 907,
913-4, 1371, 1856, 1889, 1939, 1946, 1961,
2090.
s) Psychological Test Specialists.
t) Psychometric Affiliates: *adapted,*
807.
u) Revere Copper & Brass Inc.:
adapted, 1170.
v) Saul Rosenzweig: *adapted,* 374.
w) Science Research Associates, Inc.:
adapted, 1384, 1968, 2914.
x) University of London Press Ltd.:
adapted, 2242.
y) Western Psychological Services:
adapted, 125.

JAPAN

Moore (Donald) Ltd., Sanshin Bldg., 6,
Kanda Mitoshiro-cho, Chiyoda-Ku,
Tokyo, Japan.
a) Chatto & Windus Ltd.
b) J. M. Dent & Sons Ltd.
c) George G. Harrap & Co. Ltd.
d) Crosby Lockwood & Son Ltd.
e) Staples Press Ltd.
f) Tavistock Publications.
Sankyobo, Publisher, 11, Imagumano
Naginomori, Kyoto, Japan.
a) Institute for Personality and Ability
Testing: *adapted,* 733b-c.

b) Saul Rosenzweig: *adapted,* 374.
Tokyo Shinri, Kabushikigaisha, 4-8
Hongo, Bunkyo, Tokyo, Japan.
a) Institute for Personality and Ability
Testing: *adapted,* 187.

KENYA

E.S.A. Bookshop, P.O. Box 30167, Nai-
robi, Kenya.
a) Oliver & Boyd Ltd.

MALAYA

Federal Publications Ltd., 111 Pudu
Road, Kuala Lumpur, Malaya.
a) Oliver & Boyd Ltd.: 471, 538, 1057,
1059, 1084, 1160, 1446, 1862.
Moore (Donald) Ltd., Tet Loke Bldg.,
Tong Shin Road, Kuala Lumpur, Malaya.
a) Chatto & Windus Ltd.
b) J. M. Dent & Sons Ltd.
c) George G. Harrap & Co. Ltd.
d) Crosby Lockwood & Son Ltd.
e) Staples Press Ltd.
f) Tavistock Publications.

MEXICO

Instituto de Personal, S.C., Nogales 29,
Mexico 7, D. F.
a) Psychological Corporation.
Psicologia Industrial de Mexico, Baja
California Despacho 501, Mexico 7,
D. F.
a) Industrial Psychology, Inc.

MISCELLANEOUS

Department of Public Instruction, Hato
Rey, Puerto Rico.
a) Psychological Corporation: *adapted,*
914.
Federal Publications Ltd., Times House,
River Valley Road, Singapore.
a) Oliver & Boyd Ltd.: 471, 538, 758,
1057, 1059, 1084, 1160, 1446, 1862.
Moore (Donald) Ltd., 707 Great China
House, Queen's Road Central, Hong
Kong; and Macdonald House, Orchard
Road, Singapore 9.
a) Chatto & Windus Ltd.
b) J. M. Dent & Sons Ltd.
c) George G. Harrap & Co. Ltd.
d) Crosby Lockwood & Son Ltd.
e) Staples Press Ltd.
f) Tavistock Publications.

NEW ZEALAND

Educational Books, 19 Park Ave., Lower
Hutt, New Zealand.

a) Australian Council for Educational
Research: 75, 398, 532, 560, 631, 706-11,
713, 721, 775, 831, 992, 1016, 1058, 1387,
1436, 1471, 1495, 1828-9, 1912-3, 1939,
1947; *adapted,* 1015, 1389.
b) Badger Tests Co. Ltd.
c) Martin M. Bruce.
d) Bureau of Publications: 537, 1495.
e) C.P.S. Co.: 329, 388.
f) California Test Bureau.
g) Consulting Psychologists Press,
Inc.
h) Cornell University Medical College.
i) Educational Test Bureau.
j) Educational Testing Service.
k) Robert Gibson & Sons (Glasgow)
Ltd.: 779.
l) Grune & Stratton, Inc.
m) Guidance Centre.
n) Harcourt, Brace & World, Inc.:
adapted, 818, 1500.
o) George G. Harrap & Co. Ltd.
p) Harvard University Press: 387.
q) Houghton Mifflin Co.
r) Institute for Personality and Ability
Testing: 289.
s) H. K. Lewis & Co. Ltd: 331, 1703.
t) Macmillan & Co. Ltd.: 1487.
u) Methuen & Co. Ltd.: 386, 809.
v) National Foundation for Educational Research in England and Wales:
613.
w) National Institute of Industrial
Psychology.
x) Newnes Educational Publishing Co.
Ltd.
y) Oliver & Boyd Ltd.: 471, 538, 758,
1057, 1059, 1084, 1446, 1862.
z) Psychological Corporation: 135, 163,
224, 389, 836, 912-4.
aa) Psychological Test Specialists.
bb) Public School Publishing Co.:
1053.
cc) Stanford University Press.
dd) C. H. Stoelting Co.
ee) Tavistock Publications: 367.
ff) University of London Press Ltd.:
121b, 798, 866, 955, 1484a.
gg) Western Psychological Services:
378.
Elphick (H. R.), Empire Bldg., Willis
St., Wellington, New Zealand.
a) George G. Harrap & Co. Ltd.
Whitcombe & Tombs Ltd., Christchurch
C. 1, New Zealand.
a) Oliver & Boyd Ltd.: all tests
stocked.

NIGERIA

C.M.S. Bookshops, P.O. Box 174, Lagos,
Nigeria.
a) Macmillan & Co. Ltd.
b) Oliver & Boyd Ltd.

NORWAY

A/S Bokhjørnet, Lille Grensen 7, Oslo, Norway.
a) American Orthopsychiatric Association, Inc.: 327a.
b) C.P.S. Co.: 329.
c) Harcourt, Brace & World, Inc.: 763, 882.
d) Harvard University Press: 387.
e) Hans Huber: 373f.
f) H. K. Lewis & Co. Ltd.: 831a-b, 1703.
g) Methuen & Co. Ltd.: 386.
h) Psychological Corporation: 163, 912, 914.
i) C. H. Stoelting Co.: 877a.
j) Test Developments.

PAKISTAN

Pakistan Psychological Centre, 7, Moti Masjid, Denso Hall, Bunder Road, Karachi 1, Pakistan.
a) Psychological Corporation: all tests stocked.

POLAND

Choynowski (M.), Psychometric Section, Polish Academy of Sciences, Polska Akademie Nark, Freta 16, Warsaw, Poland.
a) Institute for Personality and Ability Testing: *adapted*, 187, 289.

SPAIN

Technicos Especialistas Asociados, Vallehermoso, 28, Madrid 15, Spain.
a) Psychological Corporation.

SWEDEN

Skandinaviska Testförlaget AB, Oxenstiernsgatan 17, Stockholm NO, Sweden.
a) H. K. Lewis & Co. Ltd.
b) National Foundation for Educational Research in England and Wales.
c) Psychological Corporation.

d) Science Research Associates, Inc.
e) C. H. Stoelting Co.

SWITZERLAND

Boxer (Oswald and John H.), Carmenstrasse 2, Zurich 7, Switzerland.
a) George G. Harrap & Co. Ltd.
Huber (Hans), Marktgasse 9, Berne, Switzerland.
a) Australian Council for Educational Research.
b) Harvard University Press: 387.
c) Psychological Corporation: *adapted*, 913-4.

UNION OF SOUTH AFRICA

Afrikaanse Pers-Boekhandel, Posbus 845, Johannesburg, Union of South Africa.
a) George G. Harrap & Co. Ltd.
National Institute for Personnel Research, South African Council for Scientific and Industrial Research, P.O. Box 10319, Johannesburg, Union of South Africa.
a) Psychological Corporation: *adapted*, 913.
Watson (A.), 13 Kildare Crescent, Fish Hoek, Capetown, Union of South Africa.
a) Oliver & Boyd Ltd.

WEST GERMANY

Hogrefe (C. J.), Verlag fur Psychologie, Brentanoweg 10, Göttingen, West Germany.
a) C.P.S. Co.: *adapted*, 329.
b) Saul Rosenzweig: *adapted*, 374.

WEST INDIES

Jackson Marshall (K.), William Collins Sons & Co. Ltd., P.O. Box 420, Barbados, West Indies.
a) Newnes Educational Publishing Co. Ltd.
b) Oliver & Boyd Ltd.
Trinidad Book Centre, 64a Marine Square, Port-of-Spain, Trinidad, West Indies.
a) George G. Harrap & Co. Ltd.

TITLE INDEX *

* References are to test entry numbers, not to page numbers. References to out of print tests
are given in italic numbers. In the running heads of the text, entry numbers of the first and last
tests on facing pages are given next to the *outside* margins.

American Council Solid Geometry Test, 1101

American Council Trigonometry Test, Revised, 1131

American Government and Citizenship: Every Pupil Test, 1796

American Government and Civics: Comprehensive Tests in High School Subjects, *2863*

American Government: Every Pupil Scholarship Test, 1797

American Handwriting Scale, 1217

American History: Achievement Examinations for Secondary Schools, 1756

American History: Comprehensive Tests in High School Subjects, *2827*

American History: Every Pupil Scholarship Test, 1753

American History: Every Pupil Test, 1754

American History—Government—Problems of Democracy: Acorn Achievement Tests, 1706

American History: Midwest High School Achievement Examinations, 1782

American History: Multiple-Purpose Objective Tests in High School Subjects, *2828*

American History: Preliminary District-State Scholarship Test, 1757

American History: Final District-State Scholarship Test, 1755

American History Test for Catholic Elementary Schools, *2829*

American History Test: The Affiliation Testing Program for Catholic Secondary Schools, 1343k

American History Test: National Achievement Tests, 1758

American History Test: State High School Tests for Indiana, 1759

American Home Scale, 1336

American Institute of Certified Public Accountants Testing Programs, 1995

American Literature: Every Pupil Scholarship Test, 485

American Literature: Every Pupil Test, 486

American Literature: Manchester Semester-End Achievement Tests, *2285*

American School Achievement Tests, 2; Part 1, Reading, 1391; Part 2, Arithmetic, 1018; Part 3, Language and Spelling, 400; Part 4, Social Studies and Science, 1707; Arithmetic Readiness, 1017

American School Intelligence Test, 723a

American School Reading Readiness Test, 1492

American School Reading Tests, 1392

[American Transit Association Tests], 2100

Analysis of Choices, 1855

Analysis of Controversial Writing: Test 5.31, *2697*

Analysis of Relationships, **724**

Analytical Scales of Attainment in American History, *2830;* Arithmetic, 1019; Elementary Science, *2751;* Geography, *2812;* Literature, *2286*

Analytical Survey Test in Computational Arithmetic, 1020

Analytical Survey Test in English Fundamentals, 401

Ancient and Medieval History: Comprehensive Tests in High School Subjects, *2831*

Ancient and Medieval History: Every Pupil Scholarship Test, *2832*

Ancient and Medieval History: Multiple-Purpose Objective Tests in High School Subjects, *2833*

Ancient History: Every Pupil Scholarship Test, 1760

Anderson Chemistry Test, 1604

Andover School-Entrance Test, 894a

Animal Husbandry Test: State High School Tests for Indiana, 1144

Animal Puzzles, *2240*

Application of Principles in Biological Science: Test 1.33A, *2730*

Application of Principles in Physical Science: Test 1.34, *2764*

Application of Principles in Science: Test 1.3b, *2716*

Applied Reading for Junior-Senior High School: Every Pupil Test, *2698*

Aptitests, 1821

Aptitude Index, 2042b

Aptitude Index Selection Procedure, 2042

[Aptitude-Intelligence Tests], 1367

[Aptitude Inventory], 1820

Aptitude Test E51 (Revision 3) for Electronic Data-Processing Programmers, 2015

Aptitude Test for Elementary School Teachers-in-Training, 1178

Aptitude Test for Nursing: George Washington University Series Nursing Tests, 2032a

Aptitude Tests for Occupations, 1368

Aptitudes Associates Test of Sales Aptitude: A Test for Measuring Knowledge of Basic Principles of Selling, 2043

Arithmetic Computation: Public School Achievement Tests, 1021

Arithmetic Essentials Test, 1022

Arithmetic: Every Pupil Scholarship Test, 1023

Arithmetic: Every Pupil Test, 1024

Arithmetic Fundamentals Test: State High School Tests for Indiana, 1025

Arithmetic: Midland Attainment Tests, *2496*

Arithmetic: Northumberland Standardised Tests (1925 Series), 1026

Arithmetic Progress Test, 1027

Arithmetic Reasoning, 1028

Arithmetic Reasoning: Public School Achievement Tests, 1029

Arithmetic Reasoning Test: [Personnel

Detroit General Intelligence Examination, 752

[Detroit Intelligence Tests], 753

Detroit Kindergarten Test, 884

Detroit Mechanical Aptitudes Examination, Revised, 1917

Detroit Primary Intelligence Test, 753a

Detroit Reading Test, 1399

Detroit Retail Selling Inventory, 2046

Detroit Scale of Behavior Factors, 2157

Detroit Tests of Learning Aptitude, 885

Detroit Word Recognition Test, 1400

DeVault Primary Reading Test, 2662

Developmental Inventory of Background Factors, 2226

Developmental Reading Tests, 1401

Devon Interest Test, 1862

Dex-Aim Test, 1966g

Dex-Man Scale, 1966f

Diagnosis and Treatment of Pupil Maladjustment, 2158

Diagnostic and Attainment Testing, Third Edition, 1446

Diagnostic Arithmetic Tests, 1052

Diagnostic Arithmetic Tests: Easy Steps in Arithmetic, 1058a

Diagnostic Chart for Fundamental Processes in Arithmetic, 1053

Diagnostic Child Study Record, 2643

Diagnostic Counseling Form for Educational, Preventive, and Remedial Counseling, 1957

Diagnostic Fractions Tests: Easy Steps in Arithmetic, 1058c

Diagnostic Interviewer's Guide, 1977

Diagnostic Interviewer's Guide: Personnel Institute Hiring Kit, 2058c

Diagnostic Money Tests: Easy Steps in Arithmetic, 1058b

Diagnostic Performance Tests, 886

Diagnostic Reading Examination for Diagnosis of Special Difficulty in Reading, 1465

Diagnostic Reading Test: Pupil Progress Series, 1402

Diagnostic Reading Tests, 1403

Diagnostic Scale for Measuring Apprentices' Attitudes, 2911

Diagnostic Survey Test in English Fundamentals, 401

Diagnostic Teacher-Rating Scale, 1182

Diagnostic Test for Students of English as a Second Language, 619

Diagnostic Test in Arithmetic Reasoning: The Harlow Objective Tests, 2506

Diagnostic Test in Basic Algebra, 992

Diagnostic Test in Decimals, 2507

Diagnostic Test in Fractions, 2508

Diagnostic Test in Paragraph Reading: Achievement Test in Silent Reading: Dominion Tests, 1390f

Diagnostic Test in Percentage, 2509

Diagnostic Test in Practical Measurements, 2510

Diagnostic Test in Word Recognition: Achievement Test in Silent Reading: Dominion Tests, 1390d

Diagnostic Test of Letter-Writing Ability, 2280

Diagnostic Test of Whole Numbers, 2511

Diagnostic Tests and Self-Helps in Arithmetic, 1054

Diagnostic Tests in Arithmetic Fundamentals, Revised Edition: Dominion Tests, 1055

Diagnostic Tests in English Composition, 420a

Diagnostic Tests in Money, 1056

Diagnostic Tests in Vulgar Fractions, Decimal Fractions and Percentages, 1057

Diagnostic Tests of Achievement in Music, 597

Diagnostic Word-Recognition Tests: The Standard Reading Tests, Test 7, 1452g

Dictating Machine Transcription Test: National Clerical Ability Tests, 2129

Diebold Personnel Tests, 2018

Differential Ability Tests, 1370

Differential Aptitude Tests, 1371

Differential Test Battery, 1372

Dimond-Pflieger Problems of Democracy Test, 1802

"Dingwall" Test in English Usage, 2247

Diplomacy Test of Empathy, 2047

Dominion Group Test of Intelligence, 754

Dominion Higher Test, 754

Dominion Table for Converting Mental Age to I.Q., 1149

Dominion Tests, 1349

Domino Test, 906a

Doppelt Mathematical Reasoning Test, 755

Doren Diagnostic Reading Test of Word Recognition Skills, 1466

Drake Musical Aptitude Tests, 598

Drake Musical Memory Test: A Test of Musical Talent, 2346

Draw-a-Man, 763

Draw-A-Person Quality Scale, 333

Drawing Aptitude Test, 2631

Drawing-Completion Test: A Projective Technique for the Investigation of Personality, 334

Driscoll Play Kit, 335

Driver Evaluator, 1162g

Driver Scalogram, 1163

[Driver Selection Forms and Tests], 2101

Driving Attitude Inventory, 1168

Duke University Political Science Information Test (American Government), 1803

Dunlap Academic Preference Blank, 2159

Dunning Physics Test, 1634

Duplex Series of Ability Tests, 756

Durost-Center Word Mastery Test, 564

Durrell Analysis of Reading Difficulty, New Edition, 1467

Durrell-Sullivan Reading Capacity and Achievement Tests, 1468

Factored Aptitude Series, 1367
Facts About Science Test: Experimental Form for Research in Testing, 1626
Faculty Morale Scale for Institutional Improvement, 1185
Fairfield Block Substitution Test, 166
Falsification Scales, 176
Family Adjustment Test, 154
Family Relations Test: An Objective Technique for Exploring Emotional Attitudes in Children, 337
Famous Sayings, 155
Fantasy Scale, 156
Farm Shop Tools: Recognition and Use: State High School Tests for Indiana, 1145
Farnsworth Dichotomous Test for Color Blindness, 1687
Farnsworth-Munsell 100-Hue Test for the Examination of Color Discrimination, 1688
Farnum Music Notation Test, 599
Fatigue Scales Kit, 157
Feature Profile Test: Pintner-Paterson Modification, 922
Fels Parent Behavior Rating Scales, 158
Ferguson Formboards, 2465
[Fernald Weights Discrimination Test], 923
Fetler Test, 300
Fields of Occupational Interest, 1864
Fiesenheiser Test of Ability to Read Drawings, 2078
Fife Tests of Ability, 1374
Figure Reasoning Test: A Non-Verbal Intelligence Test, 759
Fiji Test of General Ability, 2432
Filing Test: United-NOMA Business Entrance Tests, 2127
Final District-State Scholarship Tests, 1362b
Final Test in Agriculture: Comprehensive Objective Tests for Seventh-Grade Pupils in Texas, 2550
Final Test in Arithmetic: Comprehensive Objective Tests for Seventh-Grade Pupils in Texas, 2515
Final Test in Civics: Comprehensive Objective Tests for Seventh-Grade Pupils in Texas, 2871
Final Test in English: Comprehensive Objective Tests for Seventh-Grade Pupils in Texas, 2260
Final Test in Fifth-Grade Arithmetic: Comprehensive Objective Tests for Fifth-Grade Pupils in Texas, 2516
Final Test in Fifth-Grade English: Comprehensive Objective Tests for Fifth-Grade Pupils in Texas, 2261
Final Test in Fifth-Grade Geography: Comprehensive Objective Tests for Fifth-Grade Pupils in Texas, 2813
Final Test in Fifth-Grade Hygiene and Health: Comprehensive Tests for Fifth-Grade Pupils in Texas, 2601
Final Test in Fifth-Grade Reading: Com-

prehensive Objective Tests for Fifth-Grade Pupils in Texas, 2664
Final Test in Fifth-Grade United States History: Comprehensive Objective Tests for Fifth-Grade Pupils in Texas, 2845
Final Test in Geography: Comprehensive Objective Tests for Seventh-Grade Pupils in Texas, 2814
Final Test in Geography: Comprehensive Objective Tests for Sixth-Grade Pupils in Texas, 2815
Final Test in Physiology: Comprehensive Objective Tests for Seventh-Grade Pupils in Texas, 2602
Final Test in Reading: Comprehensive Objective Tests for Seventh-Grade Pupils in Texas, 2665
Final Test in Sixth-Grade Arithmetic: Comprehensive Objective Tests for Sixth-Grade Pupils in Texas, 2517
Final Test in Sixth-Grade English: Comprehensive Objective Tests for Sixth-Grade Pupils in Texas, 2262
Final Test in Sixth-Grade Physiology: Comprehensive Objective Tests for Sixth-Grade Pupils in Texas, 2603
Final Test in Sixth-Grade Spelling: Comprehensive Objective Tests for Sixth-Grade Pupils in Texas, 2323
Final Test in Spelling: Comprehensive Objective Tests for Fifth-Grade Pupils in Texas, 2324
Final Test in Spelling: Comprehensive Objective Tests for Seventh-Grade Pupils in Texas, 2325
Final Test in Texas History: Comprehensive Objective Tests for Sixth-Grade Pupils in Texas, 2846
Final Test in United States History: Comprehensive Objective Tests for Seventh-Grade Pupils in Texas, 2847
Firefighter Test, 2020
First and Second Year French: Every Pupil Test, 2366
First and Second Year Spanish: Every Pupil Test, 2412
First Course in Spanish: Comprehensive Tests in High School Subjects, 2413
First Year Algebra: Comprehensive Tests in High School Subjects, 2490
First Year Algebra: Every Pupil Scholarship Test, 996
First Year Algebra: Manchester Semester-End Achievement Tests, 997
First-Year Algebra: Multiple-Purpose Objective Tests in High School Subjects, 2491
First-Year Algebra (I): Final District-State Scholarship Test, 998
First-Year Algebra (I): Preliminary District-State Scholarship Test, 999
First Year Algebra Test: National Achievement Tests, 1000
First Year Algebra Test: State High School Tests for Indiana, 1001

First Year Bookkeeping: Manchester Semester-End Achievement Tests, 62

First Year Chemistry: Manchester Semester-End Achievement Tests, 1617

First Year French: Multiple-Purpose Objective Tests in High School Subjects, *2367*

First Year French: State High School Tests for Indiana, *2368*

First Year French Test, 638

First Year German: Every Pupil Scholarship Test, *2386*

First Year German: State High School Tests for Indiana, *2387*

First Year German Test, 654

First Year Grammar and Composition: Comprehensive Tests in High School Subjects, *2263*

First Year Latin: Every Pupil Scholarship Test, 669

First Year Latin: Manchester Semester-End Achievement Tests, 670

First-Year Latin: Multiple-Purpose Objective Tests in High School Subjects, *2399*

First Year Spanish: Every Pupil Scholarship Test, *2414*

First Year Spanish: Multiple-Purpose Objective Tests in High School Subjects, *2415*

First Year Spanish Test: State High School Tests for Indiana, 691

First-Year Typewriting: Manchester Semester-End Achievement Tests, 86

Five Factor Inventory, 1959

500 Outside Reading Tests for Freshmen and Sophomores, 502

500 Outside Reading Tests for Juniors and Seniors, Revised Edition, 503

Five Task Test: A Performance and Projective Test of Emotionality, Motor Skill and Organic Brain Damage, 338

Flags: A Test of Space Thinking, 1918

Flanagan Aptitude Classification Tests, 1375

Flash-X Sight Vocabulary Test, 1482

Florida Cumulative Guidance Record, Revised, 1305

[Fluency of Association] Test, *2242*

Flu-Numb Test, 1966e

Flu-Verb Test, 1966d

Foods: Every Pupil Scholarship Test, 1261

Foods I, Food Selection and Preparation: State High School Tests for Indiana, 1262

Foods II, Planning for Family Food Needs: State High School Tests for Indiana, 1263

Foreign Language Prognosis Test, 614

Forer Structured Sentence Completion Test, 339

Forer Vocational Survey, 340

Form Relations Group Test, 1919

Foster Mazes, 924

Four Picture Test, Second Edition, 341

Fourth Grade Geography Test, *2816*

Foust-Schorling Test of Functional Thinking in Mathematics, *2478*

Fowler-Parmenter Self-Scoring Interest Record, 1865

Franck Drawing Completion Test, 342

Frear-Coxe Clothing Test, *2619*

Freeman Acuity-Tester, 1689

Freeman Anxiety Neurosis and Psychosomatic Test, 159

Freeman Protometer, 1690

French, First Year—Second Semester: State High School Tests for Indiana, 639

French Grammar Test: Dominion Tests, *2369*

French Life and Culture Test, *2370*

French I and II: Achievement Examinations for Secondary Schools, 641

French I and II: Final District-State Scholarship Test, 640

French I and II: Midwest High School Achievement Examinations, 642

French I and II: Preliminary District-State Scholarship Test, 643

French Reading Test: Dominion Tests, *2371*

French Recognition Vocabulary Test, 639

French: Teacher Education Examination Program, 644

French Test (Two-Year Course): The Affiliation Testing Program for Catholic Secondary Schools, 1343e

[French Tests for Professional Courses in Knowledge of Sports]: Physical Education Major Examinations, *2604*

French Vocabulary Test: Dominion Tests, *2372*

Friend-Critic Statement, 160

Full-Range Picture Vocabulary Test, 887

Fulmer-Schrammel Physics Test, 1635

Functional Evaluation in Mathematics, 950

Functional Readiness Questionnaire for School and College Students, 1469

Fundamentals Test: National Clerical Ability Tests, *2120*

Furbay-Schrammel Social Comprehension Test, 1213

Furness Test of Aural Comprehension in Spanish, 692

G.C. ANECDOTAL Record Form, 1306

G.C. Cumulative Record Folder, Revised Edition, 1307

G.C. Interview Record Form, 1308

G.C. Personality Development Record, 161

G.C. Self-Scoring Interest Record, Second Experimental Edition, 1865

G.C. Student Information Form, Revised, 1309

G-Z Temperament Map, 175

Garage Mechanic Test, 2079

Gardner Behavior Chart, *2164*

Garman-Schrammel Algebra Test, 1002

Garrison First Year Reading Test, *2666*
Garvey Primary Reading Test, *2667*
Gates Advanced Primary Reading Tests, 1407
Gates Basic Reading Tests, 1408
Gates Primary Reading Tests, 1409
Gates Reading Diagnostic Tests, 1470
Gates Reading Readiness Tests, 1495
Gates Reading Survey, 1410
Gates-Russell Spelling Diagnosis Test, 537
Gates Silent Reading Tests, 1408
Gates-Strang Health Knowledge Tests, *2605*
Geist Picture Interest Inventory, 1866
General Achievement Test in Fire Safety: National Fire Prevention Tests, *2562*
General Adaptability Battery, 1822
General Aptitude Test Battery, 1376
General Background in the Natural Sciences: Iowa Tests of Educational Development, Test 2, 1564
General Biology Test: National Achievement Tests, 1590
General Business: Every Pupil Scholarship Test, 50
General Chemistry Test: National Achievement Tests, 1618
General Classification Battery, 1822a
General Clerical Ability Test: ETSA Tests, Test 3A, 1821c
General Clerical: Every Pupil Test, *2119*
General Clerical Test, PCI Selection Form 20, 1847
General Education Series, *2165, 2171, 2175, 2301-2, 2703, 2706, 2712, 2727-8, 2742*
General First-Aid Test for Senior-High School Students: National Safety Education Tests, *2563*
General Goals of Life Inventory: General Education Series, *2165*
General High School Mathematics: Manchester Semester-End Achievement Tests, *2479*
General Home Economics: State High School Tests for Indiana, *2620*
General Information Survey, 1960
General Information Test: National Clerical Ability Tests, *2121*
General Intelligence: Northumberland Standardised Tests (1925 Series), 760
General Intelligence Test for Africans, *2433*
General Knowledge Test of Local, State and National Government, *2872*
General Mathematical Ability: Tests of General Educational Development, Test 5, 951
General Mathematics: Every Pupil Scholarship Test, 952
General Mathematics: Midwest High School Achievement Examinations, 953
General Mathematics III: Achievement Examinations for Secondary Schools, 954

General Mental Ability Test: ETSA Tests, Test 1A, 1821a
General Office Clerical Test (Including Filing): National Business Entrance Tests, 51
General Physics Test: National Achievement Tests, 1636
General Reading Test: [Ohio Senior Survey Tests], 1411
General Safety Education Test for Junior-High-School Pupils: National Safety Education Tests, *2564*
General Sales Ability, 1368c
General Scholarship Test for High School Seniors, 14
General Science: Comprehensive Objective Tests in High School Subjects, *2721*
General Science: Every Pupil Scholarship Test, 1555
General Science: Every Pupil Test, 1556
General Science: Final District-State Scholarship Test, 1557
General Science: Preliminary District-State Scholarship Test, 1558
General Science Scales, 1559
General Science Test for Prospective Nurses: George Washington University Series Nursing Tests, *2032d*
General Science Test: Gibson's Attainment Tests, *2722*
General Science Test: National Achievement Tests, 1560
General Science Test: State High School Tests for Indiana, 1561
General Science III: Achievement Examinations for Secondary Schools, 1562
General Science III: Midwest High School Achievement Examinations, 1563
General Shop Woodworking: Manchester Semester-End Achievement Tests, 1276
General Test of Business Information, 52
General Test on Traffic and Driving Knowledge, 1165
General Test T, 711
General Verbal Practice Tests G1 and G2, 761
General Vocabulary: Iowa Tests of Educational Development, Test 8, 568
Generalized Attitude Scales, 267
Geography Ability Test: Gibson's Attainment Tests, *2817*
Geography: Every Pupil Scholarship Test, 1745
Geography: Every Pupil Test, 1746
Geography Test: Municipal Tests: National Achievement Tests, 1747
Geography Test: National Achievement Tests, 1748
Geometry Attainment Test, 1105
Geometry: Every Pupil Test, 1106
Geometry Survey Test, 1107
George Washington University Series, 198, 291, 1183, 1208, 2032, *2354, 2438, 2595*

Group Test 81, 1921
Group Test 90A, 769
Group Test in Siddur Reading, 2390
Group Test of Intelligence, 770
Group Test of Learning Capacity: Dominion Tests, 770
Group Test of Reading Readiness: Dominion Tests, 1496
Group Test of Speed and Accuracy in Arithmetic Computation: Dominion Tests, 1061
[Guidance Cumulative Folder and Record Forms], 1310
Guidance Inventory, 170
Guidance Questionnaire, 2913
Guidance Questionnaire for Students of Speech, 2318
Guidance Summary Form for Use in Vocational and Educational Counseling, 1961
Guide to Employment Decision: For Sales Personnel Only, 2948
Guilford-Martin Inventory of Factors GAMIN, Abridged Edition, 171
Guilford-Martin Personnel Inventory, 172
Guilford-Martin Temperament Profile Chart, 173
Guilford-Shneidman-Zimmerman Interest Survey, 1868
Guilford-Zimmerman Aptitude Survey, 1377
Guilford-Zimmerman Temperament Survey, 174
Gulick Vocabulary Survey, 565a

H-T-P: HOUSE-TREE-PERSON Projective Technique, 348
Haggerty-Olson-Wickman Behavior Rating Schedules, 177
Haggerty Reading Examination, 2668
Hall Salespower Inventory, 2050
Hamilton Cumulative Record Folder, Revised Edition, 2644
Hammond Matrix Sorter, 1151
Handbook of Tests for Use in Schools, Second Edition, 3
Hand-Eye Coordination: Edmiston Motor Capacity Test, 1668a
Handicap Problems Inventory, 178
Hand-Tool Dexterity Test, 1899
Hanes-Benz Biology Test, 2738
Hanes Sales Selection Inventory, Revised Edition, 2051
Hankes' Answer Sheets, 1152
Hannaford Industrial Safety Attitude Scales, 1166
Harlow Achievement Tests for First and Second Grades, 2111
Harlow Achievement Tests for Texas, 19
Harlow Battery Achievement Test, 20
Harris Tests of Lateral Dominance, 1651
Harrison-Stroud Reading Readiness Profiles, 1497
Harrower's Group Rorschach, 373c
Harrower's Multiple Choice Test, 373d

[Hay Tests for Clerical Aptitude], 1839
Health and Safety Education Test: National Achievement Tests, 1230
Health and Safety Education Test: State High School Tests for Indiana, 1231
Health Awareness Test, 2606
Health Education and Hygiene: Every Pupil Test, 1232
Health Education Test: Knowledge and Application: Acorn National Achievement Tests, Revised Edition, 1233
Health Guidance Test, 2919
Health Inventories, 2607
Health Inventory for High School Students, 1234
Health Knowledge and Attitude: Every Pupil Scholarship Test, 2608
Health Knowledge Test, 2609
Health Knowledge Test for College Freshmen: National Achievement Tests, 1235
Health: Manchester Semester-End Achievement Tests, 1236
Health Practice Inventory, 1237
Health Test: National Achievement Tests, 1238
Healy-Fernald Puzzle Box A, 906a
Healy Pictorial Completion Tests, 925
Hearing Evaluator, 1659e
Hebrew Aptitude Test, 2391
Hebrew Intermediate Test, 2392
Hebrew Primary Test, 2393
Hebrew School Attitude Test, 2653
Helping With Food in the Home: State High School Tests for Indiana, 1264
Helping With the Housekeeping: State High School Tests for Indiana, 1265
Henderson Analysis of Interest, [Second Edition], 1869
Henmon-Nelson Tests of Mental Ability: The Clapp-Young Self-Marking Tests, 771
Hemon-Nelson Tests of Mental Ability, Revised Edition, 772
Herring Revision of the Binet-Simon Tests, 2466
Heston Personal Adjustment Inventory, 179
Hiett Simplified Shorthand Test (Gregg), 71
Hiett Stenography Test (Gregg), 2132
High School American History: Every Pupil Scholarship Test, 2848
High School Attitude Scale, 267i
High School Characteristics Index, 277a
High School Economics: Manchester Semester-End Achievement Tests, 1738
High School Fundamentals Evaluation Test, 21
High School Health: Every Pupil Scholarship Test, 1239
High School Physics: Comprehensive Tests in High School Subjects, 2771
High School Placement Test, 773
High School Reading Test: National Achievement Tests, 1412

Language Battery: National Institute for Personnel Research Normal Battery, 451

Language Essentials Tests, 452

Language Usage: Public School Achievement Tests, 453

Lankton First-Year Algebra Test, 1005

Larson-Greene Unit Tests in First-Year Algebra, 1006

Latin I and II: Achievement Examinations for Secondary Schools, 676

Latin I and II: Every Pupil Test, 674

Latin I and II: Final District-State Scholarship Test, 675

Latin I and II: Midwest High School Achievement Examinations, 677

Latin I and II: Preliminary District-State Scholarship Test, 678

Latin Test: State High School Tests for Indiana, 679

Latin Test (Two-Year Course): The Affiliation Testing Program for Catholic Secondary Schools, 1343c

Lauer Driver Reaction Inventory, 1168

Law School Admission Test, 2010

Lawshe-Kephart Personnel Comparison System, 1985

Laycock Mental Ability Test, 786

Lazerte Diagnostic Problem-Solving Test in Arithmetic, 2520

Leaderless Group Test, 1822b

Leadership Ability Evaluation, 209a

Leadership Opinion Questionnaire, 2091

Leadership Q-Sort Test (A Test of Leadership Values), 210

Leahy-Fenlason Rating Scale for Social Case Workers, 2943

Learning Methods Test, 1472

Leavell Analytical Oral Reading Test, 1486

Leavell Hand-Eye Coordinator Tests, 1652

Lee-Clark Arithmetic Fundamentals Survey Test: High School Edition, 1067

Lee-Clark Reading Readiness Test, 1951 Revision, 1498

Lee-Clark Reading Test, 1958 Revision, 1418

Lee Test of Algebraic Ability, 1007

Lee Test of Geometric Aptitude, 1111

Leiter Adaptation of Arthur's Stencil Design Test, 895

Leiter Adaptation of the Painted Cube Test, 895

Leiter Adult Intelligence Scale, 895

Leiter International Performance Scale, 896

Leiter International Performance Scale: Arthur Adaptation, 897

Leiter Nomenclature Profile, 211

Leiter-Partington Adult Performance Scale, 2468

Leiter Profile, 211

Leonard Diagnostic Test in Punctuation and Capitalization, 2268

Level of Aspiration Board, 212

Lewerenz-Steinmetz Orientation Test: Concerning Fundamental Aims of Education, 2178

Library Orientation Test for College Freshmen, 1955 Edition, 1527

Library Test for Junior High Schools, 2705

Library Usage Test, 1528

Life Adjustment Inventory, 213

Life Experience Inventory, 214

Likes and Interests Test, 142

Lincoln Diagnostic Spelling Tests, [Educational Records Bureau Edition], 543

Lincoln Diagnostic Spelling Tests, [Public School Publishing Company Edition], 544

Lincoln Intermediate Spelling Test, 543b

Lincoln-Oseretsky Motor Development Scale, 1669

Lincoln Primary Spelling Test, 543a

Linfert-Hierholzer Scale for Measuring the Mental Development of Infants During the First Year of Life, 2469

Linguistic Awareness Test, 454

Literary Information Test: American Literature: Test 3.5, 2305

Literary Information Test: English Literature: Test 3.4, 2306

Literature Appreciation Tests, 507

Literature: Every Pupil Scholarship Test, 508

Literature Questionnaire: The Drama: Test 3.21, 2307

Literature Questionnaire: The Novel: Test 3.2a, 2308

Literature Test: Municipal Tests: National Achievement Tests, 2309

Literature Test: National Achievement Tests, 509

Little Pink Tower Test, 898

Logical Reasoning, 1529

Logical Reasoning Test: General Education Series, 2706

Lorge-Thorndike Intelligence Tests, 787

Los Angeles Diagnostic Tests: Fundamentals of Arithmetic, 1068

Los Angeles Diagnostic Tests: Language (A Test in Capitalization, Punctuation and Language Usage), 2269

Los Angeles Diagnostic Tests: Reasoning in Arithmetic, 1069

Los Angeles Elementary Reading Test, 1419

Los Angeles Primary Reading Test, 2670

Lothian English Tests: Vocabulary and Comprehension, 2671

Lowenfeld Kaleidoblocs, 360

Lowenfeld Mosaic Test, 361

Lower Extension of the Inglis Tests of English Vocabulary, 571

Lowry-Lucier Reasoning Test Combination, 788

Lundeberg-Tharp Audition Test in French, 647

Lundeberg-Tharp Audition Test in German, 657

Medieval History: Every Pupil Test, *2853*

Meier Art Tests: I, Art Judgment, 593

Meier-Seashore Art Judgment Test, 593

Melbo Social Science Survey Test, *2793*

Mellenbruch Curve-Block Series, 1901

Mellenbruch Mechanical Aptitude Test for Men and Women, 1927

Mellenbruch Mechanical Motivation Test, 1927

Memory-for-Designs Test, 221

Mental Alertness: National Institute for Personnel Research High Level Battery, 791

Mental Alertness: National Institute for Personnel Research Normal Battery, 792

Mental Alertness Test: George Washington University Series, Revised Form, *2438*

Mental Health Analysis, 1959 Revision, 222

Merit Rating Series, 1987

Mental Tests, 1356

Merrill-Palmer Logarithmic Developmental Graph, 1312

Merrill-Palmer Scale of Mental Tests, 898

Metricon Decibel Meter, 1662

Metropolitan Achievement Tests, [1947 Edition], 26

Metropolitan Achievement Tests, [1960 Edition], 27; Arithmetic, 1072; Reading, 1421; Science, 1566; Social Studies, 1716

Metropolitan Primary Cursive Handwriting Scale, 1220

Metropolitan Primary Manuscript Handwriting Scale, 1220

Metropolitan Readiness Tests, 1500

Meyer Finger Mazes, 930

Miami-Oxford Curve-Block Series, 1901

Michigan Adult Profile, *2920*

Michigan Nonverbal Series, *2920*

Michigan Occupational Preference Check List, *2920*

Michigan Picture Test, 365

Michigan Pre-School T/O Vision Tests, 1702a

Michigan Speed of Reading Test, *2695*

Michigan Vocabulary Profile Test, 572

Middleton Industrial Arts Test, 1282

Midland Attainment Tests, *2252, 2297, 2334, 2496, 2663*

Midwest High School Achievement Examinations, 1357

Miles Career Evaluation Inventory, *2921*

Miller Analogies Test, 794

Miller-Davis French Test, *2373*

Mill Hill Vocabulary Scale, 793

Milne Arithmetic Test, 1073

Minnesota Assembly Test, 1928

Minnesota Check List for Food Preparation and Serving, Third Edition, 1272

Minnesota Clerical Test, 1841

Minnesota Counseling Inventory, 223

Minnesota Engineering Analogies Test, 2004

Minnesota Food Score Cards, Revised Edition, *2624*

Minnesota Home Status Index: A Scale for Measuring Urban Home Environment, 1338

Minnesota House Design and House Furnishing Test, *2625*

Minnesota Inventory of Social Attitudes, *2180*

Minnesota Manual Dexterity Test, 1902

Minnesota Mechanical Assembly Test, 1928

Minnesota Multiphasic Personality Inventory, Revised Edition, 224

Minnesota Occupational Rating Scales and Counseling Profile, *2922*

Minnesota Paper Form Board Test, 1929

Minnesota Personality Scale, *2181*

Minnesota Preschool Scale, 899

Minnesota Rate of Manipulation Test, [1933 Edition], 1903

Minnesota Rate of Manipulation Test, [1946 Edition], 1904

Minnesota Rating Scale for Personal Qualities and Abilities, [Fourth Revision], 225

Minnesota Reading Examination for College Students, 1422

Minnesota Scale for the Survey of Opinions, *2182*

Minnesota Spatial Relations Test, 1930

Minnesota Speed of Reading Test for College Students, 1516

Minnesota T-S-E Inventory, 226

Minnesota Teacher Attitude Inventory, 1191

Minnesota Vocational Test for Clerical Workers, 1841

Mitchell Vocabulary Test, 795

Modern English Usage Test, *2270*

Modern European History: Comprehensive Tests in High School Subjects, *2854*

Modern European History: Every Pupil Scholarship Test, *2855*

Modern European History: Multiple-Purpose Objective Tests in High School Subjects, *2856*

Modern Geography and Allied Social Studies, *2821*

Modern History: Every Pupil Test, *2857*

Modern Language Aptitude Test, 618

Modern School Achievement Tests: Skills Edition, 28

Modern World History: Achievement Examinations for Secondary Schools, 1777

Modern World History: Midwest High School Achievement Examinations, 1783

Modification of the Kent-Shakow Formboard, *2470*

Modified Alpha Examination Form 9, 796

Modified Ortho-Rater, 1698b

Money and Banking : Every Pupil Scholarship Test, *2810*

Monroe's Standardized Silent Reading Tests, 1423

Mooney Problem Check List, 1950 Revision, 227

Moore Eye-Hand Coordination and Color-Matching Test, 1653

Mooseheart Graphic Rating Scale for Housemothers and Housefathers, *2944*

Moray House Adult Test 1, 797d

Moray House Arithmetic Tests, 1074

Moray House English Tests, 456

Moray House Intelligence Tests, 797

Moray House Junior Arithmetic Test 2, 1074a

Moray House Junior English Test 2, 456a

Moray House Junior Reasoning Test 2 for Nine-Year-Olds, 797a

Moray House Picture Intelligence Test 1, 798

Moray House Space Tests, 1931

Moray House Test 11a, *2439*

Moray House Verbal Reasoning Test (Adv.) 10, 797c

Moray House Verbal Reasoning Test 63, 797b

Mordy-Schrammel American Government Test, 1807

Mordy-Schrammel Constitution Test, *2874*

Mordy-Schrammel Elementary Civics Test, *2875*

Morgan Achievement Test in Mathematics for Employee Selection, 969

Morgan IQ Calculator, *2554*

Morgan Spelling Test for Business and Industry, *2327*

Morgan Spelling Test for Schools and Colleges, *2327*

Morrison-McCall Spelling Scale, 545

Morrison Rating Scale Profile for Teachers, *2581*

Mother-Child Relationship Evaluation, 227a

Mother's Day Fatigue Scale, 157c

Motivation Analysis Test, Research Edition, 228

Motivation Indicator, 1876

Motor Skills Tests Adapted to the Blind, 1905

Mount Holyoke College Reading Test, *2673*

Multi-Aptitude Test, 1380

Multidimensional Scale for Rating Psychiatric Patients, Hospital Form, 229

Multi-Mental Scale, *2440*

Multiple Aptitude Tests, 1959 Edition, 1381

[Multiple Choice Attitudes Questionnaire], 371c

Multiple Purpose Self Trainer, 1158

Multi-Racial Picture Intelligence Tests Suitable for Use in African and Asian Schools, 799

Multiscore Profile Form and Scoring Codes, *2555*

Municipal Battery : National Achievement Tests, 29

Murphy-Durrell Diagnostic Reading Readiness Test, 1501

Music Education : National Teacher Examinations, 607

Musical Achievement Test, *2351*

Musical Appreciation Ability Test : Gibson's Attainment Tests, *2352*

Musical Aptitude Test : Series A, 608

Mutilated Cubes Test of Power to Visualize, *2903*

My Code : Northwestern University Citizenship Tests, *2183*

My Dog Test, 1446b

My Ideas About Religion, 1325

Myers-Briggs Type Indicator, 230

Myers-Ruch High School Progress Test, *2113*

Myokinetic Psychodiagnosis (M.K.P.), 366

[N.B. GROUP Tests], 800

N.B. Group Test for Five and Six Year Olds, 800a

N.B. Group Test for Seven and Eight Year Olds, 800b

N.I.I.P. Squares Test, 1932

N.I.P.R. Cube Construction Test, 1822a

NLN Achievement Tests for Basic Professional Nursing Program, 2033

NLN Achievement Tests for Psychiatric Aides, 2034

NLN Graduate Nurse Examination, 2035

NLN Mathematics Test, 2038c

NLN Natural Science Achievement Test, 2038d

NLN Practical Nurse Achievement Tests, 2036

NLN Pre-Admission and Classification Examination, 2037

NLN Pre-Nursing and Guidance Examination, 2038

NLN Reading Comprehension Test, 2035b, 2038b

NLN Social Studies Achievement Test, 2038e

NLN Test of Academic Aptitude, 2035a, 2038a

National Achievement Tests, 30

National Achievement Tests, [Series Entry], 1358

National Bicycle Tests, *2568*, 1162a

National Business Entrance Tests, 53; separate tests, 49, 51, 60, 65, 81, 95

National Clerical Ability Tests, 53

National Council of Geography Teachers Geography Test, *2816*

National Educational Development Tests, 31

National Fire Prevention Tests, *2562*

National Guidance Testing Program, 1359

Pain Apperception Test, 368
Paper Puzzles: A Test of Space Relations, 1935
Parents Rating Scale, *2189*
Parke Commercial Law Test, 66
Parr Skill-Ability Tests, *2708*
Parsons Social Comprehension Test, 1215
Passalong Test: A Performance Test of Intelligence, 904
Pathways Test, 895
Patient's Self-History Form, Second Edition, 1243
Pattern Perception Test, 819
Pattern Similarity Quotient, *2892*
Patterned Analytical Interview: Hiring Kit, 2052
Patterned Interview Form, 1981
Patterned Merit Review, 1980
Patterson Test or Study Exercises on the Constitution of the United States, 1808
Patterson Test or Study Exercises on the Declaration of Independence, 1809
Patterson's Tests on the Federal Constitution, 1810
Pauli Test, [N.I.P.R. Edition, Experimental Form], 236
Payne Sentence Completion Blank, 378
Peabody Library Information Test, 1530
Peabody Picture Vocabulary Test, 905
Peel Group Tests of Practical Ability, *2442*
Peltier-Durost Civics and Citizenship Test, 1811
Pennsylvania Bi-Manual Worksample, 1908
Per-Flu-Dex Tests, 1966
Per-Numb Test, 1966c
Per-Symb Test, 1966a
Per-Verb Test, 1966b
Perception of Relations Scales, *2443*
Perceptual Forms Test, 1699
Perceptual Mechanics Test, *2904*
Perceptual Speed (Identical Forms), 931a
Performance Alertness "PA" (With Pictures): Individual Placement Series (Area I), 820
Performance Record, 1989
[Performance Review Forms], 1990
Performance Tests of Intelligence: A Series of Non-Linguistic Tests for Deaf and Normal Children, Third Edition, 906
Permanent Record [National Association of Secondary-School Principals], 1314
Perrin Motor Coordination Test, 1671
Personal Adaptability Test, *2190*
Personal Adjustability Test: ETSA Tests, Test 8A, 1821h
Personal and Social Development Program, 237
Personal Audit, 238
Personal Classification Test, 821
Personal Data Blank, 1991
Personal Data Form for Scientific, Engineering, and Technical Personnel, 2041b

Personal Data Scale, *2191*
Personal Experience and Attitude Questionnaire, 239
Personal Health Inventory, *2610*
Personal History, *2946*
Personal History Record, *2192*
Personal Index, 240
Personal Inventory of Background Factors, 2070
Personal Inventory of Basic Factors, *2948*
Personal Preference Inventory: Student Form, *2193*
Personal Preference Scale, 241
Personal Preference Schedule for Student Nurses, 2030d, 2031c
Personal Reaction Test for Transit Employees, 2100b
Personal Relations Inventory, 242
Personal-Social Adjustment Inventory, 285
Personality and Interest Inventory, 243
Personality Evaluation Form: A Technique for the Organization and Interpretation of Personality Data, 244
Personality Index, 245
Personality Inventory, 246
Personality-Maturity Test, *2194*
Personality Rating Chart for Preschool Children, *2195*
Personality Rating Scale for Preschool Children, *2196*
Personality Record (Revised), 248
Personality Report, 249
Personality Report Sheet, 1310c
Personality Schedule, 1929 Edition, 250
Personality Sketches: For Individual Diagnosis, *2197*
Personality Survey, *2198*
Personnel Classification Test, [Henderson], *2444*
Personnel Institute Clerical Tests, 1845
Personnel Institute Hiring Kit, 2058
[Personnel Interviewing Forms], 1992
Personnel Reaction Blank, 251
[Personnel Record Form], *2647*
Personnel Research Institute Area Interview—Long Form, 2059
Personnel Research Institute Classification Test, 822
[Personnel Research Institute Clerical Battery], 1846
Personnel Research Institute Factory Series Test, 823
Personnel Research Institute Test of Shorthand Skills, 72
Personnel Selection and Classification Test, 1824
Personnel Service Rating Report, 2022
Personnel Tests for Industry, 824
Pertinent Questions, 932
Peters Biblical Knowledge Test, 1327
Phillips-Woody Group Tests for Reversals, *2682*
Philo-Phobe, 252
Phonograph Record Tests in Arithmetic, *2521*

Phonovisual Diagnostic Spelling Test, [1949 Edition], 548

Phonovisual Diagnostic Spelling Test, [1958 Edition], 549

Photo-Analysis Test, 352c

Physical Education Achievement Scales for Boys in Secondary Schools, *2611*

Physical Education Major Examinations, *2604*

Physical Education: National Teacher Examinations, 1244

Physical Education: Teacher Education Examination Program, 1245

Physical Education Tests, 1246

Physical Examination Record, *2612*

Physical Geography: Every Pupil Scholarship Test, 1749

Physical Geography: Multiple-Purpose Objective Tests in High School Subjects, *2822*

Physical Science Aptitude Examination, Special Edition, 1567

Physical Science: Teacher Education Examination Program, 1568

Physics: Achievement Examinations for Secondary Schools, 1644

Physics: Every Pupil Scholarship Test, 1641

Physics: Every Pupil Test, 1642

Physics: Final District-State Scholarship Test, 1643

Physics: Manchester Semester-End Achievement Tests, 1645

Physics: Midwest High School Achievement Examinations, 1646

Physics: Multiple-Purpose Objective Tests in High School Subjects, *2774*

Physics: Preliminary District-State Scholarship Test, 1647

Physics Test: The Affiliation Testing Program for Catholic Secondary Schools, 1343j

Physics Test: State High School Tests for Indiana, 1648

Physiography Test, *2823*

Physiology: Every Pupil Scholarship Test, *2613*

Pictographic Self Rating Scale, 1531

Pictorial Interest Inventory, 1883

Pictorial Study of Values: Pictorial Allport-Vernon, 253

[Picture Attitudes Test], 371a

Picture Completion Test, 906a

Picture Impressions: A Projective Technique for Investigating the Patient-Therapist Relationship, 369

Picture Intelligence Test 1, 825

Picture Interest Inventory, 1884

Picture Speech Sound Discrimination Test for Young Children, 1664b

Picture Story Completion Test, 352b

Picture Title Test, 352d

Picture Word-Recognition Test: The Standard Reading Tests, Test 9, 1452i

Picture World Test, 370

Pintner Advanced Test, 827d

Pintner-Cunningham Primary Mental Test, 827a

Pintner-Cunningham Primary Test, 827a

Pintner-Durost Elementary Test, 827b

Pintner General Ability Tests: Non-Language Series, 826

Pintner General Ability Tests: Verbal Series, 827

Pintner Intelligence Test, 827c

Pintner Intermediate Test, 827c

Pintner Non-Language Primary Mental Test, *2445*

Pintner-Paterson Scale of Performance Tests, *2472*

Placement Examination in General Engineering Drawing, Revised Edition, *2942*

Plane Geometry: Achievement Examinations for Secondary Schools, 1115

Plane Geometry: Comprehensive Tests in High School Subjects, *2541*

Plane Geometry: Every Pupil Scholarship Test, 1113

Plane Geometry: Final District-State Scholarship Test, 1114

Plane Geometry: Manchester Semester-End Achievement Tests, 1116

Plane Geometry: Midwest High School Achievement Examinations, 1117

Plane Geometry: National Achievement Tests, 1118

Plane Geometry: Preliminary District-State Scholarship Test, 1119

Plane Geometry Test: The Affiliation Testing Program for Catholic Secondary Schools, 1343g

Plane Geometry Test: State High School Tests for Indiana, 1120

Plane Trigonometry: National Achievement Tests, 1133

Plot-Completion Test, *2243*

Plumb IQ Slide Rule for Use With the Wechsler-Bellevue Intelligence Scale, *2556*

Poley Precis Test: A Test by Paragraph Summaries of Reading Comprehension, *2683*

Policeman Test, *2023*

Polyfactorial Study of Personality, 254

Porteus Maze Extension, 907c

Porteus Maze Supplement, 907d

Porteus Maze Test, 907

Porteus Maze Test (Arthur Revision), 877b

Portland Prognostic Tests for Mathematics, 970

[Position Response Form and Response Form], 255

Post-School Inventory, 1988a

Potter-Nash Aptitude Test for Lumber Inspectors and Other General Personnel Who Handle Lumber, *2024*

Potts-Bennett Tests, *2030*

Power-Achievement Tests in Gregg Shorthand, *2133*

SRA Junior Inventory, 274
SRA Language Skills, *2272*
SRA Mechanical Aptitudes, 1940
SRA Non-Verbal Classification Form, 840
SRA Non-Verbal Form, 840
SRA Primary Mental Abilities, 1384
SRA Reading Record, 1443
SRA Sales Attitudes Check List, 2060
SRA Self-Scorer, *2557*
SRA Survey of Interpersonal Values, 275
SRA Tests of Educational Ability, 841
SRA Tests of General Ability, 842
SRA Typing Adaptability Test, 89
SRA Typing Skills, 90
SRA Verbal Classification Form, 843
SRA Verbal Form, 843
SRA Youth Inventory, 276
SSRC S-A Schedule, 295
Safety Education: Manchester Semester-End Achievement Tests, 1173
Sales Aptitude Inventory, 1820c
Sales Aptitude Test: ETSA Tests, Test 7A, 1821g
Sales Comprehension Test, 2061
Sales Employee Inventory, 2062
Sales Method Index, 2063
Sales Motivation Inventory, 2064
Sales Personnel Description Form, 2065
Sales Questionnaire, *2947*
Sales Situation Test, 2066
Sangren-Reidy Survey Tests in Arithmetic, *2524*
Sangren-Woody Reading Test, 1444
Sare-Sanders Sociology Test, 1817
Scale for Evaluating the School Behavior of Children Ten to Fifteen, *2206*
Scale for Evaluating Student-Efficiency in the Home Economics Laboratory, *2627*
Scale for Measuring Attitude Toward Any Defined Group, 267b; Any Home Making Activity, 267g; Any Institution, 267c; Any Practice, 267f; Any Proposed Social Action, 267e; Any Vocation, 267b
Scale for Measuring Attitude Toward Races and Nationalities, 267d
Scale for Measuring Attitude Toward Teaching, *2585*
Scale for Measuring Developmental Age in Girls, 303b
Scale for Measuring Individual and Group "Morale," 267h
Scale for Rating Effective Teacher Behavior, *2586*
Scale of Beliefs for Junior High School: Tests 4.4 and 4.5, *2207*
Scale of Beliefs: Tests 4.21 and 4.31, *2208*
Scale of Non-Verbal Mental Ability, 804a
Scale of Problems in Commercial Arithmetic, *2525*
Scale to Measure Attitude Toward Any School Subject, 267a
Scholarship Qualifying Test, *2450*
Scholastic Achievement Series, 37; Arith-

metic, 1083; English-Spelling, 470
Scholastic Diagnostic Reading Test, 1445
Scholastic Mental Ability Tests, 844
Scholastic Reading Readiness Test, 1505
Schonell Diagnostic Arithmetic Tests, 1084
Schonell Diagnostic English Tests, 471
Schonell Reading Tests, 1446
School Adjustment Questionnaire, *2209*
School Aptitude Test: Thanet Mental Tests, 845
[School Characteristics Index], 277
School Inventory, 278
School Motivation Analysis Test, Research Edition, 279
School Practices Questionnaire: A Test of the Curriculum, *2106*
School Readiness Inventory, 1499
[School Records], 1317
Schorling-Clark-Potter Arithmetic Test, Revised Edition, 1062
Schrammel General Ability Test, 846
Schrammel-Gorbutt Personality Adjustjustment Scale, 280
Schrammel-Gray High School and College Reading Test, 1447
Schrammel-Otterstrom Arithmetic Test, 1085
Schrammel-Reed Solid Geometry Test, 1121
Schrammel-Wharton Vocabulary Test, 576
Schubert General Ability Battery, 847
Science Applications Test: Gibson's Attainment Tests, *2724*
Science Aptitude Examination, 1571
Science Background: A Science Service Test to Identify Potential Scientific and Technical Talent, 1572
Science Information Test, *2725*
Science Research Temperament Scale, 281
Scientific Attitudes, *2760*
Scientific Ingenuity and Juristic Aptitude Test, 848
Scientific Methods: Test 1, Controlled Experimentation Test in Science, *2761*
Scientific Thinking: Every Pupil Test, *2762*
Score Transmuter, *2558*
Scott Company Mental Alertness Test, 849
Scottish Council for Research in Education 1932 Mental Survey Test, *2451*
Scovill Classification Test, *2452*
Screening Audiometers, 1655e
Screening Tests for Apprentices, 1825
Seashore-Bennett Stenographic Proficiency Tests: A Standard Recorded Stenographic Worksample, 74
Seashore Measures of Musical Talents, Revised Edition, 609
Seattle Algebra Test, 1009
Seattle Plane Geometry Test, 1122
Seattle Solid Geometry Test Series, 1123
Second Course in Algebra: Comprehen-

World History: Every Pupil Scholarship Test, 1788
World History: Every Pupil Test, 1789
World History: Final District-State Scholarship Test, 1790
World History: Manchester Semester-End Achievement Tests, 1791
World History: Multiple-Purpose Objective Tests in High School Subjects, *2862*
World History: Preliminary District-State Scholarship Test, 1792
World History Test: Acorn National Achievement Tests, 1793
World History Test: The Affiliation Testing Program for Catholic Secondary Schools, 1343l
World History Test: State High School Tests for Indiana, 1794

World Test, 394
Worth of People to Each Other Inventory, 1142
Wrightstone Scale of Civic Beliefs, *2238*

YALE Educational Aptitude Test Battery, 1386
Yale Psycho-Clinic Developmental Schedules, 888
Yale Tests of Child Development, 888
Young-Estabrooks Scale for Measuring Studiousness by Means of the Strong Vocational Interest Blank for Men, *2714*
Your Activities and Attitudes, *2239*
Your Educational Plans, 1895
Ypsilanti Reading Test, *2678*

NAME INDEX *

AAHPER Youth Fitness Project: *test,* 1222
Abbott, Allan: *test,* 412
Abelson, Harold H.: *rev,* 2156, 2226
Abercrombie, Stanley A.: *test,* 1167, 1169
Aborn, Murray: *rev,* 913
Adams, Clifford R.: *test,* 238
Adams, Elizabeth C.: *rev,* 1786, 1796
Adams, Georgia Sachs: *test,* 7, 1575-6, 1594, 1750, 1784
Adams, Michael: *test,* 2009
Adams, R. H.: *test,* 758
Adcock, C. J.: *rev,* 289, 361, 852
Adkins, Dorothy C.: *rev,* 65, 1039, 1373, 1763, 1769, 1824, 2843, 2852
Adler, Dan L.: *rev,* 214, 306
Afflerbach, Janet G.: *rev,* 559, 1327, 1527; *test,* 424, 573
Afflerbach, Lois Grimes: *rev,* 1527
Agard, Frederick B.: *rev,* 692, 697, 2409
Aiken, Beulah: *test,* 699
Aiken, J. R.: *test,* 654
Aiken, Mary: *test,* 822, 1846
Ainsworth, Mary D.: *rev,* 391-2
Albright, Norma A.: *rev,* 1275, 2623
Alexander, Theron: *test,* 326
Alexander, W. P.: *test,* 436, 778, 845, 876, 904, 1036
Alft, E. C.: *test,* 1740
Aliferis, James: *test,* 595
Allen, L. W.: *test,* 1471
Allen, Richard D.: *test,* 26
Almack, John C.: *rev,* 537, 1224, 2322, 2331
Alper, Thelma G.: *test,* 559
Allport, Floyd H.: *test,* 99
Allport, Gordon W.: *test,* 99, 299
Alster, Benjamin: *test,* 107
Altus, William D.: *rev,* 887, 913
Amatora, Mary: *test,* 129, 1182
Ambco, Inc.: *test,* 1655-6
Amberson, Jean D.: *rev,* 1264, 1270
American Association for Health, Physical Education, and Recreation. See AAHPER Youth Fitness Project.
American Association for Jewish Education. See Committee on Tests.
American Association of Collegiate Registrars and Admissions Officers: *test,* 1318

American Association of University Professors: *test,* 1185
American Automobile Association. See Traffic Engineering and Safety Department.
American Chemical Society. See Examinations Committee.
American Civil Liberties Union, Illinois Division, Academic Freedom Committee: *test,* 1177
American Council on Education: *test,* 249, 477, 864, 1301, 1347, 1458, 1513-4
American Dental Association. See Committee on Aptitude Testing.
American Guidance Service, Inc.: *test,* 1300
American Institute of Certified Public Accountants. See Committee on Personnel Testing.
American Library Association. See Subcommittee on Service Ratings.
American Optical Co.: *test,* 1680
Amerson, Vera M.: *rev,* 47, 52
Ammons, Helen S.: *test,* 887
Ammons, Robert B.: *test,* 887, 1890
Amoss, Harry: *test,* 878, 903, 962
Anastasi, Anne: *rev,* 719, 722, 730, 771, 859, 865, 885, 1377-8, 1384, 1386
Anderhalter, Oliver F.: *rev,* 16; *test,* 37, 470, 773, 844, 1083, 1329, 1402, 1445, 1505
Anderson, Elizabeth: *test,* 1255, 1264
Anderson, Howard R.: *rev,* 1706, 1713, 1769, 1782, 2788, 2793, 2798, 2802, 2841, 2878, 2880; *test,* 1764
Anderson, Irving H.: *rev,* 1493, 1500, 1502, 1694, 2686, 2688-9
Anderson, James M.: *rev,* 914, 935, 2473, 2557
Anderson, Kenneth E.: *rev,* 1597, 1620-1; *test,* 1604
Anderson, L. Dewey: *test,* 1928, 1930, 1939
Anderson, Noelle: *test,* 1303
Anderson, Rose G.: *test,* 783-4
Andrade, R. D.: *test,* 627
Andrew, Dorothy M.: *test,* 1841
Andrew, Gwen: *test,* 269, 365
Andrews, Oliver, Jr.: *test,* 639
Andrus, Lawrence: *rev,* 690, 2405

---

* References are to test entry numbers, not to page numbers. The numbers following the names may be interpreted thus: "*rev,* 68" indicates authorship of an original review in *The Mental Measurements Yearbook* of test 68; "*test,* 73" indicates authorship of test 73. Authors of out of print tests are not indexed.

Buhler, Charlotte: *test*, 244, 338, 370, 373, 394
Buhler, Karl: *test*, 373
Bundy, R. D.: *test*, 2089
Burch, Robert L.: *rev*, 1043, 1072, 1090
Burdock, E. I.: *test*, 116
Bureau of Educational Measurements: *test*, 50, 54, 64, 94, 423, 485, 497, 508, 553, 579, 669, 682, 940, 952, 996, 1023, 1079, 1113, 1143, 1228, 1239, 1258, 1261, 1269, 1278, 1299, 1404, 1429, 1553, 1555, 1558, 1605, 1641, 1708, 1721, 1730, 1745, 1749, 1752-3, 1760, 1772, 1774, 1788, 1797, 1800, 1818
Bureau of Tests: *test*, 62, 86, 422, 459, 475, 670, 683, 997, 1010, 1046, 1116, 1135, 1173, 1236, 1273, 1276, 1582, 1617, 1645, 1738
Burgemeister, Bessie B.: *test*, 882
Burgess Cellulose Co., Grade-O-Mat Division, *test*, 1150a
Burgess, Ernest W.: *test*, 1289-90
Burke, Charles: *test*, 1857, 1860
Burke, Paul J.: *test*, 944, 1548, 1614, 1632
Burnett, R. Will: *rev*, 1550, 2727
Burnham, Paul S.: *rev*, 583, 1867, 2335; *test*, 1386
Burnham, Robert W.: *test*, 1681
Burns, Donald G.: *rev*, 2376-7
Burns, Robert K.: *test*, 1965, 1968, 2045
Burr, Emily T.: *rev*, 730, 865
Burt, Cyril: *rev*, 731, 747, 1384; *test*, 3, 428, 760, 1026, 1484
Buswell, Guy T.: *rev*, 2785; *test*, 1053, 1443
Butler, Margaret N.: *test*, 1890
Byers, Edward E.: *test*, 68
Byrd, Oliver E.: *test*, 1225, 1243

CAHOON, G. P.: *rev*, 1632, 1634, 1639, 2770
Caldwell, C. W.: *test*, 2083
California Test Bureau: *test*, 1146
Caligor, Leopold: *test*, 336
Calkins, E. J.: *test*, 1744, 1770
Call, Hazel: *test*, 512-3
Callis, Robert: *test*, 1191
Calvert, B.: *test*, 804
Campbell, Donald T.: *rev*, 267, 311, 2214, 2220, 2864
Campbell, J. Helen: *test*, 401
Campbell, Russell N.: *test*, 622
Cardall, Alfred J.: *test*, 2097
Carey, Gertrude L.: *test*, 592
Carl, George P.: *test*, 879
Carleton, Frederick O.: *test*, 1571
Carlile, A. B.: *test*, 247, 318
Carlsen, G. Robert: *test*, 1283
Carpenter, M. F.: *test*, 414, 444-5
Carr, W. L.: *rev*, 671, 673
Carroll, Herbert A.: *test*, 490
Carroll, John B.: *rev*, 1371, 1375, 1377, 1384; *test*, 618
Carter, Harold D.: *rev*, 198, 1459, 1827,

1873, 1875, 1887, 2895, 2897, 2919; *test*, 1522
Carter, Launor F.: *rev*, 2169
Cartwright, W. H.: *rev*, 1773, 2867, 2874
Case, Harry W.: *test*, 1945
Cassaretto, Frank P.: *rev*, 1597, 1614, 1624
Cassel, Russell N.: *test*, 125-6, 128, 130, 144, 209a, 210, 214, 307, 345, 1303a, 2075
Castka, Joseph F.: *test*, 1614
Castner, Burton M.: *rev*, 898, 2460
Cate, Charles A.: *test*, 1320
Cathcart, Robert S.: *rev*, 530
Catholic University of America. See Program of Affiliation.
Cattell, A. K. S. See Schuettler, A. K.
Cattell, Psyche: *rev*, 751, 783, 816, 884, 2445; *test*, 880
Cattell, Raymond B.: *rev*, 103, 124, 732, 748; *test*, 187-94, 228, 231, 234-5, 279, 289, 733-4
Center, Stella S.: *rev*, 2785; *test*, 492, 564
Central Institute for the Deaf: *test*, 1658
Central Surveys, Inc.: *test*, 1956
Century School Crafts: *test*, 1214
Chadderdon, Hester: *rev*, 1262, 1265, 1275, 2618
Chall, Jeanne S.: *test*, 1478
Challman, Robert C.: *rev*, 374, 2243
Chambers, E. G.: *rev*, 1837-8, 1875, 1920-1, 1941, 1945
Chambers, M. M.: *test*, 1795
Champney, Horace: *test*, 158
Chapin, F. Stuart: *test*, 1340
Chapman, J. C.: *test*, 1396, 1515
Chapple, Eliot D.: *test*, 197
Chauncey, Henry: *rev*, 25
Character Guidance Committee, Lighthouse Branch, Tuscon YMCA: *test*, 310
Checov, L.: *test*, 235
Chesler, David J.: *test*, 556, 822, 1030, 1846
Chestek, Abbie: *test*, 1042
Chittenden, E. W.: *test*, 957-8, 1567
Christensen, Paul R.: *test*, 140, 852, 916, 919-20
Christie, Richard: *test*, 295
Christofferson, H. C.: *test*, 1020
Chriswell, M. Irving: *test*, 1914
Chronicle Guidance Publications, Inc.: *test*, 1310
Churchill, Edmund P.: *rev*, 957-8, 2487
Churchill, Ruth: *rev*, 1386, 2274
Clapp, Frank L.: *test*, 407, 1045
Clark, Cherry Ann: *rev*, 336, 356
Clark, Gale W.: *rev*, 71, 89
Clark, Grace W.: *test*, 521
Clark, H. V.: *test*, 838
Clark, J. F.: *rev*, 1932, 1947
Clark, John R.: *rev*, 987, 2492; *test*, 1062
Clark, Joyce R.: *test*, 1681
Clark, Kenneth E.: *rev*, 267, 276, 1190
Clark, M. L.: *test*, 708, 831, 1436
Clark, Meribah: *test*, 1812-3

Clark, Stanley: *rev, 990, 992, 1003, 1005, 2485*
Clark, Willis W.: *test, 4-6, 124, 222, 405-6, 473, 730-2, 858, 976, 1043-4, 1067-8, 1091, 1394-5, 1418, 1455, 1498, 1654, 1824*
Clarke, H. Harrison: *rev, 1226, 2604*
Clarke, Walter V.: *test, 101*
Cleeton, Glen U.: *rev, 291, 2097, 2893; test, 1827, 1859, 2100*
Clem, Jane E.: *test, 85*
Clendenen, Dorothy M.: *rev, 225, 1182*
Clinton, R. J.: *test, 1795*
Clymer, Theodore: *test, 1401, 1479*
Coan, R. W.: *test, 191*
Cochran, Grace: *test, 615*
Cochran, Robert: *test, 2087*
Cochrane, Roy: *test, 256, 1076*
Cockerille, Clara: *test, 2, 1707*
Cofer, Charles N.: *rev, 339-40, 375, 378, 894, 937*
Coffin, Clarine: *test, 460*
Coffman, William E.: *rev, 30, 37, 222*
Cogan, E. A.: *test, 235*
Cohen, John: *rev, 471, 876, 1059, 1074*
Cohen, S. W.: *test, 631*
Cole, Lawrence W.: *test, 737*
Cole, Luella: *test, 1786*
Coleman, John H.: *test, 183*
Colestock, Ruth: *test, 1402, 1445, 1505*
College Entrance Examination Board: *test, 409, 480a, 481, 632-4, 651-3, 659-60, 662-3, 666-7, 685, 687-9, 738, 828, 941-3, 1345-6, 1586-7, 1612-3, 1629-31, 1709, 1761-2*
Collins, Mary: *test, 906*
Collins, Patricia: *test, 1888*
Color Aptitude Test Committee, Inter-Society Color Council: *test, 1692*
Colvin, Edgar S.: *test, 989*
Commins, W. D.: *rev, 267, 722, 727, 732, 840, 843, 1841, 2106, 2424, 2429*
Committee on Aptitude Testing, Council on Dental Education, American Dental Association: *test, 1996*
Committee on Biology Tests, Educational Records Bureau: *test, 1589*
Committee on Chemistry Tests, Educational Records Bureau: *test, 1615*
Committee on Cumulative Records, American Council on Education: *test, 1301*
Committee on Diagnostic Reading Tests, Inc.: *test, 1403*
Committee on Modern Languages, American Council on Education: *test, 477, 864, 1347, 1458, 1513-4*
Committee on Personnel Methods, American Council on Education: *test, 249*
Committee on Personnel Testing, American Institute of Certified Public Accountants: *test, 1994-5*
Committee on Physics Tests, Educational Records Bureau: *test, 1633*
Committee on Tests, American Association for Jewish Education: *test, 661*

Committee on Tests and Measurements, Board for Parish Education, Lutheran Church—Missouri Synod: *test, 1334*
Committee on Tests, Mathematical Association of America: *test, 946*
Committee on Tests, UBEA Research Foundation: *test, 98*
Comrey, Andrew L.: *rev, 1376, 1966*
Conant, Margaret M.: *test, 1476*
Conkling, F. R.: *test, 420a*
Connery, Robert H.: *test, 1803*
Connor, Frank: *test, 460*
Connor, William L.: *test, 26*
Conrad, Clinton C.: *rev, 1775, 2838*
Conrad, Herbert S.: *rev, 12, 28, 33, 44, 2115-6*
Contreras, María de la Soledad S.: *test, 704*
Cook, Elaine Forsyth: *rev, 1748, 2816; test, 1710-1*
Cook, Roy S.: *test, 1618, 1636*
Cook, Sidney: *test, 1515*
Cook, Walter W.: *rev, 2, 42, 536, 1192, 1205, 2326; test, 414, 424, 1191*
Coombs, Clyde H.: *rev, 971*
Cooperative Test Division: *test, 9, 482-3, 743, 974, 1284, 1359, 1449, 1573, 1719, 2006*
Cordell, Christobel M.: *test, 502-3, 516*
Corey, Stephen M.: *rev, 243, 267, 2238*
Cornell, Ethel L.: *rev, 2116; test, 232*
Cornog, Jacob: *test, 1620-1*
Cornwell, J.: *test, 809*
Corsini, Raymond J.: *test, 273, 891*
Costa, Maria Irene Leite da: *test, 1670*
Cottle, William C.: *rev, 773, 1856*
Cottrell, Alice B.: *test, 1481*
Courtis, Stuart A.: *rev, 783, 1384, 2597*
Courtney, Douglas: *rev, 45, 206, 2198*
Cowell, Charles C.: *test, 138-9*
Cox, J. W.: *test, 1915*
Cox, John A., Jr.: *rev, 620-2*
Cox, Marion Monroe: *rev, 1467-8, 1494-5, 1498, 1694, 2689, 2785; test, 1465, 1502*
Coxe, W. W.: *test, 232*
Crabtree, Margaret: *test, 524*
Crager, Richard L.: *test, 881*
Craig, Clara R.: *test, 801*
Crain, Marguerite Rice: *test, 638, 649*
Cram, Fred D.: *test, 442*
Crary, Ryland W.: *test, 1768*
Crawford, A. B.: *rev, 1875, 2008; test, 1386*
Crawford, Dorothea M.: *test, 1898*
Crawford, John E.: *test, 1898*
Crissy, William J. E.: *rev, 2177, 2523*
Criswell, R. Lenox: *rev, 2606*
Crockett, Alex C.: *test, 1369, 1917*
Croft, Kenneth: *test, 623*
Croft, Lysle W.: *rev, 131, 1867, 1872, 2234*
Cromer, S. S.: *test, 1144*
Cronbach, Lee J.: *rev, 123, 198, 267, 1191, 2159, 2450*
Crook, Frances E.: *rev, 977, 1061, 1092*

Croon, Charlotte W. See Davis, Charlotte Croon.
Cross, E. A.: *test, 420*
Crow, Alice: *test, 30, 43, 1437*
Crow, Lester D.: *test, 30, 43, 1230, 1437, 1554, 1560, 1590, 1618, 1636, 1724, 1748, 1758*
Crowder, Norman A.: *test, 1378*
Cruickshank, William M.: *rev, 314, 887*
Cummings, Howard H.: *test, 1769*
Cunningham, Bess V.: *test, 827*
Cureton, Edward E.: *rev, 1109, 1111-2, 1614, 1839, 1847, 2449, 2452, 2723; test, 1380*
Cureton, Louise Witmer: *rev, 1846; test, 1380*
Cureton, Thomas Kirk: *rev, 1237, 1249*
Curr, William: *rev, 1027, 1050*
Curtis, Francis D.: *rev, 1560, 1588, 2230, 2715*
Curtis, James W.: *test, 332, 1835, 1861, 1916*
Curtiss, Dorothy W.: *test, 1527*

DAHLSTROM, W. Grant: *rev, 125, 192*
Dailey, John T.: *rev, 725-6, 738, 764, 794*
Dale, Edgar: *rev, 563, 2335*
Dale, Reginald R.: *rev, 835, 1448*
Dallmann, Martha: *test, 465*
Damrin, Dora E.: *test, 271*
Dana, Richard H.: *rev, 374, 383*
Daniels, John C.: *rev, 418, 856, 866; test, 759, 1452*
Danzer, Herbert: *test, 424*
Darley, Frederic L.: *test, 529*
Darley, John G.: *rev, 103, 572, 1153, 1887-8, 2920*
Dartnell Corporation: *test, 2101*
Daugherty, John H.: *rev, 1614, 2750*
Davidson, Helen H.: *test, 373*
Davies, A. E.: *test, 434*
Davis, A. L.: *test, 619, 623*
Davis, Allison: *test, 747*
Davis, Charlotte Croon: *rev, 410-1, 417, 430, 438, 476, 483; test, 563, 1398, 1436, 1764*
Davis, D. Russell: *rev, 152, 167, 287, 2144*
Davis, David J.: *test, 948*
Davis, Edwin W.: *rev, 1856, 2237*
Davis, Frederick B.: *rev, 15, 738, 743, 1394, 1403, 1413, 1460, 1516, 2660, 2677; test, 493, 563, 1398, 1436*
Davis, Julian C.: *test, 373*
Davis, Lawrie F.: *test, 1794*
Davis, Parker, Jr.: *rev, 252*
Davis, Robert A.: *rev, 1711, 2705*
Davis, V. A.: *test, 494*
Davis, Vera. See Hoyum, Vera Davis.
Dawe, Helen C.: *rev, 1254, 1257*
Dawson, Shepherd: *test, 748*
Dearborn, Terry H.: *test, 1226*
Deemer, Walter L., Jr.: *test, 70*
Deese, James: *rev, 1521, 1535*
Degering, Ed. F.: *test, 1616*
De Lay, Frank P.: *rev, 457, 2244*

Delp, Harold A.: *rev, 914, 2468*
Demaree, Robert G.: *rev, 2177, 2424*
Denny, E. C.: *test, 1424-5*
Denton, John C.: *test, 1820*
DePalma, Nicholas: *test, 373*
Department of Business Education, Ball State Teachers College: *test, 61, 78, 96*
Department of Education, University of Edinburgh: *test, 456, 797, 1074, 1931*
Department of Educational Research, Ontario College of Education, University of Toronto: *test, 17-8, 575, 770, 834, 1032, 1055, 1061, 1077, 1092, 1149, 1349, 1390, 1488, 1496*
Deri, Susan K.: *rev, 385*
Derrick, Clarence: *rev, 400, 444-5, 1442; test, 413, 424, 1436, 1523*
Derryberry, Mayhew: *rev, 1225, 1234*
Derthick, Lawrence G.: *rev, 1192*
DeSilva, Harry R.: *rev, 2561, 2567*
Dewey, Joseph C.: *rev, 536, 1394, 1408, 1421, 2676*
Diack, Hunter: *test, 1452*
Dibner, Andrew S.: *test, 239*
Dickson, Gwendolen Schneidler: *rev, 1888, 2891, 2919*
Diebold (John) & Associates, Inc.: *test, 2018*
Diederich, Paul B.: *rev, 494-5, 507, 681*
Diekhoff, John S.: *rev, 409, 482, 517, 519, 2258, 2287, 2289, 2301*
Dimond, Stanley E.: *test, 1802*
Dinkel, Robert E.: *test, 1011*
Distad, H. W.: *test, 1042*
Division of Research, Northwestern University: *test, 1326*
Dodd, Catherine: *test, 424*
Dolch, Edward W.: *test, 1463*
Dole, Arthur A.: *test, 1892*
Dolio, Ardwin J.: *test, 1190*
Doll, Edgar A.: *test, 314, 921*
Doll, Ronald C.: *test, 213*
Dombrose, Lawrence A.: *test, 352*
Domincovich, H. A.: *test, 493*
Doppelt, Jerome E.: *rev, 574, 891, 1434, 1870, 2006; test, 755, 824*
Dopyera, John: *test, 277*
Doren, Margaret: *test, 1466*
Dotterer, J. E.: *test, 1126*
Douglass, Harl R.: *rev, 990, 1183, 2113, 2578*
Downing, Chester Miller: *test, 571*
Drake, Raleigh M.: *rev, 280, 605, 733, 735, 747, 836, 864, 2351, 2431; test, 598*
Drake, Richard M.: *rev, 947, 1004, 1013, 2488*
Drasgow, James: *test, 315*
Dreese, Mitchell: *test, 198*
Dresden, Arnold: *rev, 2483, 2486*
Dressel, Paul L.: *rev, 8, 941, 943, 948, 957-8, 974*
Drever, James: *rev, 904; test, 906*
Drew (H. & W. B.) Co.: *test, 1305*
Driscoll, Gertrude P.: *test, 335*
Drucker, Arthur J.: *test, 276*

Drummond, Robert: *test,* 1184
Dubois, Philip H.: *rev,* 70, 80, 84, 1109
Duggins, Lydia A.: *rev,* 1483, 1486
Dulsky, Stanley G.: *rev,* 1878, 1880, 2168, 2889-90
Dunkel, Harold B.: *rev,* 651, 656-7, 666, 668, 2380-1
Dunlap, Jack W.: *rev,* 26, 243, 722, 1567, 1856, 2210
Dunlap, Roy: *test,* 1434
Dunn, Lloyd M.: *test,* 905
Dunn, S. S.: *rev,* 1408, 1497, 1501; *test,* 75
Dunnette, Marvin D.: *test,* 2004
Dunning, Gordon M.: *test,* 1634
Durost, Walter N.: *rev,* 785, 844, 864, 2270; *test,* 12, 27, 83, 492, 564, 827, 1072, 1421, 1566, 1716, 1811
Durrell, Donald D.: *test,* 1467-8, 1501
Dvorak, August: *rev,* 771, 2113; *test,* 10, 1123, 1559
Dvorak, Beatrice J.: *rev,* 79, 95
Dvorine, Israel: *test,* 1683-4
Dyer, Henry S.: *rev,* 1392, 1870; *test,* 1202
Dykema, Peter W.: *test,* 603

EAGLE, Norman: *rev,* 807
Eakins, Lyle M.: *test,* 994
Eames, Thomas H.: *test,* 1685
Earle, Frank M.: *test,* 399, 756, 978, 1100, 1374, 1545
Easley, Howard: *rev,* 771, 859
Eaton, Harold T.: *test,* 421, 495-6
Ebel, Robert L.: *rev,* 1532, 1536, 2614, 2706
Eber, Herbert W.: *test,* 193
Edfeldt, Åke W.: *test,* 1504
Edgar, J. W.: *test,* 1541
Edgerton, Harold A.: *test,* 1571
Edmiston, R. W.: *test,* 1524, 1668, 1863
Educational Records Bureau: *test,* 949, 1589, 1615, 1633
Educational Test Bureau: *test,* 449, 656, 677, 702, 953, 980, 995, 1117, 1127, 1316, 1563, 1583, 1609, 1646, 1722-3, 1743, 1782-3
Educational Testing Service: *test,* 15, 46, 498-9, 504, 523, 586, 600, 607, 617, 620, 644-5, 648, 658, 664, 686, 693, 698, 705, 722-3, 764, 851, 956, 965-6, 1186, 1192, 1205, 1244-5, 1268, 1277, 1279, 1293-4, 1296, 1353, 1546-7, 1568, 1577, 1591, 1619, 1627, 1637, 1726-7, 1737, 1771, 1804, 1816, 1952, 2003, 2010. See also College Entrance Examination Board.
Edwards, Allen L.: *test,* 143
Edwards, Bateman: *rev,* 630, 2370
Edwards, Reginald: *rev,* 435, 1057
Eells, Kenneth: *test,* 747
Eichorn, Dorothy H.: *rev,* 244, 338
Eidsmoe, Russell M.: *test,* 1195
Eigerman, Hyman: *test,* 493
Eisenberg, Philip: *rev,* 226, 2181
Eisenson, Jon: *test,* 152
Eisner, Harry: *test,* 960

Elias, Gabriel: *test,* 154
Elliott, D. N.: *test,* 1198
Elliott, M. H.: *rev,* 2186, 2922
Elliott, Richard M.: *test,* 1928, 1930, 1939
Ellis, Albert: *rev,* 141, 151, 154, 179, 204, 224, 328, 348, 1291
Ellsworth, Robert B.: *test,* 215
Elsbree, Willard S.: *test,* 1211
Emmett, W. G.: *rev,* 756, 770, 783; *test,* 749
Engburg, Ina: *test,* 426
Engel, Anna M.: *test,* 751
Engelhart, Max D.: *rev,* 8, 1612, 2109, 2747-8, 2751
Engelmann, Hugo O.: *test,* 149
Engelson, Ieleen: *test,* 550
Engle, T. L.: *test,* 1295
English Language Institute, University of Michigan: *test,* 624
Epstein, Bertram: *rev,* 1574, 2503
Epstein, Seymour: *test,* 156
Erdmann, Albert J., Jr.: *test,* 1227
Erickson, Willard E.: *test,* 1965
Ericson, Emanuel E.: *rev,* 2633-4
Eron, Leonard D.: *rev,* 387
ErSelcuk, Rolande G.: *test,* 639
Espenschade, Anna S.: *rev,* 1669-70, 2781-2
Eurich, Alvin C.: *rev,* 1459, 2224, 2793, 2805; *test,* 1422, 1516
Evans, Catharine: *test,* 226
Examinations Committee, Division of Chemical Education, American Chemical Society: *test,* 1596-1603, 1624
Exton, Alfred H.: *test,* 823
Eyesight Conservation Committee, Winter Haven Lions Club: *test,* 1699
Eysenck, H. J.: *rev,* 135, 171, 179, 185, 201, 224, 235, 309, 324, 373; *test,* 219

FAGIN, Harold T.: *test,* 183
Falk, Nellie F.: *test,* 462
Farnsworth, Dean: *test,* 1687-8
Farnsworth, Paul R.: *rev,* 199, 593, 598, 604, 609-11, 2346
Farnum, Stephen E.: *test,* 599, 612
Faulkner, Ray: *rev,* 591, 594, 2625
Fawcett, Harold P.: *rev,* 990, 1102-3, 1117, 1122, 1124, 2540, 2543
Fay, Jay W.: *rev,* 602, 2347
Fay, Lola: *test,* 1777
Feagley, Ethel M.: *rev,* 2705, 2713; *test,* 1527
Fear, Richard A.: *test,* 1978
Fehr, Howard F.: *rev,* 975
Fehrer, Elizabeth: *rev,* 65, 81
Feinberg, Henry: *rev,* 885
Feldman, Marvin J.: *test,* 315
Feldt, Leonard S.: *rev,* 403, 1518; *test,* 31
Fensch, Edwin A.: *test,* 530
Ferguson, George A.: *rev,* 786, 808, 863, 1824, 2456, 2884, 2893
Ferguson, James T.: *test,* 182
Fernald, G. M.: *test,* 923, 929
Ferrell, Robert H.: *rev,* 1771

Ghiselli, Edwin E.: *rev,* 1904, 1908, 1910; *test,* 724
Gibb, Cecil A.: *rev,* 197, 347, 2169
Gibb, E. Glenadine: *test,* 1086
Gibson (Robert) & Sons, Ltd.: *test,* 811
Giedt, F. Harold: *test,* 216
Gilbert, Marc D.: *test,* 1060
Giles, H. H.: *rev,* 487, 509, 2803
Gill, Ethan M.: *test,* 1229
Gilliland, A. R.: *test,* 902
Gilmore, John V.: *test,* 1483
Gittinger, John W.: *rev,* 393
Glaser, Edward Maynard: *test,* 1543
Glock, Marvin D.: *rev,* 1476, 1541
Glorig, Aram: *test,* 1655
Goddard, H. H.: *test,* 111, 934
Goldburg, C. M.: *rev,* 1622
Goldman, Bernard: *test,* 168
Goldstein, Kurt: *test,* 163
Goltry, Keith: *rev,* 2245, 2264
Goodenough, Florence L.: *rev,* 898, 1384, 2459-60; *test,* 763, 899
Goodson, Margaret: *test,* 1120, 1129
Goppert, H. R.: *test,* 2083
Gorbutt, Dorothy Gale: *test,* 280
Gordon, Hans C.: *rev,* 1424, 1550, 1565, 2719, 2725
Gordon, Leonard V.: *test,* 164-5, 227, 275
Gordon, Wayne: *test,* 541
Gorham, Donald R.: *test,* 832
Gough, Harrison G.: *rev,* 125, 131, 253, 299, 306; *test,* 102, 123, 251, 562, 1298, 1337, 1960, 2012, 2014, 2017, 2026
Gourlay, Neil: *rev,* 429, 1417
Graebner, Oliver E.: *test,* 1323
Graff, Franklyn: *test,* 1860
Graham, Frances: *test,* 221
Graham, Frederick B.: *test,* 26
Graham, Grace: *rev,* 2834
Graham, Herbert B.: *test,* 1368
Grant, Albert: *test,* 1221
Grapko, Michael F.: *test,* 196
Grassi, Joseph R.: *test,* 166
Graves, Maitland: *test,* 588
Gray, Hob: *test,* 16
Gray, W. H.: *test,* 1406, 1447
Gray, William S.: *rev,* 1409, 1430, 1468, 1497, 2668; *test,* 1490-1, 1693
Grayson, Harry M.: *test,* 167
Greenberg, Jacob: *test,* 630, 636, 690
Greene, Edward B.: *rev,* 81, 89, 1376, 1859, 1953, 2092, 2170; *test,* 572
Greene, Esther: *test,* 1527
Greene, Harry A.: *rev,* 405, 420a, 433, 452; *test,* 22-3, 404, 440, 442-3, 446, 539, 546, 1004, 1006, 1038, 1109, 1110, 1413, 1415, 1450, 1544
Gregory, R. W.: *test,* 1144
Gregory, W. S.: *test,* 1867
Greig, Mary E.: *test,* 1712
Gries, Konrad: *rev,* 659, 666, 2398, 2400, 2404
Griffin, Charles H.: *test,* 2001
Griffin, Warren B.: *test,* 2085, 2088
Griffiths, Nellie L.: *test,* 1500
Griffiths, Ruth: *test,* 890

Grimsley, G.: *test,* 1373
Gross, Richard E.: *rev,* 1706, 1719
Grossnickle, Foster E.: *rev,* 1022, 1033, 1053, 1072, 2499, 2500-1, 2529
Grove, William R.: *rev,* 877, 1901, 1928, 1942, 2900
Grover, Clifford C.: *test,* 1494
Gruber, Alin: *test,* 833
Gruen, W.: *test,* 235
Grygier, T. G.: *test,* 142
Guertin, Wilson H.: *rev,* 149, 912; *test,* 100
Guetzkow, Harold: *test,* 347
Guidance Centre: *test,* 161, 1161, 1306, 1313, 1948-9
Guiler, Walter: *rev,* 543; *test,* 401, 1020
Guilford, J. P.: *rev,* 103, 187, 250, 722, 747, 764, 771, 794, 808, 2180, 2197, 2438; *test,* 140, 171-4, 201, 852, 916, 919-20, 932, 1377, 1529, 1868
Gulick, Sidney L.: *test,* 565a
Gulliksen, Harold: *rev,* 34, 984, 1004, 1008, 2238, 2796
Gummere, John Flagg: *rev,* 668, 672
Gurvitz, Milton: *test,* 836
Gustad, John W.: *rev,* 283, 1874

HABERMAN, Helen: *test,* 55, 1742
Hadley, Laura B.: *rev,* 2619, 2628
Hadley, S. Trevor: *test,* 1821
Haefner, John H.: *rev,* 1802; *test,* 1801
Hagen, Elizabeth: *rev,* 1586, 1590
Haggerty, M. E.: *test,* 177, 1422
Haggerty, M. J.: *test,* 1756, 1777
Hahn, Milton E.: *rev,* 1187, 2043, 2046, 2061, 2948
Hakerem, G.: *test,* 116
Halfter, Irma T.: *test,* 1397
Hall, Clifton W.: *test,* 2050
Hall, Prudence: *test,* 1512
Hall, W. E.: *rev,* 1509
Hamilton, B. A.: *test,* 1775
Hammond, S. B.: *test,* 1151
Hanawalt, Nelson G.: *rev,* 103, 135, 280, 282, 292, 917
Hand, Harold C.: *test,* 1190
Handschin, C. H.: *rev,* 2378, 2381
Hanes, Bernard: *test,* 2051
Hanfmann, Eugenia: *test,* 133
Hankes, E. J.: *test,* 1152
Hanna, Lavone A.: *rev,* 9-10, 25, 1765, 2867, 2870
Hanna, Paul R.: *rev,* 42
Hannaford, Earle S.: *test,* 1166
Hannum, T. E.: *test,* 1887
Hardesty, Anne S.: *test,* 116
Hardy, LeGrand H.: *test,* 1678
Hargrave, Harold: *test,* 1794
Harless, Byron B.: *test,* 868
Harlow Publishing Corporation: *test,* 19-20
Harrell, Thomas W.: *rev,* 1908, 1910
Harriman, Philip L.: *rev,* 333, 336, 343, 348, 350, 362
Harris, Albert J.: *rev,* 1433, 1700, 2681, 2691; *test,* 1651

Hovey, Nelson W.: *test,* 1625
Hovland, Carl I.: *rev,* 723, 764, 794, 860, 1543
Howard, Gertrude: *test,* 244
Howard, James W.: *test,* 351
Howard, Robert W.: *rev,* 408, 2253
Howe, Mary E.: *test,* 1189
Howie, Duncan: *rev,* 707, 1529
Howitt, C.: *test,* 18
Hoye, Monica M.: *rev,* 1067, 2513
Hoyt, Cyril J.: *rev,* 36, 808, 1103, 1124, 2535; *test,* 1401, 1479
Hoyum, Vera Davis: *test,* 441, 452, 536
Huddleston, Edith M.: *rev,* 2639, 2821
Huebert, Anna: *test,* 570
Hughes, J. L.: *test,* 2025a
Hughes, Violet: *rev,* 494
Humble, Emma: *test,* 1065, 1414
Hume, C. D.: *test,* 2084
Humm, Doncaster G.: *rev,* 99, 103, 235b, 2140; *test,* 185, 2057
Humm, Kathryn A.: *test,* 2057
Humphreys, Lloyd G.: *rev,* 1368, 1371, 1376, 1917, 1927, 1946
Hunsicker, Albert L.: *rev,* 106, 218
Hunsucker, Florise: *test,* 1805
Hunt, E. Patricia: *rev,* 778, 2441
Hunt, Howard F.: *test,* 186
Hunt, Thelma: *rev,* 1841, 1847; *test,* 291, 1183, 1208, 2032, 2073
Hunt, William A.: *rev,* 288
Hunter, G. W.: *rev,* 1549, 1560, 1588, 2725, 2739
Hurd, A. W.: *rev,* 1632, 1648, 2773
Husek, E.: *test,* 235
Hutchison, Mary H.: *test,* 430
Hutt, Max L.: *test,* 269, 327, 365
Huttner, Ludwig: *test,* 2093

ILLINOIS Council on Economic Education: *test,* 1740
Immergluck, Ludwig: *rev,* 163
Implementation Commission, National Association of Secondary-School Principals: *test,* 1988
Imus, Henry A.: *rev,* 1680, 1698
Inaba, Kay: *test,* 833
Industrial Relations Center: *test,* 2007
Inglis, Alexander: *test,* 567, 1155
Ingraham, Jessie E.: *test,* 1419
Institut pedagogique Saint-Georges: *test,* 303
International Business Machines Corporation: *test,* 1153
Irwin, Orvis C.: *test,* 524a
Ishihara, Shinobu: *test,* 1703
Ives, Margaret: *rev,* 186, 288

JACKSON, C. L.: *test,* 1280
Jackson, Harvey O.: *test,* 979
Jackson, Joseph F.: *rev,* 636, 2360, 2362, 2364
Jackson, Lydia: *test,* 386
Jackson, Robert W.: *rev,* 39
Jacobs, Alfred: *test,* 176
Jameson, Alice N.: *rev,* 1432, 1461, 2662

Jamison, Olis G.: *test,* 1813
Jastak, Joseph: *test,* 45, 1379
Jay, Edith Sherman: *test,* 120
Jean, F. C.: *rev,* 2732
Jeffery, Harold B.: *test,* 1009, 1122
Jeffrey, T. E.: *test,* 919a, 924a, 931a, 1918, 1926, 1935, 1951
Jenkins, J. W.: *test,* 419, 745, 804, 1051
Jenkins, R. L.: *test,* 229
Jenkins, Thomas N.: *test,* 183, 1870
Jennings, Charles G.: *test,* 1312
Jennings, John R.: *rev,* 1912-3
Jensen, Arthur R.: *rev,* 337, 387; *test,* 1184
Jensen, Carl Christian: *test,* 1156
Jensen, Milton B.: *test,* 926
Jessor, Richard: *rev,* 354, 356
Jewish Education Committee of New York, Inc.: *test,* 1322
John, Lenore: *test,* 1053
Johns, Edward B.: *test,* 1237
Johnson, A. Pemberton: *rev,* 1914, 2004
Johnson, B. F., Jr.: *test,* 862
Johnson, Cecil D.: *rev,* 189
Johnson, Frances L.: *test,* 526
Johnson, Helen: *test,* 696
Johnson, Hildegarde: *test,* 1271
Johnson, Laura B.: *rev,* 650, 2360
Johnson, Leland P.: *rev,* 1588, 1592
Johnson, Palmer O.: *rev,* 1548, 1573, 1597, 1624, 1630, 1635, 2483, 2726, 2728, 2770, 2775
Johnson, Roswell H.: *test,* 204
Johnston, Philip W.: *test,* 1661
Joint Committee on School-College Relations, National Association of Secondary-School Principals and American Association of Collegiate Registrars and Admissions Officers: *test,* 1318
Joint Committee on Tests, United Business Education Association and National Office Management Association: *test,* 47, 51, 53, 60, 65, 81, 95
Jolles, Isaac: *test,* 348
Jonah, H. F. S.: *test,* 972
Jones, Archie N.: *test,* 601
Jones, Carleton C.: *rev,* 414, 2286, 2290
Jones, Edward S.: *rev,* 9, 1537, 1542, 1991
Jones, F. Nowell: *rev,* 1680, 1694, 1698
Jones, Frankie: *test,* 1794
Jones, Harold E.: *rev,* 151, 177, 227, 1180, 2152, 2156
Jones, Harold J.: *test,* 205
Jones, Robert A.: *rev,* 773, 1854
Jones, Winifred E.: *test,* 623
Jones, Worth R.: *rev,* 35, 441
Jordan, A. C.: *test,* 408
Jordan, A. M.: *rev,* 29, 750
Jordan, Byron: *test,* 1978
Jordan, R. C.: *test,* 862
Jordan, Richard H.: *rev,* 2720, 2736
Jorgensen, A. N.: *test,* 1413
Judd-Safian Associates: *test,* 1992
Juhnke, Warren L.: *test,* 1237
Jurgensen, Clifford E.: *rev,* 82, 95, 1939, 1944-5, 2096; *test,* 1319

Justman, Joseph: *rev,* 1018, 1083; *test,* 1075

KAHN, Theodore C.: *test,* 345, 356, 893
Kaiser, Herbert E.: *test,* 1333
Kaldenberg, Donald E.: *test,* 110
Kalhorn, Joan: *test,* 158
Kambly, Paul E.: *rev,* 1574, 2605; *test,* 1549-50, 1588
Karn, Harry W.: *rev,* 1980
Karnes, M. Ray: *rev,* 1145
Kasanin, Jacob: *test,* 133
Kass, Walter: *rev,* 370, 384
Katz, Evelyn: *test,* 822, 1846
Katz, Martin: *rev,* 1878
Katzell, Raymond A.: *rev,* 1832, 1844, 1847, 1898, 1939, 2027, 2061
Kaufman, Herbert A., Jr.: *test,* 2092
Kaufmann, H. J.: *test,* 884
Kaulfers, Walter V.: *rev,* 477, 614, 616, 632, 635-6, 645, 690, 692, 697, 2373, 2419; *test,* 704
Kauzer, Adelaide: *test,* 88
Kayser, Kathryn: *test,* 13
Keating, T. J.: *rev,* 831, 879, 904
Keats, J. A.: *rev,* 742, 863
Keeley, William E.: *test,* 7, 1575-6, 1594
Keim, C. Ray: *test,* 1787, 1815
Keir, Gertrude: *rev,* 798, 857
Kell, Leone: *test,* 357
Keller, M. W.: *test,* 972, 1137
Kelley, Ida B.: *test,* 1188
Kelley, Truman L.: *rev,* 1384; *test,* 42, 1090, 1453, 1536, 1574, 1728
Kelley, Victor H.: *test,* 1413, 1415
Kellogg, D. E.: *test,* 836
Kellogg, Martha: *test,* 1019
Kellogg, Roy D.: *test,* 1122
Kellogg, Theodore E.: *rev,* 1003, 1070, 1103, 1124, 2535
Kelly, E. Lowell: *rev,* 179, 187, 199, 2173, 2193
Kelly, Roberta: *test,* 1257
Kelso, Paul C.: *test,* 772
Kemp, Gladys: *test,* 1065
Kemp, Thomas G.: *test,* 538a
Kendall, Barbara: *test,* 221
Kendel, Elizabeth H.: *test,* 1040
Keneally, Katherine G.: *rev,* 2669
Kenny, Douglas T.: *rev,* 214, 329
Kent, Grace H.: *rev,* 879, 904, 911, 2463-5; *test,* 358, 894
Kentucky Cooperative Counseling and Testing Service: *test,* 781
Keohane, Robert E.: *rev,* 2859
Kephart, N. C.: *test,* 1985
Kerr, Willard A.: *rev,* 1170, 1901, 1936; *test,* 147, 157, 259, 311, 1336, 1970, 2047
Kessler, Sydney: *test,* 207, 359
Keys, Noel: *test,* 240, 988
Keystone View Co.: *test,* 1694
Kilander, H. Frederick: *test,* 1241-2, 1248, 1274, 1288
Kiltz, K. W.: *test,* 1144
Kimber, George C.: *test,* 1542
Kinder, Elaine F.: *rev,* 314

King, Harold V.: *test,* 622
King, Helen B.: *test,* 908
King, Janet E.: *test,* 263
King, Joseph E.: *rev,* 572, 1954; *test,* 189, 194, 840, 1367, 1976, 1982, 1987
Kinget, G. Marian: *test,* 334
Kingsbury, Forrest A.: *rev,* 185, 1859
Kinney, L. B.: *rev,* 945, 991, 2485
Kinzer, John R.: *rev,* 1904, 1922
Kirby, Thomas J.: *test,* 448, 684
Kirkpatrick, Donald L.: *test,* 2095
Kirkpatrick, Ernest L.: *test,* 1623
Kirschner, Earl E.: *test,* 1009
Kivlin, Laura D.: *test,* 1266
Klebanoff, Seymour G.: *rev,* 186, 2144
Kline, Linus W.: *test,* 592
Klopfer, Bruno: *test,* 373
Knauber, Alma Jordan: *test,* 590-1
Knight, James: *test,* 862
Knott, Donald P.: *test,* 1794
Knowles, Lois: *test,* 1086
Knuth, William E.: *test,* 602
Kobal, Andrew: *test,* 717-8, 1342, 1831, 1873, 1923
Koch, Charles: *test,* 396
Koch, David G.: *test,* 1561
Koepke, H. F.: *test,* 1888
Kogan, Kate Levine: *rev,* 133, 163, 939; *test,* 881
Kogan, William S.: *rev,* 133
Kohs, S. C.: *test,* 918
Kopel, David: *rev,* 1491, 1694, 2687, 2785
Kosinar, William C.: *test,* 281
Kotick, M. Lela: *test,* 597
Kraeft, Walter O.: *test,* 1323
Kraft, Merwyn A.: *test,* 2100
Krathwohl, David R.: *rev,* 7, 1712
Krause, Carl A.: *test,* 650
Krey, A. C.: *rev,* 1765
Kriedt, P. H.: *test,* 1887
Krohn, Albertine: *test,* 1625
Kropp, Russell P.: *rev,* 1396, 1415
Krout, Johanna. See Tabin, Johanna Krout.
Krout, Maurice H.: *test,* 200, 241
Krugman, Arnold D.: *test,* 100
Krugman, Morris: *rev,* 105, 227, 269, 348, 365, 373
Kuder, G. Frederic: *rev,* 403, 814, 816, 818, 1369; *test,* 209, 1874-5
Kuhlmann, F.: *rev,* 732, 816; *test,* 783-4, 911
Kuhlmann, Martha J.: *test,* 1437
Kunze, Karl R.: *test,* 717-8, 1342, 1831, 1873, 1923
Kurtz, Albert K.: *rev,* 1384, 1846, 1989
Kutash, Samuel B.: *test,* 343
Kvaraceus, W. C.: *rev,* 113, 444-5, 673, 2159; *test,* 206
Kwalwasser, Jacob: *test,* 603-6
Kyte, George C.: *test,* 1189

LaBRANT, Lou: *rev,* 2290-1
Lado, Robert: *test,* 621, 626-8
Lafayette Instrument Co.: *test,* 1674
LaForge, Rolfe: *test,* 355

Merton, Elda L.: *test,* 1080
Meyer, Bernadine: *rev,* 92, 574
Meyer, Donald L.: *test,* 277
Meyer, John H.: *rev,* 2362, 2369
Meyers, Charles E.: *test,* 320
Michael, William B.: *rev,* 588, 614, 722-3, 841
Micheels, William J.: *rev,* 1281-2, 1944, 2087
Michels, Walter C.: *test,* 1649
Middleton, Jean Ellis: *test,* 1282
Middleton, William: *test,* 2073
Miles, Catherine Cox: *test,* 109
Miles, T. R.: *rev,* 152, 867, 2436
Miles, Walter R.: *test,* 1677
Milholland, John E.: *rev,* 732, 787
Miller, Ben W.: *test,* 1162a
Miller, Daniel R.: *test,* 1943-4
Miller, Ezra A.: *test,* 1611
Miller, Kenneth M.: *test,* 1886
Miller, L. W.: *test,* 445, 957
Miller, Lawrence W.: *test,* 285
Miller, Mildred: *test,* 1065
Miller, Minnie M.: *test,* 638, 649, 695, 699
Miller, Robert B.: *test,* 1989
Miller, W. S.: *test,* 720, 794
Millett, Ruth: *test,* 1216
Mills, Robert E.: *test,* 1472
Milne, F. T.: *test,* 1073
Miner, John B.: *rev,* 2890, 2895; *test,* 393
Minkler, F. W.: *test,* 18
Minnick, J. H.: *rev,* 989, 2535
Misbach, Lorenz: *rev,* 185
Mitchell, A.: *test,* 795
Mitchell, Claude: *test,* 729
Mitchell, Mary Alice: *test,* 1476
Mittlemann, Bela: *test,* 135-6
Modern Language Association of America: *test,* 617, 648, 658, 664, 686, 698
Modisette, B. R.: *test,* 2085
Moeller, George: *test,* 114
Mollenkopf, William G.: *rev,* 973, 978, 988, 2480, 2484
Monroe, Eason: *rev,* 1515, 2695-6
Monroe, Marion. See Cox, Marion Monroe.
Monroe, Walter S.: *test,* 1423
Mooney, Elizabeth: *test,* 198
Mooney, Ross L.: *rev,* 227, 260-1
Moore, B. V.: *test,* 1028, 2001
Moore, David G.: *test,* 1968
Moore, Herbert: *test,* 1830, 1848
Moore, J. H.: *test,* 1842
Moore, Joseph E.: *rev,* 16, 591, 1848, 1897-8, 2008; *test,* 1530, 1653
Mordy, Francis E.: *test,* 1807
Morgan, Antonia: *test,* 1039
Morgan, G. A. V.: *rev,* 24, 892; *test,* 434-5, 1027, 1035, 1095, 1834
Morgan, Howard K.: *test,* 245
Morgan, M. E.: *test,* 1123
Morgan, William J.: *test,* 969, 1039
Morison, Luella J.: *test,* 261
Morris, John B.: *rev,* 1927, 2027
Morrisby, J. R.: *test,* 1372
Morrison, Harriet Barthelmess: *rev,* 22, 1406, 2106, 2235, 2711

Morrison, J. Cayce: *test,* 545
Morrison, James H.: *test,* 304
Morrison, Nathan: *rev,* 1013, 2475
Morrison, Thomas F.: *rev,* 2740-1
Morse, H. T.: *rev,* 9, 2801
Mort, Paul R.: *test,* 28
Morton, N. W.: *rev,* 347, 1859, 1887, 1946, 2895; *test,* 836
Morton, R. L.: *rev,* 1019, 1034
Moser, Harold E.: *rev,* 1017, 1054
Moses, Peggy Lou: *test,* 1503
Mosier, Charles I.: *rev,* 235b, 246, 2081, 2090
Moss, F. A.: *test,* 291, 1208, 2073
Moutoux, A. C.: *test,* 2081
Moutoux, Ruth Davis: *test,* 1260
Mueller, Kate Hevner: *rev,* 604, 611
Murphy, Helen A.: *test,* 1501
Murra, Wilbur F.: *rev,* 1764, 1773, 2830, 2859
Murray, Elsie: *rev,* 1687-8, 1691
Murray, Elwood: *test,* 285
Murray, Henry A.: *test,* 387
Murray, James G.: *test,* 1590
Murray, Winifred: *test,* 426
Mursell, James L.: *rev,* 596, 598, 602, 606, 609, 2346
Myers, Charles T.: *rev,* 1941
Myers, Isabel Briggs: *test,* 230

NANASSY, Louis C.: *rev,* 1434, 2428
Nash, Elizabeth A.: *test,* 112
Nash, N.: *test,* 2024
Naslund, Robert A.: *test,* 35, 469, 1082, 1442, 1532
National Association of Secondary-School Principals: *test,* 248, 1304, 1311, 1314, 1318, 1988
National Bureau of Educational and Social Research: *test,* 104, 800, 802, 1052, 1073, 1370, 1451, 1825
National Cash Register Co.: *test,* 2015
National Foundation for Educational Research in England and Wales: *test,* 337, 431, 613, 761, 867
National Institute for Personnel Research: *test,* 450-1, 791-2, 1037, 1048, 1093-4, 1382-3, 1822, 1972
National Institute of Industrial Psychology: *test,* 765-9, 1837-8, 1919-21, 1932
National League for Nursing, Inc.: *test,* 2033-8
National Office Management Association. See Joint Committee on Tests.
National Research Council, Psychology Committee: *test,* 726
Neale, Marie D.: *test,* 1487
Nedelsky, Leo: *rev,* 1631, 1637
Neher, Gerwin: *test,* 1234
Neidt, Charles O.: *rev,* 5, 785; *test,* 257
Nel, B. F.: *test,* 379
Nelson, Charles W.: *test,* 1158, 1203
Nelson, Clarence H.: *rev,* 1229-30, 1513, 2733, 2737, 2742; *test,* 1592
Nelson, Ethel V.: *test,* 10, 1426

Nelson, M. J.: *test,* 457, 771-2, 1424-5, 1427
Nelson, Severina E.: *test,* 526
Neville, Harry R.: *test,* 1436
New York Institute of Finance: *test,* 2019
New York Times: *test,* 1732-3
New Zealand Council for Educational Research: *test,* 818, 1015, 1489, 1500
Newcomb, Theodore: *rev,* 246, 267
Newman, Joseph: *rev,* 917, 939
Newsweek Educational Division: *test,* 1734-5
Newton, Kenneth R.: *rev,* 328, 384
Neyhart, Amos E.: *test,* 1171, 2101-3
Neyhart, Helen L.: *test,* 2101
Nielson, J. R.: *test,* 615
Nila, Mary: *test,* 1507
Nisbet, John: *rev,* 538, 830, 871
Nisbet, Stanley: *rev,* 40, 429, 756, 955, 1485
Noe, Pryce: *test,* 1120, 1129
Noffsinger, Gletha Mae: *test,* 472
Noll, Victor H.: *rev,* 21, 1412, 1595, 2616, 2703, 2715, 2719, 2749, 2751, 2753, 2762
Norcross, Claude E.: *rev,* 42
Norman, J. H.: *test,* 77, 97, 301, 716, 820, 1435, 1823, 1852, 1879
Norman, Warren T.: *rev,* 224
Norris, Raymond C.: *rev,* 184, 801, 1720
Norsworthy, N.: *test,* 934
Northwestern University. See Division of Research.
North, Robert D.: *rev,* 1044, 1082
Northrop, Paul A.: *rev,* 2766, 2772, 2775
Noyes, Edward S.: *rev,* 413, 420, 2290

OAKLEY, C. A.: *rev,* 1859, 1915, 1927
Oakley, C. O.: *rev,* 1103, 2536
Oberlin College: *test,* 585
O'Brien, John: *test,* 37, 470, 1083
O'Brien, John A.: *test,* 1324
O'Connor, James P.: *test,* 265
O'Connor, Johnson: *test,* 569, 1906-7, 1933
O'Connor, K. P.: *test,* 1056-7
Odell, C. W.: *rev,* 4, 22, 26, 680, 2115, 2398
Ogawa, George Y.: *test,* 2045, 2062
Oglesby, Eliza F.: *test,* 1400
Ohio College Association: *test,* 235a
Ohio Scholarship Tests: *tests,* 11, 14, 57-9, 76, 93, 425, 427, 437, 486, 500, 551, 640, 643, 674-5, 678, 700, 703, 963-4, 981-2, 993, 998-9, 1024, 1106, 1114, 1119, 1232, 1362, 1405, 1430, 1457, 1552, 1556-8, 1579-80, 1584, 1606-7, 1610, 1642-3, 1647, 1717-8, 1729, 1746, 1754-5, 1757, 1779, 1789-90, 1792, 1796
Oliverio, Mary Ellen: *rev,* 1848, 2096
Olson, W. C.: *test,* 177
Omwake, K. T.: *test,* 291
Ontario College of Education. See Department of Educational Research.
Orata, Pedro T.: *rev,* 2224, 2797
Orbach, Charles E.: *test,* 1961, 2027
Orleans, Jacob S.: *rev,* 43, 53, 457, 1028, **1040, 1238, 1458**, 1758; *test,* 33, 41, 232,

439, 453, 554, 616, 680, 1021, 1029, 1439
Orleans, Joseph B.: *test,* 1008, 1112, 1131
O'Rourke, L. J.: *test,* 474, 578, 810, 1456, 1844, 1934
Orshansky, Bernice: *test,* 944, 947, 990-1, 1103
Osborne, Agnes E., *rev,* 2130, 2132
Osborne, Raymond L.: *test,* 239
Osburn, Worth J.: *rev,* 557, 1019, 1034, 1062, 1064-5, 1218, 1470, 1500, 2106, 2281, 2530, 2661
Oseretsky, N.: *test,* 1670
O'Steen, Alton: *rev,* 2348-9
Otis, Arthur S.: *test,* 41, 812-8, 1078, 1159
Otis, Jay L.: *rev,* 1653, 1934, 1937, 1943, 2929; *test,* 72, 556, 822-3, 1030, 1846
O'Toole, Charles E.: *test,* 1936
Ott, Vesperella E.: *test,* 7
Otterstrom, Ruth E.: *test,* 1064, 1085
Otto, Herbert A.: *test,* 1290a
Overley, H. M.: *test,* 73
Owen, H. F.: *test,* 2080, 2084
Owens, William A.: *test,* 1946, 2005, 2013

PACE, C. Robert: *rev,* 119, 311, 1206, 1509, 2165, 2220, 2875; *test,* 277
Packard, Albert Gibson: *rev,* 1908, 1910
Page, Horace A.: *test,* 156
Page, Richard M.: *test,* 2050
Painter, Inez: *test,* 679
Palmer, Orville: *rev,* 589
Palmer, Osmond E.: *rev,* 408, 440, 573
Park, John C.: *test,* 134
Parke, L. A.: *test,* 66
Parker, Claudia M.: *test,* 1399
Parkhurst, Nelson M.: *test,* 1145
Parmenter, M. D.: *test,* 1307-9, 1865
Parsek, Anna: *rev,* 2824
Parsons, Verlin: *test,* 1215
Parvis, Jeannette O.: *test,* 1259-60
Passow, A. Harry: *rev,* 12
Paterson, Donald G.: *rev,* 1831, 1833, 1842, 1853, 1991, 2042-3, 2061, 2948; *test,* 414, 563, 922, 1841, 1928-30, 1939
Patterson, D. H.: *test,* 691
Patterson, Gerald R.: *rev,* 914
Patterson, Raymond G.: *test,* 1808-10
Patty, Willard W.: *rev,* 2610
Pauli, Richard: test, 236
Payne, Loyal C.: *test,* 2013
Peacher, William G.: *rev,* 1651
Peak, Mildred: *test,* 1064
Peak, Philip: *test,* 1047, 1070, 1120, 1129
Pearce, Blythe: *test,* 420a
Pearson, Carl A.: *test,* 1548-9
Pearson, Helen: *test,* 672
Peatman, John Gray: *rev,* 1369, 2924
Peatman, Lillie B.: *test,* 908
Pedersen, Ruth A.: *test,* 90
Pederson, Walter: *test,* 701
Peel, E. A.: *rev,* 804, 841, 931, 1372, 1941
Pelser, A. J. K.: *test,* 379
Peltier, Charles L.: *test,* 1811
Pence, Raymond W.: *test,* 476
Penrose, L. S.: *rev,* 224, 2431; *test,* 819
Perideaux, Gerald G.: *test,* 1891

Renck, Richard: *test,* 1959, 1965, 2045, 2062
Research and Guidance Branch, Queensland Department of Public Instruction: *test,* 1913, 1947
Reuning, H.: *test,* 236
Revere Copper & Brass, Inc.: *test,* 1170
Reymert, Martin L.: *test,* 323
Reynolds, Maynard C.: *rev,* 1483, 1486
Reznikoff, Marvin: *test,* 371
Rhinesperger, Lois: *test,* 1270
Rich, Gilbert J.: *rev,* 2237
Rich, Vernita: *test,* 550
Richards, M. K. B.: *test,* 1834, 1941
Richards, R. C.: *test,* 1786
Richards, Roger A.: *rev,* 449
Richards, T. W.: *rev,* 350
Richardson, Bellows, Henry & Co., Inc.: *test,* 1849, 1940
Richardson, C. A.: *test,* 853-5
Richardson, J. A.: *rev,* 398, 531; *test,* 1056-7
Richardson, John S.: *rev,* 1549, 1570
Richardson, Marion W.: *rev,* 946, 1004, 1836, 2476, 2483, 2486; *test,* 90
Richardson, S. C.: *rev,* 419, 435
Ricks, James H., Jr.: *rev,* 1096, 1213, 2428, 2595
Rider, Paul R.: *rev,* 2483, 2486
Rieman, William, III: *rev,* 1601-2, 1604
Rietz, Edward G.: *rev,* 1063, 1609
Rietz, Henry L.: *rev,* 2486
Rifenburgh, S. A.: *test,* 1585
Rigg, Melvin G.: *test,* 517
Rinsland, Henry D.: *rev,* 414, 541, 550, 558-9, 563, 567, 781, 1476, 2322, 2712; *test,* 34, 468, 476
Rising, Justus: *test,* 1281
Risk, Avis: *test,* 1585
Rittler, M. Catherine: *test,* 1678
Rivlin, Harry N.: *rev,* 1186, 1192
Roahen, R. L.: *test,* 494
Roback, A. A.: *test,* 286, 741, 837, 848
Robbins, Rosa Seymour: *test,* 1664
Robbins, Samuel D.: *test,* 527, 1664
Roberts, Holland: *rev,* 492-3, 1393, 1412-3, 2259, 2270, 2302
Roberts, John R.: *test,* 1905, 1908, 1954
Robinson, Bertha: *test,* 1414
Robinson, Francis P.: *test,* 1512
Robinson, Helen M.: *rev,* 1453, 1467-8, 1492
Rock, Milton L.: *test,* 2066
Rodger, Alec: *rev,* 1848, 1915, 1922-3, 1939-40
Roeber, Edward C.: *test,* 1891
Roeder, Wesley S.: *test,* 256, 1368
Rogers, Carl R.: *rev,* 240, 2151; *test,* 306
Rogers, Cyril A.: *rev,* 804
Rogers, Frederick Rand: *rev,* 1224, 2605
Rogers, J. Lloyd: *test,* 16
Rohde, Amanda R.: *test,* 378
Rohrer, Perry L.: *test,* 735
Rorschach, Hermann: *test,* 373
Rosanoff, A. J.: *test,* 358

Rosen, Ephraim: *rev,* 341, 348
Rosen, Ned A.: *test,* 1569
Rosenzweig, Saul: *test,* 374
Rosner, Benjamin: *rev,* 1398
Ross, C. C.: *rev,* 10, 13-4, 16, 34
Ross, Charles S.: *rev,* 950, 1022, 1033, 1075, 1083
Rosskopf, Myron F.: *rev,* 960, 986
Roswell, Florence G.: *test,* 1478
Roth, Robert M.: *test,* 227a
Rothe, Harold F.: *rev,* 74, 2134; *test,* 148
Rothney, John W. M.: *rev,* 206, 213, 314, 320, 909, 2186, 2198, 2643
Rothwell, J. W.: *test,* 1886
Rotter, Julian B.: *rev,* 224, 387; *test,* 212, 375
Royse, Arthur B.: *rev,* 855, 1862
Royster, Robert F.: *test,* 2100
Royster, Salibelle: *test,* 518
Ruch, Floyd L.: *rev,* 1980-1, 2046, 2073, 2948; *test,* 1373, 1853, 1945
Ruch, G. M.: *rev,* 947, 1065, 2797; *test,* 23, 42, 606, 1090, 1453, 1536, 1574, 1728
Ruedisili, C. H.: *rev,* 1978, 2090
Rugen, Mabel E.: *rev,* 1233-4
Ruhlen, Helen: *test,* 420a
Rulon, Philip J.: *test,* 112
Rundquist, Edward A.: *rev,* 70, 80
Rushing, John R.: *test,* 1009
Russell, David H.: *rev,* 532, 1444, 1490, 1492, 1494, 1498-9; *test,* 537
Russell, Harry J.: *rev,* 690, 694, 2406, 2410
Rutledge, Aaron L.: *test,* 1287
Ryan, Loretta C.: *test,* 1230
Ryan, Teresa M.: *test,* 402-3, 488
Ryans, David G.: *rev,* 309, 1188, 2578, 2588
Ryden, Einar R.: *test,* 1531

SACKETT, Everett B.: *rev,* 1856
Saetveit, Joseph G.: *test,* 609
Salisbury, Rachel: *rev,* 1542, 2245
Sallak, V. J.: *test,* 1247
Salmi, Irene: *test,* 556, 1846
Salmon, Christine: *test,* 1266
Sammartino, Peter: *test,* 650
Sampson, Harold: *test,* 562, 1298
Sanders, Ardis: *test,* 479-80, 1012
Sanders, C.: *rev,* 706, 708, 721
Sanders, Joseph R.: *test,* 936
Sanders, Juanita: *test,* 1040
Sanders, M. W.: *test,* 402, 1776, 1806, 1817
Sanford, Nevitt: *test,* 295, 312
Sangren, Paul V.: *test,* 1444
Sapon, Stanley M.: *test,* 618
Sappenfield, Bert R.: *rev,* 338, 374
Sarbin, Theodore R.: *rev,* 103, 2175
Sare, Harold: *test,* 1817
Sargent, Helen D.: *rev,* 373; *test,* 354
Satlow, I. David: *rev,* 56, 862
Satter, G. A.: *rev,* 1847, 1849, 1934, 1946
Satterfield, Mabel S.: *test,* 515

Saunders, Aulus Ward: *rev,* 593-4
Saunders, David R.: *rev,* 174, 281; *test,* 235, 289
Scarborough, Barron B.: *test,* 1883
Scates, Douglas E.: *rev,* 16, 1530, 1537, 1541, 1802, 2224
Schaaf, William: *rev,* 1060, 2497
Schaefer, Willis C.: *rev,* 726, 843
Schaie, K. Warner: *test,* 305
Scheerer, Martin: *test,* 163
Scheier, Ivan H.: *test,* 187, 190, 231, 234
Scherer, Isidor W.: *test,* 233
Schiff, H.: *test,* 235
Schindler, Alvin W.: *rev,* 4, 10, 1549, 1632, 1635
Schlaff, Allan: *test,* 176
Schlesser, George E.: *test,* 1204
Schmidt, Austin G.: *test,* 1329
Schmieding, Alfred: *test,* 258
Schneider, Arnold E.: *rev,* 51, 63, 2127
Schneidler, Gwendolen. See Dickson, Gwendolen Schneidler.
Schnell, Leroy H.: *rev,* 1034, 1038, 1045, 1103
Schnell, William: *test,* 2073
Schnepp, Alfred: *test,* 1332
Schofield, William: *rev,* 167, 287, 375, 917
Schonell, F. Eleanor: *test,* 471
Schonell, Fred J.: *rev,* 1036, 1387-8, 1495, 2421, 2496; *test,* 538, 758, 1056-7, 1059, 1084, 1446
School Administrator's Service: *test,* 1317
Schoolfield, Lucille D.: *test,* 528, 548-9
Schoonover, Charles, Jr.: *test,* 1280
Schorling, Raleigh: *test,* 1062
Schrader, William B.: *rev,* 717-8, 847, 2004, 2457
Schrammel, H. E.: *rev,* 2115; *test,* 13, 63, 71, 88, 280, 402-3, 441, 452, 488, 494, 536, 541, 550, 570, 576, 596, 665, 671, 673, 726-7, 846, 961, 973, 989, 1002, 1064-5, 1085, 1102, 1121, 1213, 1224, 1229, 1249, 1280, 1282, 1297, 1335, 1406, 1414, 1447, 1520, 1565, 1595, 1623, 1635, 1739, 1744, 1770, 1773, 1775, 1785, 1807, 2021
Schubert, Herman J. P.: *test,* 333, 847
Schueler, Herbert: *rev,* 651, 653-4, 2381, 2383-5
Schuettler, A. K.: *test,* 189, 194, 733
Schultz, Douglas G.: *rev,* 1936, 1940
Schultz, Harold A.: *rev,* 593
Schunert, J. R.: *test.* 954
Schutter, Charles H.: *test,* 1003, 1108
Schutz, William C.: *test,* 153
Schwab, Joseph J.: *rev,* 2733
Schwartz, S. L.: *test,* 2094
Schwebel, Milton: *test,* 1887
Schwehn, Hilda: *test,* 1231
Schweickhard, Dean M.: *rev,* 1280
Schwesinger, Gladys C.: *rev,* 733, 907
Science Research Associates, Inc.: *test,* I, 32, 739, 839, 1200
Scollay, Robert W.: *test,* 807
Scott Co.: *test,* 849
Scott, David B.: *test,* 1009

Scott, Louise B.: *rev,* 530
Sea, Marcella Ryser: *test,* 320
Seagoe, May V.: *rev,* 1188, 1208
Seashore, Carl E.: *rev,* 602, 610; *test,* 609
Seashore, Harold G.: *rev,* 1170, 1295-7, 1353, 2100, 2462; *test,* 74, 1371, 2027
Seavey, Virginia: *rev,* 1407, 1430
Secondary Education Board: *test,* 777
Seeling, Kenneth D.: *test,* 1714
Seeman, William: *rev,* 238, 317
Segel, David: *rev,* 572, 722, 783, 988, 1004; *test,* 1381
Segner, Esther F.: *rev,* 2619
Seguin, E.: *test,* 934
Seitz, Clifford P.: *test,* 235b
Sell, DeWitt E.: *test,* 807, 1525
Sells, S. B.: *rev,* 189, 194
Selover, R. B.: *rev,* 1841-2
Semeonoff, Boris: *test,* 886
Seville, E. W.: *test,* 1058
Sexology Magazine Medical Advisors: *test,* 1292
Sexson, John A.: *test,* 7, 1575-6, 1594, 1750, 1784
Shacter, Helen: *rev,* 213, 2593
Shaffer, Laurance F.: *rev,* 124, 135, 141, 196, 373, 2158
Shank, Spencer: *rev,* 1460
Shaw, John H.: *test,* 1233
Shaycoft, Marion F.: *rev,* 969, 1039; *test,* 990-1, 1124
Shea, James T.: *test,* 1022
Shearer, Lois: *test,* 1720
Sheldon, William D.: *rev,* 1427, 2674
Shemwill, E. C.: *test,* 63
Shepherd, Lou A.: *test,* 446
Sherburne, J. W.: *test,* 1517, 1534
Sheridan, Mary D.: *test,* 1667, 1701
Sherman, Murray H.: *test,* 287
Shimberg, Benjamin: *rev,* 172, 245, 1827, 2607; *test,* 276
Shipley, Walter C.: *rev,* 831, 836, 2431; *test,* 288
Shneidman, Edwin S.: *rev,* 395; *test,* 363, 1868
Shoben, Edward Joseph, Jr.: *rev,* 356, 397
Shontz, Geraldine: *test,* 1561
Shooster, Charles: *test,* 253
Shores, J. Harlan: *rev,* 4
Shores, Louis: *rev,* 1520, 2712; *test,* 1530
Shover, Grace: *test,* 1538
Shumaker, L. K.: *rev,* 412, 414
Shuman, W. L.: *test,* 1554
Siceloff, L. P.: *test,* 945, 1101, 1104, 1131-2
Siebrecht, Elmer B.: *test,* 1174
Siegel, Laurence: *test,* 118
Silliman, Henrietta: *test,* 501
Simberg, A. L.: *test,* 1998
Simmons, Ernest P.: *test,* 547
Sims, Verner M.: *rev,* 21, 45, 105, 124, 248, 578, 1336, 1338, 2106, 2180, 2333; *test,* 1339
Singer, M.: *test,* 229

Strong, Edward K., Jr.: *test*, 1887-8
Strother, C. R.: *rev*, 152, 163, 285, 351, 363, 378
Stroud, James B.: *rev*, 1436, 1517; *test*, 1474, 1497
Strouse, Catherine E.: *test*, 610
Stuart, Joan E.: *test*, 825
Stucky, Philip: *test*, 1009
Stuit, Dewey B.: *rev*, 1917, 1937, 1939, 2006, 2008; *test*, 23, 445, 615, 957, 1567, 1620, 1638, 2009
Sturrock, George W.: *rev*, 1050, 1095
Stutsman, Rachel: *rev*, 899; *test*, 898
Stutz, Frederick H.: *rev*, 1768, 1775, 2842, 2876; *test*, 1765-6
Subcommittee on Mathematics Tests, Educational Records Bureau: *test*, 949
Subcommittee on Service Ratings, American Library Association Board on Personnel Administration: *test*, 2022
Suczek, Robert: *test*, 355
Sueltz, Ben A.: *test*, 950
Sullivan, Celestine: *test*, 303b
Sullivan, Elizabeth T.: *test*, 730-2, 858, 1654, 1824
Sullivan, Helen Blair: *test*, 1468
Sullivan, Robert: *test*, 773
Sumner, W. L.: *rev*, 1051, 1105
Sundberg, Norman D.: *rev*, 909
Super, Donald E.: *rev*, 1372, 1841, 1869, 1875, 1889, 2894-5, 2897
Sutcliffe, J. P.: *rev*, 125
Sutherland, John: *rev*, 1027, 1055, 1084
Swaim, Evelyn: *test*, 1265
Swanson, V. J.: *test*, 2077
Sweney, Arthur B.: *test*, 228, 279
Swensen, Clifford H., Jr.: *rev*, 273, 325
Swineford, Frances: *test*, 1523
Sykes, E. G.: *test*, 121
Symonds, Percival M.: *rev*, 103, 124, 238, 331, 339, 374, 2168, 2243; *test*, 384, 614, 1184, 1872
Szondi, Lipot: *test*, 385

TABA, Hilda: *rev*, 9, 1711, 2106, 2224, 2596, 2796
Tabin, Johanna Krout: *test*, 241, 383
Takala, Reino: *test*, 1120
Tate, Donald J.: *test*, 570, 1751
Taylor, Calvin W.: *rev*, 742
Taylor, Doris: *test*, 416
Taylor, Earl A.: *test*, 1469
Taylor, Erwin K.: *rev*, 824, 872, 1832, 1841, 1853, 1968, 2423; *test*, 2060
Taylor, Howard R.: *rev*, 291, 1376, 1871, 2097
Taylor, Stanford E.: *test*, 1477, 1482
Taylor, Wallace: *rev*, 1758, 2843, 2852; *test*, 1764, 1766, 1785
Teagarden, Florence M.: *rev*, 120, 314, 757, 880, 888, 898-9
Technisonic Studios, Inc.: *test*, 1665
Teegarden, Lorene: *rev*, 1904, 1930, 2467
Templin, Mildred C.: *rev*, 900, 902; *test*, 529

Tenney, Edward A.: *rev*, 2291, 2683
Tennyson, W. Wesley: *rev*, 36, 808
Terman, E. L.: *test*, 803
Terman, Lewis M.: *test*, 42, 109, 742, 859-60, 909-10, 1090, 1453, 1536, 1574, 1728
Tharp, James B.: *rev*, 636, 2373, 2408, 2420; *test*, 647, 657, 697
Thelen, Herbert A.: *rev*, 1550, 1565
Thibault, Paula: *test*, 424
Thiele, C. L.: *rev*, 1032, 1043, 2522, 2524
Thomas, Charles Swain: *rev*, 403, 414, 468, 2291; *test*, 571
Thomas, Cleveland A.: *rev*, 403, 435
Thompson, Albert S.: *rev*, 1859, 1904, 1906-7, 1968, 1989, 2042, 2948
Thompson, Anton: *rev*, 22, 536, 545
Thompson, Charles E.: *test*, 392
Thompson, George: *test*, 302
Thompson, John H.: *rev*, 414, 2290-1
Thomson, Edith I. M.: *rev*, 1446, 2159
Thomson, Godfrey H.: *rev*, 734, 1384; *test*, 806
Thorndike, Robert L.: *rev*, 123, 147, 259, 291, 722, 860, 1709, 2429, 2899; *test*, 581, 787
Thorpe, Louis P.: *rev*, 45; *test*, 35, 124, 222, 320, 469, 608, 1082, 1532, 1442, 1824, 1878, 1891
Thouless, Robert H.: *rev*, 471, 1543, 2247
Thurstone, L. L.: *test*, 250, 309, 722-3, 841, 843, 865, 919a, 924a, 931a, 1384, 1826, 1889, 1918, 1926, 1935, 1951, 1968
Thurstone, Thelma Gwinn: *test*, 250, 722-3, 841, 843, 865, 1384
Tiedeman, David V.: *rev*, 23, 739-40, 781
Tiedeman, H. R.: *test*, 1096
Tiegs, Ernest W.: *rev*, 2106, 2113, 2117, 2804; *test*, 4-6, 124, 405-6, 473, 730-2, 858, 976, 1043-4, 1091, 1394-5, 1455, 1654, 1824
Tiffin, Joseph: *rev*, 2785; *test*, 574, 719, 833, 1434, 1848, 1909-10, 1937, 2080, 2083-8
Timberlake, Josephine B.: *test*, 548-9
Time, Inc.: *test*, 1731
Tinker, Miles A.: *rev*, 1460, 1467, 1517, 1534, 1651, 1677, 2785; *test*, 1518
Titmus Optical Co., Inc.: *test*, 1702
Toliver, Hazel M.: *rev*, 672, 2398
Tollefson, Donald: *test*, 192
Tomkins, Silvan S.: *test*, 393
Tomlinson, T. P.: *test*, 805, 866, 873-4
Tonne, Herbert A.: *rev*, 52, 268, 1954, 2122, 2126
Toops, Herbert A.: *rev*, 1301, 1867; *test*, 808, 1538, 1928, 1930, 1939
Torgerson, T. L.: *rev*, 1408, 1470; *test*, 597
Towley, Carl: *test*, 426
Townsend, Agatha: *rev*, 1391, 1453, 1744, 2816
Trabue, M. R.: *rev*, 572, 1827, 1856, 1859, 2695, 2890, 2919-20; *test*, 723a, 1930
Traffic Engineering and Safety Depart-

ment, American Automobile Association: *test,* 1162, 1164-5
Trankell, Arne: *test,* 1675
Travers, Robert M. W.: *rev,* 1178, 1560, 1573, 1634, 1638, 2001
Travis, Lee E.: *test,* 395
Traxler, Arthur E.: *rev,* 572, 576, 732, 1153, 1445, 1859, 1875-6, 1991, 2557, 2888, 2918, 2920; *test,* 34, 558, 1041, 1459-60, 1539
Tressler, J. C.: *test,* 34, 478
Triggs, Frances Oralind: *rev,* 1443, 2891, 2896
Trist, Eric: *test,* 886
Trost, Marie E.: *rev,* 2824
Troyer, Maurice E.: *rev,* 23, 2117; *test,* 1180, 1233, 1411
Trusler, V. T.: *test,* 1249
Tryon, R. M.: *rev,* 1766, 2793, 2802
Tryon, Robert C.: *rev,* 1384
Tulchin, Simon H.: *rev,* 113, 2187, 2200, 2218
Turille, Stephen J.: *test,* 52
Turnbull, Mary E.: *rev,* 631, 638, 642, 677
Turnbull, William W.: *rev,* 36, 824, 1393, 1403, 1413, 1443
Turner, Clarence E.: *rev,* 621, 626, 639, 649, 2359, 2362, 2364, 2370
Turner, Dodds M.: *test,* 1064
Turner, Mervyn L.: *rev,* 1622, 1640
Turney, Austin H.: *rev,* 103, 723, 783, 2605-6
Turse, Paul L.: *test,* 83-4, 1854
Tuska, Shirley A.: *test,* 91
Twitchell-Allen, Doris: *test,* 397
Tydlaska, Mary: *test,* 89
Tyler, F. T.: *rev,* 770, 786, 2458
Tyler, Henry T.: *test,* 1542
Tyler, Leona E.: *rev,* 246, 772, 1271, 2165
Tyler, Ralph W.: *rev,* 1588, 1709, 1719, 2801, 2804

UBEA Research Foundation. See Committee on Tests.
Ulett, George A.: *test,* 373
Ullman, B. L.: *test,* 521, 684
United Business Education Association. See Committee on Tests; and Joint Committee on Tests.
United States Armed Forces Institute: *test,* 44, 417, 505, 951, 1508-9
United States Employment Service: *test,* 1376, 1385, 1871
University Counseling Center, University of Maryland: *test,* 264
University of Edinburgh. See Department of Education.
University of Maryland. See University Counseling Center.
University of Michigan. See English Language Institute.
University of Pittsburgh Project Talent Office: *test,* 1364
University of Toronto. See Department of Educational Research.
Upshall, C. C.: *rev,* 47, 51, 971, 2127

Utley, Jean: *test,* 1139
Uttley, Marguerite: *rev,* 1751, 2824

VAIL, Curtis C. D.: *rev,* 2379, 2381-2
Vaillant, Paul: *test,* 636
Valenti, J. J.: *test,* 1203
Valentine, C. W.: *test,* 270, 835, 892
Van Allyn, Keith: *test,* 1858, 1885, 1979
Vander Beke, G. E.: *test,* 615, 646, 694
Van der Slice, David: *test,* 1303
Van Engen, Henry: *rev,* 1041; *test,* 1086
van Lennep, D. J.: *test,* 341
Van Orsdall, Otie P.: *test,* 1009
Van Roekel, B. H.: *rev,* 1466, 1478
Van Steenberg, Neil J.: *rev,* 172, 174, 193, 309
Van Wagenen, M. J.: *test,* 10, 899, 1019, 1426
Veenker, C. H.: *test,* 1250
Vernon, Leroy N.: *test,* 807
Vernon, Magdalen D.: *rev,* 1390, 1415, 1417, 1685
Vernon, P. E.: *rev,* 107, 124, 185, 1372, 1377-8, 1384, 2242; *test,* 299, 955, 1484
Vickery, Verna L.: *rev,* 1466, 1474
Vicon Instrument Co.: *test,* 1662
Victoreen, John A.: *test,* 1663
Vincent, D. F.: *test,* 1950
Vincent, Leona E.: *test,* 737
Vinette, Roland: *rev,* 2362, 2372
Vinson, Lulu: *test,* 862
Viteles, Morris S.: *rev,* 1904, 1906-7, 2100
Voelker, Paul H.: *test,* 752, 1369, 1836, 1917, 2046
Vorhaus, Pauline G.: *test,* 390
Votaw, David F., Jr.: *test,* 1013
Votaw, David F., Sr.: *test,* 16, 21, 1013, 1210, 1503

WADSWORTH, Guy W., Jr.: *test,* 185
Wagner, Guy: *rev,* 1694
Wagner, Mazie Earle: *test,* 333, 1393
Wait, W. T.: *test,* 1123
Waite, William W.: *rev,* 2082, 2084, 2925
Waits, J. V.: *rev,* 2100
Walker, Biron: *test,* 413, 424, 1436
Walker, Helen: *rev,* 990
Wall, W. D.: *rev,* 831, 883
Wallace, F. C.: *test,* 1208
Wallace, S. Rains: *rev,* 1373, 2064, 2101, 2929
Wallace, Wimburn L.: *rev,* 53, 132; *test,* 740
Walter, Ralph W.: *test,* 567
Walton, R. D.: *test,* 1105
Walton, Ralph E.: *test,* 269, 365
Wandt, Edwin: *rev,* 1178, 2579, 2586
Wantman, Morey J.: *rev,* 458, 2011, 2876, 2878
Warburton, F. W.: *rev,* 746, 758, 830, 1963
Warren, Neil D.: *rev,* 1898-9, 1908, 1910; *test,* 1373
Warrington, Willard G.: *rev,* 1603, 1614